GenderSpeak
6th Edition

Why Use This New Edition?

GenderSpeak 6/e has been reorganized, with a more coherent three-part structure and the addition of a new chapter on nonverbal communication as affected by sex and gender. A downloadable version of the text is available from Kendall Hunt Publishers, as well as an updated, wide-ranging set of ancillary materials to assist instructors with visual aids, chapter outlines/lecture notes, and test items. The text has been thoroughly revised and updated to include the newest research on gender communication, including the following:

1. A **new chapter** on the effects of sex and gender on **nonverbal communication,** or all the ways we communicate without words;
2. Coverage of **gender communication in friendships and romantic/intimate relationships** combined into one chapter, streamlined, and updated with research and information from popular literature;
3. An **expanded discussion of gender identity diversity** in Chapter 2, including new and broadened information about **intersex, asexual, and transgender** identities;
4. A discussion of **changes to the language regarding sex and gender,** including an exploration of Facebook's 50-plus terms for sex and gender identity;
5. Updated **critiques of ad campaigns, TV programming, film and music trends, and new media** that connect to class discussion of media's influence on our thinking about gender;
6. Coverage of **Internet pornography** and **tips for avoiding deceptive pornographic websites;**
7. Discussions on **workplace harassment, the increased presence of women in the American workforce, and barriers that restrict workers** for insight into recognizing and avoiding these situations when students begin or expand their careers;
8. A concentrated focus in Chapter 7 on **abuses of power in relationships,** specifically **sexual assault** and **partner violence,** including the newest information about **consent and sexual safety;**
9. "Hot Topics" at the start of each chapter that overview key issues and **topical chapter outlines that can be used for study and review;**
10. "Case Studies" that provide context and real-life examples related to text material;
11. "Net Notes" boxed features that guide students to web-based information corresponding to or expanding text content; and
12. "Remember" boxes to help students review key terms and concepts in the study of gender communication.

i

Sixth Edition

GenderSpeak

Communicating in a Gendered World

Kendall Hunt
publishing company

Diana K. Ivy

Texas A&M University–Corpus Christi

Book Team

Chairman and Chief Executive Officer   Mark C. Falb
President and Chief Operating Officer   Chad M. Chandlee
Vice President, Higher Education   David L. Tart
Director of Publishing Partnerships   Paul B. Carty
Senior Developmental Coordinator   Angela Willenbring
Vice President, Operations   Timothy J. Beitzel
Senior Production Editor   Sheri Hosek
Senior Permissions Editor   Caroline Kieler
Cover Designer   Faith Walker

Cover image © Shutterstock.com

www.kendallhunt.com
Send all inquiries to:
4050 Westmark Drive
Dubuque, IA 52004-1840

Copyright © 2017 by Kendall Hunt Publishing Company
Copyright © 2012, 2008 by Pearson Education, Inc.

ISBN 978-1-4652-8652-9

Printed in the United States of America

DEDICATION

To Important Women
Hazel, Carol, and Karen
DKI

BRIEF CONTENTS

CONTENTS

PREFACE

The Continuously Changing World of Sex, Gender, and Communication

GenderSpeak is written primarily for college students, both at undergraduate and graduate levels, enrolled in courses that focus on the effects of sex and gender on the communication process. The text is appropriate for graduate seminars in which students arrive with varying levels of knowledge of the subject, as well as upper-division and introductory undergraduate courses. While some prior exposure to basic concepts and theories of interpersonal communication will serve readers well, it's not a prerequisite for understanding the content of this text. Some professors adopt the book (or certain chapters from it) to supplement readings in courses like interpersonal communication and relational communication.

I've long wanted to include a chapter on gender and nonverbal communication in this textbook; for this, the sixth edition, I've finally realized that goal. The book's basic organization has shifted a bit, keeping the Prologue-plus-ten-chapter organization and three-part structure, but with different themes for the parts.

The Prologue provides contextual and historical information to help students situate the content and realize how far we've come (and how far we still need to go) in terms of equality for the sexes. Part One, "Communication and Gender: The Basics," contains an overview of the communication process; a discussion of key terminology; an expansive exploration of sex and gender identity (including a critique of the sex/gender binary view); an in-depth discussion of language—language used *about* the sexes that influences our perceptions of ourselves and others, as well as language used *between* the sexes in relationships; and a new chapter on gender and nonverbal communication.

Part Two, now titled "Gender Communication and Relationships," encourages readers to explore how gender communication affects the initiation, maintenance, and sometimes termination of personal relationships, including online relationships. Chapter 5 is the most general of the three chapters in this part, with coverage of interpersonal communication as affected by sex and gender. Chapter 6 is a new combination of past chapters, providing information about gender communication in friendship and romantic/intimate relationships. Chapter 7 explores the "dark side" of relationships, in terms of power abuses related to sexual assault and partner violence.

"Gender Communication in Context" is the new title for Part Three, which begins with a chapter devoted to the influence of mediated communication on sex and gender, including an extensive, updated discussion of pornography and new media. Remaining chapters explore the effects of sex and gender on workplace communication and educational settings.

PEDAGOGICAL FEATURES

Each chapter includes nine pedagogical features, which serve as aids for instructors and students alike. *Hot Topics* are a means of helping students realize the scope of each chapter. These bulleted phrases serve as topical chapter outlines, which students can use to prepare for exams or to simply check their understanding of chapter content.

Case Studies introduce most chapters, although in Chapter 7 on power abuses, case studies are embedded in the text for the two main subtopics. In some instances, case studies represent actual events that occurred or emerged from discussions in gender communication classrooms; others are fictive. The case study device is used not only to gain attention from readers as they delve into a new topic, but also to orient or alert the reader to the nature of the discussion that lies ahead.

A popular feature retained and updated in the sixth edition is the *Celebrity Quotation*. These fascinating (and sometimes appalling) "pearls of wisdom" come from film and TV personalities, athletes, political figures, musicians, and historical figures, with content that relates to concepts discussed on the page.

Also updated are chapter-end *Conclusions*, as well as the series of *Discussion Starters* that instructors may use as a means of generating class discussion about chapter content, as actual assignments, or as thought provokers for students to consider on their own time.

Complete *References* to the updated research base cited within the text appear at the end of each chapter. Students may find these references useful as they prepare assignments and/or conduct their own research projects. Instructors may use the references to gather additional material for their own research or to supplement instruction.

The sixth edition continues to provide helpful boxed features entitled *Remember . . .*, which go beyond a simple listing of key terms to provide brief definitions for students' review. These boxes appear intermittently within each chapter as a reminder to students of important concepts they will want to retain.

The *Net Notes* feature was also retained, with updated websites related to chapter content. For example, in our discussion of gender and new media in Chapter 8, information from a website offers tips for avoiding online traps that lure users to porn sites.

Finally, the sixth edition features updated *Hot Button Issue* boxes, where ideas challenge students' thinking related to sex and gender. These boxes often raise controversial issues—not in a way that advocates a particular stance, but that encourages students to think for themselves.

ACKNOWLEDGMENTS

This project has certainly been a team effort; thus there are many people to acknowledge and thank. No words can adequately convey the gratitude Ivy feels for past co-author Phil Backlund's contributions to the original vision of this book, his efforts on four editions, and his continued support and good humor throughout the book's evolution. The author wishes to thank the folks I've been privileged to work with at Kendall Hunt, including Paul Carty and Angela Willenbring, who offered great assistance, encouragement, and suggestions.

Gratitude goes to colleagues in the field of communication whose advice and encouragement were invaluable throughout the review process over the multiple editions of this text. Reviewers over the years include: Elizabeth Altman, University of Southern California; Janis Andersen, Emerson College; Bernardo Attias, California State University, Northridge; Cynthia Begnal, Pennsylvania State University; Cynthia Berryman-Fink, formerly of University of Cincinnati; Anne E. Boyle, University of Maryland; Diana Carlin, University of Kansas; Dan Cavanaugh, formerly of Texas State University; Sheila A. Cuffy, Indiana–Purdue University, Fort Wayne; Judith Dallinger, Western Illinois University; Marsha D. Dixson, Indiana–Purdue University, Fort Wayne; Rozell R. Duncan, Kent State University; Pamela Dunkin, Southern Oregon State University; Karen Foss, University of Arizona; Marcie Goodman, University of Utah; Trudy Hanson, West Texas A&M University; Jim Hasenauer, California State University, Northridge; Karla Kay Jensen, Nebraska Wesleyan University; Naomi Johnson, University of North Carolina, Chapel Hill; Meredith Moore, Washburn University; Carol Morgan, Wright State University; Anthony Mulac, University of California, Santa Barbara; Mark P. Orbe, Western Michigan University;

Lisa M. Orick-Martinez, Central New Mexico Community College; Jamey A. Piland, Trinity Washington University; Linda M. Pledge, University of Arkansas at Little Rock; Joey W. Pogue, Pittsburg State University; Judith Pratt, California State University, Bakersfield; Pamela Schultz, Alfred University; Robert Smith, University of Tennessee, Martin; Laura Stafford, University of Kentucky; Helen Sterk, Western Kentucky University; Judith Terminin, Gallaudet University; Lynn H. Turner, Marquette University; Melinda S. Womack, Santiago Canyon College; Julia Wood, formerly of University of North Carolina, Chapel Hill.

Thanks also to colleagues in the Department of Communication at Texas A&M University–Corpus Christi, for their unwavering support and constant praise. Nada Frazier, graduate of Texas A&M University– Corpus Christi, is much appreciated for her early contribution to the Prologue. A very special thanks goes to my dear friends and support systems extraordinaire, Steve and Sue Beebe, Texas State University, for their advice, empathy, good humor, and encouragement of a fellow author.

No project for the benefit of college students has probably ever succeeded without the help of college students. Thousands deserve thanks at Texas A&M University–Corpus Christi for being sources of inspiration for the creation and revision of this textbook. Students of gender communication deserve thanks for providing the motivation to write this text and the "fuel" for a good deal of its content.

Finally, families and friends deserve thanks for their listening ears, thought-provoking questions, lively arguments, and persistent belief in this book and its author.

Diana K. Ivy

PROLOGUE

The Impact of Social Movements on Gender Communication

You Must Know Where You've Been to Know Where You're Going

What question do college students get asked more than any other, especially as they approach graduation? "So, what are you going to do *now*?" As you embark on the journey this book provides, meaning this trip into gender communication as an area of study, you'll be surrounded with topics that make you question the *present*: What am I doing? How do I talk to people of different genders? Do I have some changes to make?

So much of how we communicate, how we think and act, and how we form our visions of the future stem from or are related to the past. For example, most of today's female college students can't fathom the notion of being required to have their fathers sign a lease for them to be able to rent an apartment or cosign a loan document to buy a car. And yet, even as late as the 1960s in many parts of the U.S., the law dictated that a woman had to have either her husband or father cosign documents—she didn't have the basic credibility (because she was a woman) to go it alone. It took valiant efforts to change such sexist practices and it will take more valiant efforts to change sexist practices that persist today. To better understand what's going on today, we need to first explore the past—how we came to be where we are in this society.

In this prologue, we survey history, examine women's and men's movements, and take a look at some of the individuals who have contributed to social, economic, and political changes that have affected and will continue to affect gender communication. But it's beyond the scope of this prologue to focus on each and every social movement that has had an impact. If we fail to mention events or movements you deem significant, we hope you will use the omission as a beginning point for class discussion.

LEARNING "HERSTORY"

Regardless of whether you personally embrace feminism, much of what men and women do and enjoy today is the result of actions and advocacies of feminists. Some of you no doubt have grown up taking equality for granted; fortunately, it may be all you've ever known. But it's because of dedicated feminists that many of you are sitting in college classrooms today.

It's impossible to describe every significant feminist in American history. The truth is we simply don't know or don't have information about each significant women's rights and civil rights advocate. Those we do know about aren't representative of all who fought to get us where we are today. It's important to remember, especially with respect to women and members of minority groups, that historically, most were considered the property of privileged men. They weren't always afforded educational opportunities and often were denied a voice. Those we discuss here somehow made their way into the annals of history, but they are by no means the only ones who made valuable contributions. While history books today are much more inclusive than they've ever been, many would argue they're still "his story," as opposed to "her story." Let's begin by focusing on developments in the realm of education.

Men, Education, and Women—In That Order

When you enter your next class, look around you. Notice the number of university students who once were barred from the education you receive today. Who's responsible for education expanding and becoming accessible to everyone?

In Colonial times American women, under the guidance of men, focused on their "helpmeet" role, which centered on economically essential household production (Theriot, 1996, p. 17). In 1778 a Quaker grammar school opened to educate rural mothers responsible for teaching their children (Bernikow, 1997). Emma Hart Willard is often considered the first important female educator in the United States (Weatherford, 1994). In 1818 Willard appealed to the New York State legislature to allocate taxes for the education of young women, an outlandish concept at the time. Her requests were denied. But she later founded the Troy Female Seminary, which incorporated an unprecedented mathematics and science curriculum that sought to provide women with a comparable education to men's (Lunardini, 1994; Weatherford, 1994).

The first public high school for girls was opened in 1824 in Worcester, Massachusetts, by Quaker Prudence Crandall (Weatherford, 1994). But in 1834 the school was set ablaze and burned to the ground.

In 1837 Mary Lyon founded Mount Holyoke Female Seminary in South Hadley, Massachusetts, which was the first to educate women who weren't from the upper class. In 1837 Oberlin College began to admit women students, as did Antioch College in 1853 and Vassar College in 1865 (Bernikow, 1997). Despite these progressive steps, women's equality in education was still a distant goal.

The First Wave of Feminism

England's Mary Wollstonecraft is regarded as one of the first feminists. Her book *A Vindication of the Rights of Woman*, which called for women's equality with men, is still widely studied today. Abigail Smith Adams, wife of the second U.S. president, John Adams, and mother of the sixth president, John Quincy Adams, is considered an early feminist as well. She is credited with writing letters in 1776 to her husband while he was at the Continental Congress, prodding him to "remember the ladies" (Lunardini, 1994, p. 16). However, the Constitution originally barred women, African Americans, American Indians, and many poor people from civic participation. For years after the Constitution was adopted, women were legally subjugated to their husbands. According to the laws in most states, a married woman "literally did not own the clothes on her back"; her husband legally possessed her and everything she earned (Weatherford, 1994, p. 222). Married women couldn't sign contracts or obtain credit. The first middle-class women employed by the federal government in the patent office received paychecks made out to their husbands (Weatherford, 1994).

SUFFRAGISTS: THE EARLY EQUALITY SEEKERS Imagine that as you leave class today you go to vote in the student government elections, only to find that men are allowed to vote but the women on campus are being turned away, arrested, and imprisoned for voting. This was what the U.S. was like 100 years ago. The origins of feminism can be found in antislavery (abolitionist) and temperance campaigns (Humm, 1992; Krolokke & Sorensen, 2006). However, as

©Everett-Art/Shutterstock.com

> Women are systematically degraded by receiving the trivial attentions which men think it manly to pay to the sex, when, in fact, men are insultingly supporting their own superiority.
> —Mary Wollstonecraft, British feminist

feminist writer Rachel Fudge (2006) explains, "the centuries-long fight for women's right to vote was not just about ballot-casting, but about securing women's right to participate as full citizens: to hold property, keep their own wages, have guardianship of their children, and, yes, vote" (p. 59).

One of the initial launching grounds for women's organized efforts was in 1837 at the first national antislavery convention in New York. Celebrated female abolitionists at the time included Lucy Stone, Angelina Grimké, Sarah Grimké, Lucretia Mott, Elizabeth Cady Stanton, and Susan B. Anthony. Mott was a delegate at the World Antislavery Convention in London, where women were excluded from participation and forced to sit in the balcony behind a curtain (Greenspan, 1994). After this event Mott's and Stanton's activism for women's equality, particularly their efforts to win women's right to vote, intensified.

On July 19, 1848, the first Women's Rights Convention was held in Seneca Falls, New York, with some 300 women and men attending. Mott and Stanton, along with other early feminists, advocated for social policy changes including equality between husbands and wives and women's suffrage. Stanton wrote the "Declaration of Sentiments," modeled after the Declaration of Independence, which stated, "We hold these truths to be self evident, that all men *and women* are created equal" (Ruth, 2001, p. 460). It further listed eighteen legal grievances and called for major reform in suffrage, marriage, and inheritance laws (Greenspan, 1994).

Varying opinions on issues emerged that led to the establishment of two distinct suffrage organizations, the National Woman Suffrage Association (NWSA) founded by Susan B. Anthony and Elizabeth Cady Stanton, and the American Woman Suffrage Association (AWSA) founded by Lucy Stone (Carver, 1999). (Stone graduated first in her class in 1847 at Oberlin College, but was forced to sit in the audience while a male student read her valedictory speech.) NWSA argued that as long as women were denied their rights, all other issues had to be secondary. The AWSA disagreed with a "radical" nationwide suffrage movement and instead focused on enacting change to individual state constitutions (Lunardini, 1994).

©Everett Historical/Shutterstock.com

We want rights. The flour-merchant, the house-builder, and the postman charge us no less on account of our sex; but when we endeavor to earn money to pay all these, then, indeed, we find the difference.
—Lucy Stone, Suffragist, in her "Disappointment Is the Lot of Women" speech of 1855

PROLOGUE: The Impact of Social Movements on Gender Communication

Feminist discontent intensified in 1870 when the Fifteenth Amendment to the Constitution ensured former male slaves the right to vote, but didn't extend that right to women (Lunardini, 1994).

During the 1872 election, Susan B. Anthony and hundreds of women attempted to vote, knowing that it was against the law (Lunardini, 1994). Anthony was arrested for daring to cast a vote, tried in U.S. District court, convicted, and ordered to pay a $100 fine (Weatherford, 1994). Anthony wasn't allowed to speak at her trial, as the law deemed her incompetent to testify because she was a woman. There were other "subversive," but unsuccessful, attempts to vote.

©Everett Historical/Shutterstock.com

The true republic—men, their rights and nothing more; women, their rights and nothing less.
—Susan B. Anthony, Suffragist

Women continued to fight for the right to vote, but success wouldn't come easily. Suffragists like Alice Paul and Carrie Chapman Catt organized massive rallies and demonstrations, including the Woman Suffrage Procession in 1913, staged boycotts and hunger strikes, destroyed property, chained themselves to public buildings, and carried out other acts of civil disobedience (Krolokke & Sorensen, 2006; Miller, 2013; Neft & Levine, 1997). Thousands continued to march, the White House was picketed six days a week, and over a period of two militant years, 500 women were arrested (Bernikow, 1997).

Other notable early feminists were Harriet Tubman and Sojourner Truth. Tubman, an escaped slave, is best known for running the Underground Railroad, but she was also a feminist, a nurse, and a spy for the North during the Civil War (Ventura, 1998). Tubman is credited with leading a raid in 1863 that freed 750 slaves, and she became the first American woman to lead troops into battle in the Civil War (Greenspan, 1994). In 2016, Congress passed a bill allowing the Treasury Department to place Harriet Tubman's picture on the U.S. twenty-dollar bill. Tubman edged out other prominent women in history (including Sojourner Truth, Rosa Parks, and Eleanor Roosevelt) in a nationwide polling effort to depict a woman on either the ten- or twenty-dollar bill (Bandow, 2015). Susan B. Anthony was the first woman depicted on U.S. currency; her likeness was on dollar coins which didn't gain usage and eventually faded from circulation.

At the 1851 Women's Rights Convention, Sojourner Truth made one of her marks on history. Truth was the only woman of color in attendance, and amidst the jeers of hostile men she delivered her famous "Ain't I a

Woman" speech (Fitch & Mandziuk, 1997; Greenspan, 1994). Truth, a preacher, suffragist, and abolitionist, was born a slave, sold away from her parents, and traded numerous times. When she was an adult, her children were sold away from her (Ventura, 1998). Truth dedicated her life to activism against slavery and for integration and women's rights.

After decades of activism, finally in 1920 the Nineteenth Amendment granting women the right to vote was ratified into law. Many of you probably were unaware of the fact that white women and women of color didn't have the right to vote in this country until fifty years after black men (former slaves) were granted their right to vote. Once women obtained the right to vote, the public's interest in women's rights waned, and, collectively, feminism lay dormant for years—until World War II changed everything.

Enter "Rosie the Riveter"

©TinaImages/Shutterstock.com

"Rosie the Riveter" represented all the women who went to work during World War II.

World War II sent men off to war and motivated women to enter the workforce to fill industry jobs. More than 6 million women went to work outside the home for the first time, with the majority employed in factory or clerical jobs in war-related industries (Neft & Levine, 1997). "Rosie the Riveter" became a national symbol for women's contributions to the war effort (Colman, 1995). Some employers still refused to hire women, causing the War Department in 1943 to distribute the booklet *You're Going to Employ Women*. Women were hired as welders, electricians, mechanics, police officers, lawyers, statisticians, journalists, and boilermakers. They operated streetcars, taxis, cranes, buses, tractors, and planes.

Job opportunities for women dried up in 1945 when the war ended. Many women's jobs were terminated in order to ensure jobs for men returning home from the war. Propaganda from government and industry tried to sell women on the idea that it was their patriotic duty to return home and take care of their husbands and children. Many women who attempted to keep their wartime jobs were laid off or forced into lower-paying jobs (Cobble, 2014). Women who wanted or needed employment were encouraged to find traditional women's work as teachers, nurses, or clerical workers. The obvious message to women was that it was their role or duty to focus on husband, children, and home. And for many, home they went and home they stayed (Dicker, 2008).

The Civil Rights Movement

Life in Montgomery, Alabama, in 1955 was much different than it is today. Racism was rampant; racist and segregationist rules and practices were the norm. African Americans riding city buses had to enter the front of a bus to pay a fare, and then get off and enter the bus again from the rear door. They were also required to give up their seats if white people were standing (Lunardini, 1994). Rosa Parks, a mild-mannered African American seamstress in her mid-forties, was seated in the first row of the blacks only section when the white section filled up, leaving a white man without a seat. Parks was arrested for failing to follow the bus driver's instructions to surrender her bus seat to the white man (Lunardini, 1994; Ventura, 1998). Within three days of Parks's arrest, Alabama African Americans began a massive bus boycott that continued for a year until Alabama's state and city bus segregation policies were found unconstitutional (Lunardini, 1994).

From this point on, Martin Luther King, Jr., and other civil rights leaders began to vehemently demand overdue civil rights reforms. Women and men fought for racial progress by joining organizations such as the Student Nonviolent Coordinating Committee (SNCC) and Students for a Democratic Society (SDS). Soon Martin Luther King, Jr., Malcolm X, John F. Kennedy, and Robert Kennedy would all be assassinated. Young men would head off to fight the Vietnam War, while others would protest it by proclaiming we should "make love, not war." For many, the 1960s were about change and challenging "the establishment." For some, it was a time of sexual revolution—a revolution with profound impact on relationships and communication between women and men.

The Sexual Revolution

Later chapters in this text explore gender communication in intimate relationships, but again, relevant historical events have had a profound effect on our modern relationships. For example, women have practiced birth control in one form or another throughout history, just not always legally or safely. Obstetrics nurse Margaret Sanger was among the first to make the connection between reproductive rights and women's economic and social equality. She felt that birth control was the key to women's equality (Ayoub, 2011; Baker, 2012; Emerling Bone, 2010). In 1914 Sanger began publishing a journal entitled *Woman Rebel* (Cuklanz, 1995). Even though it contained no specific contraceptive information, it violated laws of the time and led to Sanger's arrest and indictment by an all-male grand jury. By 1938 federal courts altered obscenity laws. Sanger and associates opened a network of 300 birth control clinics nationwide, and in 1942 they established the Birth Control League, which later would become Planned Parenthood (Lunardini, 1994).

In 1960 the Food and Drug Administration approved the manufacture and sale of "the pill" as a new form of contraception, which quickly became the keystone of the so-called sexual revolution (Lunardini, 1994, p. 297). Many people believe that this one innovation in the form of a simple pill helped make the ideas of women's liberation more practical and acceptable to a wider range of American women. In 1965 the Supreme Court ruled that states couldn't ban the distribution of contraceptives to married people; in 1972 rights were extended to purchase contraceptives without regard to marital status (Weatherford, 1994).

In 2010, much was written about the 50th anniversary of the advent of the birth control pill (Kotz, 2010; Northrup, 2010). The pill is still the primary form of contraception in the United States; Americans spend billions of dollars annually on birth control pills (Tone, 2010). American Studies professor Elaine Tyler May (2010a, 2010b) describes one interesting benefit of this particular form of contraception that could be controlled by women: "Intimate personal relationships changed because women could take the pill without the approval, participation or even the knowledge of their sexual partners" (2010b, p. 40). In an article for *US News & World Report*, reporter Deborah Kotz (2010) discussed various ways the pill changed lives, with the primary effect being that the pill increased a woman's earning potential. Because women have become better able to control conception, they have worked longer outside the home (many in lucrative careers), have delayed childbearing, and thus, have become more financially secure than women in prepill generations.

The Second Wave of Feminism

In 1953 French writer and philosopher Simone de Beauvoir published *The Second Sex*, which

> argued that women—like all human beings—were in essence free but that they had almost always been trapped by particularly inflexible and limiting conditions. Only by means of courageous action and self-assertive creativity could a woman become a completely free person and escape the role of the inferior 'other' that men had constructed for her gender. (McKay, Hill, & Buckler, 2005, p. 1055)

THE SECOND-CLASS STATUS OF WOMEN In 1961 President John F. Kennedy appointed Eleanor Roosevelt to chair the Commission on the Status of Women (Weatherford, 1994). The report from this commission documented discriminatory practices in government, education, and employment and included recommendations for reform. Many states followed suit and identified discrimination at the state level. Hundreds of daily situations exemplified the second-class status of women in our society, which contributed to a movement that many refer to as "women's liberation" (Dicker, 2008; Gordon, 2014).

At the recommendation of the President's Commission on the Status of Women, Congress passed the Equal Pay Act of 1963, which was the first national legislation for women's employment since the Progressive Era. However, it has proved difficult to enforce (Lunardini, 1994). The Civil Rights Act of 1964 prohibited private employers from discriminating on the basis of race, color, religion, national origin, or sex.

THE PROBLEM THAT HAS NO NAME In 1963 American author Betty Friedan, a Smith college graduate who shortly after graduation married and began raising her family, helped awaken the feminist movement with the publication of her book *The Feminine Mystique*. Friedan wrote of the "problem that has no name," which she described as a vague feeling of discontent and aimlessness (p. 15). Friedan's book helped break the silence on issues such as unequal salaries, limited opportunities, and women's powerlessness in family and society (Deakins, 2013; Hardman, 2013; Ortega Murphy, 2013; Taylor, 2013; Turner, 2013). Friedan argued that editors of women's magazines, advertising experts, Freudian psychologists, social scientists, and educators "contributed to a romanticization of domesticity she termed 'the feminine mystique'" (Kerber, De Hart, & Dayton, 2010, p. 505). She further asserted that women should help themselves out of their malaise and take positive steps to reassert their identities (Coontz, 2011; Lunardini, 1994). Quickly, Friedan became a celebrity with a mission.

GETTING THEIR ACTS TOGETHER In 1966 Friedan and twenty-seven other women attending the Washington, D.C., Third National Conference of the Commission on the Status of Women founded the National Organization for Women, commonly referred to as NOW (NOW, 2015). NOW committed to "take action to bring women into full participation in the mainstream of American society . . ." (Friedan, 1963,

Net Notes

If you're interested in viewing documents produced during the women's liberation movement, check out Duke University's Digital Collection:

http://library.duke.edu/digitalcollections.wlmpc

p. 384). The organization clearly communicated that women were ready for action *now*. NOW's six core issues include: reproductive rights and justice; ending violence against women; economic justice; LGBT rights; racial justice; and ratifying a Constitutional Equality Amendment (NOW, 2015).

Other organizations, such as the Women's Equity Action League (WEAL), formed to further women's issues. In 1987 the Feminist Majority was founded to promote "equality for women and men, non-violence, reproductive health, peace, social justice and economic development and to enhance feminist participation in public policy" with a mission to "empower feminists, who are the majority, and to win equality for women at the decision-making tables of the state, nation, and the world" (Feminist Majority, 2015, p. 1).

MS. GLORIA STEINEM "Gloria Steinem's name is synonymous with feminism" (Ventura, 1998, p. 160). Steinem is certainly one of the most renowned feminists. She was a leading activist in the early days of NOW, and in 1971 she joined Bella Abzug and Shirley Chisholm to found the National Women's Political Caucus (Weatherford, 1994). Still active today, this group encourages women to become involved as officeholders, volunteers, political appointees, convention delegates, judges, and committee members (Lunardini, 1994). Steinem then created *Ms.* magazine, the first mainstream feminist magazine in American history (Pogrebin, 2011; Ventura, 1997). In 1971 the preview issue of *Ms.* hit the stands, and the initial 300,000 copies were sold out within ten days (Thom, 1997). The *Ms.* Foundation for Women, organized in 1972, further supports the efforts of women and girls to govern their own lives and influence the world around them (*Ms.* Foundation for Women, 2015).

Feminist activists made numerous other groundbreaking accomplishments during the second wave. In 1969 San Diego State University established the first women's studies baccalaureate degree program (Lunardini, 1994). In 1970 the first congressional hearings on sex discrimination in education were held. In 1972 Title IX of the Education Omnibus Act passed, creating penalties for educational institutions for sex discrimination in schools. In 1973 the Supreme Court's *Roe* v. *Wade* decision legalized abortion. In 1975 the Equal

© Helga Esteb/Shutterstock.com

A woman without a man is like a fish without a bicycle.

—Gloria Steinem, author and political activist

Credit Opportunity Act made credit more available to women. That same year the Rhodes Scholarship Foundation, which funded undergraduate study at Oxford University, no longer excluded women from consideration as Rhodes Scholars (Bernikow, 1997). In 1981 Sandra Day O'Connor was appointed the first female justice on the U.S. Supreme Court. In 1983 Sally Ride became the first female astronaut. In 1984 Geraldine Ferraro became the first female vice presidential candidate, as running mate in Walter Mondale's bid for the presidency. Granted, there were many changes during this second wave, but one reality remained: women still did not have the same, full equal rights as men.

THE EQUAL RIGHTS AMENDMENT (ERA) Much as gaining the right to vote had brought first-wave feminists together to focus on a common goal, the quest for ratification of the Equal Rights Amendment (ERA) united many second-wave feminists. You may not realize that the ERA was first introduced to Congress in 1923 (Andersen, 2009). For almost fifty years it lay dormant. The 1972 version of the ERA states, "equality of rights under the law shall not be denied or abridged by the United States or by any State on account of sex" (Kerber, De Hart, & Dayton, 2010, p. 547). By an overwhelming majority, both houses of Congress passed the ERA in 1972. Shortly thereafter, twenty-eight of the needed thirty-eight states had ratified the ERA (Lunardini, 1994). Phyllis Schlafly, a staunchly conservative voice of the time, rallied others in opposition to the ERA, predicting the destruction of the family, among other things.

A campaign known as STOP-ERA spread fear that women would be drafted and might have to serve in combat if the ERA passed (Andersen, 2009; Lunardini, 1994). In 1982 the ERA failed, just three states shy of the thirty-eight needed for ratification. In 1983 the amendment was reintroduced in Congress, but its passage is still pending (Kerber, De Hart, & Dayton, 2010). As of 2015, thirty-five states had ratified the ERA—still three states shy of what's required for it to become federal law—but 23 states have opted for incorporating ERA-like statements into their state constitutions, given resistance at the federal level. The drive for passage of the ERA continues, with many supporters believing that it provides a necessary tool to protect women's rights in an era in which sex discrimination and inequality still exist (Burroughs, 2015; Neuwirth, 2015).

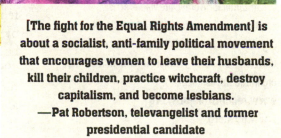

[The fight for the Equal Rights Amendment] is about a socialist, anti-family political movement that encourages women to leave their husbands, kill their children, practice witchcraft, destroy capitalism, and become lesbians.
—Pat Robertson, televangelist and former presidential candidate

No Such Thing as "THE" Feminists

© Helga Esteb/Shutterstock.com

I am a feminist. I reject wholeheartedly the way we are taught to perceive women. Women are strong and fragile. Women are beautiful and ugly. We are soft-spoken and loud, all at once. Perhaps we can make women's rights trendy. Feminism, strength, security, the power, the wisdom of the woman. Let's make that trendy.
—Lady Gaga, performer

Despite rumors to the contrary, feminism is still alive and well in the United States, as well as internationally; however, it continues to receive misunderstanding and opposition as a movement and philosophy (Collins, 2010). One way to reduce the perceived power of a movement, such as civil rights or feminism, is to suggest that members of the movement should be one cohesive group, all in agreement, all using the same rhetoric, and all dedicated to the same causes. When it's inevitably discovered that disagreement or diversity exists within the ranks, then the movement can be criticized and the causes ignored, because "they can't even agree among themselves."

There are many "feminisms," meaning different interpretations or approaches to achieving the goal of sexual equality (Andersen, 2014; Bell, 2010; McRobbie, 2009). As the editors of the book, *Fifty Shades of Feminism*, explain, "There's no one kind of feminism and no one kind of feminist" (Appignanesi, Holmes, & Orbach, 2013). It's not uncommon for feminist philosophies or viewpoints to blend or overlap at times and for various strands to share members, because, as we've stated, no one guiding perspective can be identified as *the* feminist perspective. But gender inequality has and continues to be an abiding theme within feminism (Lorber, 2011; Valenti, 2007). According to feminist author bell hooks (2000), "Simply put, feminism is a movement to end sexism, sexist exploitation, and oppression" (p. 1).

Some women felt (and still feel) alienated by the feminist movement. Women who work inside the home and enjoy more traditional family styles sometimes feel that they have little in common with feminists. Some feminists perpetuate the mistrust by not validating those women who truly want to be traditional housewives and mothers (Lunardini, 1994). While many feminists still vehemently push to further their causes and gain choice, they sometimes are perceived as having violated the feminist golden rule by devaluing the choices of women who follow more traditional paths.

The Third Wave of Feminism

Some critics have contended that feminism is dead or "stolen" (Hoff Sommers, 1994) or that we now live in a "postfeminist" existence because feminism is no longer necessary (Denfeld, 1995; Roiphe, 1993). Others document a feminist movement for the twenty-first century that emerged in the 1990s from women in their twenties and thirties who were proud to call themselves "the third wave" (Tobias, 1997, p. 252). Third-wave feminism draws from the struggles of past waves, but is not a mere extension of a past movement. Third-wave feminists emphasize collective action to effect change and embrace the diversity represented by various feminisms (Heywood & Drake, 1997). They focus on inclusion and multiculturalism and strive to address problems stemming from sexism, racism, social class inequality, and homophobia (Baumgardner & Richards, 2010; Dicker & Piepmeier, 2003; Fixmer & Wood, 2005; Fudge, 2006; Henry, 2014; Krolokke & Sorensen, 2006; Lotz, 2007; Renzetti, Curran, & Maier, 2012; Siegel, 2007). A key feature distinguishing third-wave feminism from second-wave is technological innovation that allows feminism a more global reach than past generations were able to accomplish (Whelehan, 2007).

> I call myself a feminist. Isn't that what you call someone who fights for women's rights?
> —The Dalai Lama

Just as other strains of feminism have had their critics, third-wave feminism has also been scrutinized (Hogeland, 2001; Shugart, 2001; Shugart, Waggoner, & Hallstein, 2001; Woodhull, 2007). Some question the movement's reliance on celebrity and media images and its close association with popular culture, in that some of its icons are TV characters, fashion models, musicians, and actors (Dow, 1996; Hunter College Women's Studies Collective, 2005; Shugart et al., 2001).

> It is really funny how even cool chicks are sort of like, "Our moms covered the feminism thing and now we're living in a post-that world," when that just isn't true.
> —Lena Dunham, actor and author

As we said earlier in this prologue, no matter whether you call yourself a feminist or embrace feminist ideals of any wave, you're now likely to be more aware of the opportunities and freedoms you enjoy that are a direct result of feminists' hard work, determination, and dedication to equality. None of us arrived where we are today without the help and work of others. Let's now explore the development of men's movements to see how their contributions continue to affect relationships and communication between women and men.

WHAT ABOUT "HIS STORY"?

As women's movements have progressed, men's lives have also changed significantly, often as a result of that progress. In Chapter 2, we discuss the fact that many men enjoy privilege based on their biological sex. Privilege, however, varies from man to man, depending on ethnicity, race, social class, age, physical ability, and sexual orientation (Renzetti, Curran, & Maier, 2012). Men's movements, like women's movements, aren't made up of one central group united around a common cause; they reflect a rich diversity of issues and followers. Some movements aren't really considered movements at all, more like efforts to improve the human condition through societal, political, and personal change. As we did for women's movements, we also look at men's movements from a historical standpoint since they have affected and will continue to affect gender communication.

Early Male Supporters of Women's Rights

Historically in the United States, men have benefited from a patriarchally constructed (male-dominated) society. However, exceptional men have always fought societal trends and supported women and their causes. Frederick Douglass, James Mott, and Henry Blackwell openly advocated women's suffrage when it certainly wasn't stylish to do so (Bernikow, 1997). After his passionate speech at the Seneca Falls Convention, antislavery leader Frederick Douglass was maligned in Syracuse newspapers, which first called him a "wimp," then referred to him as an "Aunt Nancy Man" (Kimmel, 2011, p. 52). James Mott, a Quaker businessperson, cochaired the women's rights meeting at Seneca Falls with his suffragist wife, Lucretia Mott. Persistent women's rights advocate Henry Blackwell helped his wife, Lucy Stone, and daughter, Alice Stone Blackwell, publish *The Woman's Journal* (Bernikow, 1997). In 1910 Columbia University philosophy instructor Max Eastman cofounded the Men's League for Woman Suffrage (Kimmel, 2011). While they weren't chaining themselves to fences for women's suffrage, the public support from these men was exceptional for the time.

Effects of the Sexual Revolution on Men

Over time male sex and gender roles have evolved, if not as dramatically or visibly as women's. Author James Doyle (1995) identified three developments that challenged traditional views of the male gender role: technological advances, distrust of established institutions, and the women's movement. As the industrial revolution changed our society from an agrarian basis to a technological, service-oriented one, men's role as providers (or "hunters," as they once were in hunter–gatherer cultures) diminished.

In the 1960s and 1970s social conflicts such as the Vietnam War, college campus antiwar protests, the beating of demonstrators at the 1968 Democratic National Convention in Chicago, and the killing of four students at Kent State University turned many against the government (Doyle, 1995). The 1960s saw a convergence of the civil rights movement, the women's movement, the antiwar movement, and the new left movement (Astrachan, 1986). When respect for the traditionally masculine role of soldier declined with America's increasing disillusionment with the military and the government, men experienced a significant shift in role. Along with the women's movement, this shift made it a confusing time to decide just what it meant to be a man. However, some believe that the process of reconsidering sex roles and opening up new avenues of communication between men and women was a very necessary, healthy development.

Men Raised Consciousness Too

We most often think of consciousness-raising as an activity of the women's liberation movement. However, the men's movement (actually more a trend than a movement per se) in the 1970s also involved consciousness-raising groups, most often focusing on individual growth. These groups "triggered changes in the lives of a few participants, but none excited people to the collective action that affected the whole society, as many women's gatherings did" (Astrachan, 1986, pp. 290–291). Up to the mid-1980s, most men actively participating in men's groups held a single guiding ideology: the elimination of the belief that one sex is superior to the other, or the eradication of sexism (Doyle, 1995). Men considered to be profeminist agreed generally with the feminist critique of patriarchy and organized themselves collectively to change men's behavior and attitudes (Mechling & Mechling, 1994). In 1975 the First National Conference on Men and Masculinity was held in Knoxville, Tennessee. Associations such as the National Organization for Men Against Sexism (NOMAS, originally called the National Organization for Changing Men) were founded during this time (Astrachan, 1986).

Profeminist men (many of whom simply call themselves feminists) are active today (Kimmel, 2011). The NOMAS group still holds conferences on men and masculinity today and publishes *Brother*, a newsletter focused on promoting and strengthening men's relationships with other men. Groups of profeminists may well be active on your campus. University profeminist men often organize Take Back the Night marches, which are programs that honor survivors of rape and sexual assault. Others present programs on sexual assault to fraternities, dorms, and athletic teams, while others teach and take courses on masculinity (Epstein, 2010).

Perhaps the most current national effort to focus on men and masculinity is The Good Men Project, founded by Tom Matlack and designed to encourage conversation about what exactly it means to be a "good man" today (Houghton, Bean, & Matlack, 2009). For more information on this organization, check out the website <goodmenproject.com> or the magazine the founders launched entitled *Good Men Magazine*. You'll find discussions of many issues confronting men today online and in the magazine, such as how men cope with pornography and the toll it can take on their relationships, sports topics, health issues, "measures" of masculinity in today's culture, and so forth.

Net Notes

For more information regarding masculinity studies and male studies programs on the collegiate level, see the following:
www.malestudies.org
www.men'sstudies.org

Fathers' Movements

Other movements of men, primarily active in the 1960s and 1970s, involve fathers' rights in divorce and child custody cases. In Colonial times fathers retained domestic control and defined and supervised their children's development; wives were expected to defer to their husbands (Furstenberg, 1988, as in Skolnick & Skolnick, 2008). Until the middle of the nineteenth century, if "marital disruption" occurred the father was typically awarded custody because fathers "were assumed to maintain control over marital property (of which the children were a part)" (Furstenberg, 1988, p. 224). During this time period women often died in childbirth, leaving their widowed husbands responsible for their children. The children were most often turned over to another woman in the family to raise. With the industrial revolution, public and private spheres became more separate—men worked in the outside world and women worked in the home attending to the needs of the children (Doyle, 1995).

By the end of the century women predominantly were awarded custody of their children because women were believed to possess superior parenting skills (Furstenberg, 1988). The courts subsequently adopted a "tender years presumption," meaning the view that during a child's younger years she or he needed a mother more than a father (Renzetti, Curran, & Maier, 2012). This view dramatically shifted custody decisions in favor of mothers and against fathers, a practice that still continues in today's courts. This trend has led some men around the country to challenge the courts for equal custody and parenting rights (Gross, 2006; Kimbrell, 1995). Support groups and activist organizations have formed over the years, such as Fathers United for Equal Rights, U.S. Divorce Reform, the Coalition Organized for Parental Equality (COPE), Divorced American Men Unite, the National Center for Men, and the Fathers' Rights Movement (Gandy, 2006).

There Are Some "Wild Men" Out There

Another social movement that emerged in the 1980s and 1990s is most often referred to simply as the men's movement, but its more elaborate name is the mythopoetic movement (Barton, 2000). The most noteworthy spokesperson for the mythopoetic movement was author and poet Robert Bly. Bly's 1990 best-selling book *Iron John* utilized mythology and Grimm's fairy tales to help men find the "community inside the psyche" (p. 227), meaning that men were encouraged to seek out different parts or roles within themselves.

Bly and other advocates of mythopoetics promoted men's self-discovery and masculinity through nature and tribal rituals. At retreats called "Wild Man Gatherings," men beat drums, tearfully hugged one another, danced in ritualistic circles, smeared one another's bodies with mud, and huddled around campfires howling (Kimbrell, 1995, p. 133; Natharius, 1992). One goal of such gatherings was to encourage men to explore the complicated relationships most had with their fathers, engaging the psychological and emotional wounds left over from childhood. In turn, the hope was that these men would become better fathers to their own children.

The Million Man March

On October 16, 1995, an estimated 400,000 men attended the Million Man March on the Federal Mall in Washington, D.C. (*USA Today*, 1996). Organized by the controversial head of the Nation of Islam, Louis Farrakhan, the march was to rally the Black community and strengthen Black families by

Net Notes

Many websites are designed to help fathers gain or retain custody rights of their children. Some sites are nothing more than mere commercials for attorneys, but a few organizations' websites have useful information. Check out:

www.just4dads.org
www.fathersrightsmovement.us
www.dadsrights.org (website for the organization formerly known as Fathers Rights & Equality Exchange)

> We are living at an important and fruitful moment now, for it is clear to men that the images of adult manhood given by the popular culture are worn out; a man can no longer depend on them. By the time a man is thirty-five he knows that the images of the right man, the tough man, the true man which he received in high school do not work in life.
>
> —Robert Bly, author

emphasizing the role of fathers. Farrakhan (1998) described the event as a "Holy Day of Atonement and Reconciliation"; he called for "one million disciplined, committed, and dedicated Black men, from all walks of life in America, to march in Washington, D.C." (p. 1). Similar marches among African American women and rallies for Black youth in Harlem occurred in the decade of the 1990s, with the goals of strengthening African Americans' self-esteem and pride and building community (Bekker, 1997).

Keeping Those Promises

The Promise Keepers, a movement based on fundamental Christian traditions and beliefs, was very influential, yet it lost a great deal of steam at the turn of the century. Bill McCartney, successful University of Colorado head football coach, and his friend Dave Wardell conceived of the organization in 1990 as they were driving to a Fellowship of Christian Athletes dinner (McCartney & Diles, 1995). The two men discussed the idea of filling a stadium with Christian men coming together for the purpose of Christian discipleship. Their idea came to fruition, and the first Promise Keepers conference was attended by over 4,000 men in July of 1991 (Kellner, 2000).

The mission of the Promise Keepers is "to ignite and unite men to become warriors who will change their world through living out the Seven Promises" (Promise Keepers, 2015). The promises these men make are intended to guide them toward Christ, transform them as people, and challenge them to assume active leadership roles within their own families (Dobson et al., 1994; Silverstein, Auerbach, Grieco, & Dunkel, 1999). While attendance at rallies has declined in recent years, the Promise Keepers organization is still alive and well, holding recent rallies with such themes as "Battle Lines." Conferences and rallies offer messages about reinforcing men's traditional roles in families and holding "battles lines" against divorce, cohabitation, and infringements on religious liberty (Promise Keepers, 2015).

Gender Communication: Looking Forward

Why have we included so much information on women's and men's movements in this prologue? Relevant historical events that shape gender communication are either skimmed over or not taught at most secondary school levels. Even in colleges and universities today, often only students enrolled in specialized courses in women's history are exposed to this important material.

It's critical to understand how our current state of gender communication came to be, to realize the historical context for why women and men relate to one another as they do. When you hear people discuss disparity in wages between the sexes or argue for fathers' rights, knowing some of the historical details that preceded the status quo facilitates more effective gender communication. When you embrace racial diversity, it's important to comprehend what people of color have historically encountered. When you participate in intimate relationships and grapple with reproductive issues, it completes your perspective to understand the history of birth control and controversies surrounding reproductive rights. When you hear a statistic cited that less than 40 percent of eligible voters in the United States actually vote these days, perhaps you'll wonder if suffragists are rolling over in their graves. When you study the theories and effective tools of gender communication we explore in this text, looking at the past will help you plan your future. After all, that "What will you do *now*?" question looms.

References

Andersen, M. L. (2014). *Thinking about women: Sociological perspectives on sex and gender* (10th ed.). Boston: Pearson.

Appignanesi, L., Holmes, R., & Orbach, S. (Eds.) (2013). *Fifty shades of feminism.* London: Virago Press.

Astrachan, A. (1986). *How men feel: Their response to women's demands for equality and power.* Garden City, NY: Anchor Press/Doubleday.

Ayoub, N. C. (2011, November 18). A life of controversy. *The Chronicle Review,* p. B15.

Baker, J. H. (2012). *Margaret Sanger: A life of passion.* New York: Hill and Wang.

Bandow, D. (2015, June 19). Put Harriet Tubman on America's currency. Retrieved from <http://www.thehuffingtonpost.com>.

Barton, E. R. (2000). *Mythopoetic perspectives of men's healing work: An anthology for therapists and others.* Santa Barbara, CA: Praeger/Greenwood Press.

Baumgardner, J., & Richards, A. (2010). *Manifesta: Young women, feminism, and the future* (Anv. Rev. ed.). New York: Farrar, Straus & Giroux.

Bekker, S. (1997, October 26). Sending a message of solidarity: Civil rights issues voiced at Million Woman March. *Corpus Christi Caller Times,* pp. A1, A14.

Bell, E (2010). Operationalizing feminism: Two challenges for feminist research. *Women and Language, 33,* 97–102.

Bernikow, L. (1997). *The American women's almanac: An inspiring and irreverent women's history.* New York: Berkley.

Bly, R. (1990). *Iron John: A book about men.* Reading, MA: Addison-Wesley.

Burroughs, G. (2015, Winter). ERA yes. *Ms.,* 34–37.

Carver, M. (1999, October). *Lucy Stone: Apostle for a "new woman."* Paper presented at the 22nd Conference of the Organization for the Study of Communication, Language, and Gender, Wichita, KS.

Cobble, D. S. (2014). More than sex equality: Feminism after suffrage. In D. S. Cobble, L. Gordon, & A. Henry (Eds.), *Feminism unfinished: A short, surprising history of American women's movements* (pp. 1–68). New York: Liveright/W. W. Norton.

Collins, G. (2010, May). The "f" word. *O: The Oprah Winfrey Magazine,* 228–229.

Colman, P. (1995). *Rosie the riveter.* New York: Crown.

Coontz, S. (2011). *A strange stirring:* The Feminine Mystique *and American women at the dawn of the 1960s.* New York: Basic Books.

Cuklanz, L. (1995). Shrill squawk or strategic innovation: A rhetorical reassessment of Margaret Sanger's *Woman Rebel. Communication Quarterly, 43,* 1–19.

Deakins, A. H. (2013). Betty Friedan and me. *Women & Language, 36,* 53–55.

Denfeld, R. (1995). *The new Victorians: A young woman's challenge to the old feminist order.* New York: Warner.

Dicker, R. C. (2008). *A history of U.S. feminisms.* Berkeley, CA: Seal Press.

Dicker, R., & Piepmeier, A. (2003). Introduction. In R. Dicker & A. Piepmeier (Eds.), *Catching a wave: Reclaiming feminism for the 21st century.* Boston: Northeastern University Press.

Dobson, J., Bright, B., Cole, E., Evans, T., McCartney, B., Palau, L., Phillips, R., & Smalley, G. (1994). *Seven promises of a Promise Keeper.* Colorado Springs: Focus on the Family.

Dow, B. J. (1996). *Prime-time feminism: Television, media culture, and the women's movement since 1970.* Philadelphia: University of Pennsylvania Press.

Doyle, J. (1995). *The male experience* (3rd ed.). Madison, WI: Brown & Benchmark.

Emerling Bone, J. (2010). When publics collide: Margaret Sanger's argument for birth control and the rhetorical breakdown of barriers. *Women's Studies in Communication, 33,* 16–33.

Epstein, J. (2010, April 8). Male studies vs. men's studies. Retrieved June 27, 2010, from <http://www.insidehighered.com>.

Farrakhan, L. (1998, November 16). Second opinion. *Minister Louis Farrakhan on the Million Man March.* Retrieved from <http://users.aol.com/camikem/eyeview/millionman.html>.

Feminist Majority. (2015). Retrieved June 21, 2015, from <http://www.feministmajority.org>.

Fitch, S. P., & Mandziuk, R. M. (1997). *Sojourner Truth as orator: Wit, story, and song.* Santa Barbara, CA: Greenwood.

Fixmer, N., & Wood, J. T. (2005). The personal is *still* political: Embodied politics in third wave feminism. *Women's Studies in Communication, 28,* 235–257.

Friedan, B. (1963). *The feminine mystique.* New York: Laurel.

Fudge, R. (2006). Everything you always wanted to know about feminism but were afraid to ask. *Bitch, 31,* 58–67.

Furstenberg, F. F., Jr. (1988). Good dad—bad dads: Two faces of fatherhood. In A. Cherlin (Ed.), *The changing American family.* New York: Urban Institute Press.

Gandy, K. (2006, Summer). Viewpoint: Father's rights . . . and wrongs. *National NOW Times,* p. 4.

Gordon, L. (2014). The women's liberation movement. In D. S. Cobble, L. Gordon, & A. Henry (Eds.), *Feminism unfinished: A short, surprising history of American women's movements* (pp. 69–146). New York: Liveright/W. W. Norton.

Greenspan, K. (1994). *The timetables of women's history: A chronology of the most important people and events in women's history.* New York: Simon & Schuster.

Gross, J. (2006). *Fathers' rights: The best interest of your child includes you.* Phoenix: Sphinx Publishing.

Hardman, M. J. (2013). On the 50th anniversary of the publication of *The Feminine Mystique* by Betty Friedan. *Women & Language, 36,* 57–61.

Henry, A. (2014). From a mindset to a movement: Feminism since 1990. In D. S. Cobble, L. Gordon, & A. Henry (Eds.), *Feminism unfinished: A short, surprising history of American women's movements* (pp. 147–226). New York: Liveright/W. W. Norton.

Heywood, L., & Drake, J. (1997). *Third wave agenda: Being feminist, doing feminism.* Minneapolis: University of Minnesota Press.

Hoff Sommers, C. (1994). *Who stole feminism? How women have betrayed women.* New York: Simon & Schuster.

Hogeland, L. M. (2001). Against generational thinking, or, some things that "third wave" feminism isn't. *Women's Studies in Communication, 24,* 107–121.

hooks, b. (2000). *Feminism is for everybody: Passionate politics.* Cambridge, MA: South End Press.

Houghton, J., Bean, L., & Matlack, T. (2009). *The Good Men Project: Real stories from the front lines of modern manhood.* Boston: The Good Men Foundation.

Humm, M. (Ed.). (1992). *Modern feminisms: Political, literary, cultural.* New York: Columbia University Press.

Hunter College Women's Studies Collective. (2005). *Women's realities, women's choices: An introduction to women's studies.* New York: Oxford University Press.

Kellner, M. A. (2000). Keeping their promises. *Christianity Today, 44,* 21.

Kerber, L., De Hart, J., & Dayton, C. H. (2010). *Women's America: Refocusing the past* (7th ed.). New York: Oxford University Press.

Kimbrell, A. (1995). *The masculine mystique: The politics of masculinity.* New York: Ballantine.

Kimmel, M. S. (2011). *Manhood in America: A cultural history* (3rd ed.). New York: Oxford University Press.

Kotz, D. (2010, May 7). Birth control pill turns 50: 7 ways it changed lives. Retrieved May 7, 2010, from <http://www.usnews.com>.

Krolokke, C., & Sorensen, A. S. (2006). *Gender communication theory and analyses: From silence to performance.* Thousand Oaks, CA: Sage.

Lorber, J. (2011). *Gender inequality: Feminist theories and politics* (5th ed.). New York: Oxford University Press.

Lotz, A. D. (2007). Theorising the intermezzo: The contributions of postfeminism and third wave feminism. In S. Gillis, G. Howie, & R. Munford (Eds.), *Third wave feminism: A critical exploration* (pp. 71–85). New York: Palgrave/Macmillan.

Lunardini, C. (1994). *What every American should know about women's history.* Holbrook, MA: Bob Adams.

McCartney, B., & Diles, D. (1995). *From ashes to glory.* Nashville: Thomas Nelson.

McKay, J., Hill, B., & Buckler, J. (2005). *A history of Western society, volume II: From absolutism to the present* (8th ed.). Boston: Bedford/St. Martin's.

McRobbie, A. (2009). *The aftermath of feminism: Gender, culture and social change.* Los Angeles: Sage.

Mechling, E., & Mechling, J. (1994). The Jung and the restless: The mythopoetic men's movement. *Southern Communication Journal, 59,* 97–111.

Miller, J. (2013, March 3). Suffrage march to be saluted. *Corpus Christi Caller Times,* p. 5A.

Ms. Foundation for Women. (2015). Retrieved June 26, 2015, from <http://www.ms.foundation.org>.

Natharius, D. (1992, October). *From the hazards of being male to fire in the belly: Are men finally getting it and, if so, what are they getting?* Paper presented at the meeting of the Speech Communication Association, Chicago, IL.

National Organization for Women (NOW). (2015). Retrieved June 21, 2015, from <http://www.now.org>.

Neft, N., & Levine, A. (1997). *Where women stand: An international report on the status of women in 140 countries, 1997–1998.* New York: Random House.

Neuwirth, J. (2015). *Equal means equal: Why the time for an Equal Rights Amendment is now.* New York: The New Press.

Northrup, C. (2010). The pill turns 50: Taking stock. Retrieved May 8, 2010, from <http://www.thehuffingtonpost.com>.

Ortega Murphy, B. (2013). Reflections on *The Feminine Mystique. Women & Language, 36,* 63–65.

Pogrebin, A. (2011, November 7). How do you spell Ms.? *New York,* 34–41, 104–105.

Promise Keepers. (2015). Retrieved June 21, 2015, from <http://www.promisekeepers.org>.

Renzetti, C. M., Curran, D. J., & Maier, S. L. (2012). *Women, men and society* (6th ed.). Boston: Pearson.

Roiphe, K. (1993). *The morning after: Sex, fear, and feminism on campus.* Boston: Little, Brown.

Ruth, S. (2001). *Issues in feminism: An introduction to women's studies* (5th ed.). Mountain View, CA: Mayfield.

Shugart, H. A. (2001). Isn't it ironic? The intersection of third-wave feminism and generation X. *Women's Studies in Communication, 24,* 131–168.

Shugart, H. A., Waggoner, C. E., & Hallstein, D. L. O. (2001). Mediating third-wave feminism: Appropriation as postmodern media practice. *Critical Studies in Media Communication, 18,* 194–210.

Siegel, D. (2007). *Sisterhood interrupted: From radical women to grrls gone wild.* New York: Palgrave/Macmillan.

Silverstein, L. B., Auerbach, C. F., Grieco, L., & Dunkel, F. (1999). Do Promise Keepers dream of feminist sheep? *Sex Roles, 40,* 665–688.

Skolnick, A. S., & Skolnick, J. H. (2013). *Family in transition* (17th ed.). Boston: Pearson.

Taylor, A. (2013). Putting *The Feminine Mystique* in context. *Women & Language, 36,* 71–76.

Theriot, N. (1996). *Mothers and daughters in nineteenth-century America: The biosocial construction of femininity.* Lexington: University of Kentucky Press.

Thom, M. (1997). *Inside Ms.: 25 years of the magazine and the feminist movement.* New York: Henry Holt.

Tobias, S. (1997). *Faces of feminism: An activist's reflections on the women's movement.* Boulder, CO: Westview.

Tone, A. (2010). Birth control pill turns 50 on Mother's Day. Retrieved May 12, 2010, from <http://www.examiner.com>.

Turner, L. H. (2013). *The Feminine Mystique* and me: 50 years of intersections. *Women & Language, 36,* 67–69.

Tyler May, E. (2010a, May 7). 50 years on the pill. *The Chronicle Review,* pp. B4–B5.

Tyler May, E. (2010b, Spring). The pill turns 50. *Ms.,* 40.

USA Today. (1996, February 16). Washington's great gatherings. *USA Today.* [Electronic version]. Retrieved from <http://www.usatoday.com>.

Valenti, J. (2007). *Full frontal feminism: A young woman's guide to why feminism matters.* Berkeley, CA: Seal Press.

Ventura, V. (1998). *Sheroes: Bold, brash, and absolutely unabashed superwomen.* Berkeley, CA: Conari.

Weatherford, D. (1994). *American women's history: An A to Z of people, organizations, issues, and events.* New York: Prentice Hall.

Whelehan, I. (2007). Foreword. In S. Gillis, G. Howie, & R. Munford (Eds.), *Third wave feminism: A critical exploration* (pp. xv–xx). New York: Palgrave/Macmillan.

Woodhull, W. (2007). Global feminisms, transnational political economies, third world cultural production. In S. Gillis, G. Howie, & R. Munford (Eds.), *Third wave feminism: A critical exploration* (pp. 156–167). New York: Palgrave/Macmillan.

ABOUT THE AUTHOR

Diana K. Ivy, Ph.D., Professor of Communication at Texas A&M University-Corpus Christi, has been teaching communication at the college level for 30 years, including undergraduate and graduate courses in gender, nonverbal, interpersonal, and instructional communication. She has co-authored two other textbooks, *Communication: Principles for a Lifetime* and *Nonverbal Communication for a Lifetime*, both in multiple editions, and has published articles in *Communication Education*, *Southern Communication Journal*, and *Women & Language*. She was Speaker of the Faculty Senate and Director of the Women's Center at her university, has held multiple offices in the National Communication Association, and was named Outstanding Gender Scholar of the Year by the Southern States Communication Association. She was a guest contributor to *Cosmopolitan* magazine, hosted a call-in talk radio show, "Call Me Ivy," and completed post-doctoral coursework at Oxford University, studying C. S. Lewis and communication.

Part One

COMMUNICATION AND GENDER: THE BASICS

CHAPTER I

TALKING THE TALK AND WALKING THE WALK
Becoming a Better Gender Communicator

WHAT IS GENDER COMMUNICATION?

Societal issues continue to perplex women and men, whether they involve situations of professional communication between coworkers, confusion over interpersonal signals, competing messages of homemaker versus careerism, or verbal exchanges that result in violence. One thing is for certain: Communication between women and men is a popular topic of conversation, study, and research—more now than ever, it seems. But is this popular topic all there is to the term gender communication? What all is encompassed by the term? Just what is this topic you're going to read about and study?

First you need to understand that we're putting the words *gender* and *communication* together to form a modern label for an ancient phenomenon. Gender communication is a unique, fascinating subset of a larger phenomenon known as communication. From our perspective, not all communication is gender communication.

Here's a simple way to understand this perspective of gender communication: **Gender communication is communication *about* and *between* men and women.** The first part of the statement—the "about" aspect—involves how the sexes are discussed, referred to, or depicted, both verbally and nonverbally. The second part of the sentence—the "between" aspect—is the interpersonal dimension of gender communication, and it's a bit harder to understand.

HOT TOPICS

- What gender communication is and why you're studying it
- Meanings for such terms as *sex, gender, identity, androgyny, sexual orientation, heterosexism, homophobia, intersex, transgender,* and *transphobia*
- What feminism and sexism mean today
- How to communicate from a receiver orientation

We believe that communication becomes *gendered* when sex or gender overtly begins to influence your choices—choices of what you say and how you relate to others. For example, two students could be talking about a project for class. The students could be both male, both female, or of opposite sexes. The sex composition of the communicators doesn't matter in a judgment of whether gender communication is going on. Thus far, the conversation about the class project doesn't necessarily involve gender communication. But what happens if the conversation topic shifts to a discussion of political issues especially relevant to women, opinions regarding parenting responsibilities, or who the interactants are dating? For these topics, the awareness of one's own sex, the other person's sex, or both may come into play; thus gender communication is occurring. Notice that we said "may come into play," because the topic doesn't always dictate whether gender communication is occurring. When sex or gender becomes an overt factor in your communication, when you become conscious of your own or another person's sex or gender, then gender communication is operating.

However, some scholars believe that gender is an all-encompassing designation, that it is so pervasive a characteristic of a person that communication cannot escape the effects of gender. In this view, all communication is gendered (Spender, 1985; Thorne, Kramarae, & Henley, 1983; Wilson Schaef, 1981). These viewpoints—our more restricted approach to gender communication and the more pervasive perspective—aren't necessarily contradictory, meaning that you can study gender communication and operate from both perspectives.

WHY STUDY GENDER COMMUNICATION?

Gender communication is . . .

🍁 *Provocative:* Gender communication is **provocative** because we're all interested in how we're perceived, how we communicate with others, and how others respond to us. We're also interested in the potential rewards that may result from effective gender communication.

🍁 *Popularized:* Gender communication is a hot topic in our culture, evidenced by the many viral videos, books, TV shows, websites, posts, films, and songs devoted to the topic. You're likely to be highly aware of pop culture's treatment of gender, so we offer a balance by reviewing research findings on the subject.

Pervasive: Gender communication is **pervasive,** meaning that interaction with women and men occurs 24/7. The sheer number of contacts we have heightens interest in the effects of sex and gender on communication. When those contacts affect us in profound ways, such as in social or work relationships, we realize the need for improved understanding of gender communication.

Problematic: Saying that gender communication is **problematic** doesn't mean that all gender communication centers around problems, but that it's complicated. In 2014, when Facebook amassed over 50 terms as "gender options," it was easy to realize added layers of complexity when it comes to sex, sexuality, gender, and relationships. Communication itself is also complex; it's not a simple process that can be accomplished just because we're human beings who learned language at some early age or because we've been talking all our lives.

Unpredictable: Gender communication is **unpredictable** in that societal norms, rules, and roles have changed dramatically and continue to change. Lessons learned while growing up come into conflict with changes in society, leaving confusion about appropriate behavior. Most gender communication courses and books, like this one, tend to change your worldview. Twenty years ago, students in gender communication classes talked about changes in heterosexual dating etiquette. Now, students are working to change their pronouns when they meet (or become) a transgender person (which is far more likely than it was even a few years ago).

Here's where we come in—your textbook author and your instructor. We not only summarize research-based and popularized information in this text and this course you're taking, but also provide practical suggestions about how to apply the knowledge to your life's experiences. We want you to not only *know* the information, but also be able to *use* the information to improve your communication skills and enhance your relationships.

GENDER JARGON

Many gender-related terms are assigned different meanings, primarily by the media. Your own experience also may give you meanings that differ from textbook terminology. So to reduce the potential for confusion, here we offer you some common gender communication terms and their most commonly used meanings. Becoming more skilled in your communication with men and women begins with the use of current, sensitive, accurate language.

Rethinking Sex and Gender

When you get to Chapter 3 on language, get ready for all those Facebook terms; for now, let's try to simplify the situation and focus on the primary terms that affect our study of gender communication. You've probably already heard the terms *sex* and *gender* used interchangeably. For the sake of clarity and accuracy, we use them in this text with exclusive meanings.

The term *sex* has traditionally meant the anatomical/biological characteristics that make us female or male (Muehlenhard & Peterson, 2011). (At some points in this text the term *sex* is used to refer to sexual activity among men and women, but it will be clear to you whether the term is meant as a categorization of persons or an activity.) In most cases, sex is binary, meaning two choices. However, you may have heard or read about people who are born with both or mixed sets of genitalia and hormonal systems, causing complexity in determining biological sex. The term used in the past for this form of biological sex was *hermaphroditism*, but the contemporary term is *intersex* (Davis & Murphy, 2013; Dreger, 2000; Feder, 2014; Preves, 2003). The Intersex Society of North America's (ISNA) goal is to bring intersex gender identity out of the shadows and into the light. Through greater awareness, parents, physicians, and intersex individuals will have more choices, rather than being forced into surgeries to align them with traditional standards of biological sex. This association and research will no doubt continue to provide insight into intersex, expanding our thinking from the traditional sex binary.

I can't stand people that can't stand one of the sexes. We've only got two. Why would you dislike one of them?—Drew Barrymore, actor

The term used most often in this text (even in the title) is *gender*. Most narrowly, gender refers to psychological and emotional characteristics of individuals. You may understand these characteristics to be masculine, feminine, or androgynous (a combination of both feminine and masculine traits). But gender encompasses more than this. According to gender scholars Perry and Ballard-Reisch (2004), gender refers to "how one is socialized to behave in relation to one's sex" (p. 18). Defined broadly, the term *gender* not only includes personality traits, but also involves psychological makeup; attitudes, beliefs, and values; sexual orientation; and gender identity (defined later).

Gender is socially and culturally constructed; it's much more extensive than the fact of being born anatomically female, male, or intersex (Andersen & Hysock, 2010; LaFrance, Paluck, & Brescoll, 2004; Marecek, Crawford, & Popp, 2004; Sloop, 2012). What is *attached* or *related* to your anatomy is taught to you through your culture, virtually from the time you are born. Culture, with its evolving customs, rules, and expectations for behavior, has the power to affect your perception of gender. For example, if you were raised in the Middle East, your views regarding the status and role of women in society would be quite different than if you were raised in the United States. When you encounter members of other cultures (or your own culture, for that matter) who do not adhere to clearly drawn gender lines or who operate from expectations different than your own, the notable difference may reinforce your original conception of gender or cause it to change.

Viewing gender as culturally constructed allows one to change or reconstruct gender. This is a powerful idea. For example, if you view sex and gender as only "male, masculine" or "female, feminine," that's not the way you *have* to see it. You can learn to see combinations of sex and gender differently and more broadly if you discover new information. This is discussed more thoroughly in Chapter 2; but for now, consider these examples: What if a guy discovers that "being a man" doesn't mean that he has to be strong and emotionally nonexpressive? He might decide that he's tired of this approach and that he'd rather express his emotions without fear of ridicule instead. A woman might realize that her ability to climb the ladder of professional success is stronger than her nurturing instinct, so she chooses a career over motherhood as her primary life's work. Might these discoveries alter one's vision of gender? Possibly, but these people don't merely replace one stereotypical trait with another; they expand their options and find new ways of seeing themselves in relation to others. That's one of the goals of this text—to give you different ways of seeing things, including gender.

Biological sex suggests several things about how people communicate and are communicated with, but biology isn't destiny, and that's the powerful potential of studying gender communication. A person's sex may not be easily changed, but a person's conception of gender is far more open to change and development.

GENDER IDENTITY, ANDROGYNY, AND SEXUAL ORIENTATION

<table>
<tr><td>

Remember...

Gender Communication:
Communication about
and between women and men

Sex: Biological designation of being
female or male

Intersex: Having anatomy, genitalia,
and hormonal systems reflective
of both biologically male and
female people

Gender: Cultural construction
that includes biological sex,
psychological characteristics,
attitudes about the sexes, and
sexual orientation

</td></tr>
</table>

In this text, we use the term *gender identity* as a subset of gender to refer to the way you view yourself—how you see yourself relative to stereotypically feminine or masculine traits. As gender scholars Andersen and Hysock (2010) explain it, "gender identity is an individual's specific definition of self, based on that person's understanding of what it means to be a man or a woman" (p. 2).

Many people are more comfortable viewing themselves as androgynous, meaning that they possess and blend traits typically associated with femininity and masculinity. *Androgyny* is a term made popular by gender scholar Sandra Bem (1974); the term is derived from the Greek *andros*, meaning man, and *gyne*, meaning woman. Androgynous women aren't necessarily masculine or sexless; likewise, androgynous men aren't necessarily effeminate, gay, or asexual. This form of gender identity simply involves a blending of sex-associated traits, rather than an adherence only to those traits associated with femininity or masculinity (Lippa, 2005).

Another component of gender is your general perception of appropriate roles for women and men in the society of which you are a member. Your gender identity thus encompasses not only your vision of self, but also your vision of the roles or functions for human beings within a given culture. While your gender identity is affected by your sex and your gender, it is within your control to change this identity. But what about a remaining element within the broad-based view of gender—an element that, in the view of many, you have no control over?

The term *sexual preference* is outdated. The word *preference* implies that people *choose* or make conscious decisions about their sexuality. The prevailing view is that one's *sexual orientation*, that is, to whom one is sexually attracted or with whom one has sexual relations, is a characteristic of a person, not a person's choice (Perry & Ballard-Reisch, 2004). Many people contend that they were born with their sexuality, not shaped into it by life experiences or societal factors. Whatever your view of choice or no choice, being inclusive, sensitive, and contemporary in language usage requires referring to a person's sexuality as an orientation, not a preference.

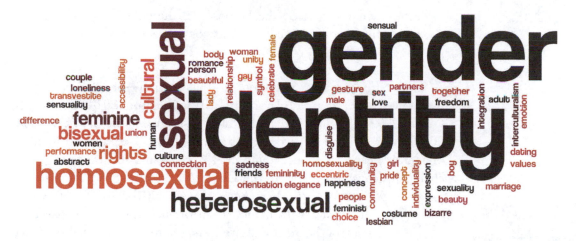

Many components make up your gender identity.

Discriminatory attitudes and behavior that communicate the belief that heterosexuality is superior to other forms of sexuality are termed *heterosexist* (Griffin, 1998). Often this form of discrimination manifests itself by omission, rather than by commission—it's not what you say, it's the assumption you communicate by what you leave out or don't say. Even in an age of increasing awareness of and openness to various sexualities, it's still common to hear students (and others) talk as though the world were only or primarily heterosexual. Students occasionally start presentations with something like this: "For the men in the room, aren't you tired of your girlfriend complaining about....?" or "Ladies, we all know the importance of looking good for your man...." Such openers assume heterosexuality in a world where sex and gender diversity are increasingly probable, recognized, and celebrated. Perhaps you attend college in a setting where such heterosexist language would never even be considered appropriate usage, but many students haven't changed their language to match the complexity of their world.

Some confusion surrounds the term *homophobia* (Kantor, 2009). We have found three usages of this term:

1. Homophobia can refer to a general fear of people who are homosexual in sexual orientation.
2. The term may also describe the fear of being labeled a homosexual.
3. Within homosexual communities, homophobia may be used to mean behavior or attitudes that indicate a self-hatred or severe loss of self-

esteem. In these cases, the homosexual individual, out of anger or hatred for her or his orientation, acts or thinks in ways that direct this anger onto the self.

A final term warrants attention in this section—people identifying themselves as *transgender* (Cavalcante, 2013; Garrison, 2014; Girshick & Green, 2009; Herman, 2009; McGrath, 2014; Valentine, 2007; Wilson, 2011). More and more is being written and discussed about this form of identity, especially since multiple TV programs feature transgender characters, most notably Laverne Cox's character of Sophia Burset on *Orange Is the New Black* (Maerz, 2014, 2015). If you're unfamiliar with or not a fan of such shows, you may have read or heard about well-known media personality Bruce Jenner's transition into Caitlyn Jenner, who is documenting her gender reassignment process on the TV show *I Am Cait* (Havrilesky, 2015; Rice, 2015a, 2015b, 2015c).

Gender scholar Carla Golden (2009) suggests: "'Trans' means *across* or *beyond*, and thus transgender means that which moves across or beyond gender (as it is defined by the culture). As applied to people, it refers to someone who moves across or beyond gender boundaries" (p. 22). In the introduction to his book on transgender identity and communication, Leland Spencer (2015) cites Susan Stryker's (2008) widely-reported definition of transgenderism, taken from her book *Transgender History*: Transgenders are "people who move away from the gender they were assigned at birth, people who cross over (trans-) the boundaries constructed by their culture to define and contain gender" (p. xi). Transgender people strive to challenge the patriarchal, traditional idea of gender, in essence, taking the gender-as-constructed notion to its fullest. While some transgender people have medical treatments and surgery so that they can more fully transition to a different identity, others opt to live outwardly as a member of a distinct sex and gender but not undergo medical procedures for a biological transformation. Still others choose to keep this form of gender identity private. Resistance to transgenderism or antagonism toward transgender persons is termed *transphobia* (Silman, 2015).

Remember...

Gender Identity: View of the self relative to feminine or masculine traits, as well as one's vision of the roles or functions for people within a given culture

Androgyny: Blending of masculine and feminine personality traits

Sexual Orientation: To whom one is sexually attracted or with whom one has sexual relations

Heterosexism: Discriminatory attitudes and behavior that communicate the belief that heterosexuality is superior to homosexuality or bisexuality

Homophobia: General fear of homosexual persons, a fear of being labeled a homosexual, and/or a homosexual's behavior or attitudes that indicate self-hatred or severe loss of self-esteem

Transgender: Unique gender identity not confined by traditional notions of masculinity or femininity

Transphobia: Fear of or antagonism toward transgender people

"Too Much Gender Diversity?"

Ah, the good old days when men were men and women were women, and you knew the difference. But were those days really that good? While some yearn for simpler times, when navigating the gender and relationship waters was less complicated, many people felt forced to suffer in silence, keeping their inner identities hidden from the rest of the world. We hope you'll fight the urge to long for sex and gender issues to be less complicated, opting instead for a reality of gender diversity being better understood and celebrated. We like the way philosophy professor and author Stephen Asma (2015) expressed it: "Instead of arguing that nothing is normal and we're just making it all up, we should learn how to celebrate diversity and uniqueness for what it is. People who do not fit into traditional gender or sex categories should be able to say, I'm different, and different is great. There are ordinary sex categories, but we should celebrate the extra-ordinary. In that way, we don't have to dismiss reality just to make sure people are treated with respect" (p. B9).

Feminism and Sexism

When you first saw the term *feminism* in the title of this section, what thoughts or images came to mind? In the prologue to this book, we overviewed feminism from its historical perspective, starting with the first wave (suffrage), then the second wave (beginning with the women's liberation movement), and the more recent third wave of feminism. For our purposes in this chapter, it's illuminating to find out what people, especially college students, know and think about feminism these days.

© Helga Esteb/Shutterstock.com

I didn't mean to become a beacon for feminism, but I'm really embracing it. I'm an unflinching feminist, so it makes sense for me. It's the cause I'm most interested in helping.
—Amy Schumer, comedian and actor

When students are asked, "Do you believe that women and men should receive equal opportunities and treatment in all facets of life?" most reply with a confident, hearty affirmative. When asked, "Are you a feminist?" the response is much more convoluted, with the most prevalent response being, "Well, no, I wouldn't call myself a feminist." Research suggests that, although people may believe in equality, which is the basic tenet of feminism, many don't consider themselves feminists and don't

want to be called such (Busis, 2014; Collins, 2010; Dahl Crossley, 2010; Martin & Sullivan, 2010; Olson et al., 2008).

Why does feminism conjure up visions, among men *and* women, of angry, radical, bra-burning, man-hating, humorless, masculine women storming out of the National Organization for Women (NOW) headquarters to try to gain superiority over men? These negative connotations in large part come from selective images the media transmitted (and continues to transmit) to the mass audience (hooks, 2000; Valenti, 2007). For example, did you know that there are no documented accounts of actual bra-burning episodes among "women's libbers" in the late 1960s? Only one incident was remotely connected—a protest of the 1968 Miss America pageant in which protesters threw their bras into a trash can! Yet the bra-burning image of feminists persists.

I'm definitely a feminist. I've never understood the negative connotation of being a feminist or why anyone would be afraid of it. I frankly don't know why anyone would not be for the equality of other people in any shape or form. I think it's a great word.
—Shonda Rhimes, TV writer and showrunner

One of the strongest feminist voices of our time is bell hooks; in her book *Feminism Is for Everybody* (2000), hooks describes another attempt in history to discredit or marginalize the feminist movement: "Embedded in the portrayal of feminists as man-hating was the assumption that all feminists were lesbians. Appealing to homophobia, mass media intensified anti-feminist sentiment among men" (p. 68). We still see evidence of this today, when students reveal that they associate feminism with lesbianism, assuming that all feminists are homosexual and, in turn, man-hating. Let's clear up the confusion: First, not all feminists are female; second, not all female feminists are lesbians; and finally, we don't know any lesbian feminists who hate men.

"Don't Call Me a Feminist!"

We realize that some of you reading this material are likely to get a negative mental image when you hear reference made to "feminism." Yet in our experience with college students, once they understand the basic tenets of the feminist movement, they find themselves in agreement with it. Is there a better term, one that is less divisive or negative? One that would rally people around the issues rather than turn them off?

In the most basic sense, a feminist is a person—of any sex or gender—who believes in equality, especially sex and gender equality. hooks (2000) calls for people to "come closer to feminism," citing her favorite definition of the term: "Feminism is a movement to end sexism, sexist exploitation, and oppression" (p. 1). The authors of *Manifesta: Young Women, Feminism, and the Future*, Baumgardner and Richards (2010), describe feminism as being "the movement for social, political, and economic equality of men and women. Feminism means that women have the right to enough information to make informed choices about their lives" (p. 56).

Discriminatory practices or attitudes are referred to as *sexist*, typically pertaining to the treatment of women. But the term *sexism* simply means the denigration of one sex and the exaltation of another or, stated another way, the valuing of one sex over another. Thus, sexism does not refer exclusively to devaluing women, just as racism does not refer exclusively to the denigration of one specific race in preference for another. Given this definition of sexism, there can be no such thing as "reverse sexism," even though some have used this term in specific reference to the discriminatory treatment of men.

Perhaps you believe that our society isn't male dominated or that sexism is okay because "that's just the way it is." Maybe you feel that no opportunities have been denied any sex or that no sex has endured particular suffering during your lifetime. But stop and think for a moment, not only on a personal level but also on a global one. Which sex is still the most underrepresented as decision makers, such as political leaders and judges, and among highly paid corporate executives? For the first time in American history, women make up half the workforce, yet they still earn, on average, 78 cents to the man's dollar (American Association of University Women, 2015; U.S. Bureau of Labor Statistics, 2015; U.S. Census Bureau, 2010). Conversely, which parent is most often denied child custody in divorce proceedings, simply because of that parent's sex? Perhaps you haven't yet seen any overt instances of sex discrimination in your personal life. But what about missed

Remember...

Feminism: Movement or philosophy based on a belief in sex and gender equality

Sexism: Denigration of one sex and the exaltation of another; valuing one sex over another

© Andrea Raffin/Shutterstock.com

There seems to be a very recent thing that you come "out" as a feminist. It's a very weird thing. I'm a feminist in as much as I'm an egalitarian about everything and I believe in meritocracy. I think anyone who isn't at this point is just swimming against the tide, just like people who are vaguely homophobic or racist or sexist or whatever it is. I just think "God, you're still keeping that up? Give it up, you've lost."
—Daniel Radcliffe, actor

opportunities—jobs, benefits and rewards, or relationships that didn't come your way merely because someone held a limited view of which sex is best suited for a certain circumstance?

Today, individuals have many options when it comes to gender communication and behavior. This relatively recent development stems from changing roles, a wider, more tolerant view of what is considered appropriate behavior, and increased opportunities for everyone. Many of the changes in societal expectations, opportunities, and relational patterns resulted (and continue to result) from the work of feminists and their supporters.

COMMUNICATION: A COMPLEX HUMAN PROCESS

Communication is a word you hear a lot, especially since technology has become so sophisticated that we can easily and quickly interact around the world. As the channels for communicating have expanded, so have the meanings of the term *communication*. In fact, two communication theorists back in the 1970s isolated 126 definitions of communication (Dance & Larson, 1976). For our purposes, here's a fairly basic perspective of communication.

Human communication isn't static; it's an ongoing and dynamic process of sending and receiving messages for the purpose of sharing meaning. To accomplish this purpose, people use both *verbal* and *nonverbal* communication (including body movement, physical appearance, facial expression, touch, and tone of voice). Communication flows back and forth simultaneously, both verbally and nonverbally, between *sender* and *receiver* (Beebe, Beebe, & Ivy, 2016).

Becoming Receiver Oriented in Your Communication

While the roles of sender and receiver in the communication process are both important, we believe the receiver 's interpretation of the sender 's message makes the difference between shared meaning and misunderstanding. Thus, the approach we advocate is termed the *receiver orientation to communication*. What the sender *intends* to convey is important, but it's less important than what the receiver *thinks is being conveyed*, or how the receiver interprets the message. You may clearly understand your intentions in what you say, but a listener may

Human communication is a dynamic process, using verbal and nonverbal messages to share meaning.

take your message in a different way than you originally intended. The result of not taking a receiver orientation can sound like this: "What do you MEAN, I'm late in calling you?! I said I'd call you AROUND five o'clock. Six-thirty IS around five o'clock!" In an instance like this, obviously the sender intended something different than the receiver 's interpretation. Taking a receiver orientation—stopping to think about how your message will be understood by a listener *before* you say it—can greatly enhance your skill as a communicator.

When one is misunderstood, a typical response is to think that the receiver is at fault for not understanding the message. This reaction becomes particularly relevant to gender communication when you consider how often women report that they don't understand men because they don't react like women. And men get frustrated with women when they don't communicate or interpret communication like men. Here's our proposition to you:

> **If people would spend more time figuring out how a listener will best hear, accept, understand, and retain a message and less time figuring out how they want to say something to please themselves, then their communication with others would vastly improve.**

This sounds like the "golden rule of communication," doesn't it? Do you currently communicate from this perspective, even though you didn't know what to call it? Think of it this way: If you talk, but no one is there to listen or receive what you say, has communication occurred? Some will say yes; at the very least the sender has communicated with the self. But others will argue that without a listener, communication does not occur, making the receiver the most necessary link for the communication process to work. Again, this is part of the receiver orientation to communication.

If communication breaks down (as it seems to regularly), whose fault is it? Rarely are breakdowns solely the sender's fault. Sometimes the best forethought, insight, experience, and skill applied to a situation still lead to misunderstanding on the part of a receiver. But, in a receiver-oriented view of communication, the sender is responsible for communicating in a manner that will be most easily understood by the receiver; the receiver's responsibility is to attempt to understand the intent of the sender. Communication researchers Beebe, Beebe, and Ivy (2016) frame the receiver orientation as a skill of adaptation, a critical skill to develop as an effective communicator. They explain, "When you adapt a message, you make choices about how best to formulate both your message content and delivery, and how to respond to someone, in order to achieve your communication goals. Adapting involves appropriately editing and shaping your responses so that others accurately understand your messages and so that you achieve your goal without coercing or using false information or other unethical methods" (p. 23).

© pixelheadphoto/Shutterstock.com

Considering in advance how a receiver will interpret your message will go a long way toward improving your skills as a communicator. This stance is especially critical for gender communication, which is highly complex. It's advisable in every situation to focus on the receiver of your message *before, during,* and *after* you communicate.

How can you effectively focus on the receiver of your message?

CONCLUSION

In this opening chapter, we offered a definition of gender communication and described it as provocative, popularized, pervasive, problematic, and unpredictable. We introduced the increasingly complex world of sex and gender to you, in the hope that you could expand your thinking on the subject to reflect the changing times. We provided contemporary explanations of key terms so that you would more fully understand the gender jargon used in the remainder of this textbook. Finally, we defined communication and explored the communication process from a receiver orientation.

DISCUSSION STARTERS

1. Think about how roles have changed for men and women in our society. What kinds of roles did your parents model for you when you were growing up? What kinds of attitudes have you developed about appropriate roles for women and men in our society? Will you assume different roles than your same-sex parent as you continue to mature?

2. What comes to mind when you hear the term *feminism?* Do you consider yourself a feminist? Why or why not?

3. Think of something you consider to be really sexist. It could be a policy or practice, or something that you saw, read, or heard. What was your reaction to this sexist stimulus at the time? What's your reaction now? If your reactions are different, why are they different?

4. Recall a situation in which your interpretation of a message (as the receiver) didn't match a person's intentions (as the sender). It could be something simple such as a miscommunication over the time or place where you were supposed to meet someone, or it could be something more serious, such as misunderstanding an instructor's explanation of an upcoming assignment. Analyze that situation: Who was involved in the conversation? What do you think the sender of the message intended to communicate? How did you, as the receiver, interpret the message? What was said or done during the conversation that was the primary cause of misunderstanding? How was the situation resolved? Using a receiver orientation to communication, what could the sender in the conversation have done to make the situation better? How could you, as the receiver, have reduced the potential for misunderstanding?

References

American Association of University Women. (2015, Spring). *A simple truth about the gender pay gap.* Retrieved June 26, 2015, from <www.aauw.org>.

Andersen, M. L., & Hysock, D. (2010). The social construction of gender. In B. Hutchinson (Ed.), *Annual editions: Gender 10/11* (pp. 2–5). New York: McGraw-Hill.

Asma, S. T. (2011, November 4). Gauging gender. *The Chronicle Review*, pp. B6-B8.

Baumgardner, J., & Richards, A. (2010). *Manifesta: Young women, feminism, and the future* (Anv. Rev. Ed.). New York: Farrar, Straus, & Giroux.

Beebe, S. A., Beebe, S. J., & Ivy, D. K. (2016). *Communication: Principles for a lifetime* (6th ed.) Boston: Pearson.

Bem, S. L. (1974). The measurement of psychological androgyny. *Journal of Consulting and Clinical Psychology, 42,* 155–162.

Busis, H. (2014, December 12). This was the year that everyone used the f-word. *Entertainment Weekly,* 12.

Cavalcante, A. (2013). Center transgender identity via the textual periphery: *TransAmerica* and the "double work" of paratexts. *Critical Studies in Media Communication, 30,* 85–101.

Collins, G. (2010, May). The "f" word. *O: The Oprah Winfrey Magazine*, 228, 230.

Dahl Crossley, A. (2010). "When it suits me, I'm a feminist": International students negotiating feminist representations. *Women's Studies International Forum*, *33*, 125–133.

Dance, F. E. X., & Larson, C. E. (1976). *The functions of human communication*. New York: Holt, Rinehart, & Winston.

Davis, G., & Murphy, E. L. (2013). Intersex bodies as states of exception: An empirical explanation for unnecessary surgical modification. *Feminist Formations*, *25*, 129–152.

Dreger, A. D. (2000). *Hermaphrodites and the medical invention of sex*. Cambridge, MA: Harvard University Press.

Feder, E. K. (2014). *Making sense of intersex: Changing ethical perspectives in biomedicine*. Bloomington: Indiana University Press.

Garrison, B. (2014, Fall). Bitch in: Transgender Law Center. *Bitch: Feminist Response to Pop Culture*, 10.

Girshick, L. B., & Green, J. (2009). *Transgender voices: Beyond women and men*. Lebanon, NH: University Press of New England.

Golden, C. (2009). The intersexed and the trans-gendered: Rethinking sex/gender. In J. W. White (Ed.), *Taking sides: Clashing views in gender* (4th ed., pp. 22–29). New York: McGraw-Hill.

Griffin, G. (1998). Understanding heterosexism— the subtle continuum of homophobia. *Women & Language*, *21*, 33–39.

Havrilesky, H. (2015, February 23-March 8). Reading Bruce Jenner: Intrusions of reality in greater Calabasas. *New York*, 11–12.

Heinz, B. (2002). Enga(y)ging the discipline: Sexual minorities and communication studies. *Communication Education*, *51*, 95–104.

Herman, J. (2009). *Transgender explained for those who are not*. Bloomington, IN: AuthorHouse.

hooks, b. (2000). *Feminism is for everybody: Passionate politics*. Cambridge, MA: South End.

Kantor, M. (2009). *Homophobia: The state of sexual bigotry today* (2nd ed.). Santa Barbara, CA: Praeger.

LaFrance, M., Paluck, E. L., & Brescoll, V. (2004). Sex changes: A current perspective on the psychology of gender. In A. H. Eagly, A. E. Beall, & R. J. Sternberg (Eds.), *The psychology of gender* (2nd ed., pp. 328–344). New York: Guilford.

Lippa, R. A. (2005). *Gender, nature, and nurture* (2nd ed.). London: Psychology Press.

Maerz, M. (2014, December 12). This was the year that TV transformed the way we think. *Entertainment Weekly*, 24.

Maerz, M. (2015, June 19). Lady liberated. *Entertainment Weekly*, 24–29.

Marecek, J., Crawford, M., & Popp, D. (2004). On the construction of gender, sex, and sexualities. In A. H. Eagly, A. E. Beall, & R. J. Sternberg (Eds.), *The psychology of gender* (2nd ed., pp. 192–216). New York: Guilford.

Martin, C. E., & Sullivan, J. C. (2010). *Click: When we knew we were feminists*. Berkeley, CA: Seal Press.

McGrath, K. (2014). Teaching sex, gender, transsexual, and transgender concepts. *Communication Teacher*, *28*, 96–101.

Muehlenhard, C., & Peterson, Z. (2011). Distinguishing between sex and gender: History, current conceptualizations, and implications. *Sex Roles, 64*, 791–803.

Olson, L. N., Coffelt, T. A., Berlin Ray, E., Rudd, J., Botta, R., Ray, G., & Kopfman, J. E. (2008). "I'm all for equal rights, but don't call me a feminist": Identity dilemmas in young adults' discursive representations of being a feminist. *Women's Studies in Communication, 31*, 104–132.

Perry, L. A. M., & Ballard-Reisch, D. (2004). There's a rainbow in the closet: On the importance of developing a common language for "sex" and "gender." In P. M. Backlund & M. R. Williams (Eds.), *Readings in gender communication* (pp. 17–34). Belmont, CA: Thomson/Wadsworth.

Preves, S. E. (2003). *Intersex and identity: The contested self*. Rutgers, NJ: Rutgers University Press.

Rice, L. (2015a, April 3). Transstories find a home on reality TV. *Entertainment Weekly*, 16.

Rice, L. (2015b, May 8). A second act—and show—for Bruce Jenner. *Entertainment Weekly*, 18–19.

Rice, L. (2015c, June 12). Keeping up with Caitlyn Jenner. *Entertainment Weekly*, 16.

Silman, A. (2015, June 24). Laverne Cox talks battling transphobia on "Orange Is the New Black." Retrieved June 26, 2015, from <www.salon.com>.

Sloop, J. M. (2012). "This is not natural": Caster Semenya's gender threats. *Critical Studies in Media Communication, 29*, 81–96.

Spencer, L. G., IV. (2015). Introduction: Centering transgender studies and gender identity in communication scholarship. In L. G. Spencer, IV & J. C. Capuzza (Eds.), *Transgender communication studies: Histories, trends, and trajectories* (pp. ix–xxii). Lanham, MD: Lexington.

Spender, D. (1985). *Man made language* (2nd ed.). London: Routledge & Kegan Paul.

Thorne, B., Kramarae, C., & Henley, N. (1983). Language, gender, and society: Opening a second decade of research. In B. Thorne, C. Kramarae, & N. Henley (Eds.), *Language, gender, and society* (pp. 7–24). Rowley, MA: Newbury.

U.S. Bureau of Labor Statistics. (2015). Employment situation summary. Retrieved June 26, 2015, from <www.bls.gov>.

U.S. Census Bureau. (2010). Income, poverty and health insurance in the United States: 2010. Available: <http://www.census.gov/hhes/www/income/incomestats.html>.

Valenti, J. (2007). *Full frontal feminism: A young woman's guide to why feminism matters.* Berkeley, CA: Seal Press.

Valentine, D. (2007). *Imagining transgender: An ethnography of a category.* Durham, NC: Duke University Press.

Wilson, R. (2011, November 18). We can help students think about who they are and who they are becoming. *The Chronicle of Higher Education*, p. A28.

Wilson Schaef, A. (1981). *Women's reality: An emerging female system in the white male society.* Minneapolis: Winston.

CHAPTER 2

GENDER IDENTITY DEVELOPMENT

Biological, Social, and Cultural Influences

CASE STUDY

Am I Masculine? Am I Feminine? What's That Mean, Anyway?

When you read or hear the words *masculine* and *feminine*, what comes to mind? What were your early lessons about femininity and masculinity? Did you grow up hearing "Act like a lady!" or "Buck up little soldier; boys don't cry!"? Did masculine and feminine stereotypes affect your thinking, or were you raised with "outside the box" views of what it meant to be feminine or masculine? Are your current views on the subject in line with your earlier thinking, or have you changed your vision as you've grown up and matured?

Your earliest teachings and thoughts about these issues are powerful, because they affect how you currently communicate and develop relationships. Remnants of those early lessons stay with us, try as hard as we may to undo what we learned about how people are supposed to behave. Your views about men, women, masculinity, femininity, sexuality, and relationships arise from and continue to be shaped by your culture and experiences. That's the subject of this chapter.

HOT TOPICS

- Sex and gender identity development
- Changing definitions of masculinity and femininity
- How social interpretations of biological sex differences affect gender identity development
- Social and psychological theories of gender identity development
- Gender transcendence
- Effects of socialization (e.g., families, clothes, toys, peers, and schools) on gender identity development
- Culture and its impact on gender identity development
- Intersections of identity—how different aspects of identity interact

In Chapter 1, we distinguished biological sex from socially constructed gender. We each develop our own identity within our cultural context. This chapter explores factors that influence our identity development and our communication. We begin with a description of the importance of self-identity and the role gender plays in identity development, then move on to three major influences on that identity development—biology, society, and culture. We conclude with an examination of what happens when these factors intersect.

HOW YOU DEVELOP YOUR IDENTITY

How do you come to understand who you are? Your *identity* is the sum total of the answers to the question "Who am I?" An interesting exercise to try some time is to jot down twenty answers to that question. For some students, twenty answers come easily; for others, it's a more difficult task. If you do the exercise, you're likely to find such responses as son/daughter, brother/sister, student, friend, and employee. You might also include a sex identifier such as male, female, or intersex, because your biological sex is very much a part of your identity.

Fundamentals of Identity Development

Let's first review some basics about how identity develops in general. A good place to start is with the long-enduring question of nature versus nurture: Do people behave the way they do because they were born that way, or because they were socialized and educated to be that way? This question has been debated for years, and you probably have an opinion about it. But it doesn't have to be an either-or question. Identity is actually the product of the fusion of your genetically determined tendencies and your culturally determined socialization. In other words, identity is created through the combination of your biology and your social environment.

This view leads to two important points regarding identity: First, no two identities are the same. This may seem like a completely obvious statement, but it has significant implications for communication. We can't ever assume that two people—whether they're from the same sex, the same group, or the same culture—will act or see the world in precisely the same way. Similarities will exist of course, but so will differences. Second, identities aren't fixed. Since identities are created through the interaction of the individual and the environment, and since both change and evolve over time, an individual's identity also is malleable and can be altered.

Identity is created through a combination of your biology and social environment.

In this chapter, we can't examine all the ways in which a person's identity develops, but let's review a few salient points.

🍁 Social groups (e.g., family, schoolmates, friends, culture) shape cultural identities. These groups might be based on sex, ethnicity, sexual orientation, social class, religion, nationality, or other factors.

🍁 Different parts of your identity are formed at different times. *Sex identity*, related to your biological properties, appears to come early, between one and three years of age (Martin & Nakayama, 2013). During this stage, most children begin to identify themselves as belonging to one sex or the other, but we emphasize the word *begin* because the process of identifying with a particular sex takes time to develop. Intersex children (people born with a mixture of female and male genitalia and hormonal systems) and their parents often struggle because of the pressure they may feel to determine a clear sex identity when the biology of a child is complex. Other children may feel that they are biologically one sex, but internally and emotionally another sex, a condition that used to be called gender identity disorder, now referred to as *gender dysphoria* (Banda, 2013; Davis & Murphy, 2013; Feder, 2014).

🍁 Sex identity is a subset of *gender identity*, just as your biological sex is a subset of your psychological, social, and cultural gender—a distinction we made in Chapter 1. Gender identity is more complex than mere biology; it includes how you see yourself in terms of sexuality or sexual orientation, how you relate to culturally defined notions of masculinity and femininity, and your views about appropriate roles for people in society.

🍁 Identity development occurs through communication. Identities are negotiated, cocreated, reinforced, and challenged through communication (Hecht, Ribeault, & Collier, 1993). As you communicate who you think you are to other people and they respond to your identity presentation, they come to form judgments about you, a process called *avowal* and *ascription* (Martin & Nakayama, 2013). *Avowal* is the identity you portray to others. *Ascription* is the process by which others attribute characteristics and identities back to you.

🍁 You learn multiple roles as part of your identity. In various contexts, different parts of your identity come to the fore. For example, in a college classroom, your student identity may be the most obvious. But in a bar or club, your sexual orientation might be the most obvious. The point is that the self you present (avow) to the world can vary widely from context to context, and you communicate differently based on which part of your identity is at the forefront.

🍁 At times, different parts of your identity may come into conflict with other parts, increasing the level of difficulty in communication. For example, a male student might try to follow the stereotypical role of being a man (e.g., "Don't ask for help or you'll appear weak"), which could conflict with his role as a student ("I have no idea what's going on in class!"). Or a woman might want to assertively confront a coworker in a meeting, but that conflicts with an age-old, cultural notion that "women are supposed to defer to others."

🍁 Identity is a bridge between your interior and your exterior (Martin & Nakayama, 2013). Your interior mind consists of the sum total of your attitudes, values, and beliefs—all the things you think are true, right, and worthwhile; your exterior involves your experiences with other people and the environment within which you operate. These aspects of identity guide and even govern how you see the world and, consequently, how you communicate with people in it.

❧ Last, your identity provides a means of interpreting reality and a perspective for understanding the social world, including the definition of other identities. How you define a group, social class, sex, or gender will subsequently govern how you will act toward members of that group. This perspective is critical if you want to understand why you communicate in particular ways to men, women, or members of other identity classifications.

Masculine and Feminine Identity Revisited

As we consider degrees of similarity and difference within sex and gender identity, we must consider the basic concepts of masculinity and femininity because they are still prevalent in our culture. By now, we hope you accept the idea that gender is a social construct based in interaction and that definitions of femininity and masculinity can and do change according to the needs of the society that created the definition. For example, when American society was organized more closely around agriculture, the differences between masculinity and femininity were less distinct (Rudman & Glick, 2010). Both women and men assumed responsibility for the family and for economic survival. Since the husband's work was in the same physical location as that of the wife (or very close to it), the two were much more interdependent. This interdependence created a sense of shared and relatively equal responsibility for the family. However, when factories emerged and men began to work outside the home, the concept of separate gender identities expanded greatly. Men's working environment and separateness led to an impersonal, public, and utilitarian attitude. Women remained at home and became more directly associated with the personal, the private, the nurturing, and the emotional. References to women as weak and decorative, inferior, negative, and trivial emerged at that time.

As society changed, so did conceptions of femininity and masculinity. Qualities that had been important to women in agricultural life such as ambition, strength, and decisiveness slowly faded from the feminine gender identity. Qualities important to men in agricultural society such as emotionality, nurturance, and interdependence (essential to family life) likewise diminished from the masculine

© s_bukley/Shutterstock.com

Every social group in this country has had an upgrade to their software except for the average white male. I think they are still playing off an antiquated rule book. Men had a clearer role in society in the earlier part of the last century. Men knew their place and were valued as soldiers, workers, husbands, caretakers, and protectors.
—Liev Schreiber, actor

gender identity. As women were confined to the private domain, femininity was redefined as nurturing, relational, and caring for others, first described by Bakan (1966, as in Rudman & Glick, 2010) as a communal fundamental modality. As men became more removed from the home, masculinity was redefined to include independence, aggressiveness, self-control, and achievement, described by Bakan as an agentic fundamental modality. These conceptions of masculinity and femininity became so prevalent that they became stereotypes. To *stereotype* is to presume that someone is like members of a particular group, rather than an individual.

Social psychologist Douglas Kenrick and his colleagues suggest, "Stereotyping is a cognitively inexpensive way of understanding others: By presuming that people are like other members of their groups, we avoid the effortful process of learning about them as individuals" (Kenrick, Neuberg, & Cialdini, 2005, p. 399). In American culture, the stereotypical woman is soft-spoken (when she speaks at all), emotional, subjective, self-effacing by reflecting uncertainty and humbleness, and compliant through submissiveness. Femininity results in warm and continued relationships, maternal instincts, interest in caring for children, and the capacity to work productively and continuously in female occupations. These descriptions imply that women be heterosexual, which in turn requires women to focus on their attractiveness to men.

The stereotypical American man is an ineffective listener, emotionally inexpressive, categorical and certain in his language use, and dominating in discussions. Psychologist Joseph Pleck (1981) suggests that one or more of the following conveys masculinity in our society:

1. Displaying success or high status in one's social group
2. Exhibiting a manly air of toughness, confidence, and self-reliance
3. Demonstrating aggression, violence, and daring
4. Avoiding anything associated with femininity

These descriptions require men to organize themselves and society in a competitive, hierarchical manner. Competition is driven by a goal of individual achievement, and it requires participants to show a degree of emotional insensitivity to others' pain or losses. This stereotype leaves little room for relationships.

The societal conditions that gave rise to the current stereotypical definitions of masculinity and femininity occurred more than a hundred years ago, and these conditions have changed a great deal in past decades.

Yet the definitions themselves have been slower to change. Femininity remains linked to the private sphere—to home, family, emotional expressiveness, and caring for others. Masculinity continues to focus on the public areas of work and is associated with power and dominance, emotional reserve, and productivity.

THE CHANGING FACE OF MASCULINITY

Men get a great deal of input on how to be men, but how good is this advice? American men's magazines such as *Men's Health* and *Details* focus on self-improvement and include topics such as diet and exercise tips, relationship columns, sex advice, health updates, and information on how to be more masculine, meaning powerful and dominant.

Views of what is masculine and what masculinity actually means continue to change (Addis, Mansfield, & Syzdek, 2010; Connell, 2005; Connell & Messerschmidt, 2005; DeVisser, 2010; Duerringer, 2015; Harris, 2010; Khan & Blair, 2013; Lockwood Harris, 2011; Messner, 2012; Reeser, 2010). One of the most prolific scholars to write about masculinity is sociologist Michael Kimmel (2011, 2015; Kimmel & Messner, 2012). In his book, *Guyland*, Kimmel (2009) describes how young men (aka, "guys") navigate gender identity and changing notions about masculinity within the period of time from adolescence to adulthood. Most guys Kimmel interviewed for his research said they heed the voices of older men, especially their fathers, when it comes to defining masculinity, and that they constantly feel policed by other men. Kimmel explains "Our peers are a kind of 'gender police,' always waiting for us to screw up so they can give us a ticket for crossing the well-drawn boundaries of manhood" (p. 47).

One interesting difference between masculinity and femininity is that masculinity seems to be something that must be "attained." Masculinity, in much of the world, is earned and achieved rather than merely socially prescribed. This is reflected in the exhortation, "Be a man!" One rarely hears

The definitions of masculinity and femininity have been slow to change.

women say to each other, "Be a woman!" with the underlying message of "you aren't there yet, so get there!" The words "be a man" come with a long list of socially prescribed role behaviors that men in training must work up to. Consequently, manhood can be revoked. A man may hear, "You're no longer a man" if he loses his job, is unable to provide for his family, can't stand up to an aggressor, exhibits a waning libido or erectile dysfunction, or experiences some other culturally determined criteria. This kind of communication can be damaging to both identity and self-esteem.

> Why do we have to take a backseat to men? Let's face it, money gives men the power to run the show. It gives men the power to define value. They define what's sexy. And men define what's feminine. It's ridiculous.
> —Beyoncé, performer

THE CHANGING FACE OF FEMININITY

Cultural definitions of femininity have a history of negative characteristics, reviewed earlier in this chapter. However, research shows that perceptions of femininity have changed in a positive direction (Holmes & Schnurr, 2006; Kehily & Nayak, 2008; Kelly, Pomerantz, & Currie, 2006). Views of what it means to be feminine continue to change, from self-definitions to ideas about body image, athleticism, clothing, and nonconformity, such that a wider range of behaviors, attitudes, and choices may be viewed as feminine (Brownmiller, 2013).

One significant factor affecting the evolution of what it means to be feminine involves the increasing number of women, particularly young women, who participate in sports (Aitchison, 2006; Billings, Butterworth, & Turman, 2015; Bruce, 2012; Mean & Kassing, 2008; O'Reilly & Cahn, 2007; Root Aulette & Wittner, 2014). While equality with male athletes clearly hasn't yet been achieved, gains have been made. According to the Women's Sports Foundation (2015), women who play sports enjoy greater physical and emotional health, are less likely to engage in a host of risky health behaviors (e.g., drug use, smoking, drinking), and have fewer incidences of breast cancer and osteoporosis later in life than non-athletes. In addition, studies show that girls who participate in high school sports are more likely to achieve higher levels of education and have greater earning potential and enhanced employment opportunities than those who don't engage in athletics (Stevenson, 2007, 2010). Girls develop skills playing sports that translate into advantages later in life, like enhanced communication skills, the ability to work well with others, competitiveness, assertiveness, and self-discipline. In general, sports participation by boys and girls affects the likelihood of becoming a productive member of society (O'Brien, 2010).

Most people simply can't live up to the ideal or stereotypical images of masculinity and femininity. The frustration and disillusionment that may set in when the ideal isn't reached can have lasting effects on self-esteem. The more you consciously learn about options in defining and living out your identity, the easier it is to select a definition that fits your own personality, needs, and goals.

THE EFFECTS OF SOCIAL INTERPRETATIONS OF BIOLOGICAL SEX ON IDENTITY

Biological sex differences continue to be hot topics these days. Some people believe that because biological differences are natural and uniquely human, they're something to be appreciated, not downplayed or resented. Others believe that biological sex differences are fairly insignificant; the real issue is the social interpretation of those differences.

Communication scholar Peter Andersen (2006) supports the notion that biology isn't destiny; he provides an interesting starting point in the consideration of sex differences. Based on the work of communication pioneer Ray Birdwhistell, Andersen describes three levels of differences:

🍁 Primary sexual characteristics are related to basic reproductive functions and behaviors such as the production of sperm, eggs, and the ability to lactate. These are the most obvious of differences between men and women, and are the ones least amenable to change. Even sex change operations do not give a person the ability to produce eggs or sperm.

🍁 Characteristics that are indirect results of reproductive roles include the amount of body hair one has, one's muscle mass, and certain behaviors that research suggests are biologically based, such as a female's apparent higher degree of nonverbal sensitivity and a male's apparent advantage in navigation and spatial visualization.

🍁 The third level of differences consists of those patterns of social behaviors that are learned, culturally based, and situationally produced.

Remember...

Identity: Sum total of answers to the question "Who am I?"

Sex Identity: Subset of gender identity; identity related to biological properties

Gender Dysphoria: A condition in which a person is biologically one sex, but internally and emotionally identifies with another sex

Gender Identity: More complex than mere biology; includes the view of self in terms of sexuality or sexual orientation, how one relates to culturally defined notions of masculinity and femininity, and one's views about appropriate roles for men and women in society

Avowal: Self-identity communicated to others

Ascription: Process by which people attribute characteristics and identities to other people

Stereotype: Presumption that someone is like members of a group, rather than an individual

According to Andersen (2006), our behavior, including communication behavior, stems from all three levels. As noted, the primary level is the most resistant to change, and these reproductive differences will likely always be with us. Of particular interest are the other two layers, especially the third level. At these two levels, are men and women completely different? Or is there some similarity and overlap?

Communication scholar Kathryn Dindia (2006) reviewed research on communication and psychological variables (Andersen's third layer) and concluded that sex differences in these areas are, on the average, small. She suggests, "The average woman is not that much different from the average man . . . approximately 85 percent of women and men overlap across various psychological variables, whereas approximately 15 percent of men and women do not overlap" (pp. 10–11).

For a number of years, gender researcher Janet Shibley Hyde (2005, 2006; Peterson & Shibley Hyde, 2010) has advanced a supposition known as the Gender Similarities Hypothesis, which holds that women and men are more alike than different. This hypothesis does not state that men and women are similar in every psychological dimension; Shibley Hyde notes that some sex differences can be detected in smiling, emotional expressiveness, sensitivity to nonverbal cues, and attitudes about casual sex. But the commonalities outweigh the differences.

While this chapter will inform you about some biological sex differences, those differences are neither our central focus nor critical to our approach to gender communication. We don't want to make too much out of biological differences because we've seen that they sometimes become a cop-out. ("That's just the way we are.") This view implies that somehow biology gives us permission to behave in a certain way—even if that way is discriminatory or inappropriate. For many of us who study gender communication, this isn't a workable stance. While we want to explore the biology, we're most interested in how identity development and communication are affected by the social translations of that biology.

"Innies" and "Outies": Social Interpretations of Anatomical Differences

Some of the biological findings described in this section may be quite familiar to you, while some may surprise you. We challenge you to think about the social interpretations of the biology in ways you might not have thought of before now. Think also about how those interpretations affect your identity, as well as how they influence the way you communicate.

SEXUAL ORGANS The human fetus starts to form internal female or external male genitalia at around three or four months into development (Crawford , 2011). Think for a moment about the consequences of that simple differentiation. Consider the interesting parallel between the sexes' genitalia and their roles in society. For centuries the male penis has been viewed as a symbol of virility—an external, outward sign of men's strength and their ability to assert themselves in the world. In contrast, the internal genitalia of women is paralleled with the more passive, submissive profiles that women have traditionally assumed—profiles endorsed by men, and often, society in general. The social interpretations of women's sexual organs identify them as reactors, receivers, followers, and beneficiaries of men's decisions.

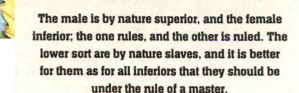

The male is by nature superior, and the female inferior; the one rules, and the other is ruled. The lower sort are by nature slaves, and it is better for them as for all inferiors that they should be under the rule of a master.
—Aristotle, Greek philosopher

REPRODUCTIVE FUNCTIONS While the sexual organs represent the more obvious anatomical sex differences, perhaps the most profound difference rests in the sexes' *reproductive functions*. What makes the sexes so different in this regard is the woman's capacity to carry a developing fetus for nine months, give birth, and nurse an infant—things that men can't do. These tasks have long been protected, even to the extent that nineteenth century medical information warned women against too much thinking or exercise so as not to divert blood away from their reproductive systems (Borisoff & Merrill, 1998; McLoughlin, Shryer, Goode, & McAuliffe, 1988). The reproductive capabilities of men and women have more profound social translations than any other biological property or function.

Sex differences exist in their current form primarily because of centuries of *hunter–gatherer cultures*. These were societies in which the men combed the land, hunted the food, and protected their families from danger, while the women had the birthing and child-rearing duties and developed tools to gather and carry the food. This separation of labor formed the basis of a social structure that worked very well; thus it continued into modern times. Did you ever think that so much might rest on the capacity to reproduce? This is a prime example of what we mean by biological factors contributing to a wide range of social norms and expectations.

Medical knowledge and technology have progressed to the point that women, in particular, can benefit from alternatives to their own biology—alternatives that continue to change our social structure. Although still able to carry and give birth to babies, women now have several methods of preventing conception. In 2010, the birth control pill turned 50, meaning that this simple but effective means of contraception has now been available to women for over 50 years in the U.S. (Kotz, 2010; Northrup, 2010). Some hold the view that the development, accessibility, and affordability of "the pill" contributed more than other events or discoveries in altering male–female dynamics in recent U.S. history (Tyler May, 2010a, 2010b, 2010c). In addition, if women do become pregnant, they don't necessarily have to be the biologically designated, primary caregivers once the baby is born. Many women choose to return to work (or have to work because of economic constraints) or pursue other endeavors. More men are now single parents, and in two-parent families, some fathers choose to take time off from their jobs after a baby's birth or even quit their jobs to care for their children (Boushey, 2009; Brott, 2008; Coontz, 2009; Gray & Anderson, 2010; Painter, 2010; U.S. Census Bureau, 2010; Winter & Pauwels, 2006). These choices affect how people view each other, as well as how they communicate.

Strong women leave big hickeys.
—Madonna, performer

THE MEASURE OF STRENGTH When the subject of biological sex differences is introduced, students are quick to comment about issues surrounding *physical strength* and endurance. Heightened by events in the U.S. campaign against terrorism and other military conflicts, such topics as biological attributes of male and female soldiers, differing fitness standards, and women in frontline combat generate provocative discussions (Cergol, 2010; Hanafin, 2010; Holland, 2006; Neary, 2010). A common theme in these discussions is whether women, whose bodies are higher in fat and lower in muscle in comparison to men's, have the strength and endurance necessary for combat or other sustained military action. Some people contend that if women are able to endure childbirth, they ought to be able to handle combat. As of January 2016, all combat positions were open to women in the U.S. military; however, the rates of women being drawn to direct combat positions tend to be about as low as the rates for men's participation in these roles (Michaels, 2015). *National Review* reporter Elaine Donnelly (2010) contends that "Women on average do not have the physical capability to lift a fully loaded male soldier who has been wounded under fire, in order to save his life. Even average-sized men have that capability; no one should have to die because women do not."

Besides men's higher concentrations of muscle, four other factors give men more physical strength than women: (1) a greater oxygen-carrying capacity, (2) a lower resting heart rate, (3) higher blood pressure, and (4) more efficient methods of recovering from physical exertion (Stockard & Johnson, 1980). Because of these characteristics, men have long been thought of as the stronger sex, women the weaker sex. But let's take a closer look at determinations of strength.

Strength is defined in Webster's dictionary as force, invulnerability, or the capacity for exertion and endurance. If you examine strength from a vulnerability or endurance angle, then the sex-typed strength argument breaks down a bit. Research documents six differences between males and females:

1. Male fetuses experience many more developmental difficulties and birth defects, average an hour longer to deliver, and have a higher death rate than female fetuses.
2. For the top fifteen leading causes of death in the United States, men have higher death rates than women.
3. Women outlive men by an average of five years.
4. Men do not tend to see themselves as ill or susceptible to disease or injury, when they actually are more susceptible.
5. Men generally drive more recklessly than women, accounting for three out of every four traffic fatalities.
6. In some sports requiring extreme levels of endurance (such as ultramarathons and dogsled racing), women have been catching up to and surpassing men (Cahn, 2015; Schmid, 2005; *Science Daily*, 2007; Stibich, 2008; Tirrito, 2010; TrafficSTATS, 2010).

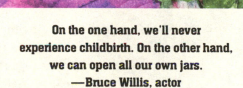

On the one hand, we'll never experience childbirth. On the other hand, we can open all our own jars.
—Bruce Willis, actor

Could it be that the notion of male strength has more to do with social interpretations than biological fact? The answer to that question is no, if you equate strength with higher muscle mass, but yes, if you equate strength with vulnerability and endurance. Most often a

"People in Combat"

For some people, the presence of women in the U.S. armed forces is still a hot button issue. Even though women have served in the American military for decades, debate continues over the roles they should play and whether holding differing standards for physical ability is fair (Cergol, 2010; Donnelly, 2010; Neary, 2010). Given laws that passed in 2016 allowing women in the U.S. armed forces to finally hold direct combat positions, is women's fitness still a hot button issue, worthy of debate, or a "done deal"?

To further complicate the issue, from time to time, talk emerges across the nation about reinstating the draft, given the strain currently placed on the all-volunteer U.S. military forces stationed around the world. If a draft were to be reinstated, should women and men alike be eligible for the draft? What if an intersex person—someone born with a mixture of male and female genitalia and hormonal systems who chooses to remain intersex—wanted to enter the military and, eventually, qualify for direct combat? How would the military house that person? What would need to change for intersex people to gain acceptance among our nation's military forces?

determination of strength depends on the individual, not the sex. We've all seen some women who were stronger (in terms of muscle strength) than some men and vice versa. But it's quite fascinating when you realize how many social expectations and stereotypes are steeped in the basic biology.

Social Interpretations of "Raging" Hormones

When people think about or comment on biological differences, most often those differences are attributed to hormones (Jacklin, 1989). However, as hormonal studies become more frequent and utilize more sophisticated methods, they produce inconsistent results. Some of the complexity stems from not knowing where genetics leave off and environment begins.

For the sake of simplicity, let's explore those hormones most associated with masculinity (androgens, more specifically, testosterone) and femininity (estrogen). We've pared some complex information down to three key elements: hormonal effects on nurturance, aggression, and cycles. These functions are the most distinctive for the sexes and have the most significant social interpretations.

NURTURANCE Stereotypically, *nurturance* is associated with women's mothering roles, but it's been defined as the "giving of aid and comfort to others" (Maccoby & Jacklin, 1974, pp. 214–215). Research by Anke Ehrhardt determined a relationship between female hormones and the inclination to nurture. Ehrhardt and colleagues (1980, 1984) examined young girls who had been prenatally "masculinized" by receiving large doses of androgens (male hormones) from drugs prescribed for their mothers. These subjects rarely fantasized or daydreamed about marriage and pregnancy, nor did they show much interest in caring for small children. They more often gave career a higher priority than marriage in discussions of future plans, generally liked to play and associate with boys more than girls, and were more likely to exhibit high levels of physical energy. These studies and other evidence led researchers to link hormones and nurturance.

But many researchers have argued that the ability to nurture goes beyond biology (Stockard & Johnson, 1980). Such experiences as participation in childbirth, early contact between parents and infants, and even whether one has younger siblings may affect one's ability to nurture. Psychologist Mary Crawford (2011) suggests that a person's tendency toward nurturance can be developed simply when the person is put into a nurturing role. Given this information, why does society tend to readily associate femininity with the ability to nurture and comfort, as though men were incapable of doing so? If a man has a stronger or equally strong nurturing tendency as his wife or partner, should his masculinity be threatened? Conversely, if a woman isn't particularly fond of children nor interested in motherhood, does this mean that she has a hormonal deficit or that she is somehow less feminine than women who want to nurture children? It's easy to see how hormonal functioning can lead to labels and stereotypes that affect our opportunities and influence our choices in communication.

AGGRESSION Aggressive behavior may be learned, but research indicates that hormones influence *aggression*, defined as the stereotypically male trait of asserting or inflicting force (Lippa, 2005; Snowbeck, 2001). Aggressiveness has long been viewed as a male characteristic related to androgens (primarily

Remember…

Reproductive Functions: Sexes' differing abilities to conceive, gestate, give birth to, and nurse offspring

Hunter–Gatherer Cultures: Ancient societies in which men's and women's roles were distinguished according to who provided food, protected the family from danger, and birthed and reared children

Physical Strength: Societally derived judgment based on physical characteristics such as muscle mass, vulnerability, and endurance

Nurturance: Stereotypically female trait of giving aid and comfort to others

Aggression: Stereotypically male trait of asserting or inflicting force

testosterone), while passivity has been related to the female system's lack of androgens (Maccoby & Jacklin, 1980). However, professor of medical science Anne Fausto-Sterling (1992) discovered that many studies attempting to link male aggression and testosterone levels produced contradictory results, meaning that the relationship between hormones and aggression was questionable. So researchers continue their attempts to better understand this relationship.

Why do we still tend to associate masculinity with aggressive behavior, femininity with passive behavior? Could it again be the case that judgments about aggression and the sexes have more to do with social influences than biological fact? Think about the messages that lots of little boys receive from their mothers and fathers, siblings, peers, and the media. In addition to those messages about strength that we discussed in an earlier section, boys are warned not to "act like a sissy" and chastised for anything resembling feminine behavior (Kimmel, 2009, 2015). Granted, things are changing and not all families raise their male children in this manner, but the notion of the male as aggressor is still around.

Many men aren't particularly proud of the legacy of aggression. In fact, they're working hard to turn this legacy around because the expectation that they will be constantly strong and aggressive constitutes a burden they'd rather not carry. They seek alternatives to expected behavior and resent the implication that being a "real man" means being aggressive, competitive, emotionally aloof or detached, and in control all the time.

How do most people react when women exhibit assertive or aggressive behavior? Unfortunately, many people react negatively, as though a woman who expresses this stereotypically masculine trait is experiencing a hormonal imbalance or simply behaving inappropriately. Occasionally, off-base, derogatory insinuations about sexual orientation are made. Some men are threatened or put off by aggressive women, because they don't welcome another context for competition. Also, some women are put off by unexpected, aggressive behavior in other women.

What about aggression and sports? Most people encourage verbal and physical aggression by women in the sporting context, as long as that aggression isn't aimed at male competitors. Apart from the occasional anomaly—such as the famous 1973 "Battle of the Sexes" tennis match between Billy Jean King and Bobby Riggs, successful NASCAR driver Danica Patrick, and female golfers who occasionally qualify to compete on the PGA tour (which is, to date, an all-male organization)—few women are given the opportunity to compete against men in either professional or collegiate sports. Perhaps a continued rise in popularity of women's sports, to the degree that they become more commonplace instead of exceptions to the rule, will affect people's stereotypical notions about aggression.

CYCLES When we think of biological cycles, we typically associate them with women's biology in general and with premenstrual syndrome (PMS) in particular. Decades ago, the medical profession largely chalked up women's menstrual discomfort to hypochondria. When enough research documented women's reports of menstrual problems over time, the medical community declared PMS a disease (Richmond-Abbott, 1992). Some scholars believe that labeling PMS a disease has added credibility to the condition, but it has also reinforced an old stereotype (Caplan, 2008). Dramatic accounts of outlandish, overemotional, even violent behavior, as well as exaggerated images of women unable to meet their responsibilities have been attributed to PMS. While diagnosing the condition legitimized women's complaints and brought folklore into reality, it gave society more impetus to question women's abilities.

The question (loaded with stereotypes) that still persists today about this issue is whether a woman who might experience PMS can be trusted to make critical decisions, like ones about going to war, using deadly weapons, and so forth. This question implies that women are such victims of their own biology that they couldn't possibly be relied on in critical situations. What's most interesting here is that the same argument could be made about men's levels of testosterone and aggressive behavior. Do men's hormonal functioning and bent toward aggression better equip them to handle conflict?

What about the notion of a male biological cycle? The male cycle is more than a mere notion, according to research (Fischman, 2001). Tracking back a bit, researchers in the mid-1970s began to investigate male hormonal functioning as evidence of a male cycle. Ramey (1976) found that men displayed regular variations in emotions over each twenty-four-hour period within a six-week time frame. Ramey also detected a thirty-day cycle for men's hormonal functioning. During these cycles, men's physical strength, emotionality, and intellectual functioning were affected. Internationally acclaimed scholar Doreen Kimura (1987) identified a tentative link between seasons of the year and men's cognitive functioning. According to Kimura, in the spring, when testosterone levels are lower, men's mathematical and analytic skills are enhanced. These abilities decrease in the fall when testosterone levels are higher. The popular press picked up on this research, having fun comparing women's monthly periods to what it called men's seasonal "commas" (Kleiman, 1992, p. 1E).

Mind Over Matter: Are Men's and Women's Brains Really Different?

Brain functions are extremely complex, tied into hormonal functioning, affected by environmental and social factors, and related to cognitive abilities (Halpern, 2012). Information regarding sex differences and brain functioning has caused more than mild controversy. Two of the more prominent and popular books on the subject of how differently male and female brains function, *The Female Brain* and *The Male Brain*, are authored by Louann Brizendine (2007, 2010), but her findings and observations aren't completely accepted. Critics suggest that Brizendine's conclusions are overly dichotomizing and divisive, leading to unhelpful sex stereotyping and notions of biology-as-destiny that aren't useful.

BRAIN FUNCTIONING Some researchers report sex differences in brain size, glucose metabolism counts, and cerebral blood flow (Gur et al., 1982; Gur et al., 1995; Halpern, 2012). But others conclude that studies in this area actually show minimal differences (indicating that the sexes' brains are actually more similar than different) and are used primarily to engender divisiveness (Bleier, 1984; Gibbons, 1991; Tavris, 1992). Prolific gender scholar Celeste Condit contends that a good deal of research on sex differences and the brain is biased in its assumptions and faulty in its methods, constituting a form of "bad science" (1996, p. 87).

Research has shown that the brain has two hemispheres that house various human capabilities. The left hemisphere is primarily responsible for the production of language, while the right hemisphere manages spatial ability. It has long been thought—and many still contend—that men perform better on tests of spatial skills while women excel on tests of verbal ability, as a result of hormonal and brain functioning, but ongoing research questions these trends (Kimura, 2000; Lenroot & Giedd, 2010; O'Grady, 2015; Witte, Savli, Holik, Kasper, & Lanzenberger, 2010).

> It was a very cool thing to be a smart girl, as opposed to some other, different kind. And I think that made a great deal of difference to me growing up.
> —Supreme Court Justice Elena Kagan, 4th woman appointed to the U.S. Supreme Court

Simon Baron-Cohen (2012), author of *The Essential Difference: Men, Women, and the Extreme Male Brain*, suggests that the male brain is predominantly hard-wired for understanding and building organizing systems, while the female brain is hard-wired mostly for empathy.

COGNITIVE ABILITY A consistent pattern emerged over decades of conducting research on gifted girls and boys: Boys outscored girls on the math portions of the SAT (Benbow & Stanley, 1980). This finding led to the conclusion that male dominance in math was related to hemispheric specialization in the brain, that is, that the right hemisphere was more fully developed in men than in women (Pinker, 2005). However, social scientists on the nurture side of the nature/nurture argument have other explanations for sex differences in cognitive functioning, insisting that social and environmental factors affect the picture (Spelke, 2005). Research shows that since boys are expected to excel in math, they're encouraged and coached by parents and teachers, while attitudes and anxiety about the difficulty of math inhibit girls' achievement (Baenninger & Newcombe, 1995; Eccles, 1989; Linn & Petersen, 1986).

Concerning verbal ability, the general opinion for decades was that females outperformed males in such capacities as language acquisition, vocabulary, spelling, writing, and verbal expressiveness. But again, research has produced findings to the contrary. Researchers now believe that, if there once was a gap in verbal abilities and math and spatial abilities between the sexes due to brain differences and hormonal functioning, this gap has all but disappeared (Crawford, 2011; Hill, Corbett, & St. Rose, 2010; Mortenson, 2008). If the human brain hasn't changed, then what explains the sexes performing more similarly in specific areas than in times past?

One explanation relates to changing times and changing parents. More parents have backed off of the old stereotypes, believing now that children of any sex can do anything, given encouragement, support, and education (Ehrensaft, 2011). Teachers who refrain from sex-biased behaviors are helping students to maximize their potential, regardless of expectations for their sex. Educational institutions that offer and encourage mathematical and spatial curricula for all children help to enhance these abilities. In sum, societal shifts are affecting students' visions of what they can accomplish, and the gender gap in cognitive ability is narrowing.

Since boys are expected to excel in math, they are encouraged more by parents and teachers.

© racom/Shutterstock.com

SOCIAL INFLUENCES ON PSYCHOLOGICAL GENDER IDENTITY

In the previous section of this chapter we talked about biological sex differences; note that here we switch the focus to psychological variables or gender identity. As we noted earlier, gender is culturally based and socially constructed out of psychological characteristics; it also contains such things as attitudes and beliefs, sexual orientation, and perceptions of appropriate roles in society.

Learning to Be Girls and Boys

The development of gender understanding in young children is fascinating because children sometimes believe gender to be changeable (Devor, 1992). (Ah, the wisdom of children.) They see gender not as being based on anatomy, but as a role that can be changed much like changing a hairstyle. As children start to understand themselves as individuals separate from others, they begin to understand that others see them and respond to them as people of a particular sex. Theories have been generated to explain this identity development process or how one becomes "gendered."

SOCIAL LEARNING THEORY Social psychologists Walter Mischel (1966) and Albert Bandura (1971, 1986) are noted for their research on social learning theory as an explanation for human development. This theory suggests that children learn gender-related behavior from their social contacts, primarily their parents and peers. Children model the thoughts, emotions, and actions of others. This role modeling has a powerful effect on how children see themselves, how they form gender identities. Because of the power of parents in this regard, resources continue to be published to assist parents who want to raise their children to be unencumbered by traditional views of male and female behavior (Ehrensaft, 2011; Lucas-Stannard, 2013; Spears Brown, 2014).

Parents, teachers, peers, and other agents of socialization reward some behaviors in little girls and boys; the same behaviors enacted by members of the opposite sex are punished. As children continue to receive positive and negative responses to their behaviors, they generalize to other situations and come to develop identities as girls or boys (Lippa, 2005; Peach, 1998). One criticism of this theory is the suggestion that children develop according to gender stereotypes, a limited or confining view of human development.

COGNITIVE DEVELOPMENT THEORY According to Lawrence Kohlberg's (1966) theory, as children's minds mature, they gain an understanding of gender roles and identity without external reinforcement (in contrast to social learning theory). Essentially children socialize themselves into feminine or masculine identities via their progress through four stages of mental ability. In stage 1, very young children begin to recognize sex distinctions, but can't attach a sex to a person. They're likely to say such things as "Daddy is a girl." In stage 2, children learn their own sexual identity, as well as how to identify other people's sex correctly. In stage 3, children learn to behave according to ground rules or guidelines for sex-typed appropriate behavior, stemming from their culture. For example, most girls want to wear ruffly, "girly" clothing and boys are appalled at the thought of playing with dolls. At this point, children begin to value and imitate those behaviors associated with their own sex, more so than behaviors associated with a different sex.

This progress continues into stage 4, when children separate their identities from those of their primary caregivers (typically their mothers). For boys, the importance of their father's identity and behavior is compounded. But because female children can't separate themselves from the mother's

During Kohlberg's stage 3, most girls want to wear frilly dresses and play with dolls.

© Melanie DeFazio/Shutterstock.com

female identity, they remain at stage 3, unlike their male counterparts who progress through all four stages. In essence, a girl's development is stunted because her sex identity is the same as her mother's. Can you anticipate any problems with this theory? A major criticism of this theory has to do with its use of a male model of development that is then generalized to all humans. The model suggests that girls' development is somehow less complete or advanced than boys'.

GENDER SCHEMA THEORY Gender schema theory, primarily advanced by psychologist Sandra Bem (1983), states that once a child learns an appropriate cultural definition of gender, this definition becomes the key structure around which all other information is organized. A schema is a cognitive structure that helps us interpret the world. In cultures that adhere closely to traditional gender differentiation, gender schemas are likely to be complex and elaborate. Gender schemas provide prescriptions for how to behave and can strongly influence a child's sense of self-esteem.

As children develop a gender schema, they increasingly use it as an organizing perspective. A schema related to a child's own sex appears to develop first, and it becomes more complex and detailed than schemas for the other sex. Using his or her own schema, a child takes in new information, plans activities, and chooses roles. The development of and subsequent adherence to gender schemas may help us understand why it's so difficult to dislodge gender-stereotypical thinking.

GILLIGAN'S GENDER IDENTITY DEVELOPMENT THEORY Carol Gilligan (1982) challenged human development theorists in her ground-breaking book *In a Different Voice: Psychological Theory and Women's Development.* Gilligan's theory expands previous views of human development to account for both female and male paths to gender identity. In a nutshell (which does not do justice to this theory), the core of identity development rests within the mother–child relationship. The female child connects and finds gender identity with the mother, but the male child must find identity by separating himself from this female caregiver. Thus—unlike male development, which stresses separation and independence—female identity revolves around interconnectedness and relationship. Gilligan's critics claim that the theory focuses too heavily on female development, implying an advantage for females who can identify with a same-sex caregiver, while merely drawing occasional comparisons to how the process works for males.

How, then, does one make sense of all these theories? Does a "best" theory of gender identity exist? While the theories reviewed here significantly contribute to our understanding, they tend to dichotomize, focusing heavily on maleness and femaleness and depleting the broader concept of gender. Another problem is that each theory tends to focus primarily on childhood development or how children discover gender and corresponding social expectations. What we believe to be more interesting for our discussion of gender communication is a model that begins with how we experience gender as children, but shifts to how we progress or transcend that experience later in life. A theory of transcendence offers real insight into how adults negotiate and renegotiate their gender identities, over time, given experiences and education.

GENDER TRANSCENDENCE AND ANDROGYNY Several researchers have developed, expanded, and refined a theory of gender identity development called *gender transcendence,* relying most heavily on the research of psychologist Joseph Pleck.

In traditional views of development, the sex role is prominent, defined as "the psychological traits and the social responsibilities that individuals have and feel are appropriate for them because they are male or female" (Pleck, 1977, p. 182). Emphasis is on two designations—masculine and feminine. Masculinity involves instrumental or task-oriented competence and includes such traits as assertiveness, self-expansion, self-protection, and a general orientation of self against the world. Femininity is viewed as expressive or relationship-oriented competence, with corresponding traits that include nurturance and concern for others, emphasis on relationships and the expression of feelings, and a general orientation of self *within* the world (Eccles, 1987).

Gender transcendence theory responds to the criticism that the prevailing theories perpetuate the dichotomy between males and females and limit individuals' options regarding identity. Pleck (1975) envisioned a three-stage sequence of gender identity development. The first two stages resemble Kohlberg's (1966) cognitive development model. However, stage 3 represents the point where transcendence theory departs from other theories. Stage 3 occurs when individuals experience difficulty because the rules of behavior no longer seem to make sense or because they begin to suspect that they possess both expressive (feminine) and instrumental (masculine) abilities.

At this point, individuals may "transcend" their understanding of the norms and expectations of sex and gender to develop "psychological androgyny in accordance with their inner needs and temperaments" (Pleck, 1975, p. 172). Communication researcher Harold Barrett (1998) described the shift in emphasis from biological sex to psychological gender this way: "The emphasis now is less on determination of role by sex—male versus female—and more on awareness of gender plurality in an individual's nature" (p. 83).

Like other theories of gender identity development, transcendence theory begins with a discussion of child development. However, it emphasizes adolescence as a period when traditional definitions of what is male and female are likely to be challenged for the first time. The theory then tracks into adult development, as changing values, social pressures, education, and life events (e.g., marriage, new jobs, parenting, retirement) cause adults to reevaluate their gender identities. Transcendence, then, may occur in adolescence and adulthood; however, not everyone experiences it. Some people continue throughout adulthood to adhere to traditional roles and definitions of what is female and male, and they manage this quite successfully.

Androgyny, which we discussed briefly in Chapter 1, is related to this notion of gender transcendence. Androgyny is more understandable if you envision a continuum with masculinity placed toward one end, femininity toward the other end, and androgyny in the middle. You don't lose masculine traits or behaviors if you're androgynous, or somehow become masculine if you move away from the feminine pole. Some androgynous individuals may have more masculine traits than feminine, and vice versa.

While their identity expands, gender-transcendent individuals' repertoire of communication behavior also has the capacity to expand. Effective communicators develop a wider range of behaviors from which to choose; they know how to analyze a situation and select the best behaviors from their repertoire, enact those behaviors, and evaluate the results. Because the process of gender transcendence causes an individual to incorporate feminine and masculine traits into a unique blend, that individual is more likely to behave in ways that aren't confined by traditional, stereotypical notions of how men and women are *supposed* to behave and to be more generally accepting and less judgmental of others whose behavior deviates from social expectations. Androgynous or gender-transcendent individuals, in general, are adaptive to situations and comfortable with communicative options—options that become extremely helpful in the complicated realm of gender communication (Johnson, Murphy, Zewdie, & Reichard, 2008; Kada, Brunner, & Maier, 2009; Pickard Leszczynski, 2009; Sidelinger, Frisby, & McMullen, 2009). We present gender transcendence to you as an option, but recognize some caution should be applied.

First, while gender transcendence and repertoire expansion fit together logically, don't take that to mean that the only way to expand the communication repertoire is to adopt a transcendent gender identity. A person who aligns himself or herself with a traditionally feminine or masculine gender identity may still expand the communication repertoire. In many situations, this individual may behave appropriately and be viewed as an effective communicator.

The second caution is sort of a reverse of the first. We don't mean to insinuate that *all* gender-transcendent people are *automatically* effective communicators in *all* situations, just because they embody and integrate masculine and feminine traits and behaviors. As you're becoming aware, easy answers and "quick fixes" don't emerge in gender communication. Gender transcendence may broaden your approach and enhance your repertoire, making it a desirable position from which to communicate with others, but it offers no guarantees.

Remember...

Gender Identity Development: Theory about how one develops one's gender, with regard to feminine traits, masculine traits, or a blend of both

Social Learning Theory: Theory about how children learn gender-related behavior from social contacts, primarily parents and peers

Cognitive Development Theory: Theory about how children socialize themselves into feminine or masculine identities as they progress through various stages of mental ability

Gender Schema Theory: Theory about how children learn appropriate cultural definitions of gender, which become key structures around which all other information is organized

Gilligan's Gender Identity Theory: Theory suggesting that the core of gender identity development rests within the mother–child relationship; involves the development of connectedness in girls and autonomy in boys

Gender Transcendence: Rejection of traditional gender identities; integration of feminine and masculine selves into a self-defined gender identity

Androgyny: Blending of feminine and masculine traits

One final note, in an effort to address potential confusion: Try not to conflate gender transcendence theory, as initiated by Pleck and discussed here, with transgenderism, as explored in Chapter 1. In today's society, transgenderism typically extends from a person's feeling that her or his gender doesn't match her or his sex—sometimes described as being "trapped in the wrong body." People who adhere to the theory of gender transcendence may or may not also be transgender, although it's likely that this theory of gender identity development lends itself readily to a person who's experienced the confusion and contemplation integral to most transgender people. However, someone could consider himself or herself divergent or non-cohesive in biology versus psychology, decide to transition into a different sex, and then embody traditional notions of identity and behaviors for that sex. In such a circumstance, post-transition, the person would not be gender transcendent, but perhaps gender adherent. Choice is key.

SOCIALIZATION AND GENDER IDENTITY DEVELOPMENT

The process of developing gender identity involves acquiring information about cultural norms and roles (a social function), then adjusting one's view of self, one's role in society, and one's behavior in response to those norms (a psychological function). Some prefer to call this *socialization*, defined as the process through which individuals learn their culture, develop their potential, and become functioning members of society (Lindsey, 2015; Martin & Ruble, 2004). The primary vehicle for socialization is communication. Socialization occurs throughout the life cycle and includes gender identity development as only one facet. Focusing on gender identity within the larger framework of socialization helps us understand how we come to develop our sense of self, our own vision of appropriate roles and behavior for women and men, and our patterns in gender communication.

The Family as a Primary Socializing Agent

Our society is never finished socializing us, and the family is by far the most significant agent of socialization (Kimmel & Aronson,

2013; Owen Blakemore & Hill, 2007). Family communication scholar Virginia Satir (1972, 1988) viewed family as a place where "peoplemaking" occurred. This is a useful perspective because families do create people, not just children. The family has the ability to influence the gender identities of the people it makes by reinforcing the status quo or by offering a broader view (Galvin, 2006; Haddock, Zimmerman, & Lyness, 2003).

Gender differences in the treatment of children begins *before* birth. While most parents indicate that their first priority is to have a healthy baby, preferences according to sex are prevalent. Across the globe, most couples prefer male over female children, especially in a first or only child—a finding that hasn't changed much since the 1930s (Grayling, 2005; Haworth, 2013; Jain, Missmer, Gupta, & Hornstein, 2005; Oomman & Ganatra, 2002; Shannon, 2004; Stein, 2004; Wiseman, 2002).

After the birth of a child, the family maintains the major responsibility for socializing the child during the critical years of life, even when other socializing influences (like schools and peers) exist. In the family, the child gains a sense of self, learns language, and begins to understand norms of interaction with parents, siblings, and significant others. Sex-typing of babies occurs; in studies over multiple decades involving infants of similar weight, length, and health, both parents described sons as big, tough, strong, firm, and alert, while daughters were cheerful, gentle, delicate, soft, and awkward (Galvin, 2006; Rubin, Provensano, & Luria, 1974; Stern & Karraker, 1989).

© Monkey Business Images/Shutterstock.com

The family is by far the most significant agent of socialization.

Sex-typed socialization continues as children grow and mature (Rudman & Glick, 2010). Fathers are significantly more likely than mothers to differentiate between their sons and daughters, encourage more traditional sex-specific behavior in their sons, and play with their children differently dependent on the sex of the child (Kane, 2006; Lindsey & Mize, 2001; Pomeranz, Ng, & Wang, 2005; Raley & Bianchi, 2006). Heterosexual fathers are especially forceful in conditioning their sons to be heterosexual (Solebello & Elliott, 2011).

Secondary Agents of Socialization

Because of parents' influence on children's understanding of gender, some modern parents are trying a nongendered approach by giving children gender-neutral toys, games, and books, and avoiding more traditional items that can perpetuate stereotypes, like Barbie, G.I. Joe, and traditional fairy tales (Ayres-Brown, 2014; Grinberg, 2012; Messner, 2000). In this section, we address the socializing effects of clothing, toys, peer relationships, and teachers as role models. The media have a significant impact on children's gender identity development too—a topic we'll save for Chapter 8. For now, think about those things you played with as a child and those relationships in the neighborhood or at school that had the greatest effect on your gender identity development.

CLOTHES AND TOYS After birth, the first things typically acquired for an infant are clothes and toys. When the sex of a baby isn't known, friends and family members try to buy sex-neutral gifts, like yellow receiving blankets or green bibs. Color-coded and sex-typed clothing of infants and young children is still quite prevalent (Ehrensaft, 2011; Fagot, Rodgers, & Leinbach, 2000; Koller, 2008).

Along with clothing, toys and play are powerful forces of socialization (Forman-Brunell & Whitney, 2015; Messner, 2000). For girls, arguably the most popular and influential toy of all time is the Barbie doll. Barbie, in her various incarnations introduced across the years, continues to be the subject of much research and discussion, in terms of the doll's impact on young girls, how they see themselves, and how they develop notions of femininity and attractiveness (Barnett & Rivers, 2005; Bulik, 2014; Kuther & McDonald, 2004; Wanless, 2001; Zaslow & Schoenberg, 2012). Years ago, the male counterpart to Barbie was G.I. Joe. That series of "action figures" (certainly not dolls) set the model for a range of action figures targeted to boys. These figures emphasize ruggedness, adventure, and large muscles, and in many ways are as unrealistic for boys as Barbies are for girls. Research has shown that gendered toys are linked to lower self-esteem and eating disorders in both male and female children (Dittmar, 2010; Grogan & Richards, 2002; Kenway & Bullen, 2001).

Toys for girls encourage domesticity, interpersonal closeness, and social orientation, whereas boys receive not only more categories of toys, but also toys that are more complex and expensive, and that foster self-reliance, problem solving, and fantasy (Owen Blakemore & Centers, 2005). Boys' toys tend to be rated higher in sociability, competitiveness, aggressiveness, and constructiveness, whereas girls' toys are rated higher in creativity, manipulability, nurturance, and attractiveness (Owen Blakemore & Centers, 2005).

Feminism promised us two things: Fatter dolls and an end to traditional gender roles.
—Tina Fey, actor, screenwriter, and author

Some scholars believe that children construct a great deal of their sense of gender through play (Messner, 2000). Much of children's play has shifted from outdoors to indoors, with the rapidly increasing popularity and accessibility of video games (Banks, 2015). It's beyond the scope of this chapter to review the large volume of publications devoted to video gaming's socialization effects; we examine this topic more in depth in Chapter 8 on media. But a few studies deserve mention here, even if the results are contradictory.

One of the earliest threads of research on video games explored whether exposure to violent games led to enhanced violent or aggressive behavior in children (Zorrilla, 2010). For every study suggesting that exposure to virtual violence, especially the victimization of girls and women, affects aggressive attitudes and enhances aggressive behavior in real life (Carnagey & Anderson, 2005; Eastin, 2006; Konijn, Nije Bijvank, & Bushman, 2007; Norris, 2004; Shibuya, Sakamoto, Ihori, & Yukawa, 2008; Williams, Consalvo, Caplan, & Yee, 2009), there's an equally well-executed study saying "video games don't kill people, people kill people," in essence, a "don't blame the messenger" type of finding (Blake, 2008; Brenick, Henning, Killen, O'Connor, & Collins, 2007; Ferguson, 2007; Williams & Skoric, 2005).

Research documents a perpetual male dominance in terms of numbers of male characters in leading roles, as well as dominant, aggressive personalities

© Keith Homan/Shutterstock.com

Barbie has been influencing girls for generations.

and behaviors of those characters, and sexualized, marginalized depictions of female characters (Behm-Morawitz & Mastro, 2009; Cassell & Jenkins, 2000; Dill & Thill, 2007; Fox & Bailenson, 2009; Ivory, 2006; Martins, Williams, Harrison, & Ratan, 2009; Miller & Summers, 2007; Yao, Mahood, & Linz, 2010). But other research notes a significant increase in strong female characters, which some view as empowering to young girls and women who play (and design) such games (Banks, 2015; Bertozzi & Lee, 2007; Glenn, 2008; Herbst, 2005; Jansz & Martis, 2007; Kafai, Heeter, Denner, & Sun, 2008).

PEERS AND SCHOOL As children get older, they're gradually introduced into the world outside the family. Parents' gender expectations at home become extended into the child's social world. Parents initiate the first relationships for their children and for the first few years of life, children prefer playing with children of a similar age, sex unspecified. Often this is related to proximity, meaning that kids tend to play with other kids from their neighborhood or building since they're close by and handy. The sex of the child doesn't matter much until kids start school—then their preference for playmates changes quickly and same-sex "packs" of friends tend to emerge. This is also a time that poses a great challenge to parents of intersex children and to the children themselves, as schools tend to still be divided (by facilities, activities, and teaching/learning approaches) according to biological sex (Banda, 2013). Activities and games in schools tend to be strongly related to gender roles and are powerful agents of socialization (Lindsey, 2015).

GENDER AND CULTURE

All cultures differentiate between female and male behavior, though not in the same ways. Ancient Greek and Roman views of men and women mirror some of the current gender stereotypes. For example, women were assumed to be naturally emotional and nurturing. Men were assumed to be naturally rational and strong. These beliefs formed the basis of the patriarchal (male-dominated) system (Learner, 1986). Once this dominance was established largely on the basis of sex, it lasted for over 2,500 years and was incorporated into most, but not all, cultures. Let us first consider culture, in general, before turning to the role that sex and gender play in culture.

Culture Considered

Defining *culture* is as problematic as defining gender or communication. According to one definition, culture is "a learned system of knowledge, behavior, attitudes, beliefs, values, and norms that is shared by a group of people and shaped from one generation to the next" (Smith, 1966). Culture includes such elements as history, religion, values, social organization, and language. Anthropologist William Haviland (2002) states "in humans, it is culture that sets the limits on behavior and guides it along predictable paths" (p. 26). Culture essentially tells us who we are and what we should do. Culture strongly influences a person's behavior, including communication behavior. Another anthropologist, Edward T. Hall (1976), suggests that communication and culture are inseparable, in that you can't talk about one without the other.

Cultural expert Claude Levi-Strauss (2004) suggests that humans are represented by two sexes and a handful of races, but literally thousands of cultures. Cultural patterns, including sex and gender roles, reflect far too much diversity to be explained by biology or any other internal, hardwired mechanism. To understand sex and gender roles, you must begin with the notion that roles are arbitrarily constructed by cultures (Cooper, Calloway-Thomas, & Simonds, 2007). It's difficult, if not impossible, to understand your own role without at least having some understanding of your culture.

Dutch anthropologist Geert Hofstede (1980, 1991, 2011) and colleagues developed four fundamental dimensions of culture: individualism/collectivism, power distribution, uncertainty avoidance, and masculinity/femininity. Of most interest to our discussion is the dimension of masculinity/femininity. Hofstede (1998) identifies cultures as existing on a continuum from masculine to feminine. He describes *masculine cultures* as societies in which men are supposed to be assertive, tough, and focused on material success, while women are supposed to be modest, tender, and concerned with the quality of life. In *feminine cultures*, both women and men are supposed to be modest, tender, and concerned with the quality of life. In one line of research, Hofstede and Hofstede (2005) rated seventy-four countries on a scale called the Masculinity Index, which measures masculine values such as assertiveness, performance, and competitiveness, and how much these values prevail over typically feminine values. Results showed that the five most masculine nations were Slovakia, Japan, Hungary,

Austria, and Venezuela. The most feminine countries were the four Scandinavian countries—Denmark, the Netherlands, Norway, and Sweden, with Slovenia and Costa Rica close behind. The United States ranked nineteenth on the Masculinity Index, meaning that our culture adheres more closely to prescribed sex roles than many other countries in the world (Hofstede & Hofstede, 2005). However, Hofstede is careful to point out that his conclusions about cultural characteristics are not absolute; his results represent tendencies, not explicit or clear-cut differences.

> Sex and race, because they are easy and visible differences, have been the primary ways of organizing human beings into superior and inferior groups. . . . We are talking about a society in which there will be no roles other than those chosen or those earned.
> —Gloria Steinem, author and political activist

In masculine cultures, both women and men express a strong preference for distinct and separate masculine and feminine roles. But in most feminine cultures, no difference exists between the responses of women and men; both indicate a preference for a tender and nurturing value system. People in masculine cultures tend to be less permissive, more formal, and more structured than people in feminine cultures, and they conduct business in a more aggressive style, viewing meetings as opportunities to express themselves and to sell ideas. People in feminine cultures tend to prefer shorter working hours to higher salaries, and meetings are viewed as opportunities for cooperative consensus building (Hofstede, 1998; Hofstede & Hofstede, 2005).

When Aspects of Identity Intersect

Internal identity conflicts (and some external ones too) are frequently caused by the intersection or overlapping of different parts of your identity. When different segments of your identity bump up against one another, you experience *intersectionality* (Yep, 2016). The conceptual origins of intersectionality emanated from the work of sociologist W. E. B. DuBois. In his influential book *The Souls of Black Folks* (1903/2004), DuBois described the intersection of race, class, and nation to explain the situation facing Black people at the time. According to sociologist Patricia Collins (2000), DuBois asserted that culture, race, gender, and economic class were not merely personal identifiers, but aspects of identity that marked or controlled how people interacted in society at large. For example, DuBois contended that Black women carried a special burden— not only were they Black, poor, and second-class citizens, but they were female as well. The ways in which these identity characteristics intersect provide keen insights into human behavior.

Collins (1998) contends that gender identities are not the same across racial groups and social classes. White women, Black women, Hispanic women, and Asian women, among others in the United States, do not have the same or even similar gender identities. Collins believes that we must examine how gender is constructed within the context of race and class, not separately as a construct unto itself. Doing so allows a complex web of understanding and social relationships to emerge. Moreover, Collins suggests that, to further our understanding of the human condition, we must move beyond race, class, and gender to encompass additional categories, such as nationality, sexuality, ethnicity, age, and religion.

We know we've tossed a great many ideas your way in this chapter on sex and gender identity development, but we trust that you'll iron out the information and find a way to make sense out of it and apply it to your life. We leave you with an interesting exercise to try, one that encapsulates what we've been talking about in this chapter: Pick someone—anyone. It could be a classmate, a dorm or apartment roommate, family member, or relational partner. Write down the factors of that person's identity you perceive to be primary, meaning those aspects that rise up in importance (from your perspective). What factors did you list? Sex? Gender? Race or ethnicity? Religion? Social class? Educational level? Sexual orientation? What came to mind first? Did you think of one primary factor and then allow that factor to overshadow others? Or could you only see the whole person, not separate facets?

After you've generated the list, ask the person to do the same thing about herself or himself, independently of your list. Then share lists and check for agreement. Significant discrepancies might mean that the person views himself or herself quite differently than others do. It might be that the person just isn't very good at self-presentation, or perhaps she or he extends only certain parts of the personality to you, saving other aspects for other people. Perhaps you focused on one part of the person's identity to the exclusion of other parts. Why might this have happened? This exercise will likely make you closer to the other person, or at least know him or her better, so choose your person with that in mind. The exercise can be extended by delving into a discussion of how people handle conflicts between various aspects of their identity, particularly as relates to the enactment of sex and gender roles.

Remember...

Socialization: Process through which individuals learn their culture, develop their potential, and become functioning members of society

Culture: A learned system of knowledge, behavior, attitudes, beliefs, values, and norms that is shared by a group of people and shaped from one generation to the next

Masculine Cultures: Cultures in which men are supposed to be assertive, tough, and focused on material success, while women are supposed to be modest, tender, and concerned with the quality of life

Feminine Cultures: Cultures in which both women and men are supposed to be modest, tender, and concerned with the quality of life

Intersectionality: When identity variables such as gender, race/ethnicity, and class collide

CONCLUSION

Learning to be a woman or man is both interesting and problematic. This chapter examined factors that influence your sex and gender identity development. What it means to be masculine and feminine in today's modern society changes—it seems like almost every day. It's important to factor in your personality attributes, experiences, and culture as you shape your view of yourself and others.

Biological influences discussed in this chapter affect your view of self. Social and cultural influences, as well as your own attitudes about appropriate roles for others to assume in society, shape your view of self. Out of these biological, social, and cultural influences, you form a psychological response—your gender identity—which is expressed in your communication with others. Sex and gender are not the only, and sometimes not the most important, aspects of a person's identity. Knowing and attending to the intersections of various dimensions of one's own identity and others' identities can do much to enhance your communication.

Improving your gender communication skills starts with introspection—a long, hard look at yourself in terms of your sex and your gender identity. As you learn more about the effects of gender on the communication process, your identity may begin to change. Or you may become more comfortable with your current view of self, so that it solidifies. We challenge you to answer the following questions for yourself, either after reading this chapter or this text, or after taking a course in gender communication: What is your current gender identity? What aspects of your biology most affect this identity? What social and cultural influences most shaped your identity? How does your communication clue people as to your gender identity? What other factors of identity (e.g., race, class, religion) intersect with your sex and gender to create your full identity? How can you become more effective in communicating who you are to others?

DISCUSSION STARTERS

1. On a sheet of paper, list ten of the most common adjectives describing women; then list ten for men. Discuss in class whether these adjectives reflect stereotypes or "real" traits. Have people's stereotypes of the sexes changed? In what ways? What does it mean now, in the twenty-first century, to be feminine? Masculine?

2. Think about reproductive capabilities. What if someday science and technology were to progress to the point where men could carry a fetus and give birth? Would they still be "men"? After all, what is the real definition of a man? A woman?

3. Of the various agents of socialization discussed in this chapter—family, clothes, toys, peers, and school—which do you think has had the greatest impact on your gender identity? If, for example, the greatest influence on you was your family, do you adhere to stereotypical masculine or feminine traits learned in your family, or has your identity transcended gender?

4. Consider the intersections of various aspects of your identity and how those aspects are viewed. Have you had internal conflicts over how to communicate your identity? If so, how did you work them out? Have you experienced conflicts about your own gender identity versus how someone significant to you views your identity? If so, how did you resolve that conflict?

References

Addis, M. E., Mansfield, A. K., & Syzdek, M. R. (2010). Is "masculinity" a problem?: Framing the effects of gendered social learning in men. *Psychology of Men and Masculinity, 11,* 77–90.

Aitchison, C. (2006). *Sports and gender identities: Masculinities, femininities, and sexualities.* New York: Routledge.

Andersen, P. A. (2006). The evolution of biological sex differences in communication. In K. Dindia & D. J. Canary (Eds.), *Sex differences and similarities in communication* (2nd ed., pp. 117–136). Mahwah, NJ: Erlbaum.

Ayres-Brown, A. (2014, April 21). McDonald's gave me the "girl's toy" with my Happy Meal. So I went to the CEO. Retrieved April 24, 2014, from <www.slate.com/blogs>.

Baenninger, M. A., & Newcombe, N. (1995). Environmental input to the development of sex-related differences in spatial and mathematical ability. *Learning and Individual Differences, 7.* [Excerpt derived from Paul, E. L. (2002). *Taking sides: Clashing views on controversial issues in sex and gender* (2nd ed., pp. 97–107). New York: McGraw-Hill/Dushkin.]

Banda, P. S. (2013, March 3). Child embraces his inner little girl. *Corpus Christi Caller Times,* p. 17A.

Bandura, A. (1971). Social-learning theory of identificatory processes. In D. A. Goslin (Ed.), *Handbook of socialization theory and research.* Chicago: Rand McNally.

Bandura, A. (1986). *Social foundations of thought and action: A social cognitive theory.* Englewood Cliffs, NJ: Prentice Hall.

Banks, J. (2015, May). Digital games as communication and culture. *Spectra,* 8–15.

Barnett, R. C., & Rivers, C. (2005). *Same difference: How gender myths are hurting our relationships, our children, and our jobs.* New York: Basic Books.

Baron-Cohen, S. (2012). *The essential difference: Men, women, and the extreme male brain.* New York: Penguin.

Barrett, H. (1998). *Maintaining the self in communication.* Incline Village, NV: Alpha & Omega.

Behm-Morawitz, E., & Mastro, D. (2009). The effects of the sexualization of female video game characters on gender stereotyping and female self-concept. *Sex Roles, 61,* 808–823.

Bem, S. L. (1983). Gender schema theory and its implications for child development: Raising gender-aschematic children in a gender-schematic society. *Signs, 8,* 598–616.

Benbow, C. P., & Stanley, J. C. (1980). Sex differences in mathematical ability: Fact or artifact? *Science, 210,* 1262–1264.

Bertozzi, E., & Lee, S. (2007). Not just fun and games: Digital play, gender, and attitudes towards technology. *Women's Studies in Communication, 30,* 179–204.

Billings, A. C., Butterworth, M. L., & Turman, P. D. (2015). *Communication and sport: Surveying the field* (2nd ed.). Los Angeles: Sage.

Blake, B. (2008, June 27). Go ahead, steal my car. *The Chronicle Review,* pp. B6–B7.

Bleier, R. (1984). *Science and gender: A critique of biology and its theories on women.* New York: Pergamon.

Borisoff, D., & Merrill, L. (1998). *The power to communicate: Gender differences as barriers* (3rd ed.). Prospect Heights, IL: Waveland.

Boushey, H. (2009). The new breadwinners. In H. Boushey & A. O'Leary (Eds.), *The Shriver report: A woman's nation changes everything.* Washington, DC: Center for American Progress.

Brenick, A., Henning, A., Killen, M., O'Connor, A., & Collins, M. (2007). Social evaluations of stereotypic images in video games. *Youth and Society, 38,* 395–419.

Brizendine, L. (2007). *The female brain.* New York: Broadway.

Brizendine, L. (2010). *The male brain: A breakthrough understanding of how men and boys think.* New York: Broadway.

Brott, A. A. (2008). *Fathering your child from the crib to the classroom* (2nd ed.). New York: Abbeville Press.

Brownmiller, S. (2013). *Femininity.* New York: Open Road Media.

Bruce, T. (2012). Reflections on communication and sport: On women and femininities. *Communication & Sport, 1,* 125–137.

Bulik, B. S. (2014). To Mattel, Barbie represents girl power—unapologetically. *Advertising Age, 85,* 24.

Cahn, S. K. (2015). *Coming on strong: Gender and sexuality in women's sport* (2nd ed.). Champaign: University of Illinois Press.

Caplan, P. J. (2008, Summer). Pathologizing your period. *Ms.,* 63–64.

Carnagey, N., & Anderson, C. (2005). The effects of reward and punishment in violent video games on aggressive affect, cognition, and behavior. *Psychological Science, 16,* 882–889.

Cassell, J., & Jenkins, H. (Eds.) (2000). *From Barbie to Mortal Kombat.* Cambridge, MA: MIT Press.

Cergol, G. (2010, March 11). Women in combat: What's the impact? Retrieved August 11, 2010, from <http://www.nbcnewyork.com>.

Collins, P. H. (1998). On book exhibits and new complexities: Reflections on sociology as science. *Contemporary Sociology, 27*, 7–11.

Collins, P. H. (2000). Gender, black feminism, and black political economy. *The Annals of the American Academy of Political & Social Science, 568*, 41–53.

Condit, C. (1996). How bad science stays that way: Brain sex, demarcation, and the status of truth in the rhetoric of science. *Rhetoric Society Quarterly, 26*, 83–109.

Connell, R. L. (2005). *Masculinities* (2nd ed). Oakland: University of California Press.

Connell, R. L., & Messerschmidt, J. W. (2005). Hegemonic masculinity: Rethinking the concept. *Gender and Society, 19*, 829–859.

Coontz, S. (2009). Sharing the load: Quality marriages today depend on couples sharing domestic work. In H. Boushey & A. O'Leary (Eds.), *The Shriver report: A woman's nation changes everything*. Washington, DC: Center for American Progress.

Cooper, P. J., Calloway-Thomas, C., & Simonds, J. (Eds.) (2007). *Intercultural communication: A text with readings*. Boston: Pearson.

Crawford, M. (2011). *Transformations: Women, gender, and psychology* (2nd ed.). New York: McGraw-Hill.

Davis, G., & Murphy, E. L. (2013). Intersex bodies as states of exception: An empirical explanation for unnecessary surgical modification. *Feminist Formations, 25*, 129–152.

DeVisser, R. O. (2010). I'm not a very manly man: Qualitative insights into young men's masculine subjectivity. In B. Hutchinson (Ed.), *Annual editions: Gender 10/11* (pp. 39–41). Boston: McGraw-Hill.

Devor, H. (1992). Becoming members of society: Learning the social meanings of gender. In M. Schaum & C. Flanagan (Eds.), *Gender images: Readings for composition* (pp. 23–33). Boston: Houghton Mifflin.

Dill, K. E., & Thill, K. P. (2007). Video game characters and the socialization of gender roles: Young people's perceptions mirror sexist media depictions. *Sex Roles, 57*, 851–864.

Dindia, K. (2006). Men are from North Dakota, women are from South Dakota. In K. Dindia & J. Canary (Eds.), *Sex differences and similarities in communication* (2nd ed., pp. 3–21). Mahwah, NJ: Erlbaum.

Dittmar, H. (2010). *Consumer culture, identity and well-being: The search for the "good life" and the "body perfect."* London: Psychology Press.

Donnelly, E. (2010, February 16). Women in combat, ctd. Retrieved August 11, 2010, from <http://www.nationalreview.com>.

DuBois, W. E. B. (1903/2004). *The souls of black folks*. Boulder, CO: Paradigm Publishers. (Original work published in 1903)

Duerringer, C. (2015). Be a man—buy a car! Articulating masculinity with consumerism in *Man's Last Stand*. *Southern Communication Journal, 80*, 137–152.

Eastin, M. (2006). Video game violence and the female game player: Self- and opponent-gender effects on presence and aggressive thoughts. *Human Communication Research, 32*, 351–372.

Eccles, J. S. (1987). Adolescence: Gateway to gender-role transcendence. In D. B. Carter (Ed.), *Current conceptions of sex roles and sex typing* (pp. 225–241). New York: Praeger.

Eccles, J. S. (1989). Bringing young women to math and science. In M. Crawford & M. Gentry (Eds.), *Gender and thought: Psychological perspectives* (pp. 36–58). New York: Springer.

Ehrensaft, D. (2011). *Gender born, gender made: Raising healthy gender-nonconforming children*. New York: The Experiment.

Ehrhardt, A. A. (1984). Gender differences: A biosocial perspective. In T. B. Sonderegger (Ed.), *Psychology and gender* (pp. 37–57). Lincoln: University of Nebraska Press.

Ehrhardt, A. A., & Meyer-Behlburg, H. (1980). Prenatal sex hormones and the developing brain: Effects on psychosexual differentiation and cognitive functions. *Annual Progress in Child Psychology & Child Development*, 177–191.

Fagot, B. L., Rodgers, C. S., & Leinbach, M. D. (2000). Theories of gender socialization. In T. Eckes & H. Trautner (Eds.), *The developmental social psychology of gender* (pp. 65–89). Mahwah, NJ: Erlbaum.

Fausto-Sterling, A. (1992). *Myths of gender: Biological theories about women and men* (2nd ed.). New York: Basic Books.

Feder, E. K. (2014). *Making sense of intersex: Changing ethical perspectives in biomedicine*. Bloomington: Indiana University Press.

Ferguson, C. (2007). The good, the bad, and the ugly: A meta-analytic review of positive and negative effects of violent video games. *Psychiatric Quarterly, 78*, 309–316.

Fischman, J. (2001, July 30). Do men experience menopause? *U.S. News & World Report*, 47.

Forman-Brunell, M., & Whitney, J. D. (Eds.) (2015). *Dolls studies: The many meanings of girls' toys and play*. London: Peter Lang.

Fox, J., & Bailenson, J. N. (2009). Virtual virgins and vamps: The effects of exposure to female characters' sexualized appearance and gaze in an immersive virtual environment. *Sex Roles, 61*, 147–157.

Galvin, K. (2006). Gendered communication in families. In B. Dow & J. T. Wood (Eds.), *The SAGE handbook of gender and communication* (pp. 41–55). Thousand Oaks, CA: Sage.

Gibbons, A. (1991). The brain as "sexual organ." *Science, 253,* 957–959.

Gilligan, C. (1982). *In a different voice: Psychological theory and women's development.* Cambridge, MA: Harvard University Press.

Glenn, K. (2008, October 3). She's got game. *The Chronicle Review,* p. B20.

Gray, P. B., & Anderson, K. G. (2010, May 14). Darwin's daddies. *The Chronicle Review,* pp. B12–B14.

Grayling, A. C. (2005, April 9). The power to choose. *New Scientist,* 17.

Grinberg, E. (2012, August 28). When kids play across gender lines. Retrieved August 28, 2012, from <www.cnn.com>.

Grogan, S., & Richards, H. (2002). Body image: Focus groups with boys and men. *Men & Masculinity, 4,* 219–232.

Gur, R. C., Gur, R. E., Obrist, W. D., Hungerbuhler, J. P., Younkin, D., Rosen, A. D., Skolnick, B. E., & Reivich, M. (1982). Sex and handedness differences in cerebral blood flow during rest and cognitive activity. *Science, 217,* 659–661.

Gur, R. C., Mozley, L. H., Mozley, P. D., Resnick, S. M., Karp, J. S., Alavi, A., Arnold, S. E., & Gur, R. E. (1995). Sex differences in regional cerebral glucose metabolism during a resting state. *Science, 267,* 528–531.

Haddock, S. A., Zimmerman, T. S., & Lyness, K. P. (2003). Changing gender norms: Transitional dilemmas. In F. Walsh (Ed.), *Normal family processes: Growing diversity and complexity* (3rd ed., pp. 301–336). New York: Guilford.

Hall, E. T. (1976). *Beyond culture.* Garden City, NY: Doubleday.

Halpern, D. (2012). *Sex differences in cognitive abilities* (4th ed.). New York: Psychology Press.

Hanafin, R. L. (2010, March 1). Department of Defense lifting ban on women in combat but not gays. Retrieved August 11, 2010, from <http://www.veteranstoday.com>.

Harris, F., III. (2010). College men's meanings of masculinities and contextual influences: Toward a conceptual model. *Journal of College Student Development, 51,* 297–319.

Haviland, W. A. (2002). *Cultural anthropology* (10th ed.). Belmont, CA: Wadsworth.

Haworth, A. (2013, January). Where the boys are. *Marie Claire,* 58–61.

Hecht, M. L., Ribeault, S. A., & Collier, M. J. (1993). *African American communication: Ethnic identity and cultural interpretation.* Newbury Park, CA: Sage.

Herbst, C. (2005). Shock and awe: Virtual females and the sexing of war. *Feminist Media Studies, 5,* 311–324.

Hill, C., Corbett, C., & St. Rose, A. (2010). *Why so few? Women in science, technology, engineering, and mathematics: Executive summary.* Washington, DC: American Association of University Women.

Hofstede, G. (2011). Dimensionalizing cultures: The Hofstede model in context. In L. A. Samovar, R. E. Porter, & E. R. McDaniel (Eds.), *Intercultural communication: A reader* (13th ed., pp. 19–33). Belmont, CA: Wadsworth.

Hofstede, G. H. (1980). *Culture's consequences: International differences in work-related values.* Beverly Hills, CA: Sage.

Hofstede, G. H. (1991). *Cultures and organizations: Software of the mind.* London: McGraw-Hill.

Hofstede, G. H. (Ed.). (1998). *Masculinity and femininity: The taboo dimension of national cultures.* Thousand Oaks, CA: Sage.

Hofstede, G. H., & Hofstede, G. J. (2005). *Cultures and organizations: Software of the mind* (2nd ed.). New York: McGraw-Hill.

Holland, S. L. (2006). The dangers of playing dress-up: Popular representations of Jessica Lynch and the controversy regarding women in combat. *Quarterly Journal of Speech, 92,* 27–50.

Holmes, J., & Schnurr, S. (2006). "Doing femininity" at work: More than just relational practice. *Journal of Sociolinguistics, 10,* 31–51.

Ivory, J. D. (2006). Still a man's game: Gender representation in online reviews of video games. *Mass Communication and Society, 9,* 103–114.

Jacklin, C. N. (1989). Female and male: Issues of gender. *The American Psychologist, 44,* 127–134.

Jain, T., Missmer, S. A., Gupta, R. S., & Hornstein, M. D. (2005). Preimplantation sex selection demand and preferences in an infertility population. *Fertility and Sterility, 83,* 649–658.

Jansz, J., & Martis, R. G. (2007). The Lara phenomenon: Powerful female characters in video games. *Sex Roles, 56,* 141–148.

Johnson, S. K., Murphy, S. E., Zewdie, S., & Reichard, R. J. (2008). The strong, sensitive type: Effects of gender stereotypes and leadership prototypes on the evaluation of male and female leaders. *Organizational Behavior and Human Decision Processes, 106,* 39–60.

Kada, O., Brunner, E., & Maier, M. (2009). Do male nurses suffer more? Focusing masculinity, femininity, sense of coherence, and work strain. *Journal of Men's Health, 6,* 247.

Kafai, Y. B., Heeter, C., Denner, J., & Sun, J. Y. (Eds.) (2008). *Beyond Barbie and Mortal Kombat: New perspectives on gender and gaming.* Cambridge, MA: MIT Press.

Kane, E. W. (2006). "No way my boys are going to be like that!" Parents' responses to children's gender nonconformity. *Gender & Society, 20*, 149–176.

Kehily, M. J., & Nayak, A. (2008). Global femininities: Consumption, culture, and the significance of place. *Discourse: Studies in the Cultural Politics of Education, 29*, 325–342.

Kelly, D. M., Pomerantz, S., & Currie, D. H. (2006). "No boundaries?" Girls' interactive, online learning about femininities. *Youth and Society, 38*, 3–28.

Kenrick, D. T., Neuberg, S. L., & Cialdini, R. B. (2005). *Social psychology: Unraveling the mystery* (3rd ed.). Boston: Allyn & Bacon.

Kenway, J., & Bullen, E. (2001). *Consuming children: Education, entertainment, and advertising.* Buckingham, UK: Open University.

Khan, K., & Blair, D. M. (2013). Writing Bill Clinton: Mediated discourse on hegemonic masculinity and the 2008 presidential primary. *Women's Studies in Communication, 36*, 56–71.

Kimmel, M. (2015). *Angry white men: American masculinity at the end of an era.* New York: Nation Books.

Kimmel, M., & Aronson, A. (2013). *The gendered society reader* (5th ed.). New York: Oxford University Press.

Kimmel, M. S. (2009). *Guyland: The perilous world where boys become men.* New York: Harper Paperbacks.

Kimmel, M. S. (2011). *Manhood in America: A cultural history* (3rd ed.). New York: Oxford University Press.

Kimmel, M. S., & Messner, M. A. (2012). *Men's lives* (9th ed.). Boston: Pearson.

Kimura, D. (1987). Are men's and women's brains really different? *Canadian Psychology, 28*, 133–147.

Kimura, D. (2000). *Sex and cognition.* Boston: MIT Press. [Excerpt derived from Paul, E. L. (2002). *Taking sides: Clashing views on controversial issues in sex and gender* (2nd ed., pp. 94–96). New York: McGraw-Hill/Dushkin.]

Kleiman, C. (1992, January 23). Males and their raging hormones. *Raleigh News and Observer,* pp. 1E, 2E.

Kohlberg, L. (1966). A cognitive-developmental analysis of children's sex-role concepts and attitudes. In E. E. Maccoby (Ed.), *The development of sex differences* (pp. 82–173). Stanford, CA: Stanford University Press.

Koller, V. (2008). "Not just a colour": Pink as a gender and sexuality marker in visual communication. *Visual Communication, 7*, 395–423.

Konijn, E. A., Nije Bijvank, M., & Bushman, B. J. (2007). I wish I were a warrior: The role of wishful identification in the effects of violent video games on aggression in adolescent boys. *Developmental Psychology, 43*, 1038–1044.

Kotz, D. (2010, May 7). Birth control pill turns 50: 7 ways it changed lives. Retrieved May 12, 2010, from <http://usnews.com>.

Kuther, T. L., & McDonald, E. (2004). Early adolescents' experiences with and views of Barbie. *Adolescence, 39*, 39–51.

Learner, G. (1986). *The creation of patriarchy.* New York: Oxford University Press.

Lenroot, R. K., & Giedd, J. N. (2010). Sex differences in the adolescent brain. *Brain & Cognition, 72*, 46–55.

Levi-Strauss, C. (2004). Gender differences in communication: An intercultural experience. In F. Jandt (Ed.), *Intercultural communication: A global reader* (pp. 221–229). Thousand Oaks, CA: Sage.

Lindsey, E. W., & Mize, J. (2001). Contextual differences in parent-child play: Implications for children's gender role development. *Sex Roles, 44*, 155–176.

Lindsey, L. L. (2015). *Gender roles: A sociological perspective* (6th ed.). New York: Routledge.

Lindsey, L. L., & Christy, S. (1997). *Gender roles: A sociological perspective* (3rd ed.). Upper Saddle River, NJ: Prentice Hall.

Linn, M. C., & Petersen, A. C. (1986). A metaanalysis of gender differences in spatial ability: Implications for mathematics and science achievement. In J. S. Hyde & M. C. Linn (Eds.), *The psychology of gender: Advances through meta-analysis* (pp. 67–101). Baltimore: Johns Hopkins University Press.

Lippa, R. A. (2005). *Gender, nature, and nurture* (2nd ed). London: Psychology Press.

Lockwood Harris, K. (2011). "Compassion" and Katrina: Reasserting violent white masculinity after the storm. *Women & Language, 34*, 11–27.

Lucas-Stannard, P. (2013). *Gender neutral parenting: Raising kids with the freedom to be themselves.* South Africa: Verity Publishing.

Maccoby, E. E., & Jacklin, C. (1974). *The psychology of sex differences.* Stanford, CA: Stanford University Press.

Maccoby, E. E., & Jacklin, C. (1980). Sex differences in aggression: A rejoinder and reprise. *Child Development, 5*, 964–980.

Martin, C. L., & Ruble, D. (2004). Children's search for gender cues: Cognitive perspectives on gender development. *Current Directions in Psychological Science, 13*, 67–70.

Martin, J. N., & Nakayama, T. K. (2013). *Experiencing intercultural communication* (5th ed.). New York: McGraw-Hill.

Martins, N., Williams, D. C., Harrison, K., & Ratan, R. A. (2009). A content analysis of female body imagery in video games. *Sex Roles, 61*, 824–836.

McLoughlin, M., Shryer, T. L., Goode, E. E., & McAuliffe, K. (1988, August 8). Men vs. women. *U.S. News & World Report,* 50–56.

Mean, L. J., & Kassing, J. W. (2008). "I would just like to be known as an athlete": Managing hegemony, femininity, and heterosexuality in female sport. *Western Journal of Communication, 72,* 126–144.

Messner, M. (2012). Reflections on communication and sport: On men and masculinities. *Communication & Sport, 1,* 113–124.

Messner, M. A. (2000). Barbie girls versus sea monsters: Children constructing gender. *Gender & Society, 14,* 765–784.

Michaels, J. (2015, June 30). Women not clamoring to enter combat arms fields. *USA Today,* retrieved July 1, 2015, from <http://www.usatoday.com>.

Miller, M. K., & Summers, A. (2007). Gender differences in video game characters' roles, appearances, and attire as portrayed in video game magazines. *Sex Roles, 57,* 733–742.

Mischel, W. (1966). A social learning view of sex differences in behavior. In E. E. Maccoby (Ed.), *The development of sex differences* (pp. 56–81). Stanford, CA: Stanford University Press.

Mortenson, T. G. (2008, June 6). Where the boys were: Women outnumber them in colleges and the work force, and too many men are failing to keep up. *The Chronicle of Higher Education,* p. A31.

Neary, L. (2010, March 1). Ending ban on women in combat is long overdue. Retrieved August 11, 2010, from <http://www.npr.org>.

Norris, K. (2004). Gender stereotypes, aggression, and computer games: An online survey of women. *CyberPsychology and Behavior, 76,* 714–727.

Northrup, C. (2010, April 22). The pill turns 50: Taking stock. Retrieved May 12, 2010, from <http://www.thehuffingtonpost.com>.

O'Brien, K. (2010, August 1). She shoots, she scores! What sports actually do for girls—and for all of us. *The Boston Globe.* Retrieved August 11, 2010, from <http://www.boston.com/bostonglobe>.

O'Grady, C. (2015, Winter). Born this way? Why an evidence-based stance on sex and gender is good for science and for feminism. *Bitch,* 29–33.

Oomman, N., & Ganatra, B. R. (2002). Sex selection: The systematic elimination of girls. *Reproductive Health Matters, 10,* 184–188.

O'Reilly, J., & Cahn, S. K. (2007). *Women and sports in the United States: A documentary reader.* Holliston, MA: Northeastern.

Owen Blakemore, J. E., & Centers, R. E. (2005). Characteristics of boys' and girls' toys. *Sex Roles, 53,* 619–634.

Owen Blakemore, J. E., & Hill, C. A. (2007). The Child Gender Socialization Scale: A measure to compare traditional and feminist parents. *Sex Roles, 58,* 192–207.

Painter, K. (2010, June 14). New dads can be a cautious lot. *USA Today,* p. 4D.

Peach, L. J. (1998). Women in culture: Introduction. In L. J. Peach (Ed.), *Women in culture: A women's studies anthology* (pp. 1–12). Malden, MA: Blackwell.

Peterson, J. L., & Shibley Hyde, J. (2010). A meta-analytic review of research on gender differences in sexuality, 1993–2007. *Psychological Bulletin, 136,* 21–38.

Pickard Leszczynski, J. (2009). A state conceptualization: Are individuals' masculine and feminine personality traits situationally influenced? *Personality and Individual Differences, 47,* 157–162.

Pinker, S. (2005, May 16). The science of gender and science: Pinker vs. Spelke. *The Edge.*

Pleck, J. H. (1975). Masculinity-femininity: Current and alternative paradigms. *Sex Roles, 1,* 161–178.

Pleck, J. H. (1977). The psychology of sex roles: Traditional and new views. In L. A. Cater, A. F. Scott, & W. Martyna (Eds.), *Women and men: Changing roles, relationships, and perceptions* (pp. 181–199). New York: Praeger.

Pleck, J. H. (1981). *The myth of masculinity.* Cambridge, MA: MIT Press.

Pomerantz, E. M., Ng, F. F-Y., & Wang, Q. (2005). Gender socialization: A parent x child model. In A. H. Eagly, A. E. Beall, & R. J. Sternberg (Eds.), *The psychology of gender* (2nd ed., pp. 120–144). New York: Guilford.

Raley, S., & Bianchi, S. (2006). Sons, daughters, and family processes: Does gender of children matter? *Annual Review of Sociology, 16,* 401–422.

Ramey, E. (1976). Men's cycles (They have them too you know). In A. Kaplan & J. Bean (Eds.), *Beyond sex-role stereotypes.* Boston: Little, Brown.

Richmond-Abbott, M. (1992). *Masculine and feminine: Gender roles over the life cycle* (2nd ed.). New York: McGraw-Hill.

Reeser, T. W. (2010). *Masculinities in theory: An introduction.* New York: Wiley-Blackwell.

Root Aulette, J., & Wittner, J. (2014). *Gendered worlds* (3rd ed.). New York: Oxford University Press.

Rubin, J. Z., Provensano, F., & Luria, Z. (1974). The eye of the beholder: Parents' views on sex of newborns. *American Journal of Orthopsychiatry, 44,* 312–319.

Rudman, L. A., & Glick, P. (2010). *The social psychology of gender: How power and intimacy shape gender relations.* New York: Guilford.

Satir, V. (1972). *Peoplemaking.* Palo Alto, CA: Science and Behavior.

Satir, V. (1988). *The new peoplemaking.* Mountain View, CA: Science and Behavior.

Schmid, R. E. (2005, March 1). US life expectancy up to 77.6 years; gender gap narrows. Retrieved August 11, 2010, from <http://www.bostonglobe.com>.

Science Daily. (2007, January 7). Age, gender major factors in severity of auto-accident injuries. Retrieved August 11, 2010, from <http://www.sciencedaily.com>.

Shannon, T. A. (2004). *Reproductive technologies: A reader.* Lanham, MD: Rowman & Littlefield.

Shibley Hyde, J. (2005). The gender similarities hypothesis. *American Psychologist, 60,* 581–582.

Shibley Hyde, J. (2006). Epilogue. In K. Dindia & D. J. Canary (Eds.), *Sex differences and similarities in communication* (2nd ed., pp. 413–418). Mahwah, NJ: Erlbaum.

Shibuya, A., Sakamoto, A., Ihori, N., & Yukawa, S. (2008). The effects of the presence and contexts of video game violence on children: A longitudinal study in Japan. *Simulation and Gaming, 39,* 528–539.

Sidelinger, R. J., Frisby, B. N., & McMullen, A. L. (2009). The decision to forgive: Sex, gender, and the likelihood to forgive partner transgressions. *Communication Studies, 60,* 164–179.

Smith, A. G. (Ed.). (1966). *Communication and culture.* New York: Holt, Rinehart & Winston.

Snowbeck, C. (2001, September 9). The many moods of testosterone. *Pittsburgh Post-Gazette,* as in *Corpus Christi Caller Times,* p. C7.

Solebello, N., & Elliott, S. (2011). "We want them to be as heterosexual as possible": Fathers talk about their teen children's sexuality. *Gender & Society, 25,* 293–315.

Spears Brown, C. (2014). *Parenting beyond pink and blue: How to raise your kids free of gender stereotypes.* New York: Ten Speed Press.

Spelke, E. (2005, May 16). The science of gender and science: Pinker vs. Spelke. *The Edge.*

Stein, R. (2004, December 14). A boy for you, a girl for me: Technology allows choice. *The Washington Post,* p. A1.

Stern, M., & Karraker, K. H. (1989). Sex stereotyping in infants: A review of gender labeling studies. *Sex Roles, 20,* 501–522.

Stevenson, B. (2007). Title IX and the evolution of high school sports. *Contemporary Economic Policy, 25,* 486–506.

Stevenson, B. (2010). Beyond the classroom: Using Title IX to measure the return to high school sports. *Review of Economics and Statistics, 92,* 284–337.

Stibich, M. (2008, June 4). Why do women live longer than men? Retrieved August 11, 2010, from <http://longevity.about.com>.

Stockard, J., & Johnson, M. (1980). *Sex roles.* Englewood Cliffs, NJ: Prentice Hall.

Tavris, C. (1992). *The mismeasure of woman.* New York: Simon & Schuster.

Tirrito, S. J. (2010). Women as endurance athletes: What you need to know. Retrieved August 11, 2010, from <http://www.coachtroy.com>.

TrafficSTATS. (2010). Motorists get improved risk information. Retrieved August 11, 2010, from <http://www.cmu.edu>.

Tyler May, E. (2010a, May 7). 50 years on the pill. *The Chronicle Review,* pp. B4–B5.

Tyler May, E. (2010b, Spring). The pill turns 50. *Ms.,* 40.

Tyler May, E. (2010c). *America and the pill: A history of promise, peril, and liberation.* New York: Basic Books.

U.S. Census Bureau. (2010). Retrieved June 30, 2010, from <http://www.census.gov>.

Wanless, M. D. (2001). Barbie's body images. *Feminist Media Studies, 1,* 125–127.

Williams, D., Consalvo, M., Caplan, S., & Yee, N. (2009). Looking for gender: Gender roles and behaviors among online gamers. *Journal of Communication, 59,* 700–725.

Williams, D., & Skoric, M. (2005). Internet fantasy violence: A test of aggression in an online game. *Communication Monographs, 72,* 217–233.

Winter, J., & Pauwels, A. (2006). Men staying at home looking after their children: Feminist linguistic reform and social change. *International Journal of Applied Linguistics, 16,* 16–36.

Wiseman, P. (2002, June 19). China thrown off balance as boys outnumber girls. *USA Today.* Retrieved August 13, 2010, from <http://www.usatoday.com>.

Witte, A. V., Savli, M., Holik, A., Kasper, S., & Lanzenberger, R. (2010). Regional sex differences in grey matter volume are associated with sex hormones in the young adult human brain. *Neuro Images, 49,* 1205–1212.

Women's Sports Foundation. (2015). Her life depends on it III: Sport, physical activity, and the health and well-being of American girls and women. Retrieved July 30, 2015, from <http://www.womenssportsfoundation.org>.

Yao, M. A., Mahood, C., & Linz, D. (2010). Sexual priming, gender stereotyping, and likelihood to sexually harass: Examining the cognitive effects of playing a sexually-explicit video game. *Sex Roles, 62,* 77–88.

Yep, G. A. (2016). Toward thick(er) intersectionalities: Theorizing, researching, and activating the complexities of communication and identities. In K. S. Sorrells & S. Sekimoto (Eds.), *Globalizing intercultural communication: A reader* (pp. 86–94). Los Angeles: Sage.

Zaslow, E., & Schoenberg, J. (2012). Stumping to girls through popular culture: Feminist interventions to shape future political leaders. *Women & Language, 35,* 97–116.

Zorrilla, M. (2010). *Video games and gender: Game representation, gender effects, differences in play, and player representation.* Unpublished undergraduate thesis, Central Washington University, Ellensburg, WA.

CHAPTER 3

CHOOSING AND USING GENDERED LANGUAGE

CASE STUDY

"*Cis* Who? LGBTQIA+ What?"

Prior to 2014, Facebook users could identify their sex/gender with two options only: male and female. But early in 2014, Facebook published over 50 terms as user options for identifying sex/gender online (Goldman, 2014; Steinmetz, 2014). You may have seen some of this language, whether or not you're a Facebook user. Some of the more prominent terms include *cis/cisgender* (more specifically, *cis female/male* and *cis man/woman)* and *transgender* (with variations like *trans woman/trans man*).

You've probably heard the term *transgender* and may remember our discussion of this form of gender in both Chapters 1 and 2, but perhaps *cis* is new to you. According to the Basic Rights Oregon organization, *cis* derives from the Latin meaning of "on this side of" and describes "people who, for the most part, identify as the gender they were assigned at birth. In other words, 'cisgender' is used to describe people who are not transgender" (Trans 101: Cisgender, 2014).

In 2013, self-described social justice comedian Sam Killerman published a handbook of gender terminology, with an extensive glossary of more terms than likely any of us have ever heard. Killerman explains that *cis* is a more politically sensitive replacement term for *normal*, because who gets to say what's "normal" anymore?

HOT TOPICS

- The power of choosing and using language
- Nonsexist (gender-fair) language and the interrelationship between language and thought
- Reasons for using nonsexist language
- Forms of sexist language, such as man-linked terms and generic pronouns
- Sexual language and what it communicates about people
- Linguistic practices that reflect bias, such as married names and titles
- Vocal properties and linguistic constructions that communicate tentativeness
- How people manage conversation

Another term and categorization of gender is *asexual*, an identifier for people who aren't sexually attracted to either women or men (Decker, 2014). These individuals may engage in sexual activity and have meaningful relationships in their lives, but according to the Asexual Visibility and Education Network (AVEN), an asexual person "does not experience sexual attraction" (Asexual Visibility and Education Network, 2015). Don't confuse asexuality with agender, defined as a people who don't necessarily see themselves as lacking a gender, but they don't view gender as a central or defining part of their identity as people (Killerman, 2013). In addition, the term *bisexual* has given way to the more all-encompassing term *bigender*, which takes the emphasis off of the sexual nature of the identity. The term *queer* has been reclaimed by some people as an umbrella term for anything "non-straight," but because of its history as a derogatory term, not everyone uses it or responds to its use positively (Killerman, 2013).

Confused? Overwhelmed? Ready to throw your hands up and retreat to the past? We understand those emotions. But at least now you can consider yourself current when you see a designation like "LGBTQIA+" (St. James, 2015). (Although to some, the "Q" stands for *questioning* rather than *queer*, as in people who are questioning or in the process of better understanding their identity.) Just how well you understand and embrace the extensive terminology associated with identity is up to you, but here's something to think about: Before all these terms surfaced (with no doubt more terms to surface in coming years), people who felt "different" or "not normal" had no language to describe their sense of difference or being "other." Without language for even the most basic aspects of identity, many people retreat inward and feel invisible, which typically leads to a pretty miserable life. You might *be* one of these people, so perhaps all of this new language gives you optimism that the world is becoming less dichotomous, less black and white and more shades of gray, less male and female and more about celebrating human uniqueness.

Language is an evolving entity; the plus sign at the end of LGBTQIA+ indicates that additional language will no doubt emerge over time. We can either be rigid and irritated by changing language, or become educated and make conscious choices about the language we and others choose to use.

Have you ever thought about language—how yours originated and how it has changed and evolved over time? Why are some people so protective of language and resistant to attempts to update it, as though the words they used were a central part of their identities? Sometimes it seems we hold onto language like we hold onto old, worn-out luggage.

This chapter offers an in-depth examination of language because *the language we choose to use reveals to others who we are*. One linguist put it this way: "What we say *is* who we are" (Penelope, 1990, p. 202). Communication scholars Taylor, Hardman, and Wright (2013) suggest, "All that is human is mediated through language." In this chapter, we put language under a microscope because, as much as some people discount its importance, the language you choose to use is your primary tool of communication, your primary method of communicating who you are to others and of becoming known by them (McConnell-Ginet, 2011). That puts language at the center of what most of us find incredibly important.

CHOOSING YOUR LANGUAGE

The terms *choosing* and *using* in the chapter title refer to our view of using language by choice. Many people use language out of habit—they talk the way they've always talked, simply because they've always talked that way. These people rarely think about the influence of language on their view of self, their relationships, and their communication. After reading this chapter, maybe you won't be one of these people.

This chapter scrutinizes language in order to examine its powerful influences on communication. We explore language in two ways, which also parallel our definition of gender communication: communication *about* and *between* women and men. We first focus on how language treats us, how it's used to communicate *about* the sexes. The latter part of the chapter explores language from the *between* standpoint, how gender affects our choice of language as we communicate with others.

WHAT IS LANGUAGE? WHAT IS SEXIST LANGUAGE?

A *language* is a system of symbols (words or vocabulary) governed by rules (grammar) and patterns (syntax) common to a community of people

© Olga Besnard/Shutterstock.com

We die. That may be the meaning of life. But we do language. That may be the measure of our lives. —Toni Morrison, author

(Beebe, Beebe, & Ivy, 2016). Graddol and Swann (1989) suggest that language is both personal and social, that it's a "vehicle of our internal thoughts" as well as a "public resource" (pp. 4–5). Our thoughts take form when they're translated into language, but sometimes language is inadequate to truly express thoughts and emotions. Have you ever seen or felt something that you just couldn't put into words?

Language has power because it allows us to make sense out of reality, but that power can also be constraining. If you don't have a word for something, can you think about it? Have you ever considered that maybe your thinking might be limited by your language? A whole host of "realities" may exist that you've never thought of because there are no words in your language to describe them.

Two researchers who investigated this notion were Edward Sapir and his student Benjamin Lee Whorf. They developed what has come to be called the *Sapir–Whorf Hypothesis*, which suggests an interrelationship between language and thought. Whorf (1956) hypothesized that "the forms of a person's thoughts are controlled by inexorable laws of pattern of which he [she] is unconscious" (p. 252). In this view, human thought is so rooted in language that language may actually control (or at least influence) what you can think about.

Remember...

Language: System of symbols (words or vocabulary) governed by rules (grammar) and patterns (syntax) common to a community of people

Sapir–Whorf Hypothesis: Supposition about the interrelationship between language and thought

Sexist Language: Verbal communication conveying differential attitudes or behaviors with regard to the sexes; language revealing that one sex is valued over others

Thus, language is a powerful tool in two ways: It affects how you think, shaping your reality; and it allows you to verbally communicate what you think and feel, to convey who you are to others. In the discussion of terminology in Chapter 1, we defined *sexism* as attitudes, behavior, or both that denigrate one sex to the exaltation of others. It follows, then, that *sexist language* is verbal communication that conveys those differential attitudes or behaviors. Not surprisingly, research documents a connection between people's attitudes toward the sexes and their language usage (Budziszewska, Hansen, & Bilewicz, 2014; Cralley & Ruscher, 2005; Douglas & Sutton, 2014; Formanowicz, Bedynska, Cislak, Braun, & Sczesny, 2013; Parks & Roberton, 2005, 2008).

Sexist language reflects women's traditional lower status and the male-dominated nature of U.S. society and other societies around the world (Teso & Crolley, 2013). Some scholars contend that English and similar languages cause women to be a *muted group* (Ardener, 2005; Kramarae, 1981, 2005). Muted group theorist Cheris Kramarae (1981) explains:

> Women (and members of other subordinate groups) are not as free or as able as men are to say what they wish, when and where they wish, because the words and the norms for their use have been formulated by the dominant group, men. So women cannot as easily or as directly articulate their experiences as men can. Women's perceptions differ from those of men because women's subordination means they experience life differently. However, the words and norms for speaking are not generated from or fitted to women's experiences. Women are thus "muted." (p. 1)

The intent in this chapter is to explore the English language, wonderful and flawed as it is—not to blame anyone, not to suggest that people use language purposefully to oppress others, and not to make readers feel defensive about how they use language. We all inherited a male-dominated language, but it's not some mystical entity that can't be studied or changed. Language may control some people, but it need not control you. Think of language as something that has tremendous influence on us, but remember that we can *choose* how to use it and how to influence *it*.

WHY USE NONSEXIST (GENDER-FAIR) LANGUAGE?

Inventorying your language and making changes takes work, but the benefits you'll experience are considerable. Below are five reasons for incorporating nonsexist (sometimes called *gender-fair*) language into your communication repertoire.

Net Notes

We all could use a little vocabulary expansion—whether for speaking or writing. Here are some useful websites that focus on language:

http://www.yourdictionary.com This extensive website offers dictionaries in many languages, a thesaurus, word-of-the-day, a resource of quotations, and specialized dictionaries.

http://www.vocabulary.com This site combines dictionary definitions with an adaptive game to help users build their vocabularies.

http://www.wordsmyth.net This site provides website search features and options for kids and adult educators alike, like clues and tips for solving crossword puzzles.

http://www.word-detective.com This online version of a newspaper column addresses readers' questions about words and language.

http://www.wordspy.com This site is self-described as "the word lover's guide to new words."

http://wordnik.com This website provides "everything you want to know" about words, related words, nontraditional definitions, related images, statistics, and audio pronunciations.

http://www.wordsmith.org You can sign up for A.Word.A.Day on this site, which also offers anagramming and other tidbits of information about language.

http://www.dictionary.com If you seek a definition for a word, type the word in at this site and it will provide several definitions from multiple reputable dictionaries, so you can compare meanings. The site will also provide pronunciation tips and translate words, phrases, or an entire web page from one major European language (including English) into another.

Reason 1: Nonsexist Language Demonstrates Sensitivity

While you may believe that variations among people are worthy of respect, you may communicate in a manner that contradicts your belief—out of ignorance (you just didn't know any better), nonchalance (thinking that sexist communication is "no big deal"), or denial (thinking no one would dare deem you a sexist because of how you talk) (Mallett & Wagner, 2011). Maybe your language is just a habit you think is too hard to change. But if who you are is how you talk, it's time to make your language match your beliefs.

Reason 2: Nonsexist Language Reflects Nonsexist Attitudes

Even though we aren't sure about the exact relationship between language and thought, it's clear that a relationship exists. So if you communicate in a sexist manner—whether or not you're aware it's sexist and regardless of your intentions—it's possible you hold some sexist attitudes (Douglas & Sutton, 2014; Swim, Mallett, & Stangor, 2004). Someone could justifiably deem you a sexist, insensitive person just by your use of outdated, non-inclusive language. Coincidentally, someone could deem you a nonsexist, gender-fair person with gender equitable views because you use gender-fair language (Koeser, Kuhn, & Sczesny, 2015).

> "Homophobe. Bigot. Gay-basher. Ignorant frat boy. Fat Jewish pig." I was called all these names when I foolishly used a gay slur in a misguided attempt to be funny. Do I believe what I was called to be true? Aside from the Jewish and fat part? No, absolutely not. But I learned a valuable lesson: A word can matter, whether it's said with malice or as a joke.
> —Brett Ratner, film director

Reason 3: Nonsexist Language Is Basic to the Receiver Orientation to Communication

In Chapter 1 we described our preferred receiver orientation to communication. With regard for language, simply put, if a listener (receiver) perceives your language to be sexist, that's a legitimate judgment—one you need to think about. You may not mean anything sexist or demeaning in your message, but if your message is interpreted by a listener as sexist, you can't erase it. The communication is *out there*. Convincing a listener you meant otherwise takes a lot longer than if you'd applied a little forethought before speaking.

Reason 4: Nonsexist Language Is Contemporary

One set of goals within higher education is that students will be able to think, write, and converse in a manner befitting a highly educated person. Using outdated, sexist language undermines that goal. The roles people can fulfill in today's world have changed a great deal and are likely to keep changing, so language must evolve to reflect current society.

Reason 5: Nonsexist Language Strengthens Expression

Some students believe that nonsexist language "junks up" their speaking and writing with a bunch of extra words, just to include everybody—like it's "PC run amok." But once students learn and begin to practice simple methods of avoiding sexist, exclusive language, they readily admit it makes their communication more clear and dynamic.

SEXIST LANGUAGE: FORMS, PRACTICES, AND ALTERNATIVES

This section is divided into two main areas: *forms* of sexist language and sexist *practices* that involve language. The first area has to do with language that is sexist in and of itself. In the second area, it's not the words themselves that are sexist but the traditions inherent in how we use language.

Forms of Sexist Language

MAN-MADE EVERYTHING Words or phrases that include *man*, as though these terms should operate as generics to stand for all persons, are referred to as man-linked terminology—a form of sexist language that has diminished but not disappeared (Miller, Swift, & Maggio, 1997; Steinem, 1995). Calling a group of people that includes both men and women (or just women) "guys" is probably the most common example of sexist man-linked terminology (Earp, 2012). The term *man* or its derivative *mankind* in reference to all persons creates ambiguity and confusion when one doesn't know whether the term refers to a set of male persons or to all persons in general.

Originally, *man* was derived from a truly generic form, similar to the term *human*. Contrary to popular belief, the term *woman* didn't derive from the term *man*, nor did *female* derive from *male* (Hardman, 1999). The terms for female-men (*wifmann*) and male-men (*wermann*) developed when the culture decided it needed differentiating terms for the sexes (McConnell-Ginet, 1980). Maggio's (1988) dictionary of gender-free terminology provides Greek, Latin, and Old English terms for human, woman, and man. In Greek, the terms are *anthropos, gyne,* and *aner;* in Latin, *homo, femina,* and *vir;* and in Old English, *man, female,* and *wer* (pp. 176–177). *Wer* fell out of use, and *man* came to mean *men.* The problem is that *man* (as well as *guys*) should be a designation only for *male* persons, not *all* persons.

Even though the word *human* contains *man,* it's derived from the Latin *homo,* meaning all persons. The term *human* doesn't connote masculine-only imagery like the term *man* does (Graddol & Swann, 1989; Maggio, 1988). Man-linked terms include expressions such as *man the phones* or *manned space flight* as well as numerous words that have *man* attached to or embedded within them (e.g., *repairman*), which convert the term into a role, position, or action that an individual can assume or make (Palczewski, 1998). Unfortunately, people see the masculine part of the term and form perceptions that the word describes something masculine only.

Alternatives to *man* (e.g., *people, persons, individuals*), the simplest being *human* (and its derivatives *human being, humanity,* and *humankind*), have become more commonplace in everyday language usage. Many man-linked terms can be "nonsexed" by simply substituting *person* for the word *man; chairman* becomes *chairperson, spokesman* becomes *spokesperson,* and so forth. Other terms require more creativity, such as *postman* becoming *mail carrier, spaceman* becoming *astronaut,* etc.

ANTIMALE BIAS IN LANGUAGE Language scholar Eugene August (1992) describes three forms of antimale language in English: gender-exclusive language, gender-restrictive language, and language that evokes negative stereotypes of males. First, August explores the equating of *mother* and *parent,* suggesting that the terms are often used interchangeably, whereas the term *noncustodial parent* is almost always synonymous with *father.* He suggests that males are also excluded from terms describing victims, such as the expressions *wife abuse* and *innocent women and children.* This language implies that males can't be victims of violence, rape, and abuse. This is clearly not the case, and our language is beginning to reflect that fact. For example, *spousal abuse* or *partner abuse* is more often used today because it reflects the reality that either spouse or partner in a relationship could be the abused party.

August's second category, gender-restrictive language, refers to language that limits men to a social role. August's examples include language that strongly suggests to boys the role they're to play and chastises them if they stray from that role or don't perform as expected (e.g., *sissy*, *mama's boy*, *take it like a man*, and *impotent*). In the final category, August claims that "negative stereotyping is embedded in the language, sometimes it resides in people's assumptions about males . . ." (p. 137). As evidence of this tendency, August cites terms linked to crime and evil, such as *murderer*, *mugger*, *suspect*, and *rapist*—terms he contends evoke male stereotypes that are "insulting, dehumanizing, and potentially dangerous" (p. 132). In reference to the term *rape*, August discusses the fact that the majority of rapes are committed by males on female victims; however, the bias comes in with the assumption of a female victim, ignoring rapes perpetrated against males.

THE PERPETUAL PRONOUN PROBLEM Think about what you were taught regarding pronouns. If you were taught that the masculine pronoun *he* (and its derivatives *his*, *him*, and *himself*) was perfectly acceptable as a generic term for all people, then you got an outdated lesson. Research from the 1970s to the present provides convincing evidence that the generic *he* isn't generic at all; it's masculine and conjures masculine images (Clason, 2006; Conkright, Flannagan, & Dykes, 2000; Earp, 2012, Gabriel, 2008; Gastil, 1990; Gygax, Gabriel, Sarrasin, Oakhill, & Garnham, 2009; Hamilton, 1988; He, 2010; Krolokke & Sorenson, 2006; Lee, 2007; Moulton, Robinson, & Elias, 1978; Romaine, 1999; Stinger & Hopper, 1998). As Hopper (2003) points out, if the choice is made to say *he* not in reference to a specific man, two meanings for the word are created: a male individual and a person of undetermined sex. The listener's job then is to figure out which meaning is intended. Why give the listener that task? Why not make it clear?

One of the most illuminating early studies on this topic was conducted by Wendy Martyna (1978), who investigated college students' use of pronouns by asking them to complete sentence fragments, both orally and in writing. Students were asked to provide pronouns to refer to sex-indefinite nouns, as in the statement, "Before a judge can give a final ruling,_____." Occupations or roles depicted in the fragments included *doctor*, *lawyer*, *engineer*, *judge*, *nurse*, *librarian*, *teacher*, *babysitter*, and neutral terms like *person*, *individual*, and *student*. Participants also described images or ideas that came to mind as they chose pronouns to complete sentence fragments.

In a nutshell, college students in Martyna's research continually read sex into the subjects of sentence fragments and responded with sex-specific pronouns. The nurses, librarians, teachers, and babysitters were predominantly *she*, while the doctors, lawyers, engineers, and judges were *he*. Neutral subjects most often received the pronoun *they*. If the pronoun *he* had truly been a term indicating all persons, then *he* would have been the pronoun of choice no matter what role the sentence depicted. In conjunction with their choices of pronouns, students reported sex-stereotypical images that came to mind when they read the fragments.

If you think that Martyna's study is so dated that the results couldn't be replicated, think again. In the mid 1990s at two universities, researchers repeated and extended Martyna's study, hoping to find that contemporary college students were attuned to the problem of sexist pronouns (Ivy, Bullis-Moore, Norvell, Backlund, & Javidi, 1995). On the contrary, the results were virtually the same. For terms like *lawyer, judge,* and *engineer,* students responded predominantly with male pronouns and imagery, while *nurses, librarians,* and *babysitters* were female. The results of these and more current studies underscore the fact that people (at least in U.S. culture) can hardly function without knowing the sex of a person. If they aren't told the sex of a person, they generally assign one based on stereotypes (Earp, 2012; Flanigan, 2013; Grey, 2015). Are we passing this sex-stereotypical language down to our kids?

College students still think of doctors as 'he' and nurses as 'she'.

© Rob Marmion/Shutterstock.com

Studies show that exclusive pronoun usage (1) places undue emphasis on males; (2) maintains sex-biased perceptions; (3) shapes people's attitudes about careers that are appropriate for members of one sex but not others; (4) causes some people to believe that certain jobs and roles aren't attainable; and (5) contributes to the belief that men deserve more status in society than anyone else (Briere & Lanktree, 1983; Brooks, 1983; Burkette & Warhol, 2009; Earp, 2012; Gygax et al., 2009; Ivy, 1986; Stericker, 1981; Stinger & Hopper, 1998).

THE PRONOUN SOLUTION Does a pronoun exist that can stand for everyone? Some scholars have attempted to introduce new words, or *neologisms*, into the language, primarily for the purpose of inclusivity. Historically, such neologisms as *gen, tey, co, herm,* and *heris* didn't have much success in being adopted into common usage. However, new neutral terms like *ze* and *hir* have emerged (and are preferred by many transgender people), but we've yet to see whether these will catch on in general use (Grey, 2015; Killerman, 2013).

Right now, the best ways to avoid excluding any portion of the population in your communication are to (1) omit a pronoun altogether, either rewording a message or substituting an article (*a, an,* or *the*) for the pronoun; (2) use *you* or variations of the indefinite pronoun *one;* or (3) use the plural pronoun *they* (which may drive your English professors crazy). Using a plural pronoun in a singular sense is becoming more common and acceptable, both in written and oral forms (Grey, 2015; Madson & Shoda, 2006; Strahan, 2008).

THE LADY DOCTOR AND THE MALE NURSE A subtle form of sexist language, called *marking*, involves placing a sex-identifying adjective in front of a noun to designate the reference as somehow different or deviant from the norm (DeFrancisco & Palczewski, 2007; West, 1998). Sex-marked language is limiting, discriminatory, and unnecessary. Examples of this practice include *woman* or *lady doctor, male secretary, female boss, female soldier,* and *lady lawyer.* As more people enter in greater numbers into fields typically dominated by members of other sexes, some of these references are disappearing.

Remember...

Man-Linked Terminology: Use of words or phrases that include man in them as generics to stand for all people

Antimale Bias: Language use that excludes men, restricts the roles for and perceptions of men, and evokes negative stereotypes of men

Generic Pronoun: Use of a masculine pronoun as a term to stand for all people

Neologism: New word introduced into a language

Marking: Placing a sex-identifying adjective in front of a noun to designate the reference as somehow different or deviant from the norm

Feminine Suffix: Adding a suffix to a male term to form a female term

"Go Team!"

Do you have athletic teams at your college? Are team names differentiated by sex? It's common to find men's athletic teams named simply "Tigers" or "Longhorns," but what happens when women's teams are introduced at those schools? Are they Tigers and Longhorns too or do they become "Lady Tigers" and "Lady Longhorns"?

At many institutions, the latter is exactly what happens. Is that a sexist practice or just a matter of which team came first? Sociologist Faye Linda Wachs (2006) studied the "male universal" norm in the sports world and concluded that "women's teams are often marked with feminized nicknames, while male teams hold the general mascot name (i.e., Lady Gamecocks, Wildkittens, Lady Lions). Though this practice is decreasing over time, it remains a barrier to equality for women's sports" (p. 45). Even major tournaments and sports associations contain differentiated language; for example the men's collegiate basketball tournament is simply the NCAA tournament, whereas the women's counterpart event is marked by the term "women's" or "ladies.'"

Studies have investigated the extent of the problem among collegiate athletic teams in the South, finding that most schools used gender markings for their women's teams; 61 percent of schools used the term "lady" to distinguish women's teams from men's. None used the marker "gentleman" for men's team names (Fabrizio Pelak, 2008). Research shows that women's athleticism is stronger at schools with non–gender-marked team names and that more women serve in coaching positions at such schools (Ward, 2004). Language is, indeed, powerful. If your university has sex-marked team names, should that tradition be changed? If so, how would you go about it?

HOW'S TRIX? We have the eleventh-century French language to thank for many suffixes like -*ette*, -*ess*, -*enne*, and -*trix* still used in English to form a feminine version of a generic or masculine term, such as in *bachelor/bachelorette* and *governor/governess*. Your textbook author must admit to being an avid fan of the TV show *Shark Tank*, but cringes each time egotistical shark Kevin O'Leary disrespectfully refers to the female business moguls on the show as "sharkettes." Suffixed terms are problematic because, first, they often connote smallness, such as in reference to inanimate objects like *booklets* and *kitchenettes* (Holmes, 2001). Second, researchers have deemed it a subtle sexist practice to

Sex-marked language is limiting, discriminatory, and unnecessary.

attach suffixes to a male form of a word to establish a female form (He, 2010; Miller, Swift, & Maggio, 1997; Stahlberg, Braun, Irmen, & Sczesny, 2007). The suffix "perpetuates the notion that the male is the norm and the female is a subset, a deviation, a secondary classification. In other words, men are 'the real thing' and women are sort of like them" (Maggio, 1988, p. 178). Does the sex of the person waiting on your table at a restaurant really matter? Does someone who is admired need to be called a *hero* or a *heroine?* Such terminology makes a person's sex too important, revealing a need to know the sex to determine how to behave or what to expect.

How can sexist suffixes be avoided? Simply use the original term and omit the suffix. If there is a legitimate reason for specifying sex, a pronoun can be used, as in "The actor was performing her monologue beautifully, when someone's cell phone rang in the theatre." (Creators of the TV show *The Bachelor/The Bachelorette* will no doubt disagree.)

SPEAKING OF A HIGHER POWER . . .   Saying that the topic of sexism in religious language is "sticky" is a major understatement. It's not our intent here to uproot anyone's religious beliefs, but merely to provide food for thought.

People continue to debate the potential sexism in biblical language, as well as litany (what gets read or spoken in worship services; Bryant, 2008; Clason, 2006). Miller and Swift (1991) explain that within the Judeo-Christian tradition, religious scholars for centuries insisted that the translation of such an abstract concept as a deity into language need not involve a designation of sex. According to these researchers, "the symbolization of a male God must not be taken to mean that God really is 'male.' In fact, it must be understood that God has no sex at all" (p. 64). To one dean of the Harvard Divinity School, masculine language about God is "a cultural and linguistic accident" (Stendahl, as in Miller & Swift, 1991, p. 67). As one rabbi put it, "I think of God as an undefinable being; to talk about God in gender terms, we're talking in terms we can understand and not in terms of what God is really like" (Ezring, as in Leardi, 1997, p. H1).

The problem, at least for religions relying on biblical teachings, is that translations of scriptures from the ancient Hebrew language into Old English rendered masculine images of deity, reflecting the culture of male superiority (Kramarae, 1981; Schmitt, 1992). Thus, the literature is dominated by the pronoun *he* and such terms as *father* and *kingdom*. Linguistic scholars contend that much of the original female imagery was lost in modern translation or was omitted from consideration by the canonizers of the Bible (Miller & Swift, 1991; Spender, 1985). This point received resurgent attention when the book and movie *The Da Vinci Code* came out. The Old Testament says that humans were created in God's image—both male and female. It's interesting, then, that we have come to connect masculinity with most religious images and terms. Also interesting, as August (1992) contends, is the "masculinization of evil," the fact that male pronouns and images are most often associated with Satan, such as a reference to the *Father of Lies*. August says, "Few theologians talk about Satan and her legions" (p. 139).

Are you uncomfortable enough at this point in your reading to say to yourself, "Come on now; you're messing with religion. Enough is enough"? That's understandable, because religion is a deeply personal thing. It's something that a lot of us grew up with; thus, its images and teachings are so ingrained that we don't often question them or stop to consider where some of the traditions originated. However, questioning the language of religion doesn't mean that people are questioning their faith.

A few religions, primarily Judaism and Christianity, have begun lessening the male dominance in their communication (Jones & Mills, 2001). In some Christian sects, the masculinity *and* femininity of God are beginning to receive equal emphasis, as in one version of the Apostles' Creed which begins with "I believe in God the Father and Mother almighty, maker of heaven and earth." In 2002, publishers of the *New International Version Bible* announced that they would begin producing editions that contained more inclusive language (Gorski, 2002). Not all references to *men* were changed to *people*, nor were male references to God removed, but sex-specific language was altered when it was evident that the original text didn't intend any sex. For example, some references to *sons* were changed to *children* and *brothers* into *brothers and sisters*. Then in 2006, controversy arose again when publishers of a gender-inclusive Bible translation, *Today's New International Version*, were criticized by evangelical Christian groups who contended that the version was a feminist-driven effort to undermine Christian theology (Clason, 2006). These kinds of reforms are interesting and increasing in number, but they are unnerving to many people.

"Stay Out of Scripture?"

Our discussion of sexism in religious language may raise some hairs on the back of your neck, because religion, to many of us, is something deeply felt and rooted in tradition. Many people feel that changing the language in current translations of the Bible is akin to (or worse than) altering Shakespeare. If you're a person within the Christian tradition, which is grounded in biblical teachings, do you feel your faith or your ability to worship would be shaken if more gender-neutral terms appeared in the Bible? Would you trip over such language or see it as a welcome change? Is it political correctness gone amok, or an opportunity for more people to relate to biblical teachings?

REDUCED TO A BODY PART Language about sexuality profoundly affects perceptions, as well as communication. Most of us know that reducing people to their sexuality is a degrading practice that can be personally devastating.

Although research in the twenty-first century continues to explore sexual language usage (Braun & Kitzinger, 2001a, 2001b; Butler, 2004; Motschenbacher, 2009), we defer to the important work of linguist Robert Baker in the 1980s, who was interested in conceptions of women in American culture. Although men also are described in sexualized terms, significantly more sexual terms identify women than men (and we contend that that's still the case today). One study uncovered 220 terms for sexually promiscuous women and only twenty-two terms for sexually promiscuous men (Stanley, 1977).

Think of how many terms exist that are based on anatomy, but that may be used to describe a whole person. Over the years of teaching gender communication on the college level, students have been asked to participate in a "mature exercise" in which they provide current sexual terms—the language of their generation, even if they themselves rarely use such language. It's been interesting to see the shifts over the years, as well as the "creative" additions that inevitably make their contributions to the lexicon. Pardon the adult nature of this material, but here are some student-generated terms that describe women's anatomy or sexual behavior, many of which are interchangeable with the word *woman*: *vajayjay* (thanks to the TV show *Grey's Anatomy*), *coozie, coochie, vag, snatch, twat, pussy,*

beaver, cherry, a piece, box, easy, some (as in "getting some"), *slut, whore* (or *ho*), and a *screw, hookup,* or *lay.* Here's some male sexual lingo, again generated by research as well as college students: *wiener, dingle, schlong, peter, wanker, sausage, prick, cock, male member, dick, willy, tallywacker, johnson, dingdong, tool,* and a *screw, hookup,* or *lay.* Obviously, there are more terms than these, but we leave those to your imagination rather than putting them in print.

My mother never saw the irony in calling me a son-of-a-bitch.
—Jack Nicholson, actor

Anthropologist Michael Moffat (1989) studied university dormitory residents' use of language and found that one-third of young men in the study, in conversations with other men, consistently referred to women as "chicks, broads, and sluts," reflecting what Moffat termed a "locker-room style" of communication about women (p. 183). More recently, Hopper (2003) analyzed the speech patterns of dozens of men as they commented on women; he concluded that the degree of objectification and references to body parts was startling. Yes, we know that both men and women are capable of using sexually demeaning terminology. Hopper found that women frequently called or referred to other women in sexually objectifying terms, but they primarily used terms that implied sexual promiscuity (e.g., *slut, ho, easy*). However, in his research, subjects rarely talked about men in sexually degrading terms.

Two other studies examined college students' use and perceptions of sexual language (Murnen, 2000). In the first study, students were asked about their use of sexual language to describe others. Results showed that men were much more likely than women in the study to use (a) sexually degrading terms in reference to female genitalia, and (b) highly aggressive terms to refer to sexual intercourse. In a follow-up study, subjects listened to either two men or two women conversing about having sex with someone they'd just met the night before. Both male and female speakers who used degrading sexual language about their hookup were evaluated negatively by the listeners. However, in highly degrading conversations, the object of the degradation was judged as less intelligent and less moral than people who were spoken of in more respectful terms. Murnen concluded that use of sexual language is affected by a person's sex/gender, and that attitudes toward people of a different sex, as well as about sexual activity in general, are revealed by choice of language.

Another form of sexual language describes sexual activity, with an emphasis on verbs and their effect on the roles women and men assume

"Dirty Words"

We realize that many of you don't use the language we discuss (so bluntly) in this section of the chapter. But perhaps you've found yourself using language you wouldn't ordinarily use—only in specific situations, like when you were really down over being dumped from an important relationship or when you've been frustrated or mad. You probably know people who do use this kind of language, even if you don't use it yourself. How have you reacted when you've heard friends or acquaintances equate people with their sexual organs or body parts? Should language be an emotional release for people? Stated another way, is there a place and time for foul or degrading language? Does it depend on who's around to hear you?

sexually. Baker's synonyms for sexual intercourse, as generated by his students in the early 1980s, include *screwed, laid, had, did it, banged, slept with, humped,* and *made love to.* Feminist theorist Deborah Cameron (1985, 2009) adds the verb *poked* to the list. Author Jonathan Green (1999) offers such metaphorical language for intercourse as *jumped someone's bones* or *bod, bumped uglies, gave a tumble,* and *knocked boots.* Local students have generously contributed their own linguistic examples to the mix, including *hooked up with, got some from, got some play, made* (someone), *did the deed with, porked, boned, boinked, did the horizontal polka* (or *mambo*) *with, took,* and even *mated.* Whew, that's colorful.

According to Baker, the sexism lies in the placement of subjects preceding verbs as well as the objects that follow verbs. Sentences like "Dick screwed Jane" and "Dick banged Jane" describe men as the doers of sexual activity, while women are almost always the recipients. When a female subject of a sentence appears, the verb form changes into a passive rather than an active construction, as in "Jane was screwed by Dick" and "Jane was banged by Dick"—the woman is still the recipient (pp. 175–176). Baker debunks the argument that the tendency to describe males as active and females as passive reflects the fact that men's genitalia are external and women's are internal. If active sexual roles for women were the norm or more accepted, then Baker contends that the verb *to engulf* would be in common usage. Cameron (1985) proposes that the term *penetration* as a synonym for the sexual act suggests male origins; if a woman had set the term, it might have been *enclosure.*

Students of the twenty-first century believe that the dichotomy of male-active, female-passive sexuality is changing, as is the corresponding language. They offer a few active constructions for women's sexual behavior (largely related to women being on top in heterosexual intercourse, such as in the language *to ride*). Interesting changes will continue to take place in the sexual arena, linguistically speaking.

Sexist Linguistic Practices

THE NAME GAME Many of us believe that our names are an integral part of our identity. The long-standing practice of wives taking husbands' surnames isn't necessarily sexist; what's sexist is the expectation that a married heterosexual woman is supposed to or must take her husband's last name. For some women, assuming a husband's surname is something they've looked forward to all their lives. For others, this custom identifies the woman as property, which actually is the historic intent behind the practice.

Throughout a good deal of the twentieth century, most states in the U.S. required married women to assume their husbands' names in order to participate in such civic activities as voting (Emens, 2007). In the 1960s and '70s laws were overturned and many women kept their maiden names after marriage (Arichi, 1999; Emens, 2007; Goldin & Shim, 2004; Hopper, 2003). (There's really no such thing as a "maiden" name because most women's maiden or birth names are their fathers' last names.) Alternative naming practices became more prevalent during this time, such as adding the husband's last name to the wife's maiden name (having a two-word or hyphenated last name); the reverse of that (adding the husband's last name to the wife's birth or maiden name, although this option was far from prevalent; Stritof & Stritof, 2010); or coming up with a new hybrid last name for both spouses to adopt (Foss, Edson, & Linde, 2000; Johnson & Scheuble, 1995; Tracy, 2002). Married women who changed their names received warnings from academic sources as well as the popular press about a loss of identity and self-esteem, but research didn't detect any meaningful trends in this regard (Stafford & Kline, 1996). However, such practices were suspect in traditional social circles. Andy Rooney, late commentator for CBS' *Sixty Minutes*, was quoted as saying "women who keep their own names are less apt to keep their husbands."

Move forward into the twenty-first century and it seems as though the pendulum has swung back to the traditionalism of earlier generations, maybe more for expedience or simplicity's sake than as political commentary. Now fewer heterosexual women retain their maiden names after marriage than in the past (Black, 2009; Boxer & Gritsenko, 2005; Brightman, 1994; Kopelman, Fossen, Paraskevas, Lawter, & Prottas, 2009; Scheuble, Klingemann, & Johnson, 2000). Fewer couples choose to hyphenate; occasionally, wives may add their husbands' last name to their maiden name, but rarely do husbands follow suit. She may become Mary Smith Jones, but rarely does he become John Smith Jones; he's just John Jones.

Situational naming—using different versions of one's name depending on role or context—has become trendy. Sociologists Scheuble and Johnson (2005) surveyed 600 married women and found that in family or social situations wives tended to use their husbands' last name only, but in professional situations many preferred a hyphenated version, one that communicated a sense of independence associated with professional rather than personal life. The decision to use last names situationally was associated with level of education, type of employment (full-time versus part time), and age when first married. Similar studies found that feminist attitudes, level of career commitment, professional stature, concerns of ancestry, and value placed on motherhood were also factors that affected women's decisions about married names (Hoffnung, 2006; Laskowski, 2010).

How do same-sex, bigender, and transgender couples handle the last name issue? This decision was interesting enough when same-sex marriage was only legal in a few states in the U.S., but once the Supreme Court ruling in 2015 made same-sex marriage legal across the country, this negotiation has only become more interesting. This is an under-researched topic, at least at present, but it will no doubt receive much more attention as many more same-sex and transgender couples navigate the name dilemma. For some couples—gay, straight, and otherwise—the issue isn't important until they have or adopt children and confront decisions about children's last names (Clarke, Burns, & Burgoyne, 2008; Lannutti, 2008; Suter & Oswald, 2003). In the Clarke et al. (2008) study, one reason cited for not changing either gay spouse's last name upon marriage was resistance to heteronormativity; in other words, why do what straight people do?

When I got married my feminist friends went mad. One sniffed, "Are you going to take your husband's name?" I said, "No, because I don't think 'Dave' suits me very much."
—Jo Brand, British comedian

EUPHEMISMS AND METAPHORS The English language contains a great many expressions about the sexes that go seemingly unnoticed, but that form subtly sexist patterns. These expressions are usually in the form of *metaphors* or *euphemisms*—more comfortable substitutes for other terms (Cralley & Ruscher, 2005; Hegstrom & McCarl-Nielsen, 2002; Kovecses, 2010; McGlone, Beck, & Pfiester, 2006). One of the most influential authors on the topic of euphemistic language is Robin Lakoff, whose research from the 1970s continues to have impact today. Lakoff (1975) explored euphemisms for the word *woman*, such as *lady* and *girl*, and their connotations. While some people think of *lady* as a term of respect that puts a woman on a pedestal, to others it suggests negative qualities such as being frail, scatterbrained, sugary sweet, demure, flatterable, and sexually repressed. To illustrate, substitute *ladies* for *women* in the following organizations' titles: the National Organization for Women, the Black Women's Community Development Foundation, and the Harvard Committee on the Status of Women (Lindsey, 2005). In this context, the term *ladies* minimizes the seriousness of the group.

Connotations of the word *girl* have changed a great deal in recent years, as has its spelling in the media (*grrrl*) (Siegel, 2007). Many adult women in the '70s and '80s reported feeling patronized and disrespected when referred to as *girls*. The term connoted childishness, innocence, and immaturity—and most women don't want to be thought of in those terms. However, today more positive meanings for *girl* have emerged (especially for women in their teens and twenties). Many positive efforts and projects across the country continue to use *grrl*-language as a means of enhancing young girls' self-esteem and sense that they're not powerless in the world (Aragon, 2008; Radway, 2009; Riordan, 2001).

Some euphemistic confusion exists in the fact that there's no acceptable female equivalent term for *guy*. When males are called *guys*, females are called *girls*, rather than *gals* or *women*. Think about what would happen if you were to say to a group of men, "Good morning, boys!" It would most likely be interpreted as a condescending euphemism for men. The most appropriate terms to use depend on the context in which you find yourself.

A PARALLEL UNIVERSE *Symmetry* or *parallelism* in language refers to the use of gender-fair terms in referring to the sexes. Terms can be asymmetrical and sexist in three ways:

Words that seem parallel (equal) but aren't: An example that seems to be on its rightful way out is the statement, "I now pronounce you man and wife." This language suggests that the man is still a man, but the woman is now a wife, with the connotation that she is relegated to that one role while he maintains a complete identity. How different would the connotation be if the statement were, "I now pronounce you woman and husband"? In this category, language may seem parallel simply because it's used often and may go unnoticed, but upon inspection, the language perpetuates inequity.

Terms originally constructed as parallel, but meanings have taken on negative connotations (primarily for women) over time: Examples include *governor/governess, master/mistress, sir/madam,* and *bachelor/spinster* or *old maid.* A man who governs is a *governor,* but a *governess* has come to mean a woman who takes care of someone else's children. You can certainly see the gap between meanings in the second and third examples—*mistress* and *madam* have negative, sexual connotations while the masculine forms still imply power and authority. The last example is dramatic—as men grow older and stay single, they remain *bachelors* while women degenerate into *spinsters* and *old maids* (DeFrancisco & Palczewski, 2007; Romaine, 1999).

Acceptable words, but their usage becomes unacceptable because it alters the equality: Examples can be readily found in media, such as in news accounts when citizens encounter tragedies abroad, and a news reporter describes how "three people have been taken hostage—one is a woman." You often hear nonparallel usage in reference to soldiers killed in conflicts around the world, when special note is made of female military casualties or prisoners. The language depicts men as the norm and women as the aberrations (Lakoff, 1975; Maggio, 1988). Is a hostage or casualty situation made worse because one of the people is female?

OUT OF ORDER Have you heard the traditional saying "ladies first"? While some people still operate by this standard in things like opening doors, the "ladies first" pattern isn't predominant in the language. When you put language under the microscope, you find that male terms are almost always communicated first and female terms second, as in the following: his and hers; boys and girls; men and women; men, women, and children; male and female; husband and wife; Mr. and Mrs. Smith; the Duke and Duchess of Windsor; king and queen; brothers and sisters.

Three exceptions include the traditional greeting, "ladies and gentlemen," references to the "bride and groom," and a mention of someone's parents, as in "How are your mom and dad doing?" Putting the masculine term first gives precedence to men and implies that women were derived from men or are secondary to them (Amare, 2006; Frank & Treichler, 1989). The simple suggestion here is that you try to alternate which term you say or write first. It's a small correction in your language and few may notice, but it will make your communication more gender-fair.

TITLES AND SALUTATIONS The common male title *Mr.* doesn't reflect a man's marital status. Mr. Joe Schmoe can be single, married, divorced, or widowed. The titles for women include *Miss, Mrs.,* and *Ms.,* which have been called *nubility titles,* derived from the term *nubile,* which means sexually attractive or marriageable (Romaine, 1999). What differentiates *Miss* from *Mrs.* is marital status, but this is only a fairly recent usage. Until the nineteenth century, the two terms merely distinguished female children and young women from older, more mature women (Spender, 1985). History isn't clear about why the function of the titles changed, but some scholars link it to the beginning of the Industrial Revolution, when women began working outside the home. Supposedly, working obscured a woman's tie to the home, so the titles provided clarity (Miller & Swift, 1991). Because of the patriarchal nature of language, people deemed it necessary to be able to identify whether a woman was married, though it wasn't necessary to know a man's relationship to a woman.

To counter this practice, women began to use the neologism *Ms.* a few decades ago, although the term has existed as a title of courtesy since the 1940s (Miller & Swift, 1991). People of both sexes resisted the use of *Ms.* when it first came on the scene, claiming that it was hard to pronounce. But is it any harder to pronounce than *Mrs.* or *Mr.?* Some women today choose not to use the title because they believe it links them with feminists, a connection they consider undesirable. Others use *Ms.* just exactly for that reason—its link with feminism—and to establish their identity apart from men (Atkins-Sayre, 2005; Fuller, 2005; Kuhn, 2007). A common misconception is that *Ms.* is a title referring exclusively to divorced women (Chivero, 2009).

Regarding written salutations and greetings, for many years the standard salutation in a letter to someone you did not know (and did not know the sex of) was "Dear Sir" or "Gentlemen." If you only knew the last name of a person in an address or if the first name did not reveal the sex of the person, the default salutation was "Dear Mr. So-and-So." But that sexist practice is changing because of questions about why the masculine form should stand for all people. The terms *Sirs* and *Gentlemen* no more include women than the pronoun *he* or the term *mankind*.

What are some nonsexist options for salutations? Sometimes a simple phone call or e-mail to the organization you want to contact will enable you to specify a greeting. An easier way to fix this problem is to use terms that don't imply sex, such as: (Dear) Officers, Staff Member, Managers, Director, and the like. If it's more comfortable for you to use a sex-identified term, use inclusive references such as *Ms./Mr.* or *Sir or Madam*. Other alternatives include omitting a salutation altogether, opting for an opening line that says "Greetings!" or "Hello!" or structuring a letter more like a memo, beginning with "Regarding Your Memo of 9/7" or "TO: Friends of the Library" (Maggio, 1988, p. 184). We caution against using the trite "To Whom It May Concern"; your letter may end up in the trash simply because "no one was concerned."

Could you do me a favor? Could you say "senator" instead of "ma'am"? I worked so hard to get that title.
— Senator Barbara Boxer, to an Army Brigadier General during a Senate hearing

USING LANGUAGE: ONCE YOU CHOOSE IT, HOW DO YOU USE IT?

Now that you understand what we mean by choice in language, here comes the real challenge: the actual usage of language in everyday interactions with others. We now move on to the *between* aspect of language—communication *between* the sexes, not *about* them.

Some studies have documented linguistic sex differences (Cohen, 2009; Erlandson, 2005; Tannen, 1995) profound enough to form *genderlects,* defined as "speech that contains features that mark it as stereotypically masculine or feminine" (Hoar, 1992, p. 127). In general, female speech patterns have been viewed as being weaker, more passive, and less commanding of respect, in comparison with male styles. But other research has produced different results regarding linguistic sex patterns, with male and female styles often being indistinguishable (Brownlaw, Rosamond, & Parker, 2003). In

Remember...

Euphemism: More comfortable term that substitutes for another term

Metaphor: Use of language to draw a comparison; the nonliteral application of language to an object or action

Symmetrical or Parallel Language: Use of language that represents the sexes in a balanced and fair manner

Order of Terms: Language usage that alternates which sex appears or is said first

Titles: Designations such as *Mr.* or *Ms.* before a person's name

Salutations: Letter or memo greetings that often contain sexist, exclusively male language

various studies conducted by Anthony Mulac and his associates, subjects frequently incorrectly identified the sex of a speaker, based on written transcripts of casual conversation, as well as discussions in problem-solving groups (Mulac, 1998; Mulac, Bradac, & Gibbons, 2001; Mulac, Wiemann, Widenmann, & Gibson, 1988).

While Mulac discovered more similarities than differences in women's and men's speaking styles, he isolated some consistent male language features, which include references to quantity; judgmental adjectives (e.g., "Reading can be such a drag"); elliptical or abbreviated sentences, like "Great picture"; directives (commands); locatives (such as "in the background"); and "I" references. Female language features include intensive adverbs (such as use of the term *really*), references to emotions, dependent clauses (instead of full sentences), sentence-initial adverbials (such as use of the word *actually* to begin a sentence), longer sentences, uncertainty verbs (e.g., "It seems to be . . ."), negations (using negative terms such as *not*), hedges (e.g., "It's kind of . . ."), and questions (Mulac, Bradac, & Palomares, 2003).

An overdrawn, media-hyped linguistic sex difference garnered a lot of attention in the latter part of the 2000s; the focus was on who talked more—men or women. The ancient, enduring stereotype is that women *way* outtalk men, but does research bear this out? The controversy was launched when Louann Brizendine, author of *The Female Brain* (2006) and *The Male Brain* (2010), claimed that women use 20,000 words on average per day, whereas men only average 7,000 a day. The implication was either that women were verbose or men were reticent.

All sorts of personalities and pundits quoted the "facts," but the problem was, the numbers didn't add up. Researchers at different institutions studied the phenomenon, concluding that no such sex differences in sheer volumes of speaking were scientifically documented (Do Women Really, 2010; Newman, Groom, Handelman, & Pennebaker, 2008; Stipe, 2010). Seasoned public speaking coaches estimate that the average English (U.S.) speaker talks at a rate of about 125 words per minute (around 2 words per second). Speaking 20,000 words at that rate would take 160 minutes total—about 2.6 hours in a 24-hour day. That equates to 10 minutes per hour in a 16-hour day, meaning that the average woman is silent for 50 minutes each hour (excluding 8 hours of sleep). When you do the math for the men's statistics, the average man speaks only 56 minutes in an entire 16-hour day, or 3.5 minutes each hour. Does that seem accurate to you? Does that match your experience? Here's one of those times when getting the facts—doing just a bit of research—helped counter a stereotype.

Vocal Properties and Linguistic Constructions

Vocal properties are aspects of the production of sound related to the physiological voice-producing mechanism in humans. *Linguistic constructions* reflect speech patterns or habits; they are communicative choices people make.

HOW LOW CAN YOU GO? The *pitch* of a human voice can be defined as the highness or lowness of a particular sound due to air causing the vocal chords to vibrate (Karpf, 2006). Physiological structures related to voice production, as well as hormones, allow women to more easily produce higher-pitched sounds, while men more easily produce lower-pitched sounds (Evans, Neave, Wakelin, & Hamilton, 2008; Kooijman, Thomas, Graamans, & deJong, 2007; Krolokke & Sorensen, 2006; Tracy, 2002). But scholarly evidence suggests that differences may have more to do with social interpretations than with physiology alone. Research indicates that women and men have equal abilities to produce high pitches, but that men have been socialized not to use the higher pitches for fear of sounding feminine (Cartei & Reby, 2012; Ivy & Wahl, 2014; Viscovich et al., 2003).

In comparison to the low tones that most men are able to produce, the so-called high-pitched female whine has drawn long-standing societal criticism and even prejudice against women's voices (Cameron, 1985; Hoar, 1992; McConnell-Ginet, 2011). In patriarchal societies, men's lower-pitched voices are deemed more credible and persuasive than women's (Imhof, 2010). Examples of this can be readily found at radio and TV stations where women serving as news anchors or reporters tend to have (or develop) lower-pitched voices than women in the general population, in order to be perceived as more credible and taken more seriously by the listening or viewing public.

Men with higher-pitched voices are often ridiculed for being effeminate. Their "feminine" voices may be perceived as detracting from their credibility and dynamism, unless another physical or personality attribute somehow overpowers or contradicts that judgment. (Mike Tyson, former heavyweight boxing champion, is one example of this.)

Mike Tyson's distinctive voice contradicts his former boxing champion status.

INDICATIONS OF TENTATIVENESS Research has documented how women tend to be more *tentative* in their communication than men, and this tentativeness can reduce the power of women's messages, making them appear uncertain, insecure, incompetent, and less likely to be taken seriously than men (Carli, 1990; McConnell-Ginet, 2011). However, other research indicates that instead of interpreting weakness or tentativeness from women's speech style, politeness or a motive toward affiliation, facilitation, and inclusion of others may be the intent (Mulac, Giles, Bradac, & Palomares, 2013; Palomares, 2009; Watts, 2003). Additional studies suggest that factors such as culture, status and position in society, communication goals, and the sex-composition of the group in which communication occurs have more impact than sex on stylistic variations (Aries, 2006; Eckert & McConnell-Ginet, 2013; Mulac et al., 2001).

One vocal property that indicates tentativeness is *intonation* or "the tune to which we set the text of our talk" (McConnell-Ginet, 1983, p. 70). Research is contradictory as to whether rising intonation (typically associated with asking questions) is indicative of a female style or just a sex-based stereotype. Another tentativeness indicator is the *tag question*, as in "This is a really beautiful day, don't you think?" The primary function of the tag question is to seek agreement or a response from a listener (Blankenship & Craig, 2007). Lakoff (1975) believed that tag questions serve as an "apology for making an assertion at all" (p. 54). She attributed the use of tag questions to a general lack of assertiveness or confidence about what one is saying, more indicative of female style than male style. Older research supported a connection between women's style and the use of tag questions (Carli, 1990; Zimmerman & West, 1975), but more current research finds no evidence that tag questions occur more in female speech than in male speech, nor that tag questions necessarily indicate uncertainty or tentativeness (Hancock & Rubin, 2015).

Qualifiers, hedges, and *disclaimers* are other linguistic constructions generally interpreted as indicating tentativeness and stereotypically associated with women's speech. *Qualifiers* include *well, you know, kind of, sort of, really, perhaps, possibly, maybe,* and *of course. Hedging* devices include such terms as *I think (believe, feel), I guess, I mean,* and *I wonder* (Holmes, 1990; Winn & Rubin,

© Ovidiu Hrubaru/Shutterstock.com

2001). *Disclaimers* are typically longer hedges that act as prefaces or defense mechanisms when one is unsure or doubtful of what one is about to say; they tend to weaken or soften the effect of a message (Beach & Dunning, 1982; Hewitt & Stokes, 1975). Students often use disclaimers like "I know this is a dumb question, but . . ." and "I may be wrong here, but I think. . ." Rather than imposing a stereotype, scholars advise that interpretations of tentativeness are best made within the given context in which the communication occurs (Cameron, 1985; Holmes, 1990; Mulac et al., 2001; Ragan, 1989).

MANAGING TO CONVERSE Have you ever considered how conversation is organized or "managed"? *Conversation management* involves several variables, but one interesting vein of research surrounds indicators of conversational dominance.

Conversation typically occurs in *turns*, meaning that one speaker takes a turn, then another, and so on, such that interaction is socially organized (Sacks, Schegloff, & Jefferson, 1978). When people take turns talking, they may experience *overlaps*, defined as "simultaneous speech initiated by a next speaker just as a current speaker arrives at a possible turn-transition place" and *interruptions* or "deeper intrusions into the internal structure of the speaker's utterance" (West & Zimmerman, 1983, pp. 103–104). Interruptions and overlaps have been interpreted as indications of disrespect, restrictions on a speaker's rights, devices for controlling a topic, reflections of an attitude of dominance and authority, and as more indicative of men's speech than women's (Guerrero & Floyd, 2006; Hancock & Rubin, 2015; Weiss & Fisher, 1998). Overlaps are considered less egregious than interruptions because overlapping someone's speech may be seen as supportive—as trying to reinforce or dovetail off of someone's idea. Interruptions more often indicate dominance and power play because they cut off the speaker in midstream and suggest that the interrupter's comment is somehow more important or insightful.

In the most widely cited study of adult conversations, Zimmerman and West (1975) found few overlaps and interruptions within same-sex interactions. However, in mixed-sex conversations, more interruptions occurred than overlaps, and 96 percent of the interruptions were made by males. Other early research revealed evidence of male conversational dominance in terms of initiating topics, working to maintain conversation around those topics, talking more often and for longer durations, offering minimal responses to women's comments, and using more declaratives than questions (Edelsky, 1981; Fishman, 1983).

Remember...

Genderlects: Language containing specific, consistent features that mark it as stereotypically masculine or feminine

Vocal Properties: Aspects of the production of sound related to the physiological voice-producing mechanism in humans

Linguistic Constructions: Speech patterns or habits; communicative choices people make

Pitch: Highness or lowness of a particular sound due to air causing the vocal chords to vibrate

Tentativeness: Forms of language that indicate hesitation or speculation and that can make people appear uncertain, insecure, incompetent, powerless, and less likely to be taken seriously

Intonation: Use of pitch that creates a pattern or that sends a specific message, such as a rising pitch to indicate a question

Tag Question: Linguistic construction related to tentativeness, which involves adding a brief question onto the end of a statement

Qualifier, Hedge, and Disclaimer: Linguistic constructions related to tentativeness, which preface or accompany a message so as to soften its impact or deflect attention away from the statement

Conversation Management: How a conversation is organized or conducted in a series of turns

Overlap: Linguistic construction typically associated with conversational dominance, in which one person begins speaking just as another person finishes speaking

Interruption: Linguistic construction typically associated with conversational dominance, in which one speaker intrudes into the comments of another speaker

More recent studies have gone beyond sex effects to examine the complexity of dominance in such contexts as face-to-face interaction, same-sex and mixed-sex dyads and groups, marital dyads, and online conversations (Palomares, 2010). Researchers now suggest that many nonverbal, contextual, and cultural factors, such as perceptions of power and status, seating arrangements, and sex-typed topics affect judgments of dominant or powerless styles (Aries, 2006; Guerrero & Floyd, 2006).

News talk shows on television, such as MSNBC's *Hardball* and Fox News' *The O'Reilly Factor*, are prime opportunities to observe conversation management (or, many times, mismanagement). Displays of vocal dominance and competitiveness among male and female hosts and guests are fascinating in these forums. The more seasoned guests have learned techniques to control the topics they respond to and raise with hosts, hold their turns at talk longer, and minimize interruptions from other guests or the host.

CONCLUSION

In this chapter on language, we've given you more than a few things to think about, because when you put something under a microscope, you see it in a whole new way. We've tossed a lot at you for one main reason—so that you won't use language by default or habit but instead *choose* to use language that accurately reflects who you are and how you think.

This chapter has challenged you to consider more fully how communication is used to talk *about* the sexes, as well as why and how communication occurs *between* them. We first explored the nature of language and some reasons for using nonsexist or gender-fair language; then we reviewed several forms and practices related to sexist language usage, as well as nonsexist alternatives. Regarding communication *between* the sexes, we examined vocal properties and linguistic constructions that continue to be studied for what they reveal about gender communication. As we said in the introduction to this chapter, the goal of this chapter was to focus on language and its important role in gender communication, to offer ways that you can expand your linguistic options, and to challenge you to *choose* and *use* language in a more inclusive, unbiased, and contemporary manner.

DISCUSSION STARTERS

1. What were you taught in middle school or high school about sexist language? If you received no such instruction, why do you think this information wasn't included in your education? Have you been taught anything in college English classes about sexist language?

2. Sexism in religious language is one of the more difficult topics to explore and discuss. For some people, it's an affront to put the language used to convey their deeply personal religious beliefs under the microscope. What are your views on this subject?

3. Think about sexual language, as discussed in this chapter. We all know times have changed in regard to sexual activity, but has the language changed to keep pace? What changes do you think still need to be made in this area?

4. In light of the information in this chapter on conversation management, assess your own style of communication. Are you more likely to be interrupted or to interrupt someone else? How do you respond to others' overlaps and interruptions? Do you have a lot of tag questions, qualifiers, hedges, and disclaimers in your communication? Think about classroom communication: Do you find yourself saying things like, "This might be a dumb question, but . . ." or "I could be wrong, but . . ."? If so, what effect do these disclaimers have on how you're perceived?

References

Amare, N. (2006). Finding Dickinson: Linguistic sexism and inconsistent indexing in *Masterplots. Women & Language, 29,* 37–42.

Aragon, J. (2008). The lady revolution in the age of technology. *International Journal of Media and Cultural Politics, 4,* 71–85.

Ardener, S. (2005). Muted groups: The genesis of an idea and its praxis. *Women & Language, 28,* 50–54.

Arichi, M. (1999). Is it radical? Women's right to keep their own surnames after marriage. *Women's Studies International Forum, 22,* 411–415.

Aries, E. (2006). Sex differences in interaction: A reexamination. In K. Dindia & D. J. Canary (Eds.), *Sex differences and similarities in communication* (2nd ed., pp. 19–34). Mahwah, NJ: Erlbaum.

Atkins-Sayre, W. (2005). Naming women: The emergence of "Ms." as a liberatory title. *Women & Language, 28*, 8–16.

Asexuality Visibility and Education Network (AVEN). (2015). Retrieved July 4, 2015, from <www.asexuality.org>.

August, E. R. (1992). Real men don't: Anti-male bias in English. In M. Schaum & C. Flanagan (Eds.), *Gender images: Readings for composition* (pp. 131–141). Boston: Houghton Mifflin.

Baker, R. (1981). "Pricks" and "chicks": A plea for "persons." In M. Vetterling-Braggin (Ed.), *Sexist language: A modern philosophical analysis* (pp. 161–182). New York: Rowman & Littlefield.

Beach, W. A., & Dunning, D. G. (1982). Pre-indexing and conversational organization. *Quarterly Journal of Speech, 67*, 170–185.

Beebe, S. A., Beebe, S. J., & Ivy, D. K. (2016). *Communication: Principles for a lifetime* (6th ed.). Boston: Pearson.

Black, R. (2009, August 11). What women's lib? 70 percent of Americans think women should take spouse's name after marriage. Retrieved July 2, 2010, from <http://www.nydailynews.com>.

Blankenship, K. L., & Craig, T. Y. (2007). Language and persuasion: Tag questions as powerless speech or as interpreted in context. *Journal of Experimental Social Psychology, 43*, 112–118.

Boxer, D., & Gritsenko, E. (2005). Women and surnames across cultures: Reconstituting identity in marriage. *Women & Language, 28*, 1–11.

Braun, V., & Kitzinger, C. (2001a). "Snatch," "hole," or "honey-pot"? Semantic categories and the problem of nonspecificity in female genital slang. *Journal of Sex Research, 38*, 146–158.

Braun, V., & Kitzinger, C. (2001b). Telling it straight? Dictionary definitions of women's genitals. *Journal of Sociolinguistics, 5*, 214–232.

Briere, J., & Lanktree, C. (1983). Sex-role related effects of sex bias in language. *Sex Roles, 9*, 625–632.

Brightman, J. (1994). Why Hillary chooses Rodham Clinton. *American Demographics, 16*, 9–11.

Brizendine, L. (2006). *The female brain.* New York: Broadway.

Brizendine, L. (2010). *The male brain.* New York: Broadway.

Brooks, L. (1983). Sexist language in occupational information: Does it make a difference? *Journal of Vocational Behavior, 23*, 227–232.

Brownlaw, S., Rosamond, J. A., & Parker, J. A. (2003). Gender-linked linguistic behavior in television interviews. *Sex Roles, 49*, 121–132.

Bryant, C. J. (2008). Concerns of faith inclusive language: Will it solve the problems? *Language in India, 8*, 2.

Budziszewska, M., Hansen, K., & Bilewicz, M. (2014). Backlash over gender-fair language: The impact of feminine job titles on men's and women's perception of women. *Journal of Language and Social Psychology, 33*, 681–691.

Burkette, A., & Warhol, T. (2009). "The bush was no place for a woman": Personal pronouns and gender stereotypes. *Women & Language, 32*, 70–76.

Butler, J. (2004). *Undoing gender.* London: Routledge.

Cameron, D. (1992). *Feminism and linguistic theory* (2nd ed.). New York: Palgrave/Macmillan.

Cameron, D. (2009). *The myth of Mars and Venus: Do men and women really speak different languages?* New York: Oxford University Press.

Carli, L. L. (1990). Gender, language, and influence. *Journal of Personality and Social Psychology, 59*, 941–951.

Cartei, V., & Reby, D. (2012). Acting gay: Male actors shift the frequency components of their voices toward female values when playing homosexual characters. *Journal of Nonverbal Behavior, 36*, 79–93.

Chivero, E. (2009). Perceptions of "Ms." as title of address among Shona-English bilinguals in Harare. *NAWA: Journal of Language and Communication, 3*, 174–186.

Clarke, V., Burns, M., & Burgoyne, C. (2008). "Who would take whose name?" Accounts of naming practices in same-sex relationships. *Journal of Community & Applied Social Psychology, 18*, 420–439.

Clason, M. A. (2006). Feminism, generic "he," and the *TNIV* Bible translation debate. *Critical Discourse Studies, 3*, 23–35.

Cohen, S. J. (2009). Gender differences in speech temporal patterns detected using lagged co-occurrence text-analysis of personal narratives. *Journal of Psycholinguistic Research, 38*, 111–127.

Conkright, L., Flannagan, D., & Dykes, J. (2000). Effects of pronoun type and gender role consistency on children's recall and interpretation of stories. *Sex Roles, 43*, 481–499.

Cralley, E. L., & Ruscher, J. B. (2005). Lady, girl, or woman: Sexism and cognitive busyness predict use of gender-biased nouns. *Journal of Language and Social Psychology, 24*, 300–314.

Decker, J. S. (2014, September 20). How to tell if you are asexual. Retrieved October 1, 2014, from <www.time.com>.

DeFrancisco, V. P., & Palczewski, C. H. (2007). *Communicating gender diversity: A critical approach*. Los Angeles: Sage.

Do women really talk more than men? (2010). Retrieved February 3, 2010, from < http://www.amazingwomenrock.com>.

Douglas, K. M., & Sutton, R. M. (2014). "A giant leap for mankind," but what about women? The role of system-justifying ideologies in predicting attitudes toward sexist language. *Journal of Language and Social Psychology, 33,* 667–680.

Earp, B. D. (2012). The extinction of masculine generics. *Journal for Communication & Culture, 2,* 4–19.

Eckert, P., & McConnell-Ginet, S. (2013). *Language and gender* (2nd ed.). New York: Cambridge University Press.

Edelsky, C. (1981). Who's got the floor? *Language in Society, 10,* 383–421.

Emens, E. F. (2007). Changing name changing: Framing rules and the future of marital names. *University of Chicago Law Review, 74,* 761–863.

Erlandson, K. (2005). Gender differences in language use. *Communication Teacher, 19,* 116–120.

Evans, S., Neave, M., Wakelin, D., & Hamilton, C. (2008). The relationship between testosterone and vocal frequencies in human males. *Physiology & Behavior, 93,* 783–788.

Fabrizio Pelak, C. (2008). The relationship between sexist naming practices and athletic opportunities at colleges and universities in the southern United States. *Sociology of Education, 81,* 189–213.

Fishman, P. M. (1983). Interaction: The work women do. In B. Thorne, C. Kramarae, & N. Henley (Eds.), *Language, gender, and society* (pp. 89– 101). Rowley, MA: Newbury.

Flanigan, J. (2013). The use and evolution of gender neutral language in an intentional community. *Women & Language, 36,* 27–41.

Formanowicz, M., Bedynska, S., Cislak, A., Braun, F., & Sczesny, S. (2013). Side effects of gender-fair language: How feminine job titles influence the evaluation of female applicants. *European Journal of Social Psychology, 43,* 62–72.

Foss, K., Edson, B., & Linde, J. (2000). What's in a name? Negotiating decisions about marital names. In D. O. Braithwaite & J. T. Wood (Eds.), *Case studies in interpersonal communication* (pp. 18–25). Belmont, CA: Wadsworth.

Frank, F. W., & Treichler, P. A. (1989). *Language, gender, and professional writing: Theoretical approaches and guidelines for non-sexist usage.* New York: Modern Language Association.

Fuller, J. M. (2005). The uses and meanings of the female title *Ms. American Speech, 80,* 180–206.

Gabriel, U. (2008). Language policies and in-group favoritism: The malleability of the interpretation of generically intended masculine forms. *Social Psychology, 39,* 103–107.

Gastil, J. (1990). Generic pronouns and sexist language: The oxymoronic character of masculine generics. *Sex Roles, 23,* 629–641.

Goldman, R. (2014, February 13). Here's a list of 58 gender options for Facebook users. Retrieved February 17, 2014, from <http://abcnews.go.com>.

Goldin, C., & Shim, M. (2004). Making a name: Women's surnames at marriage and beyond. *Journal of Economic Perspectives, 18,* 143–160.

Gorski, E. (2002, February 3). Christian leaders debate new gender-neutral Bible translation. Knight Ridder Newspapers, as in *Corpus Christi Caller Times.*

Graddol, D., & Swann, J. (1989). *Gender voices.* Cambridge, MA: Basil Blackwell.

Green, J. (1999). *The big book of filth.* London: Cassell.

Grey, S. (2015, Winter). Track changes. *Bitch,* 50–54.

Guerrero, L. K., & Floyd, K. (2006). *Nonverbal communication in close relationships.* Mahwah, NJ: Erlbaum.

Gygax, P., Gabriel, U., Sarrasin, O., Oakhill, J., & Garnham, A. (2009). Some grammatical rules are more difficult than others: The case of the generic interpretation of the masculine. *European Journal of Psychology of Education, 24,* 235–246.

Hamilton, L. C. (1988). Using masculine generics: Does generic "he" increase male bias in the user's imagery? *Sex Roles, 19,* 785–799.

Hancock, A. B., & Rubin, B. A. (2015). Influence of communication partner's gender on language. *Journal of Language and Social Psychology, 34,* 46–64.

Hardman, M. J. (1999). Why we should say "women and men" until it doesn't matter any more. *Women & Language, 22,* 1–2.

He, G. (2010). An analysis of sexism in English. *Journal of Language Teaching and Research, 1,* 332–335.

Hegstrom, J. L., & McCarl-Nielsen, J. (2002). Gender and metaphor: Descriptions of familiar persons. *Discourse Processes, 33,* 219–234.

Hewitt, J. P., & Stokes, R. (1975). Disclaimers. *American Sociological Review, 40,* 1–11.

Hoar, N. (1992). Genderlect, powerlect, and politeness. In L. A. M. Perry, L. H. Turner, & H. M. Sterk (Eds.), *Constructing and reconstructing gender: The links among communication, language, and gender* (pp. 127–136). Albany: State University of New York Press.

Hoffnung, M. (2006). What's in a name? Marital name choice revisited. *Sex Roles, 55,* 817–825.

Holmes, J. (1990). Hedges and boosters in women's and men's speech. *Language & Communication, 10,* 185–205.

Holmes, J. (2001). A corpus based view of gender in New Zealand English. In M. Hellinger & H. Bussmann (Eds.), *Gender across languages: Volume 1: The linguistic representation of women and men* (pp. 115–133). Philadelphia: John Benjamins Publishing Company.

Hopper, R. (2003). *Gendering talk.* East Lansing: Michigan State University Press.

Imhof, M. (2010). Listening to voices and judging people. *International Journal of Listening, 24,* 19–33.

Ivy, D. K. (1986, February). *Who's the boss?: He, he/she, or they?* Paper presented at the meeting of the Western Speech Communication Association, Tucson, AZ.

Ivy, D. K., Bullis-Moore, L., Norvell, K., Backlund, P., & Javidi, M. (1995). The lawyer, the babysitter, and the student: Inclusive language usage and instruction. *Women & Language, 18,* 13–21.

Ivy, D. K., & Wahl, S. T. (2014). *Nonverbal communication for a lifetime* (2nd ed.). Dubuque, IA: Kendall Hunt.

Johnson, D. R., & Scheuble, L. K. (1995). Women's marital naming in two generations: A national study. *Journal of Marriage and the Family, 57,* 724–732.

Jones, K. T., & Mills, R. (2001). The rhetoric of heteroglossia of Jewish feminism: A paradox confronted. *Women & Language, 24,* 58–64.

Karpf, A. (2006). *The human voice: How this extraordinary instrument reveals essential clues about who we are.* New York: Bloomsbury.

Kennedy, D. (1992). Review essay: She or he in textbooks. *Women & Language, 15,* 46–49.

Killerman, S. (2013). *The social justice advocate's handbook: A guide to gender.* Austin: Impetus Books.

Koeser, S., Kuhn, E. A., & Sczesny, S. (2015). Just reading? How gender-fair language triggers readers' use of gender-fair forms. *Journal of Language and Social Psychology, 34,* 343–357.

Kooijman, P. G. C., Thomas, G., Graamans, K., & deJong, F. I. C. R. S. (2007). Psychosocial impact of the teacher's voice throughout the career. *Journal of Voice, 21,* 316–324.

Kopelman, R. E., Fossen, R. J. S-V., Paraskevas, E., Lawter, L., & Prottas, D. J. (2009). The bride is keeping her name: A 35-year retrospective analysis of trends and correlates. *Social Behavior and Personality: An International Journal, 37,* 687–700.

Kovecses, Z. (2010). *Metaphor: A practical introduction* (2nd ed.). New York: Oxford University Press.

Kramarae, C. (1981). *Women and men speaking.* Rowley, MA: Newbury.

Kramarae, C. (2005). Muted group theory and communication: Asking dangerous questions. *Women & Language, 28,* 55–61.

Krolokke, C., & Sorensen, A. S. (2006). *Gender communication theories & analyses: From silence to performance.* Thousand Oaks, CA: Sage.

Kuhn, E. D. (2007). Rethinking Ms. *Women & Language, 30,* 4.

Lakoff, R. (1975). *Language and woman's place.* New York: Harper & Row.

Lannutti, P. (2008, May). *Tying the knot? Couples' deliberations regarding legally recognized same-sex marriage.* Paper presented at the meeting of the International Communication Association, Montreal, Canada.

Laskowski, K. A. (2010). Women's post-marital name retention and the communication of identity. *Names: A Journal of Onomastics, 58,* 75–89.

Leardi, J. (1997, September 28). Is God male or female? For some, issue of God and gender is subject to debate. *Corpus Christi Caller Times,* pp. H1, H3.

Lee, J. F. K. (2007). Acceptability of sexist language among young people in Hong Kong. *Sex Roles, 56,* 285–295.

Lindsey, L. (2005). *Gender roles: A sociological perspective* (4th ed.). Upper Saddle River, NJ: Pearson/Prentice Hall.

Madson, L., & Shoda, J. (2006). Alternating between masculine and feminine pronouns: Does essay topic affect readers' perceptions? *Sex Roles, 54,* 275–285.

Maggio, R. (1988). *The nonsexist word finder: A dictionary of gender-free usage.* Boston: Beacon.

Maggio, R. (1992). *The bias-free word finder: A dictionary of nondiscriminatory language.* Boston: Beacon.

Mallett, R. K., & Wagner, D. E. (2011). The unexpectedly positive consequences of confronting sexism. *Journal of Experimental Social Psychology, 47,* 215–220.

Martyna, W. (1978). What does "he" mean? Use of the generic masculine. *Journal of Communication, 28,* 131–138.

McConnell-Ginet, S. (1980). Linguistics and the feminist challenge. In S. McConnell-Ginet, R. Borker, & N. Furman (Eds.), *Women and language in literature and society* (pp. 3–25). New York: Praeger.

McConnell-Ginet, S. (1983). Intonation in a man's world. In B. Thorne, C. Kramarae, & N. Henley

(Eds.), *Language, gender, and society* (pp. 69 -88). Rowley, MA: Newbury.

McConnell-Ginet, S. (2011). *Gender, sexuality, and meaning: Linguistic practice and politics.* New York: Oxford University Press.

McGlone, M. S., Beck, G., & Pfiester, A. (2006). Contamination and camouflage in euphemisms. *Communication Monographs*, 73, 261-282.

Miller, C., & Swift, K. (1988). *The handbook of non-sexist writing* (2nd ed.). New York: Harper & Row.

Miller, C., & Swift, K. (1991). *Words and women: New language in new times.* New York: HarperCollins.

Miller, C., Swift, K., & Maggio, R. (1997, September–October). Liberating language. *Ms.*, 50–54.

Moffat, M. (1989). *Coming of age in New Jersey.* New Brunswick, NJ: Rutgers University Press.

Motschenbacher, H. (2009). Speaking the gendered body: The performative construction of commercial femininities and masculinities via body-part vocabulary. *Language in Society, 38*, 1–22.

Moulton, J., Robinson, G. M., & Elias, C. (1978). Sex bias in language use: "Neutral" pronouns that aren't. *American Psychologist, 33*, 1032–1036.

Mulac, A. (1998). The gender-linked language effect: Do language differences really make a difference? In D. J. Canary & K. Dindia (Eds.), *Sex differences and similarities in communication* (pp. 127–155). Mahwah, NJ: Erlbaum.

Mulac, A., Bradac, J. J., & Gibbons, P. (2001). Empirical support for the gender-as-culture hypothesis: An intercultural analysis of male/female language differences. *Human Communication Research, 27*, 121–152.

Mulac, A., Bradac, J. J., & Palomares, N. (2003, May). *A general process model of the gender-linked language effect: Antecedents for and consequences of language used by men and women.* Paper presented at the meeting of the International Communication Association, San Diego, CA.

Mulac, A., Giles, H., Bradac, J. J., & Palomares, N. A. (2013). The gender-linked language effect: An empirical test of a gender process model. *Language Sciences, 38*, 22–31.

Mulac, A., Wiemann, J. M., Widenmann, S. J., & Gibson, T. W. (1988). Male/female language differences and effects in same-sex and mixed sex dyads: The gender-linked language effect. *Communication Monographs, 55*, 315–335.

Murnen, S. K. (2000). Gender and the use of sexually degrading language. *Psychology of Women Quarterly, 24*, 319–327.

Newman, M., Groom, C. J., Handelman, L. D., & Pennebaker, J. W. (2008). Gender differences in language use: An analysis of 14,000 text samples. *Discourse Processes, 45*, 211–236.

Palczewski, C. H. (1998). "Tak[e] the helm," man the ship . . . and I forgot my bikini! Unraveling why woman is not considered a verb. *Women & Language, 21*, 1–8.

Palomares, N. A. (2009). Women are sort of more tentative than men, aren't they? How men and women use tentative language differently, similarly, and counterstereotypically as a function of gender salience. *Communication Research, 36*, 538–560.

Palomares, N. A. (2010). Virtual gender identity: The linguistic assimilation to gendered avatars in computer-mediated communication. *Journal of Language and Social Psychology, 29*, 5–23.

Parks, J. B., & Roberton, M. A. (2005). Explaining age and gender effects on attitudes toward sexist language. *Journal of Language and Social Psychology, 24*, 401–411.

Parks, J. B., & Roberton, M. A. (2008). Generation gaps in attitudes toward sexist/nonsexist language. *Journal of Language and Social Psychology, 27*, 276–283.

Penelope, J. (1990). *Speaking freely: Unlearning the lies of the fathers' tongues.* New York: Pergamon.

Radway, J. (2009, May). *Girls, zines, and the limits of the body.* Paper presented at the meeting of the International Communication Association, Chicago, IL.

Ragan, S. L. (1989). Communication between the sexes: A consideration of sex differences in adult communication. In J. F. Nussbaum (Ed.), *Life-span communication: Normative processes* (pp. 179–193). Hillsdale, NJ: Erlbaum.

Riordan, E. (2001). Commodified agents and empowered girls: Consuming and producing feminism. *Journal of Communication Inquiry, 25*, 279–297.

Roger, D., & Nesshoever, W. (1987). Individual differences in dyadic conversational strategies: A further study. *British Journal of Social Psychology, 26*, 247–255.

Romaine, S. (1999). *Communicating gender.* Mahwah, NJ: Erlbaum.

Sacks, H., Schegloff, E. A., & Jefferson, G. (1978). A simple systematic for the organization of turn taking for conversation. In J. Schenkein (Ed.), *Studies in the organization of conversational interaction* (pp. 7–55). New York: Academic.

Scheuble, L. K., & Johnson, D. R. (2005). Married women's situational use of last names: An empirical study. *Sex Roles, 53*, 143–151.

Scheuble, L. K., Klingemann, K., & Johnson, D. R. (2000). Trends in women's marital name choices: 1966–1996. *Names: A Journal of Onomastics, 48*, 105–114.

Schmitt, J. J. (1992). God's wife: Some gender reflections on the Bible and biblical interpretation. In L. A. M. Perry, L. H. Turner, & H. M. Sterk (Eds.), *Constructing and reconstructing gender: The links among communication, language, and gender* (pp. 269–281). Albany: State University of New York Press.

Siegel, D. (2007). *Sisterhood, interrupted: From radical women to grrls gone wild.* New York: Palgrave/Macmillan.

Spender, D. (1985). *Man made language* (2nd ed.). London: Routledge & Kegan Paul.

Stafford, L., & Kline, S. L. (1996). Married women's name choices and sense of self. *Communication Reports, 9,* 85–92.

Stahlberg, D., Braun, F., Irmen, L., & Sczesny, S. (2007). Representation of the sexes in language. In K. Fiedler (Ed.), *Social communication* (pp. 163–187). New York: Psychology Press.

Stanley, J. P. (1977). Paradigmatic woman: The prostitute. In D. L. Shores (Ed.), *Papers in language variation.* Birmingham: University of Alabama Press.

Steinem, G. (1995, September–October). Words and change. *Ms.,* 93–96.

Steinmetz, K. (2014, February 14). A comprehensive guide to Facebook's new options for gender identity. Retrieved February 18, 2014, from <http://techland.time.com>.

Stericker, A. (1981). Does this "he or she" business really make a difference? The effect of masculine pronouns as generics on job attitudes. *Sex Roles, 7,* 637–641.

Stinger, J. L., & Hopper, R. (1998). Generic *he* in conversation? *Quarterly Journal of Speech, 84,* 209–221.

Stipe, B. (2010). Why can't he hear what you're saying? Retrieved February 3, 2010, from < http:// lifestyle. msn.com/relationship>.

St. James, J. (2015, June 24). 4 reasons why expecting LGBTQIA+ people to come out is problematic (and how inviting in is better). Retrieved June 26, 2015, from <http://everydayfeminism.com>.

Strahan, T. (2008). "They" in Australian English: Non-gender-specific or specifically non-gendered? *Australian Journal of Linguistics, 28,* 17–29.

Stritof, S., & Stritof, B. (2010). Changing your name after marriage: A look at your options. Retrieved July 2, 2010, from <http://marriage.about.com>.

Suter, E. A., & Oswald, R. F. (2003). Do lesbians change their last names in the context of a committed relationship? *Journal of Lesbian Studies, 7,* 71–83.

Swim, J. K., Mallett, R., & Stangor, C. (2004). Understanding subtle sexism: Detection and use of sexist language. *Sex Roles, 51,* 117–128.

Tannen, D. (1995). *Talking 9 to 5: Women and men at work.* New York: Harper.

Taylor, A., Hardman, M. J., & Wright, C. (2013). *Making the invisible visible: Gender in language.* Bloomington, IN: iUniverse.

Teso, E., & Crolley, L. (2013). Gender-based linguistic reform in international organisations. *Language Policy, 12,* 139–158.

Tracy, K. (2002). *Everyday talk: Building and reflecting identities.* New York: Guilford.

Trans 101: Cisgender. (2011, October 9). Retrieved February 18, 2014, from <www.basicrights.org>.

Viscovich, N., Borod, J., Pihan, H., Peery, S., Brickman, A. M., & Tabert, M. (2003). Acoustical analysis of posed prosodic expressions: Effects of emotion and sex. *Perceptual and Motor Skills, 96,* 759–777.

Wachs, F. L. (2006). "Throw like a girl" doesn't mean what it used to: Research on gender, language, and power. In L. K. Fuller (Ed.), *Sports, rhetoric, and gender: Historical perspectives and media representations* (pp. 43–52). New York: Palgrave/Macmillan.

Ward, R. E., Jr. (2004). Are doors being opened for the "ladies" of college sports? A covariance analysis. *Sex Roles, 51,* 697–708.

Watts, R. J. (2003). *Politeness.* Cambridge, UK: Cambridge University Press.

Weiss, E. H., & Fisher, B. (1998). Should we teach women to interrupt? Cultural variables in management communication courses. *Women in Management Review, 13,* 37–44.

West, C. (2011). When the doctor is a "lady": Power, status and gender in physician-patient encounters. In J. Coates & P. Pichler (Eds.), *Language and gender: A reader* (2nd ed., pp. 468–482). Malden, MA: Wiley-Blackwell.

West, C., & Zimmerman, D. H. (1983). Small insults: A study of interruptions in cross-sex conversations between unacquainted persons. In B. Thorne, C. Kramarae, & N. Henley (Eds.), *Language, gender, and society* (pp. 102–117). Rowley, MA: Newbury.

Whorf, B. L. (1956). Science and linguistics. In J. B. Carroll (Ed.), *Language, thought, and reality.* Cambridge: Massachusetts Institute of Technology Press.

Winn, L. L., & Rubin, D. L. (2001). Enacting gender identity in written discourse: Responding to gender role bidding in personal ads. *Journal of Language & Social Psychology, 20,* 393–418.

Zimmerman, D. H., & West, C. (1975). Sex roles, interruptions and silences in conversation. In B. Thorne & N. Henley (Eds.), *Language and sex: Difference and dominance* (pp. 105–129). Rowley, MA: Newbury.

CHAPTER 4

CATCHING A CLUE
Nonverbal Communication and Gender

CASE STUDY

The Rush of Attraction

It's the first week of a new semester and Sam is sitting in his first class for his newly declared communication major. He scans the room to see if he knows anyone; when he doesn't recognize any faces, he takes a seat in the back and gets ready for class to start.

In walks "Ms. Right" (or "Ms. Right Now" or "Ms. Perfect-for-me-where-have-you-been-all-my-life"). Sam looks at her—it's hard not to notice her—and she looks back at him and smiles, then blushes and takes a seat near the front of the room. "Whoa, this could get interesting," Sam thinks to himself. Then the panic sets in: What do I do next? Do I do anything or do I need more information? Is she interested in me? Is she involved with anyone? What's her number? How can I meet her? What would I say?

HOT TOPICS

- Effects of sex and gender on nonverbal communication
- Nonverbal cues associated with initiating, maintaining, and terminating relationships
- Nonverbal cues and sexuality
- The role of nonverbal communication in sexual activity

Not every first encounter with an attractive person makes everyone this unnerved, but it likely has happened (or will happen) to almost everyone reading this book. Even those of us with a great deal of confidence may doubt or question ourselves, like Sam, when that rush of attraction sweeps over us. What do you think happened to Sam when the classmate made eye contact with him and then blushed—do you think he kept looking at her, quickly looked down or away, smiled, or just went blank?

This simple example illustrates the power and complexity of nonverbal communication—those ways we communicate our thoughts, emotions, desires, insecurities, and so forth *without* the use of words. Yes, language is your primary tool to communicate with others, but you communicate volumes more nonverbally than verbally. And that's the subject of this chapter.

In the last chapter, we explored the power of language to communicate sex, gender, identity, orientation, and so forth. We described language as our primary tool to communicate who we are to others, to be known by them and to know them as well. While language is incredibly important, nonverbal communication is more pervasive than language, meaning that you communicate far more to others nonverbally than you do verbally. Scholar Ray Birdwhistell (1970) contended that as much as 65 percent of the way human beings convey meanings in their messages is accomplished through nonverbal channels.

> We respond to gestures with an extreme alertness and, one might say, in accordance with an elaborate and secret code that is written nowhere, known by none, and understood by all. —Edward Sapir, American anthropologist and linguist

Nonverbal communication is "all those ways we communicate without words" (Ivy & Wahl, 2014, p. 5). More specifically, nonverbal communication is "communication other than written or spoken language that creates meaning for someone" (Beebe, Beebe, & Ivy, 2016, p. 75). What do your nonverbal cues convey to others about such things as your biological sex, psychosocial gender, sexual orientation, and attitudes toward members of your culture and the roles they should play?

WOMEN, MEN, AND NONVERBAL COMMUNICATION CODES

Are women and men more alike when it comes to nonverbal communication, or are the differences more pronounced? How can we possibly address the huge generalizations inherent in this topic?

Let's explore research findings on the most prominent nonverbal codes or categories of cues pertinent to our study of sex and gender. But first, a caveat: Most of the research on nonverbal communication focuses on biological sex (binary perspective), not psychological/cultural gender. One reason for this is because gender, with all its interesting complications, is harder to study than binary sex. Imagine you're a researcher: Is it easier to categorize a group of people by sex—female or male—or by gender, which involves many variables? Research is widening now to reflect the broader gender spectrum, but we'll have to look to the future for a more in-depth understanding of gender and nonverbal communication. For now, we ask you to tolerate the predominance of research on nonverbal communication that focuses on merely maleness and femaleness, masculinity and femininity, in the hopes that we'll soon have a richer base of research from which to draw.

NONVERBAL SENDING AND RECEIVING ABILITY Research on this topic has shown consistently that the sexes have varying abilities when it comes to sending (encoding) and receiving (decoding) nonverbal cues, with women having the edge, in general. At least three explanations can be offered for the variation: (1) genetics, (2) brain functioning, and (3) modeling (i.e., socialization). In terms of genetics, biological factors affect our development, which affects our nonverbal behavior (Richmond, McCroskey, & Hickson, 2011). For example, our physicality in terms of body shape, type, and structure is genetically determined, and these characteristics affect how our physical appearance communicates to others, as well as our walk, stance, gesturing behavior, and facial expression. A second explanation comes from studies that suggest that our brains function differently, in terms of how men and women process and interpret stimuli, as well as how we respond verbally and nonverbally to others, although this area of research is controversial (Baron-Cohen, 2004; Halpern, 2012; Hines, 2010; Lenroot & Giedd, 2010). (We refer you to Chapter 2 for information on the sexes' brain functioning.)

In terms of the third explanation, modeling (social learning theory), as we mentioned in Chapter 2, researchers contend that children model the thoughts, emotions, and actions of others, and that this role-modeling has a powerful effect on how children see themselves in terms of sex and gender (Bandura, 1986; Lippa, 2006; Schofield, Parke, Castaneda, & Coltrane, 2008). These modeling experiences are most potent in childhood and adolescence, but they continue to affect us as adults, as we continue to redefine ourselves.

You'll recall also from Chapter 2 our discussion of masculinity or an instrumental orientation and femininity or an expressive orientation (Gilligan, 1982). To recap, in American culture, women and femininity are more associated with affiliation, meaning that women are socialized to emphasize connectedness and culturally shaped to behave in ways that enhance social interaction (Mehrabian, 1981). Women are generally more expressive of emotion than men are, which relates to approachability and the skills of listening, responding, and connecting with others (Ellis, 2006; Hess, Adams, & Kleck, 2005; Weisfeld & Stack, 2002). In general, women's nonverbal behaviors come from a motivation to be congruent with other people. Studies have found women and girls to be better encoders of emotional information, meaning they more readily display nonverbal cues of emotion than do men and boys (Burgoon & Bacue, 2003; Hall, 2006; Woodzicka, 2008).

In contrast, men are socialized toward independence (versus interdependence), and masculinity is associated with status, power, and dominance. Men's nonverbal behaviors primarily serve the purpose of commanding attention and asserting their ideas and identities (Guerrero, Jones, & Boburka, 2006; Hess, Adams, Grammer, & Kleck, 2009). These socialization trends affect a great deal of what we're taught, from very young ages, regarding appropriate behavior for a person of our sex.

In addition to being more nonverbally expressive than men, women tend to be more sensitive receivers and decoders of others' nonverbal cues, especially those associated with emotions (Baron-Cohen, Wheelwright, Hill, Raste, & Plumb, 2001; Hall, 1998; Scherer, Banse, & Wallbott, 2001; Vogt & Colvin, 2003). On various tests of nonverbal receiving ability measured over decades of studies, girls and women typically outscore boys and men—a differential that begins in grade school and continues into adulthood. What this means is that a female advantage exists not only when it comes to expressing one's own emotions but also when interpreting others' nonverbal cues, such as processing micro eye and facial expressions, attending to subtle changes in vocal cues, and remembering people's appearance (Hall, Andrzejewski, & Yopchick, 2009; McClure, 2000; Rosip & Hall, 2004; Schmid Mast & Hall, 2006). This sex difference is consistent across U.S. and non-U.S. subjects and across age groups (Dickey & Knower, 1941; Hall, 1978; Horgan, Schmid Mast, Hall, & Carter, 2004; Izard, 1971; Rosenthal, Hall, DiMatteo, Rogers, & Archer, 1979). However, two exceptions have been documented in research: Women tend to be less adept than men when it comes to decoding nonverbal expressions of anger (Rotter & Rotter, 1988; Wagner, MacDonald, & Manstead, 1986) and nonverbal cues of deception (Hurd & Noller, 1988; Zuckerman, DePaulo, & Rosenthal, 1981).

PROXEMICS "The way distance and space play a communicative role in everyday life" is termed *proxemics* (Ivy & Wahl, 2014, p. 115). While proxemic behavior reflects our culture more than it does our sex, some interesting differences exist in how women and men tend to use and relate to space. Research for more than four decades has consistently shown that, in general, women's personal space bubble seems to be smaller than men's (Basu, 2011; Hall, 2006; Li & Li, 2007; Maguire & Kinney, 2010; Morman & Whitely, 2012). Research conducted in public settings shows that female dyads stand and sit closer together than male dyads, with the male–female dyad standing and sitting the closest (Santilli & Miller, 2011). Women and girls interact with others more closely than do men and boys, and are less likely to view intrusions into their personal space as violations.

Various explanations for proxemic differences have been rendered over the years. One is that males tend to be physically larger than most females and thus require more space. Another explanation relates to how children play and what they play with (Blakemore & Centers, 2005). Typically, girls play with dolls and small objects, which don't take up much room; conversely, boys play with trucks, balls, and larger objects, which encourage play away from the home and often occupy more space. Yet another explanation relates to traditional sex roles in U.S. culture—meaning that, even in this day and age, women's connection to the home and men's to the workplace affect our spatial behavior (Riesman, 1990; Wood, 1994). A final explanation is this: Since expansive, highly protected and defended spaces are correlated with higher power and status, particularly in U.S. culture, the tendency is for men to be afforded more personal space, since they typically hold more economic, political, and social power than do women (Henley, 2001).

PHYSICAL APPEARANCE, ATTRACTIVENESS, CLOTHING, AND ARTIFACTS A person's physical appearance is a major nonverbal communicator (much as we might like it not to be). Some obvious differences exist in terms of cultural displays of biological sex. For example, in most cultures, men don't wear dresses or skirts, but there are always exceptions (such as Scottish kilts or tribal sarongs worn by members of both sexes). What's more interesting for our discussion are men's and women's attitudes toward attractiveness and how their choices regarding physical appearance, clothing, and *artifacts* (temporary aspects of physical adornment other than clothing—e.g., jewelry, eyeglasses, cologne, makeup) serve as nonverbal communication.

© Hdcg Esteb/Shutterstock.com

What you look like on the outside is not what makes you cool at all. I mean, I had a mullet and wore parachute pants for a long, long time, and I'm doin' okay. —Ellen DeGeneres, comedian and TV talk show host

What's the first question most people ask when they learn a baby has been born—10 fingers and 10 toes? No, usually they ask, "Boy or girl?" After the sex of the baby is determined, pink and blue clothing and accessories are often lavished on the infant (as well as a whole array of sex-typed behavior; Fagot, Rodgers, & Leinbach, 2000; Koller, 2008).

In U.S. culture, as well as many cultures around the world, more emphasis is placed on the physical attractiveness of females than males. Girls are given toys related to appearance more often than boys are. Grooming sets (toy brushes, combs, and mirrors), makeup and fingernail kits, tutus and other dress-up items, and dolls with endless outfits and accessories can communicate an "appearance is everything" message to young girls (Aliakbari & Abdollahi, 2013; Dittmar, 2010; Kuther & McDonald, 2004; Messner, 2000). Is the most important thing about G.I. Joe the outfits he wears? Target may be an innovator on this front: In August of 2015 the company announced that it was doing away with its gender-marked labels and signs for such products in its stores as toys, kids' bedding, and clothing (Cunha, 2015).

While clothing has become more generic, fashions for men and women still differ significantly in most cultures around the world. Clothing for men primarily serves as body protection, cultural display, and, for many, an extension of their personalities. Men's clothing and artifacts are less often chosen for their conveyance of masculinity and ability to attract others, but for women, clothing can be an extension of their sexuality and a device for attracting attention. This emphasis has an obvious downside: compromised safety. As gender communication scholar Julia Wood (2012) explains, "Women's shoes are designed to flatter legs at the cost of comfort and

From the moment of birth, a baby is dressed in either pink or blue.

© Patryk Kosmider/Shutterstock.com

safety—how fast can you run in stilettos?" (p. 144). Researchers continue to examine the connection between general appearance, clothing choices, the pressure women feel to conform to current standards, and women's physical and sexual safety (Amon, 2015; Crawford & Unger, 2004; Farris, Treat, Viken, & McFall, 2008).

Volumes have been written on the subject of the sexes and the pressure to be physically attractive; it's beyond our parameters here to explore this topic fully. But think about the heat men and women take in American culture when it comes to their appearance: For example, are we as critical of overweight men as we are of overweight women? Granted, anyone can be made to feel bad about her or his weight, fitness, health, and attractiveness nowadays, but research suggests that women feel more intense pressure to be physically attractive than do men (Agthe, Sporrle, & Maner, 2010; Arroyo & Harwood, 2012; Bodey & Wood, 2009; Darlow & Lobel, 2010; Quick, McWilliams, & Byrd-Bredbenner, 2013; Shu-Yueh, 2014).

© Photology1971/Shutterstock.com

How fast can a woman run in stiletto heels?

KINESICS As a category or code of nonverbal communication, *kinesics* involves human movement, gestures, and posture (Ivy & Wahl, 2014). With regard to movement in general, researchers have obtained mixed results when observing the sexes. Some studies have found that men tend to be more active (or restless), in that they move and gesture more than women, which runs opposite to the stereotype that most women couldn't talk if you tied their hands together. Yet other studies have found that women tend to use more gestures than men do (Hall, 2006). What may be the differentiator here isn't the amount of gesturing but the type of gesture or the intention behind its use. Men often use commanding gestures for the purpose of indicating dominance, while women more often use gestures in acquiescence or affiliation with other people (Richmond et al., 2011). For example, you're more likely to see a man use a pointing gesture to emphasize a statement,

© Tinseltown/Shutterstock.com

I'm afraid to start plastic surgery. And my breasts are so versatile now, I can wear them down, up, and side to side.
—Cybill Shepherd, actor

while a woman is more likely to use a palms-up or other less confrontational gesture to say the same thing.

In terms of walking behavior, some sex differences have been detected (Moore, Hickson, & Stacks, 2009). For example, nonverbal communication scholar Peter Andersen (2004) explains that men's bodies are somewhat motionless while walking, in that their hips and torso tend to stay facing frontward, their feet move about one foot apart in stride, and their arms swing significantly. In contrast, women have more sway or side-to-side motion in their walks. Women's hips tend to move more than men's, mostly due to the fact that women often put one foot in front of the other when walking, which engages the hips more.

Sex differences in sitting behavior have also been observed with regularity in American culture. Typically, men assume open sitting positions, meaning that their legs are often extended and spread apart rather than close together. A man is more likely to cross his leg over his other knee in a 90-degree angle to the floor, while a woman is more likely to cross her legs at the knee, with the crossed leg hanging down, or to cross her legs at the ankles (Andersen, 2004; Hall, 2006). While some women like the comfort of the 90-degree, crossed-leg position, sitting this way tends to give off a masculine vibe.

How do men and women typically sit?

© michaeljung/Shutterstock.com

FACIAL AND EYE EXPRESSIONS A subset of kinesics, facial and eye expressions have long been a fascination of nonverbal research. A key difference between women and men has been detected in how often and why they smile. A comprehensive review of more than 400 studies revealed that women smile more than men (LaFrance, Hecht, & Levy Paluck, 2003). Women tend to use more facial animation than men do; they smile as a common facial expression in social interaction, whereas men's smiles are more purposeful and used to reveal their emotions (Ellis, 2006; Guéguen, 2008; Hess et al., 2005; Hess et al., 2009; Vatsa & Lata, 2012; Weisfeld & Stack, 2002; Woodzicka, 2008). Apparently, women smile more, even when they're alone (Trees & Manusov, 1998), and they receive more smiles from others than men do (Hall, Carney, & Murphy, 2002; Hinsz & Tomhave, 1991). Watch a group in interaction sometime and note the smiling behavior. Might you see more of the men using rather blank expressions until they wish to make a point or convey a particular emotion, whereas the women smile seemingly for no reason?

In terms of eye contact, research with American subjects shows some sex differences in that women tend to maintain more eye contact in conversation than men do; men tend to hold eye gaze while they're speaking but not while listening (Bate & Bowker, 1997; Hall, 2006; Hall & Halberstadt, 1986; McCormick & Jones, 1989). In research terms this is called the *visual dominance ratio* or the amount of time spent looking while speaking, versus looking while listening (Hall, 2006; Koch, Baehne, Kruse, Zimmermann, & Zumbach, 2010). People who wish to assert dominance will make eye contact when they have something to say but break eye contact when spoken to.

TOUCH (HAPTICS) Touch behavior in humans and animals is referred to as *haptics* (Ivy & Wahl, 2014). Studies document some sex differences in terms of how women and men give and receive touch. Research has produced mixed results regarding affection between parents and male versus female children. While some research has found that, in general, parents extend more affection to daughters than to sons and that touches they extend to daughters are more gentle (Condry, Condry, & Pogatshnik, 1983; Lindsey & Mize, 2001), other research hasn't detected this differential, nor has it seen any differences in benefits for male or female children who receive affection from either a same-sex or opposite-sex parent (Schrodt, Ledbetter, & Ohrt, 2007).

Many nonverbal researchers have deemed touch more of a "female-appropriate" behavior, primarily because studies from the 1970s to the present have concluded the following: (1) Women express more nonverbal affection than men do; (2) women receive more touch, from both men and other women, than men do; (3) women engage in more frequent and more intimate same-sex touch than men do; (4) women are more comfortable with touch in general and same-sex touch in specific than men are; (5) women in heterosexual stable or married relationships are more likely to initiate touch than their male partners are; and (6) women perceive themselves as being more affectionate than men (Burgoon & Bacue, 2003; Derlega, Lewis, Harrison, Winstead, & Costanza, 1989; Emmers & Dindia, 1995; Floyd, 1997, 2000; Floyd & Morman, 1997; Greenbaum & Rosenfeld, 1980; Guerrero & Floyd, 2006; Hall & Veccia, 1990; Harrison & Shortall, 2011; Jones, 1986; Major, Schmidlin, & Williams, 1990; Miller, Denes, Diaz, & Buck, 2014; Roese, Olson, Borenstein, Martin, & Shores, 1992; Wallace, 1981; Willis & Rawdon, 1994).

VOCALICS (PARALANGUAGE) The ways people express themselves through their voices is termed *vocalics*, sometimes referred to as *paralanguage* (Ivy & Wahl, 2014). Some sex differences in vocal production can be attributed to physiology, meaning how vocal anatomy is structured and the influence of hormones on its functioning. But physiology doesn't tell the whole story. Granted, men's typically thicker vocal folds produce lower pitches; women's hormonal changes (the depletion of estrogen as women age) deepen the average pitch of female voices (Feinberg et al., 2006; Frank, Maroulis, & Griffin, 2013; Krolokke & Sorensen, 2006; Stathopoulos, Huber, & Sussman, 2011). But cultural/societal factors (and resulting stereotypes) affect voice production as well; men have been socialized not to use higher pitches, lest they be ridiculed for sounding feminine (Cartei & Reby, 2012; Henley, 2001; Viscovich et al., 2003). Masculinity is associated with greater volume, while femininity is associated with a softer-sounding voice, but men and women are equally capable of generating volume when they want to or the situation demands. See how the stereotypes come into play?

Remember...

Nonverbal Communication: Communication without words that creates meaning for someone

Proxemics: The way distance and space play a communicative role in everyday life

Artifacts: Temporary aspects of physical adornment other than clothing (e.g., jewelry, eyeglasses, cologne, makeup)

Kinesics: Human movement, gestures, and posture

Visual Dominance Ratio: Amount of time spent looking while speaking, versus looking while listening

Haptics: Touch behavior in humans and animals

Vocalics (Paralanguage): How people express themselves through their voices

A significant challenge transgender people face relates to having a voice that corresponds to their new sex/gender. Physical transformations are daunting, but the voice is typically one of the last elements to be tackled; speech therapy and surgery are options that help the voice align with other identity cues (Hancock & Garabedian, 2013; Hancock & Haskin, 2015; Sawyer, Perry, & Dobbins-Scaramelli, 2014).

INTERSECTIONS: GENDER, NONVERBAL, AND RELATIONAL COMMUNICATION

In Chapter 6, we explore the role of sex and gender in relationships—primarily in friendships and romantic or intimate relationships. Here, let's examine the intersections of research on sex/gender, nonverbal communication, and relationship building.

Relationship Initiation

It may sound old-fashioned, but the activity of getting a relationship going is termed *courtship* in research (Moore, 2010; Stafford, 2010). First we go back in time a bit to rely on the longstanding work of Albert Scheflen (1965), who studied interpersonal encounters and noted patterns of nonverbal behavior over time—patterns that formed into a courtship ritual. (Scheflen's observations were about Western cultures in particular, so understand that courtship in African or Middle-Eastern cultures, for example, is enacted differently.)

Scheflen distinguished between *courtship*, which he defined as romantic attraction and an interest in some form of sexual intimacy, and *quasi-courtship behavior*, which he was much keener on and known for among nonverbal scholars. To make it confusing, the same set of behaviors can indicate courtship—a more serious level of interest—as well as quasi-courtship, in which behavior is flirtatious and not to be taken seriously. Scheflen believed that quasi-courtship behavior is useful, in that it can breathe life into dull interactions or settings, or reinvigorate someone's waning attention. More recent research has focused on the problems that arise if someone interprets nonverbal cues as courtship while someone else views the behavior as harmless flirtation or seduction—with no intention of forming a deeper connection (Yeomans, 2009). The onus is on the receiver of such nonverbal cues to judge the motivation or intent of the behavior, as to whether it indicates serious interest or "just kidding around" or "having fun." In their book on nonverbal communication in relationships, Guerrero and Floyd (2006) explain that "there is often little distinction in the flirtation behaviors used by courters and quasi-courters; where the groups differ is often only in the eventual outcomes they seek" (p. 81).

Scheflen's quasi-courtship ritual includes four categories or stages:

- *Courtship readiness* cues communicate that we're open to being approached. Women and men alike convey such cues as erect posture (no slouching), alert eyes and a lifted chin, heightened muscle tone, and a tucked-in stomach. In this phase, we accentuate our best physical features instead of camouflaging or downplaying them, so as to attract people to us.

- *Preening behavior* comes next, which involves adjustment behaviors toward the self, such as stroking, twirling, or moving our hair; fixing makeup (especially when women reapply lipstick); smoothing or rearranging clothing (e.g., tugging on a bra strap, adjusting a tie); checking ourselves in a mirror; and unbuttoning or leaving unbuttoned parts of shirts or blouses.

- *Positional cues* partition us toward someone and away from others. At social gatherings people use proxemics as well as their arms, legs, and sitting/standing positions to section themselves off from a group, thereby signaling interest in each other and creating a barrier to ward off intruders.

- *Actions of appeal or invitation* is Scheflen's fourth category. These actions typically occur later in the courtship ritual and involve more engaged behaviors, such as holding eye gaze longer; looking at a partner flirtatiously; exposing more of the skin; rolling the pelvis forward (which sounds odd but is a subtle, subconscious move that reveals attraction); and flexing muscles or moving in a way that emphasizes those body parts we're most proud of or that will arouse our partner.

In Chapter 5, we discuss *flirting*, or the act of attracting romantic attention, and how flirting plays a role in relationship initiation. For our focus on nonverbal communication in this chapter, just realize that a great deal of flirtation is accomplished nonverbally. Several decades of studies on heterosexual flirtation have found upwards of 50 gestures and related nonverbal cues that people use to signal their interest (Grammer, Kruck, Juette, & Fink, 2000; Hall, Carter, Cody, & Albright, 2010; Kaspar & Krull, 2013; Knox & Wilson, 1981; McCormick & Jones, 1989; Moore, 1985, 1995; Muehlenhard, Koralewski, Andrews, & Burdick, 1986/2008; Perper & Weis, 1987; Renninger, Wade, & Grammer, 2004; Weber, Goodboy, & Cayanus, 2010). Among the top flirting cues are smiling; surveying a crowded room with the eyes; increased proxemics; prolonged and mutual eye gaze; brief, darting glances; looking at specific body features of another person; animated facial expressions; touches (both purposeful and accidental); head tosses (sometimes including the infamous "hair flip"); caressing objects such as a glass or keys; movement to music; animated vocal inflection, increased speech rate, and volume changes; and the adjustment of clothing.

> **Remember...**
>
> **Courtship:** Process of trying to get a relationship going; romantic attraction and an interest in some form of sexual intimacy
>
> **Quasi-Courtship Behavior:** Patterns of nonverbal communication that form a ritual of flirtatious behavior
>
> **Flirting:** Act of attracting romantic attention

Research has found that men tend to view flirting as more sexual than women do, with heterosexual men often misinterpreting women's friendly behaviors as signs of sexual attraction and interest (Farris et al., 2008; Haselton, 2003; Henningsen, 2004; Henningsen, Henningsen, & Valde, 2006; Henningsen, Kartch, Orr, & Brown, 2009; Koeppel, Montagne, O'Hair, & Cody, 1999; Koukounas & Letch, 2001; LaFrance, Henningsen, Oates, & Shaw, 2009; Mongeau, Serewicz, & Thierren, 2004; Moore, 2002). Studies have also noted that the likelihood of this kind of misinterpretation greatly increases as alcohol consumption increases (Abbey, Zawacki, & Buck, 2005; Delaney & Gluade, 1990).

Relationship Maintenance

Once a relationship has been launched, it's equally (if not more) challenging to maintain it. The nonverbal code most critical to romantic or intimate relational success is touch (Andersen, Guerrero, & Jones, 2006; Bello, Brandau-Brown, Zhang, & Ragsdale, 2010; Bodie & Villaume, 2008; Gulledge, Gulledge, & Stahmann, 2003; Hall, 2011; Horan & Booth-Butterfield, 2010, 2013; Jones & Yarbrough, 1985; Le Poire, Shepard, Duggan, & Burgoon, 2002).

Research suggests that touch and several other nonverbal cues tend to be more prevalent in the beginning stages of a relationship, as opposed to the middle or later stages (Emmers & Dindia, 1995; McDaniel & Andersen, 1998; Punyanunt-Carter, 2004). People in long-term relationships, including marriages, tend to touch each other less frequently and less intimately than people who are working to establish a romantic relationship or to repair one that's in trouble (Guerrero & Andersen, 1991, 1994; Koerner & Fitzpatrick, 2002; Noller, 2006; Patterson, Gardner, Burr, Hubler, & Roberts, 2012). A decrease in affection doesn't necessarily signal a relationship in decline.

Becoming more comfortable or used to a partner can be a positive sign that the relationship is maturing, that the outward signals of closeness are no longer necessary or are less important (Spott, Pyle, & Punyanunt-Carter, 2010). Many of us have parents who've been together for many years; some of those parents stopped sleeping in the same bed (or even the same room) years ago, but that change in behavior doesn't necessarily signal something's wrong in the relationship. But if the outward or public displays of affection as well as the inward or private displays change, such that one or both partners feel decreasing intimacy, that might indicate a problem.

In *My Guy: A Gay Man's Guide to a Lasting Relationship*, psychiatrist Martin Kantor (2002) discusses one particular change in an intimate relationship—sexual dissatisfaction (more specifically, boredom) in a gay male relationship:

> Boredom with sex is not inherent in gay relationships, new or old. Overfamiliarity is often cited as the culprit, but with good relationships sex gets less, not more, boring. When a relationship is solid, lust, although not necessarily in its original form, actually increases over the days, months, and years. In simple behavioral terms, having your cake makes you want another slice. (p. 183)

Other nonverbal codes are important in intimate relationships. Four key proxemic cues are interpersonal distance, body lean, body orientation, and physical plane (Andersen et al., 2006). Research shows that people tend to sit closer to their romantic partners than to their friends (Guerrero, 1997). Forward lean, a face-to-face body orientation, and interacting on the same physical plane (as opposed to above or below someone) are all associated with enhanced intimacy (Andersen et al., 2006). Kinesic behaviors such as smiling, facial animation, general facial pleasantness, increased eye contact, and synchronized gestures of immediacy, affection, closeness, and warmth are all important in an intimate relationship (Burgoon & Newton, 1991; Kleinke, 1986; Tickle-Degnen, 2006). As people remain intimate over time, they tend to mimic or acquire each other's nonverbal behaviors, such that they come to look, sound, and behave alike.

Certain vocal behaviors are associated with intimacy and demonstrations of affection between partners (Farinelli, 2008). Research shows that high-pitched female voices and low-pitched male voices communicate affection, rather than the reverse; varying the pitch (i.e., avoiding a monotone delivery) conveys affection as well (Collins & Missing, 2003; Floyd & Ray, 2003). Vocal pleasantness and warmth, as well as laughter, communicate affection between intimates (Farley, Hughes, & LaFayette, 2013; Guerrero, 2004).

Relational Conflict and Termination

Nonverbal communication plays a role in relationships on the decline, as well as those being initiated and maintained. More information exists on nonverbal communication and relationship initiation than termination, perhaps because people like to look on the bright side. We approach this topic in two parts: First, let's examine nonverbal cues and conflict, with the understanding that conflict is inevitable and can be constructive in a relationship; it doesn't necessarily signal a relationship's demise (Beebe, Beebe, & Ivy, 2016). But conflict is usually present in a relationship that's on its last legs. Second, let's focus on nonverbal communication and the "parting of ways."

RELATIONAL CONFLICT Nonverbal cues are ever-present in conflict situations, often appearing prior to verbal cues (Guerrero, 2013; Patterson et al., 2012). If we were to ask you what romantic relational partners look and sound like when they argue, you might begin with the nonverbal category of proxemics, because couples in conflict use distance in interesting ways. The most obvious use of proxemic cues is to put physical distance us and our partner (Guerrero & Floyd, 2006). The reverse behavior—getting in someone's face when arguing—is also prevalent, as we decrease distance to appear menacing or gain some sort of advantage. Sometimes we leave the scene of the conflict altogether, preferring time and distance before we can approach our partners again. However, a withdrawal or avoidant response to conflict is seldom effective (Gross, Guerrero, & Alberts, 2004).

Another relevant nonverbal cue related to proxemics is touch—its decrease or absence, or touch that is increasingly controlling, overbearing, or even abusive. When we're in conflict with an intimate partner, most of us decrease our affectionate touch with that person as we increase our distance from him or her (Guerrero, 2013). In terms of touch turned abusive in a conflict, we refer you to Chapter 7 on power abuses in relationships.

© auremar/Shutterstock.com

Conflict situation behavior is highly individualistic and depends on the circumstances of the conflict.

For now, it's important to note that in the heat of an argument, men and women alike may let touch escalate into physical violence and abuse when their emotions get out of control (Christopher & Lloyd, 2000).

What other nonverbal cues are typically present in conflict situations? Research shows that some conflict partners exhibit animated gestures, head shaking, and random movement in the heat of battle (Newton & Burgoon, 1990). For some of us, our energy builds in an argument to such a degree that our gestures fly about uncontrollably; others of us pace and gesture in a repetitive fashion, often pointing accusingly at our partner while placing a hand on our chest to signify that we're blameless. Some of us can't sit and argue—we have to stand, as though towering over our partners will give us an edge.

Facial expressions are usually animated in conflict, although some of us put on a stony face and stay that way until the conflict is over. Some of us use continuous eye contact—staring as though we want to burn a hole into our partner—while others break eye contact in an argument, preferring to look down or stare off into space. These behaviors are highly individualistic; they depend on the person, the situation, the relationship, and the level of intensity of the conflict.

Vocalic behaviors in conflict are very revealing but, again, quite individualistic. Some of us are vocally aggressive; the more intense the conflict, the faster our rate of speaking, the greater the volume, the more varied the pitch, and the longer our turns at talk. Heightened vocalic cues rarely diffuse a conflict; they tend to escalate it. Others of us have learned the value of the pause and use a dramatic volume, pitch, and rate decrease to reveal the intensity of our emotions. Still others "suffer in silence," preferring not to engage vocally at all in an argument (Cheng & Tardy, 2010; Wilmot & Hocker, 2013). But sometimes an even, calm way of speaking can enrage a partner because it seems manipulative and controlling.

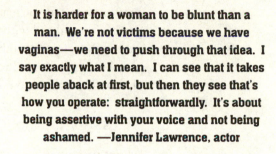

It is harder for a woman to be blunt than a man. We're not victims because we have vaginas—we need to push through that idea. I say exactly what I mean. I can see that it takes people aback at first, but then they see that's how you operate: straightforwardly. It's about being assertive with your voice and not being ashamed. —Jennifer Lawrence, actor

RELATIONSHIP TERMINATION So what happens, nonverbally speaking, when a relationship tanks? Communication scholars Knapp, Vangelisti, and Caughlin (2013) provide a five-stage framework for relationship termination or de-escalation. Realize that a couple may enter one or more stages of the de-escalation process, only to revive their relationship and save it from termination.

- *Differentiating* occurs when the differences between relational partners begin to outweigh the similarities. Partners' individual identities become more important than their identity as a couple. Nonverbally, partners begin to increase physical distance, use fewer affirming cues (e.g., smiling, head nodding, forward body lean, direct body orientation), and decrease both public and private touch.

- *Circumscribing* occurs when partners' communication becomes superficial and nonverbal expressions of emotion and affection are restrictive. If we were at a party and saw a couple in this phase of de-escalation, we could hardly tell they were a couple.

- *Stagnating* is the third stage, in which communication virtually stops and nonverbal behaviors of closeness and affiliation (e.g., eye contact, physical proximity, touch, facial expressiveness, vocal engagement) shut down.

- *Avoiding* is the fourth stage. Couples physically separate and aren't seen in public together anymore. They tend to avoid going places where they might run into each other; almost all communication ceases.

🍁 *Terminating* is the final stage in which couples end their relationship. While we don't encourage that you stage a breakup just to study the relevant nonverbal cues, it's fascinating to explore how nonverbal cues change as a relationship unravels.

NONVERBAL CUES AND SEXUALITY

In this section of the chapter, we hit some high points regarding nonverbal cues and the communication of sexuality—this is by no means an exhaustive treatment of the subject. Some of the language you'll read in this section may not be what you're used to seeing in your college textbooks, but we ask you to forge ahead with us for the greater purpose of learning something, rather than feeling embarrassed, shocked, or offended by language you may be unaccustomed to reading. Let's begin by defining a few key terms that will be critical to our discussion.

Sexuality, Sexual Orientation, and Gaydar

Many meanings for sexuality exist, but for the sake of clarity, we view *sexuality* as including sexual behavior, as well as cognitive, emotional, and psychosociocultural factors. Most human beings are sexual creatures, but the choice of how to communicate our sexuality, if we choose to do so at all, is very individualistic. How do we convey the sexual part of our being? Granted, some of us believe in abstinence, meaning we hold the belief that sexual activity should occur only within the confines of a monogamous, committed partnering, such as marriage. Just because we're not *having* sex doesn't necessarily mean we don't express our sexuality. But how does a person nonverbally convey who she or he is sexually?

This won't surprise you one bit: Physical appearance is the most central nonverbal code related to sexuality. Physical features that we're born with, that we influence by eating right (or not) and working out (or not), that may be altered by illness or accident, and that we accentuate are key conveyors of sexual information. Secondarily, all the things we do to enhance our physical appearance and attractiveness—from clothing choices to alterations of our hair, skin, and bodies, and adornments such as tattoos, piercings, and jewelry—send sexual messages to other people, whether we intend to do so or not.

Other nonverbal codes can relate to sexuality as well. For example, aspects of kinesics such as our walk, stance, and posture may attract others to us because we look confident. Or these cues may repel others because we look as though we're carrying the weight of the whole world on our shoulders. Some nonverbal cues are flirtatious, such as the way we use eye contact to show interest in another person, how closely we sit or stand by someone in conversation, how we animate our facial expressions, what kind of touch occurs between us and other people, and how our vocal inflection reveals our interest. All these elements reveal our sexuality, even if acting sexy or seeking sexual activity isn't our intent.

A key element within the larger construct of sexuality is *sexual orientation*, defined in Chapter 1 as related to the sex of people to whom we're attracted or with whom we wish to have sexual activity. Since people who aren't heterosexual are still discriminated against in U.S. culture and other cultures around the world, many gay, lesbian, bisexual/bigender, transgender, intersex, and asexual people feel they must be closeted to function safely in society. We talk a great deal in this book about how U.S. culture, laws, and attitudes have changed regarding orientations other than heterosexual, yet even with all the changes, the fear of being rejected, ostracized, ridiculed, and victimized because of one's orientation are still quite real.

Because of the danger—perceived and real—a way of perceiving someone's sexual orientation continues to operate. You've probably heard the term *gaydar*, referring to an ability to detect the sexual orientation of another person using indirect cues, sometimes referred to as the gay sixth sense (Colzato, van Hooidonk, van den Wildenberg, Harinck, & Hommel, 2010; Leap, 2007; Rieger, Linsenmeier, Gygax, Garcia, & Bailey, 2010; Woolery, 2008). But did you know that gaydar, which is based primarily on nonverbal cues, developed within the homosexual community first and was then co-opted by heterosexuals as a way of detecting whether someone was gay?

Is gaydar—this uncanny way of detecting that someone is gay—something intuitive, like extrasensory perception (ESP), something a few blessed individuals are born with? Yes and no. While some people may have a natural sixth sense about such things, most gaydar is based on keen nonverbal observation, enhanced listening skills, and experience over time in varied social encounters. Scholar Cheryl Nicholas (2004) defines gaydar as "a folk concept used within the gay community to name the recognition of verbal and non-verbal behavior associated with gay identity" (p. 60). Nicholas contends that gaydar is necessary for homosexual people's survival in a world where heterosexuality is the dominant paradigm for relationships. Gaydar protects the invisibility many homosexuals feel is necessary to survive in a discriminatory world. Nicholas adds, "Gaydar is possible because gay people believe that it is possible" (p. 66).

Scholars have studied gaydar for some time, but they're divided as to its usefulness. While some researchers argue against a distinct set of behaviors for gays and lesbians that would distinguish them from heterosexuals (Van Newkirk, 2006), other studies have produced results that speak to the existence and utility of gaydar (France, 2007; Reuter, 2002).

Johnson, Gill, Reichman, and Tassinary (2007) investigated how body shape and motion affect perceptions of sexual orientation. In two experiments, they used computer-generated animations, manipulated for body shape and motion, and found that both nonverbal behaviors affected subjects' perceptions of female figures' sexual orientation. Female figures with hourglass bodies that moved with hips swaying were perceived as heterosexual, whereas female figures that didn't look or move this way were perceived as homosexual. For men, body shape wasn't as much a factor as movement; male animated figures that moved with "shoulder swagger" were perceived as heterosexual, while those that didn't were perceived as homosexual (p. 321). In a third study, the researchers replicated the earlier studies but used outlines of real people and achieved the same results. People perceived sexual orientation based on body shape and movement, which doesn't mean they were accurate in these perceptions but only that people make inferences from what they observe. Are stereotypes operating here or patterns of behavior that can feed into gaydar?

Other studies have investigated whether observation of nonverbal cues enhances the accuracy of judgments regarding sexual orientation (Ambady & Hallahan, 2002; Ding & Rule, 2012; Gowen & Britt, 2006; Knofler & Imhof, 2007; Lawson, 2005; Mack & Munson, 2012; Shelp, 2002). In one study, subjects indicated which characteristics they relied on when attempting to identify a person as straight or gay (Carroll & Gilroy, 2002). The most predominant cue was eye contact; other cues included clothing style and fit, jewelry, facial expressions, body type, and kinesic cues.

Female figures with an hourglass shape are perceived as heterosexual.

© Nestor Rizhniak/Shutterstock.com

Sexual Activity

Nonverbal cues are a critical part of how we view ourselves as sexual beings, how we communicate our sexuality to other people, and how we express how we feel about certain people in our lives. As we mentioned earlier (but it bears repeating), we know that not all of us are currently sexually active. Some are celibate by choice, believing that sexual activity is appropriate only in a committed, monogamous partnering. Others are celibate for certain periods of time, such as those times when they're not in a relationship, their relational partner is at a distance, or they're simply concentrating on other aspects of life. Sexual expression ebbs and flows for most people (even married people and committed partners); this discussion of nonverbal behavior, gender, and sexual activity can be applicable to whatever period of life we experience.

> **Remember...**
>
> **Sexuality:** Sexual behavior, as well as cognition, emotion, and psychosociocultural factors that affect one's sexual being
>
> **Sexual Orientation:** Related to the sex of persons to whom one is attracted or with whom one wishes to engage in sexual activity
>
> **Gaydar:** Ability to detect the homosexual orientation of a person

We realize that our focus in this chapter is on nonverbal communication, but when it comes to the realm of sex, it's wise to rely more on *verbal* information than on *nonverbal* cues. In this section, we explore some nonverbal cues related to sexual interest and activity, but in the sexual context, *verbal communication is key*, and here's why: While nonverbal cues are important, too much sexual behavior involves reading signals, looking for "body language," "getting vibes," sensing what our partner wants, giving our partner exactly what we perceive is needed, and so forth. The mythology suggests that people are supposed to be so in tune with their own and their partner's bodies that they can somehow read nonverbal cues accurately (while in the midst of their own arousal) and interpret the cues appropriately so that they respond perfectly. Sorry, but what world are these folks living in?

Sexual experience and education can help us develop enhanced nonverbal sending and receiving abilities so we can send clear signals of interest, attraction, and arousal to a potential sexual partner, as well as receive and interpret such cues more accurately (LaFrance, 2010). But the opportunity for misunderstanding is so great and the consequences so dire that we encourage a little more talking, a little less guessing. (And more verbal communication means more than such statements as, "Ouch! You're on my hair.") Even if it's awkward or embarrassing, talking about such things as sexual needs and wants, boundaries, what sexual activity means in the greater context of a relationship, and suggestions about sexual behaviors or positions can open the door to deeper intimacy (Faulkner & Lannutti, 2010; Holmberg & Blair, 2009).

Communication about such "clinical" subjects as birth control methods, including condom use (i.e., who's responsible for supplying condoms, demanding their use, and actually putting them on before sexual contact), HIV/STI prevention methods, and number of sexual partners (past and present) can greatly enhance the sexual activity and the relationship (Bowleg, Valera, Teti, & Tschann, 2010; Boyle & O'Sullivan, 2010; Humphreys & Newby, 2007; Meston & Buss, 2009; Zukoski, Harvey, & Branch, 2009). If more talk about, during, and after sexual activity sounds unromantic to you, we encourage you to think again, because we still advocate for clear communication over media-concocted romance any day. *Real* romance can be highly communicative. Spontaneity and "picking up a vibe" have their definite downsides.

NONVERBAL CUES: BEFORE SEXUAL ACTIVITY

Which nonverbal codes are most related to sexual arousal, meaning the stage before sexual activity might take place or as it is beginning to occur? Certainly physical appearance, sometimes referred to as sex appeal, is a primary factor (Regan, 2004). In the U.S., as well as other cultures around the world, many people go to great lengths to enhance their physical attractiveness. Kantor (2002), whose book on gay male relationships we cited earlier, devotes an entire chapter to "Step Six: Look Great for Mr. Wonderful." He describes in detail physical appearance concerns that gay men should attend to if they want to attract a wonderful mate—from paying attention to hygiene, complexion, physical fitness, and style, down to specific nonverbal behaviors to avoid so one doesn't draw unnecessary attention.

In addition to physicality, the way people adorn their bodies can provide clues of sexuality. But here's a caution we've all probably heard before, about assumptions regarding appearance and sexual interest: *Just because someone is dressed in what we deem to be a sexy manner, that doesn't mean the person is looking for sexual activity.* We emphasize this point because the justification, "She was asking for it," is common in relation to sexual assault and rape trials, when perpetrators of these crimes often claim that a victim was dressed or acting provocatively, thereby somehow asking for sex. We can dress in a sexy manner because we want to feel sexy, because we want to express that part of our personality; that doesn't mean we give our consent or want to engage in sexual activity. *Dressing and behaving in a sexy way doesn't equate to an invitation.*

Other nonverbal cues, including kinesic behaviors such as walk, posture, and sitting position, may reveal sexual arousal as well, such as when heterosexual women sometimes exaggerate their hip sway when they walk past men so as to indicate sexual interest, get men's attention, and possibly arouse the men sexually. Likewise, men may accentuate their body parts and move in ways that emphasize their masculinity, hoping to attract attention and sexual interest from onlookers. You may not have thought of dancing as a form of nonverbal communication, but people often reveal their sexuality and attraction to others through the way they move to music.

Interactive synchrony, defined as a coordination of speech and body movement or a social rhythm between people, is another means of conveying attraction and sexual interest (Knapp, Hall, & Horgan, 2013). It's fun to watch a couple who appear interested in each other; as their interest and attraction develop over time, their body positions, gestures, touch, facial expressions, and eye behavior will mirror each other, such that they develop a rhythm of behaving (Lakens & Stel, 2011; Schmidt, Morr, Fitzpatrick, & Richardson, 2012; Wilt, Funkhouser, & Revelle, 2011).

Proxemics reveal attraction, too, in that decreased distance between people can be a signal of sexual interest, but it's just as likely that the music is too loud to converse at a greater distance. We have to be careful about leaping to an interpretation of sexual interest just because someone gets close to us.

Eye behavior is a fascinating thing to watch among persons of all sexual orientations, because it's a key indicator of interest and attraction. We've already talked about eye contact and its role in gaydar, but in U.S. culture, we rarely give our attention to people without looking at them. When people "undress someone with their eyes," it certainly communicates a pointed message, but this can backfire, making the receiver of this action feel objectified and degraded. (Women get tired of men who make eye contact with only their breasts.) Eye contact—both continuous and the kind that stops and starts (the double take)—often reveals interest and sexual attraction.

Increased frequency and intimacy of touch may indicate arousal as well, but again we emphasize the word *may*. As we've mentioned elsewhere, research over several decades shows that heterosexual men tend to misinterpret women's touches as being more intimate than women intend (Abbey, 1982, 1987, 1991; Henningsen, 2004; Koukounas & Letch, 2001; LaFrance et al., 2009; Moore, 2002). While women may intend their touches to be an indication of friendship or warmth, men may interpret those touches as indications of romantic interest and attraction, leading to sexual arousal. Part of the problem is that some heterosexual men believe that women send mixed signals regarding intimacy, and we grant that this does happen. Women may believe they're just flirting harmlessly and "having a good time," but when their actions are viewed differently than they intend, the results can be devastating.

NONVERBAL CUES: DURING SEXUAL ACTIVITY Sexual intimacy is a significant development within a relationship (Mongeau, Serewicz, Henningsen, & Davis, 2006). But saying that this topic is "ticklish" isn't just a pun; it's the reality of delving into such personal waters. It's important to discuss this subject for many reasons, most of which we've already articulated (e.g., misunderstanding, embarrassment, hurt feelings, abusive behavior). Here's another reason: quality. We wholeheartedly believe, as research, therapists, and self-help books suggest, that sexual activities will be of better quality for both partners if the communication between them is enhanced (Bowleg et al., 2010; Cupach & Metts, 1991; Humphreys & Newby, 2007; Meston & Buss, 2009).

So what nonverbal codes are most important in a sexual encounter? Research reveals that the following nonverbal cues are related to courtship and seduction: flashing an eyebrow, licking the lips, touching a thigh, tossing the head, presenting one's neck, coming close, making continuous eye contact, and flipping one's hair (Abbey & Melby, 1986; Anolli & Ciceri, 2002; Grammer, 1990; Kendrick & Trost, 1987; Moore, 1985, 1995). One of the more obvious codes is haptics (touch behavior). Probably touch is the most integral nonverbal behavior between sexual partners, but some of us assume things about touch, and you know the problem with assumptions. Three common assumptions are (1) that our current partner will behave and react as our previous partner did, (2) that what we've read or heard about sex works the same way for every partner, and (3) that our partner wants what we want. Granted, we can learn some things from books, Internet sites, and other people's experiences, but we also have to learn to treat our partner as a unique human being who will likely desire and react to us differently than other people do, than what the books say, or than we would. That lack of predictability can be viewed as a positive, not a negative.

For some people, eye contact and facial expressions during sexual activity are very important. Most of us would agree that making love to someone who won't look at us would be a major turnoff (or a dead giveaway that the person would rather be somewhere else or with someone else). What if someone cries during sex? In nonsexual situations, people may cry because they're sad or afraid, but some people cry when they're happy. How do we know what's going on with a sexual partner who's crying if we don't ask? Should we ignore the crying or assume we did something wrong? Some people—men and women alike—cry when they climax, but if we don't understand this reaction, it can be confusing and disconcerting (to say the least).

In terms of kinesics, body positioning and movement are other central aspects of the sexual encounter. Those of us who are comfortable enough to talk about our preferred sexual positions or what feels best to us are more likely to have positive sexual encounters than those of us who just hope for the best or are too afraid or intimidated to discuss our preferences (Sprecher & Cate, 2004). Again, nonverbal cues are important, but they don't replace the power of the good old-fashioned conversation. Studies show that, in general, the more partners talk about sex (and we mean a *quality* conversation), the greater their satisfaction with both the sexual and the nonsexual aspects of their relationship (Boyle & O'Sullivan, 2010; Faulkner & Lannutti, 2010; Zukoski et al., 2009).

One final word on this topic: If certain nonverbal cues heighten our sexual arousal and pleasure, it's important to learn to ask for them rather than expecting or hoping that a partner will read our mind. If we like to be touched in a certain way, how will our partner know? Touching him or her the way we like to be touched may have an impact, but this form of hinting or indirect method often doesn't work. It's better to be explicit and verbalize our desires, but not like a drill sergeant barking out orders, either. Too much instruction can kill the mood, but too little can kill the enjoyment. Nonverbal cues are important, but we shouldn't rely on them to carry sexual messages for us; clear verbal communication is critical.

NONVERBAL CUES: AFTER SEXUAL ACTIVITY People are as varied in their preferences and approaches for after-sex activity as they are in other phases, so it isn't wise to assume or buy into such stereotypical notions as

"All women like to be held" and "If you don't sleep over after sex, it's rude." The intent here isn't to take all the spontaneity out of sexual activity—before, during, or after—but, again, we shouldn't try to read our partner's mind if we're unsure of what to do after sexual activity has subsided. It's okay to ask a few simple questions, keeping in mind our own desires and preferences, because then we'll know better how to behave.

One of the things you may not have thought of regarding the after-effects of sex is this: Being in the throes of passion takes many of us to a different plane, where logic and the best advice pounding in our head have to fight to be heard. But once that passion and lust subsides, reality sets back in and things can get *really* awkward. (Talk about nonverbal cues becoming strange.) So, while we don't want to provide a laundry list of dos and don'ts regarding sexual activity and its aftermath, it's important to take some time to think about these issues, whether or not you're currently sexually active or imagine yourself someday becoming sexually active. Ask yourself, What kind of sexual encounter do I want? How do I want to nonverbally communicate my sexuality, before, during, and after sexual activity? How do I want to verbally communicate? What kind of nonverbal and verbal communication do I want, need, and expect from my partner?

HOT button issue

Jamie was ready for a night on the town with her friends. She'd had a tough week—papers, exams, her boss bugging her to take on more hours at work—it had been crazy. So, while she was "between boyfriends" at the time, nonetheless she was feeling in a sexy mood, so she dressed accordingly for a fun night out with her girlfriends. But at each place Jamie and her group of friends went that night, they got what they perceived as "unwanted attention" from men, to the point where being in the clubs just wasn't fun anymore, so they went to breakfast.

During the meal, the group of friends discussed the challenge of dressing cute and sexy when you just want to express yourself, and then being accused of "asking for it" or being a tease. If a woman dresses sexy because she feels sexy, does she have the right to get irritated or mad when she receives too much attention from people in a social setting? If a woman dresses sexy, but doesn't want sex, is she sending mixed signals?

Can someone express a healthy sexuality without people thinking she or he is a tease or is trying to get a hook up? Does a healthy expression of sexuality necessarily involve the responses of other people? Is it reasonable to expect that heterosexual men can simply enjoy the sexuality of women without expecting or wanting sex with them as the outcome of an evening?

CONCLUSION

In this chapter, we explored the intersections of gender, nonverbal communication, and relationship development. We began by overviewing key research findings regarding how the sexes are both similar and different in their displays of nonverbal codes of behavior.

Since relationships are what give most of us life's greatest joy, we turned our attention in this chapter to the role of nonverbal cues in the initiation, maintenance, and sometimes termination of intimate relationships. Most of us would agree that conflict is inevitable in intimate relationships, but it can also be healthy or constructive if partners are attuned to their own and each other's nonverbal communication. Not all relationships are successful, so we concluded this section of the chapter by looking at predominant nonverbal cues associated with relationship termination.

Finally, we explored the important subject of nonverbal cues and the expression of sexuality. We first defined some key terms, including *sexuality* and *sexual orientation*, then explored the phenomenon of *gaydar*, since these perceptions rely predominantly on nonverbal cues. We closed the chapter with a discussion of the most critical nonverbal codes of behavior that typically occur before, during, and after sexual activity.

DISCUSSION STARTERS

1. In your experience, are men and women more alike than different, nonverbally? If you believe the sexes are different, what nonverbal behaviors differ the most, from your perspective and observation?

2. If you've had an intimate relationship in the past, think about the nonverbal cues present when that relationship first began. Then think about how those nonverbal cues changed, if they diminished or disappeared over time. What do you believe caused the change in behavior? Did your behavior change more than your partner's? Why or why not? What do you want to try to do differently the next time?

3. In your experience, does gaydar exist? What nonverbal cues are most integral to gaydar? How reliable is gaydar, in general, and *your* gaydar, in specific? Is there an equivalent "sixth sense" to detect if someone is transgender? Intersex? Asexual? Should we even be wondering about detecting someone's orientation or sexuality?

4. In this chapter, we discussed the role of nonverbal communication in sexual activity. What things might you have discovered about yourself in reading this part of the chapter, in terms of how you nonverbally express your sexual self (or not) to other people? What changes do you think you need to make in this regard?

References

Abbey, A. (1982). Sex differences in attributions for friendly behavior: Do males misperceive females' friendliness? *Journal of Personality and Social Psychology, 42,* 830–838.

Abbey, A. (1987). Misperception of friendly behavior as sexual interest: A survey of naturally occurring incidents. *Psychology of Women Quarterly, 11,* 173–194.

Abbey, A. (1991). Misperception as an antecedent of acquaintance rape: A consequence of ambiguity in communication between men and women. In A. Parrot & L. Bechhofer (Eds.), *Acquaintance rape: The hidden crime* (pp. 96–111). New York: Wiley.

Abbey, A., & Melby, C. (1986). The effects of nonverbal cues on gender differences in perceptions of sexual interest. *Sex Roles, 15,* 283–298.

Abbey, A., Zawacki, T., & Buck, P. O. (2005). The effects of past sexual assault perpetration and alcohol consumption on reactions to women's mixed signals. *Journal of Social and Clinical Psychology, 25,* 129–157.

Agthe, M., Sporrle, M., & Maner, J. K. (2010). Don't hate me because I'm beautiful: Anti-attractiveness bias in organizational evaluation and decision making. *Journal of Experimental Social Psychology, 46,* 1151–1154.

Aliakbari, M., & Abdollahi, K. (2013). Does it matter what we wear? A sociolinguistic study of clothing and human values. *International Journal of Linguistics, 5,* 34–45.

Ambady, N., & Hallahan, M. (2002). Using nonverbal representations of behavior: Perceiving sexual orientation. In A. M. Galaburda & S. M. Kosslyn (Eds.), *The languages of the brain* (pp. 320–332). Cambridge, MA: Harvard University Press.

Amon, M. J. (2015). Visual attention in mixed-gender groups. *Frontiers in Psychology, 5,* 1–10.

Andersen, P. A. (2004). *The complete idiot's guide to body language.* New York: Alpha.

Andersen, P. A., Guerrero, L. K., & Jones, S. M. (2006). Nonverbal behavior in intimate interactions and intimate relationships. In V. Manusov & M. L. Patterson (Eds.), *The SAGE handbook of nonverbal communication* (pp. 259–277). Thousand Oaks, CA: Sage.

Anolli, L., & Ciceri, R. (2002). Analysis of the vocal profiles of male seduction: From exhibition to self-disclosure. *Journal of General Psychology, 129,* 149–169.

Arroyo, A., & Harwood, J. (2012). Exploring the causes and consequences of engaging in fat talk. *Journal of Applied Communication Research, 40,* 167–187.

Bandura, A. (1986). *Social foundations of thought and action: A social cognitive theory.* Englewood Cliffs, NJ: Prentice Hall.

Baron-Cohen, S. (2004). *The essential difference: Male and female brains and the truth about autism.* New York: Basic Books.

Baron-Cohen, S., Wheelwright, S., Hill, J., Raste, Y., & Plumb, I. (2001). The "Reading the Mind in the Eyes" Test Revised Version: A study with normal adults, and adults with Asperger syndrome or high-functioning autism. *Journal of Child Psychology and Psychiatry, 42,* 241–251.

Basu, A. (2011). HIV/AIDS and subaltern autonomous rationality: A call to recenter health communication in marginalized sex worker spaces. *Communication Monographs, 78,* 391–408.

Bate, B., & Bowker, J. (1997). *Communication and the sexes* (2nd ed.). Prospect Heights, IL: Waveland.

Beebe, S. A., Beebe, S. J., & Ivy, D. K. (2016). *Communication: Principles for a lifetime* (6th ed.). Boston: Pearson.

Bello, R. S., Brandau-Brown, F. E., Zhang, S., & Ragsdale, J. D. (2010). Verbal and nonverbal methods for expressing appreciation in friendships and romantic relationships: A cross-cultural comparison. *International Journal of Intercultural Relations, 34,* 294–302.

Birdwhistell, R. L. (1970). *Kinesics and context: Essays on body motion communication.* Philadelphia: University of Pennsylvania Press.

Blakemore, J. E. O., & Centers, R. E. (2005). Characteristics of boys' and girls' toys. *Sex Roles, 53,* 619–634.

Bodey, K. R., & Wood, J. T. (2009). Whose voices count and who does the counting? *Southern Communication Journal, 74,* 325–337.

Bodie, G. D., & Villaume, W. A. (2008). Men and women holding hands revisited: Effects of mutual engagement and hand dominance on attributions of cross-sex handholding. *Communication Research Reports, 25,* 243–254.

Bowleg, L., Valera, P., Teti, M., & Tschann, J. M. (2010). Silences, gestures, and words: Nonverbal and verbal communication about HIV/AIDS and condom use in black heterosexual relationships. *Health Communication, 25,* 80–90.

Boyle, A. M., & O'Sullivan, L. F. (2010). General and sexual communication in established relationships: An exploration of possible links to condom use among young adults. *Canadian Journal of Human Sexuality, 19,* 53–64.

Burgoon, J. K., & Bacue, A. E. (2003). Nonverbal communication skills. In J. O. Greene & B. R. Burleson (Eds.), *Handbook of communication and social interaction skills* (pp. 179–219). Mahwah, NJ: Erlbaum.

Burgoon, J. K., & Newton, D. A. (1991). Applying a social meaning model to relational message interpretations of conversational involvement: Comparing observer and participant perspectives. *Southern Communication Journal, 56,* 96–113.

Carroll, L., & Gilroy, P. J. (2002). Role of appearance and nonverbal behaviors in the perception of sexual orientation among lesbians and gay men. *Psychological Reports, 91,* 115–122.

Cartei, V., & Reby, D. (2012). Acting gay: Male actors shift the frequency components of their voices towards female values when playing homosexual characters. *Journal of Nonverbal Behavior, 36,* 79–93.

Cheng, C.-C., & Tardy, C. (2010). A cross-cultural study of silence in marital conflict. *China Media Report Overseas, 6,* 95–105.

Christopher, F. S., & Lloyd, S. A. (2000). Physical and sexual aggression in relationships. In C. Hendrick & S. S. Hendrick (Eds.), *Close relationships* (pp. 331–343). Thousand Oaks, CA: Sage.

Collins, S. A., & Missing, C. (2003). Vocal and visual attractiveness are related in women. *Animal Behaviour, 65,* 997–1004.

Colzato, L. S., van Hooidonk, L., van den Wildenberg, W. P. M., Harinck, F., & Hommel, B. (2010). Sexual orientation biases attentional control: A possible gaydar mechanism. *Frontiers in Psychology, 1*(13).

Condry, S. M., Condry, J. C., & Pogatshnik, L. W. (1983). Sex differences: A study of the ear of the beholder. *Sex Roles, 9,* 697–704.

Crawford, M., & Unger, R. (2004). *Women and gender: A feminist psychology* (4th ed.). New York: McGraw-Hill.

Cunha, D. (2015, August 10). Target's decision to remove gender-based signs is just the start. Retrieved September 16, 2015, from <www.time.com>.

Cupach, W. R., & Metts, S. (1991). Sexuality and communication in close relationships. In K. McKinney & S. Sprecher (Eds.), *Sexuality in close relationships* (pp. 93–110). Hillsdale, NJ: Erlbaum.

Darlow, S., & Lobel, M. (2010). Who is beholding my beauty? Thinness ideals, weight, and women's responses to appearance evaluation. *Sex Roles, 63,* 833–843.

Delaney, H. J., & Gluade, B. A. (1990). Gender differences in perception of attractiveness of men and women in bars. *Journal of Personality and Social Psychology, 16,* 378–391.

Derlega, V. J., Lewis, R. J., Harrison, S., Winstead, B. A., & Costanza, R. (1989). Gender differences in the initiation and attribution of tactile intimacy. *Journal of Nonverbal Behavior, 13,* 83–96.

Dickey, E. C., & Knower, F. H. (1941). A note on some ethnological differences in recognition of simulated expressions of emotions. *American Journal of Sociology, 47,* 190–193.

Ding, J., & Rule, N. O. (2012). Gay, straight, or somewhere in between: Accuracy and bias in the perception of bisexual faces. *Journal of Nonverbal Behavior, 36,* 165–176.

Dittmar, H. (2010). *Consumer culture, identity and well-being: The search for the "good life" and the "body perfect."* London: Psychology Press.

Ellis, L. (2006). Gender differences in smiling: An evolutionary neuroandrogenic theory. *Physiology and Behavior, 88,* 303–308.

Emmers, T. M., & Dindia, K. (1995). The effect of relational stage and intimacy on touch: An extension of Guerrero and Andersen. *Personal Relationships, 2,* 225–236.

Fagot, B. L., Rodgers, C. S., & Leinbach, M. D. (2000). Theories of gender socialization. In T. Eckes & H. Trautner (Eds.), *The developmental social psychology of gender* (pp. 65–89). Mahwah, NJ: Erlbaum.

Farinelli, L. (2008). The sounds of seduction and affection. In L. K. Guerrero & M. L. Hecht (Eds.), *The nonverbal communication reader* (3rd ed., pp. 160–168). Long Grove, IL: Waveland.

Farley, S. D., Hughes, S. M., & LaFayette, J. N. (2013). People will know we are in love: Evidence of differences between vocal samples directed toward lovers and friends. *Journal of Nonverbal Behavior, 37,* 123–138.

Farris, C., Treat, T. A., Viken, R. J., & McFall, R. M. (2008). Sexual coercion and the misperception of sexual intent. *Clinical Psychology Review, 28,* 48–66.

Faulkner, S. L., & Lannutti, P. J. (2010). Examining the content and outcomes of young adults' satisfying and unsatisfying conversations about sex. *Qualitative Health Research, 20,* 275–285.

Feinberg, D. R., Jones, B. C., Law Smith, M. J., Moore, F. R., DeBruine, L. M., Cornwall, R. E., et al. (2006). Menstrual cycle, trait estrogen level, and masculinity preferences in the human voice. *Hormones and Behavior, 46,* 215–222.

Floyd, K. (1997). Communicating affection in dyadic relationships: An assessment of behavior and expectancies. *Communication Quarterly, 45,* 68–80.

Floyd, K. (2000). Affectionate same-sex touch: The influence of homophobia on observers' perceptions. *Journal of Social Psychology, 140,* 774–788.

Floyd, K., & Morman, M. T. (1997). Affectionate communication in nonromantic relationships: Influences of communicator, relational, and contextual factors. *Western Journal of Communication, 61,* 279–298.

Floyd, K., & Ray, G. B. (2003). Human affection exchange: VI. Vocalic predictors of perceived affection in initial interactions. *Western Journal of Communication, 67,* 56–73.

France, D. (2007, June 25). The science of gaydar. *New York Magazine*, 31–99.

Frank, M. G., Maroulis, A., & Griffin, D. J. (2013). The voice. In D. Matusomo, M. G. Frank, & H. S. Hwang (Eds.), *Nonverbal communication: Science and application* (pp. 53–74). Thousand Oaks, CA: Sage.

Gilligan, C. (1982). *In a different voice: Psychological theory and women's development*. Cambridge, MA: Harvard University Press.

Gowen, C. W., & Britt, T. W. (2006). The interactive effects of homosexual speech and sexual orientation on the stigmatization of men: Evidence for expectancy violation theory. *Journal of Language and Social Psychology, 25*, 437–456.

Grammer, K. (1990). Strangers meet: Laughter and nonverbal signs of interest in opposite-sex encounters. *Journal of Nonverbal Behavior, 14*, 209–236.

Grammer, K., Kruck, K., Juette, A., & Fink, B. (2000). Nonverbal behavior as courtship signals: The role of control and choice in selecting partners. *Evolution and Human Behavior, 21*, 371–390.

Greenbaum, P. E., & Rosenfeld, H. M. (1980). Varieties of touching in greetings: Sequential structure and sex-related differences. *Journal of Nonverbal Behavior, 5*, 13–25.

Gross, M. A., Guerrero, L. K., & Alberts, J. K. (2004). Perceptions of conflict strategies and communication competence in task-oriented dyads. *Journal of Applied Communication Research, 32*, 249–270.

Guéguen, N. (2008). The effect of a woman's smile on men's courtship behavior. *Social Behavior and Personality, 36*, 1233–1236.

Guerrero, L. K. (1997). Nonverbal involvement across interactions with same-sex friends, opposite-sex friends, and romantic partners: Consistency or change? *Journal of Social and Personal Relationships, 14*, 31–58.

Guerrero, L. K. (2004). Observer ratings of nonverbal involvement and immediacy. In V. Manusov (Ed.), *The sourcebook of nonverbal measures: Going beyond words* (pp. 221–235). Mahwah, NJ: Erlbaum.

Guerrero, L. K. (2013). Emotion and communication in conflict interaction. In J. G. Oetzel & S. Ting-Toomey (Eds.), *The SAGE handbook of conflict communication: Integrating theory, research, and practice* (pp. 105–131). Thousand Oaks, CA: Sage.

Guerrero, L. K., & Andersen, P. A. (1991). The waxing and waning of relational intimacy: Touch as a function of relational stage, gender, and touch avoidance. *Journal of Social and Personal Relationships, 8*, 147–165.

Guerrero, L. K., & Andersen, P. A. (1994). Patterns of matching and initiation: Touch behavior and touch avoidance across romantic relationship stages. *Journal of Nonverbal Behavior, 18*, 137–153.

Guerrero, L. K., & Floyd, K. (2006). *Nonverbal communication in close relationships*. Mahwah, NJ: Erlbaum.

Guerrero, L. K., Jones, S. M., & Boburka, R. R. (2006). Sex differences in emotional communication. In D. J. Canary & K. Dindia (Eds.), *Sex differences and similarities in communication* (2nd ed., pp. 241–261). Mahwah, NJ: Erlbaum.

Gulledge, A., Gulledge, M., & Stahmann, R. (2003). Romantic physical affection types and relationship satisfaction. *American Journal of Family Therapy, 31*, 233–242.

Hall, J. A. (1978). Gender effects in decoding nonverbal cues. *Psychological Bulletin, 85*, 845–857.

Hall, J. A. (1998). How big are nonverbal sex differences? The case of similarity and sensitivity to nonverbal cues. In D. Canary & K. Dindia (Eds.), *Sex differences and similarities in communication: Critical essays and empirical investigations of sex and gender in interaction* (pp. 155–178). Mahwah, NJ: Erlbaum.

Hall, J. A. (2006). Women's and men's nonverbal communication: Similarities, differences, stereotypes, and origins. In V. Manusov & M. L. Patterson (Eds.), *The SAGE handbook of nonverbal communication* (pp. 201–218). Thousand Oaks, CA: Sage.

Hall, J. A. (2011). Gender and status patterns in social touch. In M. J. Hertenstein & S. J. Weiss (Eds.), *The handbook of touch: Neuroscience, behavioral, and health perspectives* (pp. 329–350). New York: Springer.

Hall, J. A., Andrzejewski, S. A., & Yopchick, J. E. (2009). Psychosocial correlates of interpersonal sensitivity: A meta-analysis. *Journal of Nonverbal Behavior, 33*, 149–180.

Hall, J. A., Carney, D. R., & Murphy, N. A. (2002). Gender differences in smiling. In M. H. Abel (Ed.), *An empirical reflection on the smile: Mellen studies in psychology* (Vol. 4, pp. 155–185). Lewiston, NY: Edwin Mellen.

Hall, J. A., Carter, S., Cody, M. J., & Albright, J. M. (2010). Individual differences in the communication of romantic interest: Development of the Flirting Styles Inventory. *Communication Quarterly, 58*, 365–393.

Hall, J. A., & Halberstadt, A. G. (1986). Smiling and gazing. In J. S. Hyde & M. Linn (Eds.), *The psychology of gender: Advances through meta-analysis* (pp. 136–158). Baltimore, MD: Johns Hopkins University Press.

Hall, J. A., & Veccia, E. M. (1990). More "touching" observations: New insights on men, women, and interpersonal touch. *Journal of Personality and Social Psychology, 59*, 1155–1162.

Halpern, D. F. (2012). *Sex differences in cognitive abilities* (4th ed.). New York: Psychology Press.

Hancock, A. B., & Garabedian, L. M. (2013). Transgender voice and communication treatment: A retrospective chart review of 25 cases. *International Journal of Language & Communication Disorders, 48*, 54–65.

Hancock, A. B., & Haskin, G. (2015). Speech-language pathologists' knowledge and attitudes regarding lesbian, gay, bisexual, transgender, and queer (LGBTQ) populations. *American Journal of Speech-Language Pathology, 24*, 206–221.

Harrison, M., & Shortall, J. (2011). Women and men in love: Who really feels it and says it first? *Journal of Social Psychology, 151*, 727–736.

Haselton, M. G. (2003). The sexual overperception bias: Evidence of a systematic bias in men from a survey of naturally occurring events. *Journal of Research in Personality, 37*, 34–47.

Henley, N. M. (2001). Body politics. In A. Branaman (Ed.), *Self and society: Blackwell readers in sociology* (pp. 288–297). Malden, MA: Blackwell.

Henningsen, D. D. (2004). Flirting with meaning: An examination of miscommunication in flirting interactions. *Sex Roles, 50*, 481–489.

Henningsen, D. D., Henningsen, M. L. M., & Valde, K. S. (2006). Gender differences in perceptions of women's sexual interest during cross-sex interactions: An application and extension of cognitive valence theory. *Sex Roles, 54*, 821–829.

Henningsen, D. D., Kartch, F., Orr, N., & Brown, A. (2009). The perceptions of verbal and nonverbal flirting cues in cross-sex interactions. *Human Communication, 12*, 371–381.

Hess, U., Adams, R. B., Jr., Grammer, K., & Kleck, R. E. (2009). Face gender and emotion expression: Are angry women more like men? *Journal of Vision, 9*, 1–8.

Hess, U., Adams, R. B., Jr., & Kleck, R. E. (2005). Who may frown and who should smile? Dominance, affiliation, and the display of anger and happiness. *Cognition and Emotion, 19*, 515–536.

Hines, M. (2010). Sex-related variation in human behavior and the brain. *Trends in Cognitive Sciences, 14*, 448–456.

Hinsz, V. B., & Tomhave, J. A. (1991). Smile and (half) the world smiles with you, frown and you frown alone. *Personality and Social Psychology Bulletin, 17*, 586–592.

Holmberg, D., & Blair, K. L. (2009). Sexual desire, communication, satisfaction, and preferences of men and women in same-sex versus mixed-sex relationships. *Journal of Sex Research, 46*, 57–66.

Horan, S., & Booth-Butterfield, M. (2010). Investigating affection: An investigation of affection exchanges theory and relational qualities. *Communication Quarterly, 58*, 394–413.

Horan, S., & Booth-Butterfield, M. (2013). Understanding the routine expression of deceptive affection in romantic relationships. *Communication Quarterly, 61*, 195–216.

Horgan, T. G., Schmid Mast, M., Hall, J. A., & Carter, J. D. (2004). Gender differences in memory for the appearance of others. *Personality and Social Psychology Bulletin, 30*, 185–196.

Humphreys, T., & Newby, J. (2007). Initiating new sexual behaviours in heterosexual relationships. *Canadian Journal of Human Sexuality, 16*, 77–88.

Hurd, K., & Noller, P. (1988). Decoding deception: A look at the process. *Journal of Nonverbal Behavior, 12*, 217–233.

Ivy, D. K., & Wahl, S. T. (2014). *Nonverbal communication for a lifetime* (2nd ed.). Dubuque, IA: Kendall Hunt.

Izard, C. E. (1971). *The face of emotion.* New York: Appleton-Century-Crofts.

Johnson, K. L., Gill, S., Reichman, V., & Tassinary, L. G. (2007). Swagger, sway, and sexuality: Judging sexual orientation from body motion and morphology. *Journal of Personality and Social Psychology, 93*, 321–334.

Jones, S. E. (1986). Sex differences in touch communication. *Western Journal of Speech Communication, 50*, 227–241.

Jones, S. E., & Yarbrough, A. E. (1985). A naturalistic study of the meanings of touch. *Communication Monographs, 52*, 19–56.

Kantor, M. (2002). *My guy: A gay man's guide to a lasting relationship.* Naperville, IL: Sourcebooks Casablanca.

Kaspar, K., & Krull, J. (2013). Incidental haptic stimulation in the context of flirt behavior. *Journal of Nonverbal Behavior, 37*, 165–173.

Kendrick, D. T., & Trost, M. R. (1987). A biosocial theory of heterosexual relationships. In K. Kelley (Ed.), *Females, males, and sexuality: Theories and research* (pp. 59–100). Albany: State University of New York Press.

Kleinke, C. L. (1986). Gaze and eye contact: A research review. *Psychological Bulletin, 100*, 78–100.

Knapp, M. L., Hall, J. A., & Horgan, T. G. (2013). *Nonverbal communication in human interaction* (8th ed.). Belmont, CA: Cengage/Wadsworth.

Knapp, M. L., Vangelisti, A. L., & Caughlin, J. (2013). *Interpersonal communication and human relationships* (7th ed.). Boston: Pearson.

Knofler, T., & Imhof, M. (2007). Does sexual orientation have an impact on nonverbal behavior in interpersonal communication? *Journal of Nonverbal Behavior, 31,* 189–204.

Knox, D., & Wilson, K. (1981). Dating behaviors of university students. *Family Relations, 30,* 255–258.

Koch, S. C., Baehne, C. G., Kruse, L., Zimmermann, F., & Zumbach, J. (2010). Visual dominance and visual egalitarianism: Individual and group-level influences of sex and status in group interactions. *Journal of Nonverbal Behavior, 34,* 137–153.

Koeppel, L. B., Montagne, Y., O'Hair, D., & Cody, M. J. (1999). Friendly? Flirting? Wrong? In L. K. Guerrero, J. A. DeVito, & M. L. Hecht (Eds.), *The nonverbal communication reader* (2nd ed., pp. 290–297). Prospect Heights, IL: Waveland.

Koerner, A. F., & Fitzpatrick, M. A. (2002). Nonverbal communication and marital adjustment and satisfaction: The role of decoding relationship relevant and relationship irrelevant affect. *Communication Monographs, 69,* 33–51.

Koller, V. (2008). "Not just a colour": Pink as a gender and sexuality marker in visual communication. *Visual Communication, 7,* 395–423.

Koukounas, E., & Letch, N. M. (2001). Psychological correlates of perception of sexual intent in women. *Journal of Social Psychology, 141,* 443–456.

Krolokke, C., & Sorensen, A. S. (2006). *Gender communication theories and analyses: From silence to performance.* Thousand Oaks, CA: Sage.

Kuther, T. L., & McDonald, E. (2004). Early adolescents' experiences with and views of Barbie. *Adolescence, 39,* 39–51.

LaFrance, B. H. (2010). What verbal and nonverbal communication cues lead to sex? An analysis of the traditional sexual script. *Communication Quarterly, 58,* 297–318.

LaFrance, B. H., Henningsen, D. D., Oates, A., & Shaw, C. M. (2009). Social–sexual interactions? Meta-analyses of sex differences in perceptions of flirtatiousness, seductiveness, and promiscuousness. *Communication Monographs, 76,* 263–285.

LaFrance, M., Hecht, M. A., & Levy Paluck, E. (2003). The contingent smile: A meta-analysis of sex differences in smiling. *Psychological Bulletin, 129,* 305–334.

Lakens, D., & Stel, M. (2011). If they move in sync, they must feel in sync: Movement synchrony leads to attributions of rapport and entitativity. *Social Cognition, 29,* 1–14.

Lawson, W. (2005, November–December). Gay men and women really do find it easier to spot other gays. *Psychology Today,* 30.

Le Poire, B., Shepard, C., Duggan, A., & Burgoon, J. K. (2002). Relational messages associated with nonverbal involvement, pleasantness, and expressiveness in romantic couples. *Communication Research Reports, 19,* 195–206.

Leap, W. (2007). Language, socialization, and silence in gay adolescence. In K. E. Lovaas & M. M. Jenkins (Eds.), *Sexualities and communication in everyday life: A reader* (pp. 95–106). Thousand Oaks, CA: Sage.

Lenroot, R. K., & Giedd, J. N. (2010). Sex differences in the adolescent brain. *Brain and Cognition, 72,* 46–55.

Li, S., & Li, Y. (2007). How far is far enough? A measure of information privacy in terms of interpersonal distance. *Environment & Behavior, 39,* 317–331.

Lindsey, E. W., & Mize, J. (2001). Contextual differences in parent-child play: Implications for children's gender role development. *Sex Roles, 44,* 155–176.

Lippa, R. A. (2006). *Gender, nature, and nurture* (2nd ed.). Mahwah, NJ: Erlbaum.

Mack, S., & Munson, B. (2012). The influence of /s/ quality on ratings of men's sexual orientation: Explicit and implicit measures of the "gay lisp" stereotype. *Journal of Phonetics, 40,* 198–212.

Maguire, K. C., & Kinney, T. A. (2010). When distance is problematic: Communication, coping, and relational satisfaction in female college students' long-distance dating relationships. *Journal of Applied Communication Research, 38,* 27–46.

Major, B., Schmidlin, A., & Williams, L. (1990). Gender patterns in social touch: The impact of setting and age. *Journal of Personality and Social Psychology, 58,* 634–643.

McClure, E. B. (2000). A meta-analytic review of sex differences in facial expression processing and their development in infants, children, and adolescents. *Psychological Bulletin, 126,* 424–453.

McCormick, N. B., & Jones, A. J. (1989). Gender differences in nonverbal flirtation. *Journal of Sex Education and Therapy, 15,* 271–282.

McDaniel, E. R., & Andersen, P. A. (1998). International patterns of tactile communication: A field study. *Journal of Nonverbal Behavior, 21,* 59–75.

Mehrabian, A. (1981). *Silent messages: Implicit communication of emotions and attitudes* (2nd ed.). Belmont, CA: Wadsworth.

Messner, M. (2000). Barbie girls versus sea monsters: Children constructing gender. *Gender and Society, 7,* 121–137.

Meston, C. M., & Buss, D. M. (2009). *Why women have sex: Understanding sexual motivations—from adventure to revenge (and everything in between)*. New York: Henry Holt.

Miller, M. J., Denes, A., Diaz, B., & Buck, R. (2014). Attachment style predicts jealous reaction to viewing touch between a romantic partner and close friend: Implications for Internet social communication. *Journal of Nonverbal Behavior, 38*, 451–476.

Mongeau, P. A., Serewicz, M. C. M., Henningsen, M. L. M., & Davis, K. L. (2006). Sex differences in the transition to heterosexual romantic relationship. In K. Dindia & D. J. Canary (Eds.), *Sex differences and similarities in communication* (2nd ed., pp. 337–358). Mahwah, NJ: Erlbaum.

Mongeau, P. A., Serewicz, M. C. M., & Thierren, L. F. (2004). Goals for cross-sex first dates: Identification, measurement, and the influence of contextual factors. *Communication Monographs, 71*, 121–147.

Moore, M. M. (1985). Nonverbal courtship patterns in women: Context and consequences. *Ethology and Sociobiology, 6*, 237–247.

Moore, M. M. (1995). Courtship signaling and adolescents: "Girls just wanna have fun?" *Journal of Sex Research, 32*, 319–329.

Moore, M. M. (2002). Courtship communication and perception. *Perceptual and Motor Skills, 94*, 97–105.

Moore, M. M. (2010). Human nonverbal courtship behavior—a brief historical review. *Journal of Sex Research, 47*, 171–180.

Moore, N.-J., Hickson, M., III, & Stacks, D. W. (2009). *Nonverbal communication: Studies and applications* (5th ed.). New York: Oxford University Press.

Morman, M. T., & Whitely, M. (2012). An exploratory analysis of critical incidents of closeness in the mother/son relationship. *Journal of Family Communication, 12*, 22–39.

Muehlenhard, C. L., Koralewski, M. A., Andrews, S. L., & Burdick, C. A. (2008). Verbal and nonverbal cues that convey interest in dating: Two studies. In L. K. Guerrero & M. L. Hecht (Eds.), *The nonverbal communication reader* (3rd ed., pp. 353–359). Long Grove, IL: Waveland. (Original work published in 1986)

Newton, D. A., & Burgoon, J. K. (1990). Nonverbal conflict behaviors: Functions, strategies, and tactics. In D. D. Cahn (Ed.), *Intimates in conflict: A communication perspective* (pp. 77–104). Hillsdale, NJ: Erlbaum.

Nicholas, C. L. (2004). Gaydar: Eye-gaze as identity recognition among gay men and lesbians. *Sexuality and Culture: An Interdisciplinary Quarterly, 8*, 60–86.

Noller, P. (2006). Nonverbal communication in close relationships. In V. Manusov & M. L. Patterson (Eds.), *The SAGE handbook of nonverbal communication* (pp. 403–420). Thousand Oaks, CA: Sage.

Patterson, J., Gardner, B. C., Burr, B. K., Hubler, D. S., & Roberts, M. K. (2012). Nonverbal behavioral indicators of negative affect in couple interaction. *Contemporary Family Therapy, 34*, 11–28.

Perper, T., & Weis, D. L. (1987). Proceptive and rejective strategies of U.S. and Canadian college women. *Journal of Sex Research, 23*, 455–480.

Punyanunt-Carter, N. M. (2004). Reported affectionate communication and satisfaction in marital and dating relationships. *Psychological Reports, 95*, 1154–1160.

Quick, V., McWilliams, R., & Byrd-Bredbenner, C. (2013). Fatty, fatty, two-by-four: Weight-teasing history and disturbed eating in young adult women. *American Journal of Public Health, 103*, 508–515.

Regan, P. C. (2004). Sex and the attraction process: Lessons from science (and Shakespeare) on lust, love, chastity, and fidelity. In J. H. Harvey, A. Wenzel, & S. Sprecher (Eds.), *The handbook of sexuality in close relationships* (pp. 115–133). Mahwah, NJ: Erlbaum.

Renninger, L. A., Wade, T. J., & Grammer, K. (2004). Getting that female glance: Patterns and consequences of male nonverbal behavior in courtship contexts. *Evolution and Human Behavior, 25*, 416–431.

Reuter, D. F. (2002). *Gaydar: The ultimate insider guide to the gay sixth sense*. New York: Crown.

Richmond, V. P., McCroskey, J. C., & Hickson, M. L., III. (2011). *Nonverbal behavior in interpersonal relations* (7th ed.). Boston: Pearson.

Rieger, G., Linsenmeier, J. A. W., Gygax, L., Garcia, S., & Bailey, J. M. (2010). Dissecting "gaydar": Accuracy and the role of masculinity–femininity. *Archives of Sexual Behavior, 39*, 124–140.

Riesman, C. (1990). *Divorce talk: Women and men make sense of personal relationships*. New Brunswick, NJ: Princeton University Press.

Roese, N. J., Olson, H. M., Borenstein, M. N., Martin, A., & Shores, A. L. (1992). Same-sex touching behavior: The moderating role of homophobic attitudes. *Journal of Nonverbal Behavior, 16*, 249–259.

Rosenthal, R., Hall, J. A., DiMatteo, M. R., Rogers, P. L., & Archer, D. (1979). *Sensitivity to nonverbal communication: The PONS test*. Baltimore, MD: Johns Hopkins University Press.

Rosip, J. C., & Hall, J. A. (2004). Knowledge of nonverbal cues, gender, and nonverbal decoding accuracy. *Journal of Nonverbal Behavior, 28*, 267–286.

Rotter, N. G., & Rotter, G. S. (1988). Sex differences in the encoding and decoding of negative facial emotions. *Journal of Nonverbal Behavior, 12,* 139–148.

Santilli, V., & Miller, A. N. (2011). The effects of gender and power distance on nonverbal immediacy in symmetrical and asymmetrical power conditions: A cross-cultural study of classrooms and friendships. *Journal of International and Intercultural Communication, 4,* 3–22.

Sawyer, J., Perry, J. L., & Dobbins-Scaramelli, A. (2014). A survey of the awareness of speech services among transgender and transsexual individuals and speech-language pathologists. *International Journal of Transgenderism, 15,* 146–163.

Scheflen, A. E. (1965). Quasi-courtship behavior in psychotherapy. *Psychiatry, 28,* 245–257.

Scherer, K. R., Banse, R., & Wallbott, H. G. (2001). Emotion inferences from vocal expression correlate across languages and cultures. *Journal of Cross-Cultural Psychology, 32,* 76–92.

Schmid Mast, M., & Hall, J. A. (2006). Women's advantage at remembering others' appearance: A systematic look at the why and when of a gender difference. *Personality and Social Psychology Bulletin, 32,* 353–364.

Schmidt, R. C., Morr, S., Fitzpatrick, P., & Richardson, M. J. (2012). Measuring the dynamics of interactional synchrony. *Journal of Nonverbal Behavior, 36,* 263–279.

Schofield, T. J., Parke, R. D., Castaneda, E. K., & Coltrane, S. (2008). Patterns of gaze between parents and children in European American and Mexican American families. *Journal of Nonverbal Behavior, 32,* 171–186.

Schrodt, P., Ledbetter, A. M., & Ohrt, J. K. (2007). Parental confirmation and affection as mediators of family communication patterns and children's mental well-being. *Journal of Family Communication, 7,* 23–46.

Shelp, S. G. (2002). Gaydar: Visual detection of sexual orientation among gay and straight men. *Journal of Homosexuality, 44,* 1–14.

Shu-Yueh, L. (2014). The effects of cosmetic surgery reality shows on women's beliefs of beauty privileges, perceptions of cosmetic surgery, and desires for cosmetic enhancements. *American Communication Journal, 16,* 1–14.

Spott, J., Pyle, C., & Punyanunt-Carter, N. M. (2010). Positive and negative nonverbal behaviors in relationships: A study of relationship satisfaction and longevity. *Human Communication, 13,* 29–41.

Sprecher, S., & Cate, R. M. (2004). Sexual satisfaction and sexual expression as predictors of relationship satisfaction and stability. In J. H. Harvey, A. Wenzel, & S. Sprecher (Eds.), *The handbook of sexuality in close relationships* (pp. 235–256). Mahwah, NJ: Erlbaum.

Stafford, L. (2010). Geographic distance and communication during courtship. *Communication Research, 37,* 275–297.

Stathopoulos, E. T., Huber, J. E., & Sussman, J. E. (2011). Changes in acoustic characteristics of the voice across the life span: Measures from individuals 4–93 years of age. *Journal of Speech, Language, and Hearing Research, 54,* 1011–1021.

Tickle-Degnen, L. (2006). Nonverbal behavior and its functions in the ecosystem of rapport. In V. Manusov & M. L. Patterson (Eds.), *The SAGE handbook of nonverbal communication* (pp. 381–399). Thousand Oaks, CA: Sage.

Trees, A. R., & Manusov, V. (1998). Managing face concerns in criticism: Integrating nonverbal behaviors as a dimension of politeness in female friendship dyads. *Human Communication Research, 24,* 564–583.

Van Newkirk, R. (2006). "Gee, I didn't get that vibe from you": Articulating my own version of a femme lesbian existence. *Journal of Lesbian Studies, 10,* 73–85.

Vatsa, S., & Lata, P. (2012). The role of gender in interpreting subtleties of facial expressions. *Journal of Arts and Culture, 3,* 87–91.

Viscovich, N., Borod, J., Pihan, H., Peery, S., Brickman, A. M., & Tabert, M. (2003). Acoustical analysis of posed prosodic expressions: Effects of emotion and sex. *Perceptual and Motor Skills, 96,* 759–777.

Vogt, D., & Colvin, C. R. (2003). Interpersonal orientation and the accuracy of personality judgments. *Journal of Personality, 71,* 267–295.

Wagner, H. L., MacDonald, C. J., & Manstead, A. S. R. (1986). Communication of individual emotions by spontaneous facial expressions. *Journal of Personality and Social Psychology, 50,* 737–743.

Wallace, D. H. (1981). Affectional climate in the family of origin and the experience of subsequent sexual-affectional behaviors. *Journal of Sex and Marital Therapy, 7,* 296–396.

Weber, K., Goodboy, A. K., & Cayanus, J. (2010). Flirting competence: An experimental study on appropriate and effective opening lines. *Communication Research Reports, 27,* 184–191.

Weisfeld, C. C., & Stack, M. A. (2002). When I look into your eyes: An ethnological analysis of gender differences in married couples' nonverbal behaviors. *Psychology, Evolution, and Gender, 4,* 125–147.

Willis, F. N., & Rawdon, V. A. (1994). Gender and national differences in attitudes toward same-gender touch. *Perceptual and Motor Skills, 78,* 1027–1034.

Wilmot, W. W., & Hocker, J. L. (2013). *Interpersonal conflict* (9th ed.). New York: McGraw-Hill.

Wilt, K., Funkhouser, K., & Revelle, W. (2011). The dynamic relationships of affective synchrony to perceptions of situations. *Journal of Research in Personality, 45*, 309–321.

Wood, J. T. (1994). Engendered identities: Shaping voice and mind through gender. In D. R. Vocate (Ed.), *Intrapersonal communication: Different voices, different minds* (pp. 145–168). Hillsdale, NJ: Erlbaum.

Wood, J. T. (2012). *Gendered lives: Communication, gender, and culture* (10th ed.). Boston: Cengage/Wadsworth.

Woodzicka, J. A. (2008). Sex differences in self-awareness of smiling during a mock job interview. *Journal of Nonverbal Behavior, 32*, 109–121.

Woolery, L. M. (2008). Gaydar: A social-cognitive analysis. *Journal of Homosexuality, 53*, 9–17.

Yeomans, T. (2009, November). *Communicating initial interest and attraction: Quasi-courtship versus courtship behaviors.* Paper presented at the meeting of the National Communication Association, Chicago, IL.

Zuckerman, M., DePaulo, B. M., & Rosenthal, R. (1981). Verbal and nonverbal communication of deception. In L. Berkowitz (Ed.), *Advances in experimental social psychology* (Vol. 14, pp. 1–59). New York: Academic Press.

Zukoski, A. P., Harvey, S. M., & Branch, M. (2009). Condom use: Exploring verbal and nonverbal communication strategies among Latino and African American men and women. *AIDS Care, 21*, 1042–1049.

Part Two

GENDER COMMUNICATION AND RELATIONSHIPS

CHAPTER 5

GENDER AND RELATIONSHIPS

Developing Potential into Reality

CASE STUDY

Choosing Relationships: A Proactive Approach

Visit any website, turn on a TV news show, or tune into your favorite talk radio station and you'll likely hear something that used to be relegated to tabloid newspapers and gossip outlets: news of the latest celeb hookup or breakup. Much as we might protest to the contrary, American culture is saturated with information about "all things celeb." From Taylor and (insert male name here) coupling and uncoupling, to Kanye and Kim having more babies, to the latest bit of celeb gossip, if Americans didn't have an appetite for this stuff, we wouldn't hear about it.

What topic seems to grab people's interest more than others? Relationships and all the human tragedies and triumphs that go with them. Rather than focusing on celebrities, let's bring the discussion down to a more local level—have you seen your friends making good or bad relational choices lately? What about your choices?

HOT TOPICS

- The role of information in the choosing and being chosen process
- Barriers or roadblocks to relational success
- The ups and downs of initiating relationships online
- The role of attraction, physical appearance, proximity, and similarity in relationship initiation
- Initial contact, first conversations, and flirting
- The role of communication skills such as self-disclosure, empathy, and listening in relationship development

Maybe you believe that relational circumstances are more about fate, destiny, or dumb luck than choice; maybe you should think again. In this chapter, we challenge you to look at your own relationships—family, coworkers, bosses, friends, acquaintances, dates, romantic partners—in terms of *choice*. What choices do you make every day in regard to the people you come into contact with— the people regularly in your life, as well as occasional acquaintances?

Which people did you proactively *choose* to have a relationship with, versus those who chose you? How do you *choose* to manage those relationships through communication and shared activities?

For most of us, relationships are what brings us life's greatest satisfaction. Probably more than anything else in life, relationships bring us our highest highs and, sad to say, our lowest lows. This chapter examines the bases of relationship choices and the forms of communication that facilitate those choices. Rather than hoping or believing that if you wait long enough or experiment enough, the perfect friends, dating partners, or mates will find their way to you, this chapter suggests a more proactive (rather than reactive) strategy. Relationship initiation and development are based on *choice—choosing* and *being chosen*. You clearly can't have close, personal relationships with everyone, so you must choose. On the flip side, it is very flattering to be chosen and can be very painful not to be.

BETTER INFORMATION = BETTER CHOICES

It is our choices that show what we really are, far more than our abilities.
—J. K. Rowling, from *Harry Potter and the Chamber of Secrets*

In talking with students about relationship choice or who chooses whom and why, it seems to come down to one thing: not physical appearance, not opposites attract, but *information*. Most of the time, people choose people they *know the most about*. And what is the source of this information? *Communication*. The information you gather may be based on verbal or nonverbal, conscious or unconscious, or intentional or unintentional communication. The better and more complete your information, the better your choices. Initiating relationships depends more on information gathered through the communication process than on any other factor, even physical appearance (no matter what the media and the fashion industry would have you believe).

The basic process works like this: You observe, you communicate, you evaluate, you make choices, you act. And other people are looking at you, doing exactly the same thing. How relationships develop and change and who takes responsibility for these tasks are questions many students have pondered, yet most aren't fully aware of the information they use to make their choices or send to others to help them make their choices. Understanding how the process works and, more important, understanding how people deal with relational issues are critical.

At various stages in a developing relationship, you'll make decisions or *choice points* about the future of the relationship. Imagine that you have a superficial friendship with someone at work. However, you think the person is interesting and decide a more personal friendship might be possible. By making that decision, you've exercised some control over the direction of the relationship and have accelerated it from one level to another. We all face relationship decisions at times, such as whether to turn an acquaintance into a friend, a friendship into something deeper, or a romantic relationship back to a friendship (good luck with that). Choice points like these occur frequently, and the decisions that arise from them have an obvious impact on the quality of the relationship.

Before going further, let's clarify our use of the terms *relationship* and *relational partner*. All kinds of relationships exist, and the word *relationship* is widely used. When using the word *relationship* in gender communication classes, students typically think of dating or romantic relationships rather than other kinds. We discuss in this chapter some elements that pertain more to dating or romantic relationships, but many concepts and research findings apply to relationships in general—all kinds of relationships. When we use the term *relational partner*, it doesn't necessarily suggest a romantic relationship, nor does it imply the same permanence implied by the term *marital partner*. It's simply a means of identifying two people in a relationship.

What kinds of relationships are you involved in?

RELATIONSHIP ROADBLOCKS

Sometimes relationships work very well; other times, they don't go well at all. Before exploring aspects of gender communication that enhance relationship initiation and maintenance, let's examine eight common barriers to healthy, satisfying relationships.

Roadblock 1: High Expectations

Websites, movies, TV shows, and romance novels often set us up for unrealistic expectations when it comes to relationships, especially romantic ones. The media frequently depict attractive, glamorous people engaged in fun, seemingly worry-free, highly physical romantic relationships. But they less frequently show these relationships six months or a year later, nor do they typically depict the work necessary to make relationships successful. We may fantasize about the perfect mate, but we know nobody's perfect. So sometimes when we set unrealistically high expectations for others and our relationships, we set ourselves up for a fall.

Roadblock 2: This Should Be Easy

You know by now that communication isn't a natural thing you can do successfully just because you've been communicating all your life. So why do we sometimes think it ought to be so easy to just relax and talk to someone? Why do attraction and nervousness sometimes get the better of us and the wrong things come out of our mouths or we can't say anything at all? Communication in relationships is a challenge, whether we're in those initial stages or later on as relationships develop.

Roadblock 3: Fear of Failure

The fear of failing at relationships so stymies some people that they don't even try to make friends or extend themselves to coworkers, much less date. The person they talk to the most is their dog. Failure is part of the relational process, however painful it might be. And, even though it's a cliché, we do learn from failure.

Roadblock 4: If I Just Relax, a Good Relationship Will Find Me

Even though we believe in a proactive approach to relationships, there are those rare times when things just happen. You aren't thinking about dating anyone, you don't expect to meet someone wonderful, and—bingo—Incredible Person comes into the picture. There's no outguessing this process, but you may be setting yourself up for some lonely times if you merely wait and expect friendship or romance to find you. A proactive, balanced approach of introspection, planning, patience, communication skill development, and maybe a bit of faith is likely to generate better results than just waiting for something to happen.

Roadblock 5: Weighed Down by Baggage

No one arrives at a new relationship with a clean slate; we all carry our past experiences with us into new situations and relationships. Some of us have troubled pasts—maybe our parents' relationship wasn't the best model or we've been burned in past relationships, making us fearful or hesitant about new ones. Are those just experiences or are they "baggage"? Most of us view baggage as a negative, something that weighs us down, something we have to overcome in a new relationship. Perhaps we should reframe our view of our baggage to see our past experiences, choices, and outcomes as lessons learned, as a road map of our relational history—one that informs the next situation and enables us make better choices. We definitely aren't "doomed" to repeat the past.

Roadblock 6: It's Got to Happen Now!

Some people want a remote control for relationships, so they can zip and zap, getting what they want when they want it. All of us could use a bigger dose of patience in our relationships. Solid, successful relationships of all kinds take time to nurture and develop. Wanting too much too soon (and sometimes getting it) can be a big problem. Not taking adequate time to nurture a relationship can sabotage a potentially wonderful connection before it's had its chance.

Roadblock 7: Giving Up Too Much Just to Have a Dating Relationship

University residence advisors describe a problem they see regularly, the fact that some students are too willing to compromise themselves sexually or in other ways in order to get a dating relationship started or keep one going. Are women more prone than men to want dating or romantic relationships, or is this just a stereotype? Heterosexual women often feel a tension between the traditional message that they should have a man in their lives and modern messages of careerism and independence. Sometimes a desire for acceptance causes people to do things they really don't want to do. No one should have to bend to pressure or be motivated by the desire to impress another person or to achieve some form of social status.

Roadblock 8: Looking Over Someone's Shoulder

Diving into a relationship, especially a romantic one, is a leap of faith for most of us. Some people deny themselves good relationships because they think someone better will come along. They'll look you in the eye at the beginning of a conversation, but soon start scanning the area for someone more interesting or attractive. They don't want to commit to working on a relationship because of a fear that they'll miss out on something better, someone more right for them, someone they believe can give them more self-esteem, rewards, or status. People do this with friendships sometimes too—holding off developing a friendship because they think they deserve a "higher class" of friend or that having higher-status friends will garner them more respect, inclusion, perks, and so forth. The "Is there something better" question is deadly for relationships and can leave you alone—friendless and dateless. People tend not to like comparisons, both to real or imagined other people.

STAGE 1: IS THERE A RELATIONSHIP GOLD MINE OUT THERE? PROSPECTING AND BEING A PROSPECT

Initiating relationships is a process similar to prospecting for gold. Like a prospector, you're looking for something that will add value to your life. Like a prospector, you go out into the "field" and examine "samples" for possible value to you. If a sample looks interesting, you can examine it more closely. But here's one big difference—while you're examining prospects, they could be examining you.

Prospecting for a relationship is an active process, quite different from the wait-for-something-to-happen belief epitomized by the expression, "If it's meant to be, it will be." The proactive approach we recommend puts you in charge of your relational life; you neither wait for something to happen nor blame something or someone if it doesn't happen. In your lifetime, you have the potential to initiate and develop hundreds of relationships. Whether you entered college right out of high school or started your college career later in life, college is a prime time for experiencing various kinds of relationships.

Seeing and Being Seen

The first part of stage 1 in relationship development, normally, is seeing others and being seen. Information gathered through observations guides your first choices, but when people go prospecting, what do they look for? What features catch the eye and spark the imagination? Research suggests that we form impressions and make judgments about people in the first 10 seconds of meeting them (Burch, 2001). What kind of first impression do *you* make?

We like to ask our students what they look for in potential dating partners; their responses are amazingly similar. They mostly look for people who are physically appealing (but not so exceptionally gorgeous that they're unapproachable), who look nice (nonthreatening, well-groomed, etc.), who show an appropriate degree of self-confidence, who smile a lot and have a good sense of humor, who aren't too afraid or too macho to show interest, and who will impress their parents and friends. It's interesting that this list doesn't usually contain comments about being "Joe Stud" or looking like a Victoria's Secret model.

Not Being Seen: Prospecting Online

Obviously, seeing a person face to face is not the only way a relationship can begin. Not only has technology vastly increased opportunities for relationship development, it's also had an impact on our understanding of how relationships function (Asiedu, 2012; Craig & Wright, 2012; Stafford & Hillyer, 2012).

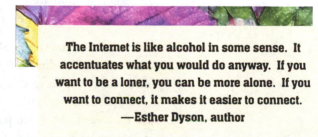

The Internet is like alcohol in some sense. It accentuates what you would do anyway. If you want to be a loner, you can be more alone. If you want to connect, it makes it easier to connect.
—Esther Dyson, author

It's hard to imagine a world without the Internet; for many of you, you've never lived without instant access to all kinds of information and people via the Internet. Marc Prensky (2001) calls you "digital natives"—those of you who've grown up in a digital age and are so comfortable with technology that you make little distinction between your online and offline lives (Palfrey & Gasser, 2010; Prensky, 2010, 2012). Web pages, blogs, and social media sites provide opportunities for people to connect without first (or ever) meeting face to face (Barnes, 2008; Grill, 2011). Video chatting through technologies like FaceTime or Skype makes it possible to talk as well as see people and check them out before deciding if you want to meet face to face (Taylor, Hester, & Wilson, 2011).

Many people find electronically mediated relationships just as satisfying as face-to-face relationships (Grieve & Kemp, 2015; Li, Chen, & Popiel, 2015; Tidwell & Walther, 2002). Some of the advantages of developing relationships online are:

- the availability of people who seek companionship

- the ability to learn basic information about people (for example, someone's status and photos on Facebook) before revealing anything about oneself or meeting in person

- getting to know someone through lower-risk means, like texts, video chats, or e-mail exchanges, before deciding to choose other, more risky and involved forms of contact

- the ease of contacting someone (versus the dreaded task of asking for a phone number)

- the protection of one's identity

- an enlarged pool of available companions not hindered by physical geography

- less expense compared to what face-to-face dating costs (Drouin & Landgraff, 2012; West & Turner, 2011).

Research suggests that some sex differences typically found in face-to-face conversation tend to diminish in electronically mediated communication (Lipinski-Harten & Tafarodi, 2012). One study found that women benefited from online communication more than face-to-face communication because they could be more participative and direct (McConnell, 1997). Other research determined that, besides reducing the importance of physical traits, online communication increases the significance of rapport and similarity and allows more freedom from gender constraints (Cooper & Sportolari, 1997; Gibbs et al., 2006).

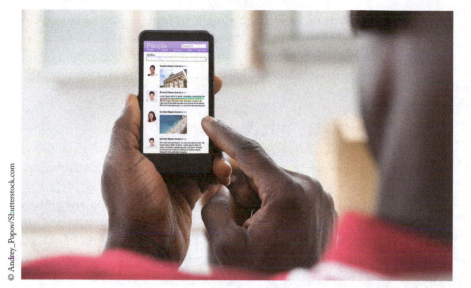

Many people find electronically mediated relationships just as satisfying as face-to-face relationships.

© Andrey_Popov/Shutterstock.com

One of the most interesting aspects of Internet communication is the potential for identity alteration and gender bending (Walther et al., 2011; Yurchisin, Watchravesringkan, & McCabe, 2005). It's possible for people to take on totally different identities online and to "walk on the wild side" in relative safety. The downside is, you may never know exactly with whom you're communicating (catfishing, anyone?); you and the other person may both be experimenting.

Being Attracted to a Prospect

Just what is attraction? According to students, it can be "lust," "a sort of chemistry between you and another person," "wanting to have sexual contact with another person," "liking someone—not just physically, but for personality traits." You can see from these responses that some people use the term *attraction* to apply to platonic friendships, in which one person is attracted to another on a nonphysical, nonsexual basis, whereas others associate attraction with sexual interest.

Attraction is a motivational state that causes someone to think, feel, and behave in a positive manner toward another person (Berscheid, 1985). More specifically, *sexual attraction* is defined as being drawn to another person because you want to have sexual contact with that person. You may or may not actually fulfill that desire, but the attraction is felt nonetheless. For our purposes in this chapter, let's use a broader interpretation of the term attraction: *interpersonal attraction* is the degree to which you desire

Not sure what you're attracted to? Maybe you're initially drawn to certain qualities of a person, only to find that that sort of person isn't right for you over the long haul. Maybe you're not interested in the long haul right now, but you'd like some guidance when it comes to attraction. Would it surprise you to know that all sorts of web quizzes are available to help you narrow down what you're attracted to and interested in? Sites like **quizplz.com** and **gotoquiz.com** offer batteries of questions to help you better understand your likes and dislikes when it comes to attracting a potential date or long-term partner.

to form and possibly maintain an interpersonal relationship with another person (Beebe, Beebe, & Ivy, 2016). That relationship might be a friendship, a coworker relationship, a romantic relationship (nonsexual), or a sexual relationship.

CHECKING OUT THE PROSPECTS One prospecting strategy for gathering information about other people is to observe them. You look at others; they look at you. You check out each other's physical appearance. Are people different, in terms of how much importance they place on physical appearance as a determinant of attraction? As odd as it sounds, we all tend to be attracted to signals of physical health in another person (Li, Bailey, Kenrick, & Linsenmeier, 2002). Surprising no one, physical appearance is a major factor in attraction (Geary, Vigil, & Byrd-Craven, 2004). Part of the popularity with the phone app Tinder is that people can be "swiped left" or "swiped right," solely depending on a person's perception of their physical attractiveness. However, positive social interactions with others may enhance our view of someone's physical attractiveness (Albada, Knapp, & Theune, 2002). Have you ever talked with someone and then thought, "Did you just get cuter or *what*?" A great conversation may increase and even generate attraction in the first place. Of course, this works in the reverse too. Ever talk to people you thought were "hotties," only to have that perception altered when they opened their mouths?

Another interesting point regarding attraction is that you may see someone you deem physically attractive but remain unattracted to that person. Haven't you ever seen someone who was beautiful, but the person didn't stir you in any way? Social psychological research in the 1970s produced a fascinating observation of human behavior that has stood the test of time and has come to be known as the *matching hypothesis* (Bar-Tal & Saxe, 1976). This research indicates that, while you may appreciate the appearance of someone who is stunningly good looking, you usually have relationships with people whom you feel are similar in physical attractiveness to you. An average-looking heterosexual man may appreciate the physical appearance of a very good-looking woman, but he's more likely to be attracted to, date, and even marry a woman he believes is at a level of attractiveness similar to his own.

The *matching hypothesis* has stood the test of time.

ATTRACTIVE TERRITORY NEARBY Some of us are drawn to people because they're cool, they seem different from us, or they're interesting for a variety of reasons. (Remember, we're talking about all kinds of attraction here, not just romantic or sexual.) Sometimes we're drawn to people simply because they're drawn to us, and we find that flattering.

One concept integral to attraction is *proximity*, which has two meanings. First, it relates to the space around you and the physical distance between you and someone else, the amount of time you spend physically near that person, how easily you can gain access to the person, and how physical closeness affects your relationship. Research shows you're more likely to be attracted to someone if you think you'll have opportunities to spend time with that person (Guerrero, Andersen, & Afifi, 2013; Kenrick, Neuberg, & Cialdini, 2005; Knapp, Hall, & Horgan, 2013). Sometimes, we create proximity by generating opportunities to connect with someone we find attractive. For example, we may join the same club or gym as the person or just happen to be in the hallway when a certain someone's class lets out. Relational partners or friends who were once in close physical proximity but who experience geographical separation know firsthand the challenges that nonproximity to a partner can create, even in a highly technological age (Dainton & Aylor, 2001; Rhodes, 2002; Sahlstein, 2006; Stafford, Merolla, & Castle, 2006).

Proximity in a relationship has a second sense, again because of technological advancements. *Everyone's close in cyberspace.* We can now communicate across the globe with such ease and speed that we can act on our attraction and develop a feeling of closeness that has nothing to do with geography or the physical realm (Shonbeck, 2011). You may become attracted to people, for a variety of purposes, by reading their blogs, e-mailing with them at work, or being introduced as a friend of a friend through social media. You may find their ideas interesting, their sense of humor engaging, or their intellect compelling, and your attraction begins and possibly grows the more you learn about them. Or, in the case of relationships that were once physically close but circumstances have separated the partners, such as military families in which one or more family members are deployed, being able to communicate through e-mail, text message, and video chat may keep the attraction alive, so to speak (Maguire, Heinemann-LaFave, & Sahlstein, 2013).

Remember...

Attraction: Motivational state that causes someone to think, feel, and behave in a positive manner toward another person

Sexual Attraction: Feeling drawn to another person because you want to have sexual contact with that person

Interpersonal Attraction: Degree to which you desire to form and possibly maintain an interpersonal relationship with another person

Matching Hypothesis: Tendency to form relationships, particularly romantic relationships, with people you feel are similar in physical attractiveness to you

Proximity: Space (territory) around you; physical and psychological distance between you and others

Similarity: Tendency to be more interested in someone whose upbringing, attitudes, beliefs, and values are more similar to yours than different

LIKING PEOPLE WHO ARE LIKE YOU Perhaps you have heard the cliché, "opposites attract." Some people may be interested in others who are radically different from them—differences can be intriguing. But while opposites may attract, often "opposites don't last" because, as the initial intrigue fades, the differences become obstacles, sometimes insurmountable ones.

Most of us prefer *similarity* over difference in our relationships. Research indicates that under most circumstances, we'll generally be more interested in someone whose upbringing, attitudes, beliefs, and values are more similar to ours than different (Amodio & Showers, 2005; Bleske-Recheck, Remiker, & Baker, 2009; Montoya, Horton, & Kirchner, 2008; Sprecher, 2014).

How do you turn this information into a strategy—both for choosing and being chosen? It's a good idea to place yourself in the company of people who are similar to you and to learn to what extent those similarities exist. For example, if you think that bar or club scenes are great opportunities for socializing with fun people, you're more likely to find someone with similar attitudes if you look for them in a bar or club than elsewhere. If your religious values are such that you believe attending church is important, then your chances of finding someone with similar values and beliefs are greater in a church setting than other places.

STAGE 2: ENGAGING THE PROSPECT— CONVERSATIONS

No clear-cut line exists between the first and second stages; they merely have some identifying characteristics. Stage 2 consists of the opening interactions of a relationship, where people expend a good deal of energy trying to get the other person to think well of them. Here are a few strategies that help accomplish that goal.

Digging In and Discovering More

Most decisions about whether to act further on one's attraction are made in the first few minutes of a conversation (online or face to face), so a lot rides on that first encounter. Your interest—and we use the word *interest* as an extension of attraction—now demands that you verbally communicate. What are the best ways to begin and develop an effective conversation?

CONVERSATION STARTERS Conversations have to start somewhere, and there has to be an opening verbalization. Everyone laughs at the old pickup lines of the 1960s and 1970s, lines like "What's your sign?" "Haven't I seen you somewhere before?" and "What's a nice girl like you doing in a place like this?" While those lines are pretty laughable, the advice given to heterosexual men regarding "picking up women" has become increasingly sophisticated—and sometimes troubling. For example, a book called *The Game: Penetrating the Secret Society of Pickup Artists* (Strauss, 2005) is devoted to giving advice to straight men on how to pick up as many women as possible. The goal is not a long-standing, loving relationship, but as many short-term relationships as a man can generate.

Reducing effective communication down to a gimmick and packaged opening lines is obviously inconsistent with the principles underlying the receiver orientation to communication because it generally ignores the process of adapting one's communication to the receiver of the message and treating the receiver as a person, not an object. So why would someone use a line? Sometimes it's simply easier—people who might be nervous sometimes resort to trite beginnings just to get the ball rolling. For these reasons, we grant that lines or conversational openers may be useful at times, but not necessarily as efforts to pick up or hit on someone. Conversational beginnings that reflect a thoughtful, sincere attempt at interaction can serve as icebreakers between you and someone you're interested in.

Daniel Menaker (2010), author of *A Good Talk: The Story and Skill of Conversation*, believes that neither person in an encounter should initiate conversation by talking about themselves or the other person; instead, Menaker suggests that a third subject, a third person, or object should start the conversation. Perhaps you've observed something about the other person that you can comment on, such as a book the person's carrying that might lead into a conversation about college classes, or a T-shirt the person's wearing from a place you've visited or a favorite sports team. In an online context, perhaps responding to someone's post or photos on a social media site might be a good conversational opening.

As a means of getting to know someone or getting a potential relationship off the ground, most of us resort to the good old-fashioned question-and-answer sequence, where we ask an easy, innocuous question, which is followed by an equally easy response, like asking where people are from, what their hobbies are, and so forth. This back-and-forth exchange of information is typical of the initiating stage of relationship development (Knapp, Vangelisti, & Caughlin, 2013). Research continues to show that initiating conversations in the early stages of relationships is perceived as an equally appropriate activity for men and women in American culture (Kankiewicz, 2007; Kleinke, Meeker, & Staneski, 1986; Smith, 2006). Try to keep questions and answers light and simple in the beginning; you don't want to "grill" someone or make them feel like they're on a stressful job interview, being barraged by questions.

> When I think of talking it is of course with a woman. For talking at its best being an inspiration, it wants a corresponding divine quality of receptiveness, and where will you find this but in a woman? —Oliver Wendell Holmes, Associate Justice of the U.S. Supreme Court

ASKING GREAT QUESTIONS If you wonder what makes a good conversationalist, the best answer we can provide is this: Learn to ask great questions (Beebe, Beebe, & Ivy, 2016). Notice we said "great" questions, not just questions. A great question is, first, tailored as much as possible to the recipient of the question. Unlike a job interview in which an interviewer may bombard an applicant with as many questions as time allows, a social encounter requires a kinder, gentler approach. Use whatever you can observe from the person and the situation to help you formulate questions that will draw the other person out. Basic informational questions (e.g., "Where are you from?" "What do you do for a living?") help break the ice, but "yes–no" questions that can be answered with a single word don't extend a conversation. Also, avoid questions that might be perceived as too personal.

The second skill that helps develop conversational ability relates to listening. Many people go through the motions of asking questions, but don't really listen to the answers. They may find themselves repeating questions they've already asked, embarrassing themselves and turning off the person they're trying to impress. It's important to listen intently when someone responds to your question, then pose a follow-up question that shows you're really listening and interested—not a statement that takes the focus away from the other person. Although some people become uncomfortable talking about themselves or their views, most of us enjoy the attention and feel like genuine interest is being shown.

Studies have found that more women than men ask questions to generate conversation in social situations (Coates, 2005; Lindsey & Zakahi, 1996, 2006). But we all need to develop and hone our conversational skills so that one person isn't responsible for getting a conversation off the ground and keeping it going. The skill of asking great questions doesn't happen like magic or overnight—time, maturity, and experience will help you improve your conversational ability.

The Art and Skill of Flirting

Is it typical of you to be unaware that someone really does like you? How do you detect that someone's interested in you, either on a friendship or romantic level? How do you show your interest in another person? Are you likely to reveal your interest through nonverbal means first, rather than coming right out and declaring undying love and affection? What exactly does it mean to flirt?

Flirting is a popular term for a long-standing phenomenon: showing attraction to and interest in another person (Metts, 2006). We suggest caution here, however, because not all flirting is an indication of interest. Researchers have found that "people may flirt because they see it as innocent fun, they want to make a third party jealous, they want to develop their social skills, or they are trying to persuade someone to do something for them" (Guerrero et al., 2013, p. 191).

Flirting shows an attraction and interest in another person.

© antoniodiaz/Shutterstock.com

No matter what type of relationship is being initiated, most of us usually convey our interest in others nonverbally, rather than strolling up to someone and saying, "I find you interesting" (Beres, Herold, & Maitland, 2004; Hall, Cody, Jackson, & Flesh, 2008). Decades of research reveal common flirtation cues:

- smiling

- surveying a room with the eyes

- prolonged and mutual eye contact

- eyebrow flash

- sidelong glances and darting glances

- increased physical proximity

- preening (e.g., adjusting clothing, fidgeting with hair, altering posture)

- animated facial expressions

- increased touching behavior (both accidental and purposeful)

- head tosses; and

- animated vocal inflection, increased rate of speaking, and changes in volume (Daly, Hogg, Sacks, Smith, & Zimring, 1999; Eibl-Eibesfeldt, 1975; Grammer, Kruck, Juette, & Fink, 2000; Grammer, Kruck, & Magnusson, 1998; Hall, Carter, Cody, & Albright, 2010; Hall & Xing, 2015; Kaspar & Krull, 2013; Moore, 1985; Scheflen, 1965; Weber, Goodboy, & Cayanus, 2010).

As for research specific to heterosexual courtship, the general conclusion is that women are more dominant or in control of the flirting process than men (Henningsen, Braz, & Davies, 2008). Specifically, research is consistent in four findings: (1) women are more skilled at encoding and decoding flirtatious nonverbal behaviors; (2) women exhibit a wide variety of flirting behaviors that are used to signal their interest to men they desire to attract; (3) women have a widely developed repertoire of rejection strategies; and (4) women who exhibit flirtatious behaviors typically will be approached by men (Frisby, Dillow, Gaughan, & Nordlund, 2011; Hall et al., 2008; Trost & Alberts, 1998, 2006). Women's approaches to flirtation may be affected by their cycles of ovulation; research has found that women display more flirting behaviors at times of high fertility in their cycles than at low fertility times (Cantu et al., 2014).

"Flirting Is a Tricky Business"

Flirting is a tricky business because one person's flirtation is another person's sexual harassment. These days, you have to be very careful when you show romantic interest in another person. Since Americans' working lives take up increasingly significant amounts of time, it would follow that many people now find their social and romantic outlets through coworkers (Work & Family Facts & Statistics, 2015). But developing a romantic relationship with a colleague is a delicate endeavor, particularly if the colleague is your boss, you are his or her boss, or status differences exist for other reasons. Flirting at the office might seem perfectly harmless to you, but the more important point is if the object of your flirtation sees it as harmless, too.

Many experts on professional behavior will warn you to stay away from romantic entanglements at the office—period. We understand this suggestion, but realize that sometimes office liaisons just happen—and they can lead to wonderful relationships. We know of many colleagues who met their spouses at work or through professional circles. But the advice on flirting at the office is sound: Be very, very careful with any kind of public demonstrations of interest. You never know who's looking and how that behavior may come back to haunt you (Knight & Wiedmaier, 2015). Apply caution to cyberflirting with colleagues and clients as well (Bruni, 2012; McCulloch, 2013; Whitty, 2004; Whitty & Carr, 2003).

Remember that most employees don't own the computer systems, office phones, or cell phones given to us by the companies we work for. The company owns these devices and all the messages we deliver and receive on them, so a simple flirtatious e-mail with a coworker in the next cubicle is the property of the company and could legally be read by your boss!

Once you've put yourself out there so as to see and be seen, you've been attracted and attractive, you've flirted, you've opened a conversation—perhaps with some well-thought-out questions—you've listened to responses to your questions, and you've followed up those responses with other questions or comments. Now what? If those first conversations were successful enough to make you feel there is real potential with someone, congratulations! Now you have more work to do.

© Featureflash Photo Agency/ Shutterstock.com

A study in the Washington Post says that women have better verbal skills than men. I just want to say to the authors of that study: Duh.
—Conan O'Brien, TV talk show host

STAGE 3: DEVELOPING THE CLAIM AND ESTABLISHING THE RELATIONSHIP

As a relationship develops, a judgment of *communicative competence* (meaning how effectively and appropriately one communicates) appears to outweigh other factors, such as appearance, proximity, or similarity, in determinations of relationship satisfaction (McEwan & Guerrero, 2010; Miczo, Segrin, & Alspach, 2001). It's important to work to establish effective communication behaviors and patterns if you want a relationship to succeed—any kind of relationship.

Opening a New Vein: Intimacy and Self-Disclosure

Intimacy is something most people long for in relationships—whether in family relationships, friendships, or romantic relationships. What exactly is intimacy? Relationship experts Harvey and Weber (2002) provide such descriptions as bonding, closeness, and emotional connection, all based on sharing personal, private information and experiences over time. Our particular favorite definition comes from couples therapist Jeffrey Fine (2001): "To be intimate is to be totally transparent, emotionally naked in front of another who is equally transparent. You want to see into the other's heart. What people should mean when they say *intimacy* is in-to-me-see" (p. 225).

It's hard to deepen a relationship and develop intimacy without accurate and useful information. The most common means of actively sharing information to develop intimacy is known as *self-disclosure*, originally researched by psychologist Sidney Jourard (1971). Jourard suggests that self-disclosure occurs when we voluntarily provide information to others

© 2016 Zits Partnership. Distributed by King Features Syndicate.

that they wouldn't learn if we didn't tell them. For example, your height and weight are generally noticeable aspects of your being, but your exact height and (especially) weight won't likely be known by people unless you choose to tell them. Research suggests that closeness and satisfaction in relationships of all types are closely tied to the level and quality of disclosure (Afifi & Steuber, 2009; Derlega, Winstead, & Greene, 2008; Dindia, 2002).

Some of our thinking about the sexes and self-disclosure is based on stereotypes, but the stereotypes have been supported by research. Consistent findings over a few decades indicate that women tend to like disclosure more and disclose more than men, especially about their relationships; women tend to take more risks in disclosure by relating sensitive feelings and personal problems (Burleson, 2003; Dindia, 2002; Shaffer, Pegalis, & Bazzini, 1996). Women are also much more often the recipient of others' disclosures (Aries, 2006; Petronio, Martin, & Littlefield, 1984).

Jourard (1971) addressed male–male disclosure (or the lack of it) and the consequences to men's physical health in a book chapter entitled, "The Lethal Aspects of the Male Role." He suggested that men who have difficulty expressing their thoughts and feelings also have higher levels of stress-related diseases compared to men who are able to disclose more fully. Other research supports this finding; stress associated with the male role hasn't significantly declined since Jourard's work was published (Copenhaver & Eisler, 1996; Kimmel, 2015; Reeser, 2010). For many men, expressing their thoughts and feelings suggests weakness and vulnerability, as though men give up power and control by revealing themselves. Lack of disclosure, however, can hamper the development of all sorts of relationships; a balance between power and disclosure facilitates relationship development.

> I find that, in general, the amount of sharing men do with each other in one year is about the same as what I share with my female friends while we wait for our cars at the valet.
> —Amy Poehler, comedian and actor

Wait a minute: Does disclosure only mean words? Many men disclose themselves through what they *do* in relationships, expressing intimacy more nonverbally than verbally. Research has called into question earlier findings on the sexes and disclosure, and the stereotypes that may accompany them (Borisoff, 2001; Galvin & Bylund, 2001; Reis, 1998). For example, Wood and Inman (1993) make a case for considering joint activities (working on hobbies, playing or watching sports together, etc.)

as a path to closeness in male friendships. While women's friendships with other women more often develop and deepen through communication, particularly self-disclosure, rather than shared experiences, we shouldn't make the judgment that men's relationships with other men are superficial because they involve more *doing* than *talking*. It's important to avoid measuring intimacy or relationship satisfaction with a feminine yardstick. However, men shouldn't use this argument as a reason to avoid appropriate disclosure.

One final aspect of disclosure warrants brief mention here: the disclosure of sexual desires, preferences, fears, and experiences (Byers, 2011; Peterson, 2011). Why do many of us find it difficult to talk about sex with our sexual partners? We may banter about sex in the locker room with members of our same sex or "dish" with friends over happy hour about a sexual conquest or a fantasy. But when it comes down to having open, frank conversations with a sexual partner about the sexual activity we're having (or not having) in our relationship, we often find ourselves at a loss for words, embarrassed to even address the subject, or inept in our communication, stumbling until we simply give up.

Research suggests that the discomfort has many roots: overtones of shame and guilt associated with sexuality; sensationalistic and unrealistic media depictions of sexual activity; a perpetual belief in the unequal sexual power of women and men; the view that sex should be "natural" and "automatic," so talking about it should be unnecessary; a belief that talking about sexuality "kills the mood"; fear of rejection or being labeled nerdy, should one partner bring up sexual concerns or questions to another; and heterosexual women's fears that talking about sex will be perceived as unfeminine by a male partner (Humphreys, 2004; Powell, 2010).

As difficult as it is to do, sexual self-disclosure is linked to relationship satisfaction (Badr & Carmack Taylor, 2009; Byers, 2011; Faulkner & Lannutti, 2010; Litzinger & Gordon, 2005). Studies show that the more sexual disclosure in a relationship, the more satisfied the partners are with their relationship and the communication within it (Holmberg & Blair, 2009; LaFrance, 2010; MacNeil & Byers, 2005). People with higher levels of self-esteem, specifically views of themselves sexually, tend to be more sexually disclosive and assertive, as well as more satisfied with the sexual activity they experience in their relationships (Menard & Offman, 2009). When people disclose more openly to their partners about a range of topics and the partner reciprocates, they're also more likely to talk about their sex life. Research on sex differences parallels studies on general self-

152

PART TWO—Gender Communication and Relationships

disclosure: Women tend to sexually self-disclose more than men; however, the disclosure by both parties tends not to be as full or complete as it is for nonsexual topics (Byers, 2011; Byers & Demmons, 1999). Part of the issue here parallels the trend for mothers to be more likely to discuss sex with their children (particularly female children) than fathers (Coffelt, 2010; Dennis & Wood, 2012; Heisler, 2005; Jerman & Constantine, 2010; Wilson & Koo, 2010).

The Big "E": Empathy

Empathy is one of the "hallmarks of supportive relationships" (Beebe, Beebe, & Ivy, 2016, p. 68). To empathize means that you try to understand and feel what another person is feeling; you try to step into the shoes of the other person, to experience as closely as you can what she or he experiences (Krznaric, 2014; McLaren, 2013). Even if you haven't gone through exactly what another person experiences, you can still relate to that person's emotion; empathy matches emotion to emotion, *not* experience to experience. For example, you may not yet have experienced the death of a parent, but if one of your friends loses a parent, you can relate to your friend's sadness and fear, if not to the actual experience itself. Research underscores the power of empathy to enhance the quality of close relationships (Clark, 2010; Devoldre, Davis, Verhofstadt, & Buysse, 2010; Hakansson & Montgomery, 2003; Johnson, 2011; Levesque, Lafontaine, Caron, Flescha, & Bjornson, 2014; Trout, 2009).

Can empathy be taught, or do some people just have "natural" empathy, while others of us only watch and wish we could respond this way? Some people are more empathic than others. But it remains to be seen whether they have an "empathy gene." Empathy definitely can be a communication skill taught and learned, just like we can learn to become better listeners or public speakers (Barone et al., 2005).

Beebe, Beebe, and Ivy (2016) offer the following suggestions for developing and demonstrating empathy: First, stop focusing on yourself, your messages, and

I view that quality of empathy, of understanding and identifying with people's hopes and struggles, as an essential ingredient for arriving at just decisions and outcomes. We need somebody on the court with the empathy to recognize what it's like to be a young, teenaged mom, the empathy to understand what it's like to be poor or African American, or disabled or gay or old. And that's the criteria by which I'm going to be selecting my judges. —President Barack Obama, before selecting Sonia Sotomayor and Elena Kagan as Supreme Court Justices

© Frederic Legrand - COMEO/Shutter-stock.com

Empathy can be demonstrated by focusing on the other person and asking appropriate questions.

your thoughts; focus instead on the other person. Next, pay attention to nonverbal cues as you try to understand the person's emotions. Then concentrate and listen to what the person is telling you; imagine how you would feel if you were in her or his situation. Finally, ask appropriate questions and, when suitable, paraphrase the person's communication to demonstrate your understanding of the situation and how the person feels about it.

Notice that we didn't include "give helpful advice" in our list. Many people believe, incorrectly, that the way to show empathy is to offer advice, to suggest something someone can do to respond to or improve a situation (Harvey & Weber, 2002; Johnson, 2011). They bypass empathy altogether and try to move the person into action, typically before that person is ready. When people need empathy, they don't need advice (although advice may come later). Remember that empathy meets people at their emotional level. It doesn't talk them out of what they are feeling, distract them from their emotions or the situation, move them to act, or downplay events with a "Well, it'll all blow over soon."

How do women and men show empathy in relationships? The stereotype suggests that women are more empathic than men; however, research has found mixed results regarding differences, according to both gender and sex. Some research found no significant differences between the sexes' empathic ability (Graham & Ickes, 1997), whereas other studies found women more empathic than men (Reis, 1998; Staats, Long, Manulik, & Kelley, 2006; Toussaint & Webb, 2005). Fong and Borders (1985) focused on gender rather than sex and found that androgynous individuals were more empathic, regardless of sex. Perhaps this is another one of those situations where talking is emphasized over doing. Perhaps men show empathy by just being there—being present and in the moment with someone—whereas women express empathy more though conversation.

A final, troubling trend regarding empathy warrants brief mention: A three-decade analysis of 72 studies of American college students showed a decline in empathy over the last 40 years, as measured by various scientific instruments and surveys (Konrath, O'Brien, & Hsing, 2011). The greatest decline occurred during the first decade of the twenty-first century. These results parallel a general research trend of today's college students reporting significantly more narcissism and competitiveness than previous generations. No matter the trends, we continue to stress the importance of learning and enhancing empathy skills as a critical component of successful relationships. The ability to feel and express empathy is a fundamental skill to add to your communication repertoire or to exercise more fully.

Are You Listening?

Although many factors come into play during relationship development, one seems to make the most difference: listening. Estimates are that more than 70 percent of adults' waking time is spent in some act of communication. On average, 30 percent of one's communicative energy is engaged in speaking, while 45 percent is spent listening (Galvin & Cooper, 2006). As we explained earlier in our section on asking great questions, being deemed a successful conversationalist lies more in your listening skill than your speaking skill. Effective listening and appropriate responding are critical skills in relationship development and success (Hackenbracht & Gasper, 2013; Harris & Sherblom, 2011; Wolvin, 2010).

© Denis Makarenko/Shutterstock.com

My parents taught me how to listen to everybody before I made up my own mind. When you listen, you learn. You absorb like a sponge and your life becomes so much better than when you are just trying to be listened to all the time.
—Steven Spielberg, filmmaker

Evidence suggests that men and women can be equally good listeners, but they may listen differently or for different purposes (Burleson et al.,

2011; Kirtley Johnston, Weaver, Watson, & Barker, 2000; Pearce, Johnson, & Barker, 2003; Sargent & Weaver, 2003; Tannen, 1990). Here's a chart that summarizes key research findings on listening styles and the sexes.

Listening Styles and the Sexes

	Feminine Style	Masculine Style
Different listening focus	• Tends to search for the relationships among separate pieces of information • Tends to identify individual facts and other isolated pieces of information • Tends to shift listening from one idea to another or from one person to another when people speak at the same time	• Tends to look for a new structure or organizational pattern • Tends to listen for the "big picture" and seek the major points being communicated • Tends to hone in on one specific message without shifting attention among different conversations
Different listening goals	• More likely to listen to new information to gain new understanding and insights • Tends to use information to develop relationships with listening partners • Tends to have more ability and motivation to listen to provide supportive, positive feedback	• More likely to listen to new information to solve a problem • Tends to listen to reach a conclusion; shows less concern about relationship cues and more concern about using the information gained • Tends to have less ability and motivation to listen in situations where supportive feedback is needed or expected
Differences in attending to non-verbal cues	• Tends to emphasize meaning communicated through nonverbal cues • Typically uses more eye contact with the other person when listening	• Tends to emphasize the meaning of words and information exchanged • Typically uses less eye contact with the other person when listening

Adapted with permission from Beebe, S. A., Beebe, S. J., & Ivy, D. K. (2016). *Communication: Principles for a lifetime* (6th ed.). Boston: Pearson.

In expanding their repertoire of communication behaviors, the sexes can learn from each other's listening tendencies and unlearn some habits and sex-typed conditioning. While listening to show support is admirable, women can expand their listening ability to more thoroughly track facts and comprehend information, rather than trying to "take the emotional temperature" of another person (Beebe, Beebe, & Ivy, 2016). Men can demonstrate more active listening by using more nonverbal signals like head nodding and eye contact and by offering vocal cues such as "uh-huh," "Tell me more," and "How did you feel about that?" These *back-channel cues* reinforce and draw out more information from a speaker (Guerrero et al., 2013; Ivy & Wahl, 2014). Research shows that women tend to offer more nonverbal signals of interest in a conversation than men (Aries, 2006). For example, as we discussed in Chapter 4, a nonverbal cue called the *visual dominance ratio* is the amount of eye contact one makes while speaking versus while listening (Knapp, Hall, & Horgan, 2013; Koch, Baehne, Kruse, Zimmerman, & Zumbach, 2010). Men tend to look more at others when they're speaking, then look elsewhere when others are speaking, which can be interpreted as a sign that one has lost interest or isn't listening. Again, expanding one's range of behavior—in this case, different listening patterns—goes a long way toward enhancing gender communication effectiveness.

Effective use of the three communication skills just discussed—self-disclosure, empathy, and listening—will likely lead to greater feelings of closeness and less psychological distance between partners in a relationship. When choice points arise that cause you to make decisions about a relationship, these basic communication skills can help you implement effective choices.

Remember...

Flirting: Means of showing attraction to and interest in another person

Communicative Competence: How effectively and appropriately one communicates

Intimacy: Sharing personal, private information and experiences over time for the purposes of bonding, developing closeness, and forming an emotional connection

Self-Disclosure: Voluntarily providing information to others that they wouldn't learn if you didn't tell them

Empathy: Understanding and feeling what another person is feeling

Back-Channel Cues: Vocalizations such as "uh-huh" and "yeah," which indicate listening and can reinforce and draw out more information from a speaker

Visual Dominance Ratio: Amount of eye contact made while speaking versus while listening

CONCLUSION

The topics explored in this chapter represent a significant challenge for most of us—the challenge of turning relationship potential into reality. The relationships that come into your life can change you in powerful and significant ways. Friendships, workplace relationships, romantic relationships, and committed partnerings all have a significant impact on you. This chapter has explored the other side of that process—your influence on relationship initiation and development through the choices you make. A consistent theme in this text is the acquisition of awareness—awareness of how various factors (e.g., biology, sociology, culture, language, media) influence you and your choices; awareness of how you can gain control over or manage those influences; and, in this chapter, awareness of how choices may influence your relationships.

Improving your ability to create the relationships you desire is a worthwhile, important goal. In this chapter, we began with a view of relationship development as "prospecting" and followed through with thoughts on finding prospects, testing a prospect, and developing a "claim." Understanding the skills associated with moving a relationship from one level to another and understanding women's and men's tendencies in such changes can give you greater insight into how positive change might be brought about. It can also keep you from getting the relationship "shaft."

The final section of this text connects these concepts to some specific contexts in your life—friendships, romance, work, and education. Effective gender communication in these contexts involves applying the concepts described in the chapters you have just read.

DISCUSSION STARTERS

1. Think about the role of information in the initiation of relationships. What information do you use to make decisions about people when initiating a friendship? Do you need different kinds of information when initiating a dating relationship than a friendship with someone? What information about yourself as a potential relational partner do you think is most important? What's the most important information to learn about someone else as a potential partner?

2. Some people still believe that the initiation of a heterosexual dating or romantic relationship should be men's work. Do you think our culture has evolved to the point where women can and do initiate dating relationships in the same ways men can? If you're a straight guy who's been "chosen" by a woman, how did you feel when she initiated a relationship with you?

3. Do you know men who disclose more than the typical amount of personal information? What are some reactions to these men? Is the reaction the same or different than the reaction a woman gets when she discloses more than is expected?

4. In your experience, how do people signal that they want to deepen a relationship? Do men use different signals than women? Do people typically just come out and say, "I'd like to change our relationship"? Have you ever said that to a relational partner? If so, what was the result?

References

Afifi, T., & Steuber, K. (2009). The Revelation Risk Model (RRM): Factors that predict the revelation of secrets and the strategies used to reveal them. *Communication Monographs, 76,* 144–176.

Albada, K. F., Knapp, M. L., & Theune, K. E. (2002). Interaction appearance theory: Changing perceptions of physical attractiveness through social interaction. *Communication Theory, 12,* 8–40.

Amodio, D. M., & Showers, C. J. (2005). "Similarity breeds liking" revisited: The moderating role of commitment. *Journal of Social and Personal Relationships, 22,* 817–836.

Aries, E. (2006). Sex differences in interaction: A reexamination. In K. Dindia & D. J. Canary (Eds.), *Sex differences and similarities in communication* (2nd ed., pp. 21–37). Mahwah, NJ: Erlbaum.

Arliss, L. P. (2001). When myths endure and realities change: Communication in romantic relationships. In L. P. Arliss & D. J. Borisoff (Eds.), *Women and men communicating: Challenges and changes* (2nd ed., pp. 115–131). Prospect Heights, IL: Waveland.

Asiedo, C. (2012). Information communication technologies for gender and development. *Information, Communication, & Society, 15,* 1186–1216.

Badr, H., & Carmack Taylor, C. L. (2009). Sexual dysfunction and spousal communication in couples coping with prostate cancer. *PsychoOncology, 18,* 735–746.

Bar-Tal, D., & Saxe, L. (1976). Perceptions of similarity and dissimilarity of attractive couples and individuals. *Journal of Personality and Social Psychology, 33,* 772–781.

Barnes, S. B. (2008). Understanding social media from the media ecological perspective. In E. A. Konijn, S. Utz, M. Tanis, & S. B. Barnes (Eds.), *Mediated interpersonal communication* (pp. 14–33). New York: Routledge.

Barone, D. F., Hutchings, P. S., Kimmel, H. J., Traub, H. L., Cooper, J. T., & Marshall, C. M. (2005). Increasing empathic accuracy through practice and feedback in a clinical interviewing course. *Journal of Social and Clinical Psychology, 24,* 156–171.

Beebe, S. A., Beebe, S. J., & Ivy, D. K. (2016). *Communication: Principles for a lifetime* (6th ed.). Boston: Pearson.

Beres, M. A., Herold, E., & Maitland, S. B. (2004). Sexual consent behaviors in same-sex relationships. *Journal of Sexual Behavior, 33,* 475–486.

Berscheid, E. (1985). Interpersonal attraction. In G. Lindzey & E. Aronson (Eds.), *Handbook of social psychology* (3rd ed.). New York: Random House.

Berscheid, E., & Reis, H. T. (1998). Attraction and close relationships. In D. T. Gilbert, S. T. Fiske, & G. Lindzey (Eds.), *The handbook of social psychology* (4th ed., vol. 2, pp. 93–281). New York: McGraw-Hill.

Bleske-Recheck, A., Remiker, M. W., & Baker, J. P. (2009). Similar from the start: Assortment in young adult dating couples and its link to relationship stability over time. *Individual Differences Research, 7,* 142–158.

Borisoff, D. E. (2001). The effect of gender on establishing and maintaining intimate relationships. In L. P. Arliss & D. E. Borisoff (Eds.), *Women and men communicating: Challenges and changes* (2nd ed., pp. 15–31). Prospect Heights, IL: Waveland.

Bruni, F. (2012, November 18). Our hard drives, ourselves. *New York Times.* Retrieved July 25, 2015, from <www.newyorktimes.com>.

Burch, P. (2001, July 15). Silent judgment: Experts say you have 10 seconds to project your true image. Scripps Howard News Service, as in *Corpus Christi Caller Times,* pp. C4, C5.

Burleson, B. R. (2003). The experience and effects of emotional support: What the study of cultural and gender differences can tell us about close relationships, emotion, and interpersonal communication. *Personal Relationships, 10,* 1–23.

Burleson, B. R., Hanasono, L. K., Bodie, G. D., Holmstrom, A. J., McCullough, J. D., Rack, J. J., & Gill Rosier, J. (2011). Are gender differences in responses to supportive communication a matter of ability, motivation, or both? Reading patterns of situation effects through the lens of a dual-process theory. *Communication Quarterly, 59,* 37–60.

Byers, E. S. (2011). Beyond the birds and the bees and was it good for you?: Thirty years of research on sexual communication. *Canadian Psychology, 52,* 20–28.

Byers, E. S., & Demmons, S. (1999). Sexual satisfaction and sexual self-disclosure within dating relationships. *Journal of Sex Research, 36,* 180–189.

Cantu, S. M., Simpson, J. A., Griskevicius, V., Weisberg, Y. J., Durante, K. M., & Beal, D. J. (2014). Fertile and selectively flirty: Women's behavior toward men changes across the ovulatory cycle. *Psychological Science, 25,* 431–438.

Clark, A. J. (2010). Empathy and sympathy: Therapeutic distinctions in counseling. *Journal of Mental Health Counseling, 32,* 95–101.

Coates, J. (2005). *Women, men, and language: A sociolinguistic account of gender differences in language* (3rd ed.). New York: Longman.

Coffelt, T. A. (2010). Is sexual communication challenging between mothers and daughters? *Journal of Family Communication, 10,* 116–130.

Cooper, A., & Sportolari, L. (1997). Romance in cyberspace: Understanding online attraction. *Journal of Sex Education & Therapy, 22,* 7–14.

Copenhaver, M. N., & Eisler, R. M. (1996). Masculine gender role stress: A perspective on men's health. In P. M. Kato & T. Mann (Eds.), *Handbook of diversity issues in health psychology* (pp. 219–235). New York: Plenum.

Craig, E., & Wright, K. B. (2012). Computer-mediated relational development and maintenance on Facebook. *Communication Research Reports, 29,* 119–129.

Dainton, M., & Aylor, B. (2001). A relational uncertainty analysis of jealousy, trust, and maintenance in long-distance versus geographically close relationships. *Communication Quarterly, 49,* 172–188.

Daly, J. A., Hogg, E., Sacks, D., Smith, M., & Zimring, L. (1999). Sex and relationship affect social self-grooming. In L. K. Guerrero, J. DeVito, & M. L. Hecht (Eds.), *The nonverbal communication reader: Classic and contemporary readings* (2nd ed., pp. 56–61). Prospect Heights, IL: Waveland.

Dennis, A. C., & Wood, J. T. (2012). "We're not going to have this conversation, but you get it": Black mother-daughter communication about sexual relations. *Women's Studies in Communication, 35,* 204–223.

Derlega, V. J., Winstead, B. A., & Greene, K. (2008). Self-disclosure and starting a close relationship. In S. Sprecher, A. Wenzel, & J. Harvey (Eds.), *Handbook of relationship initiation* (pp. 153–194). New York: Psychology Press.

Devoldre, I., Davis, M. H., Verhofstadt, L. L., & Buysse, A. (2010). Empathy and social support provision in couples: Social support and the need to study the underlying processes. *Journal of Psychology, 144,* 259–284.

Dindia, K. (2002). Self-disclosure research: Knowledge through meta-analysis. In M. Allen, R. W. Preiss, B. M. Gayle, & N. A. Burrell (Eds.), *Interpersonal communication research: Advances through meta-analysis* (pp. 169–185). Mahwah, NJ: Erlbaum.

Douglas, W. (1990). Uncertainty, information-seeking, and liking during initial interaction. *Western Journal of Speech Communication, 54,* 66–81.

Drouin, M., & Landgraff, C. (2012). Texting, sexting, and attachment in college students' romantic relationships. *Computers in Human Behavior, 28,* 444–449.

Eibl-Eibesfeldt, I. (1975). *Ethology: The biology of behavior* (2nd ed.). New York: Holt, Rinehart, & Winston.

Faulkner, S. L., & Lannutti, P. J. (2010). Examining the content and outcomes of young adults' satisfying and unsatisfying conversations about sex. *Qualitative Health Research, 20,* 375–385.

Felmee, D. H. (2001). From appealing to appalling: Disenchantment with a romantic partner. *Sociological Perspectives, 44,* 263–280.

Fine, J. (2001, October). Intimacy. *O: The Oprah Winfrey Magazine,* 225.

Fong, M. L., & Borders, L. D. (1985). Effects of sex role orientation and gender on counseling skills training. *Journal of Counseling Psychology, 32,* 104–110.

Frisby, B., Dillow, M., Gaughan, S., & Nordlund, J. (2011). Flirtatious communication: Experimental examination of perceptions of social-sexual communication motivated by evolutionary forces. *Sex Roles, 64,* 682–694.

Galvin, K. M., & Bylund, C. (2001). First marriage families: Gender and communication. In L. P. Arliss & D. E. Borisoff (Eds.), *Women and men communicating: Challenges and changes* (2nd ed., pp. 132–148). Prospect Heights, IL: Waveland.

Galvin, K. M., & Cooper, P. (Eds.) (2006). *Making connections: Readings in relational communication* (4th ed.). Los Angeles: Roxbury.

Geary, D. C., Vigil, J., & Byrd-Craven, J. (2004). The evolution of human mate choice. [Electronic version] *Journal of Sex Research, 41,* 27–43.

Gibbs, J. L., Ellison, N. B., & Heino, R. D. (2006). Self-presentation in online personals: The role of anticipated future interaction, self-disclosure, and perceived success in Internet dating. *Communication Research, 33,* 152–177.

Graham, T., & Ickes, W. (1997). When women's intuition isn't greater than men's. In W. Ickes (Ed.), *Empathic accuracy* (pp. 117–143). New York: Guilford.

Grammer, K., Kruck, K. B., & Magnusson, M. S. (1998). The courtship dance: Patterns of nonverbal synchronization in opposite sex encounters. *Journal of Nonverbal Behavior, 22,* 3–25.

Grammer, K., Kruck, K., Juette, A., & Fink, B. (2000). Nonverbal behavior as courtship signals: The role of control and choice in selecting partners. *Evolution and Human Behavior, 21,* 371–390.

Grieve, R., & Kemp, N. (2015). Individual differences predicting social connectedness derived from Facebook: Some unexpected findings. *Computers in Human Behavior, 51,* 239–243.

Grill, B. D. (2011). From Telex to Twitter: Relational communication skills for a wireless world. In K. M. Galvin (Ed.), *Making connections: Readings in relational communication* (5th ed., pp. 89–96). New York: Oxford University Press.

Guerrero, L. K., Andersen, P. A., & Afifi, W. A. (2013). *Close encounters: Communicating in relationships* (4th ed.). Los Angeles: Sage.

Hackenbracht, J., & Gasper, K. (2013). I'm all ears: The need to belong motivates listening to emotional disclosure. *Journal of Experimental Social Psychology, 49,* 915–921.

Hakansson, J., & Montgomery, H. (2003). Empathy as an interpersonal phenomenon. *Journal of Social & Personal Relationships, 20,* 267–284.

Hall, J. A., Carter, S., Cody, M. J., & Albright, J. M. (2010). Individual differences in the communication of romantic interest: Development of the Flirting Styles Inventory. *Communication Quarterly, 58,* 365–393.

Hall, J., Cody, M., Jackson, G., & Flesh, J. (2008, May). *Beauty and the flirt: Attractiveness and approaches to relationship initiation.* Paper presented at the meeting of the International Communication Association, Montreal, Canada.

Hall, J. A., & Xing, C. (2015). The verbal and nonverbal correlates of the five flirting styles. *Journal of Nonverbal Behavior, 39,* 41–68.

Harris, T. E., & Sherblom, J. C. (2011). Listening and feedback: The other half of communication. In K. M. Galvin (Ed.), *Making connections: Readings in relational communication* (5th ed., pp. 61–76). New York: Oxford University Press.

Harvey, J. H., & Weber, A. L. (2002). *Odyssey of the heart: Close relationships in the 21st century* (2nd ed.). Mahwah, NJ: Erlbaum.

Heisler, J. M. (2005). Family communication about sex: Parents and college-aged offspring recall discussion topics, satisfaction, and parental involvement. *Journal of Family Communication, 5,* 295–213.

Henningsen, D. D., Braz, M., & Davies, E. (2008). Why do we flirt? *Journal of Business Communication, 45,* 483–502.

Herring, S. C., & Martinson, A. (2004). Assessing gender authenticity in computer-mediated language use: Evidence from an identity game. *Journal of Language and Social Psychology, 23,* 424–446.

Holmberg, D., & Blair, K. L. (2009). Sexual desire, communication, satisfaction, and preferences of men and women in same-sex versus mixed-sex relationships. *Journal of Sex Research, 46,* 57–66.

Humphreys, T. P. (2004). Understanding sexual consent: An empirical investigation of the normative script for young heterosexual adults. In M. Cowling & P. Reynolds (Eds.), *Making sense of sexual consent* (pp. 209–227). Surry, UK: Ashgate Publishing Ltd.

Ivy, D. K., & Wahl, S. T. (2014). *Nonverbal communication for a lifetime* (2nd ed.). Dubuque, IA: Kendall Hunt.

Jerman, P., & Constantine, N. A. (2010). Demographic and psychological predictors of parent-adolescent communication about sex: A representative statewide analysis. *Journal of Youth and Adolescence, 39,* 1164–1174.

Johnson, D. (2011). Helpful listening and responding. In K. M. Galvin (Ed.), *Making connections: Readings in relational communication* (5th ed., pp. 70–76). New York: Oxford University Press.

Jourard, S. (1971). *The transparent self.* Princeton, NJ: Van Nostrand.

Kankiewicz, K. (2007, May 10). 50 questions you haven't already asked your date. Retrieved February 7, 2011, from <http://www.suite101.com>.

Kaspar, K., & Krull, J. (2013). Incidental haptic stimulation in the context of flirt behavior. *Journal of Nonverbal Behavior, 37,* 165–173.

Kenrick, D. T., Neuberg, S. L., & Cialdini, R. B. (2005). *Social psychology: Unraveling the mystery* (3rd ed.). Boston: Allyn & Bacon.

Kimmel, M. (2015). *Angry white men: American masculinity at the end of an era.* New York: Nation Books.

Kirtley Johnston, M., Weaver, J. B., III, Watson, K. W., & Barker, L. B. (2000). Listening styles: Biological or psychological differences? *International Journal of Listening, 14,* 32–46.

Kleinke, C. L., Meeker, F. B., & Staneski, R. A. (1986). Preference for opening lines: Comparing ratings by men and women. *Sex Roles, 15,* 585–600.

Knapp, M. L., Hall, J. A., & Horgan, T. G. (2013). *Nonverbal communication in human interaction* (8th ed.). Belmont, CA: Wadsworth.

Knapp, M. L., Vangelisti, A. L., & Caughlin, J. P. (2013). *Interpersonal communication and human relationships* (7th ed.). Boston: Pearson.

Knight, K., & Wiedmaier, B. (2015). Emerging adults' casual sexual involvements and the ideal worker norm. In A. R. Martinez & L. J. Miller (Eds.), *Gender in a transitional era: Changes and challenges* (pp. 151–165). Lanham, MD: Lexington.

Koch, S. C., Baehne, C. G., Kruse, L., Zimmerman, F., & Zumbach, J. (2010). Visual dominance and visual egalitarianism: Individual and group-level influences of sex and status in group interactions. *Journal of Nonverbal Behavior, 34,* 137–153.

Konrath, S. H., O'Brien, E. H., & Hsing, C. (2011). Changes in dispositional empathy in American college students over time: A meta-analysis. *Personality and Social Psychology Review, 15,* 180-198.

Krznaric, R. (2014). *Empathy: Why it matters and how to get it.* New York: Perigee Books.

LaFrance, M., Hecht, M. A., & Levy Paluck, E. (2003). The contingent smile: A meta-analysis of sex differences in smiling. *Psychological Bulletin, 129*, 305–334.

Levesque, C., Lafontaine, M-F., Caron, A., Flescha, J. L., & Bjornson, S. (2014). Dyadic empathy, dyadic coping, and relationship satisfaction: A dyadic model. *Europe's Journal of Psychology, 10*, 118–134.

Li, N. P., Bailey, J. M., Kenrick, D. T., & Linsenmeier, J. A. (2002). The necessities and luxuries of mate preferences: Testing the tradeoffs. *Journal of Personality and Social Psychology, 82*, 947–955.

Li, X., Chen, W., & Popiel, P. (2015). What happens on Facebook stays on Facebook? The implications of Facebook interaction for perceived, receiving, and giving social support. *Computers in Human Behavior, 51*, 106–113.

Lindsey, A. E., & Zakahi, W. R. (1996). Women who tell and men who ask: Perceptions of men and women departing from gender stereotypes during initial interaction. *Sex Roles, 34*, 767–786.

Lindsey, A. E., & Zakahi, W. R. (2006). Perceptions of men and women departing from conversational sex role stereotypes. In K. Dindia & D. J. Canary (Eds.), *Sex differences and similarities in communication* (2nd ed., pp. 281–298). Mahwah, NJ: Erlbaum.

Lipinski-Harten, M., & Tafarodi, R. W. (2012). A comparison of conversational quality in online and face-to-face first encounters. *Journal of Language and Social Psychology, 31*, 331–341.

Lippa, R. A. (2006). *Gender, nature, and nurture* (2nd ed.). Mahwah, NJ: Erlbaum.

Litzinger, S., & Gordon, K. C. (2005). Exploring relationships among communication, sexual satisfaction, and marital satisfaction. *Journal of Sex and Marital Therapy, 31*, 409–424.

MacNeil, S., & Byers, E. S. (2005). Dyadic assessment of sexual self-disclosure and sexual satisfaction in heterosexual dating couples. *Journal of Social & Personal Relationships, 22*, 169–181.

Maguire, K. C., Heinemann-LaFave, D., & Sahlstein, E. (2013). "To be so connected, yet not at all": Relational presence, absence, and maintenance in the context of a wartime deployment. *Western Journal of Communication, 77*, 249–271.

McConnell, D. (1997). Interaction patterns of mixed sex groups in educational computer conferences. *Gender and Education, 9*, 345–363.

McCulloch, S. (2013). Is flirting with clients taboo? *In Practice, 35*, 222–223.

McEwan, B., & Guerrero, L. K. (2010). Freshmen engagement through communication: Predicting friendship formation strategies and perceived availability of network resources from communication skills. *Communication Studies, 61*, 445–463.

McLaren, K. (2013). *The art of empathy: A complete guide to life's most essential skill.* Louisville, CO: Sounds True Publishers.

Menaker, D. (2010, January). How to break the ice. *O: The Oprah Winfrey Magazine*, 121.

Menard, A. D., & Offman, A. (2009). The interrelationships between sexual self-esteem, sexual assertiveness, and sexual satisfaction. *Canadian Journal of Human Sexuality, 18*, 35–45.

Metts, S. (2006). Gendered communication in dating relationships. In B. J. Dow & J. T. Wood (Eds.), *The SAGE handbook of gender and communication* (pp. 25–40). Thousand Oaks, CA: Sage.

Miczo, N., Segrin, C., & Allspach, L. E. (2001). Relationship between nonverbal sensitivity, encoding, and relational satisfaction. *Communication Reports, 14*, 39–48.

Montoya, R. M., Horton, R. S., & Kirchner, J. (2008). Is actual similarity necessary for attraction? A meta-analysis of actual and perceived similarity. *Journal of Social and Personal Relationships, 25*, 889–922.

Moore, M. M. (1985). Nonverbal courtship patterns in women: Context and consequences. *Ethology and Sociobiology, 6*, 237–247.

Palfrey, J., & Gasser, U. (2010). *Born digital: Understanding the first generation of digital natives.* New York: Basic Books.

Pearce, C. G., Johnson, I. W., & Barker, R. T. (2003). Assessment of the Listening Styles Inventory. *Journal of Business and Technical Communication, 17*, 84–113.

Peterson, V. V. (2011). *Sex, ethics, and communication.* San Diego: Cognella.

Petronio, S., Martin, J., & Littlefield, R. (1984). Prerequisite conditions for self-disclosing: A gender issue. *Communication Monographs, 51*, 268–272.

Powell, A. (2010). *Sex, power, and consent: Youth culture and the unwritten rules.* Cambridge, UK: Cambridge University Press.

Prensky, M. (2001). Digital natives, digital immigrants. *On the Horizon, 9*. Retrieved October 2, 2010, from <http://www.twitchspeed.com>.

Prensky, M. R. (2010). *Teaching digital natives: Partnering for real learning.* Newbury Park, CA: Corwin.

Prensky, M. R. (2012). *From digital natives to digital wisdom: Hopeful essays for 21st century learning.* Newbury Park, CA: Corwin.

Reeser, T. W. (2010). *Masculinities in theory: An introduction.* New York: Wiley-Blackwell.

Reis, H. T. (1998). Gender differences in intimacy and related behaviors: Context and process. In D. J. Canary & K. Dindia (Eds.), *Sex differences and similarities in communication* (pp. 203–231). Mahwah, NJ: Erlbaum.

Rhodes, A. R. (2002). Long-distance relationships in dual-career commuter couples: A review of counseling issues. *The Family Journal: Counseling and Therapy for Couples and Families, 10,* 398–404.

Sahlstein, E. (2006). Making plans: Praxis strategies for negotiating uncertainty-certainty in long-distance relationships. *Western Journal of Communication, 70,* 147–165.

Sargent, S. L., & Weaver, J. B., III. (2003). Listening styles: Sex differences in perceptions of self and others. *International Journal of Listening, 17,* 5–18.

Scheflen, A. E. (1965). Quasi-courtship behavior in psychotherapy. *Psychiatry, 27,* 245–257.

Shaffer, D. R., Pegalis, L. J., & Bazzini, D. G. (1996). When boy meets girl (revisited): Gender, gender-role orientation, and prospect of future interaction as determinants of self-disclosure among same- and opposite-sex acquaintants. *Personality and Social Psychology Bulletin, 22,* 495–506.

Shonbeck, K. (2011). Communicating in a connected world. In K. M. Galvin (Ed.), *Making connections: Readings in relational communication* (5th ed., pp. 393–400). New York: Oxford University Press.

Smith, T. J. (2006, March 2). 100 dating conversation starters. Retrieved February 7, 2011, from <http://www.searchwarp.com>.

Sprecher, S. (2014). Effects of actual (manipulated) and perceived similarity on liking in get-acquainted interactions: The role of communication. *Communication Monographs, 81,* 4–27.

Staats, S., Long, L., Manulik, K., & Kelley, P. (2006). Situated empathy: Variations associated with target gender across situations. *Social Behavior and Personality, 34,* 431–441.

Stafford, L., & Hillyer, J. D. (2012). Information and communication technologies in personal relationships. *Review of Communication 12,* 290–213.

Stafford, L., Merolla, A. J., & Castle, J. D. (2006). When long-distance dating partners become geographically close. *Journal of Social & Personal Relationships, 23,* 901–919.

Strauss, N. (2005). *The game: Penetrating the secret society of pickup artists.* New York: Regan.

Tannen, D. (1990). *You just don't understand: Women and men in conversation.* New York: William Morrow.

Taylor, T., Hester, E., & Wilson, L. S. (2011). Video conferencing vs. talking face-to-face: Is video suitable for supportive dialogue? *International Journal of Therapy and Rehabilitation, 58,* 392–403.

Tidwell, L. C., & Walther, J. B. (2002). Computer-mediated communication effects on disclosure, impressions, and interpersonal evaluations: Getting to know one another a bit at a time. *Human Communication Research, 28,* 317–348.

Toussaint, L., & Webb, J. R. (2005). Gender differences in the relationship between empathy and forgiveness. *Journal of Social Psychology, 145,* 673–685.

Trost, M. R., & Alberts, J. K. (1998). An evolutionary view on understanding sex effects in communicating attraction. In D. Canary & K. Dindia (Eds.), *Sex, gender, and communication: Similarities and differences* (pp. 233–255). Mahwah, NJ: Erlbaum.

Trost, M. R., & Alberts, J. K. (2006). How men and women communicate attraction: An evolutionary view. In K. Dindia & D. J. Canary (Eds.), *Sex differences and similarities in communication* (2nd ed., pp. 317–336). Mahwah, NJ: Erlbaum.

Trout, J. D. (2009). *The empathy gap: Building bridges to the good life and the good society.* New York: Viking.

Walther, J. B., Liang, Y., DeAndrea, D. C., Tong, S., Carr, C. T., Spottswood, E. L., et al. (2011). The effect of feedback on identity shift in computer-mediated communication. *Media Psychology, 14,* 1–26.

Weber, K., Goodboy, A. K., & Cayanus, J. (2010). Flirting competence: An experimental study on appropriate and effective opening lines. *Communication Research Reports, 27,* 184–191.

West, R., & Turner, L. H. (2011). Technology and interpersonal communication. In K. M. Galvin (Ed.), *Making connections: Readings in relational communication* (5th ed., pp. 379–386). New York: Oxford University Press.

Whitty, M. T. (2004). Cyber-flirting: An examination of men's and women's flirting behaviour both offline and on the Internet. *Behaviour Change, 21,* 115–126.

Whitty, M. T., & Carr, A. N. (2003). Cyberspace as potential space: Considering the web as a playground to cyber-flirt. *Human Relations, 56,* 869–891.

Wilson, E., & Koo, H. (2010). Mothers, fathers, sons, and daughters: Gender differences in factors associated with parent-child communication about sexual topics. *Reproductive Health, 7,* 7–31.

Wolvin, A. D. (2010). Listening engagement: Intersecting theoretical perspectives. In A. D. Wolvin (Ed.), *Listening and human communication in the 21st century* (pp. 7–30). Oxford, UK: Wiley-Blackwell.

Wood, J. T., & Inman, C. C. (1993). In a different mode: Masculine styles of communicating closeness. *Journal of Applied Communication Research, 21,* 279–295.

Work and family facts and statistics. (2015). Retrieved July 25, 2015, from <http://www.aflcio.org/issues/factsstats/>.

Yurchisin, J., Watchravesringkan, K., & McCabe, D. B. (2005). An exploration of identity recreation in the context of Internet dating. *Social Behavior and Personality, 33,* 735–750.

CHAPTER 6

FRIENDS AND LOVERS
Gender Communication in Key Relationships

CASE STUDY

Friends? Talking? Hanging Out? Dating? Seeing Each Other? Hooking Up? The Increasingly Complicated Language of Relationships

Relationships have never been simple things—to initiate, develop, deepen, or even terminate. But it seems, now more than ever, there's an increasing number of ways to connect with people.

If you say you're *friends*, most people agree as to what that means—it means pretty much what it's always meant. But what does it mean when two people say they're *talking*? This language is often used by today's college students. As best we can tell, *talking* means two people are attracted to or interested in each other beyond friendship; they have private conversations (and text/e-mail exchanges), but nothing's official. They don't hang out in public solely with each other, but people can generally tell something's going on between them. Do we have that about right?

Talking seems to have more exclusivity to it than *hanging out*, which generally means two people show up at the same events or activities and pay a bit of attention to each other, but it's not as advanced as *talking*. Each interested party knows the other is there—perhaps the two people have class together and occasionally sit in proximity to each other, or talk before or after class—but there's no implication that they'll do this regularly, nor no particular attachment to each other or shared activities.

HOT TOPICS

- Friendship development and sex segregation
- Functions, characteristics, and communication in same-sex friendships
- Factors that inhibit and enhance cross-sex friendship
- Unique challenges that emerge in transgender friendship
- The language of romance and the pressure to partner
- Tensions in romantic relationships
- Relational talk, metacommunication, and couple communication patterns
- Conflict and breakups
- Communication about sexual activity

Talking with one person doesn't necessarily mean someone won't *talk* with any others. (Describing these relationships technically is a bit nerdy, but bear with us. Language matters.)

So is *dating* truly a thing of the past, like something quaint your parents once did (or *you* did in high school, if you're now an older college student)? Perhaps at some point people move past *hanging out* and *talking*, to actually start making plans with each other and attending events or activities together, rather than just arriving separately at the same event around the same time. Would you call such a shift *dating*? When we ask college students about dating, it's still a concept they recognize, perhaps even a phase or definition they want to have with someone, but they're slow to use that term to describe a deeper phase of a relationship. They don't get asked as often as people used to, "Are you two dating?" People just don't know what that means anymore, perhaps because the old rules of asking someone out, ushering the person through a pre-planned evening, and paying for the expenses of the evening seem not to fit today's modern process of coupling. Many people find dating way too stressful, with too many rules about who's supposed to do what and when, and expectations about outcomes.

Seeing each other? This language seems to beg for a joking follow-up line, like "Yeah, we're seeing each other; she's (he's) *right over there.*" College students used to use this language because it seemed more comfortable than to declare one was actually *dating* someone—*seeing* someone left it less tangible, more casual. But it seems now that *hanging out* or perhaps *talking* has replaced *seeing*.

Probably the term with the clearest, most widely agreed upon meaning is *hooking up*, which has a sexual connotation and isn't viewed as acceptable to use as a relational definition or to declare in public, as in "we hooked up." Most of us learned that bragging about or being too public with sexual liaisons was in bad taste, so bringing someone home to meet one's parents and declaring, "Hey mom and dad, let me introduce you to my *hook up*"—well, that's not likely to happen (thankfully).

Why bother to examine all of this language? Here are two reasons: (1) What two people in a relationship *call* the relationship speaks volumes about what state or phase the relationship is in, as well as its quality. It can be very telling if one partner believes the relationship is a friendship, but the other partner thinks it's something more. What if one person thinks it's in the *talking* stage, but the other believes it's just in the *hanging out* stage? Viewing a relationship differently is common, but can be painful. (2) Language is your primary tool to communicate who you are, as well as *who you are with* in a relationship. Language fulfills that basic need to communicate clearly to others about all sorts of things, including who we relate to, how, and why.

In this chapter we explore two important categories of connections we make with others: friendships and romantic relationships. Gender communication, not surprisingly, plays a critical role in forming, deepening, and sometimes terminating both types of relationships

FROM ME TO YOU: AUTHOR'S NOTE

This chapter made me crazy. It was BY FAR the toughest chapter to revise of them all, for the sixth edition of this book. Here's why: This chapter is a combination of two relationship areas: friendship and romantic relationships. So much has changed in our culture regarding these forms of relationships that past approaches to both topics just didn't work this time around.

Here's an example to illustrate the challenge: Friendship used to be covered in its own chapter, separate from the chapter on romantic relationships. The friendship chapter was divided into two major sections: communication in same-sex friendships and communication in cross-sex friendships. But let's say you're a gay male college student who has more and better friendships with straight women than with gay women, bisexuals, and straight men—are research findings on same-sex friendships relevant to you? Are research findings on cross-sex friendships relevant to you? Does your psychological and emotional gender trump your biological sex in this context?

Take this a step further: Let's say you're a transwoman, meaning you're in the process of transitioning from being a biological male to becoming a woman, because you feel that is your true gender. As a transwoman, just who are your same-sex friends—your male friends? Your female friends? Your newly acquired transgender friends? Who is a cross-sex friend to you? The sex binary of "same" and "cross" just seems ridiculous here—like something from a past century.

The problem is, the vast societal changes we've made on the sex/gender front are emerging faster than the research necessary to document the changes. What if you, as that transwoman I just mentioned, were married to a ciswoman (a biological female who is not transgender)—and you stay married to that ciswoman after you transition—are you now in a same-sex marriage? Transgender people vary in how they go through their transitions; they vary in how well they've adopted their new sex/gender and accepted all the changes that go with the new identity. Same-sex friends may not relate to someone who transitions into a different sex/gender identity, so the communication dynamics may not be the same as before the person transitioned.

In Chapter 1, we discussed intersex identity—people born with both or mixed sets of genitalia and hormonal systems. If you're intersex (as more people are nowadays, since parents are now being advised about the pros and cons of "correcting" the anatomy and physiology of an intersex baby), who is a same-sex friend to you? Who is a cross-sex friend to you?

Research on transgenderism is a challenge to find, but it's starting to blossom and will only increase in the near future. In this chapter on relationships, I overview a key piece of research by two excellent scholars, Michael Monsour and William Rawlins (2014), that helps us understand transgender friendship. Locating studies on communication about and between intersex people is still quite the challenge, but we can all remain hopeful for more research in the future.

So we're all—including me, your textbook author—going to have to deal with the fact that, at the point in time this revision occurred, what I wrote and what the research says may feel a bit out of date, given how fast our culture is evolving. What's being published in 2016 may seem quaint and antiquated in 2017 because a good deal of what we've believed about sex, gender, and communication is changing and changing fast. Our goal is to be inclusive of everyone and respectful of people's choices and struggles. The state of the research right now is not inclusive, but it soon will be. So let's make a deal—you, dear reader, and me, your author: Let's do the best we can, learn as much as we can at present, and vow to stay open to constantly being re-educated on these topics.

FRIENDSHIP: A SINGLE SOUL IN TWO BODIES

> The meeting of two personalities is like the contact of two chemical substances: if there is any reaction, both are transformed.
> —Carl Jung, Swiss psychotherapist

Aristotle defined a friend as "a single soul who resides in two bodies." Modern definitions are a bit less poetic. Ellen Goodman and Patricia O'Brien (2000), friends and coauthors of a book on women's friendships, ask: "What's a friend? If the Eskimos have twenty-six different words for snow, Americans have only one word commonly used to describe everyone from acquaintances to intimates. It is a word we have to qualify with adjectives: school friends, work friends, old friends, casual friends, good friends" (p. 18). Friendships are a unique class of relationships; friends are vital in our lives.

LEARNING TO BE FRIENDS

Our early patterns of forming friendships reveal sex segregation, reinforced by how most schools operate (Kalmijn, 2002; Maccoby, 1998; Romaine, 1999). Neighborhood kids may play together, but at school they're categorized first by age, then by sex. Children often form separate lines for boys and girls to go to the restroom, cafeteria, auditorium, and so forth. Granted, the sex separation for toilet use has a basis in reality, in that most schools have separate facilities for females and males. But this practice marks school as a different context for children because in a typical home, toilets aren't sex segregated.

Further sex segregation occurs on playgrounds when students engage in team sports. School athletic activities (particularly in high school) are, almost exclusively, sex segregated. For families raising intersex and transgender children, things like school restrooms and gym class pose serious challenges (Davis, 2013; Feder, 2014; Preves, 2003). Simple traditions within schools facilitate a dichotomizing, segregating pattern that affects people's choice of friends, their understanding of people of a different sex, and their behavior with friends.

Beginning about age seven, boys form extended friendship networks with other boys while girls tend to cluster into exclusive same-sex friendship dyads (Rawlins, 2001). In those dyads, girls acquire the social skills of communicating their feelings and being nurturing. In contrast, boys learn to follow rules and get along with groups of people. To varying degrees, these tendencies remain through adolescence and into adulthood (Chow, Roelse, Buhrmeister, & Underwood, 2011). One explanation that may seem simple, but that has received considerable research attention, relates to similarity: We tend to gravitate toward and develop friendships with people we perceive to be similar to ourselves, more so than to those we perceive to be different from us (Fehr, 2008; Foster, 2005; Pinel, Long, Landau, Alexander, & Pyszczynksi, 2006; Rushton & Bons, 2005). Biological sex is one form of basic similarity.

COMMUNICATION IN SAME-SEX FRIENDSHIPS

To many people's thinking, same-sex friendships require less work to maintain than cross-sex friendships. Same-sex friendships do not, for the most part, experience the same tensions as cross-sex friendships, such as romance versus friendship, sexuality, jealousy, emotional intensity, and how others perceive the relationship. Another assumption about same-sex friendships is that friends are equals; power dynamics that may play a role in cross-sex friendships are absent or less of a factor.

Male–Male Friendship: Functions and Characteristics

Friendships between men have evolved, just like many other types of relationships. Although still occasionally the subject of popular culture's ridicule, like teasing about "male bonding" and being in a "bromance," men's friendships have been studied in terms of their significance, the communication or shared experiences that launch such connections, and what's necessary to sustain them (Castillo & Mack, 2015; Chen, 2012; Rawlins, 2009; Way, 2011).

For many men, male friends are important but replaceable; men tend to have more numerous but less intimate same-sex friendships than women (Greif, 2008). While men and women typically spend similar amounts of time with friends, men's friendships with other men tend to serve different purposes than women's friendships with other women (Bentall, 2004; Garfield, 2015).

Men often form friendships through groups because it satisfies a need to belong to something or to other people. For centuries, men have used group belongingness as a source of power and connection. Historically male-dominated religious ceremonies, fraternity rituals, and male-only discussions (like locker-room conversations, for example) have an air of secrecy about them and a code of correct behavior that controls access to these groups and marks women as outsiders (Spain, 1992).

In some instances, male friendships form out of conflict. While we tend to think of conflict as separating people, it can also be quite cathartic and can clear the air toward greater understanding and feelings of closeness. Conflict experienced by people on the same side—be it in war situations, sporting events, or interpersonal disagreements—can generate significant closeness as well.

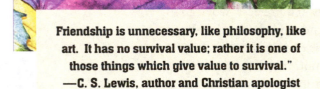

Friendship is unnecessary, like philosophy, like art. It has no survival value; rather it is one of those things which give value to survival."
—C. S. Lewis, author and Christian apologist

"DOING" VERSUS "TALKING" Men's friendships tend to be more about "doing," while women's tend to be more about "talking." Yes, women also do things together and men also talk, but the activity-orientation of men's friendships is one of its primary characteristics.

Many men's friendships begin with, are sustained by, and sometimes dissolve over doing things together and sharing (or enduring) experiences (Fisher, 2009; Martin, 1997; Rawlins, 2001). Through these shared experiences and activities, men develop feelings of closeness and express their commonality with male friends. Friendship rituals like watching sports or "going out with the guys" are important because they create a familiar, structured pattern to a friendship that facilitates the relationship without the need for a great deal of conversation (Bruess & Pearson, 1997; Garfield, 2015).

INTIMACY IN MALE–MALE FRIENDSHIP Feelings of closeness are important in any friendship, and the expression of closeness between men has changed (Rawlins, 1992, 2009). In Chapter 5, we defined intimacy as bonding, closeness, and emotional connection, based on sharing personal, private information and experiences over time. We offered Jeffrey Fine's (2001) version of intimacy, as "in-to-me-see" (p. 225). Intimacy is something most people long for in their relationships, but is intimacy actually the goal in male–male friendship?

If you think of male intimacy as the pouring of one's heart out in conversation, then no, that version of intimacy doesn't typify male-male friendship. But are we applying the wrong measurement of intimacy here? Older research on this issue is still relevant to how we view and judge male intimacy. Communication scholars Wood and Inman (1993) explored

For many men, watching sports together facilitates friendship without the need for a lot of conversation.

communication and intimacy in relationships and determined that traits like having long, emotional conversations may better describe female friendship than male. It's not that male-male friendships aren't intimate, but that we've been pronouncing them non-intimate using a feminine standard. Male subjects in Wood and Inman's study regarded practical help, mutual assistance, and companionship as marks of caring and closeness. In a subsequent study, Inman (1996) discovered that men characterize their friendships with other men as being based on "continuity, perceived support and dependability, shared understandings, perceived compatibility, having fun together, intermingled lives, and assumed significance" (p. 100).

Female–Female Friendship: Functions and Characteristics

Many women can attest to the fact that since the earliest days they can remember as girls, same-sex friendships have been sustaining, highly significant forces in their lives. Research suggests that women are, in general, more likely than men to form very close same-sex friendships and to value those friendships highly (Rose, 2007; Wright, 2006). However, until only recently, little research on female friendship was available—possibly because of the stereotype that women are too competitive, catty, and jealous to have meaningful friendships (Bleske-Rechek & Lighthall, 2010; Johnson, 1996). More recent academic and popular attention has been paid to female friendships and the communication that sustains them (Castaneda & Burns-Glover, 2008; Galupo, 2007; Greif & Sharpe, 2010; Huling, Murray, & Houston, 2012; Samter & Burleson, 2005).

INTIMACY IN FEMALE–FEMALE FRIENDSHIP Two schools of thought exist on intimacy in women's friendships versus men's. One body of information claims that women's friendships are generally more intimate and close than men's (Eichenbaum & Orbach, 2014; Miller, 2014; Rawlins, 1993). Women's conversations with male friends tend to focus more on ideas or problem solving than on shared feelings; if women want advice, suggestions, or a "fix-it" approach, they're likely to receive that from male friends. However, women most often seek out other women for a listening, sympathetic ear or for empathy in regard for what they're going through or feeling.

Another school of thought contends that intimacy differences in male–male versus female–female friendships is not so great as previous research suggests (Wright, 2006). Some scholars contend that the "women talk,

In general, women are more likely than men to form very close same-sex friendships.

men do" characterization is an overgeneralization, because women enjoy and place significant value on shared activities with their female friends.

SELF-DISCLOSURE IN FEMALE–FEMALE FRIENDSHIP
Self-disclosure is a prime source of intimacy in friendships (Derlega, Winstead, & Greene, 2008; Fehr, 2004, 2008). Disclosing one's thoughts, fears, concerns, and emotions with a same-sex friend is something most women cherish and rely on.

Research shows, in general, that women tend to be more self-disclosing in their same-sex friendships than men (Martin, 1997; Rawlins, 2001, 2009). These differences hold for online communication as well. Bane, Cornish, Erspamer, and Kampman (2010) studied over 300 female bloggers' perceptions of "real-life" same-sex friendships versus online friendships, in terms of self-disclosure, perceptions of intimacy, and relationship satisfaction. Online self-disclosure was correlated with satisfaction, meaning that women who offered and received online friends' disclosures were highly positive about these relationships.

Net Notes

The Friendship Page, located at **www.friendship.com.au**, is an Australian-based website "devoted to exploring the topic of friendship in a positive and friendly manner." The site contains such information as quotes from specialists and site visitors, poetry, tributes, interactive advice, and a chat room. If you think you'd like to expand your circle of friends—at least your circle of cyberfriends—check out this site.

CROSS-SEX FRIENDSHIP: BEING "JUST FRIENDS"

Just a few decades ago, men and women only socialized together as dates—rarely if ever as friends. American culture has experienced a social change related to friendship, because friendships between multiple sexes and genders are prevalent and common now (Galupo, 2009; Guerrero & Chavez, 2005; Monsour & Rawlins, 2014; Rawlins, 2009).

"My Gay"

Erika, a former research assistant for this book, believes that relationships beween heterosexual women and gay men are unique, wonderful, and increasingly common, especially among people of college age. She and her now-husband were talking about doing some activity together when he said, "Oh that's right—you can't because you're having a night out with your gay." Erika often called her best friend, an openly gay man, "her gay" or "my gay" as a form of affectionate shorthand. Her gay male friend didn't take offense, viewing it as a term of endearment.

Is this language offensive? Some people might think so, mainly because of the use of possessive pronouns like "her" or "my" that could connote ownership or dominance. Others might be affronted by use of the noun gay to stand for a whole person.

We do know heterosexual women who highly value their relationships with self-identified gay men, sometimes over other friendships. One explanation for the draw is that straight women and gay men are both attracted to men as sexual partners, so that commonality creates a bond. Another notion is that gay men are perceived as being able to offer insight into straight men, since they share a biological sex, so their insight is valuable.

Even though many more people are accepting of homosexuality today than in times past, it's still the case that some gay men choose to appear socially and publicly with straight women (aka, "beards") as a way to conceal their gay identity. This practice can be hurtful if the woman has been deceived about the man's sexuality and merely thinks she's out on a date.

Research continues to explore this form of friendship in more depth (Bartlett, Patterson, Vander-Laan, & Vasey, 2009; Gaiba, 2008). If you'd like to read more, we refer you to Lisa Tillmann's (2014) book, *In Solidarity: Friendship, Family, and Activism Beyond Gay and Straight* and Robert Hopcke and Laura Rafaty's (2001) *Straight Women, Gay Men: Absolutely Fabulous Friendships.*

What Gets in the Way of Cross-Sex Friendships?

One challenge to a successful cross-sex friendship may exist in the minds of the friends before they ever meet and decide to become friends. Studies over multiple decades reveal that many heterosexual men, in contrast to heterosexual women, consistently report difficulty developing cross-sex friendships that are free of romantic implications and sexual activity (Bleske & Buss, 2000; Messman, Canary, & Hause, 2000). In fact, some men have reported in studies that they're often motivated to form friendships with women because they believe these relationships will lead to "something else" (Halatsis & Christakis, 2009; Rawlins, 2001). We all know that women are capable of such motivations, too.

Some research suggests that a pervasive current of attraction and sexuality underlies most, if not all, heterosexual cross-sex friendships (Afifi & Faulkner, 2000; Halatsis & Christakis, 2009; Hughes, Morrison, & Asada, 2005; Monsour, 2006). In some ways, these findings reflect a remnant attitude of past generations—that relationships with women are for one thing, and that one thing is not friendship.

People in cross-sex friendships tire of the badgering they get from family, coworkers, and other friends about the true nature of their friendship—the hints people drop about becoming a "couple." People frequently use the word *platonic* to describe a friendship they suspect is something else altogether. Over time and with repeated input from others, such pressure can increase and erode the friendship, or it can cause the friends to reassess their connection (Guerrero & Mongeau, 2008). Some friendships do successfully change definitions and evolve into romantic relationships because many people believe that the seed or root of a successful intimate relationship is friendship (Hendrick & Hendrick, 2000; Mongeau, Serewicz, Henningsen, & Davis, 2006).

But what happens if one friend starts giving into societal pressure or if romantic feelings start to develop on one side of the friendship, but not the other? Researchers have explored the fate of friendships after one friend discloses romantic interest toward the other friend, but the romantic overture isn't reciprocated (sometimes called "unrequited romance"; Motley, Faulkner, & Reeder, 2008, p. 27). Motley

Net Notes

Friendship Force International (FFI) is a nonprofit international cultural exchange organization, headquartered in Atlanta, Georgia. The organization's mission is "to promote global understanding across the barriers that separate people." FFI has active chapters in over seventy countries, and its members seek to promote goodwill through homestay exchange programs. For those of you who think you might like to travel abroad and have friendly faces of people to stay with, visit the FFI site, located at **www.friendshipforce.org.**

et al. (2008) found that unrequited romantic disclosure was awkward for the friends, at best, and completely disruptive to the friendship, at worst.

Another source of difficulty in cross-sex friendships arises from communication patterns. Men often view female friends as emotional outlets—"safe harbors" to turn to (as opposed to romantic partners), friends to whom they can self-disclose and express personal problems, knowing they'll most likely receive supportive, empathic responses (Aries, 2006; Burleson, 2003; Dindia, 2002). Problem is, women also turn to female friends for that listening ear, that caring and empathy, so women are the supportive sources *for everyone*. This dynamic can create a sort of imbalance within friendship.

What Enhances Cross-Sex Friendships?

Cross-sex friends often make great romance advisors! It's common for heterosexual men to ask their female friends to help them understand women. At times, women are a mystery to men, so they may feel that a female friend can help them understand romantic partners more so than a male friend can. Men tend not to want to disclose their problems, insecurities, or concerns to other men for fear of appearing weak or vulnerable, so they find female friends to be valuable confidantes. Likewise, heterosexual women who are puzzled or troubled by some situation with a boyfriend or husband often find their male friends a source of support, strength, and insight.

Thus far in the chapter, we've been operating under the assumption that cross-sex friendships are platonic, meaning they don't include sexual activity. But increasingly nowadays, friends become sexual partners with little to no effect on the friendship nor expectation of romantic involvement. Among college-aged people "friends with benefits relationships" (FWBRs), sometimes called (in PG-13 language) "f-buddies," are more common now than they were even a few short years ago. Surveys at different universities have found that anywhere from over half to a majority of students responding to surveys report having been in at least one FWBR, more men than women (Bisson & Levine, 2009; McGinty, Knox, & Zusman, 2007; Owen & Fincham,

> This is a gross generalization, but I think women pay more attention to details—of their relationships, emotions, and things in the room in which they're sitting. Women are constantly wondering what men are thinking, when the answer is that we're not thinking at all.
> —Mike Greenberg, ESPN anchor and author of *All You Could Ask For*, a book about female friends battling breast cancer

Often cross-sex friends can offer good romance advice.

2012; Puentes, Knox, & Zusman, 2008). FWBRs aren't just heterosexual either; gay, lesbian, bisexual/bigender, and transgender individuals also enjoy the "benefits" of this form of friendship.

Hughes, Morrison, and Asada (2005) define the FWBR as a relationship that emerges from a preexisting friendship but that evolves to include sexual activity. The sex doesn't change the friendship into a romance or imply a commitment. However, Mongeau, Knight, Williams, Eden, and Shaw (2013) found variation in how students defined FWBRs, with some reporting having an emotional connection with their friend/sex partner (i.e., the friends truly care about each other), whereas others' connections were more like serial hookups. Perhaps some people feel guilty about repeated hookups, so they label their connection an FWBR to ease the guilt.

One view holds that an FWBR is a positive extension of a friendship; people can still enjoy sexual activity, just without the hassle of a romantic entanglement. But others wouldn't dream of having FWBRs because it goes against their moral code, religious beliefs, or simply their preference for restricting sexual activity to only their romantic partners.

Researchers continue to explore the nature of FWBRs, how people negotiate them, and the communication involved in the maintenance of such friendships (Braithwaite, Aaron, Dowdle, Spjut, & Fincham, 2015; Green & Morman, 2011; Gusarova, Fraser, & Alderson, 2012; Owen & Fincham, 2011; Paik, 2010). However, a troubling sex difference has emerged. In some studies, heterosexual women and men differ in their basic conception of the FWBR and motivations for getting into such an arrangement (Calterone Williams, & Jovanovic, 2015). Women tend to emphasize the "friends" aspect, viewing the FWBR as more involved and emotional, whereas men view the relationship as casual and place more emphasis on the sexual "benefits" (McGinty et al., 2007). One of the toughest experiences in an FWBR occurs when one friend starts to develop romantic feelings or intentions toward the other, and the other partner simply wants a friendly, yet sexual connection, and nothing more.

Hughes et al. (2005) offer some guidelines to help FWBRs function effectively (provided both friends follow them):

1. Friends with benefits must maintain their original friendship, meaning that sexual activity doesn't change the friendship and the participants continue to do things together that they typically did as friends.
2. Emotions don't become involved or the friendship will be at risk.
3. The friends with benefits relationship is maintained in secret, even if this means that their romantic or sexual partners don't know about it.
4. The relationship may be renegotiated, with either participant opting out at any time.

A NEW LANDSCAPE FOR FRIENDSHIP

The author's note earlier in this chapter foreshadows the discussion here, but to briefly recap: Things are changing on the friendship landscape. A person's sex or gender doesn't seem to be as much of a deciding factor as to if or how you'll form a friendship as it once was, even only a few years ago. Similarly to how a person's race or ethnicity has less relevance attached to it than it used to, when it comes to finding people we like, want to hang out with, and can talk easily with, a person's sex, gender, sexual orientation, and so forth don't factor much anymore into whether we will befriend someone or not, or they will befriend us. This can only be seen as a positive development, because it widens our reach; it enlarges the potential for each of us to develop important friendships. In addition, only having friends who look like and act like us limits our ability to change and grow as people.

Most college students (straight, gay, bi, etc.) now have gay and lesbian friends who are open about their sexuality. Being homosexual isn't the stigma it once was, but we must remember that many gay and lesbian people still feel the need to be closeted about their sexuality. Less frequent, but more frequent than in years past, is the potential for many college students to have friends who are openly bisexual/bigender. Perhaps where you attend college, there's a chapter of GLAAD (Gay and Lesbian Alliance Against Defamation) that offers educational programming; maybe your school also has a student organization for transgender students, faculty, and staff. It's safe to say that we're now living in a friendship landscape that is much more diverse than even a few years ago.

Research is trying to keep pace with these changes. While studies are a challenge to find (and to conduct), we want to bring one to your attention—co-authored by two of the best friendship and communication scholars in the business—Michael Monsour and William Rawlins (whose research, separate and together, is cited frequently in this book). In 2014, Monsour and Rawlins published a piece that challenges all of us, when we are thinking about friendship, to dispense with the sex/gender binary we've discussed in different chapters of this text.

Monsour and Rawlins (2014) explain: "The four decades of research addressing cross-sex friendships is limited by a hetero-normative bias and an exclusive focus on cisgendered individuals. We propose the designation 'postmodern cross-gender friendship' as a more inclusive perspective on friendships between differently gendered persons" (p. 11). In quick review, you'll recall from Chapter 3 that cisgender refers to people who aren't transgender, meaning people who identify with the gender they were assigned at birth. Since most research on cross-sex friendship has assumed a sex binary (male and female) and a heterosexual orientation, Monsour and Rawlins focused on transgender friendship in an effort to bring some unique challenges to the fore.

Their study specifically examines friendships in the lives of four transgender individuals—two self-identified as transitioning from female to male and two transitioning from male to female. Each subject in the study described their friends as members of the "other sex," not the "opposite sex," so this choice of language is important. Monsour and Rawlins explain, "Transgender individuals and their friendships with members of the 'other sex' raise new questions, transform older ones, and offer alternative possibilities for living and understanding 'cross-sex' friendships" (p. 14).

Interesting themes emerged from extensive interviews with the four subjects. First, transgender people know that their bodies aren't the defining factor in their gender identity, but their internal identities or feelings about themselves are key. However, their friends and acquaintances struggle with the body issue, meaning simply how the person looks, compared to how he or she used to look. For example, in the TV show *I Am Cait*, documenting the transition of Caitlyn Jenner (formerly Bruce Jenner) from male to female, one episode focused on Cait's challenges with male friends—former "same-sex friends" when she was Bruce and not Cait. In the show, it appears that female friends don't have as much difficulty accepting Cait's transition as male friends. Much is made of Cait's developing meaningful new friendships with other transgender people, which can be critical to a successful transition.

Another theme emerging from Monsour and Rawlins' (2014) study was the importance of retaining friends from before one's transition, because these friends are validating and important to a transgender person's ability to live authentically and integrate her or his transition into his or her longer life story. Yet another theme surrounded the use of language, both by the transitioning person and his or her friends. It's important to most transgender persons that people begin, or at least make attempts, to use language that reflects the new identity, like pronouns and a new first name. In one early *I Am Cait* episode, Jenner's mother struggles to use female pronouns when referring to Cait, but is determined to meet the challenge, telling the viewing audience that "pronouns are important."

Finally, the fluidity of the gender experience described by the four subjects in Monsour and Rawlin's (2014) study provided them a broader perspective on friendship. The conclusion was that their transgender subjects "negotiated relationships that were simultaneously same- and cross-gendered at varying moments and degrees" (p. 34).

Some of you reading this material are already very "on board" with all of these issues and likely have friends of diverse sexes, gender, identities, orientations, and so forth. But for others of you, these issues of gender identity and their effects on all sorts of relationships—friends, lovers, etc.—no doubt represent challenges to your world view and how you operate, day to day. Here's what to keep in mind: All perspectives and reactions are valued; no students are judged for their responses to societal changes. Just hang in there and don't stop trying to understand; keep the communication flowing.

AH, LOVE AND ROMANCE (AND GENDER)

Romantic relationships bring their own unique communication challenges to the people who venture into them. But even when we are in the midst of a breakup, when a relationship seems doomed and we wonder why we ever wandered into such uncharted territory, we'd probably say we'd do it all over again if given the chance. Humans are romantic creatures and, for many of us, the opportunity for romance and love is one of life's greatest experiences. Because romantic relationships tap such strong emotions and because our culture has such a strong interest in them, communication within them is critical and complex.

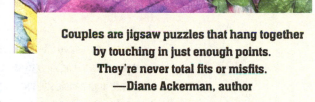

Couples are jigsaw puzzles that hang together by touching in just enough points. They're never total fits or misfits.
—Diane Ackerman, author

THE LANGUAGE OF ROMANCE

Romantic relationships are complicated (an understatement). Consider the terms used to describe a romantic relationship and the two people in it. The term *romantic relationship* reflects a range of couplings, from dating relationships to longer-term, committed relationships and nonmarital relationships that include sexual activity. (We don't mean to insinuate that marital relationships are somehow not romantic; we're just trying to be clear.) On occasion, we use the term *monogamous relationship* in reference to a romantic relationship in which the partners are exclusive, meaning they "date" or "see" only each other.

For heterosexual couples (and some lesbian couples), the term *girlfriend* is still the most common usage of traditionally aged male students, but *boyfriend* seems to be on the decline, for both straight women and gay men. Instead, straight college women often say "the guy I'm seeing." Unmarried homosexual couples most often refer to each other as *partners,* a term that some heterosexual, bisexual, and transgender couples have co-opted, because it communicates the sense of equality and cooperativeness inherent in a partnership. In this chapter, the term *relational partner* is used most often; if research findings pertain only to married partners (spouses), we'll use more specific language to be clear.

THE PRESSURE TO PARTNER

In our modern-day culture, love is the overwhelming motive for people to enter into long-term relationships. But love, as a reason for partnering, is a relatively recent occurrence in our culture (Hendrick & Hendrick, 2000). In the early twentieth century in American history, economic and social reasons were more important than love in choosing a mate. In many

Net Notes

The number of specialized Internet dating sites has expanded dramatically in recent years. It's a time saver to use a specialty site if you're interested in online coupling, although people still sing the praises of larger, long-established sites like **match.com** or **eharmony.com.**

Here are some prominent specialty sites that might catch your interest, if you're in the market:
jdate.com and **jmatch.com:** Sites for people of the Jewish faith or tradition
christianmingle.com: A site that offers shortcuts for Christians to find other Christians
girldates.com: One of many online dating services for lesbians
mypartner.com: A site that focuses on longer-term gay male relationships
farmersonly.com: Self explanatory!
ourtime.com: A site for people 50 years of age and older
seniorpeoplemeet.com: A site for people 55 years of age and older
blackpeoplemeet.com: A dating site aimed at African Americans
singleparentmeet.com: Also self explanatory!
professionalmatch.com: Site aimed at people 35 years of age and older who wish to employ the services of professional matchmakers (No, this is not a site for meeting prostitutes.)
peoplewithpurplenosesandredeyes.com: Yes, we made this up, although it sounds interesting

Many people, regardless of their circumstances, would like to be in a committed relationship.

© Lopolo/Shutterstock.com

parts of the world, love and romance aren't significant parts of marriage; business opportunities, the furtherance of family, and tradition override love as motivations for marrying.

People still feel the pressure to partner or couple, as though they can't be taken seriously or haven't really arrived until they're in a committed, monogamous relationship. Students may not feel pressure to settle down with one person while pursuing their degrees, but they often feel such pressure once they've graduated and starting working career-type jobs. Even in the twenty-first century, heterosexual women generally pay more attention to relationship dynamics than heterosexual men, plus they feel more pressure to marry than men and report a willingness to make more sacrifices in order to marry (Blakemore, Lawton, & Vartanian, 2003; Metts, 2006). While gay, lesbian, bisexual, and transgender couples experience both the stereotype and the reality of pressure to play the field, the people who tend to receive the most respect and envy among members of LGBT communities are those in committed, monogamous relationships (Isay, 2006; Lehmiller, 2010).

RELATIONAL TENSIONS

In comparison to friendships, romantic relationships engender a different set of issues, perhaps more aptly described as *tensions* within a relationship. *Relationship tensions* arise from the decision making a couple faces in developing and defining their relationship (Baxter, 2011; Baxter & Erbert, 2000; Baxter & Montgomery, 2000; Faulkner & Ruby, 2015; Turner & West, 2011).

Relationships aren't static but dynamic; they involve contradiction, change, and interdependence (Baxter, 2011). If partners can recognize the presence and shifting nature of these relationship tensions, they can talk about them and resolve them more easily. Or partners may decide that the tensions are too great to overcome and they just aren't suited for each other. The earlier couples talk about these issues, the sooner they can make wise decisions. Below are some of the more prominent relational tensions that research continues to examine, primarily stemming from relational dialectics theory (RDT; Baxter, 2011; Baxter & Montgomery, 1996; Pederson, 2014; Rudick & Golsan, 2014).

Remember...

Romantic Relationship: Nonmarital relationship that may range from dating to a more long-term, committed relationship, which may or may not include sexual activity

Monogamous Relationship: Romantic relationship in which the partners only date one another and not others; may also imply a sexual relationship in which partners are involved sexually only with each other

Relational Partner: Preferred term for someone involved in a romantic, nonmarried relationship

Autonomy Versus Connection

A defining characteristic of love is the declaration of *we;* the primary feature of *we* is the close *connection* of one person's well-being with that of another person (Nozick, 1993). The connection has a trade-off: it comes with limits on *autonomy*, or the extent to which a person values individual pursuits apart from the relationship (Peplau, 1994; Sahlstein & Dun, 2008; Semlak & Pearson, 2011; Stephenson-Abetz & Holman, 2012). The amount of autonomy partners desire within a relationship varies widely, making it one of the most difficult issues to confront.

Cell phone use—both talking and texting—has an impact on the autonomy–connection tension (Duran, Kelly, & Rotaru, 2011; Hall & Baym, 2011; Jin & Pena, 2010). Cell phone use between relational partners can be a source of conflict, meaning it doesn't mediate this particular tension; it can make it worse. Mobile phones are more often used by people who already know each other than people making a first contact, so relational partners rely considerably on this form of communication to coordinate time together and keep each other informed of what they're doing (Igarashi, Takai, & Yoshida, 2005). But conflict can arise as to *how* (calling versus texting) and *how often* partners use their phones, meaning who calls who and how often, who texts who, how quickly does one partner respond to the other's texts, and what does a nonresponse mean (time spent with someone else?). Some partners experience conflict as a result; few set ground rules on cell phone use (Duran et al., 2011).

Because each partner in a relationship may have her or his own sense of how the relationship should develop, it can be awkward when one partner wants togetherness and the other wants separation. Will it surprise you to learn that we recommend *communication* to assist with this situation? Although it doesn't always prevent this tension from arising and causing difficulty in a relationship, this is one topic couples should discuss (preferably face to face, not via text), without fear that such a discussion will wreck the romance or seem nerdy.

The notion that heterosexual women are more likely to have problems with men's assertion of autonomy than the reverse may be more a myth than a reality. As more women pursue career goals, as they continue to explore the range of options open to them, and as they enjoy fulfilling friendships, their dependence on men and the significance they attach to relationships with them have decreased (Tichenor, 2005; A Woman's Nation Changes Everything, 2009).

Power Versus Empowerment

Another source of tension is the pattern of control or *power* in a relationship. For many couples, this boils down to decision making, ranging from the simplest of things (e.g., where to eat?) to the future of the relationship. At the root of decision making is a measure of power, control, or influence over another person.

Traditional stereotypes suggest that men hold more power than women in heterosexual relationships, because of men's generally higher status in society (Kalbfleisch & Herold, 2006). But to many people, financial success confers greater power than general status in society. In many couplings, the breadwinner controls more of the decision making. However, this too is changing; financial accomplishment isn't as much of a basis for power or control as it once was. In many modern relationships, the person who manages the household, in terms of caring for children, handling food purchases and preparation, paying the bills, and generally keeping the household running smoothly is viewed as the more powerful person in the couple, because without that person's efforts, the household and structure of the family might fall apart (Boushey, 2009; O'Leary & Kornbluh, 2009).

We believe that a pattern of equality of control in a relationship, particularly a committed relationship, is the most effective for both people. This type of coupling has been termed *egalitarian*, in that partners have equal power and authority and share responsibilities equally, without regard for gender roles, income levels, job demands, and so forth (Guerrero, Andersen, & Afifi, 2013). Egalitarian relationships are characterized by *empowerment*— power *to* rather than power *over*—which involves a shared approach that capitalizes on the strengths of each partner (Amichai-Hamburger, McKenna, & Tal, 2008; Gill & Ganesh, 2007; Green, 2008).

Acceptance Versus Change

One unfortunate belief that often exists in romantic relationships is, "I can change this person. I know she or he has faults, but I can fix those faults." This is such a part of relational folklore that, even though your friends may warn you that you can't change a person, deep down inside you might be saying, "I'll be the exception; I'll be the one to do it." It may be a stereotype, but it's safe

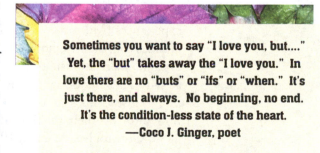

Sometimes you want to say "I love you, but...." Yet, the "but" takes away the "I love you." In love there are no "buts" or "ifs" or "when." It's just there, and always. No beginning, no end. It's the condition-less state of the heart.
—Coco J. Ginger, poet

to say that more heterosexual women declare that they will change their men than the reverse. Some straight women look at their male partners as "projects." You rarely overhear two men talking about a relationship when one friend says, "My honey has her faults, but over time, I can change them."

The importance of acceptance in a romantic relationship can hardly be overemphasized. It's a great feeling to have confidence in another person, and it's quite disconcerting when your belief in another person is lacking. Psychologist Carl Rogers (1970) based his highly successful counseling strategy on what he called "unconditional positive regard." In describing how human beings change, Rogers pointed out the paradox that real change in people seems to be possible only when a person feels completely secure and accepted in a relationship.

Comparable Views of Intimacy

One thing most people can agree on is that intimacy—however you define it—is the goal of committed romantic relationships (Andersen, Guerrero, & Jones, 2006; Burleson, 2003; Jarvis, 2009; Metts, 2006; Sanderson, Keiter, Miles, & Yopyk, 2007). Research shows that women and men often have differing views of what intimacy is and how much intimacy is desirable in a relationship (Fisher, 2009; Harvey & Weber, 2002). In fact, one partner may view a relationship as highly intimate but the other partner doesn't; at the root of this common problem may be a difference in the basic perception of what intimacy is (Gore, Cross, & Morris, 2006; Laurenceau, Barrett, & Rovine, 2005; Reis, Clark, & Holmes, 2004).

One source of basic misunderstanding arises when one partner equates intimacy with physical or sexual closeness, whereas the other believes intimacy also involves shared feelings, thoughts, and experiences (Meston & Buss, 2009; Motley, 2008a). Research over a few decades consistently shows that women and men, whether in opposite-sex or same-sex relationships, tend to have differing views of the role of sexual activity and emotional involvement in judgments of intimacy. Women more closely link emotions with sexual activity in their perceptions of how intimate their relationships are (Bailey, Gaulin, Agyei, & Gladue, 1994; Christopher & Cate, 1984; Hill, 2002; Motley, 2008b; O'Sullivan & Gaines, 1998).

The simple words "I love you" have different meanings for different people.

Shared definitions of intimacy are critical to relationship satisfaction. One way to decide on what constitutes intimacy is to use *relational currencies*— recognized and agreed-upon ways of conveying affection, information, caring, and closeness (Chapman, 2004; Wilkinson & Grill, 2011).

Expressions of Love

One of the clearest expressions of a desire to move a relationship to a more intimate level is saying the words "I love you," but these words have different meanings for different people (Migerode & Hooghe, 2012). So, expressing love can be seen as a relational tension.

Who is more likely to express love and under what circumstances? Contrary to romance novels, movies, and stereotypes, which tend to cast women as the first to say "I love you," research shows that heterosexual men more often declare their love before their female partners do (Booth-Butterfield & Trotta, 1994; Brantley, Knox, & Zusman, 2002; Brehm, 2001; Metts, 2006; Owen, 1987).

Communication scholars Dainton, Stafford, and Canary (1994) found that saying "I love you" was positively associated with long-term love, along with assuring the other person of feelings, keeping a positive outlook, being patient and forgiving, being cooperative during disagreements, and avoiding criticism. Another difficult issue in all relationships concerns whether you'll hear "I love you, too" in response to a declaration of love. Not having the sentiment reciprocated may signal an imbalance of emotion or level of commitment in a relationship (Blomquist & Giuliano, 2012).

Making a Commitment

Commitment involves the decision to stay in a relationship, but it also implies a coordinated view of the future of the relationship. In many ways, being in a relationship is largely a coordination problem—a meshing of the language, gestures, and habits of daily life, primarily through attentiveness, courtesy, and a mutual desire to make the relationship work.

Commitment also represents a level of seriousness about one's relational partner and a deeper level of regard and intimacy (Pytlak, Zerega, & Houser, 2015). Achieving a matched or equal level of commitment within romantic relationships appears to be related to how well couples handle *turning points*—critical moments in the life of a relationship that alter the relationship in some way (Baxter & Pittman, 2001; Graham, 1997; Mongeau, Serewicz, Henningsen, & Davis, 2006).

An important communication element related to this tension of commitment has been termed *relational talk,* or conversation about the relationship itself (Acitelli, 1988, 1992, 2002, 2008; Knobloch, Solomon, & Theiss, 2006; Thiess & Nagy, 2013). Research shows that more mature relationships with higher levels of commitment involve a greater amount of this form of communication (Crawford, Feng, Fischer, & Diana, 2003; Knobloch & Theiss, 2011). Relational talk and commitment feed off each other; positive relational talk increases commitment, which increases positive relational talk, and so on.

The long-standing stereotype about commitment suggests that women are more willing to commit than men. Do you think the stereotype holds true in relationships today? Are men just as likely as women to desire a committed relationship and work to maintain one? Extending the stereotype a bit, does this mean that lesbian partners are more likely to commit to each other and sustain that commitment than gay male couples?

Research is limited on this topic; one study found that gay men's commitment to their romantic relationship was more related to such intangibles as time and effort expended in the relationship and the level of disclosure beween partners, whereas straight men's commitment was more tied to tangible or measurable elements, like possessions and money

If women are more willing to commit than men, are lesbian partners more likely to commit than gay male couples?

(Lehmiller, 2010). Given that the Supreme Court ruled in support of gay marriage in 2015, we'll no doubt have more research on the commitment levels of lesbian, gay, and transgender couples.

TALKING ABOUT COMMUNICATION, OR COMMUNICATING ABOUT TALKING

Not surprisingly, highly satisfied couples communicate more than less satisfied couples (Burleson & Denton, 1997; Richmond, 1995; Teichner & Farnden-Lyster, 1997). Every relationship develops its own communication patterns, which generate predictability and security in the relationship (Driver, Tabares, Shapiro, Nahm, & Gottman, 2003; Koesten, 2004; Waite Miller, 2011). Communication patterns are especially critical in first marriages, because the patterns of each spouse's family of origin tend to be incorporated into the new marriage (sometimes causing conflict), spouses' interaction patterns often reflect sex differences, and these patterns tend to change over the developmental stages of a family, as affected by peers and culture (Galvin & Bylund, 2001).

In relationships of any kind, but especially romantic relationships, it's important to *talk about talking* or to engage in *metacommunication*. Marriage researchers and therapists have researched the value of this type of conversation and have found significant increases in marital satisfaction for couples who talk openly about their communication patterns (Bodermann, 1997; Hickmon, Protinsky, & Singh, 1997; Worthington, McCullough, Shortz, & Mindes, 1995). It takes courage to sit down and carefully examine the communication patterns of your relationship, especially if the patterns engender defensiveness or are ineffective (Becker, Ellevold, & Stamp, 2008; Hocker & Wilmot, 2013).

The stereotype, backed up by research, is that women are typically the ones in romantic partnerings to raise the issue of communication, specifically discussions about communication preferences and patterns. In lesbian relationships, partners tend to share this responsibility, meaning that lesbian couples are more likely to discuss how communication functions in their relationship than heterosexuals or gay male partners (Canary & Wahba, 2006; Messman & Mikesell, 2000).

CONFLICT: THE INEVITABLE IN A RELATIONSHIP

Why do we say conflict is inevitable in a relationship? We've simply never witnessed a healthy relationship free from conflict; in fact, a relationship may achieve its apparent health because partners cope with conflict in an effective way. *Conflict* arises when two people can't agree on a way to meet their needs (Beebe, Beebe, & Ivy, 2016; Hocker & Wilmot, 2013). Needs may simply be incompatible or too few resources may exist to satisfy the needs; however, often conflict arises or intensifies because relational partners compete rather than cooperate to resolve the difference. Conflict may also arise when a transgression (breaking the spoken or unspoken rules of the relationship) is committed (Emmers-Sommer, 2003; Kelley, 2011). The more important the relationship, the greater the potential for conflict because more is at stake. To put this another way, we're less likely to get into conflicts with people who don't matter much to us.

Might as well try to drink the ocean with a spoon as argue with a lover. —Stephen King, author

It's extremely important that conflict be handled effectively because of the potential to damage the relationship, but also because of the potential for real growth to emerge (Avtgis & Rancer, 2010; Canary & Lakey, 2011; Donohue & Cai, 2014; Segrin, Hanzal, & Domschke, 2009; Vangelisti, Middleton, & Ebersole, 2013). The ability to discover negative conflict patterns in a relationship and change them toward more positive ones is

critical to long-term relationship success (Driver et al., 2003; Hocker & Wilmot, 2011; Stone, Patton, & Heen, 2011).

Are there gender differences in approaches to conflict? Studies are mixed on this issue. Research has shown that masculine people (of both sexes) are more likely to avoid conflict than feminine people; when conflict can't be avoided, men are more likely to resort to competitive, unilateral (one-sided) conflict resolution strategies (Stafford, Dutton, & Haas, 2000). Women tend not to be as comfortable as men in negotiating to resolve a conflict, preferring to defer or compromise (Babcock & Laschever, 2003; Jones & Brinkert, 2008).

Research has identified one very interesting conflict pattern in particular—the *demand–withdraw pattern* (Burrell, Kartch, Allen, & Hill, 2014; Littlejohn & Domenici, 2007; Schrodt, Witt, & Shimkowski, 2014). One partner brings up a problem, criticizes and blames the other partner for the problem, and asks for or demands a change. The other partner tries to avoid the discussion, becomes defensive against the criticism and blame, and eventually withdraws from the conflict altogether (Anderson, Umberson, & Elliott, 2004; Berns, Jacobson, & Gottman, 1999; Kelly, Fincham, & Beach, 2003). In most research on this pattern in heterosexual relationships, men are more likely to avoid conflict

The demand-withdraw pattern in conflict is common, but not effective if the goal is to resolve a conflict between romantic partners.

and women more likely to approach it; the predominant pattern is woman-demand/man-withdraw, rather than the reverse (Caughlin, Vangelisti, & Mikucki-Enyart, 2013; Klinetob & Smith, 1996). Breaking out of such a negative pattern is quite difficult, especially if this approach to conflict works well for the dominant person in the relationship.

ENDING A RELATIONSHIP

Not all relationships can be salvaged. We realize a discussion of ending relationships can be depressing, but you're probably realistic and experienced enough to know that not all relationships make it. So it's wise to consider some effective communication strategies for ending romantic relationships.

> Why do we suffer so? Why can't we just skip on with life and instantly forget the devil who has abandoned us? Because loving is the most important thing we do.
> —Helen Fisher, relationship expert, author, and anthropology professor

Who Does the Breaking Up?

Breakups can cause stress and anguish for both persons involved—and that may be the understatement of the year! Who is more likely to end a heterosexual romantic relationship? The stereotype suggests that women are more interested in relationships and, thus, suffer more than men when a relationship ends; however, that stereotype isn't supported by research. Research shows that men more often initiate relationships while women more often terminate them (Cullington, 2008; Davis, Shaver, & Vernon, 2003; Metts, 2006). Women tend to foresee a breakup sooner than men, but men tend to be more deeply affected by relationship strain and termination, sometimes with serious consequences to their physical and mental health, as well as their self-concept (Koenig Kellas & Manusov, 2003; Simon & Barrett, 2010; Slotter, Gardner, & Finkel, 2010; Sutherland, 2010).

Communicating to End a Relationship

That heading may seem strange to you, because many people *don't* communicate when they end a relationship—they just walk (or move!) away, stop taking their former partner's calls or texts, and avoid communication at all costs. Not surprisingly, we don't advocate this approach—it's a chicken's way out, in most situations. But we can imagine that, in certain rare circumstances, partners may feel the need to simply avoid the other person and the breakup conversation altogether, hoping the person will get the hint. Most of us feel lousy when we take this approach or have it taken against us.

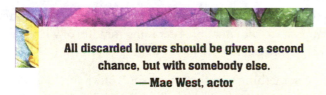

> All discarded lovers should be given a second chance, but with somebody else.
> —Mae West, actor

One study examined college students' preferred delivery method for breaking up with someone (Levine & Fitzpatrick, 2005). Of the different methods students reported using, 43 percent of breakups were accomplished through a face-to-face conversation, followed by phone calls (32%), Instant Messages (10%), e-mail messages (8%), voice mail messages (3%), written letters (2%), and using a third party, like a friend, to deliver the bad news (2%). About a third of students said that they'd used two methods in combination to get the message across, whereas some students reported using up to six different methods of delivering their bad news. (Talk about a barrage!) Surprisingly, students didn't report breaking up via text message, but some of our students have revealed that they've been broken up with via text, which made them angrier and more upset than if they'd been told to their face. Those who've gotten the "Dear John text" from someone say that the method is so rude and "chicken" that they'd never use that approach to break up with someone.

Author Kathryn Matthews (2007) calls breakups "dreaded conversations," and she offers some helpful hints for how to manage this particularly tricky form of communication. Believing that breakups should always be done in person, she suggests that relational partners avoid breaking up on a special occasion (like a holiday, birthday, or anniversary). The conversation should be held in a public location rather than a private one, but not one that's so public it's embarrassing, with no way to make a graceful exit. The person breaking up should practice what he or she wants to say ahead of time, but not so much as to sound canned or overly rehearsed. Matthews also believes that the person forcing the breakup shouldn't think of himself or herself as "the bad guy," but as someone who doesn't want to hurt others; these conversations are tough on both parties. If the person breaking up can find a genuine way to subtly praise the person they're breaking up with, that can be helpful; then time is needed to allow the other

Remember...

Commitment: Decision to stay in a relationship; a level of seriousness about one's partner

Turning Points: Critical moments in the life of a relationship that alter the relationship in some way

Relational Talk: Conversation between relational partners about the relationship itself

Metacommunication: Talking about communication; having a conversation about how one communicates, one's preferences in communicating and being communicated to, and how communication functions

Conflict: Communication that arises when people cannot agree on a way to meet their needs

Demand–Withdraw Pattern: Relational conflict pattern in which one partner raises a problem, criticizes and blames the other partner for the problem, and asks for or demands a change; the other partner tries to avoid the discussion, becomes defensive against the criticism and blame, and eventually withdraws from the conflict

person to react to the hurt and rejection. Finally, Matthews suggests adding a healthy dose of empathy to the situation, becoming mindful of what it feels like to be in each other's shoes.

Can we all agree on something? Telling a person you've just dumped "I still want to be friends" is terrible! Let that line die its overdue death. For most of us in the position of being dumped, the last thing we want to try to do, or can even conceive of, is to act like friends with our former romantic partners. A request that a relationship regress into something less intimate is understandable if you're doing the dumping, because you may genuinely want a friendship with your former romantic partner and offering friendship makes you feel as though you're easing the sting of the breakup. But it's self-serving and unreasonable to expect that someone will be able to shift relationship definitions as quickly as you'd like.

Research has examined how people communicate to renegotiate their relationships to a different level after the romantic aspect has ended (Busboom, Collins, Givertz, & Levin, 2002; Koenig Kellas, Bean, Cunningham, & Cheng, 2008; Koenig Kellas & Sato, 2011; Lambert & Hughes, 2010; Lannutti & Cameron, 2002). Sure, research on divorced couples' communication has been prevalent for decades, but research is now exploring *postdissolution relationships*, meaning situations where romantic partners (gay and straight) simply morph into a different kind of relationship, or actually agree to go back to being friends once the romance is gone. Some couples who break up still have to work together or may have the same circle of friends they're not willing to give up, so they must find a way to function even though they've broken up.

Communication scholar Rene Dailey and various colleagues study something many students (and our contemporaries) experience—the *on-again, off-again relationship* (Dailey, Hampel, & Roberts, 2010; Dailey, Jin, Pfiester, & Beck, 2011; Dailey, Middleton, & Green, 2011; Dailey, Rossetto, McCracken, Jin, & Green, 2012; Dailey, Rossetto, Pfiester, & Surra, 2009). Some people "break up to make up," and the back and forth iterations of their relationship can be dizzying to track and exhausting for the people involved, and yet they keep coming back to the same person, over and over.

The tensions we've discussed in this section are by no means *all* of the issues relational partners may have to face, but they represent some of the more prominent, common, and troublesome ones examined by research. One remaining issue connected to romantic relationships surrounds the presence of sexual activity—more specifically, how gender communication plays a significant role in a relationship that becomes sexual.

Net Notes

Transgender people in romantic relationships face unique challenges. For example, let's say that a man and woman are married, but the male spouse has always felt "in the wrong body"—which is how many transgender people describe the feeling of being one sex physically, but another sex psychologically, emotionally, etc. If the husband "comes out" as transgender and decides to start transitioning to live life as a woman, the wife may decide to remain in the marital relationship. Many spouses love the person they married, not the sex of the person they married. If these two people stay married, is this now a homosexual relationship? A trans relationship? How are they (and we) to view this relationship? What language is appropriate? This issue is morphing as we speak and we continue to learn more, so it's understandable that the language of these new relationships will need to morph as well.

Transgender romantic relational partners may need advice and counseling as they weigh their options. Even though same-sex marriage is now legal in every state in the United States, in some states it is still illegal for a transgender person to change her or his legal sex (meaning for official or legal documents). If the transgender former husband in the marriage example above lives in a state that outlaws changing one's sex for legal purposes, would the marriage become a same-sex marriage, just not "on paper"? But what if the marriage was a same-sex marriage in the first place, and one partner transitioned into a person of the opposite sex—would the marriage have to be declared something else?

Yes, this is confusing—just try being one of the transgender people we speak of or their spouses. It's important to try to understand all of this so that we can better appreciate and celebrate people's relationships, and so that the partners can better understand their relationship and each other as well. But it's even more critical when it comes to each person's legal rights, for example in the case of divorce, especially divorce made more complicated if custody of children is in play. What exactly is legal and who has what legal rights become critically important in such situations.

Thankfully, there are resources to turn to for advice and experience in such matters, with more resources being generated every day, as the transgender experience becomes more commonplace and visible. We suggest these websites as resources:

www.hrc.org: website for the Human Rights Campaign, with several articles on legal issues and ramifications, to help all sorts of couples, especially transgender couples.

www.glaad.org: website for GLAAD, the longstanding Gay and Lesbian Alliance Against Defamation, offering resources for gay, lesbian, transgender, and bisexual people. (Many college campuses in the U.S. and abroad host GLAAD chapters.)

www.transgenderlawcenter.org: This group works on securing equal rights for transgender persons by monitoring and working to change laws.

GENDER ISSUES SURROUNDING SEXUAL ACTIVITY

Passionate love is one of the most intense feelings a person can experience. It's difficult to separate considerations of passionate love from considerations of sex; Freud, in fact, believed they were one and the same (as in Hendrick & Hendrick, 2000). At the very least, the two are deeply intertwined.

As we stated earlier, romantic relationships experience a number of turning points, of which sexual intimacy is one of the most significant (Mongeau, Serewicz, Henningsen, & Davis, 2006). Thus at some point in a romantic relationship, the issue of sexual activity will probably develop (Guerrero, Andersen, & Afifi, 2013). Then the questions become, "What does sex mean to us?" and "What do we do about it?" Hendrick and Hendrick (2000) point out that for some individuals, sex without love is unthinkable, while for others sex is intrinsically good and can be an end in itself. Most couples are likely to have different meanings for sex within their relationship. The communication of a clear and mutually agreed-upon decision about what course to take is what's critical.

In Chapter 7, we explore the downside of sexual activity, specifically when sex is used as a weapon or power play. But to close this chapter, we focus on the positive side of consensual sex, in an attempt to better understand varying attitudes toward sexual activity, learn more effective ways of talking about sex with a relational partner, and develop a broader repertoire of communication behavior in dealing with problematic sexual situations.

Sexual Activity: Attitudes and Options

Many factors affect our views of sex and sexuality: cultural values, upbringing (primarily in terms of lessons our parents or other family members taught us), childhood experimentation, exposure to media, peer group influences, and self-esteem. Research shows that, at early ages, when we're first thinking about ourselves as sexual creatures, and during other stages of our development, the likelihood that we will engage in sexual activity is highly influenced by whether we perceive that our peers are having sex (Diamond, 2007; Fisher, 2004; Regnerus & Uecker, 2011).

In considering your options, it may be helpful to know what some research over a couple of decades has said about the sexes' attitudes toward sexual activity. One of the most widely cited series of studies of misperceptions of sexual interest was produced by Antonia Abbey and various colleagues (Abbey, 1982, 1987, 1991; Abbey & Melby, 1986; Abbey, Zawacki, & Buck,

2005). In her first study, opposite-sex dyads conversed for five minutes while hidden male and female subjects observed the interaction. Results indicated that, in comparison to female observers, male observers more often perceived female friendliness as seduction, made more judgments that female interactants were promiscuous, and frequently reported being sexually attracted to female interactants. Male observers also rated male interactants' behavior as sexual in nature, whereas female observers did not perceive as much sexuality in male subjects' behavior. From these results and those of other studies, Abbey contends that men are more likely to view the world through a sexual lens and to read more sexuality into

"Risky Sex"

If you had to guess which "slice" of the population was experiencing significantly increased risk, sexually speaking, who would you guess? High school teens? Tweens? College students? All those answers would be wrong. STI and HIV rates of infection have increased dramatically over the last decade for older adults, primarily aged 45 and older (Ilea et al., 2010; Kuehn, 2008; Lekas, Scrimshaw, & Siegel, 2005). Studies conducted in different countries document that middle-aged and elderly people are having unprotected sex at a rate faster than younger folks who've been warned most of their lives about sexual risks, and they are paying the price with their health (Ball, 2010; Sharples, 2008).

Although you may not want to think about it, many people feel that the ability to be sexually active longer in life is a gift! Reasons for the trend include better health information, healthier and longer life spans, Viagra and other erectile dysfunction drugs, and online dating that leads to enhanced opportunities to form relationships that become sexual (Hillman, 2007, 2008; Karlovsky, Lebed, & Mydio, 2004). However, along with the "gift" of an extended sex life may come another "gift"—a sexually transmitted infection.

Because they're no longer able to become pregnant, many older adult women don't practice safe sex, believing that they don't need protection. Older men and women alike may equate protection with birth control, not realizing they can catch and spread STIs and HIV (Lovejoy et al., 2008; Sadeghi-Nejad, Wasserman, Weidner, Richardson, & Goldmeier, 2010). Some women also hold onto the view that they developed while growing up in a different generation that condoms were only for "dirty girls," ones who slept around. Such attitudes motivate people like Jane P. Fowler (2015), Founder and Director of HIV Wisdom for Older Women, to get the word out about sexual safety.

perceptions of people's behavior than women. What's your assessment of this perspective?

Research has produced consistent findings regarding motives for engaging in sexual activity: women (of all sexual identities or orientations) are more likely to connect sex with emotional involvement, intimacy, and commitment, whereas men (of all sexual identities or orientations) more often connect sex with lust, physical gratification, and conquest (Allen, Emmers-Sommer, D'Alessio, Timmerman, Hanzal, & Korus, 2007; Meston & Buss, 2009; Peter & Valkenburg, 2010; Tolman, 2002, 2004; Voh, Catanese, & Baumeister, 2004). This doesn't mean that women don't use sex to fulfill their lustful needs or that men don't view sex as building intimacy and closeness in a relationship, but the trend persists in research. Given findings that reveal potential differences in women's and men's approaches to sexual activity in their relationships, it seems to be even more critical for relational partners to communicate openly and honestly about sex—preferably *before* they engage in it.

Women, Men, Communication, and Sex

Communicating directly about sexual activity represents a proactive approach to what can be a critical turning point in a relationship, although some people may see it as taking the romance out of the act. Interaction on sexuality is encouraged because research consistently finds that the quality of a couple's communication about sexuality is linked to the quality of their relationship, and an individual's skill in communicating about sexuality is central to successful relationships (Faulkner & Lannutti, 2010; Holmberg & Blair, 2009).

Couples who can talk effectively about sex in their relationship have higher levels of sexual satisfaction; an inability to talk about sex leads to serious problems (Byers & Demmons, 1999; LaFrance, 2010; Litzinger & Gordon, 2005; MacNeil & Byers, 2005, Menard & Offman, 2009). Honest communication is preferable to trying to read each other's minds (and nonverbal cues), or expecting sexual activity to be like it's portrayed on TV or in the movies, or taking the plunge only to discover that one's haste was a real mistake—one that may cost a relationship.

Even for people who have taken a vow of abstinence or who choose to remain celibate

It seems that talking about sex requires more intimacy than actually doing it.
—Jane Fonda, actor and political activist

even while in a romantic relationship, we advocate open and honest communication about sex—what it means, how both partners view sexual activity, and so on. But while we advocate this approach, we also recognize that most of us find this topic hard to talk about. One of the problems in conversations about sex is the fact that our language doesn't provide much help; in fact it often works against honest, serious discussion. What language can you use in a frank discussion with a partner about sex? Here are your options:

1. Clinical, scientific language, such as "You believe that sexual intercourse and oral sex should be postponed until marriage, but heavy petting of clothed genitalia is okay?"
2. Speaking in *euphemisms* (terms that serve as more comfortable alternatives for other terms), which may sound immature or condescending, as in "When I get close to you, my 'thing' reacts."
3. Using "gutter" or "street" terms for sexual acts and body parts, examples of which you're probably well aware.

Many of us are uncomfortable using clinical terms for fear we'll come off sounding like someone's therapist or a character out of *Grey's Anatomy*. Euphemisms can bring about such embarrassment or laughter that the discussion goes off-track, plus they can be extremely ambiguous (e.g., Just what "thing" are you referring to?). Gutter terms may be acceptable (even enjoyable), but are usually more appropriate once a relationship has become sexual or is further along, rather than at the beginning of development. "Street" sexual slang can make sex sound crude and unappealing, but—like everything—it depends on the person.

The sexual-help gurus, therapists, books, workshops, and courses all stress the importance of clear communication when it comes to sexual protection—protection from infection as well as pregnancy. Schools and universities are doing a better job of confronting the realities of sexuality and educating students on sexual issues than in decades past. The media, particularly film and TV, are now more realistically portraying those moments where couples have the "do you have a condom" discussion. The phrase "no glove, no love" is more prevalent now than in decades past, which shows that we're at least learning how to talk about protection, even if coarsely.

Research has explored how these conversations about sex occur (and ought to occur), particularly with regard to condom use (Bowleg, Belgrave, & Reisen, 2000; Boyle & O'Sullivan, 2010; Hadley et al., 2009; Zukoski, Harvey, & Branch, 2009). However, we still have much work to do in this area, given

In Moore and Rosenthal's (2006) study, only half of 18-year-olds reported that they would buy, carry, or talk about condoms.

research like the study conducted by psychologists Moore and Rosenthal (2006), which found that only half of 18-year-olds reported that they would buy condoms at a store, would feel comfortable carrying a condom with them, and would have a discussion with a sexual partner about condom use.

Although we, as a society, are more "on board" and aware of the importance of frank conversations about sex, that doesn't make the topic any easier to discuss. Research on college women's communication about sex shows that heterosexual women are still highly unlikely to discuss their sexual histories, ask a new partner about other or previous sex partners, explore tough but important topics like risk and protection, and share openly their sexual desires and preferences for activity (Moore & Davidson, 2005). Part of the problem is that a good deal of sexual activity, especially hookups and first-time sexual encounters, occurs between partners under the influence of alcohol or drugs—impediments to effective, clear communication (Flack et al., 2007; Krebs, Lindquist, Warner, Fisher, & Martin, 2009; Lannutti & Monahan, 2004; Meyer, 2010; Palmer, McMahon, Rounsaville, & Ball, 2010; Testa, VanZile-Tamsen, Livingston, & Buddie, 2006; Wente, 2014).

Would it surprise you to know that older adults also have difficulty talking about sex? (It likely won't surprise those of you who are nontraditional college students.) Much of the research on older, sexually active adults' conversations about sex focuses on health problems, life changes (like pregnancy and menopause), and sexual dysfunction (Badr & Carmack Taylor, 2009; Burgess, 2004; Dourado, Finamore, Barroso, Santos, & Laks, 2010; Meston & Buss, 2009). Less frequently explored is how to have healthy, open conversations about the role of sexual activity in one's relationship, how sex often changes as people age, how partners' preferences about sexual activity may have changed, and so forth. Compounding the problem, older adults may be more conservative in their upbringing and their views of sex, unused to the sexual openness that characterizes younger generations, making it harder to have a comfortable conversation about sex. And yet, if you read the Hot Button Issue box a few pages back, you understand why it's more important than ever for older, sexually active adults to have frank conversations about sex.

Given all these challenges, what do we recommend? Sorry—there's no quick, easy fix we can offer, but we have a few suggestions:

1. Realize that language is part of the problem; have metacommunication with your partner, meaning talk about talking about sex. If you have a

good laugh over how difficult it is to talk about sex without sounding clinical, nerdy, or vague, it can open the door for further discussion.

2. Technology might help this situation. Some people find that e-mailing or texting about sex is more comfortable than talking in person (Mark, 2011). (We said *texting*, not *sexting*.) Just remember that mediated communication works better as a supplement, not a substitute for face-to-face communication. Apply caution and common sense, however, because using your workplace e-mail system or work phone for sexual communication is asking for trouble (Cooper, McLoughlin, & Campbell, 2004).

3. Practice doesn't make perfect when it comes to talking about sex, but it does help. We hope we've convinced readers to try (and try again) to use their knowledge and communication skills to overcome their fears, apprehensions, and discomfort because open, honest, ongoing communication will only help you enhance your sex life and relationships.

Remember...

Postdissolutional Relationships: Situations in which romantic partners morph into a different kind of relationship, once the romance ends

On-again/Off-again Relationships: Romantic relationship in which partners break up, then make up, perhaps to break up again; repetitive partnering with the same person

Euphemisms: Terms that serve as more comfortable alternatives for other terms

CONCLUSION

No doubt, the nature of and value placed on relationships are changing. We first explored in this chapter how we learn, as children, what friendship means; we examined gender-related friendship patterns that begin in childhood and both persist and change as we progress into adolescence and adulthood.

We then explored the unique functions and characteristics of male–male friendships, as compared with female–female friendships. While these relationships are more similar than different, some aspects such as the development of intimacy and the role of self-disclosure in the relationship do differ.

Next we examined cross-sex friendship, in terms of factors that impede as well as enhance the success of this kind of friendship. We discussed the research that continues to provide insight into the friends with benefits relationship. The friendship section of this chapter closed with a discussion of issues involved in transgender friendship.

Then our discussion moved to romantic relationships—how they're initiated, maintained, deepened, and sometimes terminated.

Gender communication in love, romance, and sex is complicated by a wide range of sociological, physiological, linguistic, and relational factors. Success in these relationships is never guaranteed, but the chances for success can be increased by broadening the range of communication behaviors that you bring to these contexts.

Autonomy, change, power, commitment, intimacy, conflict—these are just some of the integral issues or tensions within a romantic relationship.

Patterns of communication within intimate relationships are particularly critical because effective patterns lead to success and feelings of satisfaction, whereas ineffective patterns lead to any number of destructive outcomes.

DISCUSSION STARTERS

1. In your experience, what forms of communication are the most critical when first making friends? What forms become more important as a friendship progresses?
2. Some researchers propose that the intimacy men achieve through doing things together is of the same quality as the intimacy achieved by women through conversation. Do you believe men and women are equally capable of forming intimate same-sex friendships? Intimate cross-sex friendships?
3. What's your view of "friends with benefits" relationships (FWBRs)? Does communication play a key role in establishing and maintaining successful FWBRs?
4. Think of an example—in your own life or the life of someone close to you—that epitomizes the tension of autonomy versus connection. If you're married or in a committed romantic relationship, was it difficult when you and your partner experienced that first rift of independence? How did you both handle it? Do you think this issue is more easily negotiated between marital partners, as compared to people who are only steadily dating?
5. Review chapter material on communication and breakups. Do the research findings about breaking up with a relational partner via text message surprise you? Or do you think more people actually break up through

a text, but tend not to be honest when asked by researchers about this breakup method? What's the best way to handle a breakup conversation if you're the one getting dumped versus the one initiating the breakup?

6. What's the best pattern of communication you've seen in a marriage? What made it effective? Did the two people involved develop this consciously or did the pattern tend to evolve out of trial and error? Should decisions be 50–50 propositions, or should different partners take the lead on different things?

7. Do you think that negotiating the sexual waters with a relational partner is a difficult communication challenge? If so, why is it that women and men may have difficulty openly discussing sexual activity in their relationships? Do you think that same-sex partners have an easier time discussing sexual activity, since they have similar physiology? What are the barriers to a successful discussion of this kind?

References

Abbey, A. (1982). Sex differences in attributions for friendly behavior: Do males misperceive females' friendliness? *Journal of Personality and Social Psychology, 42,* 830–838.

Abbey, A. (1987). Misperception of friendly behavior as sexual interest: A survey of naturally occurring incidents. *Psychology of Women Quarterly, 11,* 173–194.

Abbey, A. (1991). Misperception as an antecedent of acquaintance rape: A consequence of ambiguity in communication between men and women. In A. Parrot & L. Bechhofer (Eds.), *Acquaintance rape: The hidden crime* (pp. 96–111). New York: Wiley.

Abbey, A., & Melby, C. (1986). The effects of nonverbal cues on gender differences in perceptions of sexual interest. *Sex Roles, 15,* 283–298.

Abbey, A., Zawacki, T., & Buck, P. O. (2005). The effects of past sexual assault perpetration and alcohol consumption on reactions to women's mixed signals. *Journal of Social and Clinical Psychology, 24,* 129–157.

Acitelli, L. K. (1988). When spouses talk to each other about their relationship. *Journal of Social and Personal Relationships, 5,* 185–199.

Acitelli, L. K. (1992). Gender differences in relationship awareness and marital satisfaction among young married couples. *Personality and Social Psychology Bulletin, 18,* 102–110.

Acitelli, L. K. (2002). Relationship awareness: Crossing the bridge between cognition and communication. *Communication Theory, 12,* 92–112.

Acitelli, L. K. (2008). Knowing when to shut up: Do relationship reflections help or hurt relationship satisfaction? In J. P. Forgas & J. Fitness (Eds.), *Social relationships: Cognitive, affective, and motivational processes* (pp. 115–129). New York: Psychology Press.

Afifi, W. A., & Faulkner, S. L. (2000). On being "just friends": The frequency and impact of sexual activity in cross-sex friendships. *Journal of Social and Personal Relationships, 17,* 205–222.

Allen, M., Emmers-Sommer, T. M., D'Alessio, D., Timmerman, L., Hanzal, A., & Korus, J. (2007). The connection between the physiological and psychological reactions to sexually explicit materials: A literature summary using meta-analysis. *Communication Monographs, 74,* 541–560.

Amichai-Hamburger, Y., McKenna, K. Y. A., & Tal, S.-A. (2008). E-empowerment: Empowerment by the Internet. *Computers in Human Behavior, 24,* 1776–1789.

Andersen, P. A., Guerrero, L. K., & Jones, S. M. (2006). Nonverbal behavior in intimate interactions and intimate relationships. In V. Manusov & M. L. Patterson (Eds.), *The SAGE handbook of nonverbal communication* (pp. 259–277). Thousand Oaks, CA: Sage.

Anderson, K. L., Umberson, D., & Elliott, S. (2004). Violence and abuse in families. In A. L. Vangelisti (Ed.), *Handbook of family communication* (pp. 629–646). Mahwah, NJ: Erlbaum.

Aries, E. (2006). Sex differences in interaction: A re-examination. In K. Dindia & D. J. Canary (Eds.), *Sex differences and similarities in communication* (2nd ed., pp. 21–37). Mahwah, NJ: Erlbaum.

Avtgis, T., & Rancer, A. S. (2010). *Arguments, aggression, and conflict: New directions in theory and research.* New York: Routledge.

Babcock, L., & Laschever, S. (2003). *Women don't ask: Negotiation and the gender divide.* Princeton, NJ: Princeton University Press.

Badr, H., & Carmack Taylor, C. L. (2009). Sexual dysfunction and spousal communication in couples coping with prostate cancer. *PsychoOncology, 18,* 735–746.

Bailey, J. M., Gaulin, S., Agyei, Y., & Gladue, B. A. (1994). Effects of gender and sexual orientation on evolutionarily relevant aspects of human mating psychology. *Journal of Personality and Social Psychology, 66,* 1081–1093.

Ball, H. (2010). Death of a spouse may be associated with increased STD diagnosis among older men. *Perspectives on Sexual and Reproductive Health, 42,* 64.

Bane, C. M. H., Cornish, M., Erspamer, N., & Kampman, L. (2010). Self-disclosure through weblogs and perceptions of online and "real-life" friendships among female bloggers. *Cyberpsychology, Behavior, and Social Networking, 13,* 131–139.

Bartlett, N. H., Patterson, H. M., VanderLaan, D. P., & Vasey, P. L. (2009). The relation between women's body esteem and friendships with gay men. *Body Image, 6,* 235–241.

Baxter, L. A. (2011). *Voicing relationships: A dialogic perspective.* Thousand Oaks, CA: Sage.

Baxter, L. A., & Erbert, L. A. (2000). Perceptions of dialectical contradictions in turning points of development in heterosexual romantic relationships. *Journal of Social & Personal Relationships, 16,* 547–569.

Baxter, L. A., & Montgomery, B. M. (1996). *Relating: Dialogues and dialectics.* New York: Guilford.

Baxter, L. A., & Montgomery, B. M. (2000). Rethinking communication in personal relationships from a dialectical perspective. In K. Dindia & S. Duck (Eds.), *Communication and personal relationships* (pp. 31–53). New York: Wiley.

Baxter, L. A., & Pittman, G. (2001). Communicatively remembering turning points of relational development in heterosexual romantic relationships. *Communication Reports, 14,* 1–17.

Becker, J. A. H., Ellevold, B., & Stamp, G. H. (2008). The creation of defensiveness in social interaction II: A model of defensive communication among romantic couples. *Communication Monographs, 75,* 86–110.

Beebe, S. A., Beebe, S. J., & Ivy, D. K. (2016). *Communication: Principles for a lifetime* (6th ed.). Boston: Pearson.

Bentall, D. C. (2004). *The company you keep: The transforming power of male friendship.* Minneapolis: Augsburg Fortress Publishing.

Berns, S. B., Jacobson, N. S., & Gottman, J. M. (1999). Demand-withdraw interaction patterns between different types of batterers and their spouses. *Journal of Marital and Family Therapy, 25,* 337–348.

Bisson, M. A., & Levine, T. R. (2009). Negotiating a friends with benefits relationship. *Archives of Sexual Behavior, 38,* 66–73.

Blakemore, J. E. O., Lawton, C. A., & Vartanian, L. R. (2003). I can't wait to get married: Gender differences in drive to marry. *Sex Roles, 53,* 327–335.

Bleske-Rechek, A., & Lighthall, M. (2010). Attractiveness and rivalry in women's friendships with women. *Human Nature, 21,* 82–97.

Bleske, A. L., & Buss, D. M. (2000). Can men and women be just friends? *Personal Relationships, 7,* 131–151.

Blomquist, B. A., & Giuliano, T. A. (2012). Do you love me, too? Perceptions of responses to I love you. *North American Journal of Psychology, 14,* 407–418.

Bodermann, G. (1997). Can divorce be prevented by enhancing the coping skills of couples? *Journal of Divorce & Remarriage, 27,* 177–194.

Booth-Butterfield, M., & Trotta, M. R. (1994). Attributional patterns for expressions of love. *Communication Reports, 7,* 119–129.

Boushey, H. (2009). Women breadwinners, men unemployed. In H. Boushey & A. O'Leary (Eds.), *The Shriver report: A woman's nation changes everything.* Washington, DC: Center for American Progress.

Bowleg, L., Belgrave, F. Z., & Reisen, C. A. (2000). Gender roles, power strategies, and precautionary sexual self-efficacy: Implications for Black and Latina women's HIV/AIDS protective behaviors. *Sex Roles, 42,* 613–635.

Boyle, A. M., & O'Sullivan, L. F. (2010). General and sexual communication in established relationships: An exploration of possible links to condom use among young adults. *The Canadian Journal of Human Sexuality, 19,* 53–64.

Braithwaite, S., Aaron, S., Dowdle, K., Spjut, K., & Fincham, F. D. (2015). Does pornography consumption increase participation in friends with benefits relationships? *Sexuality & Culture, 19,* 513–532.

Brantley, A., Knox, D., & Zusman, M. E. (2002). When and why: Gender differences in saying "I love you" among college students. *College Student Journal, 36,* 614–615.

Brehm, S. S. (2001). *Intimate relationships* (3rd ed.). New York: McGraw-Hill.

Burgess, E. O. (2004). Sexuality in midlife and later life couples. In J. H. Harvey, A. Wenzel, & S. Sprecher (Eds.), *The handbook of sexuality in close relationships* (pp. 437–454). Mahwah, NJ: Erlbaum.

Burleson, B. R. (2003). The experience and effects of emotional support: What the study of cultural and gender differences can tell us about close relationships, emotion, and interpersonal communication. *Personal Relationships, 10,* 1–23.

Burleson, B. R., & Denton, W. H. (1997). The relationship between communication skill and marital satisfaction: Some moderating effects. *Journal of Marriage & the Family, 59*, 884–902.

Burns, S. M., & Lohenry, K. (2010). Cellular phone use in class: Implications for teaching and learning: A pilot study. *College Student Journal, 44*, 805–810.

Burrell, N. A., Kartch, F. F., Allen, M., & Hill, C. B. (2014). A meta-analysis of demand/withdraw interaction patterns. In N. A. Burrell, M. Allen, B. M. Gayle, & R. W. Preiss (Eds.), *Managing interpersonal conflict: Advances through meta-analysis* (pp. 297–312). New York: Routledge.

Busboom, A. L., Collins, D. M., Givertz, M. D., & Levin, L. A. (2002). Can we still be friends? Resources and romantic barriers to friendship after romantic relationship dissolution. *Personal Relationships, 9*, 215–223.

Buss, D. M. (2003). *The evolution of desire: Strategies of human mating* (Rev. ed.). New York: Basic Books.

Byers, E. S., & Demmons, S. (1999). Sexual satisfaction and sexual self-disclosure within dating relationships. *The Journal of Sex Research, 36*, 180–189.

Calterone Williams, J., & Jovanovic, J. (2015). Third Wave Feminism and emerging adult sexuality: Friends with benefits relationships. *Sexuality & Culture, 19*, 157-171.

Canary, D. J., & Lakey, S. (2011). *Strategic conflict.* New York: Routledge.

Canary, D. J., & Wahba, J. (2006). Do women work harder than men at maintaining relationships? In K. Dindia & D. J. Canary (Eds.), *Sex differences and similarities in communication* (2nd ed., pp. 359–378). Mahwah, NJ: Erlbaum.

Castaneda, D., & Burns-Glover, A. L. (2008). Women's friendships and romantic relationships. In F. L. Denmark & M. A. Paludi (Eds.), *Psychology of women: A handbook of issues and theories* (2nd ed., pp. 332–350). Westport, CT: Praeger.

Castillo, R., & Mack, A. N. (2015). Isn't that bromantic?: Rearticulating male emotionality and homosocial intimacy in Hollywood's bromcom. In A. R. Martinez & L. J. Miller (Eds.), *Gender in a transitional era: Changes and challenges* (pp. 79-96). Lanham, MD: Lexington Books.

Caughlin, J. P., Vangelisti, A. L., & Mikucki-Enyart, S. L. (2013). Conflict in dating and marital relationships. In J. G. Oetzel (Ed.), *The SAGE handbook of conflict communication* (2nd ed., pp. 161–186). Thousand Oaks, CA: Sage.

Chapman, G. (2004). *The five love languages: How to express heartfelt commitment to your mate.* Chicago: Northfield Publishing.

Chen, E. J. (2012). Caught in a bad bromance. *Texas Journal of Women and the Law, 21*, 241-266.

Chow, C. M., Roelse, H., Buhrmeister, D., & Underwood, M. K. (2011). Transformations in friend relationships across the transition into adulthood. In B. P. Larsen & W. A. Collins (Eds.), *Relationship pathways: From adolescence to young adulthood* (pp. 91-112). Thousand Oaks, CA: Sage.

Christopher, F. S., & Cate, R. M. (1984). Factors involved in premarital sexual decision-making. *The Journal of Sex Research, 20*, 363–376.

Clark, M., & Reis, H. T. (1988). Interpersonal processes in close relationships. *Annual Review of Psychology, 39*, 609–672.

Cooper, A., McLoughlin, I. P., & Campbell, K. M. (2004). Sexuality in cyberspace: Update for the 21st century. In M. S. Kimmel & R. F. Plante (Eds.), *Sexualities: Identities, behaviors, and society* (pp. 285–299). New York: Oxford University Press.

Crawford, D. W., Feng, D., Fischer, J. L., & Diana, L. K. (2003). The influence of love, equity, and alternatives on commitment in romantic relationships. *Family and Consumer Sciences Research Journal, 31*, 253–271.

Cullington, D. (2008). *Breaking up blues: A guide to survival.* New York: Routledge.

Dailey, R. M., Hampel, A. D., & Roberts, J. B. (2010). Relational maintenance in on-again/off-again relationships: An assessment of how relational maintenance, uncertainty, and commitment vary by relationship type and status. *Communication Monographs, 77*, 75–101.

Dailey, R. M., Jin, B., Pfiester, A., & Beck, G. (2011). On-again/off-again dating relationships: What keeps partners coming back? *Journal of Social Psychology, 151*, 417–440.

Dailey, R. M., Middleton, A. V., & Green, E. W. (2011). Perceived relational stability in on-again/off-again relationships. *Journal of Social & Personal Relationships, 28*, 1–25.

Dailey, R. M., Rossetto, K. R., McCracken, A. A., Jin, B., & Green, E. W. (2012). Negotiating breakups and renewals in on-again/off-again dating relationships: Traversing the transitions. *Communication Quarterly, 60*, 165–189.

Dailey, R. M., Rossetto, K. R., Pfiester, A., & Surra, C. A. (2009). A qualitative analysis of on-again/off-again romantic relationships: "It's up and down, all around." *Journal of Social & Personal Relationships, 26*, 443–466.

Dainton, M., Stafford, L., & Canary, D. (1994). Maintenance strategies and physical affection as predictors of love, liking, and satisfaction in marriage. *Communication Reports, 7*, 88–98.

Davis, D., Shaver, P. R., & Vernon, M. L. (2003). Physical, emotional, and behavioral reactions to breaking up:

The roles of gender, age, emotional involvement, and attachment style. *Personality and Social Psychology Bulletin, 29,* 871–884.

Davis, G., & Murphy, E. L. (2013). Intersex bodies as states of exception: An empirical explanation for unnecessary surgical modification. *Feminist Formations, 25,* 129-152.

Derlega, V. J., Winstead, B. A., & Greene, K. (2008). Self-disclosure and starting a close relationship. In S. Sprecher, A. Wenzel, & J. Harvey (Eds.), *Handbook of relationship initiation* (pp. 153–174). New York: Psychology Press.

Diamond, L. M. (2007). "Having a girlfriend without knowing it": Intimate friendships among adolescent sexual-minority women. In K. E. Lovaas & M. M. Jenkins (Eds.), *Sexualities and communication in everyday life: A reader* (pp. 107–115). Thousand Oaks, CA: Sage.

Dindia, K. (2002). Self-disclosure research: Knowledge through meta-analysis. In M. Allen, R. W. Preiss, B. M. Gayle, & N. A. Burrell (Eds.), *Interpersonal communication research: Advances through meta-analysis* (pp. 169–185). Mahwah, NJ: Erlbaum.

Donohue, W. A., & Cai, D. A. (2014). Interpersonal conflict: An overview. In N. A. Burrell, M. Allen, B. M. Gayle, & R. W. Preiss (Eds.), *Managing interpersonal conflict: Advances through meta-analysis* (pp. 22–41). New York: Routledge.

Dourado, M., Finamore, C., Barroso, M. F., Santos, R., & Laks, J. (2010). Sexual satisfaction in dementia: Perspectives of patients and spouses. *Sexuality and Disability, 28,* 195–203.

Driver, J., Tabares, A., Shapiro, A., Nahm, E. Y., & Gottman, J. M. (2003). Interactional patterns in marital success or failure: Gottman laboratory studies. In F. Walsh (Ed.), *Normal family processes: Growing diversity and complexity* (pp. 493–513). New York: Guilford.

Duran, R. L., Kelly, L., & Rotaru, T. (2011). Mobile phones in romantic relationships and the dialectic of autonomy versus connection. *Communication Quarterly, 59,* 19–36.

Eichenbaum, L., & Orbach, S. (2014). *Between women: Love, envy, and competition in women's friendships.* New York: CreateSpace Publishing.

Emmers-Sommer, T. M. (2003). When partners falter: Repair after a transgression. In D. J. Canary & M. Dainton (Eds.), *Maintaining relationships through communication: Relational, contextual, and cultural variations* (pp. 185–208). Mahwah, NJ: Erlbaum.

Faulkner, S. L., & Lannutti, P. J. (2010). Examining the content and outcomes of young adults' satisfying and unsatisfying conversations about sex. *Qualitative Health Research, 20,* 375–385.

Faulkner, S. L., & Ruby, P. D. (2015). Feminist identity in romantic relationships: A relational dialectics analysis of e-mail discourse as collaborative found poetry. *Women's Studies in Communication, 38,* 206–226.

Feder, E. K. (2014). *Making sense of intersex: Changing ethical perspectives in biomedicine.* Bloomington: Indiana University Press.

Fehr, B. (2004). Intimacy expectations in same-sex friendships: A prototype interaction-pattern model. *Journal of Personality and Social Psychology, 86,* 265–284.

Fehr, B. (2008). Friendship formation. In S. Sprecher, A. Wenzel, & J. Harvey (Eds.), *Handbook of relationship initiation* (pp. 29–54). New York: Psychology Press.

Fine, J. (2001, October). Intimacy. *O: The Oprah Winfrey Magazine,* 225.

Fisher, H. (2009, October). Intimacy: His & hers. *O: The Oprah Winfrey Magazine,* 138.

Fisher, T. D. (2004). Family foundations of sexuality. In J. H. Harvey, A. Wenzel, & S. Sprecher (Eds.), *The handbook of sexuality in close relationships* (pp. 385–409). Mahwah, NJ: Erlbaum.

Flack, W. F., Daubman, K. A., Caron, M. L., Asadorian, J. A., D'Aureli, N. R., Gigliotti, S. N., et al. (2007). Risk factors and consequences of unwanted sex among university students: Hooking up, alcohol, and stress response. *Journal of Interpersonal Violence, 22,* 139–157.

Foster, G. (2005). Making friends: A nonexperimental analysis of social pair formation. *Human Relations, 58,* 1443–1465.

Fowler, J. P. (2015). HIV wisdom for older women. Retrieved August 7, 2015, from <http://www.hivwisdom.org>.

Gaiba, F. (2008). Straight women and gay men friends: A qualitative study. *Dissertation Abstracts International: Section A. Humanities and Social Sciences, 69* (1–A), 262.

Galupo, M. P. (2007). Women's close friendships across sexual orientation: A comparative analysis of lesbian-heterosexual and bisexual-heterosexual women's friendships. *Sex Roles, 56,* 473–482.

Galupo, M. P. (2009). Cross-category friendship patterns: Comparison of heterosexual and sexual minority adults. *Journal of Social & Personal Relationships, 26,* 811–831.

Galvin, K. M., & Bylund, C. (2001). First marriage families: Gender and communication. In L. P. Arliss & D. E. Borisoff (Eds.), *Women and men communicating: Challenges and changes* (2nd ed., pp. 132–148). Prospect Heights, IL: Waveland.

Garfield, R. (2015). *Breaking the male code: Unlocking the power of friendship.* New York: Gotham Books.

Gill, R., & Ganesh, S. (2007). Empowerment, constraint, and the entrepreneurial self: A study of white women entrepreneurs. *Journal of Applied Communication Research, 35,* 268–293.

Goodman, E., & O'Brien, P. (2000). *I know just what you mean: The power of friendship in women's lives.* New York: Simon & Schuster.

Gore, J. S., Cross, S. E., & Morris, M. L. (2006). Let's be friends: Relational self-construal and the development of intimacy. *Personal Relationships, 13,* 83–102.

Graham, E. E. (1997). Turning points and commitment in post-divorce relationships. *Communication Monographs, 64,* 350–368.

Green, J. H. (2008). Measuring women's empowerment: Development of a model. *International Journal of Media and Cultural Politics, 4,* 369–389.

Green, K. J., & Morman, M. T. (2011). The perceived benefits of the friends with benefits relationship. *Human Communication, 14,* 327-346.

Greif, G. L. (2008). *Buddy system: Understanding men's friendships.* New York: Oxford University Press.

Greif, G. L., & Sharpe, T. L. (2010). The friendships of women: Are there differences between African-Americans and whites? *Journal of Human Behavior in the Social Environment, 20,* 791–807.

Guerrero, L. K., Andersen, P. A., & Afifi, W. A. (2013). *Close encounters: Communicating in relationships* (4th ed). Thousand Oaks, CA: Sage.

Guerrero, L. K., & Chavez, A. M. (2005). Relational maintenance in cross-sex friendships characterized by different types of romantic intent: An exploratory study. *Western Journal of Communication, 69,* 339–358.

Guerrero, L. K., & Mongeau, P. A. (2008). On becoming "more than friends": The transition from friendship to romantic relationship. In S. Sprecher, A. Wenzel, & J. Harvey (Eds.), *Handbook of relationship initiation* (pp. 175–194). New York: Psychology Press.

Gusarova, I., Fraser, V., & Alderson, K. G. (2012). A quantitative study of "friends with benefits" relationships. *Canadian Journal of Human Sexuality, 21,* 41-59.

Hadley, W., Brown, L. K., Lescano, C. M., Kell, H., Spalding, K., DiClemente, R., Donenberg, G., & Project STYLE Study Group. (2009). Parent-adolescent sexual communication: Associations of condom use with condom discussions. *AIDS and Behavior, 13,* 997–1004.

Halatsis, P., & Christakis, N. (2009). The challenge of sexual attraction within heterosexuals' cross-sex friendships. *Journal of Social & Personal Relationships, 26,* 919–937.

Hall, J. A., & Baym, N. K. (2011). Calling and texting (too much): Mobile maintenance expectations, (over)dependence, entrapment, and friendship satisfaction. *New Media & Society, 14,* 316–331.

Harvey, J. H., & Weber, A. L. (2002). *Odyssey of the heart: Close relationships in the 21st century* (2nd ed.). Mahwah, NJ: Erlbaum.

Hendrick, S. S., & Hendrick, C. (2000). Romantic love. In C. Hendrick & S. S. Hendrick (Eds.), *Close relationships: A sourcebook* (pp. 203–215). Thousand Oaks, CA: Sage.

Hickmon, W. A., Jr., Protinsky, H. O., & Singh, K. (1997). Increasing marital intimacy: Lessons from marital enrichment. *Contemporary Family Therapy: An International Journal, 19,* 581–589.

Hill, C. A. (2002). Gender, relationship stage, and sexual behavior: The importance of partner emotional investment within specific situations. *The Journal of Sex Research, 39,* 228–240.

Hillman, J. (2007). Knowledge and attitudes about HIV/AIDS among community-living older women: Reexamining issues of age and gender. *Journal of Women and Aging, 19,* 53–67.

Hillman, J. (2008). Sexual issues and aging within the context of work with older adult patients. *Professional Psychology: Research and Practice, 39,* 290–297.

Hocker, J. L., & Wilmot, W. W. (2011). Collaborative negotiation. In K. M. Galvin (Ed.), *Making connections: Readings in relational communication* (5th ed., pp. 215–222). New York: Oxford University Press.

Hocker, J. L., & Wilmot, W. (2013). *Interpersonal conflict* (9th ed.). New York: McGraw-Hill.

Holmberg, D., & Blair, K. L. (2009). Sexual desire, communication, satisfaction, and preferences of men and women in same-sex versus mixed-sex relationships. *The Journal of Sex Research, 46,* 57–66.

Hopcke, R., & Rafaty, L. (2001). *Straight women, gay men: Absolutely fabulous friendships* (2nd ed). Berkeley, CA: Wildcat Canyon Press.

Hughes, M., Morrison, K., & Asada, K. J. K. (2005). What's love got to do with it? Exploring the impact of maintenance rules, love attitudes, and network support on friends with benefits relationships. *Western Journal of Communication, 69,* 49–66.

Huling, N., Murray, C., & Houston, M. (2012). Sister-friends: Reflections on black women's communication in intra- and intercultural friendships. In A. Gonzalez, M. Houston, & V. Chen (Eds.), *Our voices: Essays in culture, ethnicity, and communication* (5th ed., pp. 85-92). New York: Oxford University Press.

Igarashi, T., Takai, J., & Yoshida, T. (2005). Gender differences in social network development via mobile phone text messages: A longitudinal study. *Journal of Social & Personal Relationships, 22*, 691–713.

Ilea, L., Echenique, M., Jean, G. S., Bustamente-Avellaneda, V., Metsch, L., Mendez-Mulet, L., Eisdorfer, C., & Sanchez-Martinez, M. (2010). Project Roadmap: Reeducating older adults in maintaining AIDS prevention: A secondary intervention for older HIV-positive adults. *AIDS Education and Prevention, 22*, 138–147.

Inman, C. (1996). Friendships among men: Closeness in the doing. In J. T. Wood (Ed.), *Gendered relationships* (pp. 95–110). Mountain View, CA: Mayfield.

Isay, R. A. (2006). *Commitment and healing: Gay men and the need for romantic love.* New York: Wiley.

Jarvis, T. (2009, January). Bridging the intimacy gap. *O: The Oprah Winfrey Magazine,* 107–108.

Jin, B., & Pena, J. F. (2010). Mobile communication in romantic relationships: Mobile phone use, relational uncertainty, love, commitment, and attachment styles. *Communication Reports, 23*, 39–51.

Johnson, F. L. (1996). Friendships among women: Closeness in dialogue. In J. T. Wood (Ed.), *Gendered relationships* (pp. 79–94). Mountain View, CA: Mayfield.

Jones, T. S., & Brinkert, R. (2008). *Conflict coaching: Conflict management strategies and skills for the individual.* Los Angeles: Sage.

Kalbfleisch, P. J., & Herold, A. L. (2006). Sex, power, and communication. In K. Dindia & D. J. Canary (Eds.), *Sex differences and similarities in communication* (2nd ed., pp. 299–318). Mahwah, NJ: Erlbaum.

Kalmijn, M. (2002). Sex segregation of friendship networks: Individual and structural determinants of having cross-sex friends. *European Sociological Review, 18*, 101–117.

Karlovsky, M., Lebed, B., & Mydio, J. H. (2004). Increasing incidence and importance of HIV/AIDS and gonorrhea among men aged over 50 years in the U.S. in the era of erectile dysfunction. *Scandinavian Journal of Urology and Nephrology, 38*, 247–252.

Kelley, D. L. (2011). Communicating forgiveness. In K. M. Galvin (Ed.), *Making connections: Readings in relational communication* (5th ed., pp. 200–211). New York: Oxford University Press.

Kelly, A. B., Fincham, F. D., & Beach, S. R. H. (2003). Communication skills in couples: A review and discussion of emerging perspectives. In J. O. Greene & B. R. Burleson (Eds.), *Handbook of communication and social interaction skills* (pp. 723–752). Mahwah, NJ: Erlbaum.

Klinetob, N. A., & Smith, D. A. (1996). Demand withdraw communication in marital interaction: Tests of interpersonal contingency and gender role hypotheses. *Journal of Marriage & the Family, 58*, 945–957.

Knobloch, J. K., Solomon, D. H., & Theiss, J. A. (2006). The role of intimacy in the production and perception of relationship talk within courtship. *Communication Research, 33*, 211–241.

Knobloch, J. K., & Theiss, J. A. (2011). Relational uncertainty and relationship talk within courtship: A longitudinal actor-partner interdependence model. *Communication Monographs, 78*, 3–26.

Koenig Kellas, J., Bean, D., Cunningham, C., & Cheng, K.Y. (2008). The ex-files: Trajectories, turning points, and adjustment in the development of post-dissolutional relationships. *Journal of Social & Personal Relationships, 25*, 23–50.

Koenig Kellas, J., & Manusov, V. (2003). What's in a story? The relationship between narrative completeness and adjustment to relationship dissolution. *Journal of Social & Personal Relationships, 20*, 285–307.

Koenig Kellas, J., & Sato, S. (2011). "The worst part is, we don't even talk anymore": Post-dissolutional communication in break-up stories. In K.M. Galvin (Ed.), *Making connections: Readings in relational communication* (5th ed., pp. 297–309). New York: Oxford University Press.

Koesten, J. (2004). Family communication patterns, sex of subject, and communication competence. *Communication Monographs, 71*, 226–244.

Krebs, C. P., Lindquist, C. H., Warner, T. D., Fisher, B. S., & Martin, S. L. (2009). College women's experiences with physically forced, alcohol- or other drug-enabled and drug-facilitated sexual assault before and since entering college. *Journal of American College Health, 57*, 639–649.

Kuehn, B. M. (2008). Time for "the talk"—again: Seniors need information on sexual health. *Journal of the American Medical Association, 300*, 1285–1287.

LaFrance, B. H. (2010). Predicting sexual satisfaction in interpersonal relationships. *Southern Communication Journal, 75*, 195–214.

Lambert, A. N., & Hughes, P. C. (2010). The influence of goodwill, secure attachment, and positively toned disengagement strategy on reports of communication satisfaction in non-marital post-dissolution relationships. *Communication Research Reports, 27*, 171–183.

Lannutti, P. J., & Cameron, K. A. (2002). Beyond the breakup: Heterosexual and homosexual post-dissolutional relationships. *Communication Quarterly, 50*, 153–170.

Lannutti, P. J., & Monahan, J. L. (2004). "Not now, maybe later": The influence of relationship type, request persistence, and alcohol consumption on women's refusal strategies. *Communication Studies, 55*, 362–378.

Laurenceau, J.-P., Barrett, L. F., & Rovine, M. J. (2005). The interpersonal process model of intimacy in marriage: A daily-diary and multilevel modeling approach. *Journal of Family Psychology, 19*, 314–323.

Lehmiller, J. J. (2010). Differences in relationship investments between gay and heterosexual men. *Journal of Personal Relationships, 17*, 82–96.

Lekas, H.-M., Scrimshaw, E., & Siegel, K. (2005). Pathways to HIV testing among adults aged fifty and older with HIV/AIDS. *AIDS Care, 17*, 674–682.

Levine, T., & Fitzpatrick, S. L. (2005, May). *You know why, the question is how? Relationships between reasons and methods in romantic breakups.* Paper presented at the meeting of the International Communication Association, New York City, NY.

Littlejohn, S. W., & Domenici, K. (2007). *Communication, conflict and the management of difference.* Long Grove, IL: Waveland.

Litzinger, S., & Gordon, K. C. (2005). Exploring relationships among communication, sexual satisfaction, and marital satisfaction. *Journal of Sex and Marital Therapy, 31*, 409–424.

Lovejoy, T. I., Heckman, T. G., Sikkema, K. J., Hansen, N. B., Kochman, A., Suhr, J. A., Garske, J. P., & Johnson, C. J. (2008). Patterns and correlates of sexual activity and condom use behavior in persons 50-plus years of age living with HIV/AIDS. *AIDS and Behavior, 12*, 943–956.

Maccoby, E. E. (1998). *The two sexes: Growing up apart, coming together.* Cambridge, MA: Harvard University Press.

MacNeil, S., & Byers, E. S. (2005). Dyadic assessment of sexual self-disclosure and sexual satisfaction in heterosexual dating couples. *Journal of Social & Personal Relationships, 22*, 169–181.

Mark, K. (2011, February 28). How to talk about sex. Retrieved March 5, 2011, from <http://www.goodinbed.com>.

Martin, R. (1997). "Girls don't talk about garages!" Perceptions of conversations in same- and cross-sex friendships. *Personal Relationships, 4*, 115–130.

Matthews, K. (2007, August). The Dear John talk and other dreaded conversations. *O: The Oprah Winfrey Magazine*, 144–146.

McGinty, K., Knox, D., & Zusman, M. E. (2007). Friends with benefits: Women want "friends," men want "benefits." *College Student Journal, 41*, 1128–1131.

Menard, A. D., & Offman, A. (2009). The interrelationships between sexual self-esteem, sexual assertiveness, and sexual satisfaction. *The Canadian Journal of Human Sexuality, 18*, 35–45.

Messman, S. J., Canary, D. J., & Hause, K. S. (2000). Motives to remain platonic, equity, and the use of maintenance strategies in opposite-sex friendships. *Journal of Social & Personal Relationships, 17*, 67–94.

Messman, S. J., & Mikesell, R. L. (2000). Competition and interpersonal conflict in dating relationships. *Communication Reports, 13*, 21–34.

Meston, C. M., & Buss, D. M. (2009). *Why women have sex: Understanding sexual motivations—from adventure to revenge (and everything in between).* New York: Times Books/Henry Holt and Company.

Metts, S. (2006). Gendered communication in dating relationships. In B. J. Dow & J. T. Wood (Eds.), *The SAGE handbook of gender and communication* (pp. 25–40). Thousand Oaks, CA: Sage.

Meyer, A. (2010). "Too drunk to say no": Binge drinking, rape, and the *Daily Mail. Feminist Media Studies, 10*, 19–34.

Migerode, L., & Hooghe, A. (2012). "I love you." How to understand love in couple therapy? Exploring love in context. *Journal of Family Therapy, 34*, 371–386.

Miller, R. (2014). *Intimate relationships* (7th ed.). New York: McGraw-Hill.

Mongeau, P. A., Knight, K., Williams, J., Eden, J., & Shaw, C. (2013). Identifying and explicating variations among friends with benefits relationships. *Journal of Sex Research, 50*, 37–47.

Mongeau, P. A., Serewicz, M. C. M., Henningsen, M. L. M., & Davis, K. L. (2006). Sex differences in the transition to a heterosexual romantic relationship. In K. Dindia & D. J. Canary (Eds.), *Sex differences and similarities in communication* (2nd ed., pp. 337–358). Mahwah, NJ: Erlbaum.

Monsour, M. (2006). Communication and gender among adult friends. In B. J. Dow & J. T. Wood (Eds.), *The Sage handbook of gender and communication* (pp. 57–69). Thousand Oaks, CA: Sage.

Monsour, M., & Rawlins, W. K. (2014). Transitional identities and postmodern cross-gender friendships: An exploratory investigation. *Women & Language, 37*, 11–39.

Moore, N. B., & Davidson, J. K., Sr. (2005). Communicating with new sex partners: College women and questions that make a differences. In J. K. Davidson, Sr., & N. B. Moore (Eds.), *Speaking of sexuality: Interdisciplinary readings* (2nd ed., pp. 117–123). Los Angeles: Roxbury.

Moore, S., & Rosenthal, D. (2006). *Sexuality in adolescence: Current trends.* New York: Routledge.

Motley, M. T. (2008a). Unwanted escalation of sexual intimacy: Pursuing a miscommunication explanation. In M. T. Motley (Ed.), *Studies in applied interpersonal communication* (pp. 121–143). Los Angeles, CA: Sage.

Motley, M. T. (2008b). Verbal coercion to unwanted sexual intimacy: How coercion messages operate. In M. T. Motley (Ed.), *Studies in applied interpersonal communication* (pp. 185–203). Los Angeles, CA: Sage.

Motley, M. T., Faulkner, L. J., & Reeder, H. (2008). Conditions that determine the fate of friendships after unrequited romantic disclosures. In M. Motley (Ed.), *Studies in applied interpersonal communication* (pp. 27–50). Thousand Oaks, CA: Sage.

Motley, M. T., Reeder, H., & Faulkner, L. J. (2008). Behaviors that determine the fate of friendships after unrequited romantic disclosures. In M. Motley (Ed.), *Studies in applied interpersonal communication* (pp. 71–93). Thousand Oaks, CA: Sage.

Nardi, P. M. (1992). *Men's friendships.* Newbury Park, CA: Sage.

Nozick, R. (1993). Love's bond. In A. Minas (Ed.), *Gender basics: Feminist perspectives on women and men* (pp. 152–159). Belmont, CA: Wadsworth.

O'Connor, P. (1992). *Friendships between women: A critical review.* New York: Guilford.

O'Doughtery Wright, M., Norton, D. L., & Matusek, A. (2010). Predicting verbal coercion following sexual refusal during a hookup: Diverging gender patterns. *Sex Roles, 62,* 647–660.

O'Leary, A., & Kornbluh, K. (2009). Family friendly for all families. In H. Boushey & A. O'Leary (Eds.), *The Shriver report: A woman's nation changes everything.* Washington, DC: Center for American Progress.

O'Sullivan, L. F., & Gaines, M. E. (1998). Decision-making in college students' heterosexual dating relationships: Ambivalence about engaging in sexual activity. *Journal of Social & Personal Relationships, 15,* 347–363.

Owen, J., & Fincham, F. D. (2011). Effects of gender and psychosocial factors on friends with benefits relationships among young adults. *Archives of Sexual Behavior, 40,* 311-320.

Owen, J., & Fincham, F. D. (2012). Friends with benefits relationships as a start to exclusive romantic relationships. *Journal of Social and Personal Relationships, 29,* 982-996.

Owen, W. F. (1987). The verbal expression of love by women and men as a critical communication event in personal relationships. *Women's Studies in Communication, 10,* 15–24.

Paik, A. (2010). "Hookups," dating, and relationship quality: Does the type of sexual involvement matter? *Social Science Research, 39,* 739–753.

Palmer, R. S., McMahon, T. J., Rounsaville, B. J., & Ball, S. A. (2010). Coercive sexual experiences, protective behavioral strategies, alcohol expectations, and consumption among male and female college students. *Journal of Interpersonal Violence, 25,* 1563–1578.

Paul, E. L., & Hayes, K. A. (2002). The casualties of "casual" sex: A qualitative exploration of the phenomenology of college students' hookups. *Journal of Social & Personal Relationships, 19,* 639–661.

Paul, E. L., McManus, B., & Hayes, K. A. (2000). "Hookups": Characteristics and correlates of college students' spontaneous and anonymous sexual experiences. *The Journal of Sex Research, 37,* 76–88.

Pederson, J. R. (2014). Competing discourses of forgiveness: A dialogic perspective. *Communication Studies, 65,* 353–369.

Peplau, L. A. (1994). Men and women in love. In D. L. Sollie & L. A. Leslie (Eds.), *Gender, families, and close relationships* (pp. 19–49). Newbury Park, CA: Sage.

Perry, L. A. M., Turner, L. H., & Sterk, H. M. (Eds.) (1992). *Constructing and reconstructing gender: The links among communication, language, and gender.* Albany: State University of New York Press.

Peter, J., & Valkenburg, P. M. (2010). Adolescents' use of sexually explicit Internet material and sexual uncertainty: The role of involvement and gender. *Communication Monographs, 77,* 357–375.

Pinel, E. C., Long, A. E., Landau, M. J., Alexander, K., & Pyszczynski, T. (2006). Seeing I to I: A pathway to interpersonal connectedness. *Journal of Personality and Social Psychology, 90,* 243–257.

Preves, S. E. (2003). *Intersex and identity: The contested self.* Rutgers, NJ: Rutgers University Press.

Puentes, J., Knox, D., & Zusman, M. E. (2008). Participants in "friends with benefits" relationships. *College Student Journal, 42,* 176–180.

Pytlak, M. A., Zerega, L. M., & Houser, M. L. (2015). Jealousy evocation: Understanding commitment, satisfaction, and uncertainty as predictors of jealousy-evoking behaviors. *Communication Quarterly, 63,* 310–328.

Rawlins, W. K. (1992). *Friendship matters: Communication, dialectics, and the life course.* Hawthorne, NY: Aldine de Gruyter.

Rawlins, W. K. (1993). Communication in cross-sex friendships. In L. P. Arliss & D. T. Borisoff (Eds.), *Women and men communicating: Challenges and changes* (pp. 51–70). Fort Worth, TX: Harcourt, Brace, & Jovanovich.

Rawlins, W. K. (2001). Times, places, and social spaces for cross-sex friendship. In L. P. Arliss & D. E. Borisoff (Eds.), *Women and men communicating: Challenges and changes* (2nd ed., pp. 93–114). Prospect Heights, IL: Waveland.

Rawlins, W. K. (2009). *The compass of friendship: Narratives, identities, and dialogues.* Los Angeles: Sage.

Reeder, H. M. (2000). "I like you . . . as a friend": The role of attraction in cross-sex friendship. *Journal of Social & Personal Relationships, 17,* 329–348.

Reeder, H. M. (2003). The effect of gender role orientation on same- and cross-sex friendship formation. *Sex Roles, 49,* 143–152.

Regnerus, M., & Uecker, J. (2011). *Premarital sex in America: How young Americans meet, mate, and think about marrying.* New York: Oxford University Press.

Reis, H. T. (1998). Gender differences in intimacy and related behaviors: Context and process. In D. J. Canary & K. Dindia (Eds.), *Sex differences and similarities in communication* (pp. 203–231).

Reis, H. T., Clark, M. S., & Holmes, J. G. (2004). Perceived partner responsiveness as an organizing construct in the study of intimacy and closeness. In D. J. Mashek & A. Aron (Eds.), *Handbook of closeness and intimacy* (pp. 201–225). Mahwah, NJ: Erlbaum.

Richmond, V. P. (1995). Amount of communication in marital dyads as a function of dyad and individual marital satisfaction. *Communication Research Reports, 12,* 152–159.

Rogers, C. (1970). *On becoming a person.* Boston: Houghton Mifflin.

Romaine, S. (1999). *Communicating gender.* Mahwah, NJ: Erlbaum.

Rose, S. M. (2007). Enjoying the returns: Women's friendships after 50. In V. Muhlbauer & J. C. Chrisler (Eds.), *Women over 50: Psychological perspectives* (pp. 112–130). New York: Springer Science + Business Media.

Rubin, Z., Peplau, L. A., & Hill, C. T. (1980). Loving and leaving: Sex differences in romantic attachments. *Sex Roles, 6,* 821–835.

Rudick, C. K., & Golsan, K. B. (2014). Revisiting the relational communication perspective: Drawing upon relational dialectics theory to map an expanded research agenda for communication and instruction scholarship. *Western Journal of Communication, 78,* 255–273.

Rushton, J. P., & Bons, T. A. (2005). Mate choice and friendship in twins: Evidence for genetic similarity. *Psychological Science, 16,* 555–559.

Sadeghi-Nejad, H., Wasserman, M., Weidner, W., Richardson, D., & Goldmeier, D. (2010). Sexually transmitted diseases and sexual function. *Journal of Sexual Medicine, 7,* 389–413.

Sahlstein, E., & Dun, T. (2008). "I wanted time to myself and he wanted us to be together all the time": Constructing breakups as managing autonomy-connection. *Qualitative Research Reports in Communication, 9,* 37–45.

Samter, W., & Burleson, B. R. (2005). The role of communication in same-sex friendships: A comparison among African Americans, Asian Americans, and European Americans. *Communication Quarterly, 53,* 265-283.

Sanderson, C. A., Keiter, E. J., Miles, M. G., & Yopyk, D. J. A. (2007). The association between intimacy goals and plans for initiating dating relationships. *Personal Relationships, 14,* 225–243.

Schrodt, P., Witt, P. L., & Shimkowski, J. R. (2014). A meta-analytical review of the demand/withdraw pattern of interaction and its associations with individual, relational, and communicative outcomes. *Communication Monographs, 81,* 28–58.

Segrin, C., Hanzal, A., & Domschke, T. J. (2009). Accuracy and bias in newlywed couples' perceptions of conflict styles and the association with marital satisfaction. *Communication Monographs, 76,* 207–233.

Semlak, J. L., & Pearson, J. C. (2011). Big Macs/peanut butter and jelly: An exploration of dialectical contradictions experienced by the sandwich generation. *Communication Research Reports, 28,* 296–307.

Sharples, T. (2008, July 2). More midlife (and older) STDs. Retrieved March 5, 2011, from <http://www.time.com>.

Shea, E. J. (2009, September 28). Tips for successful online dating. Retrieved February 27, 2011, from <http://www.oprah.com/relationships>.

Sherrod, D. (1989). The influences of gender on same-sex friendships. In C. Hendrick (Ed.), *Close relationships* (pp. 164–186). Newbury Park, CA: Sage.

Sillars, A., Shellen, W., McIntosh, A., & Pomegranate, M. (1997). Relational characteristics of language: Elaboration and differentiation in marital conversations. *Western Journal of Communication, 61,* 403–422.

Simon, R. W., & Barrett, A. E. (2010). Nonmarital romantic relationships and mental health in early adulthood: Does the association differ for women and men? *Journal of Health and Social Behavior, 51,* 168–182.

Sinclair, I., & McCluskey, U. (1996). Invasive partners: An exploration of attachment, communication and family patterns. *Journal of Family Therapy, 18,* 61–78.

Slotter, E. B., Gardner, W. L., & Finkel, E. J. (2010). Who am I without you? The influence of romantic breakups on the self-concept. *Personality and Social Psychology Bulletin, 36,* 147–160.

Spain, D. (1992). The spatial foundations of men's friendships and men's power. In P. M. Nardi (Ed.), *Men's friendships* (pp. 59–73). Newbury Park, CA: Sage.

Stafford, L. (2003). Maintaining romantic relationships: A summary and analysis of one research program. In D. J. Canary & M. Dainton (Eds.), *Maintaining relationships through communication: Relational, contextual, and cultural variation* (pp. 51–77). Mahwah, NJ: Erlbaum.

Stafford, L., Dutton, M., & Haas, S. (2000). Measuring routine maintenance: Scale revision, sex versus gender roles, and the prediction of relational characteristics. *Communication Monographs, 67,* 306–323.

Stephenson-Abetz, J., & Holman, A. (2012). Home is where the heart is: Facebook and the negotiation of "old" and "new" during the transition to college. *Western Journal of Communication, 76,* 175–193.

Stone, D., Patton, B., & Heen, S. (2011). Difficult conversations: How to discuss what matters most. In M. Galvin (Ed.), *Making connections: Readings in relational communication* (5th ed., pp. 223–231). New York: Oxford University Press.

Strikwerda, R. A., & May, L. (1992). Male friendship and intimacy. *Hypatia, 7,* 110–125.

Sutherland, A. (2010, April). The science of heartbreak. *Women's Health,* 70.

Teichner, G., & Farnden-Lyster, R. (1997). Recently married couples' length of relationship, marital communication, relational style, and marital satisfaction. *Psychological Reports, 80,* 490.

Testa, M., VanZile-Tamsen, C., Livingston, J. A., & Buddie, A. M. (2006). The role of women's alcohol consumption in managing sexual intimacy and sexual safety motives. *Journal of Studies in Alcohol, 67,* 665–674.

Theiss, J. A., & Nagy, M. E. (2013). A relational turbulence model of partner responsiveness and relationship talk across cultures. *Western Journal of Communication, 77,* 186–209.

Thorne, B. (1994). *Gender play: Girls and boys in school.* New Brunswick, NJ: Rutgers University Press.

Tichenor, V. (2005). Maintaining men's dominance: Negotiating identity and power when she earns more. *Sex Roles, 53,* 191–205.

Tiger, L. (1969). *Men in groups.* New York: Random House.

Tillmann, L. M. (2001). *Between gay and straight: Understanding friendship across sexual orientation.* Walnut Creek, CA: AltaMira Press.

Tillmann, L. M. (2014). *In solidarity: Friendship, family, and activism beyond gay and straight.* New York: Routledge.

Tolman, D. L. (2002). *Dilemmas of desire: Teenage girls talk about sexuality.* Cambridge, MA: Harvard University Press.

Tolman, D. L. (2004). Doing desire: Adolescent girls' struggles for/with sexuality. In M. S. Kimmel & R. F. Plante (Eds.), *Sexualities: Identities, behaviors, and society* (pp. 87–99). New York: Oxford University Press.

Tracy, J. (2011). 5 best dating sites of 2011. Retrieved February 27, 2011, from <http://www.onlinedatingmagazine.com>.

Turner, L. H., & West, R. (2011). Theories of relational communication. In K. M. Galvin (Ed.), *Making connections: Readings in relational communication* (5th ed., pp. 30–45). New York: Oxford University Press.

Vangelisti, A. L., Middleton, A. V., & Ebersole, D. S. (2013). Couples' online cognitions during conflict: Links between what partners think and their relational satisfaction. *Communication Monographs, 80,* 125–149.

Veniegas, R. C., & Peplau, L. A. (1997). Power and the quality of same-sex friendships. *Psychology of Women Quarterly, 21,* 279–297.

Vogel-Bauer, S., Kalbfleisch, P. J., & Beatty, M. J. (1999). Perceived equity, satisfaction, and relational maintenance strategies in parent-adolescent dyads. *Journal of Youth and Adolescence, 287,* 27–49.

Voh, K. D., Catanese, K. R., & Baumeister, R. F. (2004). Sex in "his" versus "her" relationships. In J. H. Harvey, A. Wenzel, & S. Sprecher (Eds.), *The handbook of sexuality in close relationships* (pp. 455–474). Mahwah, NJ: Erlbaum.

Waite Miller, C. (2011). Irresolvable interpersonal conflicts: Students' perceptions of common topics, possible reasons for persistence, and communication patterns. In K. M. Galvin (Ed.), *Making connections: Readings in relational communication* (5th ed., pp. 240–247). New York: Oxford University Press.

Way, N. (2011). *Deep secrets: Boys' friendships and the crisis of connection.* Cambridge, MA: Harvard University Press.

Weger, H., & Emmett, M. C. (2009). Romantic intent, relationship uncertainty, and relationship maintenance in young adults' cross-sex friendships. *Journal of Social & Personal Relationships, 26,* 964–988.

Wente, M. (2014, March 1). Can she consent to sex after drinking? Retrieved September 15, 2014, from <www.theglobeandmail.com>.

Werking, K. J. (1994, May). *Barriers to the formation of cross-sex friendship*. Paper presented at the meeting of International Network for Personal Relationships, Iowa City, IA.

Werking, K. J. (1997a). Cross-sex friendship research as ideological practice. In S. Duck (Ed.), *Handbook of personal relationships: Theory, research, and interventions* (2nd ed., pp. 391–410). Chichester, UK: Wiley.

Werking, K. J. (1997b). *We're just good friends: Women and men in nonromantic relationships.* New York: Guilford.

Wilkinson, C. A., & Grill, L. H. (2011). Expressing affection: A vocabulary of loving messages. In K. M. Galvin (Ed.), *Making connections: Readings in relational communication* (5th ed., pp. 164–173). New York: Oxford University Press.

Wood, J. T., & Inman, C. C. (1993). In a different mode: Masculine styles of communicating closeness. *Journal of Applied Communication Research, 21,* 279–295.

Worthington, E. L., McCullough, M. E., Shortz, J. L., & Mindes, E. J. (1995). Can couples' assessment and feedback improve relationships? Assessment as a brief relationship enrichment procedure. *Journal of Counseling Psychology, 42,* 466–475.

Wright, P. (1982). Men's friendships, women's friendships, and the alleged inferiority of the latter. *Sex Roles, 8,* 1–19.

Wright, P. (1998). Toward an expanded orientation to the study of sex differences in friendships. In D. J. Canary & K. Dindia (Eds.), *Sex differences and similarities in communication* (pp. 41–63). Mahwah, NJ: Erlbaum.

Wright, P. (2006). Toward an expanded orientation to comparative study of women's and men's same-sex friendships. In K. Dindia & D.J. Canary (Eds.), *Sex differences and similarities in communication* (2nd ed., pp. 41–63). Mahwah, NJ: Erlbaum.

Zukoski, A. P., Harvey, S. M., & Branch, M. (2009). Condom use: Exploring verbal and nonverbal communication strategies among Latino and African American men and women. *AIDS Care, 21,* 1042–1049.

CHAPTER 7

POWER ABUSES IN HUMAN RELATIONSHIPS

A NON-CASE STUDY

The information in this chapter is difficult to write about, and it's going to be difficult to read. Certainly it isn't the first time you've read or heard about sexual and partner violence. But it may be the most concentrated presentation of these topics you've been assigned in college. This chapter focuses on power abuses in human relationships, the downside of interacting with others, and how communication plays a role in these situations.

Rather than start with a case study, we prefer to tell some survivors' stories in context, along with the information on each topic. Here's why: It's very hard to focus on how people abuse one another; it takes us out of our comfort zones to think or talk about it. Even when we do decide to think or talk about it, we still tend to distance ourselves from it—to view it as a social problem, a bunch of statistics, or something that happens to someone else. These are understandable reactions, but you don't really understand a problem until you put a face on it. The cases in this chapter make these issues real by putting human faces on them. Sadly, you may be able to put the face of a relative, friend, or coworker into the situations we describe. But some of you *are* those human faces—your case could be in this chapter. We hope none of you has experienced sexual or partner violence, but it's very likely some of you have, so reading this chapter may bring up unpleasant reminders for you. But perhaps you'll gain a deeper understanding of what you went through or a comparison for how you coped with your situation. If you're currently in an abusive situation, our sincere hope is that this information will help you realize that you haven't caused the abuse, you don't deserve it, and you have options.

NOT-SO-HOT TOPICS

- The communication of power in abusive situations
- The changing language of sexual assault and rape
- The prevalence of date rape and date rape drugs
- Myths about rape
- Communicating consent—the core of sexual safety
- The changing language of partner violence
- Statistics and myths about partner violence, including gay, lesbian, bisexual, and transgender partner abuse
- Battered woman syndrome, one explanation of why victims stay with abusers
- What to do and how to help

AT THE CENTER OF ABUSIVE SITUATIONS: COMMUNICATING POWER

What do sexual assault and partner (domestic) violence have in common? Like sexual harassment, neither is primarily about sex, but instead they're about power. An abuser's behavior reflects an attempt to control, influence, and/or dominate another person (Angier, 2000). The role of power is obvious in stranger rape, because a stranger must render a target powerless in order to assault. Here's how power emerges when the assaulter is someone the target knows: When sexual expectations and interests in a romantic or social situation differ, when one person's sexual intentions or desires don't match another's, then the sexual motive becomes a power motive. It becomes a case of someone getting his or her way no matter the cost or the wishes of the other person.

Another common thread in abusive situations is that they usually involve communication. Acquaintance sexual assault or rape and partner violence usually involve a context of communication that precedes the assault and sometimes follows it. Most important, full recovery from these abuses involves communication. Not talking about an experience doesn't make it go away or allow the survivor to get past it. One of the worst things a survivor can do, but something that happens frequently, is to hide in shame and guilt and not tell anyone what happened. Communication makes an experience real, which is frightening but necessary for recovery. So these abuses are things that communication people—especially people with an interest in gender communication—should study.

At its most repugnant, the belief that women must be subjugated to the wishes of men excuses slavery, violence, forced prostitution, genital mutilation, and national laws that omit rape as a crime. But it also costs many millions of girls and women control over their own bodies and lives, and continues to deny them fair access to education, health, employment, and influence within their own communities.
—Jimmy Carter, former President of the United States

CASE STUDY

An Evening Out with Annie and Kris

A communication professor was asked by a dorm resident assistant (RA) to do a workshop for about twenty residents. The discussion started informally about gender communication, but then fairly quickly turned to issues about sexual activity. The RA said that a friend of hers (whom we'll call Annie) was studying and couldn't come to the session, but had a question she was going to call in.

Annie did call in and her question was about "blue balls." She said that at the end of a date, she'd been making out with her boyfriend (whom we'll call Kris) and things went a bit further than usual, at which point she resisted. She told Kris, "You know I'm not into that; I'm not ready to do it with you yet." He got flustered, as she said was typical of him, but this time he became angry as well. Kris said Annie was responsible for him having a "permanent case of blue balls" and that she had to have sex with him or it would hurt his health. He said Annie owed it to him not to tease him, and he knew she wanted sex as much as he did.

The professor then explained that blue balls was a state of pressure, swelling, and discomfort that can develop in men as a result of arousal that doesn't consummate in ejaculation. It can cause the testicles to take on a pale blueish tint, but the condition isn't permanent, as Kris claimed. It goes away shortly, as the buildup of fluid due to arousal retreats, is absorbed, or is ejaculated via masturbation. But here's the main point the professor tried to get across to Annie: Blue balls was in no way a justification for sexual coercion or aggression. Kris had no right to make Annie feel guilty for arousing him by making out and then not giving in to his insistence on sex because of the threat of some debilitating condition. On hearing this, Annie started to cry over the phone.

There was more to the story. Annie said she felt bad about making Kris angry, she cared about him, and she didn't want to do something that would hurt him physically because she'd never heard of blue balls. She'd had sex before in a prior relationship, but wasn't ready to have sex with Kris. But it turned out that Annie did have intercourse with Kris that night. In Annie's perception, she didn't really say yes, she didn't say no—she just didn't resist when Kris started in again. But she kept saying no all the time in her head. She didn't enjoy the experience and later started to question what had happened. The relationship didn't last.

Was this a case of consensual sex or date rape? One could argue this was date rape because Annie felt coerced into sex; although she complied with Kris's desires, she didn't really consent because she kept saying no in her head. But what about Kris's point of view? Kris wasn't a mind reader. He first got a "no" to sex, but later

Annie didn't resist or say no, so he continued. Kris may have thought he was just fulfilling some male role—that it's up to the guy to make the first move and the woman to resist. Then when the man keeps pressing, the woman gives in and gets what she really wanted all along. Whose interpretation is the right one? Is there a right one?

At the core of this example, and so many like it, is the issue of consent. Communication—and the lack of it—is also central to this problem.

THE CHANGING LANGUAGE OF SEXUAL VIOLENCE

Naming or labeling something takes it out of the shadows and gives us a way to talk about experiences, especially traumatic experiences, so understanding the language surrounding sexual violence is important (Gay, 2007; Harned, 2004; Young & Maguire, 2003). Let's start with the difference between *sexual assault* and *rape*—a distinction without much difference, in our opinion (which is why we tend to use the terms interchangeably in this book).

Sexual assault is the broader term; it encompasses a range of offenses. Some definitions include unwanted sexual intercourse; others describe a range of sexual behaviors, but don't include intercourse. Definitions from the National Institute of Justice (NIJ, 2015) as well as the Bureau of Justice (2015) exclude penetration by a sexual organ (which they define exclusively as rape). According to the NIJ, sexual assault may occur without any actual contact between people. Its definition is broad enough to include exposure to exhibitionism, undesired exposure to pornography, voyeurism, and public displays of images taken in private or when the victim was unaware (such as distributing photos over the Internet without a person's knowledge or agreement).

In 2012 the Federal Bureau of Investigation changed its 83-year-old definition of rape, which was "the carnal knowledge of a female forcibly and against her will" (FBI, 2009). The FBI explained that the old definition omitted "a long list of sex offenses that are criminal in most jurisdictions, such as offenses involving oral or anal penetration, penetration with objects, and rapes of males" (FBI, Frequently Asked Questions, 2014). The new FBI definition is "penetration, no matter how slight, of the vagina or anus with any body part or object, or oral penetration by a sex organ of another person, without the consent of the victim" (FBI, Frequently Asked

Questions, 2014). Feminists and other activists view the changing FBI definition as a victory in a long-fought battle, particularly over the inclusion of oral sex, male victims, and the words "however slight" in the definition, as well as deletion of the term "forcible." In the new definition, the key issue is a person's lack of consent, not if the act was forcible (Hallett, 2012).

The word *rape* can be a *trigger word* for people who've experienced it, meaning that simply hearing the term can remind targets of the trauma they went through, sometimes making them feel victimized again. This is one of the primary reasons you hear the term *sexual assault* instead of *rape.* The impact of trigger words for our readers who have survived rape is a concern, but part of the healing process may be to call an act what it is rather than using a euphemism that can dilute or trivialize the experience. People who've experienced sexual violence tend to avoid static labels when talking about their experiences, which reveals the challenges the language presents (Young & Maguire, 2003).

Stranger rape is just what the term says—rape by a person unknown to the victim. *Date rape* (also termed *acquaintance rape*) occurs in the context of people who know each other, even if they've just met. This form occurs far more frequently than stranger rape; 80 percent of rapes are committed by someone known to the victim (Rape, Abuse, and Incest National Network, RAINN, 2015; Raphael, 2013). We spend a good deal of time in this chapter on this form, because it's the most common sexual offense college students experience. While more cases of same-sex date rape are being

©Sergei Bachlakov/Shutterstock.com

Hundreds of women and men marched during a protest against sexual assault in Vancouver, Canada, on July 7, 2014.

> I think even when life begins in that horrible situation of rape, that's something God intended to happen. —Indiana State Treasurer Richard Mourdock, while running for U.S. Senate in 2012

reported and documented, far fewer targets of date rape are male than female (National Institute of Justice, 2015; Tewksbury, 2010). Bear in mind that statistics about same-sex rape are based on *reported* cases; many cases go unreported.

Legal sources predominantly refer to people who've been sexually assaulted as *victims*. However, conversationally and in most of the research, the preferred term for people who've lived through the ordeal is *survivors*—a term that signals respect and hope (Young & Maguire, 2003). Rape also occurs among marital or committed partners (together or separated) and between people who used to be married or legally committed; these forms are usually referred to as *spousal rape* or *partner rape*. Sexual violence happens to people who identify as straight, gay, lesbian, bisexual, queer, and transgender (National Coalition of Anti-Violence Programs, 2011). Although not presently included in many category listings of targets of sexual violence, sexual assault also happens to intersex and asexual people.

FACTS ABOUT SEXUAL ASSAULT AND RAPE

According to the FBI's *Uniform Crime Report* (2013–2014), incidences of violent crime (the category that includes rape) have trended downward in recent years. Yet it's still the case that one rape occurs in the U.S. every 107 seconds, resulting in nearly 300,000 victims each year (RAINN, 2015). Native American women are two-and-a-half times more likely to be sexually assaulted than other women in this country, primarily by non-Native American men (Law, 2015).

As we said previously, remember that statistics on rape and sexual assault reflect *reported* cases; approximately 70 percent of sexual assaults are not reported to police (RAINN, 2015). Only 12 percent of college rapes get reported to law enforcement authorities (Heldman & Dirks, 2014). The crime least likely to be reported and least likely to result in a conviction in the U.S. is rape (Crawford & Unger, 2004; Koss, as in Dusky, 2003).

Determining rates of sexual assaults among college students is difficult because of underreporting (Burnett et al., 2009; Karjane, Fisher, & Cullen, 2010; Karns, 2015; Lipka, 2009). In 2015, the results of one of the most comprehensive surveys of campus sexual assault were released (Mangan, 2015). The survey was conducted by the Association of American

Universities; 27 institutions responded, which resulted in a subject pool of over 150,000 college students. Findings indicated that one in four (not the previously believed statistic of one in five) female undergraduates reported having survived sexual assault or misconduct. Less than a third of these assault survivors reported the incident to campus or local authorities, which reinforces the trend toward non-reporting of sexual violence. When asked why they didn't report their assaults, most indicated that they didn't think their experiences were serious enough to warrant reporting.

In recent years some U.S. colleges and universities have been forthcoming in documenting an increase in sexual crime on campus (Anderson, 2014; Breiding et al., 2014)—at least those institutions whose officials don't have their heads in the sand about the problem. A good deal of controversy swirled in 2014 and 2015 surrounding some prominent universities' attempts to cover up sexual crimes, downplay the problem, or discourage students from reporting sexual violence (How We're Doing, 2015; Krakauer, 2015; C. Murphy, 2015; W. Murphy, 2014, 2015; Perez-Pena & Taylor, 2014). The documentary film by Kirby Dick and Amy Ziering, *The Hunting Ground*, addresses this subject.

Due to the extent of the problem, researchers have begun to explore how much students know about sexual violence when they arrive at our campuses and how many students report knowing people involved in sexual crimes. Sorenson, Joshi, and Sivitz (2014) found that 65 percent of subjects in their study knew one or more women who were targets of sexual assault; over half of subjects reported knowing one or more men who perpetrated sexual assaults.

In January of 2014, The White House Council on Women and Girls released a report entitled *Rape and Sexual Assault: A Renewed Call to Action*. The project and resulting report were in response to the growing campus rape problem in the U.S. Here are some facts contained in the report:

1. Nearly 1 in 5 women are sexually assaulted while in college.
2. Men are also at risk; nearly 1 in 71 men are sexually assaulted during their lifetimes (many during college years).

Remember...

Sexual Assault: Wide range of victimizations, including attacks or attempted attacks involving unwanted sexual conduct

Rape: Penetration, no matter how slight, of the vagina or anus with any body part or object, or oral penetration by a sex organ of another person, without the consent of the victim

Trigger Word: Use of a term that can remind a target of past trauma, sometimes making her or him feel victimized again

Stranger Rape: Rape by a person unknown to the target

Date/Acquaintance Rape: Rape by a person who is known by the target, even if they have just met

Survivor: Term for a person who has survived sexual assault, rape, or partner violence

Spousal/Partner Rape: Rape between married or committed partners, or between people who used to be married or committed, including partners who are separated

Alcohol use increases the risk of sexual assault.

© MonkeyBusinessImages/Shutterstock.com

Net Notes

Campus sexual assault is a problem, but so is the response to sexual violence on some college and university campuses in the U.S. Many institutions do a great job of responding to, documenting, and reporting sexual violence on campus, plus offering survivors assistance. But other institutions may be in denial, have antiquated policies and approaches to handling this form of campus crime, and attempt to cover up incidents or discourage survivors from going on record with what happened to them.

Empower yourself and your campus by joining or establishing a group devoted to preventing sexual assault and rape and ensuring that reports of sexual crimes are appropriately handled. Check out: Know Your IX, **www.knowyourix.org** End Rape on Campus,
   www.endrapeoncampus.org Black Women's Blueprint,
   www.blackwomensblueprint.org

3. Dynamics of college life (e.g., drug and alcohol use) fuel the problem.
4. Most victims know their assailants.
5. The vast majority (nearly 98%) of perpetrators are male.
6. Repeat victimization is common.
7. Despite the prevalence of rape and sexual assault, many offenders are neither arrested nor prosecuted. (pp. 1–2)

The most common factors that increase the risk of sexual assault for female college students include alcohol use, sorority membership, numerous sexual partners, days of the week (more assaults occur on weekends than weekdays), and attendance at off-campus parties (National Institute of Justice, 2015). In addition, being in one's first or second year of college increases the risk; the first few months of the academic year are the highest risk periods, with more documented sexual violence occurring in fall than spring semesters (Carey, Durney, Shepardson, & Carey, 2015). Survivors who experience sexual assault and rape before entering college are at higher risk for revictimization once they become college students (Carey et al., 2015).

Blaming Oneself

Date rape situations are extremely difficult for survivors to understand and grapple with, because many people who are victimized by someone they know are especially reluctant to call what happened rape. They often call it a "bad date."

Survivors tend to blame themselves for getting into the situation in the first place, not seeing it coming, using substances that

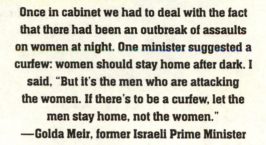

Once in cabinet we had to deal with the fact that there had been an outbreak of assaults on women at night. One minister suggested a curfew: women should stay home after dark. I said, "But it's the men who are attacking the women. If there's to be a curfew, let the men stay home, not the women."
—Golda Meir, former Israeli Prime Minister

altered their judgment or impaired their ability to resist, and being generally unable to prevent the assault. Just as the White House report showed, research over four decades consistently documents how alcohol and/or drugs are involved in most date rape situations (Abbey, Ross, McDuffie, & McAuslan, 1996; Krebs, Lindquist, Warner, Fisher, & Martin, 2009; Lannutti & Monahan, 2004; Meyer, 2010; Muehlenhard & Linton, 1987; Palmer, McMahon, Rounsaville, & Ball, 2010; Testa, VanZile-Tamsen, Livingston, & Buddie, 2006; Wente, 2014). Blaming the self is a common and understandable response to sexual assault, but such a reaction impedes the reporting and prosecuting of sex crimes, plus it rarely leads to a full recovery for the survivor.

Slip 'Em a Mickey: Date Rape Drugs

Most of you are too young to know what "slipping a Mickey" means, but it's a reference to a Mickey Finn, a substance used to involuntarily sedate someone for the purpose of assaulting or taking advantage of her or him. The old phrase "get her drunk and take advantage of her" has a twenty-first century incarnation in the form of date rape drugs.

You've probably heard or read about date rape drugs, because many universities offer programs to educate students about the problem. According to the Women's Health (2012) government website, the most commonly used, easily obtained drugs are (street names included): Rohypnol (Circles, Roofies, Roachies, La Rochas, Lunch Money, the Forget Pill); Gamma Hydroxybutyrate or GHB (Grievous Bodily Harm, Bedtime Scoop, Easy Lay, Liquid Ecstasy); and Ketamine (Black Hole, Special K, Super Acid). Rohypnol is a medication prescribed internationally for people with severe and debilitating sleep disorders. It's illegal in the United States, but continues to be smuggled in and sold as a street drug.

The Swiss-based company that manufactures Rohypnol reformulated the drug so that it releases a blue dye when dissolved in a liquid. While this is a step in the right direction, the problem is that the blue dye is difficult to detect in dark drinks and dark settings, such as bars and clubs.

"Bystander Intervention Programs: Pros & Cons"

Have you heard about bystander intervention? Similar to the push by Mothers Against Drunk Driving (MADD) and others to educate the public on the need for a designated, sober driver to accompany people when they "party," bystander intervention is friends watching out for other friends. This means having people with you socially who are aware of their surroundings, who monitor their own alcohol or drug intake, who stay vigilant of where their friends are and who they're talking to, plus how much the friends are drinking (or using), and who'll intervene if their friends are threatened or placed into unsafe situations (or if friends place themselves in unsafe situations).

Bystander intervention programs on college campuses have produced positive results; while rates of sexual assault and rape have been climbing on U.S. college campuses in recent years, rates of *reporting* sexual violence have increased, mainly due to bystander efforts (Bennett, Banyard, & Garnhart, 2014; Hust et al., 2013; Repko, 2015; White & Malkowski, 2014; Winerip, 2014). One such bystander and anti-sexual assault campaign, "It's On Us," was launched in 2014 by President Obama (Grasgreen, 2014).

So that's the "pro" side of the situation—what's the "con"? *Campus sexual violence keeps happening.* Bystander intervention has no doubt prevented a portion of sexual violence from happening. If these efforts weren't successful, we'd have an even *higher* rate of sexual violence, so these programs and individual bystanders should be applauded. But bystanding isn't enough to stop campus sexual violence from happening in the first place— we still have a huge problem.

That leads to this question: Are the people doing the assaulting and raping getting educated about these crimes? That sounds overly simplistic, but here's our question: Should it be the responsibility of people who want to go out and have a fun evening to secure a sober bystander, in the event that something bad happens or to ward off the likelihood of it happening in the first place? Does bystander intervention take the phrase "you are your brother's (sister's) keeper" too far? Or is it just a wise approach to have a friend remain vigilant so that others can party? Do bystanders exist just to help victims or to stop someone from becoming a victim of assault, or might they also stop a perpetrator from assaulting someone?

When one of these drugs is slipped into a person's drink, within twenty to thirty minutes the person will show symptoms of being sedated. Limited motion and voice production are two common effects; drugged rape survivors report feeling like they were in a daze, as though they were too heavy to move or call out. But perhaps the most devastating effect of the drug is its memory impairment. When we first began to become more aware of these drugs, the D.C. Rape Crisis Center (1998) described their effects this way: "Because survivors will have been heavily sedated, they may not have complete recall of the assault. It is likely that they will be uncertain about exactly what happened and who was involved. The unknowns may create tremendous anxiety as survivors are left to fill in the gaps with their imagination" (pp. 4–5). Some people who've been drugged have no memory of the incident; they wake up, sometimes in a hospital, to learn they've been raped, but can't remember how it happened or who raped them.

Date rape drugs are used to involuntarily sedate someone for the purpose of assaulting or taking advantage of him or her.

If you or a friend think you've been drugged because you feel dizzy or confused after drinking something, try to get to a hospital. If you believe you've been raped, crisis centers recommend that you get to a safe place and call a crisis center or 911. If you decide to report the assault to the police, don't shower, bathe, douche, urinate or defecate, brush your teeth, eat, drink, change clothes, or straighten up the area where you suspect the rape took place until medical and legal evidence is collected. Then go to a hospital or other facility where you can receive treatment for injuries, tests for STIs (and pregnancy, for female victims), an immediate urine test, and counseling. The urine test is important because GHB only stays in the system about twelve hours; however, Rohypnol can be found in urine up to seventy-two hours after ingestion, depending on a person's metabolism and the dose of the drug (D.C. Rape Crisis Center, 2006; Women's Health, 2012). The Drug-Induced Rape Prevention and Punishment Act, passed in October 1996, punishes people who commit rape by administering a controlled substance without the target's knowledge.

Who Are the Rapists?

The normal, gentle, nice-looking person sitting next to you in class could be a rapist. Does that sound paranoid or absurd? The point we're trying to make is that people capable of committing date or partner rape look just like all of us (Sela-Shayovitz, 2015). Their profiles cross racial and ethnic, class, age, sexual orientation, and religious lines. Research has isolated a number of characteristics more common among date rapists, such as the use or abuse of alcohol, athletic affiliation, fraternity affiliation, a history of family violence, and early and varied sexual experience (Crawford & Unger, 2004). But a date rapist *could be anybody.*

We don't want to make you so suspicious that you see potential rapists everywhere you look, but we do want you to realize that the "crazed man jumping out of the bushes" to rape is much more the exception than the rule. Most rapists are people you know: family members, friends of the family, neighbors, classmates, boyfriends, teachers, coworkers, bosses, doctors, lawyers, ministers.

Common Myths about Rape

Research conducted by psychologist Martha Burt (1980) generated a set of *rape myths*, beliefs people hold about rape that aren't based in fact. While these myths emerged many years ago, people still adhere

A date rapist could be anybody.

© MonkeyBusinessImages/Shutterstock.com

to them in surprising numbers today (Bonnes, 2013; Hust et al., 2013; Kahlor & Eastin, 2011; O'Hara, 2012; Vonderhaar & Carmody, 2015). In fact, acceptance of rape myths by college students, as well as reporting procedures and responses to rape, have led to descriptions of campus "rape culture" (Blaney, 2014; Buchwald, Fletcher, & Roth, 2005; Burnett et al., 2009; Dirks, 2015; Harding, 2015).

These myths include the following:

1. Women say "no" when they mean "yes" to avoid being seen as promiscuous.
2. Men must overcome women if they resist.
3. Some women deserve to be raped.
4. Some women actually enjoy rape, because it fulfills one of their sexual fantasies.
5. Some men just can't help themselves when they're aroused; they *have* to have sexual intercourse, even if they have to be aggressive to get it.
6. "Good girls" don't get raped—a myth related to prior sexual activity. A man may believe that if a woman has been sexually active, she will willingly have sex with anyone, including him. The "only virgins can be raped" myth suggests that sexually active women cannot be raped.
7. If a woman has had sex before with a man, but refuses to have sex with him again, it's not rape if he forces her. In other words, prior sexual involvement precludes an act of rape.
8. Not hearing "yes" or "no" means yes; in the absence of verbalized consent, one can infer that consent has been given.

As a next step in this research program, Burt developed the Rape Myth Acceptance Scale, an instrument that asks subjects questions about their experiences with sexual violence and determines to what level an individual accepts or believes certain

If it's a legitimate rape, the female body has ways to try to shut that whole thing down.
—Missouri State Representative Todd Akin, while running for U.S. Senate in 2012

myths about rape. Subsequent studies measuring rape myth acceptance find that men who perceive themselves as traditionally masculine, hold traditional attitudes about gender roles, are resistant to learning about sexual risk, and view feminism negatively are likely to believe in rape myths and to describe past or future aggression toward women (Good, Heppner, Hillenbrand-Gunn, & Wang, 1995; Meyer, 2010; Paul, Gray, Elhai, & Davis, 2009; Truman, Tokar, & Fischer, 1996; Yeater, Treat, Viken, & McFall, 2010). Interestingly enough, research shows that when men are asked out on dates by women—women who also pay for the date—those men have more general acceptance of rape myths than men who do the asking and paying for dates (Emmers-Sommer et al., 2010).

COMMUNICATING CONSENT: THE CORE OF SEXUAL SAFETY

If you read nothing else in this chapter, read this: *Communication is at the core of each person's sexual safety. Communicating consent is everything.*

As straightforward as it might be to say that sexual activity without consent is sexual assault, sometimes consent is hard for people to understand. Here's the most clear and direct way we can explain it:

1. You must have a person's *verbal* consent for sexual activity to be consensual.
2. If your sexual partner says "no," you don't have consent.
3. If your sexual partner says "I don't know" or "maybe," you don't have consent.
4. If your sexual partner doesn't say anything at all, you don't have consent.
5. If your sexual partner is passed out drunk, asleep, or hampered by drug use, sickness, or some other factor, that person is too incapacitated to verbally consent, so you don't have consent.
6. "Reading a vibe" of nonverbal cues that seem to convey willing participation, getting a sense that someone is "into it," and other such iffy indications of consent *constitute no consent at all.*
7. If you don't have verbal consent and you proceed with sexual activity, your actions may be construed by your partner (and the law) as sexual assault—a crime.

Here's part of what makes this issue difficult: Counter to the best advice, people usually indicate their consent to sexual activity nonverbally, rather than verbally (Beres, Herold, & Maitland, 2004; Ivy & Wahl, 2014; Kramer Bussel, 2008). From reading the chapter in this book on nonverbal communication and gender, you now know that nonverbal cues are quite often misunderstood, particularly by people in the throes of their own sexual arousal. For several decades, research on heterosexual interaction has consistently shown that men tend to interpret sexual messages from flirtatious behavior, while women tend to distinguish between behavior that is flirtatious or playful versus sexual (Abbey; 1982; Farris, Treat, Viken, & McFall, 2008; Guerrero & Floyd, 2006; Henningsen, 2004;

Koeppel, Montagne, O'Hair, & Cody, 1999; Koukounas & Letch, 2001; LaFrance, Henningsen, Oates, & Shaw, 2009).

Verbal statements of consent are required or you can't claim you have consent to any sexual activity (Beres, 2014; Hust et al., 2014; Jozkowski, Peterson, Sanders, Dennis, & Reece, 2014; Peterson & Muehlenhard, 2007; Powell, 2010). This is a tall order, we realize, because it can feel nerdy, contrived, or like a "mood breaker" to speak up and ask a sexual partner if you have consent to proceed or to tell a sexual partner to stop (Humphreys, 2004). Nerdy or awkward or not, assertive yet thoughtful communication only facilitates sexual encounters, it doesn't detract from them.

Here are two excellent tools that will help you on the consent front: First, one of the best, most realistic educational aids we've come across in years are the videos by sex education activist Laci Green. Green was a college student at Cal Berkeley in 2008 when she began posting vlogs (video blogs) on her various views about sexuality, sexual activity, how to voice consent or non-consent without sounding nerdy, rude, unsure, and so forth. The vlogs were so popular that in 2014, Green became host of MTV's first YouTube series, *Braless* (for which she won awards). On this show, Green discusses sexual consent, as well as topics like fraternity culture and slut shaming. She offers clear, realistic, and, most important, communicatively effective ways to voice consent and non-consent in sexual encounters. We encourage you to check out her excellent videos on her website, <www.lacigreen.tv> or on YouTube.

Second, two professors and a group of students at Texas Tech University created the Define Your Line program, "a student-driven campaign designed to erase the confusion and lack of communication regarding sexual consent" (Watson, 2015). Students and faculty members Rebecca Ortiz and Autumn Shafer talk to students one-on-one and give presentations to campus organizations, like fraternities and sororities (Barton, 2015; Sanoff, 2015; Terry, 2015). Educational videos on how

Net Notes

Thankfully, tons of information can be found online to help people better understand sexual assault and rape and to assist survivors. We recommend the following websites and programs:

www.rainn.org The website for Rape, Abuse, and Incest National Network, the nation's largest anti-sexual assault organization, offers an online hotline and a phone hotline, 1-800-656-HOPE.

www.ncpc.org The National Crime Prevention Council site offers current, easy-to-access information on the crimes of rape and sexual assault. The extensive section on date rape is especially useful for survivors, family members, and friends.

www.xris.com This website provides helpful information to male survivors of rape and sexual assault who are often stigmatized because of societal ignorance and denial about male victimization.

www.oneinfourusa.org This rape prevention organization educates men and women about rape, employing college students who travel and make presentations on campuses across the country.

Good consent is basically just checking in. It's paying attention to someone's body language, how they're doing. It's keep those lines of communication open so that everyone's on the same page and everyone feels safe and comfortable. —Laci Green, sex education activist

to communicate sexual boundaries and desires were created, as well as a website that offers a safe space for students to anonymously ask questions about sexual activity, and then to receive peer comments in response to their questions. For more information, check out the website, <www.defineyourline.org>.

PARTNER VIOLENCE

© Helga Esteb/Shutterstock.com

A primary commonality among the two areas discussed in this chapter is that sexual assault and rape and partner violence are both extreme abuses of power. They involve one person's attempt to control, dominate, and render powerless another person. Another commonality is privacy, meaning that most abusive episodes occur behind closed doors, not in front of witnesses. Partner violence is a bit different in that it may occur within earshot or eyeshot of children or other family members. But a closed-doors quality exists here too, in that violence in the home may be kept within the family and rarely spoken about outside the home. As you'll see from the case study below, this closed-doors quality is one of the main problems in situations of domestic violence.

> You start thinking, "What could I possibly have said to make him hit me and do this?" I didn't talk about it to anyone. To no one. Not my friends, not my family. I didn't want people looking at me and feeling sorry for me, like "There goes the victim."
> — Rihanna, singer and actor

THE CHANGING LANGUAGE OF PARTNER VIOLENCE

Family violence is probably the broadest term describing this form of abuse because it encompasses child, spousal, and elderly abuse (Hammons, 2004). Family violence can be defined as "an act carried out by one family member against another family member that causes or is intended to cause physical or emotional pain or injury to that person" (Heffernan, Shuttlesworth, & Ambrosino, 1997, p. 364). Our focus is on abuse between adults, so terms such as *domestic violence, marital abuse, spousal abuse,* and *battering* are more descriptive, but not without their problems.

CASE STUDY

Living Happily Ever After

Leah (not her real name) was an attractive woman in her mid-30s who came back to school to get her degree after her divorce. One day in gender communication class, the session focused on issues of violence and abuse. The instructor encouraged some of the students who hadn't yet entered the discussion to speak up if they had something to say or ask. At that point Leah started to tell her story, definitely putting a face to the problem.

Leah talked of her "picture perfect" courtship with her now ex-husband (whom we'll call Matt), how he had seemed like the perfect man. The couple was the envy of their friends and made their parents proud when they married. But less than a year into the marriage, when their first child was six weeks old, Leah's husband erupted during a disagreement. She didn't see it coming; she had no hints he was capable of being brutal. Before that night he'd never raised a hand to her. But it happened with her infant son just down the hall in their home.

Matt's anger was made worse by his drinking. Episodes became more frequent; many days he'd leave work early and head to a bar, drink for the rest of the afternoon, and arrive home that night in an abusive rage. A typical evening involved Matt slapping and punching Leah, yelling and calling her obscene names, and threatening to "teach her a lesson" if she left him. She learned how to cover bruises with makeup. A day or two later, Matt would show typical batterer's remorse and Leah would try to convince herself it wouldn't happen again. But it did happen again; she never knew what would trigger a violent episode. Her self-esteem plummeted; she constantly questioned herself about what she was doing wrong and what she could do better to stave off Matt's anger. She tiptoed through her life, but it seemed nothing she tried worked.

Finally, Leah contacted Matt's parents and told them what was going on. They denied that their precious son could be capable of such horrible behavior. They downplayed it, calling it a "misunderstanding," "a show of temper," and "having a bad day." They blamed Leah, saying she must have done something to make Matt act this way.

The instructor in the class, knowing that Leah was divorced, asked how Leah managed to get out of the relationship. She said, "Well, after about ten years of this, I decided—" The instructor had to interrupt because most everyone in the class was thinking, "*Ten* years?" Leah said, "Yes, I put up with it for ten years, all the while thinking it would stop." It took her another year to untangle from the relationship. She still has tremendous emotional scars from the experience, not only from Matt but from his parents as well for their role in protecting the abuser and leaving their daughter-in-law and grandchild in a life-threatening situation.

Leah experienced battered woman syndrome (discussed later in this chapter)—mixed emotions that allowed her to tolerate a terrible situation for ten years. She received a divorce and custody of their son and began putting her life back together. She told everyone in class that she would never, never again tolerate a man who tried to control her. If she stayed single the rest of her life, if she never had another romantic relationship with a man, that was fine. She hoped she might meet someone wonderful and was open to the possibility, but she didn't feel less of a woman because she wasn't in a relationship or marriage.

Net Notes

Parents are often the last to know if their daughter or son is experiencing violence at the hands of a boyfriend or girlfriend. Dating or courtship violence is a very real problem, one that groups across the country continue to address. One helpful resource is **www.breakthecycle.org**, the website for the national nonprofit organization whose mission is to "inspire and support young people to build healthy relationships and create a culture without abuse." We recommend their *Dating Violence 101* guide which offers an easy-to-follow, step-by-step approach to understanding a pattern of violent behavior. Another helpful resource is **www.loveisnotabuse.com**, founded by Liz Claiborne, Inc. The site offers materials and tools to help fight "the epidemic of domestic violence and dating abuse."

The U.S. Department of Justice (2014) defines *domestic violence* as "a pattern of abusive behavior in any relationship that is used by one partner to gain or maintain control over another intimate partner. Domestic violence can be physical, sexual, emotional, economic, or psychological actions or threats of actions that influence another person."

A problem some people have with this language is that the term *domestic* tends to sanitize the abuse. As feminist scholar bell hooks (2000) explains, "For too long the term 'domestic violence' has been used as a 'soft' term which suggests it emerges in an intimate context that is private and somehow less threatening, less brutal, than the violence that takes place outside the home" (p. 62). *Battering* is a term you still hear occasionally but its usage has lessened because it implies physical abuse rather than including other forms. The terms *marital* or *spousal abuse* aren't as inclusive as *intimate partner violence* because people in heterosexual, homosexual, bisexual, and transgender non-marital relationships (those who cohabitate, date, or are separated or divorced) also suffer abuse (Dutton & Goodman, 2005; Johnson, 2006).

Yet another form of abuse is *courtship violence*, also known as *dating violence* or *premarital violence* (Banyard & Cross, 2008; Helm, Baker, Berlin, & Kimura, 2015; Kaukinen, 2014). About 1.5 million high school students report experiencing physical abuse from dating partners each year in the U.S.; one in three girls experiences physical, emotional, or verbal abuse from a dating partner in the U.S.—a rate that far exceeds rates of other forms of youth violence (Love Is Respect, 2014; Teen Dating Violence Month, 2014). Research finds that almost half of U.S. female college students report being a target of violent and abusive dating behavior (Teen Dating Violence Month, 2014).

Because the previous section of the chapter focused heavily on date rape, we're going to emphasize intimate partner abuse rather than dating or courtship violence in this last section. Many of the patterns and problems inherent in intimate partner abuse apply to dating violence as well.

Intimate partner abuse is usually discussed in two forms: *physical* and *psychological.* Physical abuse ranges from a push or slap to a beating to the use of a weapon. Psychological abuse is a broad category that subsumes emotional and verbal abuse. Verbal abuse is aggressive communication; it emerges in many forms, including severe criticism, intimidation, threats, humiliation (private and public), isolation, degradation, and profanity/vulgarity (Rancer & Avtgis, 2014; Vangelisti, Maguire, Alexander, & Clark, 2007). Verbal abuse is a beginning stage for some batterers, while other verbal abusers don't escalate into physical violence (McCloskey, Lee, Berman, Noblett, & Coccaro, 2008; Olson, 2002). While psychological abuse is more harmful and long-lasting than physical abuse, in most instances, the two go hand in hand. Psychological abuse destroys self-esteem and leaves devastating emotional scars; physical abuse often leaves more than emotional scars (Crawford & Unger, 2004).

FACTS ABOUT INTIMATE PARTNER VIOLENCE

Like sexual assault, domestic violence is an underreported crime, mainly because of attitudes people hold about this form of violence, as well as embarrassment and social pressures that can be roadblocks for survivors who need help. While it's still the case that the majority of targets of abuse are female, a

Remember...

Family Violence: Act perpetrated by one family member against another family member that causes or is intended to cause physical or emotional pain or injury

Domestic Violence: Pattern of abusive behavior in any relationship; actions are used to gain or maintain power and control over an intimate partner; may include physical, sexual, emotional, economic, or psychological actions or threats of actions

Battering: Term for domestic violence that tends to imply only physical abuse rather than other forms

Intimate Partner Violence: Broadest term, which can encompass a range of violent actions occurring among married, separated, divorced, unmarried, cohabitating, homosexual, and transgender people

Courtship/Dating/Premarital Violence: Form of domestic violence that involves people who are dating or in committed romantic relationships, but who haven't yet legally formalized those relationships

Physical Abuse: Violent behavior that ranges from a push or slap to a beating to the use of a weapon

Psychological Abuse: Broad category of behavior that includes emotional and verbal abuse

growing percentage of domestic violence cases involves female abusers and male targets (Hoff, 2012; Rhymes, 2014; Schwartz, 2005).

Same-sex, bisexual, and transgender relational partners also commit and experience abuse (Ard & Makadon, 2011; Blosnich & Bossarte, 2009; Brown, 2008; Rohrbaugh, 2006). The Centers for Disease Control and Prevention (CDC), in partnership with the National Institute of Justice and the Department of Defense, conducted the National Intimate Partner and Sexual Violence Survey (NISVS) in 2010, then updated the results for 2013. The survey found that 44 percent of lesbians, 61 percent of bisexual women, 26 percent of gay men, and 37 percent of bisexual men reported experiencing intimate partner violence (CDC, NISVS, 2010, 2013). The study didn't include people identifying as transgender, but in a survey done earlier, 35 percent of people identifying as transgender reported experiencing intimate partner violence (National Institute of Justice, 2000).

Common Myths about Battering

Statistics for intimate partner violence, like those for sexual assault and rape, are much lower than the reality because so much of it goes unreported. A high degree of shame and guilt is associated with partner violence, on both the part of the batterer and the battered. But a primary reason for underreporting this crime relates to *battering myths*—outdated, nonfactual beliefs about relationships and the violence that can occur within them.

Sure relationships include arguments, but pain is not a side-effect of love.
—Tyler Oakley, YouTube and podcast personality

MYTH #1: EVERYBODY DOES IT You'd be surprised at how many people still believe that physical abuse is a normal part of a relationship. Some men still joke about their wives "asking for it," and how they need to "give the old lady a pop" and keep a woman in line by "smacking her around a bit." Only fairly recently has society begun to treat intimate partner violence as a crime and to decry those who batter their partners. Some of you are old enough to remember or have watched reruns of the greatly loved TV series *The Honeymooners*. While no physical domestic violence was portrayed on that show, Jackie Gleason's character, Ralph Cramden, used to pump his fist near his wife's face and yell, "To the moon, Alice!" Lots of us thought that bit was hilarious, but would it be hilarious now? Would it even get on the air?

MYTH #2: THE VICTIM IS TO BLAME, AGAIN Another myth about intimate partner abuse is that the person being abused deserves it or is to blame for the abuse. This parallels the blame-the-victim attitude in sexual assault, but it's probably most often heard in relation to battering (Schoellkopf, 2012; Thapar-Bjorkert & Morgan, 2010).

From time to time, as our society has continued to evolve on the issue of domestic violence, a few researchers have interviewed male batterers for their accounts of how domestic violence occurred in their homes. It's common for male abusers to describe their wives or partners as the abusers, rather than themselves, as they attempt to justify, excuse, minimize, or deny their own abusive behavior (Stamp & Sabourin, 1995). Sociologists Anderson and Umberson (2001) interviewed men in court-mandated domestic violence educational programs. These men believed they were victims of a biased judicial system and their female partners were responsible for the violence in their relationship. Researchers, psychologists, social workers, community activists, and others continue to work to find effective therapies and treatment programs for batterers and survivors (Holtrop et al., 2015; Walker, Bowen, Brown, & Sleath, 2015).

MYTH #3: ONLY THE POOR ARE ABUSIVE Some people believe that intimate partner abuse only occurs in low-income and minority families or couplings. While more abuse does occur among lower-income families in which one or both partners are unemployed, partner abuse extends across all social classes, races, and ethnicities (Activist dialogues, 2005; Bograd, 2006; Sokoloff & Dupont, 2005). One need only remember the O. J. Simpson case to be reminded that partner violence can occur within the wealthiest of households and among marriages of people from different racial groups.

ABUSED PARTNERS: HOW DO THEY STAND IT? WHY DO THEY STAY?

Explanations of the dynamic between an abuser and a target vary. Professionals who work in shelters know better than anyone the various reasons why people stay with their abusers. The Women's Shelter of South Texas provides the following information that offers insight into the thought processes of a battered person:

At first people stay because:

- They're told it won't happen again
- They remember the good times with the person and think things are getting better
- They're in love
- They think the person will grow up and change
- They think they can stop the beatings by doing the right thing
- They think jealousy will end if only they can convince the person of their love
- They think it is up to them to make the relationship work
- They're afraid of what will happen if the police get involved

Later, people stay because:

- They're in love, just a little less
- They still hope for change or that the abuser will get help
- Family and friends pressure them to stay
- They believe they're loved or needed
- They believe their abuser's promises of change and of having the life of their dreams
- They're increasingly afraid of the abuser's violence

Finally, people stay because:

- Fear: The abuser has become tremendously powerful
- The abuser threatens to kill them, their family, or their pets
- They've developed low self-esteem
- They believe no one else can love them
- They believe they can't survive alone
- They're confused and blame themselves, and think they must have done something to deserve the abuse

🍁 They feel helpless and hopeless (Nelson, 2008, p. 4B).

It's very hard for those who haven't experienced battering to understand the dynamic between abuser and abused. Important contributions in this area have been made by Lenore Walker, whose research coined the terms *learned helplessness* and *battered woman syndrome*. (While Walker's early research focused only on women who experienced partner violence, the phenomenon of "battered woman syndrome" has since been extended to apply to other profiles of survivors, like male targets and transgenders.) Walker (1979, 1984, 1993, 2006) describes battered woman syndrome as including a feeling of helplessness when battered women realize they cannot change their partners or their relationships with them. When a violent episode is followed by the batterer's guilt and begging for forgiveness, followed by acts of kindness, followed again by more brutality, battered women feel they have no way of protecting themselves or escaping. Many also fear that their partners will kill them (and possibly their children) if they leave, have their partners arrested, or attempt to get a restraining order. This is a very real fear, because many abusive husbands threaten to kill their wives if they leave. For many women, economic pressures and commitments to children heighten the perception that they can't leave the abusive relationship. This cycle creates a learned helplessness which is so overpowering that some battered women see no solution but to kill their abusers or themselves.

The phenomenon of "battered woman syndrome" includes a feeling of helplessness.

Battered woman syndrome helps us understand why people remain in abusive relationships. Abused people often believe they're so stupid, worthless, and unlovable that they deserve the anger and violent displays their partners perpetrate on them (Enander, 2010). They tear themselves down psychologically, saying things like, "If I was just prettier (thinner, sexier, younger), he wouldn't be so disgusted with me" and "If I just say and do the right things, if I become a better housekeeper and cook and mother, he won't treat me this way." If you're thinking, "How pathetic that someone could let themselves get so low," think again. Even people with the strongest of self-concepts and most optimistic of dispositions are susceptible to power abuses from ones they love.

In abusive episodes, targets tend not to panic or fly into an uncontrolled rage, but to exhibit what's been termed "frozen fright," a hysterical, emotional state of numbness or paralysis (Graham, Rawlings, & Rimini, 1988, p. 220). The most important thing is survival. When targets realize that their abuser holds power over their very lives, and when abusers allow targets to live, the targets' response is often a strange sort of gratitude. The chronic physical and psychological trauma battered people experience often leads to *posttraumatic stress disorder,* not unlike victims of catastrophes, hostage crises, or other forms of violence report.

What Do I Do? How Can I Help?

If you know someone who's in an abusive relationship, what do you do and how can you help? We don't have a great answer for you because the best answer is: It all depends. It depends on the situation, your relationship with the abuser and/or the target, and how you learn that the abuse is happening in the first place. While many of us have the instinct to just remove the victim from the situation and offer him or her a safe haven—the rush in and rescue response—that's typically not a realistic or effective approach. Another instinct is to dismiss or ignore our vibe that something is wrong. Sometimes we just don't want to get involved or don't want to snoop or get in someone's business where we don't belong. These are all understandable reactions, but not very helpful.

Here's our best advice: Watch and listen. Watch how someone behaves (nonverbal communication) and listen to how she or he talks (or is reluctant to talk). Watch and listen for differences, for behavior that's out of the norm for the person; try not to jump too quickly to the conclusion that abuse is the cause of a change in behavior. It *might* be, but then again it might not. A next step might be to ask a gentle question, like "Is everything okay with you?" A question can give someone an opening to divulge what's happening. Don't get too nosy or demand that the person tell you everything—such an approach could send the person deeper into a spiral or worsen an already bad situation. Try not to say bad things about the abuser (much as you might want to), because this often engenders defensiveness in the target. Allow the person to clue you in (if he or she can), as to what's wanted or needed, rather than asserting yourself into the situation, thinking you're taking over or doing the right thing. That approach is about *you*, not about the person you want to help. Tons of excellent resources can be easily found online, including information about programs on your campus and shelters in your community, so avail yourself of some expert local help in determining the best way to be of assistance to someone.

As you now realize, partner violence is an enormous problem that crosses boundaries of sex, gender, sexual orientation, race and ethnicity, class, educational level, age, and nationality. It's becoming less and less a silent destroyer of families and lives as survivors emerge, tell their stories, and give other abused people hope. From outsiders' perspectives, none of us can truly know the depth of despair this kind of victimization causes. We'll have to take the word of people who have experienced it—and there are far more of them than we'd like to think. The challenge is for all of us—men and women alike—to give our attention to this issue and decide what we can do about it. If you're in an abusive relationship, perhaps the information in this chapter will give you options and maybe some hope. If you know someone who's being abused, perhaps you now know more about the problem, what to do, and how to help.

Remember...

Battering Myths:
Beliefs about partner violence that aren't based in fact

Learned Helplessness: Sense that one cannot escape or protect oneself from an abusive partner, which causes self-esteem to plummet and dependency on the batterer to increase

Battered Woman Syndrome:
Condition that battered women often experience that makes them feel they cannot escape or protect themselves; a result of repeatedly going through a cycle of being battered by a partner, begged for forgiveness, extended acts of kindness, followed by more acts of brutality, and so on

Posttraumatic Stress Disorder:
Psychological stress-related disorder, characterized by nightmares, muscle tremors, cold sweats, hallucinations, and flashbacks

CONCLUSION

You're probably glad you made it through this chapter; we realize it's a drain to consider the terrible things people do to one another. It was a drain to research these topics and write about them, but we're sure you'll agree they're extremely important. We provided statistics and research findings in an effort to bring you the most relevant information possible, but we also put a face on each of these problems. Many of you were probably able to substitute a more familiar face for the people in our stories— Annie and Kris, Leah and Matt. The faces of the people who've suffered abuse are more real, more meaningful than all the statistics and research in the world.

We have to think about ways people use and abuse power in our society and across the world. Burying our heads in the sand, not wanting to believe that our fellow human beings commit such atrocities, not wanting to do anything to stop it, makes us part of the problem, not the solution. The author of this text often uses this adapted phrase, "Pick ye rebellions where ye may." Perhaps one of your own personal rebellions against injustice may be to see that sexual assault and rape and intimate partner violence never happen to you and the ones you love.

DISCUSSION STARTERS

1. Imagine that you (and an organization you belong to on campus) were asked to present a date rape awareness and prevention program on campus. Knowing what you now know about this serious problem, what would you choose to highlight in such a program? Who would be in your audience— men, women, both? Students, faculty, staff?

2. Why do you think people continue to adhere to myths about rape and battering? Are these forms of abuse just too terrible to face, so we manufacture false ideas about them? Knowing that these myths exist because somebody believes them, how can you expose and debunk them?

References

Abbey, A. (1982). Sex differences in attributions for friendly behavior: Do males misperceive females' friendliness? *Journal of Personality and Social Psychology, 42,* 830–838.

Abbey, A., Ross, L. T., McDuffie, D., & McAuslan, P. (1996). Alcohol and dating risk: Factors for sexual assault among college women. *Psychology of Women Quarterly, 20,* 147–169.

Activist dialogues: How domestic violence and child welfare systems impact women of color and their communities. (2005). Family Violence Prevention Fund. Retrieved July 15, 2010, from <http://www.endabuse.org>.

Anderson, K. L., & Umberson, D. (2001). Gendering violence: Masculinity and power in men's accounts of domestic violence. *Gender & Society, 15,* 358–380.

Anderson, N. (2014, July 1). Sex offense statistics show U.S. college reports are rising. Retrieved October 9, 2014, from <www.washingtonpost.com>.

Angier, N. (2000, June–July). Biological bull. *Ms.,* 80–82.

Ard, K. L., & Makadon, H. J. (2011). Addressing intimate partner violence in lesbian, gay, bisexual, and transgender patients. *Journal of General Internal Medicine, 26,* 930–933.

Banyard, V. L., & Cross, C. (2008). Consequences of teen dating violence: Understanding intervening variables in ecological context. *Violence Against Women, 14,* 998–1013.

Barton, K. (2015, March 23). Define Your Line campaign launched. Retrieved August 29, 2015, from <http://www.dailytoreador.com>.

Bennett, S., Banyard, V. L., & Garnhart, L. (2014). To act or not to act, that is the question? Barriers and facilitators of bystander intervention. *Journal of Interpersonal Violence, 29,* 476–496.

Beres, M. A. (2014). Rethinking the concept of consent for anti-sexual violence activism and education. *Feminism & Psychology, 24,* 373–389.

Beres, M. A., Herold, E., & Maitland, S. B. (2004). Sexual consent behaviors in same-sex relationships. *Archives of Sexual Behavior, 33,* 475–486. Cresskill, NJ: Hampton.

Blaney, B. (2014, October 2). Student group protests "rape culture" on campus. *The Dallas Morning News*, p. 2A.

Blosnich, J. R., & Bossarte, R. M. (2009). Comparisons of intimate partner violence among partners in same-sex and opposite-sex relationships in the United States. *American Journal of Public Health, 99,* 2182–2184.

Bograd, M. (2006). Strengthening domestic violence theories: Intersections of race, class, sexual orientation, and gender. In N. J. Sokoloff & C. Pratt (Eds.), *Domestic violence at the margins: Readings on race, class, gender, and culture* (pp. 25–38). Piscataway, NJ: Rutgers University Press.

Bonnes, S. (2013). Gender and racial stereotyping in rape coverage. *Feminist Media Studies, 13,* 208–277.

Breiding, M. J., Smith, S. G., Basile, K. C., Walters, M. L., Jieru, C., & Merrick, M. T. (2014). Prevalence and characteristics of sexual violence, stalking, and intimate partner violence victimization: National Intimate Partner and Sexual Violence Survey, United States, 2011. *MMWR Surveillance Summaries, 63,* 1–18.

Brown, C. (2008). Gender-role implications on same-sex intimate partner abuse. *Journal of Family Violence, 23,* 457–462.

Buchwald, E., Fletcher, P., & Roth, M. (Eds.). (2005). *Transforming a rape culture* (Rev. ed.). Minneapolis: Milkweed Editions.

Bureau of Justice. (2015). Statistical tables index. Retrieved August 24, 2015, from <http://www.bjs.gov>.

Burnett, A., Mattern, J. L., Herakova, L. L., Kahl, D. H., Jr., Tobola, C., & Bornsen, S. E. (2009). Communicating/muting date rape: A cocultural theoretical analysis of communication factors related to rape culture on a college campus. *Journal of Applied Communication Research, 37,* 465–485.

Burt, M. R. (1980). Cultural myths and supports for rape. *Journal of Personality and Social Psychology, 38,* 217–230.

Carey, K. B., Durney, S. E., Shepardson, R. L., & Carey, M. P. (2015). Incapacitated and forcible rape of college women: Prevalences across the first year. *Journal of Adolescent Health, 56,* 678–680.

Centers for Disease Control and Prevention. (2010/2013). National Intimate Partner and Sexual Violence Survey. Retrieved August 29, 2015, from <www.cdc.gov>.

Crawford, M., & Unger, R. (2004). *Women and gender: A feminist psychology* (4th ed.). New York: McGraw-Hill.

D.C. Rape Crisis Center. (1998). *Myths about rape.* Retrieved from <www.dcrcc.org>.

D.C. Rape Crisis Center. (2006). Turning anger into change. Retrieved from <www.dcrcc.org>.

Dirks, D. (2015). *Confronting campus rape: Legal landscape, new media, and networked activism. (Framing 21st century issues).* New York: Routledge.

Dusky, L. (2003, Spring). Harvard stumbles over rape reporting. *Ms.,* 39–40.

Dutton, M. A., & Goodman, L. A. (2005). Coercion in intimate partner violence: Toward a new conceptualization. *Sex Roles, 52,* 743–756.

Emmers-Sommer, T. M., Farrell, J., Gentry, A., Stevens, S., Eckstein, J., Battocletti, J., & Gardener, C. (2010). First date sexual expectations: The effects of who asked, who paid, date location, and gender. *Communication Studies, 61,* 339–355.

Enander, V. (2010). "A fool to keep staying": Battered women labeling themselves stupid as an expression of gendered shame. *Violence Against Women, 16,* 5–31.

Farris, C., Treat, T. A., Viken, R. J., & McFall, R. M. (2008). Sexual coercion and the misperception of sexual intent. *Clinical Psychology Review, 28,* 48–66.

Federal Bureau of Investigation. (2014, December 11). Frequently asked questions about the change in the UCR definition of rape. Retrieved August 23, 2015, from <http://www.fbi.gov>.

Federal Bureau of Investigation. (2013-2014). *Uniform crime report.* Retrieved August 23, 2015, from <http://www.fbi.gov>.

Federal Bureau of Investigation. (2009). *Uniform crime report.* Retrieved July 12, 2010, from <http://www.fbi.gov>.

Gay, W. C. (2007). Supplanting linguistic violence. In L. L. O'Toole, J. R. Schiffman, & M. L. Kiter Edwards (Eds.), *Gender violence: Interdisciplinary perspectives* (2nd ed., pp. 435–442). New York: New York University Press.

Good, G. E., Heppner, M. J., Hillenbrand-Gunn, T. L., & Wang, L. (1995). Sexual and psychological violence: An exploratory study of predictors in college men. *Journal of Men's Studies, 4,* 59–71.

Graham, D. L. R., Rawlings, E., & Rimini, N. (1988). Survivors of terror. In K. Yello & M. Bograd (Eds.), *Feminist perspectives on wife abuse* (pp. 217–233). Newbury Park, CA: Sage.

Grasgreen, A. (2014, September 19). White House: "It's On Us" campaign targets culture of sexual assault on campus. Retrieved September 22, 2014, from <www.politico.com>.

Guerrero, L. K., & Floyd, K. (2006). *Nonverbal communication in close relationships.* Mahwah, NJ: Erlbaum.

Hallett, S. (2012, Winter). Victory over violence: The FBI finally recognizes that "rape is rape." *Ms.*, 12–13.

Hammons, S. A. (2004). "Family violence": The language of legitimacy. *Affilia, 19*, 273–288.

Harding, K. (2015). *Asking for it: The alarming rise of rape culture—and what we can do about it.* Boston: DaCapo Lifelong Books.

Harned, M. (2004). The relationship between labeling unwanted sexual experiences and distress. *Journal of Consulting and Clinical Psychology, 72*, 1090–1099.

Harvey, J. H., & Weber, A. L. (2002). *Odyssey of the heart: Close relationships in the 21st century* (2nd ed.). Mahwah, NJ: Erlbaum.

Heffernan, J., Shuttlesworth, G., & Ambrosino, R. (1997). *Social work and social welfare* (3rd ed.). New York: West.

Heldman, C., & Dirks, D. (2014, Winter/Spring). Blowing the whistle on campus rape. *Ms.*, 32–37.

Helm, S., Baker, C. K., Berlin, J., & Kimura, S. (2015). Getting in, being in, staying in, and getting out: Adolescents' descriptions of dating and dating violence. *Youth Society.* doi: 10.1177/0044118X15575290.

Henningsen, D. D. (2004). Flirting with meaning: An examination of miscommunication in flirting interactions. *Sex Roles, 50*, 481–489.

Hoff, B. H. (2012, February 12). CDC study: More men than women victims of partner abuse. Retrieved August 29, 2015, from <www.saveservices.org>.

Holtrop, K., Scott, J. C., Parra-Cardona, J. R., Smith, S. M., Schmittel, E., & Larance, L. Y. (2015). Exploring factors that contribute to positive change in a diverse, group-based male batterer intervention program: Using qualitative data to inform implementation and adaptation efforts. *Journal of Interpersonal Violence.* doi: 10.1177/0886260515588535.

hooks, b. (2000). *Feminism is for everybody: Passionate politics.* Cambridge, MA: South End.

How we're doing: Rape denial. (2015, Spring). *Ms.*, 7.

Humphreys, T. P. (2004). Understanding sexual consent: An empirical investigation of the normative script for young heterosexual adults. In M. Cowling & P. Reynolds (Eds.), *Making sense of sexual consent* (pp. 209–227). Surrey, UK: Ashgate Publishing Ltd.

Hust, S. J. T., Lei, M., Ren, C., Chang, H., McNab, A. L., Marett, E. G., & Willoughby, J. F. (2013). The effects of sports media exposure on college students' rape myth beliefs and intentions to intervene in a sexual assault. *Mass Communication and Society, 16*, 762–786.

Hust, S. J. T., Marett, E. G., Ren, C., Adams, P. M., Willoughby, J. F., Lei, M., Ran, W., & Norman, C.

(2014). Establishing and adhering to consent: The association between reading magazines and college students' sexual consent negotiation. *Journal of Sex Research, 51*, 280–290.

Ivy, D. K., & Wahl, S. T. (2014). *Nonverbal communication for a lifetime* (2nd ed.). Dubuque, IA: Kendall Hunt.

Johnson, M. P. (2006). Gendered communication and intimate partner violence. In B. J. Dow & J. T. Wood (Eds.), *The SAGE handbook of gender and communication* (pp. 71–87). Thousand Oaks, CA: Sage.

Jozkowski, K. N., Peterson, Z. D., Sanders, S. A., Dennis, B., & Reece, M. (2014). Gender differences in heterosexual college students' conceptualizations and indicators of sexual consent: Implications for contemporary sexual assault prevention education. *Journal of Sex Research, 51*, 904–916.

Kahlor, L. A., & Eastin, M. S. (2011). Television's role in the culture of violence toward women: Cultivation of rape myth acceptance in the United States. *Journal of Broadcasting & Electronic Media, 55*, 215–231.

Karjane, H. M., Fisher, B. S., & Cullen, F. T. (2010). Sexual assault on campus: What colleges and universities are doing about it. In B. Hutchinson (Ed.), *Annual editions: Gender 10/11* (pp. 215–221). Boston: McGraw-Hill.

Karns, M. E. (2015). Reporting of sexual assault: Institutional comparisons 2013 [electronic version]. Report retrieved August 7, 2015, from Cornell University ILR.

Kaukinen, C. (2014). Dating violence among college students: The risk and protective factors. *Trauma Violence Abuse, 15*, 283–296.

Koeppel, L. B., Montagne, Y., O'Hair, D., & Cody, M. J. (1999). Friendly? Flirting? Wrong? In L. K. Guerrero, J. DeVito, & M. L. Hecht (Eds.), *The nonverbal communication reader* (pp. 290–297). Prospect Heights, IL: Waveland.

Koukounas, E., & Letch, N. M. (2001). Psychological correlates of perception of sexual intent in women. *Journal of Social Psychology, 141*, 443–456.

Krakauer, J. (2015). *Missoula: Rape and the justice system in a college town.* New York: Doubleday.

Kramer Bussel, R. (2008). Beyond yes or no: Consent as sexual process. In J. Friedman & J. Valenti (Eds.), *Yes means yes! Visions of female sexual power and a world without rape* (pp. 43–51). Berkeley, CA: Seal Press.

Krebs, C. P., Lindquist, C. H., Warner, T. D., Fisher, B. S., & Martin, S. L. (2009). College women's experiences with physically forced, alcohol- or other drug-enabled and drug-facilitated sexual assault before and since entering college. *Journal of American College Health, 57,* 639–649.

LaFrance, B. H., Henningsen, D. D., Oates, A., & Shaw, C. M. (2009). Social-sexual interactions? Meta-analyses of sex differences in perceptions of flirtatiousness, seductiveness, and promiscuousness. *Communication Monographs, 76,* 263–285.

Lannutti, P. J., & Monahan, J. L. (2004). Resistance, persistence, and drinking: Examining goals of women's refusals of unwanted sexual advances. *Western Journal of Communication, 68,* 151–169.

Law, V. (2015, Spring). Law of the land: An interview with legal scholar and MacArthur genius Sarah Deer. *Bitch, 66,* 51–53.

Lipka, S. (2009, January 30). In campus-crime reports, there's little safety in the numbers. *The Chronicle of Higher Education,* pp. A1, A15–A17.

Love Is Respect. (2014). Too common. Retrieved August 29, 2015, from <www.loveisrespect.org>.

Mangan, K. (2015, October 2). One in 4 college women faces sexual assault or misconduct. *The Chronicle of Higher Education,* p. A4.

McCloskey, S., Lee, R., Berman, M. E., Noblett, K. L., & Coccaro, E. F. (2008). The relationship between impulsive verbal aggression and intermittent explosive disorder. *Aggressive Behavior, 34,* 51–60.

Meyer, A. (2010). "Too drunk to say no": Binge drinking, rape, and the *Daily Mail. Feminist Media Studies, 10,* 19–34.

Muehlenhard, C. L., & Linton, M. A. (1987). Date rape and sexual aggression in dating situations: Incidence and risk factors. *Journal of Counseling Psychology, 24,* 186–196.

Murphy, C. (2015, June 26). Still another challenge on campus assaults: Getting minority students to report them. *The Chronicle of Higher Education,* p. A15.

Murphy, W. (2014, December 2). Harvard gets it right on sexual assault. Retrieved December 2, 2014, from <http://www.bostonglobe.com>.

Murphy, W. (2015, January 13). Win in Harvard case will ripple across campuses. Retrieved January 14, 2015, from <http://womensenews.org>.

National Coalition of Anti-Violence Programs. (2011). *Hate violence against lesbian, gay, bisexual, transgender, queer, and HIV-affected communities in the United States in 2010.* Retrieved August 24, 2015, from <www.avp.org>.

National Institute of Justice. (2015). *Rape and sexual violence.* U.S. Department of Justice. Retrieved August 23, 2015, from <http://www.nij.gov>.

National Institute of Justice. (2000). *Full report of the prevalence, incidence, and consequences of violence against women: Findings of the National Violence Against Women Survey.* Retrieved August 29, 2015, from <www.nij.gov>.

Nelson, A. (2008, June 8). Breaking the cycle: Women's shelter lends helping hand. *Corpus Christi Caller Times,* pp. 1B, 4B.

O'Hara, S. (2012). Monsters, playboys, virgins and whores: Rape myths in the news media's coverage of sexual violence. *Language & Literature, 21,* 247–259.

Olson, L. N. (2002). Exploring "common couple violence" in heterosexual romantic relationships. *Western Journal of Communication, 66,* 104–128.

Palmer, R. S., McMahon, T. J., Rounsaville, B. J., & Ball, S. A. (2010). Coercive sexual experiences, protective behavioral strategies, alcohol expectations, and consumption among male and female college students. *Journal of Interpersonal Violence, 25,* 1563–1578.

Paul, L. A., Gray, M. J., Elhai, J. D., & Davis, J. L. (2009). Perceptions of peer rape myth acceptance and disclosure in a sample of college sexual assault survivors. *Psychological Trauma: Theory, Research, Practice, and Policy, 1,* 231–241.

Perez-Pena, R., & Taylor, K. (2014, May 3). Fight against sexual assaults holds colleges to account. Retrieved September 1, 2014, from <http://www.nytimes.com>.

Peterson, Z. D., & Muehlenhard, C. L. (2007). Conceptualizing the "wantedness" of women's consensual and nonconsensual sexual experiences: Implications for how women label their experiences with rape. *Journal of Sex Research, 44,* 72–88.

Powell, A. (2010). *Sex, power, and consent: Youth culture and the unwritten rules.* Cambridge, UK: Cambridge University Press.

Rancer, A. S., & Avtgis, T. A. (2014). *Argumentative and aggressive communication: Theory, research, and application* (2nd ed.) Thousand Oaks, CA: Sage.

Rape, Abuse, and Incest National Network (RAINN). (2015). Statistics. Retrieved August 23, 2015, from <www.rainn.org>.

Raphael, J. (2013). *Rape is rape: How denial, distortion, and victim blaming are fueling a hidden acquaintance rape crisis.* Chicago: Chicago Review Press.

Repko, M. (2015, March 17). SMU program helps students prevent assaults. *The Dallas Morning News,* pp. 1B, 8B.

Rhymes, E. (2014, September 19). Woman as aggressor: The unspoken truth of domestic violence. Retrieved August 29, 2015, from <www.mintpressnews.com>.

Rohrbaugh, J. (2006). Domestic violence in same-gender relationships. *Family Court Review, 44,* 287–299.

Sanoff, R. (2015, April 15). "Define Your Line" is a sexual consent campaign run by Texas Tech University students, and it's awesome. Retrieved August 29, 2015, from <http://www.bustle.com>.

Schoellkopf, J. C. (2012). Victim-blaming: A new term for an old trend. Lesbian Gay Bisexual Transgender Queer Center, University of Rhode Island. Retrieved August 29, 2015, from <http://digitalcommons.uri.edu>.

Schwartz, M. D. (2005). The past and future of violence against women. *Journal of Interpersonal Violence, 20,* 7–11.

Sela-Shayovitz, R. (2015). "They are all good boys." *Feminist Media Studies, 15,* 411–428.

Sokoloff, N. J., & Dupont, I. (2005). Domestic violence at the intersections of race, class, and gender: Challenges and contributions to understanding violence against marginalized women in diverse communities. *Violence Against Women, 11,* 38–64.

Sorenson, S. B., Joshi, M., & Sivitz, E. (2014). Knowing a sexual assault victim or perpetrator: A stratified random sample of undergraduates at one university. *Journal of Interpersonal Violence, 29,* 394–416.

Teen Dating Violence Month. (2014). Why focus on teens? Retrieved August 29, 2015, from <www.teendvmonth.org>.

Terry, A. (2015, March 11). Define Your Line campaign encourages open sexual communication. Retrieved August 29, 2015, from <http://www.ttuhub.net>.

Testa, M., VanZile-Tamsen, C., Livingston, J. A., & Buddie, A. M. (2006). The role of women's alcohol consumption in managing sexual intimacy and sexual safety motives. *Journal of Studies in Alcohol, 67,* 665–674.

Tewksbury, R. (2010). Effects of sexual assaults on men: Physical, mental, and sexual consequences. In B. Hutchinson (Ed.), *Annual editions: Gender 10/11* (pp. 230–236). Boston: McGraw-Hill.

Thapar-Bjorkert, S., & Morgan, K. J. (2010). "But sometimes I think . . . they put themselves in the situation": Exploring blame and responsibility in interpersonal violence. *Violence Against Women, 16,* 32–59.

Truman, D. M., Tokar, D. M., & Fischer, A. R. (1996). Dimensions of masculinity: Relations to date rape supportive attitudes and sexual aggression in dating situations. *Journal of Counseling & Development, 74,* 555–562.

United States Department of Justice. (2014). Domestic violence. Retrieved August 28, 2015, from <www.justice.gov>.

Vangelisti, A. L., Maguire, K. C., Alexander, A. L., & Clark, G. (2007). Hurtful family environments: Links with individual, relationship, and perceptual variables. *Communication Monographs, 74,* 357–385.

Vonderhaar, R. L., & Carmody, D. C. (2015). There are no "innocent victims": The influence of just world beliefs and prior victimization on rape myth acceptance. *Journal of Interpersonal Violence, 30,* 1615–1632.

Walker, K., Bowen, E., Brown, S., & Sleath, E. (2015). Desistance from interpersonal partner violence: A conceptual model and framework for practitioners for managing the process of change. *Journal of Interpersonal Violence, 30,* 2726–2750.

Walker, L. E. A. (1979). *The battered woman.* New York: Harper Colophon.

Walker, L. E. A. (1984). *The battered woman syndrome.* New York: Springer.

Walker, L. E. A. (1993). The battered woman syndrome is a psychological consequence of abuse. In R. J. Gelles & D. R. Loseke (Eds.), *Current controversies on family violence* (pp. 133–153). Newbury Park, CA: Sage.

Walker, L. E. A. (2006). Violence and exploitation against women and girls. *Annals of the New York Academy of Sciences, 1087,* 142–157.

Watson, G. (2015, March 30). Sharpening the focus of sexual consent. *Texas Tech Today.* Retrieved April 4, 2015, from <http://today.ttu.edu>.

Wente, M. (2014, March 1). Can she consent to sex after drinking? Retrieved September 15, 2014, from <www.theglobeandmail.com>.

White, C. H., & Malkowski, J. (2014). Communicative challenges of bystander intervention: Impact of goals and message design logic on strategies college students use to intervene in drinking situations. *Health Communication, 29,* 93–104.

The White House Council on Women and Girls. (2014, January). *Rape and sexual assault: A renewed call to action.* Retrieved September 1, 2014, from <https://www.whitehouse.gov>.

Winerip, M. (2014, February 7). Stepping up to stop sexual assault. Retrieved September 15, 2014, from <http://www.nytimes.com>.

Women's Health. (2012, July 16). *Date rape drugs fact sheet.* Retrieved August 24, 2015, from <www.womenshealth.gov>.

Yeater, E. A., Treat, T. A., Viken, R. J., & McFall, R. M. (2010). Cognitive processes underlying women's risk judgments: Associations with sexual victimization history and rape myth. *Journal of Consulting and Clinical Psychology, 78,* 375–386.

Young, S. L., & Maguire, K. C. (2003). Talking about sexual violence. *Women & Language, 26,* 40–52.

Part Three

GENDER COMMUNICATION IN CONTEXT

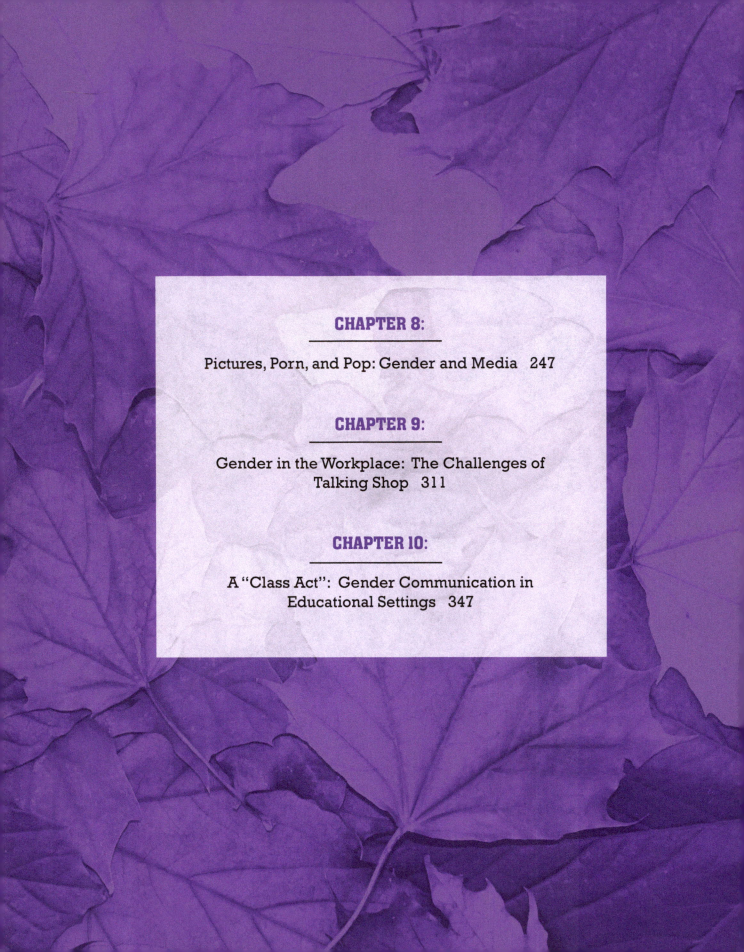

CHAPTER 8

PICTURES, PORN, AND POP: GENDER AND MEDIA

CASE STUDY

Where Were You 25 Years Ago? (Were you even born yet?!?)

- The year was 1990.
- There were only three TV networks. (Fox was so fledgling at that time that no one dared call it a network.)
- Only a few cable TV options existed with very limited programming. (No HGTV, no Bravo, no Golf Channel.)
- You watched movies on videocassettes via a VCR; there were no DVDs in 1990.
- Your "laptop" was part of your anatomy, not a personal computer.
- The independent film industry had barely started.
- No MP3s. No streaming. No downloading. No file sharing (unless you handed a manila folder to a friend).
- No such thing as a months-long Oscar season—just good movies that you hoped someone in show business remembered and nominated.
- "Second screen" meant you moved a second TV set into the living room so you could watch two football games at once.
- "Bingeing" signaled an eating disorder, not an activity where you holed up in your room watching every episode of *Lost*.
- No one but birds "live tweeted."
- "Social media" meant screaming at your TV set.
- "Tinder" and "tumblr" were helpful things to have around the house.

- Only the military knew about the Internet, so there virtually was no Internet. No web (except those produced by spiders), no surfing (except in the ocean), no website development, no Google, no browsers (except for people milling about in libraries or bookstores).
- "Meme" was a typo or a pet name for your grandmother.
- "Smart phones" were push button phones in different styles and colors, some with extra-long coiled cords.
- A discussion about "pop culture" meant debriefing with your friends at Sunday lunch at The Sizzler, about the skits in the previous night's episode of *Saturday Night Live*.
- *Time* and *Newsweek* were weighty magazines, heavily funded by ads (that most people actually read).
- Newspapers arrived at most people's front doorsteps (or in their flower beds) with a satisfying thud early each morning. And people actually read (or read through) them. Cartoon strips got torn out and stuck on the refrigerator door with magnets.

Fast forward 25 years and you arrive at 2015. Take stock of how much has changed in your lifetime, especially with regard for how women and men relate to each other. All of the societal, global, and technological changes impact people—how we view ourselves, how we perceive each other, and how we communicate.

THE POWER OF MEDIATED COMMUNICATION: EFFECTS ON OUR LIVES

Perhaps no other force influences our daily lives more than media. Parents are hugely important, teachers have significant impact, friends and romantic partners affect us in profound ways but, over time, media may have the strongest effect of all. Consider how often you compare real life—work, family, relationships—to how these things are depicted in various media. It's common to hear someone refer to something on TV, such as, "I don't trust that guy I went out with last night; he reminds me of that guy on (insert show here)" or "I feel like I've stepped into a sad country-and-western tune." Media are highly influential in how they communicate messages about people.

Mediated communication is prevalent in your day-to-day existence.

© ra2studio/Shutterstock.com

A Bombardment of Media

Your modern existence is jammed full of mediated communication every sunrise to sunset, but just how are you affected by it? You're literally bombarded with media every day, and the effects of this bombardment are dramatic (Chia & Gunther, 2006; Harris, 2011; Strasburger, 2005; Ziegler, 2007).

As a college-educated person, you're probably an above-average critical consumer of media, meaning you consciously select mediated messages to take in and filter out. However, a great deal of mediated information is absorbed unconsciously, even by the most critical of consumers. Few of us have time in our busy lives to focus concentrated attention on all the mediated messages we receive in a typical day and make conscious decisions about their effects. This critical thinking process becomes a skill we use less often as we take in more and more mediated information. Just how this absorption affects us has been the subject of a good deal of attention among media researchers.

Approaches to Studying the Effects of Media Consumption

In the 1970s, media scholar Gaye Tuchman (1979) described an explosion of media research, as mass media grew exponentially during the years between World War II and the beginning of the 1980s. Several research approaches and theories emerged at that time and since then, in an attempt to explain how media affect consumers.

HYPODERMIC NEEDLE OR DIRECT-EFFECTS THEORY This early theory viewed the mass audience as passively and directly consuming mediated messages. The imagery was that of a hypodermic needle that injected mass communication directly into the veins of its noncritical consumers (Campbell, Martin, & Fabos, 2015). This theory offered an inadequate, overly simplistic explanation of media effects because it ignored how other factors might influence the process, but it was a start.

MINIMAL-EFFECTS MODEL With increasing sophistication in social scientific techniques came dissatisfaction with direct-effects theory. Media theorists began to argue that consumers were only minimally affected by mediated messages, and that they selectively exposed themselves to media messages and selectively retained those messages that reinforced or were consistent with behaviors, attitudes, and values they already held. This theory suggested that consumers were less at the power of persuasive media than previously thought (Campbell et al., 2015).

USES AND GRATIFICATIONS THEORY Media expert John Vivian (2011) describes the uses and gratifications approach as a theory that no longer views mass audiences as passive sponges, but rather as active users of media. The theory describes how consumers are motivated to use various media and what gains, rewards, or gratifications they receive from such consumption (Sundar & Limperos, 2013). Researchers have employed

The uses and gratifications approach explains how consumers are motivated to use various media.

© Eugenio Marongiu/Shutterstock.com

uses and gratifications theory to better understand the satisfaction people derive from such activities as migrating from one medium to another (like watching TV, then migrating to a laptop computer, then to a mobile phone; Shade, Kornfield, & Oliver, 2015); using cell phones and tablets (Chen, Liang, & Leung, 2015; Magsamen-Conrad, Dowd, Abuljadail, Alsulaiman, & Shareefi, 2015); and watching reality TV (Barton, 2009).

AGENDA-SETTING RESEARCH The seeds of this approach date back to the 1920s and the early work of Walter Lippmann, who suggested that media "create pictures in our heads" (as in Campbell et al., 2015, p. 524). A contemporary of Lippmann's, Robert Park, proposed that the media don't merely report, reflect, or dramatize what's important in society, media actually guide what we think is important (Vivian, 2011). The media generate awareness of issues; thus, media may not be dictating attitudes or stances on issues, but they have the power to affect what we think *about*. In essence, viewers may allow a media outlet to set an agenda for what should be most important to them (Douglas, 2009; McCombs, Shaw, & Weaver, 2014).

CULTIVATION THEORY This theory suggests that media consumption, especially heavy TV viewing, "leads individuals to perceive the world in ways that are consistent with television portrayals" (Campbell et al., 2015, p. 525). Essentially, the theory contends that the more consumers absorb viewpoints and depictions on TV and from other media outlets, the more their views of reality are "cultivated" or distorted by those images (Croteau & Hoynes, 2014; Potter, 2014).

Media scholar George Gerbner and various colleagues originally developed cultivation theory to better understand the relationship between the social reality of violence and crime and media's depiction of it (Gerbner, 2003; Gerbner, Gross, Morgan, & Signorielli, 1980; Signorielli & Morgan, 1990). This line of research continues (Hetsroni & Lowenstein, 2013). The theory has proven insightful, such as in instances where children have harmed (and even killed) other children by replicating wrestling moves and other forms of aggression seen on TV, believing that the targets of their violence will spring back up, unharmed. As another example of research utilizing cultivation theory, Lewis and Shewmaker (2011) analyzed teen celebrity websites, finding that female celebrities were much more highly sexualized in images on websites than male celebrities, cultivating potential sexist attitudes in consumers of such sites.

CULTURAL STUDIES APPROACHES Just as minimal-effects approaches developed in reaction to earlier techniques, cultural studies approaches developed out of a reaction to what was perceived to be too much data gathering, number crunching, and trend charting in social scientific research. Cultural studies approaches are more interpretive and intuitive; researchers "try to understand how media and culture are tied to the actual patterns of communication in daily life" (Campbell et al., 2015, p. 527). Everyday cultural symbols, as found in print and visual media, are analyzed for their power to make meaning, to create and communicate reality, and to help people understand their daily existence (Kellner, 2015). Researchers are particularly interested in issues of race, gender, class, and sexuality, and the inequities therein. For example, cultural studies scholars have examined TV depictions of families in which social class and ethnicity are emphasized (Butsch, 2015; Esposito, 2011; Lipsitz, 2015).

ADVERTISING: SELLING A PRODUCT OR SELLING SEXISM?

Advertisers are getting craftier and more desperate to get their products and services into our view. Ads come through unprompted on our phones, precede movies we see in theatres, pop up to clog our computer or tablet screens, and appear as product placements in TV shows and films, such as when a character uses a particular brand of computer or drinks a name-brand beer (deGregorio & Sung, 2010; Scott & Craig-Lees, 2010; Wiles & Danielova, 2009). Ads are digitized to appear behind the batter's box or in the middle of a football field, with changing images and products while we watch. Ads line the walls of buses and subways and provide often-unwanted distraction on a road trip, in the form of billboards.

Advertising has a powerful effect that goes well beyond the purpose of selling products to consumers; it affects our culture and our views (Cortese, 2016; Jhally, 2015). A great deal of research has been conducted on the ways people are depicted in print and electronic advertisements, as well as the messages these ads communicate to media consumers.

A good deal of these depictions evoke stereotypes, but there are a few exceptions and positive trends.

Babes in Bras: Female Depiction in Advertising

Groundbreaking programmatic research by marketing professors Alice Courtney and Thomas Whipple (1974, 1980, 1983, 1985) forms the basis for the claim that advertising has a major impact on individuals' views of gender. From the compiled results of numerous studies,

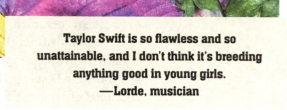

Taylor Swift is so flawless and so unattainable, and I don't think it's breeding anything good in young girls.
—Lorde, musician

Courtney and Whipple produced a list of trends and female *gender stereotypes* prevalent in advertising; researchers expanded their work (Artz, Munger, & Purdy, 1999; Browne, 1998; Lin, 1997; Simonton, 1995). Unfortunately, the abundance of recent research confirms that little has changed in terms of gender stereotyping in ads (Cogan, 2014; Eisend, Plagemann, & Sollwedel, 2014; Fairclough, 2015; Hentges, Bartsch, & Meier, 2007; LaWare & Moutsatsos, 2013; Monk-Turner, Kouts, Parris, & Webb, 2007; Yoder, Christopher, & Holmes, 2008). Read the following list and see if you have any stereotypes to add.

1. Fewer depictions of women, in general, than men
2. Women in isolation, particularly from other women
3. Women depicted as sex objects, more often in sleepwear, underwear, and lingerie than in professional clothing
4. Young girls and women portrayed as passive and in need of men's help and protection
5. Women as kitchen and bathroom product representatives
6. Women appearing more than men in ads for personal hygiene products
7. An abundance of women serving men and boys
8. Medical ads depicting male physicians interacting with hysterical female hypochondriacs
9. Women more often depicted in family- and home-oriented roles than in professional roles
10. Young housewives shown performing household duties, whereas older men act as product representatives who give advice to housewives
11. Women portrayed as decorative, nonfunctioning entities incapable of making important decisions
12. Women depicted as being obsessed with physical attractiveness
13. Fewer depictions of older women than older men

14. Fewer depictions of minority women than minority men
15. Fewer women than men advertising expensive luxury products
16. Few women depicted actively engaged in sports
17. Ads overtly critical of feminist rights and issues
18. Women's body parts, especially breasts and genitalia, featured in ads, rather than the whole body
19. Frequent decapitated images of women, meaning women often pictured only from the mouth or neck downward (as though they don't have brains)
20. Women in bondage depictions, such as being embedded in inanimate objects or bound with tape, fabric, or rope.

Perhaps you're familiar with the work of Jean Kilbourne, particularly her educational film series, *Killing Us Softly*. Kilbourne produces research and films that support her assertion that advertising presents women almost exclusively in one of two roles: housewife or sex object. In *Killing Us Softly 4* (Kilbourne, 2010a), Kilbourne's ad examples depict women's bodies turned into objects (like beer bottles and machinery) and thin, tall, long-legged mannequin-like women with perfect skin and no signs of aging. Kilbourne (2010b) has countless examples of how ruthlessly and fiercely advertisers have clung to their use of sexualized, often demoralized images of women to sell all kinds of products.

Women of color fare poorly in ads, both in the quantity of depictions and the quality of the roles (Brooks & Hebert, 2006; Cortese, 2016; Martinez, 2015). Hispanic, Asian American, and Native American women are less represented in ads than African American women, who are less represented than white women. When women of color appear, often they're expected to conform to standards of white beauty (McKay & Johnson, 2015; Mueller, 2011; Wilson & Gutierrez, 2003).

Although an abundance of research findings show perpetual female stereotyping in ads, one study detected a slight shift over time. Mager and Helgeson (2011) analyzed American magazine ads over a 50-year period and found "a trend toward objective role portrayals of women fairly equal to men" (p. 238). They didn't see evidence of Courtney and Whipple's finding that women are primarily depicted in the home, nor that women in ads appear as though they don't do important things or make critical decisions. Ads did persist in their portrayals of women as dependent and in need of men's protection; their depiction as sexual objects for the pleasure of men, rather than as whole and capable people, increased over the 50-year span.

Some manufacturers have changed their approach to advertising products for female consumers—the operant word being *some*. The Dove "Campaign for Real Beauty," launched in 2004, represented a departure from how women were typically depicted in ads. Print ads showed American women of different body shapes, ages, and ethnicities who didn't weigh what models weigh; women wore underwear that real women wear, not sexy lingerie. In some ads, women who didn't possess perfect bodies posed discreetly in the nude (private parts masked by body positioning). These ads (including enlarged images attached to buildings in Times Square) starred "real women with real bodies and real curves" in an attempt to "make more women feel beautiful every day, celebrating diversity and real women by challenging contemporary stereotypical views of beauty" (Cortese, 2016, p. 88). The Dove campaign sparked other efforts around the country, including projects to help girls develop better body image and self-esteem.

However, the Dove campaign (and later efforts, like its "Choose Beautiful" campaign) has its critics (Duffy, 2010; Gill, 2007; Givhan, 2005; Persis Murray, 2015). Early criticism related to the product the original campaign was designed to sell—slimming body cream! Some criticism comes from the "enough already" feeling; one writer complained, "I have Dove Real Fatigue" (Molloy, 2015, p. 5). Another criticism surrounds the fact that women in Dove ads tend to be in good shape; none are extremely thin, none are significantly overweight, and none are physically disabled, so how "real" is "real"?

ADVERTISING'S EFFECTS ON WOMEN Sexist and stereotypical ad portrayals have severe negative effects on women and girls (Aubrey, 2007; Durham, 2009; Harper & Tiggemann, 2007; Levine & Murnen, 2009; Stankiewicz & Rosselli, 2008; Zimmerman & Dahlberg, 2008). Women and girls who compare themselves to air-brushed images in magazines or other forms of advertising may view themselves as lacking, as constantly being measured against a standard they can never achieve, and as being judged for external rather than internal qualities. The constant objectification and self-esteem dives while viewing these images take their toll.

Studies continue to document our culture's obsession with women's thinness and beauty, as reflected in advertising (Cortese, 2016; Gill, 2015; Raiten-D'Antonio, 2010). We've all heard the phrase "sex sells," but women's sex *really* sells, as ads prove time and time again. Many of us have grown weary of women's bodies and sexuality being used in every possible way to draw attention and sell a product—*any* product.

MIXED SIGNALS CREATE CONFUSION People are confused by images in the media; at times, this confusion has consequences for our relationships and communication. Many wonder if women want to be treated as equals and professionals, as traditional helpmates and caregivers, or as sex kittens, because the media readily provide continuous, seemingly acceptable images of each.

One source of confusion is the cover pictures on women's magazines and the contradictory headlines describing the magazine's contents. Extremely thin female models, their breasts squeezed into outfits to create or exaggerate cleavage, appear on the covers—opposite headings such as "How to Get Your Boss to Take You Seriously."

© Helga Esteb/Shutterstock.com

When the covers change, that's when culture changes. —Lady Gaga, performer

The most insidious example of mixed-signal advertising was perpetrated by Philip Morris, former manufacturer of Virginia Slims cigarettes, whose ads first emerged in the 1960s during the heyday of the women's liberation movement. Early TV and print ads were done in sepia tones, to look like old-fashioned movie reels or still photographs. In the TV ads, a male voice-over described how some women in history got into trouble for being rebellious and smoking. These ads then cut to modern-day images of women, accompanied by the motto (originally sung) "You've come a long way, baby, to get where you got to today!" The point was to illustrate how women's status had improved in American society because women were finally allowed to smoke.

Slims' ads in the '80s and '90s depicted women doing fun, active things (as active as you could be with a cigarette in your hand), while employing the language of liberation. This approach is called *commodity feminism*, the "co-opting of feminist language and imagery in order to create an association between a product and the desire for women's liberation" (McIntyre, 2015, p. 5). While this approach to advertising is used to hawk other products and services, tobacco ads stand out. These ad campaigns have been criticized by healthcare officials, media critics, political activists, and feminists outraged by the fact that tobacco companies attempt to show concern over health issues, all the while packaging their products to epitomize liberation, adventure, and youthfulness (Morrison, Krugman, & Park, 2008; Murphy-Hoefer, Hyland, & Rivard, 2010). In point of fact, their products actually enslave, age, and ultimately kill people.

Studs in Suits: Male Depiction in Advertising

Just as there are female stereotypes in advertising, male stereotypes appear as well (Duerringer, 2015; Katz, 2011; MacKinnon, 2003). More research has been conducted on women's depictions, but several studies provide interesting revelations about men in advertisements.

CORPORATE SUCCESS, GREAT DAD, AND ANGRY GUY Studies in the 1980s showed that men were typically portrayed in ads as dominant, successful professionals in business settings or engaged in fun activities in settings away from home (Courtney & Whipple, 1983). They were still portrayed this way in 1990s ads, but a new trend depicted men involved in domestic tasks such as taking care of children, preparing family meals, and doing household chores (Craig, 1992; Richmond-Abbott, 1992). In addition, men were more often presented as sex objects and in decorative, nonfunctional roles that had no relation to the product being sold (Lin, 1997).

Researcher Philip Patterson (1996) identified some themes in '90s male advertising, such as *power babe commercials* in which "women enjoy the upper hand over men" (p. 93). He critiqued two prominent stereotypes of men in advertising at the time, calling them *Rambo* and *Himbo depictions*: "The image of men in advertising is either that of a 'Rambo,' solo conqueror of all he sees, or a 'Himbo,' a male bimbo" (p. 94). These stereotypical, overdrawn images of men persist today.

Eminem epitomizes the "angry white male with attitude," a stereotype often present in advertising.

Media scholar Jackson Katz (2011) expands the list into the twenty-first century by adding the "angry guy" portrayal, a trend toward depictions of violent white males in advertising for a wide range of products. Katz detects recurring themes in magazine advertising: "The angry, aggressive, white, working-class male as antiauthority rebel; violence as genetically programmed male behavior; the use of military and sports symbolism to enhance the masculine identification and appeal of products; and the association of muscularity with ideal masculinity" (p. 263). He cites examples such as white rap artist Eminem, who epitomizes the angry white male with attitude, shown most often scowling, overly serious, or in violent poses. Other common depictions include men in uniforms with their weapons or gear—both military and sporting.

A few years ago, we got a letter from a professor whose class used this textbook and found an omission in the media chapter. They didn't see a list of male stereotypes that corresponded to Courtney and Whipple's list of depictions of women. So the class created one, and we think it's well worth reprinting. According to Lynn Wells' students at Saddleback College in Mission Viejo, California (to whom we're grateful), male depictions in ads include the following:

1. Stud Cowboy, like the Marlboro Man
2. Jock, who can perform in all sports
3. Handyman, who can fix anything
4. Young and hip, as in sports drinks ads
5. Handsome ladies' man, as in beer commercials
6. Kind and grandfatherly, as in insurance ads
7. Professional, knowledgeable
8. Couch potato man
9. Blue-collar worker, sometimes seen as a sex symbol
10. Androgynous, as in Calvin Klein ads
11. Romantic, drink coffee man
12. Fonzie type, Joe Cool
13. Helpless, as in the "Got Milk" commercials
14. Just a kid, who needs a woman to save him

Because Mager and Helgeson's (2011) research we cited earlier found some subtle shifts in women's depictions in magazine ads over the last 50 years, let's revisit this study for what can be learned about men's depictions. Although women still appear in sexually suggestive poses in ads with more frequency, men's appearance in such poses is rising, generating an increased sexualization of men in advertising.

Mager and Helgeson also studied ads that display only body parts, rather than the entire figure of a person; for many years it's been quite typical for women to appear in what's commonly termed *decapitation ads,* where their bodies are shown, but not their heads. Sometimes only limbs or other limited sections of women's bodies are depicted, emphasizing their sexuality or vulnerability. Media scholar Anthony Cortese (2016) terms these "body chopping" or *dismemberment ads,* where bodies are separated into parts or body parts are shown immersed in or emerging from inanimate objects (p. 71). Interestingly enough, male decapitation or dismemberment ads didn't increase over the 50-year period Mager and Helgeson examined; perhaps the American public is still squeamish about seeing a man's genitalia highlighted in an ad or his head cut off, such that the focus is on his body. Perhaps advertisers don't believe such a depiction will sell a

"Old Spice Ads: Sexual Stereotypes or Humor?"

The day after the 2010 Super Bowl, Old Spice (a long-standing men's aftershave brand) debuted its "Old Spice Man" in the form of Isaiah Mustafa, a deep-voiced, well-toned, usually shirtless or towel-clad, light-skinned African American male (and former NFL player). The first ads were inexpensive to create, as ads go, but received such acclaim and exposure that a series of them were developed and launched through all sorts of media, including viral video (Neff, 2010a, 2010b). The ads proved popular with the general public, mainly because of odd, unexpected depictions, like Old Spice Man riding a horse backwards, appearing out of a pile of sand (guitar in tow, puppies inside guitar), or stepping out of the shower with chain saw in hand. In each ad, he generally looked perfect because, of course, he used Old Spice body wash. Some of the ads aimed at heterosexual female consumers suggested that the Old Spice Man was "the man your man could smell like" if only he'd "stop using lady-scented body wash." Part of the comedic effect of the ads is the pretense that Old Spice Man is a "man's man," shaming other men into trying to smell better and have better hygiene. Some believe he represents hypermasculinity, while others view the ads as parody, in some ways mocking masculinity and encouraging women to take charge and buy the products they want their men to use. In more recent years, African American male body builder Terry Crews is also depicted (scantily clad, muscles bulging) in ads for the Old Spice shaver. No matter your take on the ads, the campaign's success is undeniable, with dramatic increases in sales for Old Spice products (Harris, 2012; Vaynerchuk, 2011).

What do you think of the ads? Do they reinforce male stereotypes or make fun of them? Do they represent a smart departure from traditional ad campaigns, or just the latest retreads of ads we've seen for years, ones that exploit sexuality to sell a product?

product, whereas focusing on women's breasts or crotches and depicting them headless (sending a message that a woman's body is more important than her brain) are still perceived as effective ad techniques.

Mager and Helgeson found that, while depictions of men in executive roles still occurred more frequently than such depictions of women, the rate of occurrence decreased over time. In the past, men were often shown in dominant positions, as authorities, alongside women who received their instruction. This dynamic is less obvious in today's ads. In a more recent study of men's role depiction in ads, Fowler and Thomas (2015) found the following: (a) men were less likely to be depicted as leading characters in ads than in times past; (b) male roles in ads became more congruent with changing gender roles in society, primarily through an increased depiction of men as fathers; and (c) ads included more depiction of men with idealized physiques, counter to the trend in U.S. culture of increasing male obesity.

ADVERTISING'S EFFECTS ON MEN Most people prefer not to relate to men as though they were stereotypes. But it's hard not to wonder if men actually want such treatment, given that so many macho images of men still pervade many forms of media, from magazine ads depicting rugged men in their pickup trucks to infomercials pushing the latest exercise equipment (Cortese, 2016; Gentry & Harrison, 2010).

If you're a male reader, what's your reaction to an ad in which a scantily clad man is depicted as a sex object, as some would argue Abercrombie & Fitch, Calvin Klein, Versace, and other companies' ads do? Do you notice male-objectifying ads more or in a different way than, for example, Victoria's Secret lingerie ads, which began appearing on TV in the late 1990s? Do these ads make you feel badly about yourself in comparison to some stud people swoon over? Or do you find them refreshing and realistic because men are shown as sexy and people's attention to them shows their "appreciation"?

Can you watch TV for any length of time and not see an ad for erectile dysfunction products?

© Sean Nel/Shutterstock.com

Some scholars believe that men are now the targets of an all-out assault on self-esteem, mainly because the market for assaulting women's self-esteem—which forces them to buy products and services ranging from simple beauty remedies to full-scale plastic surgery—is saturated, with profits maxed out (Lin, 1997). We continue to see a significant increase in ads showing barely clothed men with perfect bodies, skin, hair, and teeth, touting the products and services that can get men that way (Cortese, 2016; Feasey, 2009). These ads encourage men to think of themselves as sex objects (Cottle, 2003; Dobosz, 1997).

Even more perplexing are the increasing number of ads for erectile dysfunction products, such as Viagra and Cialis. One particularly bizarre TV ad that ran in the early 2000s featured macho man and former NFL coach Mike Ditka, who encouraged men to "get back in the game"—meaning the game of having sex. The warnings that tend to come with such ads—the suggestion that men taking the drug and maintaining an erection for more than four hours should go to an emergency room—are jarring, if not a bit humorous.

You may find you've become so desensitized to sexually objectifying ads—of both men and women—that you hardly notice them anymore. Since sexually objectifying female ads don't seem to be going away, do you think it's a form of equality to sexually objectify men in ads? Do ads like these develop or increase in men an irrational concern with appearance, image, and sex appeal?

LESSONS FROM THE SMALL SCREEN: TELEVISION AND GENDER

According to media experts, the life cycle of TV, as a mass medium, has now entered its fourth stage, characterized by *convergence* or the "merging of media content across various platforms" (Campbell et al., 2015, p. G-3). Innovations like DVRs, streaming, and second screen viewing experiences (watching shows on computers, tablets, or phones) have greatly expanded television's impact (Chase, 2013). It seems reasonable that TV's depiction of the sexes will continue to have an impact on the viewing audience.

Television: Mirroring Reality or Creating It?

It's likely that some of the TV shows we refer to in this chapter will be off the air when you read this material. But one thing will remain—a chicken-or-egg argument about whether the media merely reflect what is happening in society or actually create the issues and trends that then become relevant in society. Perhaps it's a bit of both.

On the "media reflect reality" side, one could argue that economic pressures and changing lifestyles in the twenty-first century are reflected in TV programming, in efforts to stay "on trend." On the other hand, many researchers support the "media drive or create culture" view, believing that TV consumption actually expands viewers' range of behaviors. Yet another school of media thought contends that TV programming neither reflects nor creates reality; rather, its exaggerated portrayals and overly dramatized situations (including reality TV drama) are nowhere near the realities of

Remember...

Gender Stereotypes: Recurring media depictions of men and women that place them into narrowly defined roles

Commodity Feminism: Co-opting feminist language and imagery to create an association between a product and the desire for women's liberation

Power Babe Commercials: Ads that depict women objectifying or enjoying the upper hand over men

Rambo Depiction: Male stereotype in advertising, in which a man is depicted as a conquering hero

Himbo Depiction: Male stereotype in advertising, in which a man is depicted as a bumbling idiot or fool—a male bimbo

Decapitation Ads: Ads in which people's bodies are shown, but without heads or with their heads cut out of the picture

Dismemberment Ads: Ads in which only people's limbs or sections of their bodies are shown

most people's lives. In this view, TV programs and other forms of media serve purely as escapism and entertainment for consumers, as uses and gratifications theory suggests.

Men & Television Programming

Have men's depictions in TV changed much in recent years? Our best answer is "yes and no." While current TV programs that draw the largest audiences and the highest ad revenues still tend to portray men in narrow (traditional) gender roles, male roles have also broadened as the methods of producing, delivering, and consuming TV programming have diversified. Let's examine some of the more prominent characterizations of men in scripted TV programs, then explore some trends in reality programming.

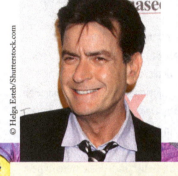

A 22-year-old girl is like a good carpenter.
No wood gets wasted.
—Charlie Sheen, actor

© Helga Esteb/Shutterstock.com

SCRIPTED MEN Media scholar Marvin Moore (1992) surveyed family depictions in American prime-time television from 1947 to 1990 and found that 94 percent of families in the programs were white and two-thirds involved the traditional profile of a married couple, with or without children.

A kinder, gentler heterosexual male character took prominence in the 1990s and 2000s in prime-time TV, which some deemed a "feminized" version of men (Beynon, 2004; MacKinnon, 2003). These male characters weren't buffoons or wimps, but likable, masculine men who struggled to understand themselves, communicate with the women in their lives, and be better parents. These depictions proved popular with male and female viewers alike, but the trend mostly reflected an effort to reach women viewers since they were (and still are) the primary shoppers for households.

At the same time, another trend emerged—one that media scholar Robert Hanke (1998) termed the *mock-macho sitcom*. In these shows, male characters made fun of machismo and ridiculed their own lack of self-awareness, but also preserved masculinity. Prevalent in sitcoms, these depictions reflected a main heterosexual male character who was typically a devoted husband and father and an equal partner to his wife, but who often goofed up and admitted he didn't understand women (Stark, 2000a). This characterization was termed the *playful patriarch* and was prominent in such sitcoms as *Home Improvement* and *Roseanne*, but still exists today (Traube, 1992; Walsh,

Fursich, & Jefferson, 2008). Might the male characters in *The Big Bang Theory* be younger, geekier extensions of a kinder, gentler male TV character? Could the overweight, bumbling-in-love character of police officer Mike in the sitcom *Mike & Molly* be today's playful patriarch?

Media scholars have found few changes in the general profile of TV scripted programs in the twenty-first century. Sitcoms and dramas are still primarily about white, young to middle-aged, middle-class America, with male roles still outnumbering female roles (Butsch, 2015; Elasmar, Hasegawa, & Brain, 1999; Harwood & Anderson, 2002). Men on TV are still portrayed primarily in work-related roles, whereas women's roles still focus more on relationships than professional situations (Lauzen, Dozier, & Horan, 2008). Scripted shows have always been and still are highly *heteronormative*, meaning that they present heterosexuality as the norm or predominant form of human relations, even though gay friends, family members, and coworkers are now almost a staple of scripted TV shows (Kim et al., 2007).

However, with the development of new outlets for TV consumption (e.g., Netflix, Amazon, Apple) as well as cable channels' enduring appeal, broader, more unconventional portrayals of men in American culture have emerged. Arguably, the pack of friends in HBO's hit series *Entourage* represented a newer, broader view of men, work, and friendship (Click, Holladay, Lee, & Kristiansen, 2015). Other TV shows (some which have since come and gone) emphasize men's friendships with other men, men rediscovering and redefining their relationships with brothers and other male family members (such as in the 2015 sitcom *The Grinder*), and more stay-at-home dads (displaying less angst about not having "real" jobs).

"REAL" MEN We put the word *real* in quotes because we want to use the term loosely. We're certainly not the first to suggest that reality TV programming is anything *but* real, even though it sells itself as such. Much of reality's "real" moments are scripted, rehearsed, shot, re-shot, and highly edited to create a desired effect (Pozner, 2010a; Skeggs & Wood, 2008). Critics, as well as proponents, of reality TV are everywhere, offering all kinds of contentions about this form of "manipulated reality" or "constructed fiction" and its effects on our culture (Andrejevic, 2003;

Remember...

Convergence: The merging of media content across various platforms

Mock-Macho Sitcom: Television situation comedy with a central theme of mocking or making fun of a middle-aged man's anxieties

Playful Patriarch: Male leading character in a sitcom who is typically a devoted husband and father, but who often goofs up and admits he doesn't understand women

Heteronormative: Presenting heterosexuality as the norm or predominant form of human relations

The long-running reality show *Deadliest Catch* revolves predominantly around men.

© Mat Hayward/Shutterstock.com

Dubrofsky, 2006; Funt, 2009; Moorti & Ross, 2004; Ouellette & Hay, 2008; Pozner, 2010b). But we can't escape one reality: Reality TV isn't a fad; it's a force unto itself in TV programming around the world, not just in the United States.

Some reality TV shows (past and present) revolve predominantly around men (e.g., *Cops, Dog the Bounty Hunter, Deadliest Catch*) and some around women (e.g., *The Real Housewives of* [insert city here], *Say Yes to the Dress, What Not to Wear*); many are ensemble-based (the oldest of modern reality shows, MTV's *The Real World; Survivor; Top Chef; The Bachelor/Bachelorette* series; *Jersey Shore; The Voice*; Bierly, 2011; Douglas, 2013; Jordan, 2015; Kinnick & Parton, 2005; Lee & Moscowitz, 2015). Some shows focus on family life—the roles of spouses, interactions with children, and occasional complications from extended family members (e.g., *Wife Swap, 19 Kids and Counting*; Ferguson, 2010; Palmer, 2015).

Perhaps nowhere are stereotypical gender roles more obvious than in reality dating shows. Media scholar Dana Cloud (2010) describes these shows as an "irony bribe," meaning that viewers can see the programs as both "'real' and 'not-real,' and therefore worth viewing and worthless at the same time" (p. 413). A viewer can be the ultimate fly on the wall, participating in the fantasy of romance while voyeuristically standing apart or outside the fantasy, not taking it seriously. Cloud cites *The Bachelor* as a case in point. In *The Bachelor*, men *act* while women *appear*; the bachelor has his pick among a bevy of young, attractive women (which Cloud calls the "harem") who clamor for his attention and compete to be his final selection. The power dynamic is apparent, in that the bachelor gets to choose, whereas "the women's role is that of supplicant, waiting passively for the redemption of romance" (p. 420).

Of course, when a woman takes the lead, as in seasons of *The Bachelorette*, the roles are reversed, with a bachelorette as chooser and a group of men as chosen (or rejected). But the power dynamics don't seem to be parallel, meaning the power of public rejection by the bachelorette seems somehow different than when the bachelor dismisses the women. Perhaps the difference lies in the postrejection confessionals—the brief self-disclosures by rejected contestants as they exit the house or ride off in the backseat of a limo. Rejected female contestants tend to be very emotional, with tears and declarations of themselves as "losers." In contrast, rejected male contestants' speeches tend toward demonstrations of anger and protestations of bravado (as in, "she doesn't know what she's missing"), with only a very few "what's wrong with me" speeches.

Women & Television Programming

In the 1970s, media scholar Gayle Tuchman and colleagues described women's presence on prime-time television as a "symbolic annihilation" (Tuchman, Daniels, & Benet, 1978). As we alluded to previously in our discussion of men on television, male roles still outnumber female roles on TV and women are still primarily portrayed interpersonally, meaning in connection to other people, rather than their work or social/political issues (Butsch, 2015; Harwood & Anderson, 2002; Lauzen, Dozier, & Horan, 2008). But again, as the delivery methods for TV programming continue to expand, so will female characters' depictions. One could argue that the highly sexual millennial women portrayed on HBO's hit *Girls* represent departures from how women typically are depicted on TV, even cable TV (Fuller & Driscoll, 2015).

SCRIPTED WOMEN Media scholars have explored women's roles in prime-time television for several decades, noting various trends. We referred to Moore's (1992) analysis of TV families in the 1980s in the previous section; Moore was also critical of how women were portrayed during this time period. While TV programs began to depict men in some nontraditional roles, women's changing roles in society were largely ignored.

The reality was that huge numbers of women entered the workforce during the '80s, but televised representations of them were few and far between.

Greenberg and Collette (1997) examined thirty years worth of TV programming, noting women's underrepresentation, traditional depictions (e.g., wives and mothers), and general youthfulness. Olson and Douglas (1997) analyzed the top ten most popular prime-time American sitcoms over a forty-year span and found that both the quantity and quality of women's roles in these programs declined. Signorielli and Bacue (1999) focused on TV dramas airing from 1967 through 1998. They found that although women's presence in prime-time programming increased over time, women were still greatly underrepresented compared to their numbers in the U.S. population, were depicted as younger than their male counterparts, and appeared more in sitcoms than dramas, which was a disadvantage, given that dramas garner more respect and are taken more seriously by the viewing public. Signorielli and Bacue (1999) found one departure from earlier studies: In the more recent years under investigation, more women were presented as employed outside the home, in more prestigious occupations, and more frequently in traditionally male jobs (e.g., law enforcement, medicine) than in the past.

Research also examined how the few contemporary working female characters on TV dealt with the tension between their personal and professional lives—the "juggling" issue (Douglas, 1995; Dow, 1996; Vande Berg & Streckfuss, 1992). Although many female characters were depicted as having both successful careers and personal lives, plot lines centered around their love lives with men (Japp, 1991; Steenland, 1995). *Desperate Housewives* best exemplified this trend, in that its depictions of working women focused more on their personal lives and intrigue on Wisteria Lane than their careers (Hill, 2010; Hopeck & Ivic, 2014; Merskin, 2011; Sharp, 2011). Although the tension between personal and professional constitutes a reality for many contemporary women (even more so today), the relational elements in female TV characters' lives receive more emphasis, sending a message that no matter how professional or successful a woman becomes, what matters most and makes a woman acceptable or unacceptable in American consciousness is her relationship with a man (Douglas, 2009). Most of this TV programming was heteronormative as well.

Some breakthrough roles emerged for women on TV during this period but probably no other depictions represented breakthroughs like the four female characters of *Sex and the City* (Gerhard, 2011; Oria, 2014; Schwartz, 2009). Scholars and media critics view this show as an example of mixed-

© Everett Collection/Shutterstock.com

Sex and the City was viewed by many as an example of mixed-signal TV programming.

signal TV programming (Baxter, 2009; Lorie, 2011; Paglia, 2008). On the one hand, viewers got strong messages of women's liberation—that it's fine (even preferable) to be single and sexually active, even experimental; to have and raise a baby on your own (or choose not to have children); to break up with men who aren't right for you instead of feeling pressure to marry; and to divorce if you're unhappy (Soll, 2008). On the other hand, the four central characters focused more on their romances than their careers or other aspects of their lives—again, a throwback to a more conventional depiction of women. Although friendship was the primary focus of the show, the almost constant subject of conversation and plot lines was men—how to get them, what to do with them, whether or not to keep them, and when it was time to move on to the next one. By the time the first full-length *Sex and the City* movie came out, all four characters were in committed heterosexual relationships, albeit in various stages of success.

Research has documented other changes in how women are portrayed on TV. Media scholars Shanahan, Signorielli, and Morgan (2008) examined prime-time TV programming over a three-decade period and found that women's presence on TV had increased. Women were more likely to be portrayed in traditionally male professions and the number of married female characters approached that of male characters (opposite the past trend). Examples include many of writer Shonda Rhimes' characters,

Meredith Grey on *Grey's Anatomy*, Olivia Pope on *Scandal*, and Annalise Keating on *How to Get Away with Murder* (Klein Modisett, 2015). Another trend emerged: "bad" women acting and speaking "badly," meaning female characters who broke laws and used foul, sexual language were more prevalent in this new century of TV than ever before. Examples include leading female characters on *Weeds, Nurse Jackie,* and *Saving Grace* (and pretty much anyone on *Orange Is the New Black)* (Bednarek, 2015).

Media and social critic Sarah Sahim (2015) documents another trend in which a female TV (or film) character is presented as an "American woman-child" (p. 7), the female counterpart to the characters Seth Rogen often portrays in films. The (typically white) woman-child is portrayed as being on a personal journey that ends up with her achieving nothing, emotionally or financially. Examples include Hannah on *Girls*, Mindy on *The Mindy Project* (whose Indian cultural background is downplayed and who doesn't struggle financially, but interpersonally and romantically), and the two female leads on *Two Broke Girls*. Sahim concludes: "The rise of the woman-child gestures to Hollywood's slow learning curve toward representing the experience of millennial women, but until big studios acknowledge the diversity and nuances of women of color as well, we are only getting part of the picture" (p. 7).

"REAL" WOMEN Let's begin this discussion by focusing on one of the older, yet still popular, forms of reality (or unscripted) TV programming: the talk show. Because there are between twenty and thirty nationally syndicated talk shows on the air in any given year in the United States, the impact of these shows cannot be denied (Cragin, 2010; Peck, 2006; Wood, 2009). Although talk show audiences were and are still dominated by women viewers, particularly daytime shows, the male audience has grown steadily since the 1990s (Albiniak, 2010; Henson & Parameswaran, 2008; Shattuc, 2004). Some suggest that this growth relates to the inclusion of more conflict and controversy on such programs as *The Jerry Springer Show*, but it is also likely related to recession-induced unemployment rates for men in the first decade of the new century, and the rise in stay-at-home fathers.

The original modern TV talk show, *The Phil Donahue Show*, revolutionized by *The Oprah Winfrey Show* (and others), provided a platform for discussions of social issues; some would argue that these shows, and daytime talk shows in general, are more about women's issues than social issues (Heaton & Wilson, 1995; Shattuc, 1997; Stark, 2000b). Feminist media critic Roseann Mandziuk (1991) studied daytime TV talk shows, discovering that the intimacy of the topics, discussion, and revelations from guests, hosts, and audience members paralleled a cultural feminine stereotype of women as sensitive, nurturing, relational, and responsive. In addition, Mandziuk exposed an agenda-setting function, concluding that such shows actually instruct women as to what they should worry about. Topics like "the husband who likes to wear his wife's lingerie" or "the girl who flirts with her sister's boyfriend" trivialize the more critical issues facing contemporary women. A greater problem ensues when the larger, general public ghettoizes important issues (e.g., equal pay, reproductive rights, sexual harassment, child care) by labeling them women's issues rather than societal or human issues. Treatments of the bigger issues often get suppressed in favor of topics that appeal to a wider base of audience.

But TV talk shows have morphed over time; they may still be primarily the province of women, but their scope has broadened and their reach has extended. Few will doubt the power of Oprah Winfrey to transform many people's lives, especially women's lives. Helen Wood (2009), author of *Talking with Television*, suggests that many viewers don't just absorb TV talk shows, they personalize and interact with them, talking back to their TVs while watching. This more active approach to TV viewership creates a heightened familiarity as well as a faux intimacy with shows, guests, and hosts. In the case of *Ellen*, audience members get to dance with Ellen DeGeneres as she weaves through the crowd; no doubt many at-home viewers also dance and develop a sense that Ellen is a trusted friend (Moore, 2015; Skerski, 2007).

A whole host of reality TV programs beyond the talk show communicate images of women in our society. From dating shows, cooking contests, model competitions, and portrayals of frustrated, newly divorced moms, rampaging brides, and dramatic housewives to MTV's offerings about teen pregnancy (*16 and Pregnant* and *Teen Mom*), "reality" is everywhere (Armstrong, 2010; Casper & Gilmour, 2014; Dubrofsky, 2009; Givhan, 2009; Mesaros-Winckles, 2014; Sung, 2013; Ward, 2015). We explored men in reality TV a few pages back; it's probably not surprising for you to learn that a great deal of research has explored women and reality TV. One trend found in research surrounds a focus on women's bodies and attractiveness, including cosmetic surgery makeover shows (Banet-Weiser & Portwood-

When you are one of two girls who have really big breasts and a great hot body with six other women who aren't, you can say that is a handicap. —Jeff Probst, host of *Survivor*

Stacer, 2006; Hasinoff, 2008; Marwick, 2010; Nabi, 2009; Stern, 2009; Tait, 2011).

Communication scholar Carolyn Davis (2008) examined perceptions of reality TV personalities, specifically contestants across several seasons of *Survivor*. Although four trends or categories emerged for male contestants, only one emerged for the women—what Davis termed "Beauty and the Beast" (p. 14). Subjects' perceptions of the women on *Survivor* focused mainly around their appearance and level of physical strength. On the "beauty" end of the scale, female contestants who were perceived as highly physically attractive were also perceived to be highly feminine, passive, and emotional; they were the ones who cried the most on the show. On the "beast" side of the equation, these women tended to be the older cast members who were perceived as masculine, less physically attractive, and more rugged looking, but who were deemed capable of performing well in challenges and surviving rough conditions. Few female contestants fell between these two polar characterizations, from the perspectives of participants in the study. These results represent a trend in perceptions of TV personalities (and, many would argue, in real life in our culture): Women are judged more harshly for their looks and attractiveness than men, whereas their intelligence or other factors are diminished.

Other media scholars critique the fact that women on reality TV programs often use their sexuality and flirtatiousness to accomplish their goals, whether the goal is landing a fiancé (as on *The Bachelor*), winning lots of money (as on *The Amazing Race* and many other shows), or having a major event go as planned, where one is the center of attention (enter *Bridezillas*). From one viewpoint, the women in such a show as WEtv's *Bridezillas* represent a combination of femininity and control (Engstrom, 2009); from another view, they represent an unfortunate gender stereotype (Brown, 2005; Egley Waggoner, 2004). Is using whatever skills and talents you possess to achieve a desired outcome an example of being empowered to succeed, even if manipulation, deception, and narcissism emerge along the way? Is such an approach merely strategy and competitiveness, or is it a throw-back to a gender stereotype—using "feminine wiles" to trick others, to outpower them?

How empowering is reality TV for women? Researchers Cato and Dillman Carpentier (2010) explored that issue, but looked at empowerment from more of a third-wave feminist perspective that focuses more on individual choice than a social movement for the good of all women. In their study, college-aged women who held positive attitudes about reality TV embraced a form of sexual empowerment, which the authors describe as feeling good about one's sexual self and one's ability to make sexual choices, no matter what those choices are. Subjects also endorsed stereotypical roles for women in society, relating sexuality with hyperfemininity, and reported being more sexually permissive. In a nutshell, this study showed that the more favorable a woman is toward reality TV and the more she embraces notions of sexual empowerment, the more sexually permissive she tends to be, which, in turn, affects her preferences for certain reality TV shows.

TV and LGBTQ(IA+?)

Whether TV programs are scripted or reality, daytime or prime-time, the inclusion of gays, lesbians, bisexuals/bigenders, transgenders, and people identifying as queer (LGBTQs) is more frequent; their portrayals are generally more positive and a great deal more open than in times past.

When do you suspect that the first gay male character appeared in American television programming? 1960s? 1980s? It'll likely surprise you to learn that the answer is a wrestler named Gorgeous George, who was one of the biggest media stars of the 1940s (Capsuto, 2000). The first major sitcom to address the subject of homosexuality was *All in the Family* in 1971, when Archie Bunker learned that his buddy, a former pro football player, was gay. The first gay recurring cast member of a TV show was played by Billy Crystal on *Soap;* Crystal's character wanted a sex change operation so he could live openly with his closeted lover, who was also a pro football player. Before the first episode of *Soap* aired (but after Crystal's story line was made public), the ABC network received 30,000 letters demanding cancellation (Tropiano, 2002).

Another TV milestone that received much scholarly and popular attention occurred in 1997, when Ellen DeGeneres' character on the sitcom *Ellen* disclosed she was gay, as well as on the cover of *Time* magazine—Ellen came out both as Ellen Morgan on the show and as herself (Dow, 2001; Hubert, 2003; Moore, 2015; Reed, 2005, 2011; Shugart, 2001; Sloop, 2006). Prior to that time, gay, lesbian, and bisexual/bigender identities were implied, portrayed by secondary or ensemble characters, or depicted in ways that suggested sexuality, but without blatantly showing homosexual affection. (Transgender characters were virtually nonexistent on TV, save the poorly drawn, overly dramatized cross-dresser or prostitute on the occasional cop show.) One of the most popular prime-time dramas of the 1980s was *thirtysomething*, which broadcast a controversial scene of two bare-chested men sharing a bed, having a conversation after sex. The drama survived, even after losing $1.5 million in ad revenues after the episode aired (Tropiano, 2002). Yet another significant development was the 1998 premier of *Will &*

Grace, a sitcom deemed groundbreaking for its depiction of a close friendship between a gay man and a straight woman, plus the contrasting personalities of the two central gay male characters, Will and Jack (Battles & Hilton-Morrow, 2002; Hart, 2003; Linneman, 2008; Shugart, 2003).

Fast-forward into the 2000s to witness a proliferation of TV programming featuring gay and lesbian characters, plotlines, and issues, primarily on cable TV, such as Showtime's *Queer as Folk* and *The L Word*. The two dramas garnered much scholarly and popular press attention during their runs, perhaps because their inclusion on a pay cable channel's lineup granted them liberties and an openness not seen on network television. *Queer as Folk,* derived from a successful British series of the same name, focused primarily on a group of young, white male friends, their lovers, and a lesbian couple in a committed relationship who were friends with the men (Noble, 2007; Peters, 2011; Porfido, 2011). Besides this show's groundbreaking depiction of nonheterosexual relationships and sexuality, it also proved to be maverick in its featuring of the word *queer* in its title.

Receiving even more notoriety than *Queer as Folk* after its debut in 2004, *The L Word* was praised (and criticized) for its portrayal of lesbian relationships (Aaron, 2006; Dove-Viebahn, 2011; Farr & Degroult, 2008; Pratt, 2011; Wolfe & Roripaugh, 2006).

Reality TV shows have included lesbian, gay, and, on occasion, bisexual/bigender and transgender cast members for some time, such as openly gay

Many say that it was the "Fab Five" who changed the presence of non-heterosexual people in reality TV.

© Featureflash Photo Agency/Shutterstock.com

Richard Hatch, winner of the first season of *Survivor*, and Adam Lambert (who didn't fully out himself as a gay man until after his season of *American Idol* concluded; Wypijewski, 2009). But many argue that it was the "Fab Five" of Bravo's *Queer Eye for the Straight Guy* who broke the doors wide open for nonheterosexual presence in reality TV (Clarkson, 2005; Pullen, 2007; Streitmatter, 2009). Just like *Queer as Folk* and *The L Word*, *Queer Eye* was both acclaimed and denounced (Gallagher, 2004; Hart, 2004; Pearson & Reich, 2004; Sender, 2006; Weiss, 2005; Westerfelhaus & Lacroix, 2006).

In the decade of the 2000s, gays, lesbians, bisexuals/bigenders, and transgenders were depicted on TV less frequently than they are now, but the emphasis was clearly on their nonheterosexual identities (Fisher, Hill, Grube, & Gruber, 2007; Ivory, Gibson, & Ivory, 2009). In 2006 an episode of *Queer Eye for the Straight Guy* entitled "Transform This Trans-man" focused on a fashion makeover of a transman named Miles Goff, which was a first for reality TV at that time (Booth, 2015). In contrast, now the majority of casts on TV (reality or scripted) includes gay couples (such as *Modern Family*), or lesbian, gay, bisexual/bigender, and transgender characters (such as *Empire; Orange Is the New Black; How to Get Away with Murder*, in which the second season revealed a past lesbian relationship for the lead character of Annalise Keating; *Transparent*, in which the family patriarch undergoes gender transition; and ABC Family's *Becoming Us*, a reality show about a teenager with a transgender parent; Armstrong, 2011; Dove-Viebahn, 2015; Harris, 2015; Maerz, 2014, 2015a).

And then there was Cait.... No doubt you've read or heard about Olympic champion Bruce Jenner's transition into Caitlyn Jenner, made fully public on April 24, 2015, in his (becoming "her") lengthy on-air interview with Diane Sawyer (Havrilesky, 2015). In July of 2015, Caitlyn was introduced via the cover of *Vanity Fair* magazine (depicted with long flowing hair and perfectly airbrushed skin, and wearing a bathing suit complete with cleavage; Rice, 2015). The transition, or more accurately, the new life of Caitlyn Jenner as transwoman continues to be explored on the cable network E!'s reality series, *I Am Cait* (Maerz, 2015b).

While other transgender actors and media personalities have appeared in multiple media formats in recent years, Caitlyn Jenner's connection to the Kardashian family (and their TV shows) instantly enhanced the viewership for *I Am Cait*, shining a light on transgenderism rarely seen before on TV or any other medium. Criticism abounds regarding Jenner's privileged and cocooned existence, exacerbated by shots of her house on a Malibu hilltop

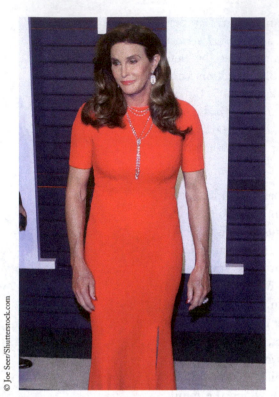

Caitlyn Jenner put a spotlight on transgenderism as TV had never before seen.

that appear in many episodes of the series. Other complaints surround the show's focus on physical beauty and fashion, with comments about how airbrushed and pampered Caitlyn Jenner appears, the frequency of cut-away shots focused on her perfectly manicured fingernails, and the use of gauzy camera lens shots, especially during "confessionals" in which Cait speaks candidly about her experiences. One of the more obvious decisions for the first season of the show, no doubt made by Jenner herself but also likely reinforced by producers, was to focus early episodes around post-transition life for Cait. However, in the second season, more information is revealed about physical and hormonal alterations Cait has undergone (and has yet to undergo) during her transition from biological man to woman.

But even given all the strategy behind this show—decision making about what to include and what to leave out, how to market the show using the massive Kardashian and E! network machinery, the near glorification of transgenderism as social change and freedom—one thing must be said from the opinion of your textbook author: The show is better than expected. Yes, it depicts economic and social privilege. Yes, it tends to be short on reality, in terms of the grueling process of physical transition (gender reassignment) and it isn't told from anything resembling a feminist perspective. But it is compelling, enlightening, and at times inspiring (again, from one person's opinion). For example, one early episode in the first season included Cait's first encounter (in her new female form) with her mother, Esther, and sisters, Pam and Lisa. The audience saw Esther's struggle to relate to her "new" child, her emotions about missing her son, and her determination to work on her language because, as she said, "pronouns are important." Research indicates that a transgender person's family relationships and family members' reactions to the transition are critical to a successful process of identity reformation (Norwood & Lannutti, 2015). Much as she'd like to be, Caitlyn Jenner isn't a spokesperson for *all* transgender people, but she is shining a huge light on something that's historically been shrouded in darkness, so perhaps that's a significant contribution to our study of sex, gender, and communication.

LESSONS FROM THE BIG SCREEN: FILM AND GENDER

Imagine you had to put together a time capsule, a snapshot of American life that represented your time on Earth, something future generations would stumble upon and use to better understand their heritage. No doubt you'd turn to media to help you fill the capsule; no doubt you'd include some movies. The question is: Which movies would you include and why? Going even further, if only three movies would fit in the capsule, which three would you make sure got in? Would you include films from different genres, such as a western, a rom-com, and a horror movie? Would you include a classic like *Casablanca*, a sci-fi film like *Star Wars*, or a movie that depicts your version of typical American life? What would your choices say to future generations about your view of sex and gender?

Gender in the Movies

Film has the power to communicate gender roles. The power may not be conveyed through blatant messages about roles women and men play in society or about how we communicate in relationships; the more subtle messages that we see and hear repeatedly are more likely to sink in on some level and affect us (Hefner & Wilson, 2013). The potential effect on children is even greater, evidenced by the significant impact of Disney and Pixar films on kids (Artz, 2015; Bell, Haas, & Sells, 2008; Davis, 2005, 2007; Gilliam & Wooden, 2008; King, 2010).

ONE FOR THE CAPSULE One memorable, outlook-altering movie is *Tootsie*, a film that to this day conjures up confused but pleasant thoughts about gender roles. Here's a synopsis of the plot: Dustin Hoffman plays Michael, an actor who desperately wants work, but whose opportunities are limited because of his reputation for being difficult. When his agent tells Michael no one will hire him, Michael sets out to prove him wrong by auditioning for a role on a popular soap opera. The twist is that the role is for a woman, so Michael auditions in drag as an actress named Dorothy Michaels. After landing the part, Michael encounters a number of sticky situations because of his hidden identity. The stickiest situation arises when Michael realizes that he's falling for Julie, another actress on the soap, played in the movie by Jessica Lange. As Michael (via Dorothy) becomes good friends with Julie, he's confronted with how to admit the deception and still have a chance with Julie.

One amazing aspect of this movie is how Dustin Hoffman's portrayal of Dorothy, through the character of Michael, becomes real to viewers, so real that when Michael reveals his true identity in one of the final scenes, audiences are sad because they're going to miss Dorothy. Another fascinating aspect of this movie was that it fulfilled a fantasy for many people—walking in a different sex's shoes, seeing how they're treated, and getting to know an attractive person without the hang-ups and pressures that often accompany romantic relationships. It was also intriguing to think about the opportunity of putting one's newfound insight to work in a relationship. As Michael explained to Julie in the last scene of the movie, "I was a better man with you, as a woman, than I ever was as a man. I've just got to learn to do it without the dress."

The film *Tootsie* frames the rest of our discussion nicely, because it exemplifies the theme of *gender bending*, a term referring to media depictions in which characters' actions belie or contradict what is expected of members of their sex (Benshoff & Griffin, 2009; Daughton, 2010; Gatewood, 2001). But our use of this term is not limited only to people who have masqueraded in films as members of a different sex. The example of *Tootsie* serves to start our thinking, but gender bending doesn't necessarily mean actors in drag.

BUDDIES ON A DEAD-END ROAD *Thelma & Louise* was a groundbreaking gender-bending film on many counts; it was an open-road, buddy film, but with female instead of male buddies (Glenn, 1992; Welsch, 2001). One of the most laudable effects of this film was that it sparked a great deal of discussion. In fact, it still sparks discussion. Although the film opened in May of 1991, people still talk about it, and media critics and scholars still write about it.

Female audiences for this movie had complex emotions and varied reactions (Cooper, 2000). Some cheered what they perceived to be payback, especially in a scene with a piggish trucker. At the same time, many felt odd to be applauding revenge. Besides the dominant images and "radical" behaviors of the female leads, male characters in *Thelma & Louise* were portrayed in an atypical fashion for movies at that time. These portrayals led to claims of male bashing, based on contentions that the male characters were unrealistic and exaggerated, particularly because they were repeatedly vanquished by the two women.

What messages about women and men did audiences get from this movie? Some people came away thinking that women were winning some kind of war against male oppression and retaliating against unacceptable male behavior in like fashion. This is a gender-bender message taken to an extreme. However, while believing that the movie made a significant statement about relationships in the '90s, some film scholars contend that *Thelma & Louise* wasn't a triumphant women's rights movie. They point out that the film depicts women's desperation—women who counter the powerlessness they feel with extreme actions, but who, in the long run, are still out of power in a patriarchal system (Cook, 2007; Fournier, 2006; Sturken, 2008).

GENDER BENDING OR SOCIETY SHIFTING? It's often a point of contention as to whether a film portrayal is truly gender bending or if it simply represents evolution or a societal shift in how men and women behave, see themselves, and relate to each other. While one could argue that the characters Melissa McCarthy tends to portray in her films, like *Spy*, *Tammy*, and *The Heat*, are indicative of gender bending, these roles might also be merely reflective of a broader view of how women behave (for good and for ill) in contemporary society (Valby, 2014).

> Being a sexual object is mortifying and irritating, yet it's giving you power—an awful power that you've done nothing to deserve, a powerless power. I think some young women fall in love with that power, and it's really objectifying. And when it starts falling away, it's an incredible relief. —Helen Mirren, actor

Are Michelle Rodriguez's performances in such films as *Avatar* and the *Fast & Furious* franchise or Jennifer Lawrence's in the *Hunger Games* franchise gender bending or just depictions of badass women being bad ass? (Lee, 2015; Vilkomerson, 2013) What about Amy Schumer in *Trainwreck*, Paul Rudd in [insert many film titles here], Sandra Bullock in *Gravity* and *Our Brand Is Crisis*, Tyler Perry's Medea films, or even Elsa and Anna in *Frozen*? Are these gender bending roles or just reflections of our expanding view of what's acceptable behavior for women and men?

Critics and scholars go back and forth with this argument, but one thing's clear: Film roles for men and women of varying identities, orientations, ages, ethnicities, and abilities have never been more diverse, with more diversification no doubt to come (Burrill, 2014; J. Shaw, 2014; Means Coleman, 2012; Nashawaty, 2015; Sperling, 2015; Staskiewicz, 2015; Zoladz, 2015a). Perhaps no other film portrays gender bending (and our increasing acceptance of sex and gender diversity) more than *The Danish Girl*, in which actor Eddie Redmayne portrays Lili Elbe, long believed to be the first person to undergo gender reassignment surgery (born male in 1882 and transitioning to female in the 1920s; McGovern, 2015).

THE COMMUNICATIVE POWER OF PORNOGRAPHY

We usually don't begin our coverage on a topic with a disclaimer or apology, but this subject is different—*really* different. Pornography is a topic that continues to generate a great deal of research and writing, and there's no way we can do justice to that body of information here. What we offer is a snapshot—a highly condensed introduction to the topic—just to get you thinking about pornography, perhaps in a way you haven't before.

Pornography: Definitions and Controversy

A specific, universally agreed-upon legal definition of pornography doesn't exist. In legal contexts, *obscenity* is the term used, but not all pornographic material meets the legal standard of obscenity (deGrazia, 1992; Tedford & Herbeck, 2013). Scholars describe what all the term *pornography* can encompass, even tracing the term to its linguistic roots:

> Numerous attempts have been made to define pornography and to distinguish it from what some consider its more acceptable form—"erotica." The word pornography comes from the Greek "writings of prostitutes" (porno = prostitute and graphein = to write). In recent definitions, material has been classified as pornography when the producer's intent is to elicit erotic responses from the consumer, when it sexually arouses the consumer, or when characters are degraded or demeaned. . . . (Malamuth & Billings, 1984, pp. 117–118)

Catherine MacKinnon and Andrea Dworkin wrote about the serious negative impact of pornographic images on women's lives and American culture in general. MacKinnon and Dworkin are best known for their efforts to get an anti-pornography ordinance passed in Minnesota in the 1980s. The definition of pornography in their bill was written from the standpoint of women's victimization, which is understandable given that (still today) more women than men are victimized in pornography. MacKinnon and Dworkin's definition is as follows:

> "Pornography" means the graphic sexually explicit subordination of women through pictures and/or words . . . that also includes one or more of the following: (1) Women are presented dehumanized as sexual objects, things, or commodities. (2)

Women are presented as sexual objects who enjoy humiliation or pain . . . (3) Women are presented in postures or positions of sexual submission . . . (4) Women's body parts . . . are exhibited such that women are reduced to those parts. (5) Women are presented being penetrated by objects or animals. (6) Women are presented in scenarios of degradation, humiliation, injury, or torture . . . (as in Gillespie et al., 1994, p. 44)

MacKinnon and Dworkin contended that their definition also pertained to electronic materials, not just traditional media like magazines, films, books, and so forth. They also explained that, while their categories specifically identified women as subordinated through pornography, men, children, and transgenders could be substituted in the language of their definition.

Representing another viewpoint is Nadine Strossen (2000), outspoken critic of anti-pornography efforts. In Strossen's view, "Pornography is a vague term. In short, it is sexual expression that is meant to, or does, provoke sexual arousal or desire" (p. 18). Strossen differentiates between destructive and degrading pornography and that which is merely sexually arousing. She still considers the latter pornography, but acceptable pornography. Strossen and other anti-censorship activists believe that if you suppress women's sexuality (by suppressing the distribution and consumption of pornography), you actually oppress them. Strossen explains: "We are as committed as any other feminists to eradicating violence and discrimination against women. But we believe that suppressing sexual words and images will not advance these crucial causes. To the contrary, we are convinced that censoring sexual expression actually would do more harm than good to women's rights and safety" (p. 14).

Sarracino and Scott (2009) discuss the complexities of pornography: "Porn is not one thing. Porn is not a single color, but a whole spectrum. Therefore, its influences on the culture are similarly varied and complex" (p. xiii). They explain their view that some pornography is definitely bad, such as child pornography; other porn they describe as "toxic waste," in reference to dark and violent pornography prevalent on the Internet (p. xiii). But they also suggest that amateur home videos, for example, are a more benign form of porn that American culture readily consumes, possibly with little harmful consequence.

Types of Readily Accessible Pornography

Hard-core pornography depicts or describes intercourse and/or other sexual practices (e.g., oral sex, anal sex). In *soft-core pornography*, such acts are

implied but not fully or explicitly acted out on a screen or displayed on a page. However, Pamela Paul (2005), author of *Pornified: How Pornography Is Damaging Our Lives, Our Relationships, and Our Families*, contends that hard-core/soft-core distinctions are no longer relevant or particularly descriptive. In our casual world where pornographic images are instantly accessible and the repercussions of consuming pornography are mild, if not nonexistent, old distinctions between "soft" and "hard" may be meaningless. Moreover, many people who consume porn nowadays do so without much explanation, embarrassment, or need for secrecy (Attwood, 2011). Although people in past generations thought it wasn't nice to look at "dirty pictures," Paul (2005) suggests, "Today, pornography is so seamlessly integrated into popular culture that embarrassment or surreptitiousness is no longer part of the equation" (p. 4).

> Pornography is a huge, huge part of our media culture. The message is reducing people, especially women, to nothing but sex objects. It happens in music videos, TV shows, movies, and magazines, and so many commercials. Whether it's rated X or approved by the FCC to sell Doritos, the message is the same.
> —Joseph Gordon-Levitt, actor

Before you dismiss or downplay this discussion because you don't believe yourself to be a consumer of pornography, think again. Perhaps you only think of pornography as the hard-core version, which you might not consume. But do you consume soft-core porn? If you adopt a broad definition of pornography as material that provokes sexual desire, then what's considered pornographic takes on a much wider frame (Boyle, 2011; Caputi, 2015; Dines, 2010; Ross, 2013). What about magazines easily purchased at convenience stores? If the depictions in such publications are sexually arousing, then do they qualify as pornographic? How about a Victoria's Secret catalog or the swimsuit issue of *Sports Illustrated*? (Uh-oh, we've just treaded on some *really* sacred ground.) Some argue that the *SI* swimsuit issue actually is soft-core porn, just packaged in a sports magazine to make it appear more socially acceptable (Davis, 1997; Hopper, 2011). What about the stripping and dancing in so-called "gentleman's" clubs? Is this activity erotic, but not pornographic, even though it may be sexually arousing to the audience?

Does the swimsuit issue of *Sports Illustrated* qualify as pornography?

Just because something might be pornographic, is it necessarily harmful, degrading, and dangerous for society? Does pornography serve some useful purpose? Sexually explicit, arousing material is all around us and available for our consumption any hour of the day, especially on the Internet (Cronin & Davenport, 2010; Familysafemedia.com, 2015; Paasonen, 2015; Sevcikova, Serek, Barbovschi, & Daneback, 2014; Wright, 2012, 2013; Wright & Arroyo, 2013; Wright, Bae, & Funk, 2013). What you consume, what you believe consenting adults have the right to consume, and what adults should protect children from consuming—these are important decisions each individual should make.

Research Findings on the Effects of Pornography Consumption

Research findings continue to show that, not only does porn degrade women and reinforce sexist attitudes in cultures around the world, but the consumption of porn has other negative effects. Most studies find more male involvement with and positive responses to pornography than female, across age groups and ethnicities (Kolehmainen, 2010; Paul & Shim, 2008). Compared to their female counterparts, male adolescents exposed to sexually explicit material online perceived that the images were realistic and reported more positive, permissive attitudes about recreational sex (i.e., viewing sex as a game and for personal gratification rather than to foster a relationship; Peter & Valkenburg, 2006, 2008, 2010).

Pornographic materials that depict male dominance and female degradation have been found to arouse male viewers (Glascock, 2005). Studies have found a link between porn consumption, men's sexist attitudes, and male sexual behavior, specifically, men committing acts of sexual domination over women (Foubert, Brosi, & Bannon, 2011; Hald, Malamuth, & Lange, 2013; Hald, Malamuth, & Yuen, 2010). Foubert et al.'s (2011) study focused on fraternity men, 82% of whom reported having viewed "mainstream pornography" (e.g., films, online sources, videos, magazines, books) within the last calendar year. These college men reported higher levels of intention to rape, were significantly less likely to intervene as a bystander to stop an act of sexual violence or aggression toward a woman, and were more likely to believe rape myths, such as the myth about women secretly desiring to be raped. (See our discussion of rape myth acceptance in Chapter 7.) Regular consumption of both alcohol and pornography have also been linked to male sexual aggression (Wright, Sun, Steffen, & Tokunaga, 2015).

The Crux of the Matter: Pornography Is Personal

We have two purposes in presenting this material on pornography to you: first, to help you better understand the complexities of the issue through a discussion of diverse viewpoints; and second, to challenge you to think about the impact of pornography in your own life. The barrage of sexual images we consume daily—in song lyrics and music videos (as we explore in the next section of this chapter); TV and film images; advertisements in magazines, newspapers, and online; and images in comic books, cartoon strips, and cyberspace—simply *have* to have some effect.

Remember...

Gender Bending: Media depiction in which a character's actions belie or contradict what is expected for members of her or his sex

Obscenity: Legal term used in reference to pornographic material

Pornography: Material produced with an intent to elicit erotic responses from a consumer, to sexually arouse a consumer, to degrade or demean female characters in a sexual manner, or to portray unequal power in sexual activity

Hard-Core Pornography: Material that depicts or describes intercourse and/or other sexual practices

Soft-Core Pornography: Material in which sexual acts are implied but not fully or explicitly acted out or portrayed

Here's an example to make this stance more concrete; you might think it an extreme case, but it involves a male student, just like someone sitting in one of your classes. A few years back a TV news magazine show did a story on a pornography users' support group, a group of about thirty or so male students at Duke University that began as a small group of guys in a campus dorm having regular informal discussions about sex and the effects of pornography on their lives. The camera taped one of the weekly discussions, and the men's revelations were startlingly honest. One student's admission was particularly painful and memorable: He described a sexual encounter with a woman he was very interested in. They'd been out a couple of times but had not yet had sex. He was highly attracted to the woman and wanted to be intimate with her, but when the opportunity to have sex with her arrived, to his embarrassment he was unable to get an erection. He then explained how he enabled himself to function in the situation by imagining the woman beneath him as a pornographic image of a woman from a magazine. When he shut his eyes, tuned out the real person he was with, and vividly imagined the graphic magazine picture, only then did he become aroused. Not only was he worried that this event signaled his sexual future—that he was doomed to a life of being aroused not by real people, but by mediated images—but he was also mortified at the impersonal way he behaved with the woman. He couldn't continue the relationship after this experience and had had no other sexual encounters at the time the group met.

Net Notes

Deceptive Techniques and Internet Porn

Jerry Ropelato (2003), contributor to the Family Safe Media website, in an article entitled "Tricks Pornographers Play," describes deceptive techniques now prevalent on the Internet, designed to lure computer users to pornographic sites. Here are some of the more common techniques. (For more information on pornography, statistics about porn use, and detrimental effects on families, check out **www.familysafemedia.com**.)

Deceptive Techniques

- Porn-napping: Pornographers purchase expired domain names when the original owners forget or don't renew them; unsuspecting Internet users get redirected to porn sites.
- Cyber-squatting: Pornographers purchase domain names for legitimate topics or entities, then alter them in a way typically unnoticed by Internet users. People search for sites innocently, but then get directed to porn sites instead (example: whitehouse.gov versus whitehouse.com).
- Doorway scams: Pornographers have discovered how to carefully design websites so that they get picked up by popular search engines; the content is designed around nonpornographic themes, which places them high on a search engine's list.
- Misspellings: Pornographers buy up misspelled, trendy domain names that typically generate high traffic on the Internet (example: googlle.com, which sent people to an Asian porn site until it got shut down).
- Advertising: Pornographers create fake system errors; when users respond to error messages, they get redirected to porn sites. Other website features such as message alert boxes and false forms dupe users into clicking on buttons that activate porn sites.

Ropelato also mentions entrapment, meaning ways your computer can become altered or marked after you make any of the mistakes above and get lured into a porn site. He warns us to be careful about file sharing and downloading, because these are becoming more prevalent mechanisms for exposing Internet consumers to unexpected pornography.

What's your reaction to the Duke student's story? Do you know people who seem to be more comfortable with pornography than with real lovers? We worry about how pornographic images harm women and men, how they keep women "in their place," as sexualized commodities to be purchased and used for gratification, and how they add to the pressure men feel to be sexual performers. But we also worry about people like those former Duke students who might now be considered sex addicts. We wonder how some men can say that they respect their wives when they regularly frequent strip clubs or adult film houses, become aroused by the dancers or images, and then come home wanting to have sex with their wives. What's the role of pornography in these people's lives? And we can't help but believe that the enormous problem of sexual violence, such as date rape and sexual assault, is related somehow to the all-pervasive, ready-and-waiting-for-your-consumption pornography.

WE COULD MAKE BEAUTIFUL MUSIC TOGETHER . . .

Music is a powerful force in our culture; its influence pervades our existence. In this section of the chapter, we examine how song lyrics and music videos communicate images of men and women.

From Pop to Rock to Rap to Hip-Hop to Country: The Women and Men of Song Lyrics

Sometimes when you listen to a song you want to concentrate on the lyrics; you process the words from a more critical standpoint. But other times you simply like the rhythm, beat, or musical performance, so you tune out the lyrics. Have you ever read the lyrics to a particular song and said to yourself, "Oh *that's* what they're saying"? That's much easier to do nowadays, with full transcripts of lyrics easily found on the Internet. Sometimes, however, you find yourself humming or singing along with a song when you suddenly realize what the words really are. You become acutely aware that what you're singing with or listening to isn't something you'd like to repeat in *any* company, especially mixed company.

Just about as many different ways to process music exist as there are delivery systems for it and people who listen to it. The repetition of songs (particularly ones with hypnotic hooks) reinforces lyrics deeply into listeners' psyches. Music, specifically song lyrics depicting gender and relationships, have more impact on you than you may realize (Frisby, 2010; Timmerman, Allen, Jorgensen, Herrett-Skjellum, Kramer, & Ryan, 2008).

Studies have found a connection between listening to sexually explicit and degrading song lyrics and permissive attitudes toward premarital sex, negative attitudes toward women, distorted perceptions of peers' sexual activities, and becoming sexually active at early ages (Brown, L'Engle,

Pardun, Guo, Kenneavy, & Jackson, 2006; Fischer & Greitemeyer, 2006; Primack, Gold, Schwarz, & Dalton, 2008). So what do song lyrics communicate specifically about women and men?

GENDER TRENDS IN LYRICS Research over the past few decades has found some interesting trends in terms of gender and song lyrics. In the 1970s, Freudiger and Almquist (1978) examined images and gender-role depictions in song lyrics of three genres of popular music. They reviewed the top fifty hits on the *Billboard* country, soul, and easy listening charts and found, first, that women were more the focus of song lyrics than men across all three music genres. Second, women were rarely criticized in these lyrics, but they were described primarily in stereotypes of submissiveness, supportiveness, and dependency. In contrast, when men were mentioned in lyrics—especially songs written from a female perspective—they were portrayed in a more negative and critical light, especially in country lyrics. Men's depictions reflected stereotypical traits of aggression, consistency, action, and confidence.

In the 1980s, studies identified stereotypical portrayals of women in American popular music, portrayals still prevalent today. Butruille and Taylor (1987) detected "three recurring images of women: The Ideal Woman/Madonna/Saint, the evil or fickle Witch/Sinner/Whore, and the victim (often dead)" (p. 180). Some of these images date back to early religious customs and beliefs about the sinful versus virginal nature of woman. One explanation for the popularity of late Tejano singer Selena was her ability to combine saint and sinner, meaning that she presented a sexual, sensual image through dress and demeanor, along with a "good girl" quality and a strong connection to family (Willis & Gonzalez, 1997).

A trend in the 1990s involved female artists' lyrics that described difficult choices, abusive situations, and destructive relationships (Maxwell, 2001; Perry, 2003; Sellnow, 1999). Certainly Alanis Morissette's "You Oughta Know" fits this description. While some scholars contended that women's music of this era was just as focused on romantic relationships as it always was, others believed that women's bold representations

© Helga Esteb/Shutterstock.com

Women are really empowering themselves in politics and in every facet of life now. Music tends to represent what's going on with youth, and the youth of America felt really frustrated a few years ago, and you had these angry alterna-bands. Now you have a lot of females who are stepping up to represent women in America or women in the world, becoming role models for young girls.
—Sheryl Crow, singer and songwriter

of brutality and degradation they experienced in relationships communicated an unprecedented honesty.

In terms of trends for song lyrics and depictions of the sexes in the twenty-first century, a good deal of the research focuses on imagery in rap and hip-hop music, which we discuss next. Researchers have examined other trends, such as the following:

- the connection between exposure to violent song lyrics and aggressive behavior (Brummert Lennings & Warburton, 2011; Lozon & Bensimon, 2014);

- lyrics that challenge the scrutiny given to women's bodies and attractiveness (like Meghan Trainor's "All About That Bass"; Raymer, 2014);

- masculine identity as affected by the lyrics of heavy metal music (Rafalovich, 2006);

- lyrics and performances of breakout artists, like FKA twigs and transgender musician Shamir Bailey (Willoughby, 2015; Zoladz, 2015b);

- and the intersections of gender and race in lyrics (Brooks & Hebert, 2011; Chandler, Ross, Kolar, Kip, & Simmons, 2015; Henry, West, & Jackson, 2010).

Unfortunately, at times it feels like we're regressing to an earlier age in our country's development: Two studies of "The Hot 100" list of pop as well as country songs on *Billboard* charts found evidence of the following themes in song lyrics: men and power over women; sex as a top priority for men; objectification of women; sexual violence against women; women being defined by having a man; and women not valuing themselves (Bretthauer, Schindler Zimmerman, & Banning, 2006; Rogers, 2013).

SEX AND DEGRADATION IN SONGS In the past, pop culture scholars asserted that rock music provided the most derogatory, sexist images of women among all forms of popular music (Harding & Nett, 1984). However, in the view of many, rap and hip-hop music have overtaken rock as the most misogynistic (i.e., woman-hating) forms (Mohammed-Baksh & Callison, 2015; Tyree, 2009; Utley, 2010; Weitzer & Kubrin, 2009). Some artists continue to depict men as all-powerful aggressors and women as virtual sex slaves (Jeffries, 2009; Natalle & Flippen, 2004; Rose, 2015; Shugart &

Egley Waggoner, 2005). However, some music/pop culture scholars separate rap music from hip-hop, believing that hip-hop is a more egalitarian form of music than rap; they point to those artists who focus on racial and political issues and attempt to show positive images of relationships in their music (Chaney, 2009; Corrigan, 2009; David, 2015; Dorris, 2013; Durham, 2014; Santa Cruz Bell & Avant-Mier, 2009; Utley & Menzies, 2009).

If you can easily remember the lyrics to a popular song (as opposed to formulas for your math exam), it's clear that they're permeating your consciousness on some level. Granted, we might not regulate our relationships according to what we hear depicted in song lyrics, but those lyrics do affect all of us in some way.

Sex Kittens and He-Men in Music Videos

What happens when visual images in music videos reinforce the messages of song lyrics? What happens when they contradict images we have in our heads, based on just listening to the lyrics? Many people report in research that when they listen to a song after having seen the video for the song, their interpretation of the lyrics is significantly affected; the video's visual images dominate the imagination (Jhally, 2015; Williams, 2007).

Music video doesn't get talked about much these days or researched as much as in past decades. After MTV went on the air in 1981 and quickly infiltrated American households, the music video industry skyrocketed (Vivian, 2011). Some believe that MTV's introduction of the reality TV show *The Real World* in 1992 signaled the demise of the music video, mainly because the ratings overwhelmingly favored programming over videos (Stransky, 2011). But music videos, no matter the delivery system, still have power to impact our culture and communicate messages about men and women (Borisoff & Chesebro, 2011; Frisby & Aubrey, 2012; Ng, 2015). Case in point is the song "Blurred Lines" by Robin Thicke; the song (deemed a "rape song" by protesters) and its accompanying video prompted outrage because of what many viewed as a sexist and demeaning depiction of women (Lynskey, 2013).

In a study of music video viewers' acceptance of the objectification of women in media, sexual permissiveness, gender attitudes, and rape myth acceptance, media scholars Kistler and Lee (2010) found the following: (1) Men who watched highly sexual hip-hop music videos held a more positive view of the objectification of women; (2) they also revealed more stereotypical views of men and women; and (3) they demonstrated more acceptance of rape myths than women in the study, as well as men who

"Do You Love *Love the Way You Lie*?"

Many people have viewed the video for *Love the Way You Lie*, featuring Eminem and Rihanna; if you haven't seen this video, check it out on YouTube (just be prepared for some of the language in the song). People have different interpretations of this video, some believing that it was Rihanna's way to offer commentary on the abuse she experienced in her relationship with Chris Brown. Others are more critical, believing it's just more of the sex, violence, and angst typical of Eminem's music and videos.

Still others think it sends a powerful message in its depiction of the cycle couples in violent, abusive relationships go through—the repetitive push-pull of passion, violence, remorse, forgiveness, reconciliation, and so forth that some intimate partners experience. As Adela Garcia (2011), community educator for The Women's Shelter of South Texas, explains, "The violence carries an ensuing, desperate need to put out the fires of the explosion. This breeds the desire for a quick fix to smother the burn. The 'passion' from the violent episode is then channeled into a sexual encounter, completing the quick burning cycle. All in all, passion becomes a way out, a way to disguise and cope with the violence" (p. 10). One of the most interesting scenes in the video is when the couple enacting the volatile relationship move from room to room in a house, revealing changes in their emotions and how they relate to each other as they move.

Emotions can be confusing, and they can surprise us with how they emerge when we least expect it in our relationships, especially in those intimate, high-priority relationships. But no matter some objectionable or gritty content (especially for feminists who take Eminem and other popular musicians to task regularly), here's an example of a music video that has the ability to teach us about the complexities of relationships—the destruction, passion, and confusion that typically characterize abusive relationships. Music video may be past its heyday, but it still has instructive power and the potential to offer provocative commentary on society.

watched music videos containing no or low levels of sexual content. College women in the study were not similarly affected by exposure to sexually charged music videos.

Perhaps you've seen the documentary film *Dreamworlds 3: Desire/Sex/ Power in Music Video*, by Sut Jhally (2007), which explores music video's hypersexualized images of women. In many videos, especially rock videos, women appear as mere sex objects designed to please men—as "legs in high heels" according to Jhally.

Images of men and women in music videos today are a "mixed bag"—a one-step-forward, two-steps-back situation. While multiple studies have found sexually objectifying and degrading images of women prevalent in hip-hop videos (Conrad, Dixon, & Zhang, 2009; Turner, 2010), other research documents evidence of a progression, particularly in Black women's depictions in videos produced by African American female artists, such as Mary J. Blige, Beyoncé, Missy Elliott, Erykah Badu, Alicia Keys, and India Arie (Balaji, 2010; Perry, 2003). Although many women's images in videos are still sexual, a distinction can be made between presenting oneself as a sexual *object*, there for the pleasure of others, versus a sexual *subject*, a sexual human being worthy of respect (Perry, 2003).

Music video is still a prevalent form of media, particularly in the lives of college students. However, it's not as pervasive as music you hear through your headphones every day. Watching a music video, even on your phone or tablet, involves more conscious choice and action than merely listening to music. But think for a moment about the whole effect—the very powerful effect of combining visual images with musical sound, a beat, and lyrics. Whether you actually watch every second of the average three-minute music video or even pay attention to the lyrics of a song, you still receive the message. Somewhere your brain is processing the information, sometimes on a conscious level, but most times on a subconscious level. Because of this power, we encourage you to think about how the music you listen to and videos you see affect your view of self, your attitudes about sex/gender roles in society, the expectations you form about men and women, and your gender communication in relationships.

SEX, GENDER, AND NEW MEDIA

Just what the heck do we mean by new media? Is new media the same thing as digital media? As electronic media? Is social networking part of new media? Let's just answer these questions with a big ole' confused, "We're not sure." We cobbled together some definitions to come up with the following: *New media* refers to electronic, interactive forms of media, especially mass media, typically combined with computers and considered experimental.

Net Notes

Any simple computer search about hip-hop music will produce several websites devoted to following hip-hop artists—their lives, their music, and occasionally their scandals. But here's a website of interest if your bent is more scholarly: **hutchinscenter.fas.harvard.edu**. Established in 2002 and now firmly rooted in The Hutchins Center at Harvard University, the Hiphop Archive's mission is "to facilitate and encourage the pursuit of knowledge, art, culture, and responsible leadership through hiphop." If you want to check out more specifically the Hiphop Archive's research base, use this website: **http://hiphoparchive.org**.

As soon as we start talking about what's new, it's no longer new. Consalvo (2006) explains that "The term *new media* is ambiguous and relative—what was new in the early 1990s . . . became mundane and accepted within a decade and was quickly replaced by newer media" (p. 355). In his collection of articles on "digital cultures," "new media cultures," "Internet cultures," and "cybercultures," media scholar Pramod Nayar (2010) describes new media this way: "[The] terrain is varied, complex, and shifting. Cybercultures is a notoriously difficult and slippery 'discipline' to theorize for the simple reason that it is arguably the fastest-growing set of practices in contemporary times" (p. ix).

In our discussion of gender and new media, we draw from Consalvo's categories and themes as well as Nayar's edited volume, with supplements from other research, to help us place some parameters on a topic too elusive, changeable, and vast to conquer. We ask your indulgence here as we broach this subject rather narrowly, despite the breadth of the topic at hand.

Although social networking is a form of new media (to many people's thinking), we've made mention of social networking many other places in this book. Here we choose to cover a few underrepresented topics related to new or digital media, including online identity development, disembodiment, and gender in virtual gaming communities. Indulge us as we choose to ignore some obvious intersections, such as how people develop online identities through their use of Facebook or how Twitter followers and viral video fans can become virtual communities.

Online Identity and Gender

In the 1990s, feminists and gender scholars believed that the Internet would afford people the ability to surpass the limitations of their physical or bodily identities; thus, one's gender identity would become less a factor than in other communicative contexts, like the development of face-to-face relationships. However, studies quickly refuted these assumptions as researchers came to view online outlets, such as newsgroups, listservs, web pages, and computer games, as gendered (Consalvo, 2006).

Theorists view new media as a place for identity exploration, such as when people create onscreen identities in terms of gender, sexuality, race, class, and so on, that differ from their offscreen identities (Chesebro, McMahan, & Russett, 2014; Helsper, 2014; van Zoonen, 2002). People can explore aspects of their identity through anonymously generated, gender-neutral (or unidentified) blogs, web pages, and posts (Fieseler, Meckel, & Ranzini,

2015; Gradinaru, 2013). The anonymity and privacy that Internet usage affords encourages gender identity expression; you can blog as *anybody*. However, scholars critique such a cavalier approach, mainly because when people experiment with gender and sexuality online, some of the same, tired stereotypes emerge and get reinforced (A. Shaw, 2014; Gajjala, 2014; Reynolds, 2015). Sexism is in our culture; why would we presume that it won't exist in our cyberculture as well?

Contemporary scholars like Sherry Turkle (2011), author of *Alone Together;* Naomi Baron (2008), who wrote *Always On;* and others point to such virtual sites as *World of Warcraft* and *Second Life* (very popular with college students) as provocative outlets for identity exploration (Brookey & Cannon, 2015; Nakamura, 2015). In many ways, virtual reality is just the newest form of fantasy, like escaping into novels, films, or soap operas where most everyone is young, beautiful, able-bodied, rich, successful, and in love. It's a way to step outside one's life and "play at being other" (Turkle, 2011, p. 159). The themes are the same, but the technological innovations make the experience different.

Research into gendered identity and new media continues, with studies on such topics as the following:

- Women's use of online pro-eating disorder sites to develop a more positive online identity for people with eating disorders than depicted in regular media (Weare, 2015);

- The link between women's use of mobile phones, the development of an independent identity, and control over one's life (Doring & Poschl, 2006);

- Identity exploration via *moblogs* (blogs uploaded from mobile phones) (Doring & Gundolf, 2010);

- Website designs that foster community for women (Mitra, 2010).

Disembodiment: Virtual Versus "Real" Bodies

Disembodiment means divesting of or being freed from bodily or physical form. Initially, virtual reality (cyberspace) looked like it was going to offer people a "disembodied space," meaning a place where participants could work, play, become educated, and generally live in a way that separated

> **Remember...**
>
> **New Media:** Electronic, interactive forms of media, especially mass media, typically combined with computers and considered experimental
>
> **Moblogs:** Blogs that can be uploaded from mobile phones
>
> **Disembodiment:** Divesting of or being freed from bodily or physical form

them from the confines of their physical bodies (Consalvo, 2006, p. 359). However, theorists began to argue that just because people chose to function in virtual reality part of the time in their lives, such usage didn't actually eliminate people's bodies; it didn't disengage or separate them from their bodies as it was purported to do (Balsamo, 1996; Kramarae, 1995). Gender scholars contended that virtual reality "privileged sight over other senses, encouraged a masculine view of the world, and perpetuated a mind/body split that falsely believed gender would become irrelevant" (Consalvo, 2006, p. 359).

Researchers studying web pages and blogs have found that, rather than freeing one from one's body, bodies are often described and talked about online, thus making them real and central rather than representational or nonfactors (Currier, 2010; Gomez, 2010; Kang, 2006; Levina, 2014). Other scholars have found that designs of digital characters and *avatars* (graphical embodiments or personifications that represent people) in video games and virtual communities (like *Second Life*) often invoke gender stereotypes, especially feminine stereotypes, which can affect how online players and users relate to the characters (Banks, 2015; Ensslin & Muse, 2011; Palomares & Lee, 2010; Sanbonmatsu, 2015).

As Consalvo (2006) explains, "The body is not so easily left behind" (p. 359). Even as we create new personae or online extensions of ourselves, our creations are affected by ideal images of men and women we see evidenced in media every day. We see strong, tall, nonbalding, athletic (typically well-endowed) male bodies that represent a cultural ideal for men and shapely, buxom female bodies with great skin, long legs, perfect rear ends, and no body fat, many of whom are portrayed as overtly sexual in skimpy, provocative clothing designed to show off their physical assets, which they may or may not allow men to enjoy. The heteronormativity of many of these online sites is substantial, with the "queering" of online communities still a relatively new phenomenon (Boler, 2010; Brookey & Cannon, 2015; Friedman, 2010).

Gendered Gaming

Researchers have studied digital game usage and design in general, as well as for gender factors (Banks, 2015; Chess, 2011; Ensslin & Muse, 2011; Juul, 2010; Mortensen, 2010; Schut, 2015; Shaw, 2013, 2015). (Because avatars are often a part of video/computer games, we recognize some overlap in this section with the last theme of disembodiment.) In many studies, gender emerges as a significant factor in understanding people's approaches to game play (Cross, 2014; Nakamura, 2015; Sanbonmatsu, 2015; Taylor, 2003). For this section, we could certainly explore some of the more widely criticized, incendiary games for their sexist elements—like *Grand Theft Auto* (recently criticized for an avatar rape incident; Brown, 2015) and various "FPS" or "first-person shooter" games, like *L.A. Noire* (Royse, Lee, Baasanjav, Hopson, & Consalvo, 2010). But we're going with a more nuanced approach, choosing to highlight one fascinating study of female gamers.

Royse et al. (2010) conducted individual and focus group interviews with female college students of various levels of gaming expertise to understand "how women described their electronic gaming experiences and how they constructed their own perspectives about gaming culture" (p. 411). Three groups emerged, based on play time: nongamers; moderate gamers (one to two hours a week of play); and power gamers (three to more than ten hours a week of play).

The power gamers integrated gaming into their lives; thus they were the most comfortable with gaming technology and themes. They revealed their level of integration not just by how frequently they played, but also by how easily they used the technology and talked about their enjoyment of various types of games. They reported using games to fulfill certain desires, like being competitive and excelling into mastery of a game. These findings parallel Taylor's (2003), in that many women enjoy game combat because it allows them to challenge gender norms and act on their feelings of aggression without repercussion. Power gamers often chose character representations for themselves that outsiders might view as unfortunate, harmful feminine stereotypes, but the gamers reported that such avatar selection enhanced their pleasure of playing the game. They preferred their avatars to reflect strength as well as sexiness, at the same time being careful to keep markers of femininity, such as retaining long fingernails while gripping rocket launchers and blowing virtual competitors away.

> I saw a sad news report recently that measured average video game use by American men between the ages of twenty-five and thirty-five: twenty hours per week. Do you mean the flower of America's masculinity can't think of anything more important to do with twenty hours a week than sit in front of a video screen? Folks, this ain't normal. Can't we unplug already?
> —Joel Salatin, American farmer and author

Royse et al. (2010) suggest, "We are presented with a paradox of sorts—the gamer who embodies 'femininity,' while performing 'masculinity'" (p. 414). Power gamers acknowledged the hypersexualization of some female

"Gamergate: True Controversy or Too Much Interference into Gaming?"

Whether or not you consider yourself a video gamer, you may have heard about the controversy that began in 2013 and extended for two years, surrounding one female game developer, Zoe Quinn's, attempts to get her text-based video game *Depression Quest* published (Dewey, 2014; Hathaway, 2014). The game was partially based on Quinn's own experience with depression. But many contend that the ensuing controversy had more to do with Quinn's being a woman than the game's content, echoing concerns about harassment and assault in the online gaming community (Cote, 2015; Liebler, 2015).

The emerging term "gamergate," according to Hathaway (2014), applies to "an online movement ostensibly concerned with ethics in game journalism and with protecting the 'gamer identity.'" But in the view of one reporter for *The Washington Post*, gamergate grew into an "Internet culture war," with advocates for greater inclusion in games (many of whom are women) on one side and traditional gamers who don't want games to change on the other (Dewey, 2014). The people behind the push for ethics received their share of criticism from gamers who want the Internet to remain free from outside interference into how it conducts its business.

Quinn's address and phone number were made public and she received online death threats and harassment, including a smear campaign (generated by an ex-boyfriend) that attempted to make Quinn out to be a promiscuous headline grabber. Some of the men she was accused of having sex with were gaming journalists, so added to the accusation was the rumor that Quinn had sex with people who could get her ahead in the gaming industry. As other gamers and feminists entered the controversy, most notably feminist critic Anita Sarkeesian, the discussion shifted from negative comments about one female gamer's sex life to sexism in general within the gaming community and as expressed in games themselves. It shifted later even more broadly to discuss journalistic ethics, leading some to believe that the broader topic of ethics was a smokescreen or cover up for sexism that many gamers didn't want to admit existed or was a problem.

You can use your search engine of choice to read more about this situation, but here are some questions that many keep asking: Would a male game developer have been treated like Quinn? Did the controversy expose sexism and harassment in the gaming community that needed exposing? Are male and female characters more likely to be portrayed in video games more equitably than in years past or do sexist portrayals and practices rule the day?

images in games, as well as the sexism some male players exhibited online, but their enjoyment of computer games was connected to choice, mastery, and control. For some power gamers, their avatars represented who they'd like to be or wished they were in their offline lives—their better selves.

Moderate female gamers mentioned control as a factor, but it was more about using a game to control their circumstances or environment, not other people. Gaming was a coping mechanism, a distraction or escape from everyday life for these users. They also drew a distinction between the games they played and those they presumed men played, those they perceived as violent and fantasy based. Their gaming intent wasn't necessarily to defeat opponents; the form of competitiveness they preferred was beating the game itself or making the right moves to solve a problem or puzzle. They didn't perceive avatars as empowering for women; they viewed them as simply characters, not embodiments of unfulfilled identity.

Nongamers in this study were critical of gamers (deeming them "interpersonally inept") and games, viewing them as an antisocial activity and a waste of time (Royse et al., 2010, p. 419). They expressed concerns about the sexualized and violent content of many games, but acknowledged that these qualities were problems in other forms of media as well. They viewed themselves as traditionally female—grounded in the real world, secure in their priorities—in opposition to men who were more frequent users of computer games and less feminine women who aggressively played the games.

As a result of their research into this phenomenon, Royse et al. (2010) call for a "technologies of the gendered self" approach to further inquiry, which helps us understand how people "negotiate game play, gender expectations and roles in relation to technology use" (p. 421). This perspective factors gender into the way people design and interface with all sorts of new media, to help us better understand this relatively new frontier for communication that will no doubt play an increasingly important role in our lives.

CONCLUSION

You may not feel you have reached media expert status, but we suspect that you know more about the forms of media that surround you every day than you did before you read this chapter. When you think about the many media outlets and methods that have the potential to influence you, it's almost overwhelming. But rather than feeling overwhelmed by media influence, your knowledge can empower you to better understand the effects of media messages about gender. We hope that you not only have an increased knowledge about mediated communication, but that you are able to more critically assess the role media—traditional and new forms—play in your life. That critical assessment enables you to make thoughtful choices about just how much you will allow the media to affect you.

Think about whether you have some standards for romantic relationships and where those standards came from. Do your expectations reflect romance as portrayed in movies or between characters on TV? Now that you're more aware of the wide range of mediated images that could be considered pornographic, do you think any of those readily accessible images have affected your expectations about relationships?

When you're feeling down, are there certain songs and musical artists that either help you feel your pain more fully or that help raise your spirits? Have you ever watched TV characters go through some trauma, such as the death of a loved one, an angry exchange between friends, or the breakup of an important relationship, and then later used how the characters talked about the experience in your own life events? We encourage you to take more opportunities to consciously decipher media influence, particularly in reference to gender communication. The more you understand what's influencing you, the more ready you'll be to dive into new relationships or strengthen existing ones.

DISCUSSION STARTERS

1. Go to your favorite website and examine the ads that pop up. How many ads depict members of your same sex? How many depict members of a different sex? Are the ads tailored to you and your tastes, or are they generic? Do you deem any of these ads sexist or stereotypical?

2. What's your favorite TV show? Think of several reasons why this show is your favorite. Do your reasons have more to do with the characters, the setting or scenery, the plot lines, or something else? Now think about a show that you watched and just hated. What was so irritating about that show? Are there any gender issues affecting your decision about most and least favorite TV shows?

3. Have your views on pornography changed at all as a result of the information in this chapter? Think about the different definitions of pornography and then think about media you consume—ads, TV shows, films, music videos, and online material. How much could be classified as pornographic? What role, if any, has pornography played in your developing understanding of gender?

4. Assess your music collection. Whom do you listen to—predominantly artists of the same sex as you or of a different sex? If there's a pattern, why do you think the pattern exists?

Then pick one CD and play the cut on it that you're the least familiar with. Listen carefully and try to take in every word of the lyrics. Did you hear anything for the first time?

5. Have you experimented with computer games where you create an avatar, such as in *Second Life?* If so, did you generate an avatar that resembles you in your offline life, or did you choose to alter your identity in some way? How do you think gender identity exploration in online settings affects your view of sex and gender in other aspects of life?

References

Aaron, M. (2006). New queer cable? *The L Word,* the small screen, and the bigger picture. In K. Akass, J. McCabe, & S. Warn (Eds.), *Reading* The L Word: *Outing contemporary television* (pp. 33–42). London: I. B. Tauris.

Albiniak, P. (2010). What women want to watch. *Broadcasting and Cable, 140,* 21.

Andrejevic, M. (2003). *Reality TV: The work of being watched.* Lanham, MD: Rowman & Littlefield.

Armstrong, J. (2010, November 29). *16 and Pregnant* delivers big. *Entertainment Weekly,* 49.

Armstrong, J. (2011, January 28). Gay teens on TV. *Entertainment Weekly,* 34–41.

Artz, L. (2015). Monarchs, monsters, and multiculturalism: Disney's menu for global hierarchy. In G. Dines & J. M. Humez (Eds.), *Gender, race, and class in media: A critical reader* (4th ed., pp. 449–454). Los Angeles: Sage.

Artz, N., Munger, J., & Purdy, W. (1999). Gender issues in advertising language. *Women & Language, 22,* 20–26.

Attwood, F. (2011). No money shot? Commerce, pornography, and new sex taste cultures. In G. Dines & J. M. Humez (Eds.), *Gender, race, and class in media: A critical reader* (3rd ed., pp. 283–292). Los Angeles: Sage.

Aubrey, J. S. (2007). The impact of sexually objectifying media exposure on negative body emotions and sexual self-perceptions: Investigating the mediating role of body self-consciousness. *Mass Communication and Society, 10,* 1–23.

Aubrey, J. S., & Harrison, K. (2004). The gender-role content of children's favorite television programs and its links to their gender-related perceptions. *Media Psychology, 6,* 111–146.

Balaji, M. (2010). Vixen resistin': Redefining black womanhood in hip-hop music videos. *Journal of Black Studies, 41,* 5–20.

Balsamo, A. (1996). *Technologies of the gendered body: Reading cyborg women.* Durham, NC: Duke University Press.

Banet-Weiser, S., & Portwood-Stacer, L. (2006). "I just want to be me again!" Beauty pageants, reality television and post-feminism. *Feminist Theory, 7,* 255–272.

Banks, J. (2015, May). Digital games as communication and culture. *Spectra,* 8–15.

Baron, N. (2008). *Always on: Language in an online and mobile world.* New York: Oxford University Press.

Barton, K. M. (2009). Reality television programming and diverging gratifications: The influence of content on gratifications obtained. *Journal of Broadcasting & Electronic Media, 53,* 460–476.

Battles, K., & Hilton-Morrow, W. (2002). Gay characters in conventional spaces: *Will & Grace* and the situation comedy genre. *Critical Studies in Media Communication, 19,* 87–105.

Baxter, J. (2009). Constructions of active woman-hood and new femininities: From a feminist linguistic perspective, is *Sex and the City* a modernist or a post-modernist TV text? *Women & Language, 32,* 91–98.

Bednarek, M. (2015). "Wicked" women in contemporary pop culture: "Bad" language and gender in *Weeds, Nurse Jackie,* and *Saving Grace. Text & Talk, 35,* 431–451.

Bell, E., Haas, L., & Sells, L. (Eds.) (2008). *From mouse to mermaid: The politics of film, gender, and culture.* Bloomington: Indiana University Press.

Bennett, L. (2008, Spring). Feminist Super Bowl AdWatch finds few women, but plenty of demeaning stereotypes. *National NOW Foundation Times,* p. 11.

Benshoff, H. M., & Griffin, S. (2009). *America on film: Representing race, class, gender, and sexuality at the movies* (2nd ed.). New York: Wiley-Blackwell.

Beynon, J. (2004). The commercialization of masculinities: From the "new man" to the "new lad." In C. Carter & L. Steiner (Eds.), *Critical readings: Media and gender* (pp. 198–217). Maidenhead, Berkshire, UK: Open University Press.

Bierly, M. (2011, March 18). The *Cops* effect. *Entertainment Weekly,* 10.

Boler, M. (2010). Hypes, hopes, and actualities: New digital Cartesianism and bodies in cyberspace. In P. K. Nayar (Ed.), *The new media and cybercultures anthology* (pp. 185–208). Malden, MA: Wiley-Blackwell.

Booth, E. T. (2015). Queering *Queer Eye*: The stability of gay identity confronts the liminality of trans embodiment. In G. Dines & J. M. Humez (Eds.), *Gender, race, and class in media: A critical reader* (4th ed., pp. 409–417). Los Angeles: Sage.

Borisoff, D. J., & Chesebro, J. W. (2011). *Communicating power and gender.* Long Grove, IL: Waveland.

Boyle, K. (2011). "That's so fun": Selling pornography for men to women in *The Girls Next Door.* In G. Dines & J. M. Humez (Eds.), *Gender, race, and class in media: A critical reader* (3rd ed., pp. 293–300). Los Angeles: Sage.

Bretthauer, B., Schindler Zimmerman, T., & Banning, J. H. (2006). A feminist analysis of popular music: Power over, objectification of, and violence against women. *Journal of Feminist Family Therapy, 18*, 29–51.

Brookey, R. A., & Cannon, K. L. (2015). Sex lives in *Second Life.* In G. Dines & J. M. Humez (Eds.), *Gender, race, and class in media: A critical reader* (4th ed., pp. 398–408). Los Angeles: Sage.

Brooks, D. E., & Hebert, L. P. (2006). Gender, race, and media representation. In B. Dow & J. T. Wood (Eds.), *The SAGE handbook of gender and communication* (pp. 297–317). Thousand Oaks, CA: Sage.

Brown, A. (2015, Winter). Not playing around: Sexual assault in multiplayer online games. *Bitch,* 7.

Brown, J. D., L'Engle, L. K., Pardun, C. J., Guo, G., Kenneavy, K., & Jackson, C. (2006). Sexy media matter: Exposure to sexual content in music, movies, television, and magazines predicts black and white adolescents' sexual behavior. *Pediatrics, 117,* 1018–1027.

Brown, L. S. (2005). Outwit, outlast, out-flirt? The women of reality TV. In E. Cole & J. Henderson Daniel (Eds.), *Featuring females: Feminist analyses of media* (pp. 71–83). Washington, DC: American Psychological Association.

Browne, B. A. (1998). Gender stereotypes in advertising on children's television in the 1990s: A cross-national analysis. *Journal of Advertising, 27,* 83–96.

Brummert Lennings, H. I., & Warburton, W. A. (2011). The effect of auditory versus visual violent media exposure on aggressive behaviour: The role of song lyrics, video clips and musical tone. *Journal of Experimental Social Psychology, 47,* 794–799.

Burrill, D. A. (2014). *The other guy: Media masculinity within the margins.* London: Peter Lang.

Butruille, S. G., & Taylor, A. (1987). Women in American popular song. In L. P. Stewart & S. Ting-Toomey (Eds.), *Communication, gender, and sex roles in diverse interaction contexts* (pp. 179–188). Norwood, NJ: Ablex.

Butsch, R. (2015). Six decades of social class in Amerian television sitcoms. In G. Dines & J. M. Humez (Eds.), *Gender, race, and class in media: A critical reader* (4th ed., pp. 507–516). Los Angeles: Sage.

Campbell, R., Martin, C. R., & Fabos, B. (2015). *Media and culture: Mass communication in a digital age* (10th ed.). Boston: Bedford/St. Martin's.

Capsuto, S. (2000). *Alternate channels: The uncensored story of gay and lesbian images on radio and television, 1930 to the present.* New York: Ballantine Books.

Caputi, J. (2015). The pornography of everyday life. In G. Dines & J. M. Humez (Eds.), *Gender, race, and class in media: A critical reader* (4th ed., pp. 373-385). Los Angeles: Sage.

Casper, M. F., & Gilmour, D. (2014). The reality of television motherhood: The personal quest and feminine test of Kate Gosselin. In A. A. Ruggerio (Ed.), *Media depictions of brides, wives, and mothers* (pp. 27–38). Lanham, MD: Lexington.

Cato, M., & Dillman Carpentier, F. R. (2010). Conceptualizations of female empowerment and enjoyment of sexualized characters in reality television. *Mass Communication and Society, 13,* 270–288.

Chandler, R., Ross, H., Kolar, S., Kip, K., & Simmons, D. (2015). Considering music lyrics and imagery in the sexual health of black college students. *Journal of Black Studies, 46,* 564–586.

Chaney, C. (2009). Trapped in the closet: Understanding contemporary relationships in the African-American hip hop community. *Women & Language, 32,* 59–67.

Chase, J. (2013, May 10). Multitasking TV. *Entertainment Weekly,* 14.

Chen, Y., Liang, J., & Leung, L. (2015). Social network service use on mobile devices: An examination of gratifications, civic attitudes and civic engagement in China. *New Media & Society, 17,* 1096–1116.

Chesebro, J. W., McMahan, D. T., & Russett, P. C. (2014). *Internet communication.* London: Peter Lang.

Chess, S. (2011). A 36-24-36 cerebrum: Productivity, gender, and video game advertising. *Critical Studies in Media Communication, 28,* 230–252.

Chia, S. C., & Gunther, A. C. (2006). How media contribute to misperceptions of social norms about sex. *Mass Communication and Society, 9,* 301–320.

Clarkson, J. (2005). Contesting masculinity's makeover: *Queer Eye,* consumer masculinity, and "straight-acting" gays. *Journal of Communication Inquiry, 29,* 235–255.

Click, M. A., Holladay, H. W., Lee, H., & Kristiansen, L. J. (2015). "Let's hug it out, bitch": HBO's *Entourage,* masculinity in crisis, and the value of audience studies. *Television & New Media, 16,* 403–421.

Cloud, D. (2010). The irony bribe and reality television: Investment and detachment in *The Bachelor. Critical Studies in Media Communication, 27,* 413–437.

Cogan, M. (2014, August 7). The great Photoshop crusade: One activist's battle with the advertising industry. Retrieved August 7, 2014, from <http://www.nationaljournal.com>.

Conrad, K., Dixon, T., & Zhang, Y. (2009). Controversial rap themes, gender portrayals and skin tone distortion: A content analysis of rap music videos. *Journal of Broadcasting & Electronic Media, 53,* 134–156.

Consalvo, M. (2006). Gender and new media. In B. J. Dow & J. T. Wood (Eds.), *The SAGE handbook of gender and communication* (pp. 355–369). Thousand Oaks, CA: Sage.

Cook, B. (Ed.) (2007). *Thelma and Louise live!: The cultural afterlife of an American film.* Austin: University of Texas Press.

Cooper, B. (2000). "Chick flicks" as feminist texts: The appropriation of the male gaze in *Thelma & Louise. Women's Studies in Communication, 23,* 277–306.

Corrigan, L. M. (2009). Sacrifice, love, and resistance: The hip hop legacy of Assata Shakur. *Women & Language, 32,* 2–13.

Cortese, A. J. (2016). *Provocateur: Images of women and minorities in advertising* (4th ed.). Lanham, MD: Rowman & Littlefield.

Cote, A. C. (2015). "I can defend myself": Women's strategies for coping with harassment while gaming online. *Games and Culture, 10,* 1–20.

Cottle, M. (2003). Turning boys into girls. In A. Alexander & J. Hanson (Eds.), *Taking sides: Clashing views on controversial issues in mass media and society* (7th ed., pp. 68–74). Guilford, CT: McGraw-Hill/Dushkin.

Courtney, A. E., & Whipple, T. W. (1974). Women in TV commercials. *Journal of Communication, 24,* 110–118.

Courtney, A. E., & Whipple, T. W. (1983). *Sex stereotyping in advertising.* Lexington, MA: Lexington.

Cragin, B. (2010). Beyond the feminine: Intersectionality and hybridity in talk shows. *Women's Studies in Communication, 33,* 154–172.

Craig, R. S. (1992, October). *Selling masculinities, selling femininities: Multiple genders and the economics of television.* Paper presented at the meeting of the Speech Communication Association, Chicago, IL.

Cronin, B., & Davenport, E. (2010). E-rogenous zones: Positioning pornography in the digital economy. In P. K. Nayar (Ed.), *The new media and cybercultures anthology* (pp. 284–306). Malden, MA: Wiley-Blackwell.

Cross, K. (2014, Fall). Let's get digital: The prejudices—and the potential—of gaming and erotic roleplaying. *Bitch,* 34–39.

Croteau, D., & Hoynes, W. (2014). *Media/society: Industries, images, and audiences* (5th ed.). Los Angeles: Sage.

Currier, D. (2010). Assembling bodies in cyberspace: Technologies, bodies, and sexual difference. In P. K. Nayar (Ed.), *The new media and cybercultures anthology* (pp. 254–267). Malden, MA: Wiley-Blackwell.

Daughton, S. M. (2010). "Cursed with self-awareness": Gender-bending, subversion, and irony in *Bull Durham. Women's Studies in Communication, 33,* 96–118.

David, M. (2015). More than baby mamas: Black mothers and hip-hop feminism. In G. Dines & J. M. Humez (Eds.), *Gender, race, and class in media: A critical reader* (4th ed., pp. 187–193). Los Angeles: Sage.

Davis, A. M. (2005). The "dark prince" and dream women: Walt Disney and mid twentieth century American feminism. *Historical Journal of Film, 25,* 213–230.

Davis, A. M. (2007). *Good girls and wicked witches: Women in Disney's feature animation.* New Barnet, Herts, UK: John Libbey Publishing.

Davis, C. (2008, May). *The gender factor of "Survivor": A Q method.* Paper presented at the meeting of the International Communication Association, Montreal, Canada.

Davis, L. R. (1997). *The swimsuit issue and sport: Hegemonic masculinity in* Sports Illustrated. Albany: State University of New York Press.

deGrazia, E. (1992). *Girls lean back everywhere: The law of obscenity and the assault on genius.* New York: Random House.

deGregorio, F., & Sung, Y. (2010). Understanding attitudes toward and behaviors in response to product placement. *Journal of Advertising, 39,* 83–96.

Dewey, C. (2014, October 14). The only guide to gamergate you will ever need to read. Retrieved July 2, 2015, from <www.wp.com>.

Dines, G. (2010). *Pornland: How porn has hijacked our sexuality.* Boston: Beacon Press.

Dobosz, A. M. (1997, November–December). Thicker thighs by Thanksgiving. *Ms.,* 89–91.

Doring, N., & Gundolf, A. (2010). Your life in snapshots: Mobile weblogs. In P. K. Nayar (Ed.), *The new media and cybercultures anthology* (pp. 515–525). Malden, MA: Wiley-Blackwell.

Doring, N., & Poschl, S. (2006). Images of men and women in mobile phone advertisements: A content analysis of advertisements for mobile communication systems in selected popular magazines. *Sex Roles, 55,* 173–185.

Dorris, J. (2013, September 9). I have sung the future: Janelle Monae broke out as an R&B innovator. Now she's going full eclectic. *Time*, 52–54.

Douglas, S. J. (2013). *Jersey Shore*: Ironic viewing. In E. Thompson & J. Mittell, *How to watch television* (pp. 148–156). New York: New York University Press.

Douglas, S. J. (1995). *Where the girls are: Growing up female with the mass media.* New York: Random House.

Douglas, S. J. (2009). Where have you gone, Roseanne Barr? In H. Boushey & A. O'Leary (Eds.), *The Shriver report: A woman's nation changes everything.* Washington, DC: Center for American Progress.

Dove-Viebahn, A. (2015, Spring). What does the female gaze look like? *Ms.*, 24–25.

Dove-Viebahn, A. (2011). Fashionably femme: Lesbian visibility, style, and politics in *The L Word*. In T. Peele (Ed.), *Queer popular culture: Literature, media, film, and television* (pp. 71–84). New York: Palgrave Macmillan.

Dow, B. J. (1996). *Prime-time feminism: Television, media culture, and the Women's Movement since 1970.* Philadelphia: University of Pennsylvania Press.

Dow, B. J. (2001). Ellen, television, and the politics of gay and lesbian visibility. *Critical Studies in Media Communication, 18,* 123–140.

Dubrofsky, R. E. (2006). *The Bachelor:* Whiteness in the harem. *Critical Studies in Media Communication, 23,* 39–56.

Dubrofsky, R. E. (2009). Fallen women in reality TV. *Feminist Media Studies, 9,* 353–368.

Duerringer, C. (2015). Be a man—buy a car! Articulating masculinity with consumerism in Man's Last Stand. *Southern Communication Journal, 80,* 137–152.

Duffy, B. E. (2010). Empowerment through endorsement? Polysemic meaning in Dove's user-generated advertising. *Communication, Culture, and Critique, 3,* 26–43.

Durham, A. S. (2014). *Home with hip hop feminism: Performances in communication and culture.* London: Peter Lang.

Durham, M. G. (2009). *The Lolita effect: The media sexualization of young girls and five keys to fixing it.* New York: The Overlook Press.

Egley Waggoner, C. (2004). Disciplining female sexuality in *Survivor. Feminist Media Studies, 4,* 217–220.

Eisend, M., Plagemann, J., & Sollwedel, J. (2014). Gender roles and humor in advertising: The occurrence of stereotyping in humorous and nonhumorous advertising and its consequences for advertising effectiveness. *Journal of Advertising, 43,* 256–273.

Elasmar, M., Hasegawa, K., & Brain, M. (1999). The portrayal of women in U.S. prime-time television. *Journal of Broadcasting & Electronic Media, 44,* 20–34.

Engstrom, E. (2009). Creation of a new "empowered" female identity in WEtv's *Bridezillas. Media Report to Women, 37,* 6–12.

Ensslin, A., & Muse, E. (Eds.) (2011). *Creating second lives: Community, identity, and spatiality as constructions of the virtual.* New York: Routledge.

Esposito, J. (2011). What does race have to do with *Ugly Betty?* An analysis of privilege and postracial(?) representations on a television sitcom. In G. Dines & J. M. Humez (Eds.), *Gender, race, and class in media: A critical reader* (3rd ed., pp. 95–99). Los Angeles: Sage.

Fairclough, K. (2015). Nothing less than perfect: Female celebrity, ageing, and hyper-scrutiny in the gossip industry. In G. Dines & J. M. Humez (Eds.), *Gender, race, and class in media: A critical reader* (4th ed., pp. 297–305). Los Angeles: Sage.

Familysafemedia.com. (2015). Pornography statistics. Retrieved October 28, 2015, from <http://familysafemedia.com>.

Farr, D., & Degroult, N. (2008). Understand the queer world of the lesbian body: Using *Queer as Folk* and *The L Word* to address the construction of the lesbian body. *Journal of Lesbian Studies, 12,* 423–434.

Feasey, R. (2009). Spray more, get more: Masculinity, television advertising, and the Lynx effect. *Journal of Gender Studies, 18,* 357–368.

Ferguson, G. (2010). The family on reality television: Who's shaming whom? *Television and New Media, 11,* 87–104.

Fieseler, C., Meckel, M., & Ranzini, G. (2015). Professional personae: How organizational identification shapes online identity in the workplace. *Journal of Computer-Mediated Communication, 20,* 153–170.

Fischer, P., & Greitemeyer, T. (2006). Music and aggression: The impact of sexual-aggressive song lyrics on aggression-related thoughts, emotions, and behavior toward the same and the opposite sex. *Personality and Social Psychology Bulletin, 32,* 1165–1176.

Fisher, D. A., Hill, D. L., Grube, J. W., & Gruber, E. L. (2007). Gay, lesbian, and bisexual content on television: A quantitative analysis across two seasons. *Journal of Homosexuality, 52,* 167–188.

Foubert, J. D., Brosi, M. W., & Bannon, R. S. (2011). Pornography viewing among fraternity men: Effects on bystander intervention, rape myth acceptance and behavioral intent to commit sexual assault. *Sexual Addiction & Compulsivity, 18,* 212–231.

Fournier, G. (2006). Thelma and Louise *and women in Hollywood.* Jefferson, NC: McFarland.

Fowler, K., & Thomas, V. (2015). A content analysis of male roles in television advertising: Do traditional roles still hold? *Journal of Marketing Communications, 21*, 356–371.

Freudiger, P., & Almquist, E. M. (1978). Male and female roles in the lyrics of three genres of contemporary music. *Sex Roles, 4*, 51–65.

Friedman, E. J. (2010). Lesbians in [cyber]space: The politics of the Internet in Latin American on- and off-line communities. In P. K. Nayar (Ed.), *The new media and cybercultures anthology* (pp. 268–283). Malden, MA: Wiley-Blackwell.

Frisby, C. M. (2010). Sticks 'n' stones may break my bones, but words they hurt like hell: Derogatory words in popular songs. *Media Report to Women, 38*, 12–18.

Frisby, C. M., & Aubrey, J. S. (2012). Race and genre in the use of sexual objectification in female artists' music videos. *The Howard Journal of Communications, 23*, 66–87.

Fuller, S., & Driscoll, C. (2015). HBO's *Girls*: Gender, generation, and quality television. *Journal of Media & Cultural Studies, 29*, 253–262.

Funt, P. (2009, December 23). Reality TV is simply a microcosm of our society. *USA Today*, p. 15A.

Gajjala, R. (2014). Woman and other women: Implicit binaries in cyberfeminisms. *Communication and Critical/Cultural Studies, 11*, 288–292.

Gallagher, M. (2004). *Queer Eye* for the heterosexual couple. *Feminist Media Studies, 4*, 223–225.

Garcia, A. (2011, First Quarter). Exploring the burn: A critical look at *Love the Way You Lie. Making the difference: A publication of The Women's Shelter of South Texas*, pp. 10–11.

Gatewood, F. (2001). She-devils on wheels: Women, motorcycles, and movies. In M. Pomerance (Ed.), *Ladies and gentlemen, boys and girls: Gender in film at the end of the twentieth century* (pp. 203–216). New York: State University of New York Press.

Gentry, J., & Harrison, R. (2010). Is advertising a barrier to male movement toward gender change? *Marketing Theory, 10*, 74–96.

Gerbner, G. (2003). Television violence at a time of turmoil and terror. In G. Dines & J. M. Humez (Eds.), *Gender, race, and class in media: A critical reader* (2nd ed., pp. 339–348). Thousand Oaks, CA: Sage.

Gerbner, G., Gross, L., Morgan, M., & Signorielli, N. (1980). The "mainstreaming" of America: Violence profile no. 11. *Journal of Communication, 30*, 10–29.

Gerhard, J. (2011). *Sex and the City:* Carrie Bradshaw's queer postfeminism. In G. Dines & J. M. Humez (Eds.), *Gender, race, and class in media: A critical reader* (3rd ed., pp. 75–79). Los Angeles: Sage.

Gill, R. (2007). *Gender and the media.* Cambridge, UK: Polity Press.

Gill, R. (2015). Supersexualize me! Advertising and the "midriffs." In G. Dines & J. M. Humez (Eds.), *Gender, race, and class in media: A critical reader* (4th ed., pp. 278–284). Los Angeles: Sage.

Gillespie, M. A., Dworkin, A., Shange, N., Ramos, N., & French, M. (1994, January–February). Where do we stand on pornography? *Ms.*, 33–41.

Gilliam, K., & Wooden, S. R. (2008). Post-princess models of gender: The new man in Disney/Pixar. *Journal of Popular Film and Television, 36*, 2–8.

Giresunlu, L. (2009). Cyborg goddesses: The mainframe revisited. *At the Interface/Probing the Boundaries, 56*, 157–187.

Givhan, R. (2005, August 19). Sorry, Dove: Bigger isn't necessarily better. Retrieved March 13, 2011, from <http://www.washingtonpost.com>.

Givhan, R. (2009, April 12). "Housewives" function best on dysfunction. Retrieved December 1, 2010, from <http://www.washingtonpost.com>.

Glascock, J. (2005). Degrading content and character sex: Accounting for men and women's differential reactions to pornography. *Communication Reports, 18*, 43–53.

Glenn, R. J. III. (1992, November). *Echoes of feminism on the big screen: A fantasy theme analysis of* Thelma and Louise. Paper presented at the meeting of the Speech Communication Association, Chicago, IL.

Gomez, A. G. (2010). Disembodiment and cyberspace: Gendered discourses in female teenagers' personal information disclosure. *Discourse & Society, 21*, 135–160.

Gradinaru, C. (2013). From multitude to convergence: Contemporary trends in the study of online identity. *Argumentum: Journal of the Seminar of Discursive Logic, Argumentation Theory & Rhetoric, 11*, 95–108.

Greenberg, B. S., & Collette, L. (1997). The changing faces on TV: A demographic analysis of network television's new seasons, 1966–1992. *Journal of Broadcasting & Electronic Media, 41*, 1–13.

Hald, G. M., Malamuth, N. M., & Lange, T. (2013). Pornography and sexist attitudes among heterosexuals. *Journal of Communication, 63*, 638–660.

Hald, G. M., Malamuth, N. M., & Yuen, C. (2010). Pornography and attitudes supporting violence against women: Revisiting the relationship in nonexperimental studies. *Aggressive Behavior, 36*, 14–20.

Hanke, R. (1998). The "mock-macho" situation comedy: Hegemonic masculinity and its reiteration. *Western Journal of Communication, 62*, 74–93.

Harding, D., & Nett, E. (1984). Women and rock music. *Atlantis, 10*, 60–77.

Harper, B., & Tiggemann, M. (2007). The effect of thin ideal media images on women's self-objectification, mood, and body image. *Sex Roles, 58,* 649–657.

Harris, L. (2012). The new Old Spice: Business identities, trademarks, and social media. *Mississippi College Law Review, 31,* 309.

Harris, M. (2011, March 4). Taking multitasking to task. *Entertainment Weekly,* 29.

Harris, M. (2015, June 19). The transition will be televised. *Entertainment Weekly,* 30–33.

Hart, K.-P. R. (2003). Representing gay men on American television. In G. Dines & J. M. Humez (Eds.), *Gender, race, and class in media: A critical reader* (2nd ed., pp. 507–607). Thousand Oaks, CA: Sage.

Hart, K.-P. R. (2004). We're here, we're queer—and we're better than you: The representational superiority of gay men to heterosexuals on *Queer Eye for the Straight Guy. Journal of Men's Studies, 12,* 241–253.

Harwood, J., & Anderson, K. (2002). The presence and portrayal of social groups on prime-time television. *Communication Reports, 15,* 81–97.

Hasinoff, A. A. (2008). Fashioning race for the free market on *America's Next Top Model. Critical Studies in Media Communication, 25,* 324–343.

Hathaway, J. (2014, October 10). What is gamergate, and why? An explainer for non-geeks. Retrieved July 2, 2015, from <www.gawker.com>.

Havrilesky, H. (2015, February 23-March 8). Reading Bruce Jenner: Intrusions of reality in greater Calabasas. *New York,* 11–12.

Heaton, J. A., & Wilson, N. L. (1995, September/October). Tuning in to trouble. *Ms.,* 44–51.

Hefner, V., & Wilson, B. J. (2013). From love at first sight to soul mate: The influence of romantic ideals in popular films on young people's beliefs about relationships. *Communication Monographs, 89,* 150–175.

Helsper, E. J. (2014). Offline social identity and online chat partner selection. *Information, Communication & Society, 17,* 695–715.

Henry, W. J., West, N. M., & Jackson, A. (2010). Hip-hop's influence on the identity development of black female college students: A literature review. *Journal of College Student Development, 51,* 237–251.

Henson, L., & Parameswaran, R. E. (2008). Getting real with "tell it like it is" talk therapy: Hegemonic masculinity and the *Dr. Phil Show. Communication, Culture, and Critique, 1,* 287–310.

Hentges, B. A., Bartsch, R. B., & Meier, J. A. (2007). Gender representation in commercials as a function of target audience age. *Communication Research Reports, 24,* 55–62.

Hetsroni, A., & Lowenstein, H. (2013). Cultivation and counter cultivation: Does religiosity shape the relationship between television viewing and estimates of crime prevalence and assessment of victimization likelihood? *Psychological Reports, 112,* 303–324.

Hill, L. (2010). Gender and genre: Situating *Desperate Housewives. Journal of Popular Film and Television, 38,* 162–169.

Hopeck, P., & Ivic, R. K. (2014). Marriage, friendship, and scandal: Constructing a typology of media representation of women in *Desperate Housewives.* In A. A. Ruggerio (Ed.), *Media depictions of brides, wives, and mothers* (pp. 39–48). Lanham, MD: Lexington.

Hopper, D. (2011, February 15). *Sports Illustrated* swimsuit issue keeps getting closer to porn without being porn. Retrieved March 27, 2011, from <http://www.bestweekever.tv>.

Hubert, S. J. (2003). What's wrong with this picture? The politics of Ellen's coming out party. In G. Dines & J. M. Humez (Eds.), *Gender, race, and class in media: A critical reader* (2nd ed., pp. 608–612). Thousand Oaks, CA: Sage.

Ivory, A. H., Gibson, R., & Ivory, J. D. (2009). Gendered relationships on television: Portrayals of same-sex and heterosexual couples. *Mass Communication and Society, 12,* 170–192.

Japp, P. M. (1991). Gender and work in the 1980s: Television's working women as displaced persons. *Women's Studies in Communication, 14,* 49–74.

Jeffries, M. P. (2009). Can a thug (get some) love? Sex, romance, and the definition of a hip hop "thug." *Women & Language, 32,* 35–41.

Jhally, S. (Producer/Director). (2007). *Dreamworlds 3: Desire/sex/power in music video* [Motion picture]. United States: Media Education Foundation.

Jhally, S. (2015). Image-based culture: Advertising and popular culture. In G. Dines & J. M. Humez (Eds.), *Gender, race, and class in media: A critical reader* (4th ed., pp. 246–250). Los Angeles: Sage.

Jordan, C. (2015). Marketing "reality" to the world: *Survivor,* post-Fordism, and reality television. In G. Dines & J. M. Humez (Eds.), *Gender, race, and class in media: A critical reader* (4th ed., pp. 517-523). Los Angeles: Sage.

Juul, J. (2010). Games telling stories: A brief note on games and narratives. In P. K. Nayar (Ed.), *The new media and cybercultures anthology* (pp. 382–393). Malden, MA: Wiley-Blackwell.

Kang, S. (2006, June). *Disembodiment in online social interaction: Impact of online chat on social support and psychosocial well-being.* Paper presented at the meeting of the International Communication Association, Dresden, Germany.

Katz, J. (2011). Advertising and the construction of violent white masculinity. In G. Dines & J. M. Humez (Eds.), *Gender, race, and class in media: A critical reader* (3rd ed., pp. 261–269). Los Angeles: Sage.

Kellner, D. (2015). Cultural studies, multiculturalism, and media culture. In G. Dines & J. M. Humez (Eds.), *Gender, race, and class in media: A critical reader* (4th ed., pp. 7–19). Los Angeles: Sage.

Kilbourne, J. (Writer). (2010a). *Killing us softly 4* [Motion picture]. United States: Media Education Foundation.

Kilbourne, J. (2010b, Summer). Sexist advertising, then & now. *Ms.*, 34–35.

Kim, J. L., Sorsoli, C. L., Collins, K., Zylbergold, A., Schooler, D., & Tolman, D. L. (2007). From sex to sexuality: Exposing the heterosexual script on primetime network television. *Journal of Sex Research, 44*, 145–157.

King, C. (2010). *Animating difference: Race, gender, and sexuality in contemporary films for children.* Lanham, MD: Rowman & Littlefield.

Kinnick, K. N., & Parton, S. R. (2005). Workplace communication: What *The Apprentice* teaches about communication skills. *Business Communication Quarterly, 68*, 429–456.

Kistler, M. E., & Lee, M. J. (2010). Does exposure to sexual hip-hop music videos influence the sexual attitudes of college students? *Mass Communication and Society, 13*, 67–86.

Klein Modisett, D. (2015, Spring). The women who steal the show. *Ms.*, 20–25.

Kolehmainen, M. (2010). Normalizing and gendering affects. *Feminist Media Studies, 10*, 179–194.

Kramarae, C. (1995). A backstage critique of virtual reality. In S. Jones (Ed.), *Cybersociety: Computer-mediated communication and community* (pp. 36–56). Thousand Oaks, CA: Sage.

Lauzen, M. M., Dozier, D. M., & Horan, N. (2008). Constructing gender stereotypes through social roles in prime-time television. *Journal of Broadcasting & Electronic Media, 52*, 200–214.

LaWare, M. R., & Moutsatsos, C. (2013). "For skin that's us, *authentically* us": Celebrity, empowerment, and the allure of antiaging advertisements. *Women's Studies in Communication, 36*, 189–208.

Lee, C. (2015, April 3). This is what America looks like. *Entertainment Weekly*, 34–40.

Lee, M. J., & Moscowitz, L. (2015). The "rich bitch": Class and gender on *The Real Housewives of New York City*. In G. Dines & J. M. Humez (Eds.), *Gender,*

race, and class in media: A critical reader (4th ed., pp. 143–156). Los Angeles: Sage.

Levina, M. (2014). From feminism without bodies, to bleeding bodies in virtual spaces. *Communication and Critical/Cultural Studies, 11*, 278–281.

Levine, M. P., & Murnen, S. K. (2009). Everybody knows that mass media are a cause of eating disorders: A critical review of evidence for a causal link between media, negative body image, and disordered eating in females. *Journal of Social and Clinical Psychology, 28*, 9–42.

Lewis, S., & Shewmaker, J. (2011). Considering age and gender: A comparative content analysis of sexualization of teen celebrity websites. *The International Journal of Interdisciplinary Social Sciences, 5*, 215–224.

Liebler, R. (2015, Spring). Information superhighway patrol: For Mary Anne Franks, cyber harassment is a civil rights issue. *Bitch*, 23–25.

Lin, C. A. (1997). Beefcake versus cheesecake in the 1990s: Sexist portrayals of both genders in television commercials. *Howard Journal of Communications, 8*, 237–249.

Linneman, T. J. (2008). How do you solve a problem like Will Truman? The feminization of gay masculinities on *Will & Grace. Men and Masculinities, 10*, 583–603.

Lipsitz, G. (2015). The meaning of memory: Family, class, and ethnicity in early network television programs. In G. Dines & J. M. Humez (Eds.), *Gender, race, and class in media: A critical reader* (4th ed., pp. 20–27). Los Angeles: Sage.

Lorie, A. F. (2011). Forbidden fruit or conventional apple pie? A look at *Sex and the City*'s reversal of the female gender. *Media, Culture, and Society, 33*, 35–51.

Lotz, A. D. (2006). *Redesigning women: Television after the network era.* Champaign: University of Illinois Press.

Lozon, J., & Bensimon, M. (2014). Music misuse: A review of the personal and collective roles of "problem music." *Aggression and Violent Behavior, 19*, 207–218.

Lynskey, D. (2013, November 13). "Blurred Lines": The most controversial song of the decade. Retrieved October 30, 2015 from <www.theguardian.com.uk>.

MacKinnon, K. (2003). *Representing men: Maleness and masculinity in the media.* New York: Arnold.

Mager, J., & Helgeson, J. G. (2011). Fifty years of advertising images: Some changing perspectives on role portrayals along with enduring consistencies. *Sex Roles, 64*, 238–252.

Maerz, M. (2014, December 12). This was the year that TV transformed the way we think. *Entertainment Weekly*, 24.

Maerz, M. (2015a, June 19). Lady liberated. *Entertainment Weekly*, 24–29.

Maerz, M. (2015b, August 7). I am Cait. *Entertainment Weekly*, 52–53.

Magsamen-Conrad, K., Dowd, J., Abuljadail, M., Alsulaiman, S., & Shareefi, A. (2015). Life-span differences in the uses and gratifications of tablets: Implications for older adults. *Computers in Human Behavior, 52*, 96–106.

Malamuth, N. M., & Billings, V. (1984). Why pornography? Models of functions and effects. *Journal of Communication, 34*, 117–129.

Mandziuk, R. (1991, February). *Cementing her sphere: Daytime talk and the television world of women.* Paper presented at the meeting of the Western States Communication Association, Phoenix, AZ.

Martinez, A. R. (2015). Savvy and susceptible: Diverse American women discuss beauty, body image, and identity in media. In A. R. Martinez & L. J. Miller (Eds.), *Gender in a transitional era: Changes and challenges* (pp. 209–228). Lanham, MD: Lexington.

Marwick, A. (2010). There's a beautiful girl under all of this: Performing hegemonic femininity in reality television. *Critical Studies in Media Communication, 27*, 251–266.

Maxwell, J. P. (2001). The perception of relationship violence in the lyrics of a song. *Journal of Interpersonal Violence, 16*, 640–661.

McCombs, M. E., Shaw, D. L., & Weaver, D. H. (2014). New directions in agenda-setting theory and research. *Mass Communication & Society, 17*, 781–802.

McGovern, J. (2015, Fall Movie Preview). *The Danish Girl. Entertainment Weekly*, 63.

McIntyre, N. (2015, Winter). Sisterhood is fashionable: Chanel's pop feminism. *Bitch*, 5.

McKay, J., & Johnson, J. (2015). Pornographic eroticism and sexual grotesquerie in representations of African American sportswomen. In G. Dines & J. M. Humez (Eds.), *Gender, race, and class in media: A critical reader* (4th ed., pp. 118–127). Los Angeles: Sage.

Means Coleman, R. R. (2012). Tyler Perry: The (self-appointed) savior of black womanhood. In A. Gonzalez, M. Houston, & V. Chen (Eds.), *Our voices: Essays in culture, ethnicity, and communication* (5th ed., pp. 53–59). New York: Oxford University Press.

Merskin, D. (2011). Perpetuation of the hot-Latina stereotype in *Desperate Housewives*. In G. Dines & J. M. Humez (Eds.), *Gender, race, and class in media: A critical reader* (3rd ed., pp. 327–334). Los Angeles: Sage.

Mesaros-Winckles, C. E. (2014). Christian patriarchy lite: TLC's *19 Kids and Counting*. In A. A. Ruggerio (Ed.), *Media depictions of brides, wives, and mothers* (pp. 63–76). Lanham, MD: Lexington.

Mitra, A. (2010). Voices of the marginalized on the Internet: Examples from a website for women of South Asia. In P. K. Nayar (Ed.), *The new media and cybercultures anthology* (pp. 166–182). Malden, MA: Wiley-Blackwell.

Mohammed-Baksh, S., & Callison, C. (2015). Hegemonic masculinity in hip-hop music? Difference in brand mention in rap music based on the rapper's gender. *Journal of Promotion Management, 21*, 351–370.

Molloy, P. (2015, Summer). When Dove tries: The latest "real beauty" gimmick. *Bitch*, 5.

Monk-Turner, E., Kouts, T., Parris, K., & Webb, (2007). Gender role stereotyping in advertisements on three radio stations: Does musical genre make a difference? *Journal of Gender Studies, 16*, 173–182.

Moore, C. (2015). Resisting, reiterating, and dancing through: The swinging closet doors of Ellen DeGeneres's televised personalities. In G. Dines & J. M. Humez (Eds.), *Gender, race, and class in media: A critical reader* (4th ed., pp. 210–219). Los Angeles: Sage.

Moore, M. L. (1992). The family as portrayed on prime-time television, 1947–1990: Structure and characteristics. *Sex Roles, 26*, 41–61.

Moorti, S., & Ross, K. (2004). Reality television: Fairy tale or feminist nightmare? *Feminist Media Studies, 4*, 211–214.

Morrison, M. A., Krugman, D. M., & Park, P. (2008). Under the radar: Smokeless tobacco advertising in magazines with substantial youth readership. *American Journal of Public Health, 98*, 543–548.

Mortensen, T. E. (2010). WoW is the new MUD: Social gaming from text to video. In P. K. Nayar (Ed.), *The new media and cybercultures anthology* (pp. 394–407). Malden, MA: Wiley-Blackwell.

Mueller, B. (2011). Reaching African American consumers: African American shopping behavior. In G. Dines & J. M. Humez (Eds.), *Gender, race, and class in media: A critical reader* (3rd ed., pp. 213–219). Los Angeles: Sage.

Murphy-Hoefer, R., Hyland, A., & Rivard, C. (2010). The influence of tobacco countermarketing ads on college students' knowledge, attitudes, and beliefs. *Journal of American College Health, 58*, 373–381.

Nabi, R. L. (2009). Cosmetic surgery makeover programs and intentions to undergo cosmetic enhancements: A consideration of three models of media effects. *Human Communication Research, 35*, 1–27.

Nakamura, L. (2015). "Don't hate the player, hate the game": The racialization of labor in *World of Warcraft*.

In G. Dines & J. M. Humez (Eds.), *Gender, race, and class in media: A critical reader* (4th ed., pp. 620-626). Los Angeles: Sage.

Nashawaty, C. (2015, July 24). *Trainwreck. Entertainment Weekly*, 20.

Natalle, E. J., & Flippen, J. L. (2004). Urban music: Gendered language in rapping. In P. M. Backlund & M. R. Williams (Eds.), *Readings in gender communication* (pp. 140–149). Belmont, CA: Thomson/Wadsworth.

Nayar, P. (Ed.) (2010). *The new media and cybercultures anthology*. Malden, MA: Wiley-Blackwell.

Neff, J. (2010a). Meet the man your man could smell like. *Advertising Age, 81*, 2–3.

Neff, J. (2010b). Cracking the viral code: Look at your ads. Now look at Old Spice. *Advertising Age, 81*, 16–17.

Ng, E. (2015). Reading the romance of fan cultural production: Music videos of a television lesbian couple. In G. Dines & J. M. Humez (Eds.), *Gender, race, and class in media: A critical reader* (4th ed., pp. 610–619). Los Angeles: Sage.

Noble, B. (2007). Queer as box: Boi spectators and boy culture on Showtime's *Queer as Folk*. In M. L. Johnson (Ed.), *Third-wave feminism and television: Jane puts it in a box* (pp. 147–165). London: I. B. Tauris.

Norwood, K. M., & Lannutti, P. J. (2015). Families' experiences with transgender identity and transition: A family stress perspective. In L. G. Spencer, IV & J. C. Capuzza (Eds.), *Transgender communication studies: Histories, trends, and trajectories* (pp. 51–68). Lanham, MD: Lexington.

Olson, B., & Douglas, W. (1997). The family on television: An evaluation of gender roles in situation comedy. *Sex Roles, 36*, 409–427.

Oria, B. (2014). *Talking dirty on* Sex and the City: *Romance, intimacy, friendship*. New York: Rowman & Littlefield.

Ouellette, L., & Hay, J. (2008). *Better living through reality TV: Television and post-welfare citizenship*. New York: Wiley-Blackwell.

Paasonen, S. (2015). Diagnoses of transformation: "Pornification," digital media, and the diversification of the pornographic. In L. Coleman & J. M. Held (Eds.), *The philosophy of pornography: Contemporary perspectives* (pp. 3–16). New York: Rowman & Littlefield.

Paglia, C. (2008, May 23). In defense of the working girl. *Entertainment Weekly*, 69.

Palmer, G. (2015). *Extreme Makeover: Home Edition:* An American fairy tale. In G. Dines & J. M. Humez (Eds.), *Gender, race, and class in media: A critical reader* (4th ed., pp. 51–57). Los Angeles: Sage.

Palomares, N. A., & Lee, E.-J. (2010). Virtual gender identity: The linguistic assimilation to gendered avatars in computer-mediated communication. *Journal of Language and Social Psychology, 29*, 5–23.

Patterson, P. (1996). Rambos and himbos: Stereotypical images of men in advertising. In P. Lester (Ed.), *Images that injure* (pp. 93–96). Westport, CT: Praeger.

Paul, B., & Shim, J. W. (2008). Gender, sexual affect, and motivations for Internet pornography use. *International Journal of Sexual Health, 20*, 187–199.

Paul, P. (2005). *Pornified: How pornography is damaging our lives, our relationships, and our families*. New York: Henry Holt and Company.

Pearson, K., & Reich, N. M. (2004). *Queer Eye* fairy tale: Changing the world one manicure at a time. *Feminist Media Studies, 4*, 229–231.

Peck, J. (2006). TV talk shows as therapeutic discourse: The ideological labor of the televised talking cure. *Communication Theory, 5*, 58–81.

Perry, I. (2003). Who(se) am I? The identity and image of women in hip-hop. In G. Dines & J. M. Humez (Eds.), *Gender, race, and class in media: A critical reader* (2nd ed., pp. 136–148). Thousand Oaks, CA: Sage.

Persis Murray, D. (2015). Branding "real" social change in Dove's Campaign for Real Beauty. In G. Dines & J. M. Humez (Eds.), *Gender, race, and class in media: A critical reader* (4th ed., pp. 285–296). Los Angeles: Sage.

Peter, J., & Valkenburg, P. M. (2006). Adolescents' exposure to sexually explicit online material and recreational attitudes toward sex. *Journal of Communication, 56*, 639–660.

Peter, J., & Valkenburg, P. M. (2008). Adolescents' exposure to sexually explicit Internet material and sexual preoccupancy: A three-wave panel study. *Media Psychology, 11*, 207–234.

Peter, J., & Valkenburg, P. M. (2010). Processes underlying the effects of adolescents' use of sexually explicit Internet material: The role of perceived realism. *Communication Research, 37*, 375–399.

Peters, W. (2011). Pink dollars, white collars: *Queer as Folk*, valuable viewers, and the price of gay TV. *Critical Studies in Media Communication, 28*, 193–212.

Porfido, G. (2011). *Queer as Folk* and the spectacularization of gender identity. In T. Peele (Ed.), *Queer popular culture: Literature, media, film, and television* (pp. 57–70). New York: Palgrave Macmillan.

Potter, W. J. (2014). A critical analysis of cultivation theory. *Journal of Communication, 64*, 1015–1036.

Pozner, J. L. (2010a). Creating the illusion of popular demand. *Extra!, 23*, 14–15.

Pozner, J. L. (2010b). *Reality bites back: The troubling truth about guilty pleasure TV.* Berkeley, CA: Seal Press.

Pratt, M. (2011). "This is the way we live ... and love!" Feeding on and still hungering for lesbian representation in *The L Word.* In G. Dines & J. M. Humez (Eds.), *Gender, race, and class in media: A critical reader* (3rd ed., pp. 341–348). Los Angeles: Sage.

Primack, B. A., Gold, M. A., Schwarz, E. B., & Dalton, M. A. (2008). Degrading and non-degrading sex in popular music: A content analysis. *Public Health Reports, 123,* 593–600.

Pullen, C. (2007). *Documenting gay men: Identity and performance in reality television and documentary film.* Jefferson, NC: McFarland.

Rafalovich, A. (2006). Broken and becoming god-sized: Contemporary metal music and masculine individualism. *Symbolic Interaction, 29,* 19–32.

Raiten-D'Antonio, T. (2010). *Ugly as sin: The truth about how we look and finding freedom from self-hatred.* Deerfield Beach, FL: Health Communications Inc.

Raymer, M. (2014, August 8). "All the right junk in all the right places": Meghan Trainor's body-positive anthem "All About That Bass" has become summer's surprise hit. *Entertainment Weekly,* 14.

Reed, J. (2005). Ellen DeGeneres: Public lesbian number one. *Feminist Media Studies, 5,* 23–36.

Reed, J. (2011). The 3 phases of Ellen: From queer to gay to postgay. In T. Peele (Ed.), *Queer popular culture: Literature, media, film, and television* (pp. 9-26). New York: Palgrave Macmillan.

Reynolds, C. (2015). "I am super straight and I prefer you be too": Constructions of heterosexual masculinity in online personal ads for "straight" men seeking sex with men. *Journal of Communication Inquiry, 39,* 213–231.

Rice, L. (2015, June 12). Keeping up with Caitlyn Jenner. *Entertainment Weekly,* 16.

Richmond-Abbott, M. (1992). *Masculine and feminine: Gender roles over the life cycle* (2nd ed.). New York: McGraw-Hill.

Rogers, A. (2013, Fall). Sexism in unexpected places: An analysis of country music lyrics. *Caravel Undergraduate Research Journal.* Retrieved October 30, 2015, from <http://caravel.sc.edu/2013>.

Ropelato, J. (2003). Tricks pornographers play. Retrieved March 29, 2011, from <http://www.familysafemedia.com>.

Rose, T. (2015). There are bitches and hoes. In G. Dines & J. M. Humez (Eds.), *Gender, race, and class in media: A critical reader* (4th ed., pp. 386–390). Los Angeles: Sage.

Ross, K. (2013). *Gendered media: Women, men, and identity politics.* New York: Rowman & Littlefield.

Royse, P., Lee, J., Baasanjav, U., Hopson, M., & Consalvo, M. (2010). Women and games: Technologies of the gendered self. In P. K. Nayar (Ed.), *The new media and cybercultures anthology* (pp. 408–424). Malden, MA: Wiley-Blackwell.

Sahim, S. (2015, Fall). American woman-child: Troubling new trope. *Bitch,* 7.

Sanbonmatsu, J. (2015). Video games and machine dreams of domination. In G. Dines & J. M. Humez (Eds.), *Gender, race, and class in media: A critical reader* (4th ed., pp. 473–483). Los Angeles: Sage.

Santa Cruz Bell, J., & Avant-Mier, R. (2009). What's love got to do with it? Analyzing the discourse of hip hop love through rap balladry, 1987 and 2007. *Women & Language, 32,* 42–49.

Sarracino, C., & Scott, K. M. (2009). *The porning of America: The rise of porn culture, what it means, and where we go from here.* New York: Beacon Press.

Schut, K. (2015). Strategic simulations and our past: The bias of computer games in the presentation of history. In G. Dines & J. M. Humez (Eds.), *Gender, race, and class in media: A critical reader* (4th ed., pp. 484–490). Los Angeles: Sage.

Schwartz, M. (2009, December 11). Sarah Jessica Parker and the women of *Sex and the City. Entertainment Weekly,* 55.

Scott, J., & Craig-Lees, M. (2010). Audience engagement and its effects on product placement recognition. *Journal of Promotion Management, 16,* 39–58.

Sellnow, D. D. (1999). Music as persuasion: Refuting hegemonic masculinity in "He Thinks He'll Keep Her." *Women's Studies in Communication, 22,* 66–84.

Sender, K. (2006). Queens for a day: *Queer Eye for the Straight Guy* and the neoliberal project. *Critical Studies in Media Communication, 23,* 131–151.

Sevcikova, A., Serek, J., Barbovschi, M., & Daneback, K. (2014). The roles of individual characteristics and liberalism in intentional and unintentional exposure to online sexual material among European youth: A multilevel approach. *Sexuality Research and Social Policy, 11,* 104–115.

Shade, D. D., Kornfield, S., & Oliver, M. B. (2015). The uses and gratifications of media migration: Investigating the activities, motivations, and predictors of migration behaviors originating in entertainment television. *Journal of Broadcasting & Electronic Media, 59,* 318–341.

Shanahan, J., Signorielli, N., & Morgan, M. (2008, May). *Television and sex roles 30 years hence: A retrospective and current look from a cultural indicators perspective.*

Paper presented at the meeting of the International Communication Association, Montreal, Canada.

Sharp, S. (2011). Disciplining the housewife in *Desperate Housewives* and domestic reality television. In G. Dines & J. M. Humez (Eds.), *Gender, race, and class in media: A critical reader* (3rd ed., pp. 481–486). Los Angeles: Sage.

Shattuc, J. (1997). *The talking cure: TV talk shows and women.* New York: Routledge.

Shattuc, J. (2004). Freud vs. women: The popularization of therapy on daytime talk shows. In C. Carter & L. Steiner (Eds.), *Critical readings: Media and gender* (pp. 307–327). Maidenhead, Berkshire, UK: Open University Press.

Shaw, A. (2013). Rethinking game studies: A case study approach to video game play and identification. *Critical Studies in Media Communication, 30,* 347–361.

Shaw, A. (2014). The Internet is full of jerks, because the world is full of jerks: What feminist theory teaches us about the Internet. *Communication and Critical/Cultural Studies, 11,* 273–277.

Shaw, A. (2015). *Gaming at the edge: Sexuality and gender at the margins of gamer culture.* Minneapolis: University of Minnesota Press.

Shaw, J. (2014, March 21). Disney's new MVPs. *Entertainment Weekly,* 12–13.

Shugart, H. A. (2001). Parody as subversive performance: Denaturalizing gender and reconstituting desire in *Ellen. Text & Performance Quarterly, 21,* 93–113.

Shugart, H. A. (2003). Reinventing privilege: The new (gay) man in contemporary popular media. *Critical Studies in Media Communication, 20,* 67–91.

Shugart, H. A., & Egley Waggoner, C. (2005). A bit much: Spectacle as discursive resistance. *Feminist Media Studies, 5,* 65–81.

Signorielli, N., & Bacue, A. (1999). Recognition and respect: A content analysis of prime-time television characters across three decades. *Sex Roles, 40,* 527–544.

Signorielli, N., & Morgan, M. (1990). *Cultivation analysis: New directions in media effects research.* Newbury Park, CA: Sage.

Simonton, A. J. (1995). Women for sale. In M. Lont (Ed.), *Women and media: Content, careers, criticism* (pp. 143–164). Belmont, CA: Wadsworth.

Skeggs, B., & Wood, H. (2008). The labour of transformation and circuits of value "around" reality television. *Continuum: Journal of Media and Cultural Studies, 22,* 559–572.

Skerski, J. (2007). From prime-time to daytime: The domestication of Ellen DeGeneres. *Communication and Critical/Cultural Studies, 4,* 363–381.

Sloop, J. M. (2006). Critical studies in gender/sexuality and media. In B. J. Dow & J. T. Wood (Eds.), *The SAGE handbook of gender and communication* (pp. 319–333). Thousand Oaks, CA: Sage.

Soll, L. (2008, May 23). In her shoes. *Entertainment Weekly,* 69.

Sperling, N. (2015, May 15). Women get the last laugh. *Entertainment Weekly,* 12–14.

Stankiewicz, J. M., & Rosselli, F. (2008). Women as sex objects and victims in print advertisements. *Sex Roles, 58,* 579–589.

Stark, S. (2000a). A tale of two sitcoms. In S. Maasik & J. Solomon (Eds.), *Signs of life in the U.S.A.: Readings on popular culture for writers* (pp. 236–241). Boston: Bedford/St. Martin's.

Stark, S. (2000b). *The Oprah Winfrey Show* and the talk-show furor. In S. Maasik & J. Solomon (Eds.), *Signs of life in the U.S.A.: Readings on popular culture for writers* (pp. 241–248). Boston: Bedford/St. Martin's.

Staskiewicz, K. (2014, August 14). Is 70 the new 30? *Entertainment Weekly,* 22–23.

Steenland, S. (1995). Content analysis of the image of women on television. In C. M. Lont (Ed.), *Women and media: Content, careers, criticism* (pp. 179–189). Belmont, CA: Wadsworth.

Steinem, G. (1990, July–August). Sex, lies, and advertising. As reprinted in the Spring 2002 issue of *Ms.,* 60–64.

Stern, D. M. (2009). Consuming the fractured female: Lessons from MTV's *The Real World. Communication Review, 12,* 50–77.

Stern, S. (2002). Virtually speaking: Girls' self-disclosure on the WWW. *Women's Studies in Communication, 25,* 223–253.

Stern, S. (2004). Expressions of identity online: Adolescents' World Wide Web home pages. *Journal of Broadcasting & Electronic Media, 48,* 218–243.

Stransky, T. (2011, March 18). Apologizing for *The Real World. Entertainment Weekly,* 63.

Strasburger, V. C. (2005). Adolescents, sex, and the media: Ooooo, baby, baby—a Q & A. *Adolescent Medicine Clinics, 16,* 269–288.

Streitmatter, R. (2009). *From "perverts" to "Fab Five": The media's changing depiction of gay men and lesbians.* New York: Routledge.

Strossen, N. (2000). *Defending pornography: Free speech, sex, and the fight for women's rights.* New York: New York University Press.

Sturken, M. (2008). *Thelma and Louise.* London: British Film Institute.

Sundar, S. S., & Limperos, A. M. (2013). Uses and grats 2.0: New gratifications for new media. *Journal of Broadcasting & Electronic Media, 57,* 504–525.

Sung, C. C. M. (2013). Language and gender in a US reality TV show: An analysis of leadership discourse in single-sex interactions. *Nordic Journal of English Studies, 12*, 25–51.

Tait, S. (2011). Television and the domestication of cosmetic surgery. In G. Dines & J. M. Humez (Eds.), *Gender, race, and class in media: A critical reader* (3rd ed., pp. 509–517). Los Angeles: Sage.

Taylor, T. L. (2003). Multiple pleasures: Women and online gaming. *Convergence, 9*, 21–46.

Tedford, T. L., & Herbeck, D. A. (2013). *Freedom of speech in the United States* (7th ed.). New York: Strata.

Timmerman, L. M., Allen, M., Jorgensen, J., Herrett-Skjellum, J., Kramer, M. R., & Ryan, J. (2008). A review and meta-analysis examining the relationships of music content with sex, race, priming, and attitudes. *Communication Quarterly, 56*, 303–324.

Traube, E. (1992). *Dreaming identities: Class, gender, and generation in 1980s Hollywood movies.* Boulder, CO: Westview.

Tropiano, S. (2002). *The prime time closet: A history of gays and lesbians on television.* Milwaukee: Applause Books.

Tuchman, G. (1979). Women's depiction by the mass media. *Signs, 4*, 528–542.

Tuchman, G., Daniels, A. K., & Benet, J. (Eds.). (1978). *Hearth and home: Images of women in the mass media.* New York: Oxford University Press.

Turkle, S. (2011). *Alone together: Why we expect more from technology and less from each other.* New York: Basic Books.

Turner, J. S. (2010). Sex and the spectacle of music videos: An examination of the portrayal of race and sexuality in music videos. *Sex Roles, 64*, 173–191.

Tyree, T. C. M. (2009). Lovin' momma and hatin' on baby mama: A comparison of misogynistic and stereotypical representations in songs about rappers' mothers and baby mamas. *Women & Language, 32*, 50–58.

Utley, E. A. (2010). "I used to love him": Exploring the miseducation about black love and sex. *Critical Studies in Media Communication, 27*, 291–308.

Utley, E. A., & Menzies, A. L. (2009). Show some love: Youth responses to "Kiss Me Thru the Phone." *Women & Language, 32*, 68–77.

Valby, K. (2014, July 4). They're worth more than their weight. *Entertainment Weekly*, 20.

van Zoonen, L. (2002). Gendering the Internet: Claims, controversies, and cultures. *European Journal of Communication, 17*, 5–23.

Vande Berg, L. R., & Streckfuss, D. (1992). Prime-time television's portrayal of women and the world of work: A demographic profile. *Journal of Broadcasting & Electronic Media, 36*, 195–208.

Vaynerchuk, G. (2011, March 3). Old Spice Man marketing, redux: What went right—and what did not. Retrieved March 11, 2011 from <http://www.fastcompany.com>.

Vilkomerson, S. (2013, October 4). The $5 billion woman. *Entertainment Weekly*, 42–45.

Vivian, J. (2011). *The media of mass communication* (10th ed.). Boston: Allyn & Bacon.

Walsh, K. R., Fursich, E., & Jefferson, B. S. (2008). Beauty and the patriarchal beast: Gender role portrayals in sitcoms featuring mismatched couples. *Journal of Popular Film and Television, 36*, 123–132.

Ward, J. R. (Ed.) (2015). *Real sister: Stereotypes, respectability, and black women in reality TV.* Rutgers, NJ: Rutgers University Press.

Weare, A. M. (2015). "I wish a whole new word was used for it": Pro-ED blogging and online identity. *The Northwest Journal of Communication, 43*, 23–52.

Weiss, D. (2005). Constructing the queer "I": Performativity, citationality, and desire in *Queer Eye for the Straight Guy. Popular Communication, 3*, 73–95.

Weitzer, R., & Kubrin, C. E. (2009). Misogyny in rap music: A content analysis of prevalence and meanings. *Men and Masculinities, 12*, 3–29.

Welsch, J. R. (2001). "Let's keep goin'!" On the road with Louise and Thelma. In M. Pomerance (Ed.), *Ladies and gentlemen, boys and girls: Gender in film at the end of the twentieth century* (pp. 249–266). Albany, NY: State University of New York Press.

Westerfelhaus, R., & Lacroix, C. (2006). Seeing "straight" through *Queer Eye:* Exposing the strategic rhetoric of heteronormativity in a mediated ritual of gay rebellion. *Critical Studies in Media Communication, 23*, 426–444.

Whipple, T. W., & Courtney, A. E. (1980). How to portray women in TV commercials. *Journal of Advertising Research, 20*, 53–59.

Whipple, T. W., & Courtney, A. E. (1985). Female role portrayals in advertising and communication effectiveness: A review. *Journal of Advertising, 14*, 4–8.

Wiles, M. A., & Danielova, A. (2009). The worth of product placement in successful films: An event study analysis. *Journal of Marketing, 73*, 44–63.

Williams, L. (2007, May). *Music lyrics versus music videos: The importance of platform in assessing exposure to sexual content.* Paper presented at the meeting of the International Communication Association, San Francisco, CA.

Willis, J., & Gonzalez, A. (1997). Reconceptualizing gender through intercultural dialogue: The case of the Tex-Mex Madonna. *Women & Language, 20*, 9–12.

Willoughby, V. (2015, Fall). Screen queen: FKA twigs is a pop music gamechanger. *Bitch*, 6.

Wilson, C. G., & Gutierrez, F. (2003). Advertising and people of color. In G. Dines & J. M. Humez (Eds.), *Gender, race, and class in media: A critical reader* (2nd ed., pp. 283–292). Thousand Oaks, CA: Sage.

Wolfe, S. J., & Roripaugh, L. A. (2006). The (in)visible lesbian: Anxieties of representation in *The L Word*. In K. Akass, J. McCabe, & S. Warn (Eds.), *Reading* The L Word*: Outing contemporary television* (pp. 43–54). London: I. B. Tauris.

Wood, H. (2009). *Talking with television: Women, talk shows, and modern self-reflexivity*. Champaign: University of Illinois Press.

Wright, P. J. (2012). A longitudinal analysis of U.S. adults' pornography exposure: Sexual socialization, selective exposure, and the moderating role of unhappiness. *Journal of Media Psychology, 24*, 67–76.

Wright, P. J. (2013). U.S. males and pornography, 1973–2010. *Journal of Sex Research, 50*, 60–71.

Wright, P. J., & Arroyo, A. (2013). Internet pornography and U.S. women's sexual behavior: Results from a national sample. *Mass Communication & Society, 16*, 617–638.

Wright, P. J., Bae, S., & Funk, M. (2013). United States women and pornography through four decades: Exposure, attitudes, behaviors, individual differences. *Archives of Sexual Behavior, 42*, 1131–1144.

Wright, P. J., Sun, C., Steffen, N. J., & Tokunaga, R. S. (2015). Pornography, alcohol, and male sexual dominance. *Communication Monographs, 82*, 252–270.

Wypijewski, J. (2009, June 15). Return of the fabulous. *The Nation*, 7–8.

Yoder, J. D., Christopher, J., & Holmes, J. D. (2008). Are television commercials still achievement scripts for women? *Psychology of Women Quarterly, 32*, 303–311.

Ziegler, S. G. (2007). The (mis)education of Generation M. *Learning, Media, & Technology, 32*, 69–81.

Zimmerman, A., & Dahlberg, J. (2008). The sexual objectification of women in advertising: A contemporary cultural perspective *Journal of Advertising Research, 48*, 71–79.

Zoladz, L. (2015a, June 29–July 12). Amy Schumer is going to be a very different kind of movie star. *New York*, 82.

Zoladz, L. (2015b, April 30–May 3). The best possible version of a 20-year-old: The post-gender, post-genre charm of indie-music star Shamir Bailey. *New York*, 105–107.

CHAPTER 9

GENDER IN THE WORKPLACE
The Challenges of Talking Shop

CASE STUDY

Textual Harassment?

Josh and Chris met at work; they shared the same status at their fast-paced, high-powered advertising agency, sometimes co-created pitches and ad campaigns, and soon shared something more—a romantic relationship. Romance at this office was allowed, in fact it was fairly common.

Often Josh and Chris texted each other during work hours (when not working together on a project) and near the end of a work day or after work hours, mainly to make plans for the evening or weekend. The relationship flourished until they found themselves competing on different teams of ad execs for the most desirable project the agency had ever seen. Competition to win the prized contract caused serious friction in their relationship, such that they parted ways romantically, but stayed employed at the agency. After Josh's team landed the plum project, he was quickly promoted—an accomplishment that Chris envied. Josh felt guilty, so he started texting Chris more than usual—not in the hopes of getting back together, but more from a motivation of making sure Chris was still his friend and okay about his promotion. Chris wasn't comfortable with Josh's repeated, insistent texts—they felt more like bragging or rubbing Chris's nose in Josh's good fortune than a sincere attempt to stay in touch as friends.

HOT TOPICS

- The greater, deeper costs of the wage gap between the sexes
- How stereotypes about men and women can affect the likelihood of getting hired
- Verbal and nonverbal indications of sex and gender bias in job interviews
- Women's and men's advancement on the job
- Juggling family and career
- Managerial communication styles of men and women
- Sexual harassment in the workplace

Chris moved on romantically and told Josh that news, but Josh's increasing number of texts (and increasingly personal texts, often recalling intimate moments in their past romantic relationship) started to feel like pressure, which then started to feel like harassment. But since Josh's position in the firm was higher up than Chris's and Josh had been employed at the agency longer than Chris, Chris wasn't sure what to do or if there was a policy to consult. Since Chris and Josh had once been romantically linked, could anything be done now to stop this unwanted texting? At first, Chris responded to Josh's texts less often, ignoring most of them; then he sent Josh an email, asking him to stop texting him socially and to only text if it was work-related. One night Josh got drunk and sent Chris *more* than a text—he *sexted* him.

What's the next step for Chris? Report Josh's behavior? Have a face-to-face confrontation and clearly set boundaries with Josh? Leave the agency? Would you call Josh's behavior sexual harassment, more specifically textual harassment?

In a world where everyone walks around with cell phones glued to their hands, it probably doesn't surprise you to learn of this form of sexual harassment, termed *textual harassment*. Actually, textual harassment goes beyond text messages that someone may consider harassing; it extends to use of social media, like Facebook and Twitter. In a world of "constant connectivity," a person's "written communication that is transferred electronically via either cell phone or the Internet" may be a new context for sexual harassment (Mainiero & Jones, 2013, p. 188).

Back to the situation we describe in this case study: Even if Chris kept all of Josh's text messages, as well as the unwise "sext," Chris will have a challenge proving to the company that Josh's behavior created a hostile workplace climate and was therefore sexual harassment. Granted, from our perspective, Josh's behavior was sexual harassment, but what compromises the situation was Chris and Josh's prior romantic relationship as coworkers, plus the fact that few companies or institutions have explicitly stated policies about workplace romances nor texting and social media use, as vehicles for sexual harassment.

Mmore college students than ever are working—many full time, some with multiple jobs. Gone are the days when college students graduated with little or no work experience because they were so focused on their studies or simply didn't have to "earn while they learned." Many students layer internships on top of their school and work schedules, to gain valuable experience and networking opportunities before graduating. Given your work experience thus far, what do you think are the more pressing issues related to sex, gender, and communication in the world of work? Competing for the best jobs? Acing the interview? Facing a glass ceiling blocking your advancement? Handling an office romance? Juggling work and home? Moving up in an organization? Dealing with sexual harassment? Let's explore these topics as we examine workplace communication in this chapter.

THE COMMONPLACE REALITY OF WOMEN AND MEN WORKING TOGETHER

For many of us, our work is our livelihood, our most time-consuming activity. Americans are spending significantly greater amounts of time on the job than three decades ago (U.S. Department of Labor, 2015). Each year from 2010 to the present, Americans have worked a full week's worth of hours more per year than in the year 2000 (Work & Family Facts & Statistics, 2015). A Gallup poll conducted in 2014 showed that the average full-time work week is 47 hours, with 39 percent of Americans working full time reporting an average work week of 50 hours or more (Saad, 2014). The Bureau of Labor Statistics reports that over six million Americans currently working part-time would prefer to work full time, but those jobs are hard to get.

Work can be a rewarding experience or a real downer on the self-esteem. Many things make a job worthwhile and rewarding. However, when asked what makes their jobs enjoyable, most employees—men and women alike—say that relationships with people they work with make the most difference between job satisfaction and dissatisfaction. It used to be more rare that men and women would work alongside each other, across a variety of professions and jobs, but it's quite commonplace today, and it's becoming more commonplace for women and men alike to report to a female supervisor.

The last national census conducted in 2010 revealed that the U.S. workforce is 49.9 percent female, compared to 47 percent in 2000, 45 percent in 1990, and 43 percent in 1980 (U.S. Census Bureau, 2010). Census statistics also showed that a woman working full time earned, as an average weekly wage, about 83 cents for every dollar a man earned. In the 1970s, that figure was 59 cents; in the 1980s, the pay gap narrowed to its smallest extent, but that was because men's wages fell, not because women's wages rose (Blau & Kahn, 1997).

However, other statistics paint the wage gap between the sexes as being more dire than census data shows. In March of 2011, the Obama administration released *Women in America: Indicators of Social and Economic Well Being*. This comprehensive report showed that women made 75 cents to the man's dollar, suggesting an even greater wage gap in the country than the census revealed. Most likely, the difference is that the census statistic reflected only full-time female workers, whereas the White House report factored in part-time female workers as well.

Using that 75 cents to the dollar figure, the earnings gap between the sexes won't disappear until the year 2056! For a woman with only a high school diploma, the pay gap will cost her $700,000 in lost income over her lifetime (WAGE, Women Are Getting Even, 2015). For women who've completed college, the economic loss is closer to $1 million; for women with graduate degrees, the figure is $1.2 million. Wage discrepancies are also affected by race and ethnicity, with a general downward trend in earnings for female members of minority groups (Baker, 2012; England, Garcia-Beaulieu, & Ross, 2007; Little, 2014; O'Neill, 2015; U.S. Department of Labor, 2015).

Some notable strides have been made toward narrowing the wage gap for workers. In 2009, President Barack Obama's first signed piece of legislation was the Lilly Ledbetter Fair Pay Act; the bill overturned a Supreme Court ruling and made it easier for women to sue employers if they discover they're not being paid as much as their male colleagues (Andronici & Katz, 2008; Brazile, 2009; Katz & Andronici, 2009; Williams, 2009).

© Helga Esteb/Shutterstock.com

It's hard for me to speak about my experience as a working woman because I can safely say my problems aren't exactly relatable. When the Sony hack happened and I found out how much less I was being paid than the lucky people with dicks, I didn't get mad at Sony. I got mad at myself. I failed as a negotiator because I gave up early. —Jennifer Lawrence, actor

It's beyond the parameters of this chapter to interpret trends in workforce statistics, nor assess the impact of the fact that, as of 2009, we have a 50/50 male/female workforce in the U.S. for the first time in our nation's history (*A Woman's Nation Changes Everything*, *The Shriver Report*, 2009). We do want to explore some possible explanations for the fact that in recent years only a minuscule increase has been achieved among the ranks of female senior management. We also examine how the increased presence of women in the workplace is affecting professional communication and the dynamics between the sexes, particularly at the management level. However, before tackling these on-the-job issues, it's a good idea to understand how sex and gender may affect getting a job in the first place.

GETTING THAT ALL-IMPORTANT JOB

Sex and gender bias may hurt your chances of landing a job. Often you don't know this has happened; you just never get a response to your résumé. If and when you do get job interviews, bias may be operating as well.

Gender Issues and the Job interview

There's no doubt about it—job interviews are extremely important. Once you've landed an interview, your insight into gender communication will be helpful.

BEING TAKEN SERIOUSLY Unfortunately, a concern about being taken seriously still applies more to female than to male candidates for jobs, unless a man applies for a job in a traditionally female-dominated field. Even though women now comprise half of the workforce, their presence seems to be noted in a different way than men's. The expectation still exists that men work out of necessity—*that's just what men do*. Although the corresponding stereotype for women is diminishing, some still believe that women work outside the home for mere distraction, for a secondary supplemental income, or as an interim activity before they "settle down" and have families (Adler & Elmhorst, 2008; O'Hair, Friedrich, & Dixon, 2015). Alternative explanations given for why women work are far more

The *maternal wall* is an employer's assumption that mothers are primary parents and so a mother can't make as full a commitment to her job the way a father can.

© Sudowoodo/Shutterstock.com

numerous than the simple possibility that they work for the same reasons as men. Some women have encountered the *maternal wall*, an employer's assumption that any woman who's a mother is the primary parent, and because of that status, she'll no doubt be unable to commit to her job the way a father can (Rowe-Finkbeiner, 2013; Williams, 2004).

NONVERBAL INDICATIONS OF SEX BIAS Nonverbal communication is critical in a job interview; nonverbal cues most often carry the true, unfiltered message, rather than someone's verbal communication (Ivy & Wahl, 2014; Quintanilla & Wahl, 2014).

But just how might sex-based expectations be revealed nonverbally during a job interview? A dead giveaway comes in the opening greeting, primarily the handshake. We make judgments about someone's personality based on the simple greeting ritual of the handshake (Kish, 2009). A team of psychologists developed the *handshake index*, a determination based on strength, vigor, completeness of grip, and duration of handshake (Chaplin, Phillips, Brown, Clanton, & Stein, 2000). They studied judgments subjects made about people with high indexes versus low indexes. People with high handshake indexes communicated more favorable first impressions and were deemed extroverted and open to experience. Women with high handshake indexes were also perceived to be highly agreeable, in comparison to women with weak or poor handshakes.

Often men and women alike appear awkward when shaking hands with a woman. This situation is improving, but women still get the "cupped fingers, half handshake" (the one that translates into "You sweet, fragile thing; I couldn't possibly grasp your whole hand because it'd fall right off"). Some career placement experts call this handshake the "fingerella." A potential employer likely has no intention of conveying negative impressions regarding a female applicant's credibility; the person just has a lousy handshake or has never learned the importance of a firm one. Nonetheless, it should raise the eyebrows of a female applicant when the handshake extended to her is less firm or confidence-inducing than one extended to a male applicant or colleague. This can be a subtle indication of a sex-based value system that's tolerated and perpetuated within the organization.

Job candidates have to exercise care when they extend handshakes to company employees, especially the person doing the hiring. For women, an overly firm handshake may violate expectations and be read as unconfident, as though the woman is overcompensating by using an extreme grip (Ralston & Kinser, 2001). Management professors Stewart, Dustin, Barrick, and Darnold (2008) explored job interview handshakes and found that women received lower ratings than men for the quality of their handshake and that perceptions about hiring were more strongly

Your handshake is a very important nonverbal skill. Learn to do it well.

© Stuart Jenner/Shutterstock.com

affected by women's handshakes than men's. It's important that male and female students alike work on this very important nonverbal skill, which can make or break a job interview.

🍁 Note to women: Work on developing a firm grip in your handshake, but not an excessive one that may backfire on you or convey an unintended message. Give the same handshake to women as to men in the organization. Give the same handshake to the receptionist that you give to the boss.

🍁 Note to men: Give the same handshake to a woman that you'd give to a man—no, we're not kidding. Alternating the firmness of your grip depending on the sex of the person receiving your handshake is "old school" and sexist, even if you don't intend it to be and even if you get different handshake grips in return. Give the same handshake to the receptionist that you give to the boss.

Besides the handshake, bias may be subtly communicated through other nonverbal cues in an interview. Applicant physical appearance has an impact on impression-making and, in some cases, hiring decisions (Barrick, Shaffer, & DeGrassi, 2009; Hosada, Stone-Romero, & Coats, 2003; Johnson, Podratz, Dipboye, & Gibbons, 2010; Tsai, Huang, & Yu, 2012). Studies show that being overweight, especially for women, negatively affects a person's chances of being perceived positively in a job interview (O'Brien, Latner, Ebneter, & Hunter, 2013; Rudolph, Wells, Weller, & Baltes, 2009). It may not seem right or fair, but bias still exists in many workplaces.

VERBAL INDICATIONS OF SEX BIAS Another way sex- and gender-based stereotypes can emerge in job interviews has to do with the questioning process. If a potential employer holds some doubt as to whether a person of your sex is serious about a job or is capable of handling the job, the interviewer might reveal these doubts by asking leading questions. *Leading questions* are designed to trap the interviewee into a forced response or a no-win situation. They often take the form of a hypothetical situation followed by a question as to what the applicant would do. For example, when men apply for jobs in a currently female-dominated field such as nursing, they may receive leading questions that translate into doubts about their nurturing abilities. Or a woman applying for a position in a male-dominated office might get a leading question like "What would you do if a male colleague disagreed with one of your ideas and started to argue with you in front of your coworkers?"

One of the more overt means of communicating sex and gender bias in a job interview is an employer's use of illegal and *unethical questions*. It's illegal and unethical to ask about marital status, parental status, or sexual orientation, among other things. Most employers know this, so most of them avoid these areas. If they want to know this information before making a hiring decision, they may resort to covert means (e.g., checking out a person's background, learning information in roundabout ways from former employers or coworkers) or be indirect in how they approach these subjects during a job interview.

I only hire men who are feminists. I'm at a place where I don't have to work with men or women who don't want to share credit or who are not feminists. — Mindy Kaling, actor and author

Your textbook author experienced an awkward situation some years back. During a segment of a job interview with the vice president of an organization, the subject of transition was raised. The interviewer talked about how moving from one job and one state to another was stressful, even more so if one had a spouse and children who were uprooted in the process. After making this statement, he stopped talking, made direct eye contact, and waited for her response. Even though she knew what information he was after, she really wanted the job, so her reply revealed her current marital and parental status.

This example is fairly typical of the way an employer might attempt to learn information that can't be asked directly. In hindsight, a better response to this awkward situation would have been simple agreement, as in "Yes, transitions can be quite stressful," rather than revealing personal information. Nonconfrontational methods can be used to communicate effectively to an employer that you know what's going on, but you're not going to play along. Another option is to respond to an illegal or unethical question with a question, as though you didn't understand what the interviewer was getting at. You may decide to use more confrontational, educative responses, but you have to weigh the risks of such tactics (such as not getting the job). The main thing to think about is whether you want to work for a company whose employees would sneak illegal or unethical questions into an interview. When verbal and nonverbal indications of sex and gender bias surface in a job interview, it increases the likelihood that biased behavior and attitudes will be in evidence on the job (Quintanilla & Wahl, 2014; Ralston & Kinser, 2001).

Do you want to work for a company whose employees try to ask illegal or unethical questions during an interview?

© Andrey_Popow/Shutterstock.com

ON THE JOB AND MOVING UP

Congratulations! You got the job. You're on the job. So what gender-related variables might emerge at your job? How will you respond?

Advancement within an Organization

Given that, as of 2009, the U.S. workforce has been 50/50 in terms of the numbers of working men and women, you might conclude that the workplace is equitable. But a more careful inspection is revealing: Although women now make up half the American workforce, they don't represent half the workers in *every kind* of job. Sex segregation in the workplace greatly contributes to the wage gap.

Men hold most of the chief executive positions as well as blue-collar jobs in this country, while women hold the majority of what's come to be termed *pink-collar jobs*, meaning administrative work or care services (Albelda, 2009; Clason & Turner, 2011; U.S. Department of Labor, 2015). Of the 20 most commonly held occupations in the U.S., men are mostly employed as truck drivers, managers, and first-line supervisors, whereas women are secretaries/administrative assistants, nurses, and schoolteachers. Only four of the top 20 jobs (salespersons, first-line supervisors of retail stores, managers, and cooks) employ men and women with roughly equal frequency (Boushey, 2009; U.S. Department of Labor, 2015).

While more women are being hired than in times past, greater numbers of men than women achieve the higher, more responsible, more rewarding ranks. In 2015, only 23 women (4.6 percent) held chief executive officer (CEO) positions in the S&P's as well as Fortune's lists of top 500 U.S. companies (Fairchild, 2014; www.catalyst.org, 2015). Women held only 14 percent of the top five positions in these companies (www. money.CNN.com, 2014). Globally, women aren't faring much better; according to the *Financial Times* of London, a study of 6700 executives across 45 countries showed that women run only 12 percent of mid-level companies (up from 10 percent in 2013 and 5 percent in 2012). As for chief financial officers in these countries, women constitute 23 percent of these positions, except in China where a whopping 63 percent of CFOs are women (Groom, 2014). What factors are connected to the trends regarding advancement in U.S. companies?

GLASS CEILINGS AND STICKY FLOORS We expect you've heard the *glass ceiling* term before. It stems from a larger metaphor for working women who operate in "glass houses," whose behavior is not only scrutinized by individuals on every level of the organization, but whose success or failure affects the status of employed women everywhere. Professional women who look higher, see the possibilities, yet are unable to reach them because of a transparent barrier have encountered the glass ceiling (Ben-Galim & Silim, 2014; Hewlett, 2013; Hewlett, Peraino, Sherbin, & Sumberg, 2010; Metz & Kulik, 2014; Zhang, Schmader, & Forbes, 2009).

Another phenomenon that contributes to the picture of leadership and advancement is termed the *sticky floor*— factors that keep women in low-level, non-managerial and support roles and prevent them from seeking or gaining promotion or career development (Engberg, 1999). Some of these factors or barriers include

Remember...

Maternal Wall: Assumption by some employers that mothers are always the primary parent in a family, thus they can't commit to a job the way fathers can

Handshake Index: Perception of a handshake, based on strength, vigor, completeness of grip, and duration

Leading Question: Interviewer question that traps an interviewee into a forced or no-win response

Unethical Question: Interviewer question about personal life, such as a question about marital status, parental status, sexual orientation, religious affiliation, and so on

Pink Collar Jobs: Administrative and care service positions, primarily held by women

> As in other fields, women seem to break through the glass ceiling just as the air-conditioning is being turned off in the penthouse office suites.
> — Alessandra Stanley, columnist,
> *The New York Times*

family commitments, sexist attitudes, stereotyping, and organizational structures that aren't conducive to sex and gender equity (Arulampalam, Booth, & Bryan, 2007; Bjerk, 2008; Rainbird, 2007). The sticky floor metaphor applies also to women who are loyal to their organizations and who may be promoted, but who don't receive pay increases along with the promotions (Shambaugh, 2007).

Much more work remains to be done to achieve sex and gender equity in the workforce, both in compensation and advancement. To combat the differential in upper-level management, organizations must actively ensure that male and female employees' careers are developed with equal attention (Buzzanell & Lucas, 2006; Williams, 2006). Teachers, parents, and academic advisors and mentors should work with children at early ages to eliminate negative gender stereotypes *where they begin* (Correll, 2006; Mendelson Freeman, 2006). In addition, women should plan their careers well in advance and proactively seek the advancement of their careers, rather than waiting for a superior to notice and reward their accomplishments (Sandberg, 2013). Networking and developing mentor and sponsor relationships are excellent strategies to help women overcome barriers in the workplace (Hewlett, 2013; Sloan & Krone, 2000; Stewart, 2001).

DIFFICULT CHOICES: FAMILY, CAREER, OR BOTH? One of the most obvious factors complicating women's professional advancement is a basic biological function—the fact that women give birth to babies. As a culture we've moved forward on this front, creating more choices for families. Efforts in the '70s and '80s helped to break the constricted thinking that women would automatically choose home and family over careers. In the 1990s, women who could afford to sacrifice their paychecks to stay home and raise young children felt more free to do so without feeling that they'd violated some basic tenet of women's liberation. We've witnessed political progress through such laws as Title VII of the Civil Rights Act (1964), the Pregnancy Disability Act (1978), the EEOC's guidelines on sexual harassment (1980), and the Family and Medical Leave Act (1996; Baxter, 2015; Burk, 2014; Gerstel & McGonagle, 2006).

Toward the end of the second decade of the twenty-first century, changes in family profile and the country's workplaces continue to have sex and gender implications. Only about one-third of American families with children at home are "traditional" families in which the father is the breadwinner, while the mother is the homemaker and primary caretaker of the children (Rehel & Baxter, 2015; U.S. Department of Labor, 2015). In two-thirds of American households, women are either primary breadwinners or co-breadwinners with their spouses. Because so many American families now fit the "juggler" profile—families juggling both parents' jobs plus child rearing (in gay, straight, and transgender families)—the workplace has had to adjust to cope with changing demands (Dixon & Dougherty, 2014; Medved & Rawlins, 2011; O'Leary & Kornbluh, 2009). While the number of stay-at-home fathers is still quite small, the rate of this form of family arrangement has risen dramatically, from 1.6 percent in the early 2000s to 3.4 percent today (Medved & Rawlins, 2011; Rehel & Baxter, 2015).

Changing workplace language indicates changing attitudes toward work and family. In the 1980s, we saw the emergence of "superwomen" who were "doing it all" and "having it all" because they raised children while maintaining their careers (Friedan, 1981). Then the term *second shift* was coined to describe the work of employed women who returned home from their jobs to hours of cleaning, cooking, and child care (Hochschild, 1989, as in Saltzman Chafetz, 1997). The 1990s brought about the *mommy track* (a variation of "fast track"), which applied to women who sought advancement in the workplace at the same time as they had child-rearing responsibilities (Hill, Martinson, Ferris, & Zenger Baker, 2006; Noonan & Corcoran, 2006).

We also saw in the 1990s greater use of *flextime*, a system some organizations adopt that allows workers to come and go early or late, or to work longer hours fewer days of the week, to better respond to home and family demands (Hochschild & Machung, 2006; Meers & Strober, 2009; Welsh, 2006). We saw an effort to create more *family-friendly workplaces*, a descriptor that emerged when *Working Mother* magazine began identifying the best places in the country for women and mothers to work (Dubeck, 2006). Organizations attempted to better

© Joseph Sohm/Shutterstock.com

Expanding flexibility in the workplace, access to child care and elder care, would boost productivity and allow more parents—men as well as women—to work full days without stress and heartache. — Hillary Clinton, former U.S. Secretary of State

"Parents Who Work Outside the Home"

Do you think that the pull between family and career exerts more pressure on women than men—even in our twenty-first century world of work? If you believe women experience more of this pressure, how does this apply to lesbian couples who choose to have and raise children?

While men are assuming greater roles in child rearing than ever before, very few give up or take a break from their careers to raise children. Should it be a given that the higher-paid parent—whether in a heterosexual, transgender, or homosexual marriage or arrangement—should be more career-oriented while the other partner assumes more of the child caretaking duties?

A stereotype also exists, which some believe has a basis in genetic fact, that women are more nurturing than men, so in heterosexual relationships, mothers should naturally be the ones to tend to young children. What's your stance on this issue? Do you know any families in which the father is actually more "naturally" nurturing than the mother, and even though he makes more money, he opts to stay home with the kids while she continues her career? If a woman wants to "have it all," just like many men want to "have it all," how can our culture enable her to do that?

accommodate workers who had family issues that could affect their job performance (Dubeck & Dunn, 2002; Finnegan, 2001; O'Leary & Kornbluh, 2009).

In reaction to the pressures of juggling home and job, some people (more women than men) choose *sequencing*—temporarily dropping out of the workforce to concentrate more fully on one's children (Quinn, 2004). However, sequencing is not without its drawbacks, primarily the inability to step back in once you've stepped out. While employers can't legally penalize these workers by replacing them, they can "restructure" the organization or write new job descriptions for which the employee wanting to return to work no longer qualifies.

In 2003, another phenomenon—*opting out*—was discussed in an article in *The New York Times Magazine*, but the "trend" was later viewed as more media hype than reality. The article described a "talent drain" of highly trained women who chose not to aspire to executive positions within corporations, or who abandoned their successful careers to concentrate on their families (Belkin, 2003). The problem was that the research generalized a trend based on its small, elite sample of Princeton female graduates who were privileged enough to be able to leave their careers behind to focus on family life (Mainiero & Sullivan, 2006). The ensuing media frenzy over the so-called trend suggested that large numbers of successful professional women were failing to achieve the highest career positions because they weren't willing to work as hard as men, they were too timid or passive to claim the top spots, they simply didn't want power, and the rewards of staying at home were psychologically too compelling (Douglas Vavrus, 2007; Moe & Shandy, 2009). While some women do choose to opt out of their professional lives because their priorities shift, their situations demand that they refocus their energies, or they tire of hitting an advancement wall and wish to change their lives, women aren't opting out of careers in droves because they find professional life too challenging (Williams, Manvell, & Bornstein, 2006).

Three other relatively recent and positive workplace changes warrant mention. The first is the development of on-site child care facilities and company-sponsored programs that increase employees' access to child care (Trei, 2002; Whitehurst, 2002). The second change surrounds *telecommuting* (working online from home), which is quite commonplace now (Baird, 2013; Rapoza, 2013). A third development regards the growing number of self-employed parents, especially mothers, who decide that working for corporations or other businesses doesn't afford much flexibility (Levitz,

The option to work online from home has been a positive change for many employees.

Remember...

Glass Ceiling:
Transparent barrier in the workplace that allows professional women to look higher and see possibilities for advancement, but prevents them from attaining higher positions

Sticky Floor: Factors that keep women in low-level, support roles in the workplace and that prevent them from seeking or gaining promotion or career development

Second Shift: Work of employed women returning home from their jobs to hours of cleaning, cooking, and child care

Mommy Track: Term applied to women who seek advancement in the workplace at the same time as they have child-rearing responsibilities

Flextime: Organizational innovation that allows employees to work flexible hours, to accommodate home and family demands

Family-Friendly Workplace:
Designation that a workplace is accommodating for employees with family responsibilities

Sequencing: Temporarily dropping out of the workforce in order to raise children, then stepping back into the workforce at an organization with flexible scheduling

2010; Luna Brem, 2001). These women prefer to become entrepreneurs, mostly through the establishment of online businesses and services (Lewis, 2014). The rise in their numbers led to the coinage of the term *entrepreneurial mother*, which means, according to scholar Paige Edley (2004), "mothers who own and operate their own businesses out of their homes" (p. 255).

Women, Men, and Management

Communication researchers, organizational behavior experts, business leaders, and gender scholars alike have studied how the sexes approach management, conflict resolution, and decision making (DeLaat, 2007; Powell, 2010; Rutherford, 2001). They've attempted to separate myth from fact in perceptions about who makes better managers.

HOW ARE MALE AND FEMALE MANAGERS PERCEIVED? A meaningful discussion on this topic must be placed in the context of the changing workplace. The American workplace, as well as some international workplaces, has witnessed a shift away from traditional management approaches, typified by such stereotypical masculine attributes as aggression, competitiveness, control, and individualism. The shift has been toward an interactional management approach, reflecting such stereotypical feminine attributes as flexibility, supportiveness, empathy, connectedness, and collaborative problem solving (Eagly, Cartzia, & Carli, 2014). However, even given the shifting workplace culture, many Americans report that they still prefer a male supervisor to a female one (Newport & Wilke, 2013).

A collaborative management style indicative of many female supervisors seems to bode well for the security of U.S. companies. In an economic downturn such as the country witnessed toward the end of the first decade of the 2000s, female-dominated professions (e.g., healthcare, education, government) and female managers weathered the recession better than their male counterparts (Cauchon, 2009; Fisher, 2009). Businesses that reacted to tough economic times by exerting more control over workers and depending more heavily on male senior managers didn't fare too well. A diverse, adaptive management style that emphasizes participation and shared responsibility for decision making proved invaluable as businesses coped with economic challenges (Grashow, Heifetz, & Linsky, 2009).

Michael Gurian and Barbara Annis (2008), authors of *Leadership and the Sexes*, suggest that sex-based brain differences offer an explanation for varying management styles. For example, women's brains contain more active emotive centers linked to their language skills while men's brains are more goal- and task-directed. Thus, female managers may be more geared toward expressing emotions in words and providing empathy for employees, while male managers focus more on the task at hand and on accomplishing goals. Another difference centers around hormones and brain functioning. Men's concentration of testosterone, a hormone linked to aggression, leads them to behave more competitively, whereas women's concentration of oxytocin (a bonding chemical) influences them to build support systems around them. An overgeneralization is this: Men compete, women bond, and these differences tend to manifest themselves in our approaches to management.

> ## Remember...
>
> **Opting Out:** More media hype than trend, women choosing to abandon successful careers and aspirations of upward achievement to stay home and take care of their families
>
> **Telecommuting:** Ability to work at home with flexible hours through the use of technological advancements
>
> **Entrepreneurial Mother:** A mother who owns and operates her own business out of her home

HOW DO THE SEXES COMMUNICATE AS MANAGERS? Research has produced mixed results when it comes to sex/gender differences among the communication styles of managers. Some research suggests that, as organizations have placed more emphasis on diversity, changes in communication styles have occurred, making male and female management approaches less distinguishable (Butler, Feng, & MacGeorge, 2003). Duehr and Bono (2006) found considerable evolution over the past 30 years, in terms of stereotypical views of managers. In their study, female managers were viewed as exhibiting more task-oriented management, once deemed a more male-expected approach. Perhaps as more women have assumed positions of authority in organizations, expectations about and reactions to them have changed over time.

However, other evidence shows that communication styles and perceptions of management abilities remain as firmly connected to sex and gender as in the past (Ayman & Korabik, 2010; Barsh & Cranston, 2009; Carli & Eagly, 2007; Fine, 2009; Rudman & Phelan, 2008). Some research indicates that subordinates often perceive female supervisors to be better communicators, both verbally and nonverbally, creating more family-friendly work environments than their male counterparts, but perceive male supervisors as being superior at accomplishing tasks and goals (Everbach, 2005; Madlock, 2009).

ATTENTION? COMPLIMENTING? FLIRTING? SEXUAL HARASSMENT?

This heading may make you want to stop reading. As difficult as sexual harassment is to think about, it's important to examine this topic because many of you are nearing graduation and will be launching (or re-launching) your careers. We hope you don't encounter sexual harassment, but everyone needs to be current and knowledgeable on this topic in order to function successfully on the job. As much as you'd like to think that companies are now fully on board and educated about sexual harassment in the workplace, think again; it may surprise you that businesses and organizations you may work for during or after college may be in the dark or are, at best, less than current about sexual harassment policies and laws.

A powerful event played out in the national media about 20 years ago, as Clarence Thomas was being confirmed as a new Supreme Court justice. Those of us glued to our TV sets, watching Anita Hill claim to the Senate Judiciary Committee that she was sexually harassed by Clarence Thomas, learned a great deal about sexual harassment, as well as American culture. The hearings had profound effects. First, they empowered people who had or were experiencing harassment to come forward and seek assistance. They also sparked a great deal of discussion and research on sexual harassment. Businesses and educational institutions began scrambling to develop or update their policies on workplace conduct. Laws changed after the Hill/Thomas debacle, and people became generally more aware of how they should behave and communicate professionally.

Sexual Harassment: The Basics

Several key elements related to sexual harassment warrant discussion. Before we explore them, let's make sure we're all on the same page in how we talk about and define sexual harassment.

THE POWER OF NAMING Just exactly what *is* sexual harassment? Gloria Steinem (1983) answered that question like this: "A few years ago this was just called life" (p. 149). No term existed for this age-old problem until feminists in the 1970s coined the term *sexual harassment* (Sheffield, 2004; Spender, 1984; Wise & Stanley, 1987). You've probably heard or read this before, but let's be clear: Sexual harassment is about *power*, not about sex.

The language surrounding sexual harassment bears witness to the struggle of many people to bring this problem into the open (Lee, 2001). Harassing behavior may be described in romantic terms, such as "seduction," "overtures," "advances," "flirtation," or "passes." But as gender scholar Julia Wood (1993) suggests, "Using terminology associated with amorous contexts obscures the ugliness, unwantedness, violation, repugnance, and sheer darkness of sexual harassment" (p. 14).

Other ways to excuse sexual harassment include a "boys will be boys" attitude as well as viewing unwanted attention as merely complimenting someone. Another prime way to blame a target of harassment and direct attention away from a harasser's behavior is the "just kidding" suggestion. If you couch communication as kidding, joking, or teasing, then when it's interpreted as harassment, a harasser can blame the victim for not getting the joke or not having a sense of humor. A prime example of this blame-shifting technique is telling the recipient of harassment to "lighten up."

If your flirting strategy is indistinguishable from harassment, it's not everyone *else* that's the problem. —John Scalzi, author

Language about sexual harassment has changed since the 1980s; it's now called harassment rather than "an advance," "inappropriate behavior," "disrespect," "personal misconduct," or "poor decision making" (Ivy, 1999; Wood, 1992, 1993; Woodward, 1995). We now have "targets" and "survivors" instead of "objects of attention," "complainers," and "whiners." "Pushy" or "forward" people are now named "harassers" and in some situations, "defendants."

LEGAL DEFINITION AND TYPES OF HARASSMENT The Civil Rights Act of 1964 protects citizens from discrimination based on a variety of factors, one of which is sex. This law made sexual harassment illegal and gave the Equal Employment Opportunity Commission (EEOC) formal authority to investigate claims of workplace sexual harassment (Peach, 1998). With the passage of Title IX in 1972, educational institutions were mandated by law to avoid sex discrimination (Wood, 1992). But sexual harassment continued despite the legislation.

In 1980 the EEOC produced the following set of guidelines on sexual harassment:

Unwelcome sexual advances, requests for sexual favors, and other verbal or physical conduct of a sexual nature constitute sexual harassment when submission to such conduct is made either explicitly or implicitly a term or condition of an individual's employment, (2) submission to or rejection of such conduct by an individual is used as the basis for employment decisions affecting such individual, or (3) such conduct has the intention or effect of unreasonably interfering with an individual's work performance or of creating an intimidating, hostile, or offensive working environment. (EEOC, 1980)

Before 1980 most documented cases were *quid pro quo harassment*, which means "this for that" or "something for something." This is a more traditional or historical view of harassment, involving a threat by superiors that unless subordinates engage in some form of sexual behavior, they'll lose their jobs, be overlooked for promotions and raises, be transferred to less-desirable units or locations, lose out on key projects, and so forth (Gerdes, 1999; Mink, 2005; Wendt & Slonaker, 2002).

Quid pro quo harassment is more easily recognizable as illegal than the second form, *hostile climate harassment.* In 1986 the U.S. Supreme Court acted on the hostile climate clause of the EEOC guidelines, extending and legitimizing complaints of sexual harassment beyond quid pro quo (*Meritor Savings Bank* v. *Vinson*, as in Paetzold & O'Leary-Kelly, 1993). Hostile climate harassment is difficult to address, but far more prevalent than quid pro quo (Hill, 2002; O'Leary-Kelly, Bowes-Sperry, Arens Bates, & Lean, 2009). It also produces the most amount of confusion surrounding what actions can or cannot be regarded as sexual harassment (Berryman-Fink & Vanover Riley, 1997; Jacobs & Bonavoglia, 1998).

Hostile climate harassment often taps into sexist structures, policies, and practices long ignored, overlooked, or even accepted as a part of the organizational culture, like gathering in the workroom to tell sexual or sexist jokes (or circulating these jokes through the office e-mail system). Other behaviors, documented by research, include hanging sexual posters (pinups) on the walls of the workplace; displaying sexually suggestive screen savers on computers; sending frequent e-mail, voice mail, or text messages to coworkers; distributing pornographic or sexually explicit materials around the office; and staring at, following, or stalking a coworker (Paetzold & O'Leary-Kelly, 1993; Rosewarne, 2007). If the offending behavior falls short of actually threatening something tangible (someone's job, promotion, or raise), it may be viewed as hostile climate harassment because it pervades the target's work environment enough to create a hostile, sexualized situation.

An element that makes this situation difficult is that one person's friendly, teasing, or flirtatious behavior is another person's sexual harassment (Henningsen, 2004; Koeppel, Montagne, O'Hair, & Cody, 1999). Since Americans spend much more time at work than in decades past, more of us are likely to find friendship and romantic liaisons in our workplaces (Fine, 1996; Saad, 2014). An office romance can make you look more forward to getting out of bed and going to work each day, but it can also create huge problems. (Re-read the opening case study for this chapter.) While some organizations believe workplace romances aren't causes for concern, worry about potential liability has led some organizations to create policies warning against or banning office romance (Applebaum, Marinescu, Klenin, & Bytautas, 2007; Bercovici, 2007; Bliss Kiser, Coley, Ford, & Moore, 2006; Mainiero & Jones, 2012; Parent, 2009). It's becoming increasingly common to find "love contracts" required in workplaces—signed agreements by coworkers who choose to also have a romantic relationship (Amaral, 2006; Mainiero & Jones, 2013).

Sexual harassment occurs at all levels within organizations, regardless of the salary, status, or power of an employee (Dougherty, 2001; Fielden & Hunt, 2014). Its reach includes temporary workers and interns, who are especially vulnerable to workplace sexual harassment (Henson, 1996; Poindexter, 2014; Rogers & Henson, 2006).

Most reported sexual harassment is heterosexual, with a male-harasser/female-target profile; same-sex harassment certainly does occur, but is less often reported or litigated (Castillo, Muscarella, & Szuchman, 2011; Goldberg & Zhang, 2004; MacKinnon, 2002). These trends are relevant to yet another complicating factor about workplace sexual harassment: Consistent research findings indicate that women react more strongly to inappropriate sexual behavior and view more behaviors as sexual harassment than men (Dougherty, 2001; Ivy & Hamlet, 1996; Lucero, Middleton, & Allen, 2006; Middleton & Lucero, 2003).

Many universities are located in areas with a heavy military presence, so you may be interested in learning some facts about sexual harassment in the military. In 2014, the U.S. Department of Defense contracted a team from the RAND National Defense Research Institute to conduct an independent study of sexual assault, gender discrimination, and sexual harassment among U.S. military personnel. The RAND sample consisted of 560,000 active-duty and reserve-duty service members from four military branches. While sexual harassment rates were down from 2012, the research team concluded that "Sexual harassment is a common

"Student Interns as Targets of Sexual Harassment"

Paula Poindexter served as president of the Association for Education in Journalism and Mass Communication in 2013–2014. In March of 2014, she wrote an article for the association's newsletter entitled "Raising Awareness about the Dirty Side of Internships." Your textbook author, as the former coordinator of her communication department's internship program, was intrigued to learn about this particular "dirty side," having become aware of abuses like tasking interns with washing the boss's car or picking up dry cleaning, clearing out files or storage areas, and working long hours for no pay.

Poindexter described several abusive situations, but one in particular dealt with an intern who worked at a TV station and was sexually harassed (physically assaulted) by the bureau chief. When the intern filed a sexual harassment lawsuit, the court dismissed the claim, ruling that because the intern wasn't paid, she lacked status as an employee of the company and couldn't sue for harassment.

Just like temporary workers or "temps," student interns are in precarious positions within organizations, especially if they work in unpaid internships. Policies and procedures for dealing with harassment and other abuses on the job may not pertain to interns—*should they*? If no policy exists at an organization or company to protect interns from abuses on the job, should a student choose to intern there? Should internship programs only place student interns into situations where explicit policies and procedures protect them?

experience, especially for women in the military" (RAND Military Workplace Study, 2014, p. 3). The survey showed that 116,600 active-duty service members were sexually harassed in 2013; among this number of sexual harassment targets, 22 percent were women and 7 percent were men. The reserve-duty component of the sample reported significantly lower rates of harassment than did the active-duty component. Sexually hostile workplace climate harassment was far more prevalent than quid pro quo harassment and, of the four military branches surveyed, members of the Air Force reported the fewest occurrences of sexual harassment.

SEXUAL HARASSMENT AND TYPES OF RELATIONSHIPS Sexual harassment often occurs between people of differing statuses or power bases; these relationships are termed *status-differentiated* (such as boss–employee, teacher–student, doctor–patient). A status-differentiated relationship may be distant and impersonal, so that harassment introduced into such a relationship is bewildering. But other such relationships may be well established and trusting, like a mentor relationship in which the lower-status person looks up to, believes, and confides in the higher status person (Avtgis, Rancer, & Liberman, 2012; Lane, 2006). Harassment in these relationships is devastating; it may involve a grooming process in which the harasser slowly develops a friendly relationship with the target, winning her or his trust and admiration before attempting to extend the relationship into a sexual arena.

Peer sexual harassment, harassment between people of equal status, occurs on the job as well. In academic settings—from elementary schools to universities—it's more prevalent than status-differentiated harassment (Conroy, 2013; Ivy & Hamlet, 1996; Wernick, Kulik, & Inglehart, 2014).

Yet another form is *contrapower harassment*, which involves a person of lower rank or status sexually harassing someone of higher rank or status (Benson, 1984; DeSouza & Fansler, 2003; Lampman, Phelps, Bancroft, & Beneke, 2009; Mohipp & Senn, 2008). Sexual harassment exists in virtual reality as well, now termed *cyber harassment* (Behm-Morawitz & Schipper, 2015; Halder & Jaishankar, 2011; Ritter, 2014).

Initial Reactions to Sexual Harassment

Sexual harassment takes a serious toll on its targets—emotionally, physically, academically, professionally, and economically. The emotional harm leaves targets angry, afraid, anxious, nervous, depressed, and with extremely low self-esteem (Page & Pina, 2015; Raver & Nishii, 2010; Wolf, 2004). Professional impairment includes missing work, being less productive on the job, and feeling isolated and ostracized by coworkers (Jiang et al., 2015). Economic costs are mostly associated with changes in or the loss of employment. If a grievance or lawsuit is filed, legal costs are exacerbated by the target being out of work or placed on leave (many times without pay) until the situation is resolved. Even though they may grab headlines, frivolous claims of sexual harassment are few because the economic hardships are very real.

Remember...

Sexual Harassment: Unwelcome sexual advances, requests for sexual favors, and other verbal or physical conduct of a sexual nature which is made a condition of one's employment or advancement, or which creates a hostile or intimidating working environment

Quid Pro Quo Sexual Harassment: "This for that" harassment; one's job, promotion, raise, grades, or other inducement is the trade-off for sexual favors

Hostile Climate Sexual Harassment: Sexual conduct that creates an intimidating or offensive working or learning environment

Status-Differentiated Relationships: Relationships in which there are clear-cut lines of status between people or a well-delineated hierarchy

Peer Sexual Harassment: Sexual harassment occurring between people of equal status

Contrapower Sexual Harassment: Person of lower rank or status sexually harassing someone of higher rank or status

Cyber Harassment: Sexual harassment that occurs in virtual reality, through such channels as text messages, e-mail, chat rooms, instant messaging, and social media

CALLING IT WHAT IT IS One of the most common reactions to sexual harassment is a reluctance to call it harassment (O'Leary-Kelly et al., 2009). This is particularly true of women, who often become numb to harassment because they grew up with it. They develop a "boys will be boys" attitude because they see so much harassment around them or they discount it with a "nothing happened" response because they don't want to rock the boat or "make a big deal" out of something (Kelly & Radford, 1996).

If you're a target of sexual harassment, realize that questioning the reality of the situation and your feelings of embarrassment or shame are common, understandable reactions. Also realize that you have an empowering right to label the behavior sexual harassment. You're not exaggerating, stirring up trouble, or making something out of nothing.

BLAMING ONESELF Another common reaction is for a target to blame herself or himself for the situation (Thomae & Pina, 2015; van der Bruggen & Grubb, 2014). Targets say things like "If I'd only seen it coming" and "Did I encourage this person or bring this on myself?" The thing to remember is that sexual harassment, by its very definition, involves *unwarranted, unwelcome* behavior. If the target deserved, welcomed, or brought about the behavior, it wouldn't be considered harassment.

Subsequent Responses to Harassment

Research continues to explore personal, professional, and legal responses to harassment (Grossman, 2015; Jiang et al., 2015). Keep in mind that, particularly for female targets, the primary goal is to get a harasser to leave her alone; most targets say, "I just want it to stop."

A RANGE OF RESPONSES Sociologist James Gruber (1989) adapted conflict resolution strategies to develop a range of responses—from least assertive to most assertive—to sexual harassment. No *best* response to sexual harassment exists; a judgment of a best response is up to the target because pros and cons emerge for each.

Avoidance: Ignoring harassment or avoiding a harasser is the most common response to sexual harassment. Given targets' discomfort and feelings of powerlessness, along with perceptions of potential threats by harassers, this reponse is understandable. However, ignoring harassment doesn't usually make it stop; on the contrary, it increases the likelihood that it'll happen again to the same target, someone else, or both.

Defusion: This response is one step away from avoidance and involves distracting or attempting to take the sting out of a situation by trivializing or joking about it. Sometimes this is a knee-jerk reaction to the shock of what happened, but defusion strategies often leave targets feeling dissatisfied and anxious about the future.

Negotiation: A more communicative strategy than the first two responses, some targets may decide to attempt to negotiate with a harasser, most often directly requesting that the harassing behavior stop. But for many targets, saying anything at all (especially about the harassing incident) directly to a harasser is a tall order.

Confrontation: Gruber's fourth level involves the most communication—a direct confrontation between harasser and target, in which the target may issue an ultimatum such as "Keep your distance and stop asking me personal questions or else I'll have to talk to the boss about it." (Obviously, this doesn't work so well when your harasser *is* your boss.) Confrontation is the response least used by targets, but what's confusing is how often targets receive advice to confront their harassers. People say, "Stand up for yourself. Just tell him to back off, that you're not going to put up with that crap." Those of us who've experienced sexual harassment know just how difficult it is to take that advice. Most of the time, harassment is so surprising, disgusting, and upsetting that a target has a hard time saying *anything*, so perhaps we should all be careful about being quick or cavalier with our advice.

Net Notes

For the latest information on sexual harassment laws and procedures for filing complaints or lawsuits, one source to turn to is **www.lawguru.com**. This site offers helpful advice on how to prove your case if you're being harassed, what to do if sexual harassment occurs at work, and ways to protect yourself while you're pursuing a case.

© Mohd Shahrizan Hussin/Shutterstock.com

If you're sexually harassed and decide to respond by confronting your harasser, here are some strategies recommended by Marty Langelan (2005), a past president of the Washington D.C. Rape Crisis Center:

1. Name the behavior; state aloud to the harasser's face what the harasser is doing, call it sexual harassment, and then give a clear and direct command for the behavior to stop.

2. Interrupt the harasser with an all-purpose statement, like "No one likes sexual harassment, so stop harassing people; show some respect."

3. Pull out a notebook and write down what the harasser says or describe what she or he does, then keep a copy in a safe place for documentation, should you need it at some point. The act of documenting can be a deterrent to a harasser.

4. Ask a Socratic question of the harasser, like "What makes you think you can tell that joke and no one will be offended?" The question makes the episode into a point of discussion and depersonalizes it.

5. Become a human stop sign, putting your hands up in front of your chest, palms facing out, and saying "Stop right there" while making direct eye contact.

6. Don't get embroiled in what the harasser says or become involved in a dispute over the meaning of what was said or done. Better to simply repeat your message of "stop this" and not be dragged into further conversation.

7. Use a safety-in-numbers strategy, meaning that a group of people confronting a harasser may be more effective than one individual. While we don't advise a "group shaming," we do agree that sometimes collectives have a more powerful effect on shaping behavior.

8. People who aren't targets of harassment should become allies and speak out against the problem, expressing their boundaries and preferences for respectful communication in the workplace and insisting that organizations or companies develop effective policies and procedures about sexual harassment.

REPORTING SEXUAL HARASSMENT We don't want to lay guilt trips here by saying that targets must report their harassment. Reporting is an individual decision because costs are always involved. But a target also has to weigh the costs of *not* reporting harassment, like leaving a harasser free to harass again.

For many targets, going with an informal, internal grievance is preferable to filing a complaint with the EEOC or launching a lawsuit. With any form of reporting—informal, formal, high profile—an important first step is to inventory the whole experience, meaning to find or create a paper trail. Were any notes made about how often the harassment occurred, what was said and done, and what was said and done in response? If there aren't any notes, targets should write an account of harassing events, recalling specific dates, what was said and done, and other details with as much accuracy and information as possible. Were there any witnesses to the harassment or the target's response or later behavior?

An important second step is to consult an employee handbook for a policy on sexual harassment and procedures for filing a grievance. Targets are often unaware that some policies impose time limits for filing grievances. Most policies advise targets to report harassment to an immediate supervisor, as a first step in a multistep process. If the harasser is one's supervisor, the next option is to report the harassment claim up the chain of command or to a third party or entity, like a personnel or human resources office. Sometimes targets take their claims directly to the EEOC, bypassing local or internal processes, because they believe they'll be taken more seriously and treated with more respect than is likely in their workplace.

It's hard to imagine it, in this day and age, but some companies still don't have sexual harassment policies and procedures "on the books"—at their own peril. If you end up working for one of these companies and are in a position where you could effect positive change, we encourage you to step up. Use the resources and research presented in this chapter to craft a policy that will protect everyone in the organization, as well as send a message that respectful, professional communication is expected in your workplace (Hobson, Szostek, & Fitzgerald, 2015; Jiang et al., 2015; McDonald, Charlesworth, & Graham, 2015; Vijayasiri, 2008).

Legal recourse is costly and time consuming, and it offers no guarantee of a desired outcome. But sexual harassment is taken way more seriously now than ever before and more claims are filed each year, as targets feel more empowered to pursue justice. Laws and policies continue to be strengthened and more targets receive compensation than in times past (Grossman, 2015).

Remember...

Avoidance: Response to sexual harassment in which a target ignores harassment and avoids any form of confrontation with a harasser

Defusion: Response to sexual harassment in which a target tries to distract or "take the sting out" of a situation, through joking, changing the subject, and so on

Negotiation: Response to sexual harassment in which a target works with the harasser, harasser's boss, or other entity internal or external to an organization so as to arrive at a resolution

Confrontation: Response to sexual harassment in which a target confronts the harasser directly, usually insisting that the harassing behavior stop and possibly issuing an ultimatum

A Parting Word about Sexual Harassment

Whether we want to believe it or not, sexual harassment is still a reality in many workplaces. Sometimes it arises out of ignorance, sometimes out of sincere intentions to get acquainted or to compliment, but sometimes out of a desire to embarrass and outpower another individual.

When students ask how to avoid sexual harassment in the workplace, here's our answer: Communicate professionally—not personally or sexually—with bosses, coworkers, clients, and customers. Sexual innuendo, the dissemination of sexual material, sexist language and jokes, excessive compliments about appearance rather than professional performance, questions about private life, requests for social contact, invasive and unwelcome nonverbal behaviors—anything of this sort basically *has no place at work.*

Put your knowledge of gender communication to work to minimize the likelihood of being accused of harassment. Communicate equally and consistently at work, meaning in the same professional manner with members of all sexes and genders. If someone reacts nonverbally with embarrassment or discomfort to something you say or do, or says that he or she doesn't appreciate your behavior, try not to get defensive. Be responsible for your own behavior and try to rectify the situation, not by explaining what you meant or trying to justify your behavior, but by apologizing and offering to make amends. If the person won't accept your apology, then *leave her or him alone.* Accept the person's interpretation of the event, rather than asserting your will into the situation. Chalk up that experience and learn some lessons from it.

CONCLUSION

This chapter has presented some of the more predominant issues that challenge today's working women and men. We've explored this particular context with students in mind, considering situations and concerns that may arise when students launch, restart, or redirect their careers. We've examined interviewing, on-the-job communication, advancement opportunities and barriers, and management styles. The complicated topic of sexual harassment has also been explored for its effects on work relationships and the work environment. Are you now magically equipped with a solution for every problem and a strategy for overcoming every obstacle you might encounter at work? Will you be able to confront sex bias and sex-related communication perplexities with skill and ease? The answers are "probably not" to the first question, and "we hope so" to the second one.

Again, when it comes to gender communication, there are no magical formulas, no sure-fire remedies, no easy answers. But by ridding your professional communication of stereotypes and personal or sexual forms of communication that are inappropriate in the workplace and by assuming a flexible, communicative style with colleagues, bosses, and clients that isn't gender specific, you'll have gone a long way toward projecting a professional, successful image at work.

DISCUSSION STARTERS

1. Remember a time you interviewed for a job you really wanted. It could be any kind of job—paper route, babysitter, part-time waitperson, and so on. Now imagine yourself in that interview, but as a member of a different sex. Would the person who interviewed you treat you any differently? If so, how so? Do you think your sex had anything to do with getting or not getting that job?

2. Think of a person who holds a position of power and authority in her or his job. This person might be one of your parents, your doctor, someone you've worked for, and so on. What's the sex of that person? If that person's male, do you think he'd have as much power and respect in his job if he were female? Would he have to change his communication style or the way he deals with coworkers, subordinates, and clients if he were female? If the person is female, what kinds of barriers or challenges has she faced as she achieved that position of respect?

3. Consider the difference between quid pro quo and hostile climate sexual harassment. Have you ever known anyone who experienced quid pro quo harassment? Think about jobs you've had; was there anything in your workplace that someone could have interpreted as contributing to a hostile sexual climate?

References

Adler, R. B., & Elmhorst, J. M. (2008). *Communicating at work* (9th ed.). New York: McGraw-Hill.

Albelda, R. (2009). Up with women in the down-turn. *Ms.*, 35–37.

Amaral, H. P. (2006). Workplace romance and fraternization policies, University of Rhode Island. Retrieved August 15, 2015, from <www.uri.edu>.

Andronici, J., & Katz, D. S. (2008, Spring). Stall tactics. *Ms.*, 57.

Applebaum, S. H., Marinescu, A., Klenin, J., & Bytautas, J. (2007). Fatal attractions: The [mis]management of workplace romance. *International Journal of Business Research, 7*, 1–20.

Arulampalam, W., Booth, A., & Bryan, M. (2007). Is there a glass ceiling over Europe? Exploring the gender pay gap across the wages distribution. *Independent Labor Relations Review, 60*, 163–186.

Avtgis, T. A., Rancer, A. S., & Liberman, C. J. (2012). *Organizational communication: Strategies for success* (2nd ed.). Dubuque, IA: Kendall Hunt.

Ayman, R., & Korabik, K. (2010). Leadership: Why gender and culture matter. *American Psychologist, 65*, 157–170.

Baird, K. (2013, December 17). The top 10 facts and statistics behind telecommuting for a virtual company. Retrieved August 13, 2015, from <nimblemedia.ca>.

Baker, B. (2012, Fall). Women's lives in the balance. *Ms.*, 26-33.

Barrick, M. R., Shaffer, J. A., & DeGrassi, S. W. (2009). What you see may not be what you get: Relationships among self-presentation tactics and ratings of interview and job performance. *Journal of Applied Psychology, 94*, 1394–1411.

Barsh, J., & Cranston, S. (2009). *How remarkable women lead.* New York: Crown.

Baxter, E. (2015, June 18). Infographic: How access to paid leave helps fathers. Retrieved August 12, 2015, from <www.americanprogress.org>.

Behm-Morawitz, E., & Schipper, S. (2015). Sexing the avatar: Gender, sexualization, and cyber-harassment in a virtual world. *Journal of Media Psychology.* dx.doi.org:10.1027/1864-1105/a000152.

Belkin, L. (2003, October 26). Q: Why don't more women choose to get to the top? A: They choose not to. *The New York Times Magazine*, 42–47, 58, 85.

Ben-Galim, D., & Silim, A. (2014, December 11). Can public policy break the glass ceiling? Retrieved August 12, 2015, from <www.americanprogress.org>.

Benson, K. (1984). Comment on Crocker's "An analysis of university definitions of sexual harassment." *Signs, 9*, 516–519.

Bercovici, J. (2007). The workplace romance and sexual favoritism: Creating a dialogue between social science and the law of sexual harassment. *Southern California Interdisciplinary Law Journal, 16*, 183–214.

Berryman-Fink, C., & Vanover Riley, K. (1997). The effect of sex and feminist orientation on perceptions in sexually harassing communication. *Women's Studies in Communication, 20*, 25–44.

Bjerk, D. (2008). Glass ceilings or sticky floors? Statistical discrimination in a dynamic model of hiring and promotion. *The Economic Journal, 118*, 961–982.

Blau, F., & Kahn, L. (1997). Swimming upstream: Trends in the gender wage differential in the 1980s. *Journal of Labor Economics, 15*. Available at <http://papers.ssrn.com>.

Bliss Kiser, S., Coley, T., Ford, M., & Moore, E. (2006). Coffee, tea, or me? Romance and sexual harassment in the workplace. *Southern Business Review, 31*, 35–50.

Boushey, H. (2009). Women breadwinners, men unemployed. In H. Boushey & A. O'Leary (Eds.), *The Shriver report: A woman's nation changes everything.* Washington, DC: Center for American Progress.

Brazile, D. (2009, Summer). No more penny pinching. *Ms.*, 47.

Burk, M. (2014, Winter/Spring). States of relief: Congress may not support paid family medical leave, but California and others do. *Ms.*, 47.

Butler, G., Feng, B., & MacGeorge, E. (2003). Gender differences in the communication values of mature adults. *Communication Research Reports, 20*, 191–199.

Buzzanell, P. M., & Lucas, K. (2006). Gendered stories of career: Unfolding discourses of time, space, and identity. In B. J. Dow & J. T. Wood (Eds.), *The SAGE handbook of gender and communication* (pp. 161–178). Thousand Oaks, CA: Sage.

Carli, L. L., & Eagly, A. H. (2007). *Through the labyrinth: The truth about how women become leaders.* Boston: Harvard Business School Press.

Castillo, Y., Muscarella, F., & Szuchman, L. T. (2011). Gender differences in college students' perceptions of same-sex sexual harassment: The influence of physical attractiveness and attitudes toward lesbians and gay men. *Journal of College Student Development, 52*, 511–522.

Cauchon, D. (2009, September 3). Women gain as men lose jobs. *USA Today.* Retrieved July 9, 2010, from <http://www.usatoday.com>.

Chaplin, W. F., Phillips, J. B., Brown, J. D., Clanton, N. R., & Stein, J. L. (2000). Handshaking, gender, personality, and first impressions. *Journal of Personality and Social Psychology, 79*, 110–117.

Clason, M. A., & Turner, L. H. (2011). Communicating manufacturing as masculine domain: How women get noticed at work. *Women & Language, 34*, 41–59.

Conroy, N. E. (2013). Rethinking adolescent peer sexual harassment: Contributions of feminist theory. *Journal of School Violence, 12*, 340–356.

Correll, S. J. (2006). Gender and the career choice process: The role of biased self-assessment. In P. J. Dubeck & D. Dunn (Eds.), *Workplace/women's place: An anthology* (3rd ed., pp. 37–51). Los Angeles: Roxbury.

DeLaat, J. (2007). *Gender in the workplace: A case study approach* (2nd ed.). Thousand Oaks, CA: Sage.

DeSouza, E., & Fansler, A. G. (2003). Contrapower sexual harassment: A survey of students and faculty members. *Sex Roles, 48*, 519–542.

Dixon, J., & Dougherty, D. S. (2014). A language convergence/meaning divergence analysis exploring how LGBTQ and single employees manage traditional family expectations in the workplace. *Journal of Applied Communication Research, 42*, 1–19.

Dougherty, D. S. (2001). Sexual harassment as [dys] functional process: A feminist standpoint analysis. *Journal of Applied Communication Research, 29*, 372–402.

Douglas Vavrus, M. (2007). Opting out moms in the news: Selling new traditionalism in the new millennium. *Feminist Media Studies, 7*, 47–63.

Dubeck, P. J. (2006). Are we there yet?: Reflections on work and family as an emergent social issue. In P. J. Dubeck & D. Dunn (Eds.), *Workplace/women's place: An anthology* (3rd ed., pp. 312–323). Los Angeles: Roxbury.

Dubeck, P. J., & Dunn, D. (2002). Introduction to unit four: Work and family: Seeking a balance. In P. J. Dubeck & D. Dunn (Eds.), *Workplace/women's place: An anthology* (2nd ed., pp. 141–145). Los Angeles: Roxbury.

Duehr, E. E., & Bono, J. E. (2006). Men, women, and managers: Are stereotypes finally changing? *Personnel Psychology, 59*, 815–847.

Eagly, A. H., Gartzia, L., & Carli, L. L. (2014). Female advantage: Revisited. In S. Kumra, R. Simpson, & R. Burke (Eds.), *The Oxford handbook of gender in organizations* (pp. 153–174). New York: Oxford University Press.

Edley, P. P. (2004). Entrepreneurial mothers' balance of work and family: Discursive constructions of time, mothering, and identity. In P. M. Buzzanell, H. M. Sterk, & L. H. Turner (Eds.), *Gender in applied communication contexts* (pp. 255–273). Thousand Oaks, CA: Sage.

Engberg, K. (1999). *It's not the glass ceiling, it's the sticky floor: And other things our daughters should know about marriage, work, and motherhood.* Amherst, NY: Prometheus Books.

England, P., Garcia-Beaulieu, C., & Ross, M. (2007). Women's employment among blacks, whites, and three groups of Latinas. In M. T. Segal & T. A. Martinez (Eds.), *Intersections of gender, race, and class* (pp. 368–379). Los Angeles: Roxbury.

Equal Employment Opportunity Commission. (1980). Guidelines on discrimination because of sex. *Federal Register, 45*, 74676–74677.

Everbach, T. (2005). *The feminine culture of a woman-led newspaper: An organizational study.* Paper presented at the meeting of the International Communication Association, New York, NY.

Fairchild, C. (2014, June 3). Number of Fortune 500 women CEOs reaches historic high. Retrieved August 12, 2015, from <http://www.fortune.com>.

Fielden, S. L., & Hunt, C. (2014). Sexual harassment in the workplace. In S. Kumra, R. Simpson, & R. Burke (Eds.), *The Oxford handbook of gender in organizations* (pp. 353–370). New York: Oxford University Press.

Fine, G. A. (1996). Friendships in the workplace. In K. M. Galvin & P. Cooper (Eds.), *Making connections: Readings in relational communication* (pp. 270–277). Los Angeles: Roxbury.

Finnegan, A. (2001, October). The inside story: Are the 100 best as good as they say they are? *Working Mother Magazine.* Retrieved from <http://www.workingmother.com>.

Fisher, A. (2009, July 23). Do women do better in a recession? Retrieved July 9, 2010, from <http://www.CNNMoney.com>.

Friedan, B. (1981). *The second stage.* New York: Summit.

Gerdes, L. I. (1999). Introduction. In L. I. Gerdes (Ed.), *Sexual harassment: Current controversies* (pp. 12–14). San Diego: Greenhaven.

Gerstel, N., & McGonagle, K. (2006). Job leaves and the limits of the Family and Medical Leave Act: The effects of gender, race, and family. In P. J. Dubeck & D. Dunn (Eds.), *Workplace/women's place: An anthology* (3rd ed., pp. 340–350). Los Angeles: Roxbury.

Goldberg, C., & Zhang, L. (2004). Simple and joint effects of gender and self-esteem on responses to same-sex sexual harassment. *Sex Roles, 50*, 823–833.

Grashow, A., Heifetz, R., & Linsky, M. (2009, July–August). Leadership in a (permanent) crisis. *Harvard Business Review*, 62–69.

Groom, B. (2014, March 23). Female chief executive numbers increase. *Financial Times.* Retrieved August 12, 2015, from <http://www.ft.com>.

Grossman, J. L. (2015). Moving forward, looking back: A retrospective on sexual harassment law. *Boston University Law Review, 95,* 1029–1048.

Gruber, J. E. (1989). How women handle sexual harassment: A literature review. *Sociology and Social Research, 74,* 3–7.

Gurian, M., & Annis, B. (2008). *Leadership and the sexes: Using gender science to create success in business.* New York: Jossey-Bass.

Halder, D., & Jaishankar, K. (2011). Cyber gender harassment and secondary victimization: A comparative analysis of the United States, the UK, and India. *Victims & Offenders, 6,* 386–398.

Henningsen, D. D. (2004). Flirting with meaning: An examination of miscommunication in flirting interactions. *Sex Roles, 50,* 481–489.

Henson, K. D. (1996). *Just a temp.* Philadelphia: Temple University Press.

Hewlett, S. A. (2013). *Forget a mentor, find a sponsor: The new way to fast-track your career.* Boston: Harvard Business Review Press.

Hewlett, S. A., Peraino, K., Sherbin, L., & Sumberg, K. (2010). *The sponsor effect: Breaking through the last glass ceiling.* Boston: Harvard Business Review Press.

Hill, A. (2002, Spring). The nature of the beast: What I've learned about sexual harassment. *Ms.,* 84–85.

Hill, E. J., Martinson, V. K., Ferris, M., & Zenger Baker, R. (2006). Beyond the mommy track: The influence of new-concept part-time work for professional women on work and family. In J. W. White (Ed.), *Taking sides: Clashing views in gender* (4th ed., pp. 242–248). Boston: McGraw-Hill.

Hobson, C. J., Szostek, J., & Fitzgerald, L. E. (2015). The development of a content valid tool to assess organizational policies and practices concerning workplace sexual harassment. *TIP: The Industrial-Organizational Psychologist, 52,* 111–119.

Hochschild, A. R., & Machung, A. (2006). The second shift: Working parents and the revolution at home. In P. J. Dubeck & D. Dunn (Eds.), *Workplace/women's place: An anthology* (3rd ed., pp. 123–133). Los Angeles: Roxbury.

Hosada, M., Stone-Romero, E., & Coats, G. (2003). The effects of physical attractiveness on job-related outcomes: A meta-analysis of experimental studies. *Personnel Psychology, 56,* 431–462.

Ivy, D. K. (1999). "*Monica madness": A feminist look at language in the Clinton sex scandal.* Unpublished manuscript.

Ivy, D. K., & Hamlet, S. (1996). College students and sexual dynamics: Two studies of peer sexual harassment. *Communication Education, 45,* 149–166.

Ivy, D. K., & Wahl, S. T. (2014). *Nonverbal communication for a lifetime* (2nd ed.). Dubuque, IA: Kendall Hunt.

Jacobs, G., & Bonavoglia, A. (1998, May–June). Confused by the rules. *Ms.,* 48–55.

Jiang, K., Hong, Y., McKay, P., Avery, D. R., Wilson, D. C., & Volpone, S. D. (2015). Retaining employees through anti-sexual harassment practices: Exploring the mediating role of psychological distress and employee engagement. *Human Resource Management, 54,* 1–21.

Johnson, S. K., Podratz, K. E., Dipboye, R. L., & Gibbons, E. (2010). Physical attractiveness biases in ratings of employment suitability: Tracking down the "beauty is beastly" effect. *Journal of Social Psychology, 150,* 301–318.

Katz, D. S., & Andronici, J. (2009, Winter). Equal pay and beyond. *Ms.,* 63.

Kelly, L., & Radford, J. (1996). "Nothing really happened": The invalidation of women's experiences of sexual violence. In M. Hester, L. Kelly, & J. Radford (Eds.), *Women, violence, and male power: Feminist activism, research, and practice.* Buckingham, UK: Open University Press.

Kish, A. (2009, December). Ace the interview. *Women's Health,* 102–103.

Koeppel, L. B., Montagne, Y., O'Hair, D., & Cody, M. J. (1999). Friendly? Flirting? Wrong? In L. K. Guerrero, J. DeVito, & M. L. Hecht (Eds.), *The nonverbal communication reader* (pp. 290–297). Prospect Heights, IL: Waveland.

Lampman, C., Phelps, A., Bancroft, S., & Beneke, M. (2009). Contrapower harassment in academia: A survey of faculty experience with student incivility, bullying, and sexual attention. *Sex Roles, 60,* 331–346.

Lane, A. J. (2006, May 5). Gender, power, and sexuality: First, do no harm. *The Chronicle of Higher Education,* pp. B10, B13.

Langelan, M. (2005, Fall). Stop right there! *Ms.,* 39.

Lee, D. (2001). "He didn't sexually harass me, as in harassed for sex . . . he was just horrible": Women's definitions of unwanted male sexual conduct at work. *Women's Studies International Forum, 24,* 25–38.

Levitz, J. (2010, February 13–14). Rise in home-based businesses tests neighborliness. *The Wall Street Journal,* p. A5.

Lewis, P. (2014). Feminism, post-feminism, and emerging femininities in entrepreneurship. In S. Kumra, R. Simpson, & R. Burke (Eds.), *The Oxford handbook of gender in organizations* (pp. 107–129). New York: Oxford University Press.

Little, A. (2014, Summer). It's not a myth—it's math: The pay gap is real and persistent. *Ms.*, 12–13.

Lucero, M. A., Middleton, K. L., & Allen, R. E. (2006). *Individual severity judgments of sexual harassment incidents.* Paper presented at the meeting of the Academy of Management, Atlanta, GA.

Luna Brem, M. (2001). *The seven greatest truths about successful women: How you can achieve financial independence, professional freedom, and personal joy.* New York: G. P. Putnam's Sons.

MacKinnon, C. A. (2002). Should Title VII apply to sexual harassment between individuals of the same sex? In E. L. Paul (Ed.), *Taking sides: Clashing views on controversial issues in sex and gender* (2nd ed., pp. 152–163). Guilford, CT: McGraw-Hill/Dushkin.

Madlock, P. (2006). Do differences in displays of nonverbal immediacy and communicator competence between male and female supervisors affect subordinates' job satisfaction? *Ohio Communication Journal, 44*, 61–77.

Mainiero, L. A., & Jones, K. J. (2012). Workplace romance 2.0: Developing a communication ethics model to address potential sexual harassment from inappropriate social media contacts between coworkers. *Journal of Business Ethics, 114*, 367–379.

Mainiero, L. A., & Jones, K. J. (2013). Sexual harassment versus workplace romance: Social media spillover and textual harassment in the workplace. *The Academy of Management Perspectives, 27*, 187–203.

Mainiero, L. A., & Sullivan, S. E. (2006). Kaleidoscope careers: An alternate explanation for the "opt-out" revolution. In P. J. Dubeck & D. Dunn (Eds.), *Workplace/women's place: An anthology* (3rd ed., pp. 324–339). Los Angeles: Roxbury.

McDonald, P., Charlesworth, S., & Graham, T. (2015). Developing a framework of effective prevention and response strategies in workplace sexual harassment. *Asia Pacific Journal of Human Resources, 53*, 41–58.

Medved, C. E., & Rawlins, W. K. (2011). At-home fathers and breadwinning mothers: Variations in constructing work and family lives. *Women & Language, 34*, 9–39.

Meers, S., & Strober, J. (2009). *Getting to 50/50: How working couples can have it all by sharing it all.* New York: Bantam Books.

Mendelson Freeman, S. J. (2006). Parental influence and women's careers. In P. J. Dubeck & D. Dunn (Eds.), *Workplace/women's place: An anthology* (3rd ed., pp. 18–27). Los Angeles: Roxbury.

Metz, I., & Kulik, C. T. (2014). The rocky climb: Women's advancement in management. In S. Kumra, R. Simpson, & R. Burke (Eds.), *The Oxford handbook of gender in organizations* (pp. 175–199). New York: Oxford University Press.

Middleton, K. L., & Lucero, M. A. (2003). Why don't men get it? A comparison of male and female judgments of aggressive and sexual behaviors. *Academy of Management Proceedings*, A1–A6.

Mink, G. (2005, Fall). Stop sexual harassment now! *Ms.*, 36–37.

Moe, K., & Shandy, D. (2009). *Glass ceilings and the 100-hour couples: What the opt-out phenomenon can teach us about work and family.* Athens: University of Georgia Press.

Mohipp, C., & Senn, C. Y. (2008). Graduate students' perceptions of contrapower sexual harassment. *Journal of Interpersonal Violence, 23*, 1258–1276.

Newport, F., & Wilke, J. (2013). Americans still prefer a male boss. Retrieved August 13, 2015, from <www.gallup.com/poll/165791/americans-prefer-male-boss>

Noonan, M. C., & Corcoran, M. E. (2006). The mommy track and partnership: Temporary delay or dead end? In J. W. White (Ed.), *Taking sides: Clashing views in gender* (4th ed., pp. 249–255). Boston: McGraw-Hill.

O'Brien, K., Latner, J., Ebneter, D., & Hunter, J. (2013). Obesity discrimination: The role of physical appearance, personal ideology, and anti-fat prejudice. *International Journal of Obesity, 37*, 455–460.

O'Hair, D., Friedrich, G. W., & Dixon, L. A. (2015). *Strategic communication in business and the professions* (8th ed.). Boston: Pearson.

O'Leary, A., & Kornbluh, K. (2009). Family friendly for all families. In H. Boushey & A. O'Leary (Eds.), *The Shriver report: A woman's nation changes everything.* Washington, DC: Center for American Progress.

O'Leary-Kelly, A. M., Bowes-Sperry, L., Arens Bates, C., & Lean, E. R. (2009). Sexual harassment at work: A decade (plus) of progress. *Journal of Management, 35*, 503–536.

O'Neill, T. (2015, Spring). Wage gap denial: We can't believe we're still protesting this sh*t! *Ms.*, 37.

Paetzold, R. L., & O'Leary-Kelly, A. M. (1993). Organizational communication and the legal dimensions of hostile work environment sexual harassment. In G. L. Kreps (Ed.), *Sexual harassment: Communication implications* (pp. 63–77). Cresskill, NJ: Hampton.

Page, T. E., & Pina, A. (2015). Moral disengagement as a self-regulatory process in sexual harassment perpetration at work: A preliminary conceptualization. *Aggression and Violent Behavior, 21*, 73–84.

Parent, J. (2009). Taking out a contract on workplace romance: "Love contract" can protect employees and the company from discrimination claims. *New Hampshire Business Review, 31,* 27–29.

Peach, L. J. (1998). Sex, sexism, sexual harassment, and sexual abuse: Introduction. In L. J. Peach (Ed.), *Women in culture: A women's studies anthology* (pp. 283–301). Malden, MA: Blackwell.

Poindexter, P. (2014, March). Raising awareness about the dirty side of internships. *AEJMC News, 2,* 4.

Powell, G. N. (2010). *Women and men in management* (4th ed.). Thousand Oaks, CA: Sage.

Quinn, M. (2004, May 9). "Sequencing" parents work, leave to care for kids, then return to work. Knight Ridder Newspapers, as in *Corpus Christi Caller Times,* p. D2.

Quintanilla, K. M., & Wahl, S. T. (2014). *Business and professional communication: Keys for workplace excellence* (2nd ed.). Thousand Oaks, CA: Sage.

Rainbird, H. (2007). Can training remove the glue from the "sticky floor" of low-paid work for women? *Equal Opportunities International, 26,* 555–572.

Ralston, S. M., & Kinser, A. E. (2001). Intersections of gender and employment interviewing. In L. P. Arliss & D. J. Borisoff (Eds.), *Women and men communicating: Challenges and changes* (2nd ed., pp. 185–211). Prospect Heights, IL: Waveland.

RAND Military Workplace Study. (2014). Sexual assault and sexual harassment in the U.S. military: Volume 2. Estimates for Department of Defense service members from the 2014 RAND Military Workplace Study. Retrieved August 15, 2015, from <www.rand/org/pubs/research_reports>.

Rapoza, K. (2013, February 18). One in five Americans work from home, numbers seen rising over 60%. Retrieved August 13, 2015, from <www.forbes.com>.

Raver, J. L., & Nishii, L. H. (2010). Once, twice, or three times as harmful? Ethnic harassment, gender harassment, and generalized workplace harassment. *Journal of Applied Psychology, 95,* 236–254.

Rehel, E., & Baxter, E. (2015, February 4). Men, fathers, and work-family balance. Retrieved August 12, 2015, from <www.americanprogress.org>.

Ritter, B. A. (2014). Deviant behavior in computer-mediated communication: Development and validation of a measure of cybersexual harassment. *Journal of Computer-Mediated Communication, 19,* 197–214.

Rogers, J. K., & Henson, K. D. (2006). "Hey, why don't you wear a shorter skirt?" Structural vulnerability and the organization of sexual harassment in temporary clerical employment. In P. J. Dubeck & D. Dunn (Eds.), *Workplace/women's place: An anthology* (3rd ed., pp. 272–283). Los Angeles: Roxbury.

Rosewarne, L. (2007). Pin-ups in public space: Sexist outdoor advertising as sexual harassment. *Women's Studies International Forum, 30,* 313–325.

Rowe-Finkbeiner, K. (2013, March 15). Overcoming the "maternal wall." *The Washington Post,* retrieved August 10, 2015, from <washingtonpost.com>.

Rudman, L. A., & Phelan, J. E. (2008). Backlash effects for disconfirming gender stereotypes in organizations. *Research in Organizational Behavior, 28,* 61–79.

Rudolph, C. W., Wells, C. L., Weller, M. D., & Baltes, B. B. (2009). A meta-analysis of empirical studies of weight-based bias in the workplace. *Journal of Vocational Behavior, 74,* 1–10.

Rutherford, S. (2001). Organizational cultures, women managers, and exclusion. *Women in Management Review, 16,* 371–382.

Saad, L. (2014, August 29). The "40-hour" workweek is actually longer—by seven hours. Retrieved August 10, 2015, from <www.gallup.com/poll/175286>.

Saltzman Chafetz, J. (1997). "I need a (traditional) wife!" Employment–family conflicts. In D. Dunn (Ed.), *Workplace/women's place: An anthology* (pp. 116–124). Los Angeles: Roxbury.

Sandberg, S. (2013). *Lean in: Women, work, and the will to lead.* New York: Alfred A. Knopf.

Shambaugh, R. (2007). *It's not a glass ceiling, it's a sticky floor: Free yourself from the hidden behaviors sabotaging your career success.* New York: McGraw-Hill.

Sheffield, C. J. (2004). Sexual terrorism. In M. S. Kimmel & R. F. Plante (Eds.), *Sexualities: Identities, behaviors, and society* (pp. 419–424). New York: Oxford University Press.

Sloan, D. K., & Krone, K. J. (2000). Women managers and gendered values. *Women's Studies in Communication, 23,* 111–130.

Spender, D. (1984). Defining reality: A powerful tool. In C. Kramarae, M. Schultz, & W. O'Barr (Eds.), *Language and power* (pp. 9–22). Beverly Hills: Sage.

Steinem, G. (1983). *Outrageous acts and everyday rebellions.* New York: Holt, Rinehart, & Winston.

Stewart, G. L., Dustin, S. L., Barrick, M. R., & Darnold, C. (2008). Exploring the handshake in employment interviews. *Journal of Applied Psychology, 93,* 1139–1146.

Stewart, L. P. (2001). Gender issues in corporate communication. In L. P. Arliss & D. J. Borisoff (Eds.), *Women and men communicating: Challenges and changes* (2nd ed., pp. 171–184). Prospect Heights, IL: Waveland.

Thomae, M., & Pina, A. (2015). Sexist humor and social identity: The role of sexist humor in men's in-group cohesion, sexual harassment, rape proclivity, and victim blame. *Humor: International Journal of Humor Research, 28*, 187–204.

Trei, L. (2002, April 10). A feminist economic view of work and family. *The Stanford Report*. Retrieved from <www.stanford.edu/dept/ news/report>.

Tsai, W., Huang, T., & Yu, H. (2012). Investigating the unique predictability and boundary conditions of applicant physical attractiveness and nonverbal behaviors on interviewer evaluations in job interviews. *Journal of Occupational & Organizational Psychology, 85*, 60–79.

U.S. Census Bureau. (2010). Census 2010. Retrieved January 30, 2011, from <http://www.census.gov>.

U.S. Department of Labor. (2015). Bureau of Labor Statistics. Retrieved August 10, 2015, from <http://www.data.bls.gov>.

van der Bruggen, M., & Grubb, A. (2014). A review of the literature relating to rape victim blaming: An analysis of the impact of observer and victim characteristics on attribution of blame in rape cases. *Aggression and Violent Behavior, 19*, 523–531.

Vijayasiri, G. (2008). Reporting sexual harassment: The importance of organizational culture and trust. *Gender Issues, 25*, 43–61.

Welsh, S. (2006, May). Flex and the office. *O: The Oprah Winfrey Magazine*, 281–283.

Wendt, A. C., & Slonaker, W. M. (2002, Autumn). Sexual harassment and retaliation: A double-edged sword. *Society for the Advancement of Management (SAM) Advanced Management Journal*, 49–57.

Wernick, L. J., Kulik, A., & Inglehart, M. H. (2014). Influences of peers, teachers, and climate on students' willingness to intervene when witnessing anti-transgender harassment. *Journal of Adolescence, 37*, 927–935.

Whitehurst, T., Jr. (2002). Child care's bottom line: Employers are learning that their participation makes dollars and sense. *Corpus Christi Caller Times*, pp. D1, D4.

Williams, C. L. (2006). Gendered jobs and gendered workers. In P. J. Dubeck & D. Dunn (Eds.), *Workplace/women's place: An anthology* (3rd ed., pp. 69–72). Los Angeles: Roxbury.

Williams, J. C. (2004). Hitting the maternal wall. *Academe, 90*, 16–20.

Williams, J. C., Manvell, J., & Bornstein, S. (2006). *"Opt out" or pushed out? How the press covers work/family conflict: The untold story of why women leave the workforce*. San Francisco: University of California, Hastings College of the Law, Center for WorkLife Law.

Williams, N. (2009, Spring). Lilly's law: Ledbetter Act helps women's fight for fair pay. *Ms.*, 17.

Wise, S., & Stanley, L. (1987). *Georgie porgie: Sexual harassment in everyday life*. New York: Pandora.

Wolf, N. (2004, March 1). The silent treatment. *New York*, 23–29.

A woman's nation changes everything. (2009). *The Shriver report*. Washington, DC: Center for American Progress. Retrieved October 28, 2009, from <http://awomansnation.com/about.php>.

Women Are Getting Even (WAGE). (2015). Home page. Retrieved August 10, 2015, from <www.wageproject.org>.

Women in America: Indicators of social and economic well-being. (2011). Retrieved March 1, 2011, from <http://www.whitehouse.gov>.

Wood, J. T. (1992). Telling our stories: Narratives as a basis for theorizing sexual harassment. *Journal of Applied Communication, 20*, 349–362.

Wood, J. T. (1993). Naming and interpreting sexual harassment: A conceptual framework for scholarship. In G. L. Kreps (Ed.), *Sexual harassment: Communication implications* (pp. 9–26). Cresskill, NJ: Hampton.

Woodward, S. (1995, September 10). Packwood his own worst enemy: Case becomes a watershed event as rules change. *The Sunday Oregonian*, pp. A1, A16, A17.

Work and family facts and statistics. (2015). Retrieved August 10, 2015, from <http://www.aflcio.org/issues/factsstats/>.

www.catalyst.org. (2015, August 12). Women CEOs of the S&P 500. Retrieved August 12, 2015, from <www.catalyst.org>.

www.money.CNN.com. (2015, March 24). Still missing: Female business leaders. Retrieved August 12, 2015, from <www.money.CNN.com>.

Zhang, S., Schmader, T., & Forbes, C. (2009). The effects of gender stereotypes on women's career choice: Opening the glass door. In M. Barreto, M. K. Ryan, & M. T. Schmitt (Eds.), *The glass ceiling in the 21st century: Understanding barriers to gender equality* (pp. 125–150). Washington, DC: American Psychological Association.

CHAPTER 10

A "CLASS ACT"
Gender Communication in Educational Settings

CASE STUDY

The "Male Nurse's" Dilemma

Rusk was one of those guys who always loved helping people. He was *that* guy—the one who helped everyone move into their dorm rooms, who stuck around after the party to clean up, and who'd loan you the shirt off his back if he thought you needed it more than he did. So it surprised exactly none of Rusk's friends and family members when Rusk decided to major in nursing in college. In fact, his parents made him pledge that he'd launch his nursing career in his hometown (so he could take care of them in their old age).

But once Rusk started attending his first nursing classes, he was surprised at the unwanted attention he got from classmates. Some of it was expected—ribbing about being a "male nurse." Rusk thought, "Didn't 'male nurse' go away with that Greg Fokker character in those *Meet the Parents* movies? Aren't there enough of us now that we don't get kidded about this anymore?" The teasing and attention worsened, with some of his female classmates becoming more blatant, like quizzing Rusk about his romantic life, asking him repeatedly to join groups of female classmates for happy hours (after he'd politely declined multiple times), and flirting with him (including some inappropriate touching). Rusk became increasingly uncomfortable just going to class, which soon began to hurt his attendance and motivation toward his studies.

HOT TOPICS

- Children's ideas about gender as affected by fairy tales, nursery rhymes, and other forms of children's literature
- How gender expectations and bias impact teaching and learning
- Factors that contribute to a chilly classroom climate for women in higher education
- The problem of peer sexual harassment in educational settings

But Rusk's first move toward fixing the problem was a smart one—a step right out of the online training module students at Rusk's university were required to complete: He met privately with one of his nursing profs, explaining the problem and asking for advice. The professor's advice was this: Unwanted attention, teasing, and flirtation from female nurses to male nurses was to be expected—it happened all the time in hospitals across the country. If Rusk couldn't handle a bit of attention and kidding from classmates, how could he possibly cope with it once he landed a job? He needed to suck it up and get along as well as possible with everyone, because that was good training for his career.

What's your assessment of the advice Rusk got and the approach his professor recommended? Was the prof simply trying to prepare Rusk for "real world" challenges, or was the prof sadly out of date on the topic of sexual harassment? If you were in Rusk's shoes, what would you do next? "Man up" and go along to get along? Push the issue further and higher up?

D o you view educational institutions as havens of equality, as places where discriminatory attitudes are left outside the ivy-covered walls? While some of us who have made education our careers like to believe that academic institutions may be more sensitive to diversity issues than other types of organizations, no institution is exempt from discrimination. In this chapter, we examine a few forms of sexism lurking in the halls of education.

CHILDREN'S LITERATURE: LESSONS ABOUT GENDER

When you think back to childhood, many experiences come to mind—some good, maybe some not so good. Do your fonder memories include the stories a parent read to you before you went to sleep or stories you read with classmates when you were in grade school? Who you are as an adult—your view of self, others, relationships, and communication within those relationships—has likely been affected by the early lessons you received from children's literature at home and school. Those lessons contribute to your vision of what it means to be a man or a woman, what roles the sexes should play in society, how relationships ought to work, and the quality of communication it takes to make relationships successful.

Fairy Tales, Nursery Rhymes, and Gender

Consider the potential effects of reading or hearing stories with the same basic plot: A young, beautiful, helpless, or abandoned girl encounters a series of obstacles (events or people) that place her in jeopardy. Enter the young, handsome, usually wealthy prince or king who rescues and marries the girl. With minor deviations, this basic theme serves as the plot for such fairy tales in American folk culture as *Cinderella, Snow White and the Seven Dwarfs, Sleeping Beauty, Goldilocks and the Three Bears,* and *Rapunzel.* The attributes of female leading characters in such tales include beauty, innocence, passivity, patience (since they often have to wait a long time for the rescuer to come), dependence, and self-sacrifice (Bottigheimer, 1986). As rescuers, male characters are handsome, independent, brave, strong, action-oriented, successful, romantic, and kindhearted. Do the characters' descriptors reflect stereotypical male and female traits? What's the potential effect of these depictions? Do today's more modern tales do enough to buffer the stereotypes?

Scholars and cultural critics continue to examine gender depictions in fairy tales (Brule, 2008; Mitchell, 2010; Ruterana, 2012; Schanoes, 2014; Weingart & Jorgensen, 2013). Research focuses special attention on Disney tales, alternatively criticized for their biased depictions of gender roles and praised for their more recent themes of feminine empowerment (Asher-Perrin, 2015; Gillam & Wooden, 2008; Smith, 2013; Sumera, 2009; White, 2013).

Many fairy tales have the same basic plot and attributes for the main male and female characters.

Several gendered messages can be drawn from fairy tales:

🍁 Main characters must be physically attractive to be worthy of romance (Baker-Sperry & Grauerholz, 2003; Henneberg, 2010). In many of these stories, love is instantaneous—an uncontrollable reaction to rapturous, extraordinary beauty. Do children, especially young girls, get the message that they must be beautiful to be deserving of love and romance?

🍁 Competition is emphasized. The primary female character often must compete with other females for the attention and affection of the hero. This message runs counter to the female tendency to cooperate rather than compete to accomplish goals. It also suggests that winning a man is more important than having good relationships with other females.

Rewards for stereotypically gendered behavior include romance, marriage, wealth, and living happily ever after (Dundes, 2001). This reinforces in girls the notion that the ultimate goal in life is to marry a wonderful man who will protect them and make them completely happy. There's nothing necessarily wrong with this goal, but is it the only appropriate goal? What fairy tale speaks to your life if you're a lesbian? A gay male? A transgender person? An asexual person?

Physical attractiveness, strength, and bravery are expected characteristics of male heroes. The dashing male lead character is expected to rescue the girl and turn her unbearable life into wedded bliss. That's a lot of pressure on men! This common plot sets up men to be the rescuers and women the rescued—and many people believe in and attempt to enact these roles as adults (Brule, 2008; Gillam & Wooden, 2008). What happens when women expect princelike qualities, when they form expectations of men that are too high and all-encompassing for any man to fulfill? What happens if the "prince" turns into a "beast"?

Marriage is the be-all and end-all. The expectation is that marriage will lead to a successful "ever after," but fairy tale readers and viewers seldom see what happens after the marriage ceremony; you get only the closing line about living "happily ever after."

> Cinderella never asked for a prince.
> She asked for a night off and a dress.
> —Kiera Cass, author

Stereotypical depictions can also be found in traditional nursery rhymes written for children, but some authors have attempted to "ungenderize" this form of literature and counter the stereotypes (Ragan, 2000). For example, in the 1980s and 1990s, Doug Larche, more familiarly known as Father Gander, published several books of rewritten, unbiased nursery rhymes in an effort to alter a sexist trend that disturbed him and that he thought sent the wrong message to children about gender (Larche, 1985, 1990). In Larche's revision, *Jack and Jill Be Nimble,* Jill is encouraged to be just as athletic as Jack in their efforts to jump over a candlestick. Jack Zipes' (1986) collection of feminist fairy tales, *Don't Bet on the Prince,* opened many people's eyes to gendered and cultural messages inherent in fairy tales. Since Zipes' and other authors' groundbreaking work, many other writers have produced children's literature that avoids stereotypes about gender, sexual orientation, race/ethnicity, ability, and so forth, contributing to a trend that gives parents and schoolteachers many more options.

Gender in Children's Books

Gender bias in children's literature emerges primarily in three ways: (1) the number of depictions of and references to men versus women, (2) representation by female versus male authors, and (3) stereotypical role portrayals of characters (Diekman & Murnen, 2004; Harmon, 2000; Segal & Podoshen, 2013; Sunderland, 2012). Research shows that when children use gender-balanced readers in their schooling, they view various activities as being appropriate for all people (Friedman, 2008; Karniol & Gal-Disegni, 2009). Conversely, when children use gender-stereotyped readers—readers depicting sex-segregated activities (e.g., sports for boys, homemaking activities for girls)—children tend to develop narrow sex-typed attitudes.

Male characters, figures, pictures, and references to male authors still greatly outnumber those of females in children's books (McCabe, Fairchild, Grauerholz, Pescosolido, & Tope, 2011; Nilges & Spencer, 2002; Simonds & Cooper, 2001; Taboas-Pais & Rey-Cao, 2012). In many elementary schools, it's common for only one or two books in an entire series to contain stories about females. History books—from elementary to college levels—are notorious for focusing on men's history, with a "nod" for women's historical contributions contained in an appendix, occasional in-chapter boxed feature, or tokenized "great women in history" chapter.

In *Packaging Boyhood: Saving Our Sons from Superheroes, Slackers, and Other Media Stereotypes*, Lamb, Brown, and Tappan (2009) discuss revelations from interviewing over 600 boys and provide specific suggestions about how labels limit boys' understanding of self and create sex-based expectations. Lamb and Brown (2006) also wrote *Packaging Girlhood: Rescuing Our Daughters from Marketers' Schemes*, in which they analyzed media stereotypes bombarding today's girls. In her research on Caldecott Award-winning children's books, communication scholar Pamela Cooper (1991) found that between the years of 1967 and 1987 (strong decades for women's liberation), a mere fourteen of ninety-seven books depicted female characters who worked outside the home. A more recent study of 200 popular children's books found the same trend of underrepresentation of female characters (Hamilton, Anderson, Broaddus, & Young, 2006).

"Teaching Kids about Social Realities: Expanding Kids' Lit"

Even today, in an era of increasing openness about and awareness of gender diversity, the reading material children are exposed to in school tends to be a hot button issue, especially surrounding depictions of gay, lesbian, bisexual, and transgender individuals. Most people believe that parents should be primarily responsible for teaching children about such social realities as sexual identity, but what if parents aren't holding up their end of the deal? Should students learn some basic facts in school about "Dick and Jim" or "Doris and Jane," not just "Dick and Jane"?

Books continue to be published to help children understand family diversity, including when a child has parents of the same sex. Popular titles include *Mommy, Mama, and Me* (Newman & Thompson, 2009) and its counterpart *Daddy, Papa, and Me* (Newman, 2009); and *A Tale of Two Daddies* (Oelschlager, 2010). Current books that help children and families understand gender identity include *I Am Jazz* (Herthel & Jennings, 2014), featuring co-writer Jazz Jennings, sometimes described as a spokesperson for transkids; *Be Who You Are* (Carr, 2010); and *Jacob's New Dress* (Hoffman & Hoffman, 2014).

Children's books such as these that depict or attempt to explain adult situations are often deemed too controversial for adoption by a school district. What's your opinion? Should the decision to expose children to such reading material and enlighten them on forms of diversity in American culture best be made by schools or left to parents' discretion?

Net Notes

Have you heard about Emily the Strange? If you have young female siblings or your own daughters, you probably know about this female character popular among teenage girls. Emily is a pop cultural icon invented on the Internet, but she is much more—a voice for individualism and self-awareness, and an alter ego for many girls. Check out Emily the Strange at **www.emilystrange.com.**

Despite these trends (or perhaps in response to them) alternative reading materials continue to be produced to widen the range of experience for children (Orenstein, 2006). Author Michelle Humphrey (2005) identified over 500 titles related to the story *Peter Pan*, explaining that many female authors over the past decade have revisited the story, generating nonracist, nonsexist versions that offer a wider range of roles and accomplishments for female and nonwhite characters.

EDUCATIONAL EXPECTATIONS AND GENDER BIAS IN THE CLASSROOM

No one begins an education with a clean slate; teachers and students come to the educational setting with their own sets of beliefs, values, and opinions, and with imprints of their experiences, some of which are related to gender. When we allow these imprints to lead us to rigid expectations about the aptitude and appropriate behavior of the sexes, bias may be the result.

Expectations about Academic Achievement: The Early Years

Current thinking is that girls and boys don't have differing learning potential. Given effective instruction, equal opportunities to acquire quality education, unbiased expectations from teachers, parents, and administrators, and encouragement free from sex and gender stereotypes, boys and girls can achieve extraordinary things.

For several decades, research has explored the academic achievement of school girls and boys, from elementary through secondary grades (American Association of University Women, AAUW, 1998; Brophy, 1983; Cooper & Good, 1983; Warrington & Younger, 2000). (The AAUW is a long-standing organization of national repute, whose research on trends in education are widely cited.) Studies continue to examine sex differences

Girls and boys have the same learning potential, though old stereotypes have influenced their academic achievement.

and achievement, especially in STEM subjects (i.e., science, technology, engineering, and mathematics). Due to the efforts of educators, parents, governmental entities, educational agencies, and nonprofit groups (like the AAUW), gender gaps are narrowing in terms of girls' and boys' interest and abilities in STEM subjects (Brazile, 2014; Corbett, Hill, & St. Rose, 2008; Mortenson, 2008). However, girls' interest in STEM subjects doesn't translate into these fields being selected as majors in college nor as careers (Hill, Corbett, & St. Rose, 2010; Lindberg, 2012).

Social and environmental factors help explain the gap; remnants of stereotypes about "brainy girls" and views that girls aren't capable of achieving in "hard subjects" contribute to the problem. Girls tend to assess their own mathematical abilities lower than boys do, so self-belief plays a role. When parents and educators tell girls that their intelligence will expand as they learn, girls improve their achievement on tests, plus they say they're more likely to pursue STEM subjects at higher levels of education and as career fields (Hill et al., 2010; Schilling, 2013). So part of the challenge is to let girls know they're capable, they can achieve, and their achievement will pay off in future endeavors, in order to sustain their interest in STEM areas.

Beyond the STEM issue, another gap has emerged, both here in the U.S. and internationally: Boys lag behind girls in reading ability (Brown, 2015; Loveless, 2015). School reading material tends to appeal more to girls, regardless of subject matter, whereas boys must already be interested in the subject matter to be motivated to read (*NBC Nightly News*, 2010).

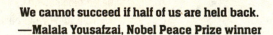

We cannot succeed if half of us are held back.
—Malala Yousafzai, Nobel Peace Prize winner

© JStone/Shutterstock.com

Expectations about Academic Achievement: The College Years

Ever sit in a classroom and feel like the teacher had formed an expectation about you before you even had a chance to open your mouth? Did you sense in high school, for example, that a teacher had labeled you a "jock," "bad girl," or "nerd" and then acted toward you based on that label? Did you ever feel that a professor thought you were a C student in a college course and that, no matter how hard you tried or what you said or did, you were going to get a C in that class? These things point to the impact of expectations on achievement and enjoyment in a classroom setting, and, once again, sex plays a role. Unfortunately, some faculty bring their expectations and biases about sex and gender into their college classrooms, and students may pay the price (Moss-Racusin, Dovidio, Brescoll, Graham, & Handelsman, 2012; Steele, James, & Barnett, 2002).

On the other side of the equation, student expectations and biases about sex and gender also play a role in the classroom (Cain Miller, 2015; Powell, 2015). Research results are mixed: For many years, male professors were perceived more positively than female professors on competence, knowledge of subject matter, educational achievement, credibility, organizational skills, level of enthusiasm, and overall effectiveness in the classroom (Arbuckle & Williams, 2003; Basow, 1998, 2000; Centra & Gaubatz, 2000; Feldman, 1992; Freeman, 1994; Hargett, 1999; Miller & Chamberlin, 2000). One study of online instruction revealed bias, in that students gave instructors of online courses higher evaluations if they believed the profs were male (MacNell, Driscoll, & Hunt, 2014).

However, other studies have found a bias in favor of female professors, both in general and on specific aspects of teaching effectiveness (Costa, Terracciano, & McCrae, 2001; Feldman, 1993). One group of researchers examined several instructional dimensions, including instructors' involvement in the teaching–learning process, student interest, classroom interaction, course demands, and organizational skills (Smith, Yoo, Farr, Salmon, & Miller, 2007). On all five dimensions, male and female students alike rated female instructors significantly higher than male instructors.

GENDER COMMUNICATION AND THE COLLEGE CLASSROOM

Through the 1950s, '60s, and '70s, men and women had very different educational opportunities at the college level in the U.S. Certain fields (for example, engineering and accounting) were completely male domains. Women were guided to elementary school teaching, nursing, and home economics. A standard joke of the time (and you still hear it some today) was that women came to college to get their "MRS" [Mrs.] degree.

How much has changed since that time? While some advances have been made, gender bias in universities still exists. For example, how many contributions by women in history are you likely to study in the typical American history course, in comparison to men's contributions? Is this because of sheer numbers, as in

Feminists understand that equality for women and girls will be sustained when government makes progressive education a national agenda. As we study and learn together we create community. Making literacy and democratic education available to everyone is the necessary foundation for responsible citizenship. Without education, diverse populations cannot communicate across boundaries.
— bell hooks, author

the assumption that there were more key men in history than women, so it's appropriate for men to be studied more than women? Were there *really* more key male figures in history than female? Perhaps the numbers stem from the fact that women in American history weren't allowed to vote, hold office, or make many political or business decisions, so their accomplishments get overlooked. Many times students aren't aware of women's contributions until they take a women's history course, which can feel like a token gesture that assumes all other history courses are men's history courses.

Female college students may not be banned from the doors of classrooms, but sex and gender bias exists nonetheless. One form of bias you might not think of surrounds students' contributions to discussion in a classroom. In the ideal college classroom, male and female students participate with about the same frequency, ask a similar number and similar types of questions, and actively engage in their own learning. While progress has been made, research over four decades indicates that student participation continues to be far from a gendered ideal.

Research in the 1970s found that men dominated class discussions (Karp & Yoels, 1977; Rich, 1979; Sternglanz & Lyberger-Ficek, 1977; Thorne, 1979). In the 1980s most classrooms favored a male approach to learning

Student participation in college classrooms still tends to be male dominated.

© Lisa F. Young/Shutterstock.com

and devalued or disconfirmed a female approach (Belenky, Clinchy, Goldberger, & Tarule, 1986; Brooks, 1982; Brophy, 1985; Gilligan, 1982; Krupnick, 1985; Treichler & Kramarae, 1983). Studies showed that male students behaved as follows, compared to female students:

- Initiated more interactions with teachers

- Talked more, talked for longer periods of time, and took more turns at speaking

- Exerted more control over the topic of discussion

- Interrupted professors and other students (especially female classmates) significantly more often, particularly in female-taught classes

- Used interruptions to introduce trivial or inappropriately personal comments—a tactic designed to bring women's discussion to an end or to change its focus

- Were more likely to control such nonverbal aspects as physical space in a classroom.

These sex differences in communication style contributed to what researchers at the time called a "chilly climate" for women on college campuses (Hall & Sandler, 1982, 1984; Sandler & Hall, 1986; Sandler, Silverberg, & Hall, 1996).

Studies in the 1990s reaffirmed the presence of the chilly climate on college campuses. A tradition of male dominance in the classroom persisted (Bowker & Regan Dunkin, 1992; Wood & Lenze, 1991). In one study, a majority of college faculty agreed that male students interrupted more frequently, assumed leadership roles more frequently, were less likely to seek outside help, and were less open to constructive criticism than female students (Condravy, Skirboll, & Taylor, 1998). However, fewer male dominance behaviors were detected than in earlier chilly climate studies, according to researchers Kopp and Farr (1999), who found that female students had begun to perceive themselves as emerging leaders in classrooms.

So what's the story in this new century? Although the chill in college classrooms may not be as blatant as it was in past generations, studies still show evidence of male dominance in college classroom communication. Research focuses on how dominance manifests itself in classrooms, with more emphasis on context and other contributing variables, like ethnicity, age, political interest, major field, and so forth (Allan, 2002; Allan & Madden, 2006; Greene & Stockard, 2010; Kramer, 2005; Morris & Daniel, 2008; O'Connor & Yanus, 2009; Salter, 2003; Schulze & Tomal, 2006; Wasburn, 2004).

Research has also focused on teacher behaviors that contribute to the chill. Instructor communication in such forms as sexist language usage, calling more on male than female students, interrupting female students, encouraging and coaching male students to get correct answers to questions, and responding more extensively to male student questions and comments have been documented in studies (Sadker & Zittleman, 2007; Simonds & Cooper, 2001).

One profile of classes doesn't fit the male-domination pattern at all—communication courses for majors. In many communication departments in colleges and universities across the country, women outnumber men as communication majors. Perhaps the old "safety in numbers" adage comes into play. Female students tend to speak up faster than male students and generally contribute more in both quantity and quality. Granted, communication majors are a different breed, in that most enjoy communicating and thus are highly interactive in the classroom. Is the interaction pattern in your communication courses different than that of other classes? Is the behavior of communication students so female dominant that we might conclude we now have a "chilly climate" for men in communication education?

SEXUAL HARASSMENT IN THE HALLOWED HALLS

In Chapter 9, we explored the problem of sexual harassment in the workplace, in particular the most complicated aspect of the Equal Employment Opportunity Commission's (EEOC) sexual harassment guidelines, the *hostile climate* clause. Many academic institutions have adapted the EEOC definition to reflect their unique concerns, the *hostile learning climate*. In this chapter, we examine two forms of sexual harassment occurring in academic institutions, from grade school through college.

Peer Sexual Harassment: Classmates Will Be Classmates?

Sexual harassment takes several forms, but the form most often documented in research involves a male harasser and a female target in a *status-differentiated relationship*, such as boss–employee, doctor–patient, or professor–student (Atvgis, Rancer, & Liberman, 2012; Buzzanell, 2004; Lane, 2006). However, harassment is more prevalent among peers than status-differentiated relationships (Conroy, 2013; Eckes, 2006; Harrington, 2004; Ormerod, Collinsworth, & Perry, 2008; Wernick, Kulik, & Inglehart, 2014). As we mentioned in Chapter 9, sexual harassment is about power, not about sex. But now we need to expand our view of power beyond thinking only about what a boss might do to an employee. Sexual harassment between people of equal status, such as coworkers, classmates, and social acquaintances, has been termed *peer sexual harassment.* In most cases, no clear power lines exist in these relationships.

Learning environments are greatly affected by peer relationships, possibly more so than relationships with teachers. The treatment you receive from your classmates directly contributes to the creation of a hostile or nonhostile learning climate (Ivy & Hamlet, 1996; Kosciw, Greytak, & Diaz, 2009; Lundy-Wagner & Winkle-Wagner, 2013). Hostile climate harassment can be even more of a problem for students who identify as LGBT (McKinley, Luo, Wright, & Kraus, 2015).

The roots of sexually harassing behavior can be found within our earliest contexts of education; unfortunately, "bad behavior" among preschoolers or kindergartners, left unchecked, can morph into harassment (sexual and otherwise, like bullying) in elementary, middle, and high school years. It's beyond the scope of this chapter to explore the decades of research on sexual harassment in schools, but here's an optimistic note: While peer sexual harassment (and other forms of sexual harassment) is still a problem in schools, more school systems, educators, administrators, students, school boards, and communities are educated about sexual harassment now than before. People are talking about how sexual harassment occurs, the laws on the books, how to develop and enforce policies, procedures for reporting, and resources to help targets, families, and personnel (Eckes, 2006; Graves & Onyeka-Crawford, 2015; Hill, 2011; Rahimi & Liston, 2011; Sandler, 2005; Smith & Gomez, 2014; Strauss, 2013a). These are positive developments, but much more work remains.

What we are learning about harassment requires recognizing this beast when we encounter it. We are learning that simply having laws against harassment on the books is not enough. The law, as it was conceived, was to provide a shield of protection for us. Yet that shield is failing us. The law needs to be more responsive to the reality of our experiences.

— Anita Hill, author and law professor

Net Notes

For sexual harassment occurring in educational settings, **www2.ed.gov**, a website from the U.S. Department of Education and Office of Civil Rights, offers information about sexual harassment that occurs at all educational levels—from elementary to university. The site explains Title IX protections, overviews current laws governing academic harassment, and provides answers to frequently asked questions about harassment.

Sexual harassment is still a problem on college campuses, despite Title IX protections and increased scrutiny on the behavior (Kattner, 2015; Smith & Gomez, 2014). The AAUW examined sexual harassment at the college level using a national sample of diverse male and female college students (American Association of University Women, 2006). Researchers found evidence of harassment on college campuses, with 62 percent of participants in the study reporting being harassed in some form. Harassing behaviors included being forced into a form of unwanted physical or sexual contact, being the target of a sexual rumor, being spied on, receiving unwanted sexual gestures and other nonverbal cues, being called gay or other homophobic terms, and being the object of sexual jokes and comments. The problem is even more pronounced at the nation's military and naval academies ("Hostile Environment," 2005; RAND Military Workplace Study, 2014). The rates of reported peer sexual harassment are dramatically high, but that's just the reported cases. The *actual* rate of occurrence is likely to be significantly higher.

Classrooms aren't exempt locales when it comes to peer sexual harassment. No simple solutions exist, except maybe for one: Treat classmates and coworkers—your peers—as individuals worthy of respect. Keep personal and sexual verbal and nonverbal communication out of your interactions. Beyond advice to the individual, we offer some suggestions for universities. First, naiveté or denial of the problem, reflected in statements such as "This doesn't happen in my classes," makes students and teachers part of the problem. Even the most well-organized, professionally run, and academically scintillating class contains students who've grown up in a society that socializes them in some negative ways. Even in this day and age some students don't know what harassment is and that their behavior might be construed as harassing.

Colleges and universities, for the most part, have become much more aware of the detrimental effect and legal liability associated with sexual harassment. They've instituted policies and procedures for reporting and responding to claims of sexual harassment, and many conduct educational programs for faculty and other campus personnel (June, 2009; Kattner, 2015; Smith & Gomez, 2014). Programs sponsored by such campus organizations as women's centers and offices of student activities, and classes like first-year seminars (how-to-survive-college type of classes) are working to educate students about sexual harassment. But a word of caution is appropriate: Just like public schools, many, if not most, university policies and programs are more attuned to harassment in status-differentiated relationships than among peers. It's important to develop programs that take a comprehensive approach to the problem.

After reading this material, you may want to do your own "campus inventory" by taking the following steps:

1. Note whether your professors include a sexual harassment policy statement in their course syllabi. Do they create and foster a classroom climate of mutual respect, one that allows for safe reporting of harassment should it occur?
2. Locate and read over your institution's sexual harassment policy. Does it contain any provisions for peer harassment? If a student is harassed by another student, whom can she or he go to for comfort and advice? Is there a procedure for reporting peer sexual harassment?
3. Inventory what entities and individuals exist on your campus to help someone who experiences sexual harassment, like a counseling center, housing officials or RAs (resident advisors) who are often regularly trained in these issues, or an ombudsperson (a knowledgeable person in a neutral position who serves as a campus resource on a whole host of issues and concerns).
4. Find out if your college mandates sexual harassment awareness training for students, faculty, staff, and administrators. If no such formalized training is available, are there outlets for informal training, such as workshops sponsored by student affairs staff?

If you find your campus lacking in awareness of the peer sexual harassment issue, that may signal it's time for you to get involved and find an avenue for volunteering your considerable knowledge on this topic.

Paying It Upward: When Students Harass Faculty

We've said in this chapter and elsewhere in this book that sexual harassment is about power, not sex. Typically, "power plays" occur when people of higher status or greater resources behave in ways that make others feel powerless or less dominant. But, as we've learned from the last section of material, power plays can be extended from peer-to-peer too. A third form of sexual harassment exists—less understood, underresearched, and occurring with less frequency than other forms, yet it can be devastating to targets.

This third form is termed *contrapower sexual harassment*, first identified by Katherine Benson in 1984. It refers to those instances in which a person of lesser status or power harasses a person of higher status or power within an organization (Holland & Cortina, 2016; Strauss, 2013b). In educational settings, contrapower sexual harassment has been studied primarily as behavior enacted by college students toward faculty, but it also occurs between other people of different statuses or power positions, such as staff members toward bosses, administrators, or faculty; students toward staff; and so forth (Attwood, 2009; Mohipp & Senn, 2008).

A few studies have been conducted on this problem, one of the earliest being a study of female faculty at Purdue University in the 1980s (Grauerholz, 1989). In this research, nearly half the faculty women participating reported experiencing at least one situation that could be considered sexual harassment from a student; most behaviors took the form of sexual or sexist comments, undue sexual attention, or suggestive nonverbal cues. In a later study conducted by DeSouza and Fansler (2003), more than half the faculty respondents (male and female) described at least one student behavior in the past two years that they deemed sexually harassing. Other studies examined sex differences and student-to-faculty sexual harassment, finding mixed results. Matchen and DeSouza (2000) as well as Lampman, Phelps, Bancroft, and Beneke (2009) found that female faculty were more upset by unwanted sexual attention from students and more likely to report harassment than male faculty. However, in other studies, male faculty were targets of student harassment as much as female faculty, revealing that they'd received such behaviors as uninvited sexual comments, suggestive or invasive nonverbal cues (e.g., staring, suggestive looks, inappropriate touch, intrusions into personal space), requests for dates, offers of sexual favors, sexual propositions, and physical advances (Carroll & Ellis, 1989; McKinney, 1990). Contrapower harassment can also be conveyed through technology—recall our discussion in Chapter 9 on *cyber harassment*. Unwanted, unwelcome sexualized e-mail or text messages, images ("sexting"), and posts on social media can now be viewed as forms of sexual harassing communication (Behm-Morawitz & Schipper, 2015; Halder & Jaishankar, 2011; Ritter, 2014).

As we've explained and documented in this book, remember that men and women often view sexual behaviors and sexual harassment differently—sometimes *quite* differently. Some behaviors that women deem uncomfortable or threatening may be viewed by men as harmless flirtation, flattery, or friendly banter. In the educational setting, female faculty may experience student behavior that they perceive as unwanted, hostile, sexist, or aggressive, but male faculty aren't necessarily upset by that same behavior, nor do they find it harassing.

Power and status aren't the same thing. A person may hold lesser status along formally recognized lines, but may feel emboldened or hostile enough to enact a power play to make a higher-status person feel embarrassed or uncomfortable, to attempt to "level the playing field" in some way, so as to make themselves seem more dominant or in control. Much as we'd all like to believe that our hallowed halls are somehow exempt from such injustice, that's simply not the reality in a lot of places. Now that you have a better understanding of this form of sexual harassment, maybe it's time to think back to any classroom experiences you've had where a student harassed a teacher—maybe at the time you just didn't know what to call it. Contrapower sexual harassment is real and just as illegal as other forms of sexual harassment; it can be proven and is actionable legally.

Remember...

Hostile Climate Sexual Harassment: Sexual conduct that has the intention or effect of interfering with an individual's work performance or creating an intimidating or offensive working environment

Hostile Learning Climate: Sexual conduct that has the intention or effect of interfering with an individual's learning or creating an intimidating or offensive learning environment

Status-Differentiated Relationship: Relationship in which the lines of status are clearly drawn; one person holds higher status than the other

Peer Sexual Harassment: Sexual harassment between persons of equal status, such as coworkers, classmates, and social acquaintances

Contrapower Sexual Harassment: Harassment directed from someone of lower status to someone of higher status

Cyber Harassment: Sexual harassment that occurs in virtual reality, through such channels as text messages, e-mail, chat rooms, instant messaging, and social media

CONCLUSION

This wraps up this final part of the text on gender communication in specific kinds of relationships and certain contexts. Intuitively, you know that the exact same thing said among family members will be taken differently by a friend, a romantic partner, a classmate, or a coworker. But intuition or what some people like to call common sense isn't common to everyone, as Benjamin Franklin once said. Some people don't realize the power of context to affect a message. We expect that, after reading these chapters, you won't be among these people. We expect that the last several pages of this text have reinforced the importance of context in gender communication.

Learning all you can about communication in educational settings, as well as about how gender communication operates in other contexts and in various types of relationships, will enhance your communication skills. Practicing what you've learned, talking with people about what you know, making mistakes but being wise enough to stare down those mistakes, learn from them, and avoid repeating them—all of these activities come highly recommended! Becoming an effective communicator in a world complicated by gender is an incredible challenge. We think you're up to it.

DISCUSSION STARTERS

1. Think about your favorite children's fairy tale, maybe a Disney or Dr. Seuss story a parent read to you when you were young. Analyze the main characters. Is a female main character the center of the story? How would you describe her character, both physically and in personality? Does her character represent a feminine stereotype? How would you describe the main male character in the story? Is he stereotypically drawn? What interpretations did you make of the story as a child? Do you have different interpretations now, as an adult?

2. This chapter discussed some of the effects of teacher expectations on students' learning and academic achievement. Can you think of a time, either in school or college, when you became acutely aware that one of your teachers held certain expectations of you? Were the expectations positive or negative, such as an instructor expecting you to excel or to fail? Were the expectations in any way related to your sex? How did the realization that those expectations were operating make you feel and affect your learning?

3. Think about the problem of peer sexual harassment on your home campus. Have you encountered any harassing experiences in college classrooms or at social events? Do you know people who believe they've been sexually harassed by a peer? Have friends told you of experiences with sexual harassment, but been reluctant to attach the label to the behavior? Knowing what you now know about the problem, will you respond to peer sexual harassment—either directed at you or at a friend—any differently?

References

Allan, E. J. (2002). Classroom climates in post-secondary education. In M. A. Aleman & K. A. Renn (Eds.), *Women in higher education: An encyclopedia* (pp. 282–287). Santa Barbara, CA: ABC-CLIO.

Allan, E. J., & Madden, M. (2006). Chilly classrooms for female undergraduate students: A question of method? *Journal of Higher Education, 77*, 684–711.

American Association of University Women. (1998). *Separated by sex: A critical look at single-sex education for girls.* Washington, DC: AAUW Educational Foundation.

American Association of University Women. (2006). *Drawing the line: Sexual harassment on campus.* Washington, DC: Author.

Arbuckle, J., & Williams, B. D. (2003). Students' perceptions of expressiveness: Age and gender effects on teacher evaluations. *Sex Roles, 49,* 507–516.

Asher-Perrin, E. (2015, January 5). *Tangled, Brave,* and *Frozen* all made the same critical mistake. Retrieved August 19, 2015, from <www.tor.com>.

Attwood, R. (2009, June 18–24). Lecturers talk of students' "shocking" abuse. *Times Higher Education,* pp. 10–11.

Avtgis, T. A., Rancer, A. S., & Liberman, C. J. (2012). *Organizational communication: Strategies for success* (2nd ed.). Dubuque, IA: Kendall Hunt.

Baker-Sperry, L., & Grauerholz, I. (2003). The pervasiveness and persistence of the feminine beauty ideal in children's fairy tales. *Gender and Society, 17,* 711–726.

Basow, S. A. (1998). Student evaluations: The role of gender bias and teaching styles. In L. H. Collins, J. C. Chrisler, & K. Quina (Eds.), *Arming Athena: Career strategies for women in academe* (pp. 135–156). Thousand Oaks, CA: Sage.

Basow, S. A. (2000). Best and worst professors: Gender patterns in students' choices. *Sex Roles, 43,* 407–417.

Behm-Morawitz, E., & Schipper, S. (2015). Sexing the avatar: Gender, sexualization, and cyber-harassment in a virtual world. *Journal of Media Psychology.* dx.doi.org:10.1027/1864-1105/a000152.

Belenky, M., Clinchy, B., Goldberger, N., & Tarule, J. (1986). *Women's ways of knowing.* New York: Basic.

Benson, K. (1984). Comment on Crocker's "An analysis of university definitions of sexual harassment." *Signs, 9,* 516–519.

Bottigheimer, R. B. (1986). Silenced women in the Grimms' tales: The "fit" between fairy tales and society in their historical context. In R. B. Bottigheimer (Ed.), *Fairy tales and society: Illusion, allusion, and paradigm* (pp. 115–132). Philadelphia: University of Pennsylvania Press.

Bowker, J. K., & Regan Dunkin, P. (1992). Enacting feminism in the teaching of communication. In L. A. M. Perry, L. H. Turner, & H. M. Sterk (Eds.), *Constructing and reconstructing gender: The links among communication, language, and gender* (pp. 261–268). Albany: State University of New York Press.

Brazile, D. (2014, Summer). Ticket out of poverty: Education is a girl's best chance for life success. *Ms., 63.*

Brooks, V. (1982). Sex differences in student dominance behavior in female and male professors' classrooms. *Sex Roles, 8,* 683–690.

Brophy, J. E. (1983). Research on the self-fulfilling prophecy and teacher expectations. *Journal of Educational Psychology, 75,* 631–661.

Brophy, J. E. (1985). Interactions of male and female students with male and female teachers. In L. C. Wilkinson & C. B. Marrett (Eds.), *Gender influence in classroom interaction* (pp. 115–142). Orlando, FL: Academic.

Brown, E. (2015, March 5). International exams show persistent achievement gaps between boys and girls. Retrieved August 20, 2015, from <www.washingtonpost.com>.

Brule, N. L. (2008). "*Sleeping Beauty* gets a makeover": Using the retelling of fairytales to create an awareness of hegemonic norms and the social construction of value. *Communication Teacher, 22,* 71–75.

Buzzanell, P. M. (2004). Revisiting sexual harassment in academe. In P. M. Buzzanell, H. M. Sterk, & L. H. Turner (Eds.), *Gender in applied communication contexts* (pp. 25–46). Thousand Oaks, CA: Sage.

Cain Miller, C. (2015, February 6). Is the professor bossy or brilliant? Much depends on gender. Retrieved May 2, 2015, from <www.nytimes.com>.

Carr, J. (2010). *Be who you are.* Bloomington, IL: AuthorHouse.

Carroll, L., & Ellis, K. (1989). Faculty attitudes toward sexual harassment: Survey results, survey process. *Initiatives, 52,* 35–41.

Centra, J. A., & Gaubatz, N. B. (2000). Is there gender bias in student evaluations of teaching? *Journal of Higher Education, 71,* 17.

Condravy, J., Skirboll, E., & Taylor, R. (1998). Faculty perceptions of classroom gender dynamics. *Women & Language, 21,* 18–27.

Conroy, N. E. (2013). Rethinking adolescent peer sexual harassment: Contributions of feminist theory. *Journal of School Violence, 12,* 340–356.

Cooper, P. J. (1991). *Women and power in the Caldecott and Newbery Winners.* Paper presented at the meeting of the Central States Communication Association, Chicago, IL.

Cooper, H., & Good, T. (1983). *Pygmalion grows up: Studies in the expectation communication process.* New York: Longman.

Corbett, C., Hill, C., & St. Rose, A. (2008). *Where the girls are: The facts about gender equity in education.* Washington, DC: American Association of University Women.

Costa, P., Jr., Terracciano, A., & McCrae, R. R. (2001). Gender differences in personality traits across cultures: Robust and surprising findings. *Journal of Personality and Cognition, 81,* 322–331.

DeSouza, E., & Fansler, A. G. (2003). Contrapower sexual harassment: A survey of students and faculty members. *Sex Roles, 48*, 529–542.

Diekman, A. B., & Murnen, S. K. (2004). Learning to be little women and little men: The inequitable gender equality of nonsexist children's literature. *Sex Roles, 50*, 373–386.

Dundes, L. (2001). Disney's modern heroine Pocahontas: Revealing age-old gender stereotypes and role discontinuity under a facade of liberation. *The Social Sciences Journal, 38*, 353–365.

Eckes, S. (2006). Reducing peer sexual harassment in schools. *The Educational Digest, 71*, 36–40.

Feldman, K. A. (1992). College students' views of male and female college teachers: Part I. Evidence from the social laboratory and experiments. *Research in Higher Education, 33*, 317–375.

Feldman, K. A. (1993). College students' views of male and female college teachers: Part II. Evidence from students' evaluations of their classroom teachers. *Research in Higher Education, 34*, 151–191.

Freeman, H. (1994). Student evaluations of college instructors: Effects of type of course taught, instructor gender and gender role, and student gender. *Journal of Educational Psychology, 86*, 627–630.

Friedman, E. G. (2008, Fall). Out-of-the-box education. *Ms.*, 59.

Gillam, K., & Wooden, S. R. (2008). Post-princess models of gender: The new man in Disney/Pixar. *Journal of Popular Film and Television, 36*, 2–8.

Gilligan, C. (1982). *In a different voice*. Cambridge: Harvard University Press.

Grauerholz, E. (1989). Sexual harassment of women professors by students: Exploring the dynamics of power, authority, and gender in a university setting. *Sex Roles, 21*, 789–801.

Graves, F. G., & Onyeka-Crawford, A. (2015). Restoring students' protections against sexual harassment in schools. *Human Rights, 41*, 20–25.

Greene, J., & Stockard, J. (2010). Is the academic climate chilly? The views of women academic chemists. *Journal of Chemical Education, 87*, 381–385.

Halder, D., & Jaishankar, K. (2011). Cyber gender harassment and secondary victimization: A comparative analysis of the United States, the UK, and India. *Victims & Offenders, 6*, 386–398.

Hall, R., & Sandler, B. (1982). *The classroom climate: A chilly one for women?* Washington, DC: Project on the Status and Education of Women, Association of American Colleges.

Hall, R. M., & Sandler, B. R. (1984). *Out of the classroom: A chilly campus climate for women?* Washington, DC: Project on the Status and Education of Women, Association of American Colleges.

Hamilton, M. C., Anderson, D., Broaddus, M., & Young, K. (2006). Gender stereotyping and under-representation of female characters in 200 popular children's picture books: A twenty-first century update. *Sex Roles, 55*, 557–565.

Hargett, J. (1999). Students' perceptions of male and female instructors' level of immediacy and teacher credibility. *Women & Language, 22*, 46.

Harmon, M. R. (2000). Gender/language subtexts as found in literature anthologies: Mixed messages, stereotypes, silence, erasure. In M. J. Hardman & A. Taylor (Eds.), *Hearing many voices* (pp. 75–85). Cresskill, NJ: Hampton.

Harrington, L. (2004). Peer sexual harassment: Protect your students and yourself. *The Delta Kappa Gamma Bulletin, 71*, 31–35.

Henneberg, S. (2010). Moms do badly, but grandmas do worse: The nexus of sexism and ageism in children's classics. *Journal of Aging Studies, 24*, 125–134.

Herthel, J., & Jennings, J. (2014). *I am Jazz.* New York: Dial Books.

Hill, C. (2011). *Crossing the line: Sexual harassment in school.* Washington, DC: American Association of University Women.

Hill, C., Corbett, C., & St. Rose, A. (2010). *Why so few? Women in science, technology, engineering, and mathematics: Executive summary.* Washington, DC: American Association of University Women.

Hoffman, S., & Hoffman, I. (2014). *Jacob's new dress.* Park Ridge, IL: Albert Whitman and Co.

Holland, K. J., & Cortina, M. (2016). Sexual harassment: Undermining the wellbeing of working women. In M. L. Connerly & J. Wu (Eds.), *Handbook on well-being of working women* (pp. 83–102). New York: Springer.

"Hostile environment" is found at academies. (2005, September 9). *The Chronicle of Higher Education,* p. A36.

Humphrey, M. (2005, Fall). Outside Neverland: Female writers reinvent *Peter Pan. Bitch,* 76–81.

Ivy, D. K., & Hamlet, S. (1996). College students and sexual dynamics: Two studies of peer sexual harassment. *Communication Education, 45*, 149–166.

June, A. W. (2009, February 20). Online programs to stop sexual harassment: Easy to use but not always enough. *The Chronicle of Higher Education,* pp. A10, A13.

Karniol, R. R., & Gal-Disegni, M. (2009). The impact of gender-fair versus gender-stereotyped basal readers on 1st-grade children's gender stereotypes: A natural experiment. *Journal of Research in Childhood Education, 23*, 411–420.

Karp, D. A., & Yoels, W. C. (1977). The college classroom: Some observations on the meanings of student participation. *Sociology & Social Research, 60*, 421–439.

Kattner, T. (2015). What to include in student Title IX training on sexual harassment. *Recruitment & Retention in Higher Education, 29*, 2–8.

Kopp, L. K., & Farr, T. (1999, October 15). *Is the chilly classroom climate still a factor for women as we close the 20th century?* Paper presented at the meeting of the Organization for the Study of Communication, Language, and Gender, Wichita, KS.

Kosciw, J. G., Greytak, E. A., & Diaz, E. M. (2009). Who, what, where, when, and why: Demographic and ecological factors contributing to hostile school climate for lesbian, gay, bisexual, and transgender youth. *Journal of Youth and Adolescence, 38*, 976–988.

Kramer, L. (2005). *The sociology of gender: A brief introduction* (2nd ed.). Los Angeles: Roxbury.

Krupnick, C. (1985). Women and men in the classroom: Inequality and its remedies. *Teaching & Learning: Journal of the Harvard Danforth Center, 1*, 18–25.

Lamb, S., & Brown, L. M. (2006). *Packaging girlhood: Rescuing our daughters from marketers' schemes.* New York: St. Martin's Press.

Lamb, S., Brown, L. M., & Tappan, M. (2009). *Packaging boyhood: Saving our sons from superheroes, slackers, and other media stereotypes.* New York: St. Martin's Press.

Lampman, C., Phelps, A., Bancroft, S., & Beneke, M. (2009). Contrapower harassment in academia: A survey of faculty experience with student incivility, bullying, and sexual attention. *Sex Roles, 60*, 331–346.

Lane, A. J. (2006, May 5). Gender, power, and sexuality: First, do no harm. *The Chronicle of Higher Education*, pp. B10, B13.

Larche, D. (1985). *Father Gander.* New York: Methuen.

Larche, D. (1990). *Father Gander's nursery rhymes for the nineteen nineties: The alternative Mother Goose.* Cambridge, UK: Oleander.

Lindberg, M. (2012, June 22). Title IX is about STEM too. Retrieved August 20, 2015, from <aauw.org>.

Loveless, T. (2015, March 24). Girls, boys, and reading: Part I of the 2015 Brown Center Report on American Education: How well are American students learning? Retrieved August 20, 2015, from <www.brookings.edu>.

Lundy-Wagner, V., & Winkle-Wagner, R. (2013). A harassing climate? Sexual harassment and campus racial climate research. *Journal of Diversity in Higher Education, 6*, 51–68.

MacNell, L., Driscoll, A., & Hunt, A. N. (2014). What's in a name: Exposing gender bias in student ratings of teaching. *Innovative Higher Education.* doi: 10.1007/S10755-014-9313-4.

Matchen, J., & DeSouza, E. (2000). The sexual harassment of faculty members by students. *Sex Roles, 41*, 295–306.

McCabe, J., Fairchild, E., Grauerholz, L., Pescosolido, B. A., & Tope, D. (2011). Gender in twentieth-century children's books: Patterns of disparity in titles and central characters. *Gender & Society, 25*, 197–226.

McKinley, C. J., Luo, Y., Wright, P. J., & Kraus, A. (2015). Reexamining LGBT resources on college counseling center websites: An over-time and cross-country analysis. *Journal of Applied Communication Research, 43*, 112–129.

McKinney, K. (1990). Sexual harassment of university faculty by colleagues and students. *Sex Roles, 23*, 421–438.

Miller, J., & Chamberlin, M. (2000). Women are teachers, men are professors: A study of student perceptions. *Teaching Sociology, 28*, 283–298.

Mitchell, M. B. (2010). Learning about ourselves through fairy tales: Their psychological value. *Psychoanalytical Perspectives, 53*, 264–279.

Mohipp, C., & Senn, C. Y. (2008). Graduate students' perceptions of contrapower sexual harassment. *Journal of Interpersonal Violence, 73*, 1258–1276.

Morris, L. K., & Daniel, L. G. (2008). Perceptions of a chilly climate: Differences in traditional and non-traditional majors for women. *Research in Higher Education, 49*, 256–273.

Mortenson, T. G. (2008, June 6). Where the boys were: Women outnumber them in colleges and the work force, and too many men are failing to keep up. *The Chronicle of Higher Education*, p. A31.

Moss-Racusin, C. A., Dovidio, J. F., Brescoll, V. L., Graham, M. J., & Handelsman, J. (2012). Science faculty's subtle gender biases favor male students. *Proceedings of the National Academy of Sciences, 109*, 16474–16479.

NBC Nightly News. (2010, March 17). Television broadcast.

Newman, L. (2009). *Daddy, papa, and me.* New York: Tricycle Press.

Newman, L., & Thompson, C. (2009). *Mommy, mama, and me.* New York: Tricycle Press.

Nilges, L. M., & Spencer, A. F. (2002). The pictorial representation of gender and physical activity level in Caldecott Medal winning children's literature (1940–1999). *Sports, Education, & Society, 7*, 135–150.

O'Connor, K., & Yanus, A. B. (2009). The chilly climate continues: Defrosting the gender divide in political science and politics. *Journal of Political Science Education, 5,* 108–118.

Oelschlager, V. (2010). *A tale of two daddies.* Akron, OH: Vanita Books.

Orenstein, P. (2006). Shortchanging girls: Gender socialization in schools. In P. J. Dubeck & D. Dunn (Ed.), *Workplace/women's place: An anthology* (3rd ed., pp. 28–36). Los Angeles: Roxbury.

Ormerod, A. J., Collinsworth, L. L., & Perry, L. A. (2008). Critical climate: Relations among sexual harassment, climate, and outcomes for high school girls and boys. *Psychology of Women Quarterly, 32,* 113–125.

Powell, A. (2015, February 16). RateMyProfessors data shows students' gender bias against professors. Retrieved August 21, 2015, from <college.usatoday.com>.

Ragan, K. (Ed.). (2000). *Fearless girls, wise women, and beloved sisters: Heroines in folk tales from around the world.* New York: W. W. Norton & Co.

Rahimi, R., & Liston, D. D. (2011). *Pervasive vulnerabilities: Sexual harassment in school.* New York: Peter Lang.

RAND Military Workplace Study. (2014). Sexual assault and sexual harassment in the U.S. military: Volume 2. Estimates for Department of Defense service members from the 2014 RAND Military Workplace Study. Retrieved August 15, 2015, from <www.rand/org/pubs/research_reports>.

Rich, A. (1979). *On lies, secrets, and silence: Selected prose 1966–1978.* New York: Norton.

Ritter, B. A. (2014). Deviant behavior in computer-mediated communication: Development and validation of a measure of cybersexual harassment. *Journal of Computer-Mediated Communication, 19,* 197–214.

Ruterana, P. C. (2012). Children's reflections on gender equality in fairy tales: A Rwanda case study. *Journal of Pan African Studies, 4,* 85–101.

Sadker, D. M., & Zittleman, K. (2007). Practical strategies for detecting and correcting gender bias in your classroom. In D. M. Sadker & E. S. Silber (Eds.), *Gender in the classroom: Foundations, skills, methods, and strategies across the curriculum* (pp. 259-275), Mahwah, NJ: Erlbaum.

Salter, D. W. (2003). Exploring the "chilly classroom" phenomenon as interactions between psychological and environmental types. *Journal of College Student Development, 44,* 110–121.

Sandler, B. R. (2005). *Student-to-student sexual harassment K–12: Strategies and solutions for educators to use in the classroom, school, and community.* New York: Rowman & Littlefield.

Sandler, B. R., & Hall, R. M. (1986). *The campus climate revisited: Chilly for women faculty, administrators, and graduate students.* Washington, DC: Project on the Status and Education of Women, Association of American Colleges.

Sandler, B. R., Silverberg, L. A., & Hall, R. M. (1996). *The chilly classroom climate: A guide to improve the education of women.* Washington, DC: National Association of Women in Education.

Schanoes, V. L. (2014). *Fairy tales, myth, and psychoanalytic theory: Feminism and retelling the tale.* Burlington, VT: Ashgate. Silber (Eds.), *Gender in the classroom: Foundations, skills, methods, and strategies across the curriculum* (pp. 259–275). Mahwah, NJ: Erlbaum.

Schilling, M. (2013, Spring). It *is* rocket science: Girls get a boost into STEM careers. *Ms.,* 16.

Schulze, E., & Tomal, A. (2006). The chilly classroom: Beyond gender. *College Teaching, 54,* 263–269.

Segal, B., & Podoshen, J. S. (2013). An examination of materialism, conspicuous consumption and gender differences. *International Journal of Consumer Studies, 37,* 189–198.

Simonds, C. J., & Cooper, P. J. (2001). Communication and gender in the classroom. In L. P. Arliss & D. J. Borisoff (Eds.), *Women and men communicating: Challenges and changes* (2nd ed., pp. 232–253). Prospect Heights, IL: Waveland.

Smith, A. (2013, November 28). Frozen in time: When will Disney's heroines reflect real body shapes? Retrieved August 19, 2015, from <www.theguardian.com>.

Smith, G. M., & Gomez, L. M. (2014). Title IX: Responding to sexual harassment and violence incidents. *University Business, 17,* 18.

Smith, S. W., Yoo, J. H., Farr, A. C., Salmon, C. T., & Miller, V. D. (2007). The influence of student sex and instructor sex on student ratings of instructors: Results from a college of communication. *Women's Studies in Communication, 30,* 64–77.

Steele, J., James, J. B., & Barnett, R. C. (2002). Learning in a man's world: Examining the perceptions of undergraduate women in male-dominated academic areas. *Psychology of Women Quarterly, 26,* 46–50.

Sternglanz, S. H., & Lyberger-Ficek, S. (1977). Sex differences in student-teacher interactions in the college classroom. *Sex Roles, 3,* 345–352.

Strauss, S. (2013a). *Sexual harassment and bullying: A guide to keeping kids safe and holding schools accountable.* New York: Rowman & Littlefield.

Strauss, S. (2013b). Sexual harassment of women in power by men who are not. In M. A. Paludi (Ed.), *Women* and management: *Global issues and promising solutions* (pp. 89–106). Santa Barbara, CA: Praeger.

Sumera, L. (2009). The mask of beauty: Masquerade theory and Disney's *Beauty and the Beast. Quarterly Review of Film and Video, 26,* 40–46.

Sunderland, J. (2012). *Language, gender, and children's fiction.* New York: Bloomsbury Academic.

Taboas-Pais, M. I., & Rey-Cao, A. (2012). Gender differences in physical education textbooks in Spain: A content analysis of photographs. *Sex Roles, 67,* 389–402.

Thorne, B. (1979). *Claiming verbal space: Women, speech, and language in college classrooms.* Paper presented at the Conference on Educational Environments and the Undergraduate Woman, Wellesley College, Wellesley, MA.

Treichler, P. A., & Kramarae, C. (1983). Women's talk in the ivory tower. *Communication Quarterly, 31,* 118–132.

Vinnedge, M. (1996, December 29). Historical novel series aimed at girl readers. *Corpus Christi Caller Times,* p. G13.

Warrington, M., & Younger, M. (2000). The other side of the gender gap. *Gender & Education, 12,* 493–508.

Wasburn, M. H. (2004). Is your classroom woman-friendly? *College Teaching, 52,* 156–158.

Weingart, S., & Jorgensen, J. (2013). Computational analysis of the body in European fairy tales. *Literary & Linguistic Computing, 28,* 404–416.

Wernick, L. J., Kulik, A., & Inglehart, M. H. (2014). Influences of peers, teachers, and climate on students' willingness to intervene when witnessing anti-transgender harassment. *Journal of Adolescence, 37,* 927–935.

White, C. (2013, November 23). Why the feminist controversy over *Frozen* misses the point. Retrieved August 19, 2015, from <www.geekmom.com>.

Wood, J. T., & Lenze, L. F. (1991). Strategies to enhance gender sensitivity in communication education. *Communication Education, 40,* 16–21.

Zipes, J. (1986). *Don't bet on the prince: Contemporary fairy tales in North America and England.* New York: Routledge.

INDEX

AUTHOR INDEX

B

Baasanjav, U., 293
Babcock, L., 191
Backlund, P., 70
Bacue, A. E., 98, 104, 266
Badr, H., 152, 200
Bae, S., 281
Baehne, C. G., 103, 157
Baenninger, M. A., 39
Bailenson, J. N., 50
Bailey, J. M., 113, 142, 186
Baird, K., 325
Bakan, D., 26
Baker, B., 314
Baker, C. K., 232
Baker, J. H., xxvii
Baker, J. P., 144
Baker, R., 75, 77
Baker-Sperry, L., 349
Balaji, M., 289
Ball, H., 197
Ball, S. A., 200, 223
Ballard-Reisch, D., 6, 8
Balsamo, A., 292
Baltes, B. B., 318
Bancroft, S., 333, 362
Banda, P. S., 23, 50
Bandow, D., xxv
Bandura, A., 41, 97
Bane, C. M. H., 173
Banet-Weiser, S., 269
Banks, J., 49, 50, 292
Banning, J. H., 286
Bannon, R. S., 281
Banse, R., 98
Banyard, V. L., 224, 232
Barbovschi, M., 281
Barker, L. B., 156
Barker, R. T., 156
Barnes, S. B., 140
Barnett, R. C., 48, 354
Baron, N., 291
Baron-Cohen, S., 39, 97, 98
Barone, D. F., 153
Barrett, A. E., 192

Barrett, H., 44
Barrett, L. F., 186
Barrick, M. R., 317, 318
Barroso, M. F., 200
Barsh, J., 327
Bar-Tal, D., 142
Bartlett, N. H., 174
Barton, E. R., xxxvii
Barton, K. M., 229, 251
Bartsch, R. B., 253
Basow, S. A., 355
Basu, A., 98
Bate, B., 103
Battles, K., 272
Baumeister, R. F., 198
Baumgardner, J., xxxiii, 13
Baxter, E., 322, 323
Baxter, J., 267
Baxter, L. A., 183, 188
Baym, N. K., 184
Bazzini, D. G., 151
Beach, S. R. H., 191
Beach, W. A., 87
Bean, D., 194
Bean, L., xxxvi
Beck, G., 80, 194
Becker, J. A. H., 190
Bednarek, M., 268
Bedynska, S., 64
Beebe, S. A., 14, 16, 64, 96, 109, 142, 146, 153, 157, 190
Beebe, S. J., 14, 16, 64, 96, 109, 142, 146, 153, 157, 190
Behm-Morawitz, E., 50, 333, 362
Bekker, S., xxxviii
Belenky, M., 357
Belgrave, F. Z., 199
Belkin, L., 324
Bell, E., xxxii, 275
Bello, R. S., 107
Bem, S. L., 8, 42
Benbow, C. P., 39
Beneke, M., 333, 362
Benet, J., 265
Ben-Galim, D., 321

Bennett, S., 224
Benshoff, H. M., 276
Bensimon, M., 286
Benson, K., 333, 362
Bentall, D. C., 170
Bercovici, J., 331
Beres, M. A., 148, 228, 229
Berlin, J., 232
Berman, M. E., 233
Bernikow, L., xxii, xxiii, xxv, xxxi, xxxiv
Berns, S. B., 191
Berryman-Fink, C., 330
Berscheid, E., 141
Bertozzi, E., 50
Beynon, J., 262
Bianchi, S., 48
Bierly, M., 264
Bilewicz, M., 64
Billings, A. C., 28
Billings, V., 278
Birdwhistell, R. L., 29, 96
Bisson, M. A., 176
Bjerk, D., 322
Bjornson, S., 153
Black, R., 79
Blair, D. M., 27
Blair, K. L., 116, 152, 198
Blake, B., 49
Blakemore, J. E. O., 99, 183
Blaney, B., 227
Blankenship, K. L., 86
Blau, F., 314
Bleier, R., 38
Bleske, A. L., 175
Bleske-Recheck, A., 144, 172
Bliss Kiser, S., 331
Blomquist, B. A., 188
Blosnich, J. R., 234
Bly, R., xxxvii, xxxviii
Boburka, R. R., 98
Bodermann, G., 190
Bodey, K. R., 101
Bodie, G. D., 107
Bograd, M., 235

Dworkin, A., 278–279
Dykes, J., 69

E

Eagly, A. H., 326, 327
Earp, B. D., 67, 69, 70
Eastin, M. S., 49, 227
Ebersole, D. S., 190
Ebneter, D., 318
Eccles, J. S., 39, 44
Eckert, P., 86
Eckes, S., 359
Edelsky, C., 87
Eden, J., 177
Edley, P. P., 326
Edson, B., 78
Egley Waggoner, C., xxxiii, 270, 287
Ehrensaft, D., 39, 41, 48
Ehrhardt, A. A., 35
Eibl-Eibesfeldt, I., 148
Eichenbaum, L., 172
Eisend, M., 253
Eisler, R. M., 151
Elasmar, M., 263
Elhai, J. D., 227
Elias, C., 69
Ellevold, B., 190
Elliott, S., 48, 191
Ellis, K., 362
Ellis, L., 97, 103
Elmhorst, J. M., 315
Emens, E. F., 78
Emerling Bone, J., xxvii
Emmers, T. M., 104, 107
Emmers-Sommer, T. M., 190, 198, 228
Enander, V., 237
Engberg, K., 321
England, P., 314
Engstrom, E., 270
Ensslin, A., 292
Epstein, J., xxxvi

Equal Employment Opportunity Commission, 329–330, 358
Erbert, L. A., 183
Erlandson, K., 83
Erspamer, N., 173
Esposito, J., 252
Evans, S., 85
Everbach, T., 328
Ezring, M., 73

F

Fabos, B., 250
Fabrizio Pelak, C., 72
Fagot, B. L., 48, 99
Fairchild, C., 321
Fairchild, E., 351
Fairclough, K., 253
Familysafemedia.com, 281, 283
Family Violence Prevention Fund, 235
Fansler, A. G., 333, 362
Farinelli, L., 109
Farley, S. D., 109
Farnden-Lyster, R., 189
Farr, A. C., 357
Farr, D., 272
Farr, T., 355
Farrakhan, L., xxxvii–xxxviii
Farris, C., 101, 107, 228
Faulkner, L. J., 175
Faulkner, S. L., 116, 119, 152, 175, 183, 198
Fausto-Sterling, A., 36
Feasey, R., 260
Feder, E. K., 6, 23, 169
Federal Bureau of Investigation, 218–219, 220
Fehr, B., 169, 173
Feinberg, D. R., 104
Feldman, K. A., 355
Feminist Majority, xxx
Feng, B., 327
Feng, D., 188
Ferguson, C., 49

Ferguson, G., 264
Ferris, M., 323
Fielden, S. L., 331
Fieseler, C., 290
Finamore, C., 200
Fincham, F. D., 176, 177, 191
Fine, G. A., 327, 331
Fine, J., 150, 171
Fink, B., 107, 148
Finkel, E. J., 192
Finnegan, A., 324
Fischer, A. R., 227
Fischer, J. L., 188
Fischer, P., 285
Fischman, J., 37
Fisher, A., 326
Fisher, B., 87
Fisher, B. S., 186, 220, 223
Fisher, D. A., 273
Fisher, H., 171
Fisher, T. D., 200
Fishman, P. M., 87
Fitch, S. P., xxvi
Fitzgerald, L. E., 337
Fitzpatrick, M. A., 108
Fitzpatrick, P., 117
Fitzpatrick, S. L., 193
Fixmer, N., xxxiii
Flack, W. F., 200
Flanigan, J., 70
Flannagan, D., 69
Flescha, J. L., 153
Flesh, J., 148
Fletcher, P., 227
Flippen, J. L., 286
Floyd, K., 87, 88, 104, 106, 109, 228
Fong, M. L., 155
Forbes, C., 321
Ford, M., 331
Forman-Brunell, M., 48
Formanowicz, M., 64
Foss, K., 78
Fossen, R. J. S-V., 79
Foster, G., 169

Foubert, J. D., 281
Fournier, G., 277
Fowler, J. P., 197
Fowler, K., 259
Fox, J., 50
France, D., 114
Frank, F. W., 82
Frank, M. G., 104
Fraser, V., 177
Freeman, H., 355
Freud, S., 196
Freudiger, P., 285
Friedan, B., xxix, 323
Friedman, E. G., 351
Friedman, E. J., 292
Friedrich, G. W., 315
Frisby, B. N., 45, 148
Frisby, C. M., 284, 287
Fudge, R., xxiv, xxxiii
Fuller, J. M, 82
Fuller, S., 265
Funk, M., 281
Funkhouser, K., 117
Funt, P., 264
Fursich, E., 263
Furstenberg, F. F., Jr., xxxvi

G

Gabriel, U., 69
Gaiba, F., 174
Gaines, M. E., 186
Gajjala, R., 291
Gal-Disegni, M., 351
Gallagher, M., 273
Galupo, M. P., 172, 174
Galvin, K. M., 47, 151, 155, 189
Ganatra, B. R., 47
Gandy, K., xxxvii
Ganesh, S., 185
Garabedian, L. M., 105
Garcia, A., 288
Garcia, S., 113
Garcia-Beaulieu, C., 314
Gardner, B. C., 108

Gardner, W. L., 192
Garfield, R., 171
Garnham, A., 69
Garnhart, L., 224
Garrison, B., 10
Gartzia, L., 326
Gasper, K., 155
Gasser, U., 140
Gastil, J., 69
Gatewood, F., 276
Gaubatz, N. B., 355
Gaughan, S., 148
Gaulin, S., 186
Gay, W. C., 218
Geary, D. C., 142
Gentry, J., 260
Gerbner, G., 251
Gerdes, L. I., 330
Gerhard, J., 266
Gerstel, N., 322
Gibbons, A., 38
Gibbons, E., 318
Gibbons, P., 84
Gibbs, J. L., 140
Gibson, R., 273
Gibson, T. W., 84
Giedd, J. N., 38, 97
Giles, H., 86
Gill, R., 185, 255
Gill, S., 114
Gillam, K., 349, 350
Gillespie, M. A., 279
Gilliam, K., 275
Gilligan, C., 43, 97, 357
Gilmour, D., 269
Gilroy, P. J., 114
Girshick, L. B., 10
Giuliano, T. A., 188
Givertz, M. D., 194
Givhan, R., 255, 269
Gladue, B. A., 107, 186
Glascock, J., 281
Glenn, K., 50
Glenn, R. J., III, 276
Glick, P., 25, 26, 48
Gold, M. A., 285

Goldberg, C., 331
Goldberger, N., 357
Golden, C., 10
Goldin, C., 78
Goldman, R., 61
Goldmeier, D., 197
Golsan, K. B., 183
Gomez, A. G., 292
Gomez, L. M., 359, 360
Gonzalez, A., 285
Good, G. E., 227
Good, T., 353
Goodboy, A. K., 107, 148
Goode, E. E., 31
Goodman, E., 168
Goodman, L. A., 232
Goran, R., 322
Gordon, K. C., 152, 198
Gordon, L., xxix
Gore, J. S., 186
Gorski, E., 74
Gottman, J. M., 189, 191
Gowen, C. W., 114
Graamans, K., 85
Graddol, D., 68
Gradinaru, C., 291
Graham, D. L. R., 238
Graham, E. E., 188
Graham, M. J., 354
Graham, T., 155, 337
Grammer, K., 98, 107, 118, 148
Grasgreen, A., 224
Grashow, A., 327
Grauerholz, E., 349
Grauerholz, I., 362
Grauerholz, L., 351
Graves, F. G., 359
Gray, M. J., 227
Gray, P. B., 32
Grayling, A. C., 47
Green, E. W., 194
Green, J., 10, 77
Green, J. H., 185
Green, K. J., 177
Green, L., 229
Greenbaum, P. E., 104

Greenberg, B. S., 266
Greene, J., 358
Greene, K., 151, 173
Greenspan, K., xxiv, xxv, xxvi
Greif, G. L., 170, 172
Greitemeyer, T., 285
Grey, S., 70, 71
Greytak, E. A., 359
Grieco, L., xxxviii
Grieve, R., 140
Griffin, D. J., 104
Griffin, G., 9
Griffin, S., 276
Grill, B. D., 140
Grill, L. H., 187
Grimké, A., xxiv
Grimké, S., xxiv
Grinberg, E., 48
Gritsenko, E., 79
Grogan, S., 49
Groom, B., 321
Groom, C. J., 84
Gross, J., xxxvii
Gross, L., 251
Gross, M. A., 109
Grossman, J. L., 334, 337
Grubb, A., 334
Grube, J. W., 273
Gruber, E. L., 273
Gruber, J. E., 334–335
Guéguen, N., 103
Guerrero, L. K., 87, 88, 98, 104,
    106, 107, 108, 109, 143, 147,
    150, 157, 174, 175, 185, 186,
    196, 228
Gulledge, A., 107
Gulledge, M., 107
Gundolf, A., 291
Gunther, A. C., 249
Guo, G., 285
Gupta, R. S., 47
Gur, R. C., 38
Gurian, M., 327
Gusarova, I., 177
Gutierrez, F., 254

Gygax, L., 113
Gygax, P., 69, 71

H

Haas, L., 275
Haas, S., 191
Hackenbracht, J., 155
Haddock, S. A., 47
Hadley, W., 199
Hakansson, J., 153
Halatsis, P., 175
Halberstadt, A. G., 103
Hald, G. M., 281
Halder, D., 333, 362
Hall, E. T., 51, 98
Hall, J. A., 98, 101, 102, 103, 104,
    107, 117, 143, 148, 157, 184
Hall, R. M., 357
Hallahan, M., 114
Hallett, S., 219
Hallstein, D. L. O., xxxiii
Halpern, D. F, 38, 97
Hamilton, C., 85
Hamilton, L. C, 69
Hamilton, M. C., 351
Hamlet, S., 331, 333, 359
Hammons, S. A., 230
Hampel, A. D., 194
Hanafin, R. L., 32
Hancock, A. B., 86, 87, 105
Handelman, L. D., 84
Handelsman, J., 354
Hanke, R., 262
Hansen, K., 64
Hanzal, A., 190, 198
Harding, D., 286
Harding, K., 227
Hardman, M. J., xxix, 63, 68
Hargett, J., 355
Harinck, F., 113
Harmon, M. R., 351
Harned, M., 218
Harper, B., 255
Harrington, L., 359

Harris, F., III, 27
Harris, L., 259
Harris, M., 249, 273
Harris, T. E., 155
Harrison, K., 50, 260
Harrison, M., 104
Harrison, R., 260
Harrison, S., 104
Hart, K.-P. R., 272, 273
Harvey, J. H., 150, 154, 186
Harvey, S. M., 116, 199
Harwood, J., 101, 263, 265
Hasegawa, K., 263
Haselton, M. G, 107
Hasinoff, A. A., 270
Haskin, G., 105
Hathaway, J., 294
Hause, K. S., 175
Haviland, W. A., 51
Havrilesky, H., 10, 273
Haworth, A., 47
Hay, J., 264
He, G., 69, 73
Heaton, J. A., 268
Hebert, L. P., 254, 286
Hecht, M. A., 103
Hecht, M. L., 24
Heen, S., 191
Heeter, C., 50
Heffernan, J., 230
Hefner, V., 275
Hegstrom, J. L., 80
Heifetz, R., 327
Heinemann-LaFave, D., 144
Heisler, J. M., 153
Heldman, C., 220
Helgeson, J. G., 254, 258–259
Helm, S., 232
Helsper, E. J., 290
Hendrick, C., 175, 181, 196
Hendrick, S. S., 175, 181, 196
Henley, N. M., 4, 99, 104
Henneberg, S., 349
Henning, A., 49

Henningsen, D. D., 107, 118, 148, 188, 196, 228, 229, 331
Henningsen, M. L. M., 107, 175
Henry, A., xxxiii
Henry, W. J., 286
Henson, K. D., 331
Henson, L., 268
Hentges, B. A., 253
Heppner, M. J., 227
Herbeck, D. A., 278
Herbst, C., 50
Herman, J., 10
Herold, A. L., 185
Herold, E., 148, 228
Herrett-Skjellum, J., 284
Herthel, J., 352
Hess, U., 97, 98, 103
Hester, E., 140
Hetsroni, A., 251
Hewitt, J. P., 87
Hewlett, S. A., 321, 322
Heywood, L., xxxiii
Hickmon, W. A., Jr., 190
Hickson, M. L., III, 97, 102
Hill, B., xxviii
Hill, C., 39, 354, 359
Hill, C. A., 47, 186
Hill, C. B., 191
Hill, D. L., 273
Hill, E. J., 323
Hill, J., 98
Hill, L., 266
Hillenbrand-Gunn, T. L., 227
Hillman, J., 197
Hillyer, J. D., 139
Hilton-Morrow, W., 272
Hines, M., 97
Hinsz, V. B., 103
Hoar, N., 83, 85
Hobson, C. J., 337
Hochschild, A. R., 323
Hocker, J. L., 111, 190, 191
Hoff, B. H., 234
Hoffman, I., 352
Hoffman, S., 352
Hoffnung, M., 79

Hoff Sommers, C., xxxiii
Hofstede, G. H., 51–52
Hofstede, G. J., 51–52
Hogeland. L. M., xxxiii
Hogg, E., 148
Holik, A., 38
Holladay, H. W., 263
Holland, K. J., 362
Holland, S. L., 32
Holman, A., 184
Holmberg, D., 116, 152, 198
Holmes, J., 28, 72, 86, 87
Holmes, J. D., 253
Holmes, J. G., 186
Holmes, R., xxxii
Holtrop, K., 235
Hommel, B., 113
Hooghe, A., 187
hooks, b., xxxii, 12, 13, 232
Hopcke, R., 174
Hopeck, P., 266
Hopper, D., 280
Hopper, R., 69, 71, 76, 78
Hopson, M., 293
Horan, N., 263, 265
Horan, S., 107
Horgan, T. G., 98, 117, 143, 157
Hornstein, M. D., 47
Horton, R. S., 144
Hosada, M., 318
Houghton, J., xxxvi
Houser, M. L., 188
Houston, M., 172
Hoynes, W., 251
Hsing, C., 155
Huang, T., 318
Huber, J. E., 104
Hubert, S. J., 271
Hubler, D. S., 108
Hughes, M., 175, 177, 178
Hughes, P. C., 194
Hughes, S. M., 109
Huling, N., 172
Humm, M., xxiii
Humphrey, M., 352

Humphreys, T. P., 116, 118, 152, 229
Hunt, A. N., 355
Hunt, C., 331
Hunter, J., 318
Hunter College Women's Studies Collective, xxxiii
Hurd, K., 98
Hust, S. J. T., 224, 227, 229
Hyland, A., 256
Hysock, D., 7, 8

I

Ickes, W., 155
Igarashi, T., 184
Ihori, N., 49
Ilea, L., 197
Imhof, M., 85, 114
Inglehart, M. H., 333, 359
Inman, C. C., 151, 171–172
Irmen, L., 73
Isay, R. A., 183
Ivic, R. K., 266
Ivory, A. H., 273
Ivory, J. D., 50, 273
Ivy, D. K., 14, 16, 64, 70, 71, 85, 96, 98, 101, 103, 104, 109, 142, 146, 153, 157, 190, 228, 316, 329, 331, 333, 359
Izard, C. E., 98

J

Jacklin, C. N., 34, 35, 36
Jackson, A., 286
Jackson, C., 285
Jackson, G., 148
Jacobs, G., 330
Jacobson, N. S., 191
Jain, T., 47
Jaishankar, K., 333, 362
James, J. B., 354
Jansz, J., 50
Japp, P. M., 266

Jarvis, T., 186
Javidi, M., 70
Jefferson, B. S., 263
Jefferson, G., 87
Jeffries, M. P., 286
Jenkins, H., 50
Jenner, E., 274
Jenner, L., 274
Jenner, P., 274
Jennings, J., 352
Jerman, P., 153
Jhally, S., 252, 287, 288
Jiang, K., 333, 334, 337
Jin, B., 184, 194
Johnson, D., 153
Johnson, D. R., 78, 79
Johnson, F. L., 172
Johnson, I. W., 154, 156
Johnson, J., 254
Johnson, K. L., 114
Johnson, M., 33, 35
Johnson, M. P., 232
Johnson, S. K., 45, 318
Jones, A. J., 103, 107
Jones, K. J., 312, 331
Jones, K. T., 74
Jones, S. E., 104, 107
Jones, S. M., 98, 107, 186
Jones, T. S., 191
Jordan, C., 264
Jorgensen, J., 284, 349
Joshi, M., 221
Jourard, S., 150, 151
Jovanovic, J., 178
Jozkowski, K. N., 229
Juette, A., 107, 148
June, A. W., 360
Juul, J., 292

K

Kada, O., 45
Kafai, Y. B., 50
Kahlor, L. A., 227
Kahn, L., 314
Kalbfleisch, P. J., 185

Kalmijn, M., 169
Kampman, L., 173
Kane, E. W., 48
Kang, S., 292
Kankiewicz, K., 146
Kantor, M., 9, 108, 116
Karjane, H. M., 220
Karlovsky, M., 197
Karniol, R. R., 351
Karns, M. E., 220
Karp, D. A., 356
Karpf, A., 85
Karraker, K. H., 47
Kartch, F. F., 107, 191
Kaspar, K., 107, 148
Kasper, S., 38
Kassing, J. W., 28
Kattner, T., 360
Katz, D. S., 314
Katz, J., 257
Kaukinen, C., 232
Kehily, M. J., 28
Keiter, E. J., 186
Kelley, D. L., 190
Kelley, P., 155
Kellner, D., 252
Kellner, M. A., xxxviii
Kelly, A. B., 191
Kelly, D. M., 28
Kelly, L., 184, 334
Kemp, N., 140
Kendrick, D. T., 118
Kenneavy, K., 285
Kenrick, D. T., 26, 142, 143
Kenway, J., 49
Kerber, L., xxix, xxxi
Khan, K., 27
Kilbourne, J., 254
Killen, M., 49
Killerman, S., 61, 62, 71
Kim, J. L., 263
Kimbrell, A., xxxvii
Kimmel, M., 151
Kimmel, M. S., xxxiv, xxxv, 27, 36, 46

Kimura, D., 37, 38
Kimura, S., 232
King, C., 275
Kinney, T. A., 98
Kinnick, K. N., 264
Kinser, A. E., 317, 319
Kip, K., 286
Kirchner, J., 144
Kirtley Johnston, M., 156
Kish, A., 316
Kistler, M. E., 287
Kitzinger, C., 75
Kleck, R. E., 97, 98
Kleiman, C., 38
Kleinke, C. L., 108, 146
Klein Modisett, D., 268
Klenin, J., 331
Kline, S. L., 78
Klinetob, N. A., 192
Klingemann, K., 79
Knapp, M. L., 111, 117, 142, 143, 146, 157
Knight, K., 149, 177
Knobloch, J. K., 188
Knofler, T., 114
Knower, F. H., 98
Knox, D., 107, 176, 177, 187
Koch, S. C., 103, 157
Koenig Kellas, J., 192, 194
Koeppel, L. B., 107, 229, 331
Koerner, A. F., 108
Koeser, S., 66
Koesten, J., 189
Kohlberg, L., 41–42, 44
Kolar, S., 286
Kolehmainen, M., 281
Koller, V., 48, 99
Konijn, E. A., 49
Konrath, S. H., 155
Koo, H., 153
Kooijman, P. G. C., 85
Kopelman, R. E., 79
Kopp, L. K., 357
Korabik, K., 327
Koralewski, M. A., 107

Littlejohn, S. W., 191
Litzinger, S., 152, 198
Livingston, J. A., 200, 223
Lloyd, S. A., 110
Lobel, M., 101
Lockwood Harris, K., 27
Long, A. E., 169
Long, L., 155
Lorber, J., xxxii
Lorie, A. F., 267
Lotz, A. D., xxxiii
Love Is Respect, 233
Lovejoy, T. I., 197
Loveless, T., 354
Lowenstein, H., 251
Lozon, J., 286
Lucas, K., 322
Lucas-Stannard, P., 41
Lucero, M. A., 331
Luna Brem, M., 326
Lunardini, C., xxii, xxiv, xxv, xxvii,
    xxviii, xxix, xxx, xxxi, xxxii
Lundy-Wagner, V., 359
Luo, Y., 359
Luria, Z., 47
Lyberger-Ficek, S., 356
Lyness, K. P., 47
Lynskey, D., 287

M

Maccoby, E. E., 35, 36, 169
MacDonald, C. J., 98
MacGeorge, E., 327
Machung, A., 323
Mack, A. N., 170
Mack, S., 114
MacKinnon, C. A., 278–279, 331
MacKinnon, K., 257, 262
MacNeil, S., 152, 198
MacNell, L., 355
Madden, M., 358
Madlock, P., 328
Madson, L., 71
Maerz, M., 10, 273

Mager, J., 254, 258–259
Maggio, R., 67, 68, 73, 81, 83
Magnusson, M. S., 148
Magsamen-Conrad, K., 251
Maguire, K. C., 98, 144, 218,
    219, 220, 233
Mahood, C., 50
Maier, M., 45
Maier, S. L., xxxiii, xxxiv, xxxvii
Mainiero, L. A., 312, 325, 331
Maitland, S. B., 148, 228
Major, B., 104
Makadon, H. J., 234
Malamuth, N. M., 278, 281
Malkowski, J., 224
Mallett, R. K., 66
Mandziuk, R. M., xxvi, 268–269
Maner, J. K., 101
Mangan, K., 220
Mansfield, A. K., 27
Manstead, A. S. R., 98
Manulik, K., 155
Manusov, V., 103, 192
Manvell, J., 325
Marecek, J., 7
Marinescu, A., 331
Mark, K., 201
Maroulis, A., 104
Martin, A., 104
Martin, C. E., 12
Martin, C. L., 46
Martin, C. R., 250
Martin, J. N., 23, 24, 151
Martin, R., 171, 173
Martin, S. L., 200, 223
Martinez, A. R., 254
Martins, N., 50
Martinson, V. K., 323
Martis, R. G., 50
Martyna, W., 69–70
Marwick, A., 270
Mastro, D., 50
Matchen, J., 362
Matlack, T., xxxvi
Matthews, K., 193–194

Maxwell, J. P., 285
May, E. T., xxviii
McAuliffe, K., 31
McAuslan, P., 223
McCabe, D. B., 141
McCabe, J., 351
McCarl-Nielsen, J., 80
McCartney, B., xxxviii
McCloskey, S., 233
McClure, E. B., 98
McCombs, M. E., 251
McConnell, D., 140
McConnell-Ginet, S., 63, 68,
    85, 86
McCormick, N. B., 103, 107
McCracken, A. A., 194
McCrae, R. R., 355
McCroskey, J. C., 97
McCulloch, S., 149
McCullough, M. E., 190
McDaniel, E. R., 107
McDonald, E., 48, 100
McDonald, P., 337
McDuffie, D., 223
McEwan, B., 150
McFall, R. M., 101, 227, 228
McGinty, K., 176, 178
McGlone, M. S., 80
McGonagle, K., 322
McGovern, J., 277
McGrath, K., 10
McIntyre, N., 256
McKay, J., xxviii, 254
McKenna, K. Y. A., 185
McKinley, C. J., 359
McKinney, K., 362
McLaren, K., 153
McLoughlin, I. P., 201
McLoughlin, M., 31
McMahan, D. T., 290
McMahon, T. J., 200, 223
McMullen, A. L., 45
McRobbie, A., xxxii
McWilliams, R., 101
Mean, L. J., 28

Means Coleman, R. R., 277
Mechling, E., xxxv
Mechling, J., xxxv
Meckel, M., 290
Medved, C. E., 323
Meeker, F. B., 146
Meers, S., 323
Mehrabian, A., 97
Meier, J. A., 253
Melby, C., 118, 196
Menaker, D., 146
Menard, A. D., 152, 198
Mendelson Freeman, S. J., 322
Menzies, A. L., 287
Merolla, A. J., 143
Merrill, L., 31
Merskin, D., 266
Mesaros-Winckles, C. E., 269
Messerschmidt, J. W., 27
Messman, S. J., 175, 190
Messner, M. A., 27, 48, 49, 100
Meston, C. M., 116, 118, 186, 198, 200
Metts, S., 118, 147, 183, 186, 187, 192
Metz, I., 321
Meyer, A., 200, 223, 227
Michaels, J., 33
Miczo, N., 150
Middleton, A. V., 190, 194
Middleton, K. L., 331
Migerode, L., 187
Mikesell, R. L., 190
Mikucki-Enyart, S. L., 192
Miles, M. G., 186
Miller, A. N., 99
Miller, C., 67, 73, 74, 82
Miller, J., xxv, 355
Miller, M. J., 104
Miller, M. K., 50
Miller, R., 172
Miller, V. D., 355
Mills, R., 74
Mindes, E. J., 190
Mink, G., 330
Mischel, W., 41

Missing, C., 109
Missmer, S. A., 47
Mitchell, M. B., 349
Mitra, A., 291
Mize, J., 48, 103
Moe, K., 325
Moffat, M., 76
Mohammed-Baksh, S., 286
Mohipp, C., 333, 362
Molloy, P., 255
Monahan, J. L., 200, 223
Mongeau, P. A., 107, 118, 175, 177, 188, 196
Monk-Turner, E., 253
Monsour, M., 168, 174, 175, 179–180
Montagne, Y., 107, 229, 331
Montgomery, B. M., 183
Montgomery, H., 153
Montoya, R. M., 144
Moore, C., 269, 271
Moore, E., 331
Moore, M. L., 262, 265
Moore, M. M., 105, 107, 118, 148
Moore, N. B., 200
Moore, N.-J., 102
Moore, S., 200
Moorti, S., 264
Morgan, K. J., 235
Morgan, M., 251, 267
Morman, M. T., 98, 104, 177
Morr, S., 117
Morris, L. K., 358
Morris, M. L., 186
Morrison, K., 175, 177
Morrison, M. A., 256
Mortensen, T. E., 292
Mortenson, T. G., 39, 354
Moscowitz, L., 264
Moss-Racusin, C. A., 354
Mothers Against Drunk Driving, 224
Motley, M. T., 175–176, 186
Motschenbacher, H., 75
Moulton, J., 69

Mourdock, R., 220
Moutsatsos, C., 253
Ms. Foundation for Women, xxx
Muehlenhard, C. L., 6, 107, 223, 229
Mueller, B., 254
Mulac, A., 84, 86, 87
Munger, J., 253
Munson, B., 114
Murnen, S. K., 76, 255, 351
Murphy, C., 221
Murphy, E. L., 6, 23
Murphy, N. A., 103
Murphy, S. E., 45
Murphy, W., 221
Murphy-Hoefer, R., 256
Murray, C., 172
Muscarella, F., 331
Muse, E., 292
Mydio, J. H., 197

N

Nabi, R. L., 270
Nagy, M. E., 188
Nahm, E. Y., 189
Nakamura, L., 291, 293
Nakayama, T. K., 23, 24
Nashawaty, C., 277
Natalle, E. J., 286
Natharius, D., xxxvii
National Coalition of Anti-Violence Programs, 220
National Institute of Justice, 218, 220, 222, 234
National Organization for Women, xxix-xxx
Nayak, A., 28
Nayar, P., 290
Neary, L., 32, 34
Neave, M., 85
Neff, J., 259
Neft, N., xxv, xxvi
Nelson, A., 237
Nett, E., 286

Sung, C. C. M., 252
Sung, Y., 269
Surra, C. A., 194
Sussman, J. E., 104
Suter, E. A., 79
Sutherland, A., 192
Sutton, R. M., 64, 66
Swann, J., 68
Swift, K., 67, 73, 74, 82
Swim, J. K., 66
Syzdek, M. R., 27
Szostek, J., 337
Szuchman, L. T., 331

T

Tabares, A., 189
Taboas-Pais, M. I., 351
Tafarodi, R. W., 140
Tait, S., 270
Takai, J., 184
Tal, S.-A., 185
Tannen, D., 83, 156
Tappan, M., 351
Tardy, C., 111
Tarule, J., 357
Tassinary, L. G., 114
Tavris, C., 38
Taylor, A., xxix, 63, 285
Taylor, K., 221
Taylor, R., 357
Taylor, T., 140
Taylor, T. L., 293
Tedford, T. L., 278
Teen Dating Violence Month, 233
Teichner, G., 189
Terracciano, A., 355
Terry, A., 229
Teso, E., 64
Testa, M., 200, 223
Teti, M., 116
Tewksbury, R., 220
Thapar-Bjorkert, S., 235
Theiss, J. A., 188

Theriot, N., xxii
Theune, K. E., 142
Thierren, L. F., 107
Thill, K. P., 50
Thom, M., xxx
Thomae, M., 334
Thomas, G., 85
Thomas, V., 259
Thompson, C., 352
Thorne, B., 4, 356
Tichenor, V., 184
Tickle-Degnen, L., 108
Tidwell, L. C., 140
Tiggemann, M., 255
Tillmann, L. M., 174
Timmerman, L. M., 198, 284
Tirrito, S. J., 33
Tobias, S., xxxiii
Tokar, D. M., 227
Tokunaga, R. S., 281
Tolman, D. L., 198
Tomal, A., 358
Tomhave, J. A., 103
Tone, A., xxviii
Tope, D., 351
Toussaint, L., 155
Tracy, K., 78, 85
Traube, E., 262
Treat, T. A., 101, 227, 228
Trees, A. R., 103
Trei, L., 325
Treichler, P. A., 82, 357
Tropiano, S., 271
Trost, M. R., 118, 148
Trotta, M. R., 187
Trout, J. D., 153
Truman, D. M., 227
Tsai, W., 318
Tschann, J. M., 116
Tuchman, G., 249, 265
Turkle, S., 291
Turman, P. D., 28
Turner, J. S., 289
Turner, L. H., xxix, 140, 183, 320
Tyler May, E., 32
Tyree, T. C. M., 286

U

Uecker, J., 196
Umberson, D., 191, 235
Underwood, M. K., 169
Unger, R., 101, 220, 226, 233
U.S. Bureau of Labor Statistics, 13
U.S. Census Bureau, 13, 32, 314
U.S. Department of Defense, 234, 331
U.S. Department of Justice, 232
U.S. Department of Labor, 313, 314, 320, 321, 323
Utley, E. A., 286, 287

V

Valby, K., 277
Valde, K. S., 107
Valenti, J., xxxii, 12
Valentine, D., 10
Valera, P., 116
Valkenburg, P. M., 198, 281
Vande Berg, L. R., 266
van den Wildenberg, W. P. M., 113
van der Bruggen, M., 334
VanderLaan, D. P., 174
Vangelisti, A. L., 111, 146, 190, 192, 233
van Hooidonk, L., 113
Van Newkirk, R., 114
Vanover Riley, K., 330
VanZile-Tamsen, C., 200, 223
van Zoonen, L., 290
Vartanian, L. R., 183
Vasey, P. L., 174
Vatsa, S., 103
Vaynerchuk, G., 259
Veccia, E. M., 104
Ventura, V., xxv, xxvi, xxvii, xxx
Verhofstadt, L. L., 153
Vernon, M. L., 192
Vigil, J., 142

INDEX

SUBJECT INDEX

nonverbal communication and, 97

breakups, 192–194

bystander intervention, 224

C

"Campaign for Real Beauty" (Dove), 255

cell phones, autonomy/connection issues of, 184

change, acceptance *versus*, 185–186

children

child custody issues, xxxvi–xxxvii

children's literature, 348–352

sex segregation patterns and friendship, 169

choice, of language, 63

choice points, 138

Christianity, Promise Keepers and, xxxviii

circumscribing, 111

cis/cisgender, 61

Civil Rights Movement, xxvii

clothing

nonverbal communication, 99–101

socialization and gender identity development, 48–50

cognitive ability, 39

cognitive development theory, 41–42, 46

collaborative management style, 326–327

college

academic achievement and expectations for, 354–356

bias in classes, 356–358

rape on college campuses, 221–222, 224 (*see also* rape)

sexual harassment in, 358–363

combat roles, in military, 34

Commission on the Status of Women, xxix

commitment, 188–189, 193

commodity feminism, 256, 261

communication, defined, 14, 16

gender and, 3-8, 14-16, 30, 43, 45, 63, 75, 100, 135-136, 157, 167-168, 194, 216-217, 231, 274, 289, 313, 315, 338, 355

communicative competence, 157

compromise, relationships and, 137–138

conflict

defined, 193

in relationships, 109–112

in romantic relationships, 190–192

confrontation, 335, 337

connection

autonomy *versus*, 184

defined, 186

consciousness-raising, xxxv–xxxvi

consent, sexual safety and, 228–230

contraception, xxvii–xxviii, 32, 116, 199–201

contrapower harassment, 333, 362–363

convergence, 261, 263

conversation

conversation management, 87–88

conversation starters, 145–149

courtship

courtship readiness cues, 106

courtship violence, 232, 233

defined, 105

flirting and, 147–149

credit, women's rights and, xxi, xxx–xxxi

cross-sex friendships

enhancement of, 176–178

overview, 174

problems of, 175–176

between straight and gay people, 174

cultivation theory, 251, 252

cultural studies approaches, to media, 252

culture and gender

culture, defined, 51, 53

intersectionality, 52–53

masculine and feminine cultures, 51–52

stereotypes, 50–51

cyber harassment, 333, 362

cycles, biological, 37–38

D

date rape, 219–220, 221

dating, relationships and, 165–166. *see also* romantic relationships

dating violence, 232, 233

decapitation ads, 258, 261

Define Your Line program (Texas Tech University), 229

defusion, 335, 337

demand-withdraw pattern, in conflict, 191–192, 193

differentiating, 111

difficulty, of relationships, 136

"digital natives," 140

direct-effects theory, 250, 252

disclaimers, 86–87, 88

disembodiment, new media and, 291–292

dismemberment ads, 258–259, 261

distance, proxemics and, 98–99

diversity

friendship and, 178–180

understanding, 11

domestic violence, 230, 232, 233

drugs, date rape, 223–225

E

educational settings, 347–369

children's literature and, 348–352

college, 355–358

expectations and bias in, 353–355

sexual harassment in, 358–363

women's rights and, xxii–xxiii

egalitarian relationships, 185, 186
electronically mediated
communication, 139–141
emotion, biological cycles and,
37–38
empathy, 153–155, 157
employment, of women. *see*
women's rights
empowerment
defined, 186
power *versus,* 185
reality television and, 270–271
entrepreneurial mothers, 326, 327
equal pay, 13–14. *see also* women's
rights
Equal Pay Act of 1963, xxix
Equal Rights Amendment, xxxi
estrogen, 34
euphemisms, 80, 201
expectations, for relationships, 136,
137
eye contact
nonverbal communication and,
103
sexual activity and, 117, 119

F

Facebook, 5, 6, 61, 140, 290, 312
face-to-face communication
for initiating relationships, 139
online communication
compared to, 139–141
terminating a relationship and,
193
facial expression
nonverbal communication and,
103
relational conflict and, 110
sexual activity and, 119
faculty, 179, 229, 354, 357,
360–363
sexual harassment of, 229,
360–363
failure, fear of, 136
fairy tales, gender identity and,
349–351

family
family-friendly workplaces,
323, 326
family violence, 230, 233
managing career and family,
322–326
parenting, 32, 46–48
socialization and gender identity
development, 46–48
fathers' movements, xxxvi–xxxvii
Federal Bureau of Investigation,
218–219, 220
female-female friendship, 172–173
feminine identity
feminine culture, 51–52, 53
gender identity development
and, 25–27, 28–29
nonverbal communication and,
97–98
sex and gender, defined, 7
feminism. *see also* men's
movements; women's rights
commodity feminism and, 256,
261
First Wave
overview, xxiii
suffragists, xxiii–xxvi, xxxiv
World War II and "Rosie
the Riveter," xxvi
future of gender
communication and,
xxxix
overview, xxii–xxiii, 11–14
Second Wave
Civil Rights Movement,
xxvii
Equal Rights
Amendment, xxxi
"feminisms," xxxii

National Organization for
Women, xxix–xxx
overview, xxviii
"problem that has no
name," xxix

second-class status of
women, xxix
sexual revolution, xxvii–
xxviii, xxxv
Steinem and, xxx–xxxi
Third Wave, xxxiii
"feminisms," xxxii
Fifteenth Amendment, xxv
film, 275–277
flextime, 323, 326
flirting, 106–107, 147–149, 157
friendship, 165–213. *see also*
romantic relationships
cross-sex friendships, 174–178
diversity and, 178–180
overview, 166–168
same-sex friendships, 169–173
sex segregation patterns in, 169
"friends with benefits
relationships," 176–178

G

"Gamergate," 294
gaming, gendered, 292–295
Gay and Lesbian Alliance Against
Defamation, 179
"gaydar," 113–114
gender
biological sex perspective *versus*
gender perspective,
96–97
defined, 6–7, 8
gender bending, 276, 282
gender communication, 3–19
communication as complex
human process, 14–16
defined, 3–4, 8
gender identity, androgyny,
sexual orientation, and,
8–14
jargon, 5–7
study of, 4–5
gender dysphobia, 29
gender dysphoria, 23
gendered gaming, 292–295

intimate partner violence
abused partners' reaction to, 235–238
definitions related to, 230–233
facts about, 233–235
helping, 238–239
intonation, 86, 88

J

jargon, 5–7

K

kinesics, 101–102, 104, 117

L

language. *see also* gendered language
about sexual harassment, 328–329
defined, 64
used to describe sexual violence, 218–220
leading questions, 318–319, 321
learned helplessness, 237, 239
lesbian gay bisexual transgender queer/questioning (LGBTQ)
cross-sex friendship between straight women and gay men, 174
friendship issues of, 178–180
LGBTQIA+ designation, 62
surnames and, 79
television and, 271–274
Lilly Ledbetter Fair Pay Act, 314
linguistic construction, 87–88
listening
receiver orientation to communication, 14–16
relationship development and, 147, 155–157
"locker-room style" of communication, 76
love
expressions of, 187–188
sexual activity and, 196

M

male-male friendship, 170–172
management, men/women in, 326–328
man-linked terminology, 67–68, 71
marital abuse, 230, 232
marking, 71
married naming, 78–79
masculine identity. *see also* media; men's movements
gender identity development and, 25–28
masculine culture, 51–52, 53
nonverbal communication and, 97–98
sex and gender, defined, 7
matching hypothesis, 142, 144
maternal wall, 315, 321
media, 247–309
advertising, 252–261
film, 275–277
growth of, 247–248
music, 284–289
new media, 289–295
pornography and, 278–284
power of mediated communication, 248–252
television, 261–274
men's movements, xxxiv–xxxix
consciousness-raising, xxxv–xxxvi
early male supporters of women's rights, xxxiv
fathers' movements, xxxvi–xxxvii
future of gender communication and, xxxix
Million Man March, xxxvii–xxxviii
Promise Keepers, xxxviii
sexual revolution and men, xxxiv–xxxv
"Wild Man Gatherings," xxxvii

menstruation, 37–38
metacommunication, 189–190, 193
metaphors, 80, 83
military
combat roles and, 34
sexual harassment in, 331–332
Million Man March, xxxvii–xxxviii
minimal-effects model, 250, 252
moblogs, 291
mock-macho sitcoms, 262, 263
modeling, 97
mommy track, 323, 326
monogamous relationships, 181, 183
movement (kinesics), 101–102, 104, 117
movies, 275–277
Ms. (magazine), xxx
"Ms." (salutation), 82
Ms. Foundation for Women, xxx
music
music videos, 287–289
song lyrics, 284–287
muted group theory, 65
myths, about battering, 234–235, 239
myths, about rape, 226–228, 230, 281

N

National Organization for Women, xxix–xxx
negotiation, 335, 337
neologisms, 71
Net Notes. *see* Web sites (Net Notes)
new media
defined, 289–290
disembodiment and, 291–292
gendered gaming, 292–295
online identity and gender, 290–291
nonsexist (gender-fair) language, 65–67

nonverbal communication, 95–129
  codes, 96–97
  consent and sexual safety,
    228–230
  defined, 14, 16, 96, 104
  facial and eye expressions, 103
  intimacy and, 151–152
  in job interviews, 316–318
  kinesics, 101–102, 104, 117
  nonverbal cues and sexuality,
    112–114
  overview, 96
  physical appearance,
    attractiveness, clothing,
    and artifacts, 99–101
  proxemics, 98–99
  relational communication,
    105–107
  relationship conflict and
    termination, 109–112
  relationship maintenance,
    107–109
  sending and receiving ability,
    97–98
  sexual activity, 115–120
  touch (haptics), 103–104,
    109–110, 117
  vocalics (paralanguage),
    104–105
nursery rhymes, gender identity
  and, 349–351
nurturance, 35

O

obscenity, 278, 282
occupations, stereotypes of, 69–70,
  71
on-again/off-again relationships,
  194, 201
online communication
  cyber harassment, 333, 362
  Internet for communicating,
    overview, 139–141
  new media, 290–295

online relationship
    development, 139–141
  terminating a relationship and,
    193
opting out, 324–325, 327
order of terms, 81–82, 83
overlaps, 87, 88

P

paralanguage, 104–105
parallel language, 80–81, 83
parenting. *see also* family
    reproductive function and, 32
    socialization and gender
        identity development,
        46–48
partnering, pressure for, 181–183
partner rape, 220, 221
partner violence, 216, 230–239
patriarchy, xxxiv, xxxv
peers, gender identity development
    and, 50
peer sexual harassment, 333, 347,
    358-363
personal relationships. *see*
    friendship; romantic
    relationships
pervasiveness, of gender
    communication, 5
physical abuse, 233
physical appearance
    initiating relationships and, 142
    nonverbal communication and,
        99–101
    sexual activity and, 116–117
    sexuality and, 112
physical strength, 32–34, 35
"pill, the," xxviii
pink-collar jobs, 320–321
pitch, 85, 88
platonic friendship, 175–176
playful patriarchs, 262–263
popularization, gender
    communication and, 4

pornography
  defined, 278–279, 282
  effects of, 281, 282–284
  types of, 279–281
positional cues, 106
postdissolution relationships, 194,
  201
"postfeminism," xxxiii
posttraumatic stress disorder, 238,
  239
power
  abuse and, 216 (*see also* abuse)
  contrapower sexual harassment,
    333, 362–363
  defined, 186
  empowerment and, 185, 186,
    270–271
power babe commercials, 257, 261
preening behavior, 106
premarital violence, 232, 233
premenstrual syndrome (PMS), 37
proactive approach, to initiating
    relationships, 137, 138–144
"problem that has no name," xxix
Promise Keepers, xxxviii
pronouns, 69–71
prospects, for relationships,
    138–144
provocation, gender
    communication and, 4
proxemics
    nonverbal communication of,
        98–99, 104
    proximity and forming
        relationships, 143–144
    relationship maintenance,
        107–108
    sexual activity and, 117
psychological abuse, 233
psychological gender identity
    theories, 40–46. *see also*
    gender identity
    cognitive development theory,
        41–42
    gender identity development
        theory, 43

gender schema theory, 42–43
gender transcendence and
androgyny, 43–46
social learning theory, 41

Q

qualifiers, 86–87, 88
quasi-courtship behavior, 105
queer, 62
questioning, 62
questions, as conversation starters,
146–147
quid pro quo sexual harassment,
330, 333

R

race. *see also* diversity
Civil Rights Movement, xxvii
Million Man March, xxxvii–
xxxviii
slavery and, xxv–xxvi
Rambo depiction, 257
rape
bystander intervention
programs, 224
on college campuses, 221–222
date rape drugs, 223–225
defined, 218–219, 221
language used to describe,
218–220
Rape Myth Acceptance Scale,
227
rape myths, 226–228, 230, 281
rapists' characteristics, 226
reported cases, 220–221
survivors' self-blame and, 223
trauma of, 219
reality television
mirroring reality *versus* creating
reality, 261–262
"real" men and, 263–265
"real" women and, 269–271
receivers
defined, 16
nonverbal communication,
97–98

receiver orientation to
communication, 14–16,
66
receiver-oriented
communication, 14–16
reciprocation, in relationships,
175–176
relational communication
conflict and termination,
109–112
relationship initiation, 105–107
relationship maintenance,
107–109
relational currencies, 186, 187
relational partners, 181, 183
relational talk, 188, 193
relationship development, 133–163
establishing, 150–157
initiating, 138–144
overview, 134–135
relationships and relational
partners, defined, 135,
138
roadblocks to, 136–138
starting conversations, 145–149
religion
gendered language and, 73–75
Nation of Islam and, xxxvii–
xxxviii
Promise Keepers and, xxxviii
reported cases, of rape, 220–221
reported cases, of sexual
harassment, 336–337
reproductive functions. *see also*
sexual activity
contraception, 116, 199–201
flirting and, 148
gender communication basics
and, 31–32, 35
Roe v. Wade, xxx
romantic relationships, 165–213.
see also friendship
conflict in, 190–192
defined, 181, 183
overview, 167–168, 180–181
partnering pressure, 181–183

relationships and relational
partners, defined, 135,
138
sexual activity and gender
issues, 196–201
talking about communicating
in, 189–190
tensions in, 183–189
termination of, 192–194
transgender, 195
"Rosie the Riveter," xxvi

S

salutations, 82–83
same-sex friendships
female-female, 172–173
male-male, 170–172
overview, 169–170
same-sex rape, 219–220
Sapir–Whorf Hypothesis, 64
school, gender identity
development and, 50
second-class status, of women, xxix
second shift, 323, 326
self-blame, 223, 334
self-disclosure, 150–153, 157, 173
self-employment, 325–326
self-esteem, advertising and, 260
senders
defined, 16
nonverbal communication,
97–98
sensitivity, language and, 66
sequencing, 324, 326
sex, defined, 6–7, 8
sex identity, 23, 24, 29
sexism, 67–83. *see also* gendered
language
antimale bias, 68–69, 71
euphemisms and metaphors, 80
man-linked terminology, 67–68
married naming, 78–79
order of terms, 81–82
overview, 11–14
parallelism in language, 80–81

pronouns, 69–71
religion and, 73–75
sexist language, defined, 64–65
sexual references, 75–78
suffixes, 72–73
team names, 72
titles and salutations, 82–83
sex segregation patterns, friendship
and, 169
sexual activity
attitudes and opinions about,
196–198
communicating directly about,
198–201
"friends with benefits
relationships," 176–178
nonverbal communication,
115–120
"risky sex," 197
in romantic relationships,
196–201
sexual assault. *see also* rape
abuse and, 216
defined, 218–219, 221
trauma of, 219
sexual attraction, 141–142, 144
sexual harassment
avoiding, 338
defined, 329, 333
in educational settings, 358–
363
of faculty, 361–363
hostile climate sexual
harassment, 358
language about, 328–329
overview, 328
by peers, 358–361
quid pro quo sexual harassment,
330, 333
reactions to, 333–336
reporting, 336–337
status-differentiated
relationships and,
332–333
types of, 329–332

sexuality
defined, 112
language about, 75–78
nonverbal cues and, 112–114
self-disclosure and, 152–153
sexually transmitted infections
(STI), 197
sexual organs, 31
sexual orientation. *see also* lesbian
gay bisexual transgender
queer/questioning
(LGBTQ)
defined, 10
gender identity and, 8–14
nonverbal communication and,
113
sexual revolution, xxvii–xxviii,
xxxiv–xxxv
sexual violence. *see* abuse; rape
similarity, 144
sitting behavior, 102
smiling, 103
social groups, identity and, 23
social interpretation of biological
sex on identity, 29–39
anatomical differences, 30–34
hormonal differences, 34–39
overview, 29–30
socialization
defined, 46, 53
gender identity development
and, 46–50
social learning theory, 41, 46, 97
soft-core pornography, 279–280,
282
song lyrics, 284–287
space, proxemics and, 98–99
sports, team names in, 72
spousal abuse, 230, 232
spousal rape, 220, 221
stagnating, 111
status-differentiated relationships,
332–333, 359
stereotypes
about commitment, 188–189
about working parents, 324

battering myths, 234–235, 239
in children's literature, 348–352
(*see also* educational
settings)
culture and gender, 50–51
defined, 29
gender stereotypes in
advertising, 253–255,
257–260, 261
job interviews and, 315–316
(*see also* workplace)
of masculinity and femininity,
25–26
in music videos, 287–289
of occupations, 69–70, 71 (*see
also* sexism)
rape myths, 226–228, 230
self-disclosure and, 151
in song lyrics, 285
sticky floor, 321–322, 326
stranger rape, 219, 221
strength, measures of, 32–34
suffixes, 72–73
suffragists, xxiii–xxvi, xxxiv
surnames, marriage and, 78–79
survivors
defined, 220, 221
self-blame by, 223
trigger words, 219, 221
symbolic annihilation, 265
symmetry, in language, 80–81, 83

T

tag questions, 86
talking
about communicating, in
romantic relationships,
189–190
"doing" *versus,* in same-sex
friendships, 170–171
importance of, in relationships,
165–166
team names, 72
telecommuting, 325, 327

television
LGBTQ and, 271–274
men and television
programming, 262–263
as mirroring reality *versus*
creating reality, 261–262
overview, 261
"real" men, 263–265
"real" women, 268–271
scripted men, 262–263
scripted women, 265–266
talk shows, 268–269
tension, in romantic relationships,
183–189
tentativeness, 86–87, 88
termination, of relationships, 109–
112, 192–194
testosterone, 34, 37–38
Title IX, 329, 360
titles, 82–83
touch (haptics)
defined, 103–104
relational conflict and, 109–110
sexual activity and, 117
toys, socialization and, 48–50
transgender persons. *see also* lesbian
gay bisexual transgender
queer/questioning
(LGBTQ)
defined, 10
friendship of, 167
gendered language, 61
romantic relationships and, 195
television depiction of, 271–274
transphobia, 10
trigger words, 219, 221
turning points, 188, 193

U

unethical questions, 319, 321
unpredictability, of gender
communication, 5
unrequited romance, 175–176
uses and gratifications theory,
250–251, 252

V

verbal communication
defined, 14, 16
sexual activity and, 115
victims
defined, 220, 221
posttraumatic stress disorder of,
238, 239
video chatting, 140
video games
gendered gaming, 292–295
gender identity development
and, 49–50
videos, music, 287–289
virtual reality, 290–291
visual dominance ratio, 103, 104,
157
vocal properties
linguistic construction, 85, 88
relational conflict and, 110–111
relationship maintenance, 109
vocalics (paralanguage),
104–105
voting, suffrage for women and,
xxiii–xxvi, xxxiv

W

walking behavior, 102
Web sites (Net Notes)
about hip-hop music, 289
about pornography and
deceptive techniques,
283
campus sexual assault, 222
dating, 182
"Emily the Strange" character,
352
friendship information, 173,
175
glass ceiling, 322
job search, 317
online quizzes about
relationships, 142
partner violence, 232

sexual harassment, 335, 360
for survivors of sexual assault
and rape, 229
talking about sex and, 116
transgender people in romantic
relationships, 195
for vocabulary expansion, 65
women's rights, xxi–xxxix
Civil Rights Movement and,
xxvii
early male supporters of, xxxiv
equal pay, 13–14
Equal Rights Amendment, xxxi
fathers' movements, xxxvi–
xxxvii
feminism, overview, xxii–xxiii
"feminisms," xxxii
First Wave feminism, overview,
xxiii
future of gender
communication, xxxvi–
xxxiii
mens' movements and, xxxvi–
xxxviii
overview, xxiii
Second Wave feminism,
overview, xxviii–xxxi
sexual revolution, xxvii–xxviii
sexual revolution and men,
xxxiv–xxxvi
suffragists, xxiii–xxvi, xxxiv
Third Wave feminism,
overview, xxxiii
"women's liberation," xix
women's studies programs, xxx
workplace, 311–345
equal pay and, 13–14
flirting in, 149
job advancement, 320–328
job search, 315–319
overview, 313–315
sexual harassment in, 328–338

CPSIA information can be obtained
at www.ICGtesting.com
Printed in the USA
LVHW061637140821
695042LV00010B/2